HANDBOOK OF THE CULTURAL FOUNDATIONS OF LEARNING

Edited by a diverse group of expert collaborators, the *Handbook of the Cultural Foundations of Learning* is a landmark volume that brings together cutting-edge research examining learning as entailing inherently cultural processes. Conceptualizing culture as both a set of social practices and connected to learner identities, the chapters synthesize contemporary research in elaborating a new vision of the cultural nature of learning, moving beyond summary to reshape the field toward studies that situate culture in the learning sciences alongside equity of educational processes and outcomes. With the recent increased focus on culture and equity within the educational research community, this volume presents a comprehensive, innovative treatment of what has become one of the field's most timely and relevant topics.

Na'ilah Suad Nasir is the sixth President of the Spencer Foundation and former Professor of Education and African American Studies at the University of California at Berkeley, USA.

Carol D. Lee is Professor Emeritus of Education and Social Policy, Learning Sciences, and African American Studies at Northwestern University, USA.

Roy Pea is David Jacks Professor of Education and Learning Sciences and Director of the Learning Sciences and Technology Design PhD program at Stanford University, USA.

Maxine McKinney de Royston is Assistant Professor in the Department of Curriculum & Instruction at the University of Wisconsin, Madison, USA.

HANDBOOK OF THE CULTURAL FOUNDATIONS OF LEARNING

*Edited by Na'ilah Suad Nasir, Carol D. Lee, Roy Pea,
and Maxine McKinney de Royston*

NEW YORK AND LONDON

First published 2020
by Routledge
52 Vanderbilt Avenue, New York, NY 10017

and by Routledge
2 Park Square, Milton Park, Abingdon, Oxon, OX14 4RN

Routledge is an imprint of the Taylor & Francis Group, an informa business

© 2020 Taylor & Francis

The right of Na'ilah Suad Nasir, Carol D. Lee, Roy Pea, and Maxine McKinney de Royston to be identified as the authors of the editorial material, and of the authors for their individual chapters, has been asserted in accordance with sections 77 and 78 of the Copyright, Designs and Patents Act 1988.

All rights reserved. No part of this book may be reprinted or reproduced or utilised in any form or by any electronic, mechanical, or other means, now known or hereafter invented, including photocopying and recording, or in any information storage or retrieval system, without permission in writing from the publishers.

Trademark notice: Product or corporate names may be trademarks or registered trademarks, and are used only for identification and explanation without intent to infringe.

Library of Congress Cataloging-in-Publication Data
Names: Nasir, Na'ilah Suad, editor. | Lee, Carol D., editor. | Pea, Roy D., editor. | McKinney de Royston, Maxine, editor.
Title: Handbook of the cultural foundations of learning / edited by Na'ilah Suad Nasir, Carol Lee, Roy Pea, Maxine McKinney de Royston.
Description: New York, NY: Routledge, 2020. | Includes bibliographical references and index. | Summary: "Edited by a diverse group of expert collaborators, the Handbook of the Cultural Foundations of Learning is a landmark volume that brings together cutting-edge research examining learning as an inherently cultural process. Conceptualizing culture as both a set of social practices and connected to learner identities, the chapters synthesize contemporary research in elaborating a new vision of the cultural nature of learning, moving beyond summary to reshape the field towards studies that situate culture in the learning sciences alongside equity of educational processes and outcomes. With the recent increase focus on culture and equity within the educational research community, this volume presents a comprehensive, innovative treatment of what has become one of the field's most timely and relevant topics"–Provided by publisher.
Identifiers: LCCN 2019058823 (print) | LCCN 2019058824 (ebook) | ISBN 9780415839044 (hardback) | ISBN 9780415839051 (paperback) | ISBN 9780203774977 (ebook)
Subjects: LCSH: Learning–Social aspects. | Cognition and culture. | Culturally relevant pedagogy. | Educational sociology. | Educational equalization.
Classification: LCC LB1060 .H34578 2020 (print) | LCC LB1060 (ebook) | DDC 370.15/23–dc23
LC record available at https://lccn.loc.gov/2019058823
LC ebook record available at https://lccn.loc.gov/2019058824

ISBN: 978-0-415-83904-4 (hbk)
ISBN: 978-0-415-83905-1 (pbk)
ISBN: 978-0-203-77497-7 (ebk)

Typeset in Bembo
by Deanta Global Publishing Services, Chennai, India

CONTENTS

List of Figures	*viii*
List of Tables	*ix*
Editors	*x*
List of Contributors	*xii*
Acknowledgments	*xv*
Introduction: Reconceptualizing Learning: A Critical Task for Knowledge-Building and Teaching	*xvii*

PART 1
Human Evolution, Physiological Processes, and Participation in Cultural Practices

1

1 The Institutional Foundations of Human Evolution, Ontogenesis, and Learning
Martin Packer and Michael Cole

3

2 The Braid of Human Learning and Development: Neuro-Physiological Processes and Participation in Cultural Practices
Carol D. Lee, Andrew N. Meltzoff, and Patricia K. Kuhl

24

3 Examining Links between Culture, Identity, and Learning
Margaret Beale Spencer, Carly Offidani-Bertrand, Keshia Harris, and Gabriel Velez

44

4 The Role of Stereotypes: Racial Identity and Learning
Leoandra Onnie Rogers, R. Josiah Rosario, and Janene Cielto

62

5 Innovation as a Key Feature of Indigenous Ways of Learning: Individuals and Communities Generating Knowledge
Francisco J. Rosado-May, Luis Urrieta Jr., Andrew Dayton, and Barbara Rogoff

79

Contents

PART 2
Discourse, Positioning, Argumentation, and Learning in Culture   97

6 Learning "How to Mean": Embodiment in Cultural Practices   99
Ray McDermott and Roy Pea

7 Positioning Theory and Discourse Analysis: An Explanatory Theory
and Analytic Lens   119
Judith L. Green, Cynthia Brock, W. Douglas Baker, and Pauline Harris

8 Hybrid Argumentation in Literature and Science for K–12 Classrooms   141
Sarah Levine, Danielle Keifert, Ananda Marin, and Noel Enyedy

9 Culture and Biology in Learning Disabilities Research: Legacies
and Possible Futures   160
Alfredo J. Artiles, David Rose, Taucia González, and Aydin Bal

10 Power, Language, and Bilingual Learners   178
Nelson Flores and Erica Saldívar García

PART 3
Learning Across Contexts   193

11 Learning Pathways: How Learning Is Culturally Organized   195
*Na'ilah Suad Nasir, Maxine McKinney de Royston, Brigid Barron,
Phillip Bell, Roy Pea, Reed Stevens, and Shelley Goldman*

12 Locating Children's Interests and Concerns:
An Interaction-Focused Approach   212
Reed Stevens

13 Communities as Contexts for Learning   230
Tryphenia B. Peele-Eady and Elizabeth Birr Moje

14 Adaptive Learning Across the Life Span   247
Shirley Heath, Michelle J. Bellino, and Maisha Winn

15 Culturally Sustaining Pedagogy: A Critical Framework for
Centering Communities   261
H. Samy Alim, Django Paris, and Casey Philip Wong

16 Multiple Ways of Knowing: Re-Imagining Disciplinary Learning   277
Beth Warren, Shirin Vossoughi, Ann S. Rosebery, Megan Bang, and Edd V. Taylor

Contents

PART 4
Reframing and Studying the Cultural Nature of Learning   **295**

17 Integrating Intersectionality into the Study of Learning   297
Subini Ancy Annamma and Angela Booker

18 Reconceptualizing the Quantitative-Qualitative Divide:
Toward a New Empiricism   314
Ezekiel J. Dixon-Román, John L. Jackson, Jr., and Maxine McKinney de Royston

19 Social Design-Based Experiments: A Utopian Methodology for
Understanding New Possibilities for Learning   330
Kris D. Gutiérrez, A. Susan Jurow, and Sepehr Vakil

20 Promoting Equitable and Just Learning Across Settings: Organizational
Forms for Educational Change   348
William R. Penuel

21 Learning at the Boundaries: Reconsidering University-District
Partnerships for Educational Change   365
Louis M. Gomez, Manuelito Biag, and David G. Imig

PART 5
Implications for Practice and Policy   **385**

22 Educating Teachers for the 21st Century: Culture, Reflection,
and Learning   387
Arnetha F. Ball and Gloria Ladson-Billings

23 Culture, Learning, and Policy   404
Linda Darling-Hammond

Index   *427*

FIGURES

1.1	Components of evolution in (a) the Modern Synthesis, (b) the Extended Evolutionary Synthesis, and (c) an approach that emphasizes reproduction	6
6.1	In the midst of the two women's first bow	100
6.2	Man begins to point to chair; seated woman joins in; standing woman about to point to chair	101
6.3	Requesting gaze of a hearer	102
6.4	Two seated people look up to find entering woman	111
6.5	Man begins to point to chair; seated woman has joined in; standing woman about to point to chair	112
6.6	In the midst of the two women's first bow	114
6.7	Woman arrives chair side; man raises hand to initiate first bow first time	114
6.8	Standing woman has glided to the front of her chair for a second bow-relevant moment; man initiates first bow for second time	114
6.9	Standing woman holds dip into bow, begins to sit down; man initiates first bow for third time; it will go to completion	114
7.1	Steps Pauline took to develop Charlie's telling case	125
7.2	Charlie's original study	126
7.3	Pauline's positioning continuum developed from TCS 1	126
7.4	History of studio art class at multiple levels of scale	135
7.5	Public interaction between teacher and Maya	136
8.1	A hybrid model of argumentation	146
12.1	Dad inspects Charlie's injury	222
12.2	Table arrangement of children	223
15.1	Six Principles of CSP	269
18.1	Cartesian dualist logics	318
19.1	Design Principles for Social Design Experiments	334
22.1	The hermeneutic cycle of critical reflection for transformative learning	396
22.2	Model of generative change	398

TABLES

6.1	Preliminaries for Two Japanese Bows	108
6.2	Chronology of a Bow Sequence Beginning	113
7.1	Contrastive analysis of Maya and James	133
20.1	Cultural Forms of Organization in Education That Can Be Appropriated to Promote Equitable Change in Education	351
21.1	Examples of Developmental Progressions at the Partnership, LEA, and IHE Levels	380

EDITORS

Na'ilah Suad Nasir is the sixth President of the Spencer Foundation. Previously, she held a faculty appointment in Education and African American Studies at the University of California, Berkeley where she also served as the Vice Chancellor for Equity and Inclusion. She also served on the faculty of the Stanford Graduate School of Education from 2000 to 2008. Nasir's research examines the racialized and cultural nature of learning and schooling, with a particular focus on the experiences of African American students in schools and communities. In her co-edited book, *We Dare Say Love: Supporting Achievement in the Educational Life of Black Boys*, Nasir explores the teaching practices and organization of the African American Male Initiative in Oakland, the first district-wide initiative of its kind focusing on supporting the achievement of Black male students. She is also the author of *Racialized Identities: Race and Achievement Among African American Youth*, published by the Stanford University Press in 2012, and co-editor of *Mathematics for Equity: A Framework for Successful Practice*, published by Teachers College Press in 2014. Her work has examined the organization of learning in cultural practices outside of school, the intersection of identity and learning, and equitable teaching in mathematics. Nasir is a member of the National Academy of Education and a Fellow of the American Educational Research Association.

Carol D. Lee is Professor Emeritus at Northwestern University, in the Learning Sciences Program of the School of Education and Social Policy. She is a former President of the American Educational Research Association (AERA), and the National Conference of Research on Language and Literacy (NCRLL). She is a member of the National Academy of Education, the American Association of Arts and Sciences, and a fellow of AERA and NCRLL and at the Center for Advanced Study in the Behavioral Sciences. Her research focuses on cultural supports for literacy including attention to the multiple-dimensions of learning, addressing identity processes, and perceptions of self, tasks, others, and settings. She has addressed these foci in the design of learning environments based on the Cultural Modeling Framework, with empirical data on multi-dimensional impacts. Her career began as a high school literature teacher in 1966 and has included teaching not only at high school, but at community college, elementary school, and university. She is a founder of three African centered schools in Chicago ranging from 21 to 47 years in operation, and still operating.

Roy Pea is David Jacks Professor of Education & Learning Sciences at Stanford University School of Education, and Computer Science (Courtesy), Director, H-STAR Institute (Human Sciences and Technologies Advanced Research), and founder and Director of Stanford's PhD program in Learning Sciences and Technology Design since 2001. His work in the learning sciences focuses on advancing theories, findings, tools, and practices of technology-enhanced learning of complex domains.

He has published extensively, with more than 225 publications including five edited volumes in K-12 learning and education, especially science, math and technology fostered by socially-augmented learning technologies including scientific visualization, online learning communities, digital video collaboratories, mobile computing, and virtual reality. Pea was co-editor on *Learning Analytics in Education* (2018), co-author on the 2010 *US National Education Technology Plan*, co-editor on *Video Research in the Learning Sciences* (2007), and NAS co-author on *How People Learn* (2000). He is a Fellow of American Academy for Arts and Sciences, National Academy of Education, Association for Psychological Science, American Educational Research Association, and Center for Advanced Study in the Behavioral Sciences. He is President of the International Society for the Learning Sciences (2004–'05) and ISLS Inaugural Fellow (2017). Pea holds seven patents advancing interactive and panoramic video technologies and received innovation awards from Apple Computer and IBM.

Maxine McKinney de Royston is an Assistant Professor in the Department of Curriculum & Instruction at the University of Wisconsin, Madison. Her research analyzes the pedagogical and interactional characteristics of learning environments, such as math classrooms, as they relate to larger discourses about race, identity, and power. Dr. McKinney de Royston's work centers around two interrelated research strands: conceptualizing the multidimensional and politicized nature of teaching and learning; and examining how learning environments operate as racialized learning spaces. Within the first strand she studies the pedagogical approaches of educators in predominately Black classrooms and schools to better understand the sociopolitical and relational nature of non-dominant theories of teaching and learning. The second strand examines how learning environments are shaped simultaneously by societal discourses, institutional and local contexts, and valued and devalued practices and norms in ways that offer up and (re)imagine the roles and identities of racially minoritized children. Among other places, Dr. McKinney de Royston's work has been published in *Teachers College Record*, *The Journal of the Learning Sciences*, *Cognition and Instruction*, and *Urban Education*.

CONTRIBUTORS

H. Samy Alim, University of California, Los Angeles

Subini Ancy Annamma, Stanford University

Alfredo J. Artiles, Arizona State University

W. Douglas Baker, Eastern Michigan University

Aydin Bal, University of Wisconsin-Madison

Arnetha F. Ball, Stanford University

Megan Bang, Northwestern University

Brigid Barron, Stanford University

Phillip Bell, University of Washington

Michelle J. Bellino, University of Michigan

Manuelito Biag, Carnegie Foundation for the Advancement of Teaching

Angela Booker, University of California, San Diego

Cynthia Brock, University of Wyoming

Janene Cielto, Northwestern University

Michael Cole, University of California, San Diego

Andrew Dayton, University of California, Santa Cruz

Linda Darling-Hammond, Learning Policy Institute and Stanford University

Ezekiel J. Dixon-Román, University of Pennsylvania

Noel Enyedy, Vanderbilt University

Nelson Flores, University of Pennsylvania

Erica Saldívar García, New York University

Contributors

Shelley Goldman, Stanford University

Louis M. Gomez, University of California, Los Angeles, Carnegie Foundation for the Advancement of Teaching

Taucia González, University of Arizona

Judith L. Green, University of California, Santa Barbara

Kris D. Gutiérrez, University of California, Berkeley

Keshia Harris, University of Chicago

Pauline Harris, University of South Australia

Shirley Heath, Stanford University

David G. Imig, University of Maryland

John L. Jackson, Jr., University of Pennsylvania

A. Susan Jurow, University of Colorado, Boulder

Danielle Keifert, University of North Texas

Patricia K. Kuhl, University of Washington

Gloria Ladson-Billings, University of Wisconsin, Madison

Carol D. Lee, Northwestern University

Sarah Levine, Stanford University

Ananda Marin, University of California, Los Angeles

Ray McDermott, Stanford University

Maxine McKinney de Royston, University of Wisconsin, Madison

Andrew N. Meltzoff, University of Washington

Elizabeth Birr Moje, University of Michigan

Na'ilah Suad Nasir, Spencer Foundation

Carly Offidani-Bertrand, University of Chicago

Martin Packer, Independent researcher, Colombia

Django Paris, University of Washington

Roy Pea, Stanford University

Tryphenia B. Peele-Eady, University of New Mexico

William R. Penuel, University of Colorado, Boulder

Leoandra Onnie Rogers, Northwestern University

Barbara Rogoff, University of California, Santa Cruz

Francisco J. Rosado-May, Universidad Intercultural Maya de Quintana Roo

R. Josiah Rosario, Northwestern University

Contributors

David Rose, Harvard University

Ann S. Rosebery, TERC

Margaret Beale Spencer, University of Chicago

Reed Stevens, Northwestern University

Edd V. Taylor, University of Colorado, Boulder

Luis Urrieta Jr., University of Texas, Austin

Sepehr Vakil, Northwestern University

Gabriel Velez, University of Chicago

Shirin Vossoughi, Northwestern University

Beth Warren, Boston University

Maisha Winn, University of California, Davis

Casey Philip Wong, University of California, Los Angeles

ACKNOWLEDGMENTS

This Handbook has been a long time coming. It began as a set of discussions about culture and diversity in learning convened by leadership in two national NSF-funded efforts. The first of these was the Learning in Formal and Informal Environments (LIFE) Center, funded as a Science of Learning Center by the National Science Foundation. The LIFE Center took up a set of research questions broadly concerned with the nature of the "social" in learning, and conducted work in three strands: research on the design of formal learning environments, research on the multiple kinds of robust learning that occurred in environments outside of school, and neuroscience research that illuminated the importance of the social nature of learning environments. The second was the Center for the Study of Culture, Learning, and Development (CHiLD), funded as a catalyst planning grant to Carol D. Lee, Beth Warren, and Kris Gutiérrez by the National Science Foundation. CHiLD focused on ecological examinations of how diverse groups of human beings learn to adapt new practices in order to tackle developmental and learning challenges over the life course. Key to this work was to understand the mutually co-constituting contributions of individual agency and the nested social contexts in which people live to the development of individuals, social networks (such as family systems), and broader communities. What these efforts held in common was a desire to theorize and study learning in more robust, inclusive, and expansive ways, beyond narrow conceptualizations of disciplinary learning, to an approach that honors the multiplicity of learning pathways, the range of settings within which powerful learning occurs.

This volume would not have come to fruition without the support and hard work of many beyond the small group of editors. We are grateful to many: the original steering committee for this project, which included James Banks, Louis Gomez, Roy Pea, Ray McDermott, Carol D. Lee, Na'ilah Suad Nasir, Luis Moll, Nora Sabelli, John Bransford, and Tiffany Lee, who convened to create the original blueprint for this volume; our original editor at Routledge, Alex Masulis, who shepherded the project through multiple job transitions and health challenges, and whose patience and kindness was instrumental; and the authors, who stepped up in ways to produce texts of quality and scope beyond our original hopes, and who stayed with us through many twists, turns, lulls, and restarts. In many cases, authors were in new writing partnerships, writing with colleagues across disciplines and perspectives that they had never written with, working through ideas that were new and tenuous. We think these writing partnerships made the final chapters incredibly rich, and model the kind of discipline-spanning work that is required to wrestle with complex ideas and concepts.

We are also incredibly grateful to the many reviewers who provided feedback on chapters, including Elaine Allensworth, James Anderson, Michael Barber, Megan Bang, John Baugh, Phillip

xv

Acknowledgments

Bowman, Lucia Braga, Angela Calabrese-Barton, Tabbye Chavous, Allan Collins, Jeannette Colyvas, Fred Erickson, Maria Falikman, Donna Ford, Vivian Gadsden, Antero Garcia, Conra Gist, Marjorie Goodwin, Rogers Hall, Victoria Hand, Lani Horn, Saadi Lahlou, Jennifer Langer-Osuna, Zeus Leonardo, Danny Martinez, Teresa McCarty, Laura Chavez Moreno, Jonathan Osborne, Leigh Patel, Barbara Rogoff, Ann Rosebery, Geoffrey Saxe, Robert Serpell, Peter Smagorinsky, Margaret Beale Spencer, Guadalupe Valdes, Vanessa Siddle Walker, Thomas Weisner, and Maisha Winn. And finally, we'd like to thank Kandyce Anderson and Emilie Homan, our editorial assistants, and Misha Kydd, Olivia Powers, and the team at Routledge for careful editorial work on the manuscript.

INTRODUCTION

Reconceptualizing Learning: A Critical Task for Knowledge-Building and Teaching

Carol D. Lee, Na'ilah Suad Nasir, Roy Pea, and
Maxine McKinney de Royston

Reconceptualizing learning is a critically important intellectual and social project at this time. Recent scientific breakthroughs reveal new and consequential insights about the brain, the complexities of thinking, and the intertwining of learning and environment that challenge much of what we thought we knew about learning, and much of the science our current educational structures and practices are built upon. This cutting-edge science can offer novel insights that can inform how we study learning and how we re-design our educational structures and practices to better cultivate learning and learners who are well-prepared for the challenges of today's world.

We take as central the proposition that understanding peoples' participation in cultural practices is *essential* to the scientific study of learning (Lee, 2017; Nasir, 2012; Pea, 1987, 2004; Rogoff, 2003). We view learning as fundamentally cultural, unfolding through multiple pathways that occur in relation to shifting social and contextual conditions, to which humans are constantly adapting. We view attention to cultural processes undergirding learning in expansive ways as a requisite subject of scientific investigation and not solely an object of political and ideological debate.

We are at a pivotal point in our efforts to understand the complexity of human learning and development. While efforts to focus on singular processes (e.g. cognitive, socio-emotional, developmental) or singular factors (e.g. motivation, executive functioning) have yielded important insights, they typically fail to account for the variation and contextual nature of such functioning. What is emerging across relevant fields that seek to understand human learning and development, albeit from different points of entry, is that human learning and development unfold within complex systems whose dynamic interactions are not fully understood. These include interactions among physiological processes, neurological processes, people's participation in cultural practices within and across time (phylogenetic time from our evolution as a species, cultural historical time, ontogenetic time in terms of where people are in the life course, and microgenetic time in terms of moment-to-moment interactions in the social and physical worlds (Lemke, 2000)), and their participation in cultural practices across spaces. And essential in this understanding of cultural practices is the understanding that people always, and often simultaneously, participate in multiple cultural communities of practice (Gutiérrez & Rogoff, 2003). Social interactions among people are as essential to learning as the artifacts (physical and ideational) are that get used in such interactions to facilitate meaning making and problem solving. While our understanding of such complex systems as the cauldron of human learning and development is still emergent, we hope in this Handbook to offer syntheses spanning multiple disciplines of what we have strong empirical evidence to support. These syntheses position participation in cultural practices as keystone and not merely an add on;

Introduction

they are grounded in seeking to account for the functionality of the diversity of pathways through which human learning unfolds.

It is vital to developing such a science of learning as cultural to be informed by interdisciplinary perspectives and research methods, including those from neuroscience, the learning sciences, developmental psychology, anthropology, cultural and gender studies, philosophy, and sociology. Therefore, we bring cutting-edge scholars and thinkers into symbiotic contact with each other within chapters and across this volume who elaborate an expanded vision of learning informed by our understandings of learning as a cultural process and by emerging and seminal scholarship across key fields. This volume offers a synthetic representation of state-of-the-art research that grapples with enduring and new questions in the learning sciences and other relevant fields. In synthesizing this research, we have been intentional about highlighting scholars whose work provides insights into how we define culture and learning, and the interplay between the two.

Limitations in the Field that Constrain Our Thinking

In taking seriously this holistic and expansive view of learning, this Handbook responds to what we view as some considerable limitations across relevant fields in how learning is conceptualized and around how culture is viewed in relation to learning. At the root of our perspective is the core notion that *to be alive as a human being is to learn*; thus, we fundamentally disagree with accounts of learning that routinely deny the humanity of some, or that view culture reductively in ways that limit how we understand and document human potential and its realizations. It is important that we take up several of these key limiting conceptions, including racial hierarchies, deficit thinking, so-called "scientific racism", the debate over nature versus nurture, the culture "container" problem, restricted notions of human possibility, and unduly restrictive ideas about what it means to learn in the disciplines.

It is an unfortunate historic fact that human communities have always found ways to demonize communities that one community deems as the "other". The "other" has been associated with nation states, with religions, with racial or ethnic groups, with gender identity, sexual orientation, and with ideological differences. This phenomenon is neither new nor limited to any one group of people or part of the world. The ways in which the demonizing and dehumanizing of the "other" gets institutionalized is a focus of this handbook, and in particular how such othering has been institutionalized through knowledge building efforts in the academy. Over the last 500 years, a particular versioning of the "other" associated with constructions of race has been particularly virulent, persistent, and taken up at one point in history as public and explicit. In more recent times, this othering has often been more implicit and masked in other ways of categorizing the other around deficit assumptions. We seek here to briefly capture this particular history of othering (powell, 2012) because it has so deeply informed developments in particular disciplines that seek to understand human learning, including psychology, human development, and anthropology.

We begin with an interrogation of the construct of race. The history of deficit theorizing emerges in European intellectual and political history as rationales for efforts to colonize populations outside of Europe, which were also taken up in intellectual and political theorizing in the Americas (Mills, 1997). Early writing and theorizing in sociology and psychology outright argued that peoples of African descent, indigenous populations in the Americas, Latinx, Asians, and women were cognitively, emotionally, and intellectually deficient, as in Herbert Spencer's (1860) social evolutionism theorizing of the hierarchy of human development that placed European whites at the top, and African descendants at the bottom. Considering patterns of immigration, particularly in the post-colonial era, the idea of European ancestry itself is complicated.

Thomas McCarthy (2009) demonstrates how these ideologies of human development relating to race and empire were integral to European-American expansion of the West. Deficit hypothesizing served as the underlying warrant for the ideology of white supremacy which provided

Introduction

presumptive moral justification for Western settler colonialism against indigenous populations outside of Europe and the enslavement of Africans (Horsman, 1986). Charles Mills in *The Racial Contract* (1997) offers a comprehensive historical documentation of such warrants, explicitly evident in policy documents, philosophical treatises, and legal and scientific texts. Indeed, the conquest and settlement of the Americas, the subjugation and extermination of indigenous peoples, and the massive expansion of the Atlantic slave trade in the early modern period were all integrally bound up with the social construction of racial differences and racial hierarchies.

Deficit theorizing about racial hierarchies of human communities based on presumedly biological explanations has a long history in Western science. "Scientific racism" is the pseudoscientific framework that suggests that empirical evidence exists to justify racial discrimination and claims of hierarchical racial inferiority or superiority[1]. Dominant in Europe, the US and across the Americas, scientific racism bases its premises on the idea that there are biological differences between "races" of people, which are meaningful and measurable. While the conception of race as a biological construct has been debunked by science (Omi & Winant, 2015), it was essential to the early formation of disciplines like psychology and anthropology. For instance, in the 1800s, the field of craniology evolved with arguments about human intellective capacity based on studies of brain size and shape. These arguments were put forward by scientists and physicians studying anatomy who claimed innate superiority of peoples from Europe over others from Africa, Asia, and indigenous populations in the Americas. Ironically, with the advent and increasing acceptance by the scientific community of Charles Darwin's theory of natural selection resulting in survival of the fittest, his findings were extrapolated by others to argue that the natural superiority of certain populations should inform social policies and practices that would ensure a survival of the fittest communities of humans. This logic was used by scientists, political theorists, and politicians to justify, for example, the colonizing enterprise by Europeans against non-Europeans.

By 1854, French writer Gobineau had published his *Essay on the Inequality of the Human Race* and by the beginnings of the 20th century, two threads of such deficit reasoning had evolved. One continued the biological arguments around racial inferiority, exemplified in the Eugenics movement. Eugenicists argued not only that there was a biological basis for inferiority but that such inferiority was inherited. Eugenicists in the US and elsewhere across Europe instituted policies and practices that included forced sterilizations for those they deemed to be feeble minded, or persons marked by class (e.g. poor), race, or disability, as well as restrictive immigration policies to keep "feeble minded" populations from entering a country. *The Races of Europe* (Ripley, 1899) distinguished the presumed superior Nordic races from the lower Mediterraneans, who were the so-called "feeble minded". Eugenic criteria were even embodied in the marriage laws of particular nations and states. Again, findings in the emergent field of genetics were used as scientific warrants, expanding from earlier work on brain size as the material embodiment of ability, to genes. A few years earlier, in 1892, the American Psychological Association had been formed by its founding president G. Stanley Hall, a eugenicist who believed in racial inferiority, as did preeminent educational psychologists Lewis Terman, Robert Yerkes, and Edward Thorndyke. By 1926, The American Eugenics Society was formed. Not ironically, Hitler and the Nazi regime studied the Eugenics movement in the US as a model and used its writings as warrants for their ideology around hierarchies of so-called races.

W.E.B. Du Bois (1897; also see Liss, 1998) argued over a century ago that race was used as a biological explanation for what he understood to be social and cultural differences between different populations of people. He spoke out against the idea of "white" and "black" as discrete groups, claiming that these distinctions ignored the scope of human diversity. Modern genetics supports Du Bois; the mainstream belief among scientists is that race is a social construct without biological meaning:

> Biological or genetic difference can be studied and quantified, but it is not race. Race is a sense-making system imposed upon the facts of difference. Races are not merely human

xix

Introduction

divisions, they are *politically salient* human dimensions [author's italics]. All classifications exist to serve a purpose; the purpose of a racial classification is to naturalize human differences—that is, to establish important categories and make their distinctions appear to be rooted in nature, rather in history or politics

(Marks, 2010, p. 271).

In the US, arguments about inherent distinctions in ability based on populations are not simply remnants of an old history but live today. Arthur Jensen, with supports from the Pioneer Fund, published "How Much Can We Boost IQ and Scholastic Achievement" in 1969's *The Harvard Educational Review*, updated in Rushton and Jensen (2005). In 1994, Richard Hernstein and Charles Murray published their controversial book *The Bell Curve*. James Traub in 2000 wrote in the *New York Times Magazine* an article entitled "What No School Can Do". Each of these pieces puts forth an argument that makes assertions about ability based on social group membership.

There are a number of thought-provoking twists and turns in this history of scientific racism. First, who is positioned as superior and inferior shifts over time and place. While Africans, and indigenous populations in the Americas, Australia, and New Zealand, are consistently placed at the bottom of the hierarchy, there are points where northern Europeans are pitted against southern Europeans, and where religion is equated with ethnicity and demonized, as was the case in the persecution of Jews across European history, culminating in the Holocaust during WWII. Second, there have historically been transitions from purely biological explanations for presumed inferiority to social and cultural explanations. For example, with both social Darwinism and Eugenics, observations of behaviors were used to attribute inferiority. Henry Goddard in 1912 published a study of the Kallikak family—a family of poor whites—who he argued epitomized the population that must be kept from reproducing in order not to continue a line of the feeble minded. Goddard claimed he could infer their inferiority from his observations of their physical presence and behaviors. Propositions about differential learning capacities with regard to particular populations— based on constructions of race, ethnicity, and SES—continue, with these early explicitly racist and deficit-oriented theories of genetic determinism giving rise to more subtle arguments that involve analyses of the "culture of poverty" (Lewis, 1966; Omi & Winant, 2015). "Culture of poverty" arguments presume that the experience of poverty is homogenous and inherently produces intellective and social deficits (Payne, 1999). While this may sound absurd, there remains educational research that implicitly and explicitly reinstantiates the idea that poverty somehow intrinsically constrains ability in ways that schools must actively work to overcome, e.g. some research on executive functioning and SES (as though executive functioning is not context dependent) and on socio-emotional learning (as if such psychological functioning is somehow apart from other psychological functioning and that poses particularly difficult challenges for children living in poverty). Much of this theorizing has implicitly and sometimes explicitly conflated class and race/ethnicity, particularly with regard to minoritized populations. Work informed by such theorizing has positioned minoritized children as academically lacking, attributing academic underperformance to "disorganization" in their families, homes, and communities, and even to "cultural deficits" (Valencia, 2012), particularly around language (Orr, 1987; Stotsky, 1999). In many ways, in our current meta-narratives, poverty has become synonymous with earlier conceptions of group identity, particularly with regard to race and ethnicity.

A third issue has been the relationships between institutions of power (e.g. universities, scientific societies, political and legislative entities) and practicing scientists to give credence to deficit biological explanations and biological explanations linked to cultural explanations of human functioning, and in so doing to enable institutional practices that harm the communities that are being demonized. The impact of the Eugenics Movement on educational practices in the US has been well documented, focusing as it has on constructions of race, ethnicity, and SES, fundamentally positing that some children were inherently not capable of complex intellectual work and that

Introduction

education should be tailored to their limited capacities. This Eugenicist influence led to policies and practices of differentiated instruction for different populations, with a basic skills focus for underachieving students, where underachievement has been based on IQ testing and more recently on skill assessments. This ideology was also mapped into the uses of microcomputers in schools, with basic skills drill activities dominating computer use in schools serving minoritized youth, not the patterns of uses of computers for writing and open-ended problem-solving activities found in more advantaged schools (OTA, 1988).

Ray McDermott and Barbara Rogoff (Gutiérrez & Rogoff, 2003; McDermott & Varenne, 1995) have made the point that typical conceptions of culture too often suffer from the "container" problem, by which they mean the false idea that cultural communities are homogenous and stable, and that people only participate in one cultural community:

> What anthropologists call culture is a much-contested term generally taken to "gloss the well-bound containers of coherence" that mark off different kinds of people living in their various ways, each kind separated from the others by a particular version of coherence, a particular way of making sense and meaning…There is a downside to the instinctive use of the term culture as a container of coherence: The container leaks.
>
> *(McDermott & Varenne, 1995, p. 325)*

The point here is that while culture tells us something about people, and how they organize their daily lives, it does not tell us everything. In reality, people live culture in incredibly rich and complex ways (Gutiérrez & Rogoff, 2003; Weisner, 1984), and importantly, they participate in multiple cultural communities simultaneously. Some of those communities may be long-standing intergenerational communities of practice associated with ethnicity, nationality, or religion, but others may have to do with traditions and practices associated with music, environmental locale, or hobbies, or other interests that people often self-select to engage in with others. To over-attribute ways of being, or ways of thinking, to any one of the multiple communities to which people belong is to reduce the complexity of human activity and experience, and in doing so, to embrace reductive notions of culture and of learning. While we do yet not fully understand this phenomenon, it is the case that the multiple communities of practice in which humans engage can have differential significance to, and consequences for them, and such significance can shift depending on the setting and depending on where one is in the life course.

Likewise, learning has been theorized within and across relevant fields utilizing limited framings of the arc of human potential. For example, scholarship on learning in the academic disciplines has been informed by narrow notions of what is entailed in such work. For instance, typical studies that document the extent or nature of learning in mathematics, or science, or literature, do not interrogate how one's identity is entailed in learning, or how learning to manage one's own emotions is a key developmental task that makes learning possible (Cantor, Osher, Berg, Steyer, & Rose, 2019; Darling-Hammond & Oakes, 2019; Lee, 2017). These omissions result in perspectives on learning that reduce learning to a purely cognitive task involving assimilating new information but which are impoverished in their ability to provide an account of the kinds of life-wide and life-deep learning that occurs in real world settings (Banks et al., 2007).

Assumptions That Undergird Our Perspective

To be sure, learning as a cultural process is deeply rooted in our biology and in our evolutionary history. We are hardwired for adaptiveness and these adaptation processes, along with developmental processes, underlie the cultural nature of learning. Recent research in the neurosciences has increasingly supported the idea that the brain is highly malleable in response to social input, thus highlighting the role of social and cultural contexts in the development of brain structures and function (Han et al., 2013; Kitayama & Park, 2010). Similarly, new advances in developmental research have found that it is not simply that culture *impacts* development, but that development itself is cultural in nature (Cole, 1996; Miller & Rodgers, 2001; Rogoff, 2003). For example, young children in the first year of life are tuned by evolution to develop competencies around learning to manipulate their bodies (crawl, walk, handle objects), to learn to read the internal states of other humans in order to achieve ego-focused goals (get to be hugged, fed, have diapers or other clothing removed when wet, etc.), and to learn to understand and begin to use language, as normative developmental milestones. They learn these competencies through their participation in cultural practices, largely in family and extended family social networks, with different kinds of supports, toward different social goals, and through engaging different cultural artifacts. These processes through which such early learning unfolds, for example, entail physiological and neurological processes responding and adapting to cultural experiences, including adapting to variability.

Among the most important developmental milestones across the life course is the development of perceptions of the self, of others, of tasks, of settings (Cantor et al., 2019; Spencer, 2006). These identity processes are essential as they propel human behavior and goal setting. From our evolutionary history, these perceptions are influenced by the emotional salience we attribute to experience, rooted in the importance of a sense of safety (Maslow, 1943). Knowledge, dispositions, and relationships as cultural experiences shape these perceptions. These perceptions are also influenced by individual variation in personality traits that have their foundations from birth, although they're clearly influenced over time and settings by the nature of cultural experiences (McAdams & Pals, 2006). Thus if we are to understand issues such as motivation, we argue, our fields must wrestle with these intertwinings of physiology and participation in cultural practices within and across time and space; and in so doing, wrestle with understanding the affordances of the multiple and diverse pathways through which such self-perceptions and meaning making unfold.

In taking up this challenge, we must confront the limited and deficit orientations that have abounded historically and today in our fields around identity, motivation, and learning. In particular, we are challenged to understand better implications for designing robust learning environments that are adaptive and responsive to the diversity of pathways through which human learning and development unfold.

In this Handbook, we examine fundamental constructs around the meaning of culture, not as a monolithic container. Culture entails routine practices, many of which are passed on across generations (Cole, 1996; Rogoff, 2003; Saxe, 1988) and within communities. Cultural communities are both homogenous and heterogenous, stable and changing (Greenfield, 2004; Rogoff, 2003). Cultural communities exist at macro levels and include communities defined by nationality, ethnicity, religion, and gender, as those that have the longest and most sustained histories (Bronfenbrenner, 1983; Cole, 1996). Routine cultural practices within families are often influenced by the communities of practice in which parents and other family adults participate, again often across generations. Cultural communities also include communities of practice that are historically situated—e.g. communities of basketball, video games, anime, dominoes, and professional communities such as teachers, engineers, painters, dairy workers, farmers, etc. (Nasir, 2002; Rogoff & Lave, 1984; Scribner & Tobach, 1997). Outside of nationality, both sets of cultural communities move across national borders, borders which shift over history (Dijink, 2002; O'Dowd, 2010). Participation in cultural communities entails participants identifying as members of such communities, where membership may be porous or closed. Participation in cultural communities provides the physical and ideational artifacts, the routine tasks that embody knowledge structures and dispositions, and the relationships of support that development across the life course requires and embodies (Saxe, 2012). Particularly important is the understanding that people participate in multiple communities of practice and as such develop intersectional identities and repertoires (Rosenthal, 2016). These identities may hold differential significance that may be influenced by the different contexts in which we operate (Spencer, 2019).

Introduction

A second essential construct of culture considers the fundamental developmental threads across what we inherit as humans from our evolutionary history—physiological processes and psychological dispositions—and our participation in cultural practices. Drawing from recent findings in cognitive science, the neurosciences, cultural psychology, human development, and the learning sciences, there is a convergence of evidence about how physiological processes around how sensory inputs from perceptions and experience are transformed into psychological processes that drive the construction of synapses in the brain, the foundation of schemas as cognitive structures and relations across cognitive structures upon which we draw to make sense of the world (Cacioppo, 2002; Cantor et al., 2019; Quartz & Sejnowski, 2002). These sensory inputs stimulate chemical reactions that trigger emotional reactions that we are hard wired to draw upon in imputing salience to experiences in the world. We are primed by our evolutionary history to attend to social relationships with other humans (Decety et al., 2004; Flavell & Miller, 1998). It is among the most consequential tasks of development across the life course to learn to read the internal states of other humans. We are disposed from our evolutionary history to seek to feel efficacious (Bandura, 1993), to seek social relationships with others that fulfill ego-related goals (Erikson, 1968), and to engage in problem solving by drawing on prior knowledge (Bransford et al. 1999).

While these foundational processes and dispositions are universal to the species, how they unfold, how they are socialized, and toward what goals they work are diverse and adaptive to differences in contexts. These contexts are cultural. Diversity of pathways of development, or cultural diversity, is normative and essential to the species. These developmental processes unfold over time. The targets of development evolve from infancy, through childhood, through adolescence and across adulthood (Bowman, 1989). While the fundamental tasks remain relatively the same within developmental periods, again how they unfold and toward what tasks are diverse based on participation in distinctive cultural communities.

Among the tasks across development is how we learn to respond to risks and supports (Spencer, 2019). Risks may be physical, social, economic, or political. Again, our perceptions of risk are triggered by chemical responses to sensory perceptions and the relationships and ideational and physical resources available to help us navigate such risks. Within and across all cultural communities, we will find sources of resilience in the face of even the most extreme and persistent risks.

Intellectual Genealogical Warrants for Centering Culture in Studies of Learning

While this Handbook draws from emerging findings across disciplines at this point in our intellectual history, it is important to acknowledge earlier work addressing the centrality of culture in human learning and development. To a large extent, philosophical traditions embody foundational belief systems that drive the organization of societies and provide the warrants that undergird human decision making in daily life. It is also the case that scientific investigations about human functioning reflect philosophical commitments or what we might think of as epistemological orientations and ontological beliefs about what it means to be human. Certainly, the history of scientific racism discussed earlier in this introduction illustrates how epistemological and ontological beliefs are taken up even in scientific investigations. In this brief review, we want to provide historical examples of research traditions and the epistemologies and ontological orientations that inform such traditions where attention to diverse processes of socialization is presumed central to human functioning. These include processes that presume human possibility as a central tenet.

Making sense of human learning and development has been a human endeavor with rich variations we are only now beginning to recognize. We consciously include traditions from different cultural communities, rather than only the Western academic canon that most often gets leveraged in studies of human learning and development. This decision is consistent with the underlying propositions undergirding this Handbook that center cultural diversity as normative and essential.

xxiii

Introduction

Here we explore the research traditions of Black psychologists and Indigenous scholars, as but two examples among many that illustrate robust epistemological and ontological belief systems about human learning and development. We begin with the field of Black psychology, or what has been termed by Azibo (2003) as African-centered psychology. This field formally began in the late 1960s and coincided with similar efforts in linguistics and sociology to interrogate cultural continuities across African and African descent populations in the diaspora. These efforts were, in part, a response to explanations of human behavior based largely on populations of European descent (Guthrie, 1976) that at the same time represented the next generation of scholarship around issues of identity and understanding resilience within African descent populations.

This earlier work included the sociological studies of scholars such as W.E.B. DuBois (1965; 2001), St. Claire Drake (Drake & Cayton, 1970), and Drusilla Dunjee Houston (1926/1985), the theorizing around education of scholars like Carter G. Woodson (1933/1969) and Mary McLeod Bethune (1939), and historians such as Anna Julia Cooper (1892/1988), John Henrik Clarke (1994), and Lerone Bennett (1964). This body of scholarship studied resilience and the role of cultural knowledge and identity in resilience based on understanding continuities in foundational belief systems and practices from across African societies. Specifically, Black psychologists from the 1960s through the 1980s examined original texts articulating propositions about what it means to be human from communities ranging from ancient Egypt (Kemet), the Niger River Valley, and Mali. They drew on the groundbreaking work of Senegalese scientist Cheik Anta Diop (1989) who documented what he called *The Cultural Unity of Black Africa*. Diop examined the melanin in the skin of mummified remains from ancient Egypt, linguistic relationships across West African languages and ancient Egypt, as well as similarities in political structures. Diop argued against the prevailing attempts to distinguish the civilizations of ancient Egypt and Ethiopia from the rest of the African continent—thus the presumed distinction between south of the Sahara and north of the Sahara. These distinctions are related to efforts, for example, to focus on Black people in the US as unconnected to their African ancestral roots, implying that as a people their history begins with enslavement.

This background is important in understanding the roots of Black psychology as a distinct field. The Association of Black Psychologists began in 1968; The Association for the Study of Classical African Civilization in 1968; The National Association of Black School Educators and the National Black Child Development Institute in 1970; the Black Caucus of the Society for the Study of Child Development in 1979; and *The Journal of Black Psychology* in 1974. It is interesting to note that developments in what would come to be called socio-cultural or cultural-historical-activity theory were unfolding during this same time period, drawing largely from the work of Soviet psychologists, particularly Lev Vygotsky and Aleksandr Luria.

Scholars such as Asa Hilliard (1995; 1998), Maulana Karenga (1984; 1993; 2006), Anderson Thompson (1998) and Jacob Carruthers (1997; 1999) translated primary source documents from ancient Kemetic (or Egyptian), Ethiopian (e.g. Geez) and the Meroitic or Nubian traditions as well as examined West African oral traditions and socialization practices. In a similar philosophical vein, beginning in the late 1960s, Sylvia Wynter (2001, 2003), inspired by Martinican psychiatrist and political theorist Franz Fanon (1963), produced many publications (literary and critical essays) arguing how social and cultural experiences intersect with biological inheritances, with particular attention to what societies determine as symbolic meanings.

There are several important takeaways from this research about foundational assumptions concerning human functioning that are consistent with the broad principles that inform this Handbook:

- A view of identity as relational—the idea that we are interconnected and inter-dependent, that development is not singularly an individual matter;
- Socialization efforts (or what we think of as education—formal or informal): should be aimed at holistic development and not compartmentalized; should productively incorporate children into a broader community; and should include moral development;

Introduction

- Beliefs in the innate and unbounded capacity of each person; belief in the Kemetic tradition that divinity exists within everyone in terms of the potential of human perfectibility.

These propositions stand in contrast with what has dominated theorizing in Western-oriented work in psychology and human development, which has focused largely on identity as individual, on socialization in schools as primarily attending to cognitive development, and long-standing efforts that assume a construct of intelligence as fixed and innate. A host of constructs (e.g. self-efficacy, grit, executive functioning, valuing an internal locus of control) presume psychological functioning as situated within the individual. We see this in places such as IQ tests that have and continue to be used as predictors or co-variates to explain educational outcomes.

In addition to the research on African philosophical traditions as a lens on positive human development, there was simultaneously substantive empirical research. This body of work in Black psychology sought to interrogate assumptions that informed empirical measures and methods for studying human learning and development, questioning both the dominant use of sampling based on white populations, but also underlying constructs used as predictors to support claims of hierarchies in human communities and of particular cultural practices (Boykin et al., 1979; Jones, 1979). Researchers developed a number of measures of relational identity orientations (Sellers et al., 1998), of resilience as an outgrowth of social supports (Spencer, 1985; 2006), and of the functionality of communal orientations for learning (Boykin et al., 1997). Jones (1996) published a groundbreaking *Handbook of Tests and Measurements for Black Populations*. We offer this brief overview of the field of Black psychology and its roots in African philosophical traditions as an example of some of the fields of research around human learning and development that have evolved out of diverse cultural traditions not rooted in Europe.

Indigenous communities, scholars and scholarship have also explored issues of human learning and development from time immemorial. Many Indigenous communities have elaborate theories of learning and development encoded in their knowledge systems and cultural ecologies, as reflected in stories, traditions, and the ways Indigenous peoples organize their families and communities. Operating from epistemological and ontological belief systems that center the well-being of the self, family, the community, the land and waters, the spirits, and the ancestors, these traditions view human learning and development within a framework of connectedness, embeddedness, and reciprocal relationships with all things past, present, and future. Within these systems, learning is understood as holistic, reflexive, reflective, and relational wherein generational roles and responsibilities must be considered. Likewise, some knowledge is appreciated as sacred and as only being able to be shared in specific situations and only with consent (First Nations Education Steering Committee, 2008).

While the purpose of this section is not to detail the entirety of Indigenous perspectives, we want to point to some of the key assertions and enduring principles that continue to be explored as central to human learning and development from Indigenous theories of human learning and development. Indigenous theories of human learning and development emerged significantly in the research literature in the '70s and '80s from scholars such as Vine Deloria, Bea Medicine, Linda Smith, Greg Cajete, Oscar Kawagley, Tsianina Lomawaima, Bryan Brayboy, and others. They articulated Indigenous processes of learning and development while carefully examining how settler-colonialism and its wake has impacted and continues to impact Indigenous peoples, including through research conducted by non-Indigenous peoples applying western or non-Indigenous frameworks and assumptions to Indigenous communities and issues.

One marker of note is the founding of the Society of Indian Psychologists (SIP) by Carolyn Attneave, a Delaware/Lenni Lenape woman in 1970. SIP was largely focused on mental health and wellbeing through research, education, and policy advocacy. Dr. Attneave's work and the work of the society named the harm that was continuing to be perpetuated on Indigenous peoples through the application of western normative assumptions. Her work expanded conceptualizations of the

Introduction

familial unit as cultural and demonstrated that Indigenous peoples' kinship networks were much more expansive than mainstream psychology constructed as important. She argued that these constructions fundamentally shaped developmental trajectories and importantly approaches to health and education that should recognize and strengthen the natural networks people depend on. Central to Dr. Attneave's work, as well as other Indigenous scholars, has been the recognition of how settler-colonialism has disrupted Indigenous developmental processes, as well as how resiliency and adaption has happened or can happen. For example, the study of language and culture in Indigenous communities has been a critical area of scholarship and one that communities themselves have been deeply focused on (e.g. Smith, 1999; McCarty & Lee, 2014; Hermes, 2007; Wilson & Kamana, 2011).

A theme across many scholars' work, including Dr. Attneave, is the role of anthropocentrism in constructions of human learning and development. In Indigenous knowledge systems kinship networks are not restricted to human beings– indeed they include the lands, waters, and more-than-human life. The body of Indigenous scholars and non-Indigenous scholars pushing to conduct scholarship that has construct validity with respect to the ontological assertions and Indigenous knowledge systems theoretically and methodological continues to expand. Consider the studies by Ananda Marin (e.g. 2013; 2020) who explores the role of land, mobilities and attentional patterns in child development and child-adult interactional patterns in ways that have the potential to expand our foundational understandings of human learning and development. The extensive programs of research briefly mentioned here are rooted in philosophies among indigenous populations in the Americas (Bang, Medin et al., 2007; Bang & Medin, 2010; Brayboy, 2005; Lomawaima, 2004; McCarty, Borgoiakova et al., 2005; San Pedro, 2015; Smith, Tuck, & Yang, 2018). There are several important takeaways from this research about foundational assumptions for human functioning consistent with the broad principles informing this handbook:

- Human learning and development fundamentally involves knowledge systems and must be understood within axiological systems of values and ethics. These systems are tied to and give shape to power, politics and societal structures.
- Human learning and development are cultural processes in which Indigenous language and linguistic structures shape identity and knowledge.
- Human learning and development are tied to place and the natural world. Thus, theories of human learning and development need to involve lands, waters, and more-than-humans as central to the study of human learning and development.
- Learning and development are fundamentally relational and evolve over the life course. The centrality of kin and extended kinship networks, including more-than-human life, forms the grounds for actualizing human developmental potential.

Just as important to the two examples presented above, distinct philosophical traditions and theories of human learning and development are organized around the epistemological and ontological systems of Latinx and Asian and Pacific Islander communities, among others (Alcoff, 2013; Bernal, 2012; Dussel, 2019; Freire, 1968/2018; Markus & Kitayama, 1991; Rowe, 2017; Uskul, Kitayama, & Nisbet, 2008). While some of this scholarship is published within educational journals and other publishing outlets, much of it gets published in other fields and has yet to be deeply integrated into educational discourse.

Another key conceptual contribution comes from the foundations of cultural-historical activity theory, drawing largely on the work of Lev Vygotsky, Aleksandr Luria, and Aleksei Leontiev, yet we think it is important to document the historical antecedents of their theorizing. Cultural-historical perspectives on learning, most notably the works of the Soviet psychologists Lev Vygotsky (1962, 1978) and his students in the 1920s–1930s, the neuropsychologist Aleksandr Luria (1976), and the activity theorist Aleksei Leontiev (1978) working in subsequent decades, were founded on the seminal writings on human nature by Vico (1688–1744) and Johann Gottfried von Herder

Introduction

(1744–1803). Vico and Herder observed that human nature is constantly changing, and thereby changing the way the world can change us. Herder said it simply if profoundly: "We live in a world we ourselves create."[2] Said another way:

> Human nature, on this view, rather than simply "being" a product of maturational and environmental forces, is of our own making and continually "becoming". A fundamental aspect of this cultural-historicism perspective is a view of human nature that, while acknowledging biological and environmental contributions, emphasizes that humankind is: "reshaped through a dialectic of reciprocal influences: Our productive activities change the world, thereby changing the ways in which the world can change us. By shaping nature and how our interactions with it are mediated, we change ourselves."
>
> *(Pea, 1985, p. 169)*

As the biologist Stephen Jay Gould observed (1980), such "cultural evolution," in contrast to Darwinian biological evolution, is defined by transmission of skills, knowledge, and behavior through learning across generations and has been our nature-transcendent innovation as a species. The collectivity of all of the cultures of the world, presuming some contact among them, makes it possible for old cultures to do new things and for new cultures to appropriate elements of previous cultures in new combinatoric relations, thus fundamentally changing humanity itself.

We owe much of our current appreciation for Vico and Herder to the Oxford philosopher Isaiah Berlin, who was concerned with the social and political implications of ideas (though also see Toulmin, 1992). Berlin was preoccupied especially with the 18th Century Enlightenment— its key writers including Hume, Kant, Montesquieu, and Voltaire—who attacked religious overreach and dogma, and promoted tolerance of diversity. But Enlightenment writings were also potentially despotic in their manifestations as a cold, narrow rationalism because reason was championed as the primary source of knowledge. Berlin particularly valued the insights of the counter-Enlightenment writers Vico and Herder, who were critical of the totalitarian edge of the Enlightenment agenda presuming all problems could be resolved with the determined application of reason.

Emphasizing the particular, historical, and evolving character of societies, cultures, and traditions, the Italian Giambattista Vico (1725: *New Science*) sought to unite the study of history with the more systematic social sciences to establish a single science of humanity to record and explain historical cycles through which societies rise and fall. Berlin writes about how these emphases were groundbreaking as a vision of the historical sciences and as a valid critique of the Enlightenment, because Vico orients our attention to the rich fullness of human life experiences, varying over historical time and place. Vico was concerned that the methods for studying nature were insufficient for studying the history of human affairs; human activity cannot, he wrote, be measured by the straight line of reason, given the uncertainties of practical social life.

Where Herder demands our attention, Berlin wrote, in his prescient arguments, is "that one must not judge one culture by the criteria of another; that different civilizations are different growths, pursue different goals, embody different ways of living, are dominated by different attitudes to life; so that to understand other cultures one must perform an imaginative act of 'empathy' into their essence, understand them 'from within' as far as possible and see the world through their eyes" (Berlin, 2000, p. 429). In Herder's *Ideas about the Philosophy of History of Mankind* (1774/1803), he argued that if we are to understand a belief or value, we can only do so by viewing it as it is viewed, valued, and assessed within the particular culture or tradition to which it belongs (thus anticipating what many today call cultural relativism). For Herder, diversity is the defining feature of human existence, and accordingly, we should avoid any temptation to rank nations and cultures. This was in contradistinction to Enlightenment writings, such as those of Voltaire, that man is the same at all times and places, and the presumption that, with humankind of a uniform nature, similar

Introduction

universal goals such as justice, happiness, and the rule of wisdom should presumably emerge, with morality that is the same among "all civilized peoples."

Karl Marx (1867/1967) in *Kapital* shared Vico's efforts to understand what it means to be human and what the potential for human life is. Berlin on Vico is equally applicable to Marx: "He conceived this study [*Scienza Nuova*] in the widest and most philosophical fashion—as being concerned with what it was for men to constitute a fully human society, more particularly, how men came to think, feel, act, live as they did" (Berlin, 1976, p. 9). Both Vico and Marx ask, "What is history?" They concur by answering that only human beings have made and make history, and that history is, accordingly, the accumulation of social actions and interactions through time. Much of importance follows. Both thinkers realized that satisfactorily answering these questions could only be achieved through an historical understanding, since human beings are products of human history. Human attributes, faculties, and capacities cannot be deduced a priori from mistakenly conceiving of a human essence as unchanging whatever the variability across all forms of human existence. There is no pre-ordained human nature.

For both Vico and Marx, human nature arises out of persons interacting with nature, with one another, and with the things that they have made in the world (from machines to theories to religions). They each realized that the key to our understanding of ourselves is to uncover the constraints on human action within which history unfolds, a science of the history of society. If we are to understand the enormous diversity across the world in the ways that human nature has been made manifest, we will have to therefore study how and why it became that way, its human history. This quest will require empirically examining the life activities of actual, concrete historical agents, functioning in human institutions and nation states. Marx wrote that the real premises of a correct theory of history "…are men, not in any fantastic isolation and rigidity, but in their actual, empirically perceptible process of development under definite conditions" (Marx & Engels, 1973, p. 47–48).

With history the product of human activity, knowledge of history will thus only be through the development of the appropriate social and cultural sciences to study human activities in situ, whenever possible. Marx expressed his appreciation of the importance for history of man–made institutions:

> Men make their own history, but they do not make it as they please; they do not make it under self-selected circumstances, but under circumstances existing already, given and transmitted from the past. The tradition of all dead generations weighs like a nightmare on the brains of the living.
>
> *(Marx, 1852, p. 5)*

It is noteworthy for our Handbook that this perspective on the sociohistorical construction of human nature has also been reflected in studies of the child as a "cultural invention" (Aries, 1962; Kessen, 1979; Siegel & Kessel, 1983):

> Children are, or become, what they are taken to be by others, and what they come to take themselves to be, in the course of their social communication and interactions with others. In this sense, I take "child" to be a social and historical kind, rather than a natural kind, and therefore also a constructed kind rather than one given, so to speak, by nature in some fixed or essential form.
>
> *(Wartofsky, 1983, p. 190)*

Building on the early work of Vygotsky (1962) and Luria (1976), work in the field of cultural psychology has studied learning and cognition in cultural practices to understand the socially organized nature of learning, and the profound influence of social context on the content and

Introduction

processes of learning (Cole, 1996; Rogoff, 1991; Scribner & Tobach, 1997). Early work in this area by Michael Cole and Sylvia Scribner (1974) argued that cognition, in many respects, was local to particular places at particular times, and efforts to measure "universal" cognitive development failed to capture the richness of thinking that occurred with the Vai community in Liberia that they studied (Scribner & Cole, 1981).

Studies in this tradition have been deeply consequential in influencing the emerging shift in attention to the situated nature of learning and development (Rogoff & Lave, 1984; Scribner & Cole, 1973; Scribner & Tobach, 1997). An early family of studies interrogated assumptions of general cognitive and memory skills (Cole & Scribner, 1974). Other studies included examining effects of schooling by comparing tasks concerning concrete operations, memory, and logical syllogism with schooled and unschooled populations. Overall, findings documented how displays of competence depended on the contexts of elicitation, where familiarity with materials, content, and assumptions undergirding the tasks mattered (Scribner, 1977). For example, Luria's studies from the 1930s on syllogistic reasoning among rural non-schooled and schooled Tadzhikistan and Uzbekistan populations showed that cultural differences around warrants for claims in making arguments mattered (Luria, 1976). While Luria interpreted his findings as evidence of impacts of schooling on syllogistic reasoning on matters beyond personal experience, later work in socio-cultural traditions interpret these findings as evidence that reasoning is not de-contextualized (Rogoff, 2003).

Some studies documented differences in displays of skills based on shifts in the contexts under which skills were elicited. For example, Serpell (1979) found differences in skills in reproducing patterns between English and Zambian children were explained by access to materials that were most familiar within each cultural community. A host of studies documented rich displays of knowledge in everyday settings from dairy factories (Scribner, 1984) to workplaces for tailors in Liberia (Lave, 1977). This family of research also included rich longitudinal studies of the social organization of everyday settings—with populations often living in poverty—documenting the distributed nature of supports for problem solving. These include studies by Carraher, Carraher, & Schliemann (1985), Saxe's (1988) studies of Brazilian children selling candy on the streets, Rogoff's studies of learning through observing among Mayan populations (Correa-Chávez & Rogoff, 2009), and Greenfield's (2004) studies of Mexican weavers.

This research has fundamentally informed what we now think of as socio-cultural theories of learning, emphasizing the situatedness of displays of competence and the centrality of understanding the social organization of a diverse array of settings in order to develop a well-grounded and ecologically rich understanding of human learning. This body of work richly documents that learning is socially organized, providing distributed supports for knowledge construction that include inter-dependent social relationships among participants, and the availability of culturally and contextually relevant artifacts as resources for problem solving, aimed at culturally specific goals. Our challenge now is to more fully understand the range of variation in such cultural socialization and the functionality of such diversity for life course outcomes, especially in an increasingly inter-dependent world.

Another important dimension of this body of work beyond cross-cultural studies is research in this tradition that examines heterogeneity within communities where people are socialized by multiple cultural communities and cultural-historical shifts in communities. Consider Saxe's (2012) pioneering longitudinal studies of the Oksapmin of Papua New Guinea where he documents the evolution of community-based mathematical representations—the construct of Fu—over decades based on the introduction of new forms of economic exchange influenced by colonial presence from Western societies, and how people's understanding of Fu depended on where in the life cycle they were when these new forms of economic exchange were introduced. Another salient body of work is Rogoff's (2011; Correa-Chávez & Rogoff, 2009) research with populations that experience both traditional Mayan family socialization and training in Western educational settings and

Introduction

how the repertoires they develop—for example in socializing their children—reflect a hybrid of resources from both sets of socialization experiences.

We take from these multiple traditions of inquiry what it means to be human and how humans learn a long-standing history of propositions about how essential understanding human variation is if we are to work from ecologically valid constructs and propositions. The fact that these foundational principles are also being validated across relevant disciplines—psychology, human development, the neurosciences, cultural & gender studies, studies of complex systems, anthropology, sociology—is important. And, thus, we can see the need for the work synthesized in this handbook.

These intellectual genealogical warrants open the door for an important rethinking of how we study and come to more deeply understand the cultural organization of learning. If human activity is fundamentally cultural, then it stands to reason that learning—as a core human activity—is also fundamentally cultural. It is not only organized by human societies in myriad ways, but those ways of organizing influence the deep structure of what gets learned under what conditions.

Organization of the Volume

This volume addresses a range of critical topics on culture and learning, including: evolutionary and developmental bases for the cultural nature of learning; language, tools, and mediation in learning; and environments and settings of learning (including both local and policy settings). Attention to methodological implications and interdisciplinary methodological innovations is woven throughout the handbook's five parts.

Part 1, Human Evolution, Physiological Processes, and Participation in Cultural Practices, synthesizes the human development and evolutionary science literature that is foundational to understanding how culture not only impacts human development and learning, but how development and learning are cultural in nature because culture is the medium through which humans adapt to the varying conditions of life. In addition to evolutionary and neuroscience perspectives, this part discusses current research on cultural developmental perspectives that include anthropological and psychological accounts of learning and issues related to learning that demonstrate how learning is culturally embedded and takes shape in interaction with learning settings and social others.

Part 2, Discourse, Positioning, Argumentation, and Learning in Culture, examines how humans use their bodies and representational systems to mediate meaning making for both reproducing and generating new cultural practices. In this section, we are defining in part what it *means* to be cultural—engaging bodily, symbolic, and interactive vehicles of meaning making and sense-making through participating in cultural practices. This part of the book first treats the foundations of this encompassing argument (Dewey, James, Vygotsky, Bakhtin, Marx, Bateson, & Mead) and then identifies several key organizing categories for scholarly analysis of language—positioning in discourse, mediation, argumentation and tools—in relation to culture and learning. It also includes considering how certain cultural forms, such as language, and certain ways of learning are differentially privileged, and how the disruption of these power hierarchies requires articulating and enacting culturally affirming and sustaining theoretical, methodological, and pedagogical approaches.

Part 3 is entitled Learning Across Contexts, in recognition of the fact that a cultural orientation to learning requires a rich and multi-layered way of thinking about spaces and places of learning. Learning necessarily occurs within and across local settings, like schools, families, and after-school settings, and research has documented the wide range of ways in which learning gets organized, and whereby access to learning is afforded in various kinds of learning arrangements in these settings. These local settings, however, are fundamentally influenced by the structures and processes of the institutions, organizations, and societies within which they are embedded, and by the policies and assumptions that guide these settings. Thus, an account of the cultural nature of learning must

xxx

Introduction

also be an account of the ways in which learning is inextricably tied to the multi-layered spaces and places within which it occurs. In this section, we summarize the research that documents the complex picture of the cultural nature of learning within and across learning environments. The chapters in this part focus on conceptual approaches to understanding learning within and across settings, the nature of learning both in schools and in out-of-school settings, and how the organization of learning environments and access to them is also deeply influenced by institutional, organizational, and policy contexts.

Part 4, Reframing and Studying the Cultural Nature of Learning, highlights the settings in which learning interactions take place and clarify what it means to engage in research when we take seriously how we think about both culture and learning. These chapters reach across the boundaries of disciplinary literatures and raise some of the key methodological issues at play in interdisciplinary research on culture and learning. Within these chapters, culture is conceptualized as both a set of traditions and practices that ethnic/racial groups have in common, but also as the various ways that daily life is organized and is fluid and changing through social interaction. These chapters also offer an overview of bodies of research on learning and diversity, surveying work on race, class, gender, and exceptionality that problematize the essentialization of groups in relation to learning. This part offers insights into the types of theoretical tools and research methods that a science of learning with culture at its core would need to utilize.

The fifth and final part of the volume, Implications for Practice and Policy, considers the implications for policy and practice of better understanding the cultural nature of learning. Specifically, chapters explore how we might think about policy solutions, teacher learning, and teacher preparation differently if we were to take seriously the ways in which learning is fundamentally a cultural process. The authors also explore and examine how a cultural view of learning adds nuance and complexity to our understanding of (as well as the practice of) educational research.

It is our hope that this Handbook, synthesizing current scientific cutting-edge research, will ignite future inquiry into the cultural nature of learning. At a time when key concerns about how educational spaces (formal and informal), systems, and teaching should be designed, funded, and assessed, this foundational work on learning is especially critical. Underneath each of these concerns are fundamental stances about what constitutes and is privileged as human ways of knowing, being, and doing. Without attention to *how* this question of "What is learning?" gets understood and changes over time comes the risk of falling into reductionist and problematic views of learning that are unfounded empirically and which further reproduce social inequities.

Notes

1 Racism can also operate independently of the wrappings of science, as an anti-democratic political discourse used to do social ranking and to rationalize social inequalities and prejudice.

2 Herder (1774). *Übers Erkennen und Empfinden in der menschlichen Seele* cited from Bernhard Suphan (ed.) *Herders sämmtliche Werke* (Berlin: Weidmann, 1877–1913) vol. 8, p. 252. Translation by Roy Pascal *The German Sturm und Drang* (Manchester: Manchester University Press, 1959), p. 136.

References

Alcoff, L. M. (2013). Educating with a (De)Colonial Consciousness. *Proceedings from the 2013 Lapes Symposium, LÁPIZ: Latin American Philosophy of Education Journal*, 1, 4–18.

Aries, P. (1962). *Centuries of Childhood: A Social History of Family Life* (R. Baldick, Trans.). New York, NY: Knopf.

Azibo, D. A. Y. (2003). *African-Centered Psychology: Culture-Focusing for Multicultural Competence*. Durham, NC: Carolina Academic Press.

Bandura, A. (1993). Perceived self-efficacy in cognitive development and functioning. *Educational Psychologist*, 28(2), 117–148.

Bang, M., & Medin, D. (2010). Cultural processes in science education: Supporting the navigation of multiple epistemologies. *Science Education*, 94(6), 1008–1026.

Introduction

Bang, M., Medin, D. L., & Atran, S. (2007). Cultural mosaics and mental models of nature. *Proceedings of the National Academy of Sciences of the United States of America*, 104(35), 13868–13874.

Banks, J. A., et al. (2007). *Learning in and Out of School in Diverse Environments: Life-Long, Life-Wide, Life-Deep.* Seattle, WA: The LIFE Center. Retrieved from http://www.life-slc.org/.

Bennett, L. (1964). *Before the Mayflower: A History of the Negro in America, 1619–1964.* Chicago, IL: Johnson Publishing Company.

Berlin, I. (1976). *Vico and Herder: Two Studies in the History of Ideas.* New York, NY: Viking.

Berlin, I. (2000). *The Proper Study of Mankind: An Anthology of Essays.* London: Macmillan.

Bernal, D., Burciaga, R., & Carmona, J. F. (2012). Chicana/Latina *testimonios*: Mapping the methodological, pedagogical, and political. *Equity and Excellence in Education*, 45(3), 363–372.

Bethune, M. M. (1939). The adaption of the history of the Negro to the capacity of the child. *Journal of Negro History*, 29, 9–13.

Bowman, P. (1989). Research perspectives on black men: Role strain and adaptation across the adult life cycle. In *Black Adult Development and Aging*, R. Jones (eds.), Berkeley, CA: Cobbs & Henry, pp. 117–150.

Boykin, A. W., et al. (1979). *Black Psychology and the Research Process: Keeping the Baby but Throwing Out the Bath Water.* New York, NY: Russell Sage Foundation.

Boykin, A. W., et al. (1997). Communalism: Conceptualization and measurement of an Afrocultural social orientation. *Journal of Black Studies*, 27(3), 409–418.

Bransford, J., et al. (1999). *How People Learn: Brain, Mind, Experience and School.* Washington, DC: National Academy Press.

Brayboy, B. M. J. (2005). Toward a tribal critical race theory in education. *The Urban Review*, 37(5), 425–446.

Brofenbrenner, U. (1983). The context of development and the development of context. In *Developmental Psychology: Historical and Philosophical Perspectives*, R. Lerner (ed.), Hillsdale, NJ: Lawrence Erlbaum.

Cacioppo, J. T. (2002). Social neuroscience: Understanding the pieces fosters understanding the whole and vice versa. *American Psychologist*, 57(11), 819–831.

Cantor, P., Osher, D., Berg, J., Steyer, L., & Rose, T. (2019). Malleability, plasticity, and individuality: How children learn and develop in context. *Applied Developmental Science*, 23(4), 307–337.

Carraher, T. N., Carraher, D., & Schliemann, A. D. (1985). Mathematics in the streets and in schools. *British Journal of Developmental Psychology*, 3(1), 21–29.

Carruthers, J. H. (1997). *African World History Project: The Preliminary Challenge.* Los Angeles, CA: The Association for the Study of Classical African Civilizations.

Carruthers, J. H. (1999). *Intellectual Warfare.* Chicago, IL: Third World Press.

Clarke, J. H. (1994). *My Life in Search of Africa.* Chicago, IL: Third World Press.

Cole, M. (1996). *Cultural Psychology: A Once and Future Discipline.* Cambridge, England: Cambridge University Press.

Cole, M., & Scribner, S. (1974). *Culture and Thought: A Psychological Introduction.* Oxford, England: John Wiley & Sons.

Cooper, A. J. (1892/1988). *A Voice from the South.* Oxford: Oxford University Press.

Correa-Chavez, M., & Rogoff, B. (2009). Children's attention to interactions directed to others: Guatemalan Mayan and European American patterns. *Developmental Psychology*, 45(3), 630–641.

Darling-Hammond, L., & Oakes, J. (2019). *Preparing Teachers for Deeper Learning.* Cambridge, MA: Harvard Education Press.

Decety, J., et al. (2004). The neural bases of cooperation and competition: An fMRI investigation. *NeuroImage*, 23(2), 744–751.

Dijink, G. (2002). *National Identity and Geopolitical Visions: Maps of Pride and Pain.* London: Routledge.

Diop, C. A. (1989). *The Cultural Unity of Black Africa: The Domains of Patriarchy and of Matriarchy in Classical Antiquity.* London: Karnak House.

Drake, S. C., & Cayton, H. R. (1970). *Black Metropolis: A Study of Negro Life in a Northern City.* Chicago: University of Chicago Press.

Du Bois, W. E. B. (1897/2006). The conservation of races. *Raisons Politiques*, 1, 117–130.

DuBois, W. E. B. (1965). *The World and Africa.* New York, NY: International Publishers.

DuBois, W. E. B. (2001). *The Education of Black People: Ten Critiques, 1906–1960.* New York, NY: NYU Press.

Dussel, E. (2019). *The Pedagogics of Liberation: A Latin American Philosophy of Education.* Brooklyn, NY: Punktum Books.

Erikson, E. (1968). *Identity, Youth, & Crisis.* New York, NY: W.W. Norton.

Fanon, F. (1963). *Black Skin, White Masks.* New York, NY: Grove Press.

First Nations Education Steering Committee. (2008). *First Peoples Principles of Learning.* Retrieved from http://www.fnesc.ca/wp/wp-content/uploads/2015/09/PUB-LFP-POSTER-Principles-of-Learning-First-Peoples-poster-11x17. pdf.

Flavell, J. H., & Miller, P. H. (1998). Social cognition. In *Handbook of Child Psychology*, D. Kuhn, & R. Siegler (eds.), Vol. 2. New York, NY: Wiley, pp. 851–898.

Introduction

Gould, S. J. (1980). Shades of Lamarck. In *The Panda's Thumb: More Reflections in Natural History*, S. J. Gould (ed.), New York, NY: Norton, pp. 76–84.

Greenfield, P. (2004). *Weaving Generations Together: Evolving Creativity in the Maya of Chiapas*. Santa Fe, NM: School of American Research Press.

Guthrie, R. (1976). *Even the Rat Was White*. New York, NY: Harper & Row.

Gutiérrez, K., & Rogoff, B. (2003). Cultural ways of learning: Individual traits of cultural repertoires of practice. *Educational Researcher*, 32(5), 19–25.

Freire, P. (1968/2018). *Pedagogy of the Oppressed*. New York, NY: Bloomsbury.

Han, S., Northoff, G., Vogeley, K., Wexler, B. E., Kitayama, S., Varnum, M. E. W. (2013). A cultural neuroscience approach to the biosocial nature of the human brain. *Annual Review of Psychology*, 64, 335–359.

Herder, J. G.V. (1774/1803). *Outlines of a Philosophy of the History of Man* (T. Churchill, Trans.). Vol. 1. London: Bergman. (Originally Published in German 1774).

Hermes, M. (2007). Moving Toward the Language: Reflections on Teaching in an Indigenous-Immersion School. *Journal of American Indian Education*, 46(3), 54–71. Retrieved March 27, 2020, from www.jstor.org/stable/24398543

Hilliard, A. (1998). *The Reawakening of the African Mind*. Gainesville, FL: Makare Publishing.

Hilliard, A. G. (1995). *The Maroon within Us: Selected Essays on African American Community Socialization*. Baltimore, MD: Black Classic Press.

Horsman, Reginald A. (1986). *Race and Manifest Destiny: The Origins of American Racial Anglo-Saxonism*. Cambridge, MA: Harvard University Press.

Houston, D. D. (1926/1985). *Wonderful Ethiopians of Ancient Cushite Empire*. Baltimore, MD: Black Classic Press.

Jones, J. M. (1979). Conceptual and strategic issues in the relationship of black psychology to American social science. In *Research Directions of Black Psychologists*, A. W. Boykin, A. J. Anderson, & J. Yates (eds.), New York, NY: Russell Sage Foundation, pp. 390–432.

Jones, R. (1996). Handbook of tests and measurement for black populations. In *Handbook of Tests and Measurements for Black Populations*, R. L. Jones (ed.), Vol. 2. Hampton, VA: Cobb & Henry.

Karenga, M. (1984). *Selections from the Husia: Sacred Writings of Ancient Egypt*. Los Angeles, CA: Kawaida Press.

Karenga, M. (1993). *Introduction to Black Studies*. Los Angeles, CA: University of Sankore Press.

Karenga, M. (2006). *Maat, The Moral Ideal in Ancient Egypt: A Study in Classical African Ethics*. Los Angeles, CA: University of Sankore Press.

Kessen, W. (1979). The American child and other cultural inventions. *American Psychologist*, 34(10), 815–820.

Lave, J. (1977). Tailor-made experiments and evaluating the intellectual consequences of apprenticeship training. *Quarterly Newsletter of the Institute for Comparative Human Development*, 1(2), 1–3.

Lee, C. D. (2017). Integrating research on how people learn and learning across settings as a window of opportunity to address inequality in educational processes and outcomes. *Review of Educational Research*, 41(1), 88–111.

Lemke, J. L. (2000). Across the scales of time: Artifacts, activities, and meanings in ecosocial systems. *Mind, Culture, and Activity*, 7(4), 273–290.

Leontyev, A. N. (1978). *Activity, Consciousness, and Personality*. Oxford: Pergamon Press.

Lewis, O. (1966). *La Vida: A Puerto Rican Family in the Culture of Poverty-San Juan and New York*, Vol. 13. New York, NY: Random House.

Liss, J. E. (1998). Diasporic identities: The science and politics of race in the work of Franz Boas and WEB Du Bois, 1894–1919. *Cultural Anthropology*, 13(2), 127–166.

Lomawaima, K. T. (2004). Educating native Americans. In *Handbook of Research on Multicultural Education*, J. Banks, & C. Banks (eds.), San Francisco, CA: Jossey-Bass, pp. 441–461.

Luriiâ, A. R. (1976). *Cognitive Development: Its Cultural and Social Foundations*. Cambridge, MA: Harvard University Press.

Marks, J. (2010). Ten facts about human variation. In *Human Evolutionary Biology*, M. P. Muehlenbein (ed.), Cambridge, England: Cambridge University Press, pp. 265–276.

Markus, H., & Kitayama, S. (1991). Culture and the self: Implications for cognition, emotion, and motivation. *Psychological Review*, 98(2), 224–253.

Marx, K. (1852). *The Eighteenth Brumaire of Louis Bonaparte*. Retrieved from https://goo.gl/wE4DCD.

Marx, K. (1867/1976). *Capital: A Critique of Political Economy* (B. Fowkes, Trans.). New York, NY: Penguin.

Marx, K., & Engels, F. (1973). *The German Ideology, Part One* (C. J. Arthur, ed.). London: International Publishers.

Maslow, A. H. (1943). A theory of human motivation. *Psychological Review*, 50(4), 370.

McAdams, D. P., & Pals, J. L. (2006). A new big five: Fundamental principles for an integrative science of personality. *American Psychologist*, 61(3), 204–217.

McCarthy, T. (2009). *Race, Empire, and the Idea of Human Development*. Cambridge, England: Cambridge University Press.

McCarty, T. L., et al. (2005). Editors' Introduction: Indigenous epistemologies and education: Self-determination, anthropology, and human rights. *Anthropology and Education Quarterly*, 86(1), 1–7.

McCarty, T. & Lee, T. (2014). Crticial culturally-sustaining/revitalizing pedagogy and Indigenous education sovereignty. *Harvard Educational Review*, 84(1), 101–124.

McDermott, R., & Varenne, H. (1995). Culture as disability. *Anthropology and Education Quarterly*, 26(3), 324–348.

Miller, W. B., & Rodgers, J. L. (2001). *The Ontogeny of Human Bonding Sysytems: Evolutionary Origins, Neural Bases, and Psychological Manifestations*. New York, NY: Springer.

Mills, C. (1997). *The Racial Contract*. Ithaca, NY: Cornell University Press.

Nasir, N. I. S. (2002). Identity, goals, and learning: Mathematics in cultural practice. *Mathematical Thinking and Learning*, 4(2–3), 213–247.

Nasir, N. S. (2012). *Racialized Identities: Race and Achievement among African American Youth*. Stanford, CA: Stanford University Press.

O'Dowd, L. (2010). From a 'borderless world' to a 'world of borders': 'bringing history back in'. *Environment and Planning D: Society and Space*, 28(6), 1031–1050. Nasir 2002.

Omi, M., & Winant, H. (2015). *Racial Formation in the United States*. (3rd edition). New York, NY: Routledge.

Orr, E. W. (1987). *Twice as Less: Black English and the Performance of Black Students in Mathematics and Science*. New York, NY: Norton.

OTA/US Office of Technology Assessment. (1988). *Power On! New Tools for Teaching and Learning* (OTA-SET-379). Washington, DC: U.S. Government Printing Office.

Payne, R. K. (1999). *A Framework for Understanding and Working with Students and Adults from Poverty*. Baytown, TX: RFT Publishing.

Pea, R. D. (1985). Beyond amplification: Using computers to reorganize human mental functioning. *Educational Psychologist*, 20(4), 167–182.

Pea, R. D. (1987). Socializing the knowledge transfer problem. *International Journal of Educational Research*, 11(6), 639–663.

Pea, R. D. (2004). The social and technological dimensions of "scaffolding" and related theoretical concepts for learning, education and human activity. *The Journal of the Learning Sciences*, 13(3), 423–451.

Powell, J. (2012). *Racing to Justice: Transforming Our Conceptions of Self and Other to Build an Inclusive Society*. Bloomington, IN: Indiana University Press.

Quartz, S. R., & Sejnowski, T. J. (2002). *Liars, Lovers, and Heroes: What the New Brain Science Reveals About How We Become Who We Are*. New York, NY: William Morrow.

Ripley, W. Z. (1899). *The Races of Europe: A Sociological Study*. New York, NY: D. Appleton and Company.

Rogoff, B. (1991). *Apprenticeship in Thinking: Cognitive Development in Social Context*. Oxford: Oxford University Press.

Rogoff, B. (2003). *The Cultural Nature of Human Development*. Oxford: Oxford University Press.

Rogoff, B. (2011). *Developing Destinies: A Mayan Midwife and Town*. Oxford: Oxford University Press.

Rogoff, B., & Lave, J. (Eds.) (1984). *Everyday Cognition: Its Development in Social Context*. Cambridge, MA: Harvard University Press.

Rosenthal, L. (2016). Incorporating intersectionality into psychology: An opportunity to promote social justice and equity. *American Psychologist*, 71(6), 474–485.

Rowe, A. C. (2017). Settler Xicana: Postcolonial and decolonial reflections on incommensurability. *Feminist Studies*, 43(3), 525–536. doi:10.15767.

Rushton, J. P., & Jensen, A. R. (2005). Thirty years of research on race differences in cognitive ability. *APA Journal of Psychology, Public Policy, and Law*, 11(2), 235–294.

San Pedro, T. J. (2015). Silence as shields: Agency and resistances among Native American students in the urban Southwest. *Research in the Teaching of English*, 50(2), 132.

Saxe, G. B. (1988). Candy selling and math learning. *Educational Rresearcher*, 17(6), 14–21.

Saxe, G. B. (2012). *Cultural Development of Mathematical Ideas: Papua New Guinea Studies*. Cambridge, England: Cambridge University Press.

Scribner, S. (1977). Thinking in action: Some characteristics of practical thought. In *Practical Intelligence: Nature and Origins of Competence in the Everyday World*, R. Wagner, & R. Sternberg (eds.), Cambridge, England: Cambridge University Press, pp. 13–30.

Scribner, S. (1984). Studying working intelligence. In *Everyday Cognition: Its Development in Social Context*, B. Rogoff, & J. Lave (eds.), Cambridge, MA: Harvard University Press, pp. 9–40.

Scribner, S., & Cole, M. (1973). Cognitive consequences of formal and informal education. *Science*, 182(4112), 553–559.

Scribner, S., & Cole, M. (1981). *The Psychology of Literacy*. Cambridge, MA: Harvard University Press.

Scribner, S., & Tobach, E. (1997). *Mind and Social Practice: Selected Writings of Sylvia Scribner*. Cambridge, England: Cambridge University Press.

Sellers, R. M., Chavous, T. M., & Cooke, D. Y. (1998). Racial ideology and racial centrality as predictors of African American college students' academic performance. *Journal of Black Psychology*, 24(1), 8–27.

Serpell, R. (1979). How specific are perceptual skills? A cross-cultural study of pattern reproduction. *British Journal of Psychology*, 70(3), 365–380.

Siegel, A. W., & Kessel, F. S. (Eds.) (1983). *The Child and Other Cultural Inventions*. New York, NY: Praeger.

Smith, L. (1999). *Decolonizing Methodologies: Research and Indigenous Peoples*. London: Zed books.

Smith, L. T., Tuck, E., & Yang, K. W. (Eds.). (2018). *Indigenous and Decolonizing Studies in Education*. New York, NY: Routledge.

Spencer, M. B. (2019). Developmental and intersectional insights about diverse children's identity. *Florida Law Review*, 71(1), 12.

Spencer, H. (1860). The social organism. *Westminster Review*, 73(143), 90–121.

Spencer, M. B. (1985). Cultural cognition and social cognition as identity factors in Black children's personal-social growth. In *Beginnings: The Social and Affective Development of Black Children*, M. Spencer, G. K. Brookins, & W. Allen (ed.), Hillsdale, NJ: Lawrence Erlbaum, pp. 59–72.

Spencer, M. B. (2006). Phenomenology and ecological systems theory: Development of diverse groups. In *Handbook of Child Psychology*, W. Damon, & R. M. Lerner (eds.), Vol. 1. New York, NY: Wiley, pp. 829–893.

Stotsky, S. (1999). *Losing Our Language: How Multiculturalism Undermines Our Children's Ability To Read, Write & Reason*. San Francisco, CA: Encounter Books.

Thompson, A. (1998). Developing an African historiography. In *African World History Project: The Preliminary Challenge*, J. H. Carruthers, & L. Harris (eds.), Los Angeles, CA: Association for the Study of Classical African Civilizations, pp. 9–30.

Toulmin, S. E. (1992). *Cosmopolis: The Hidden Agenda of Modernity*. Chicago, IL: University of Chicago Press.

Uskul, A., Kitayama, S., & Nisbet, R. (2008). Ecocultural basis of cognition: Farmers and fisherman are more holistic that herders. *PNAS*, 105(25), 8552–8556.

Valencia, R. R. (2012). *The Evolution of Deficit Thinking: Educational Thought and Practice*. New York, NY: Routledge.

Vico, G. (1725). *Scienza Nuova* (The First New Science) (Leon Pompa, Trans.). Cambridge, England: Cambridge University Press, 2002.

Vygotsky, L. S. (1962). *Thought and Language*. Cambridge, MA: MIT Press.

Vygotsky, L. S. (1978). *Mind in Society: The Development of Higher Psychological Functions* (M. Cole, V. John-Steiner, S. Scribner, & E. Souberman, Eds.). Cambridge, MA: Harvard University Press.

Wartofsky, M. (1983). The child's construction of the world and the world's construction of the child: From historical epistemology to historical psychology. In *The Child and Other Cultural Inventions*, F. S. Kessel, & A. W. Sigel (eds.), New York, NY: Praeger, pp. 188–215.

Weisner, T. S. (1984). Ecocultural niches of middle childhood: A cross-cultural perspective. In *Development During Middle Childhood: The Years From Six to Twelve*, W. A. Collins (ed.), Washington, DC: National Academy Press, pp. 335–369.

Wilson, W. H., & Kamanā, K. (2011). Insights from Indigenous language immersion in Hawai ʻi. *Immersion Education: Practices, Policies, Possibilities*, 36–57.

Woodson, C. G. (1933/1969). *The Mis-Education of the Negro*. Washington, DC: The Associated Publishers.

Wynter, S. (2001). Towards the sociogenic principle: Fanon, identity, the puzzle of conscious experience, and what it is like to be 'Black'. In *National Identities and Sociopolitical Changes in Latin America*, M. Duran-Cogan, & A. Gomez-Moriana (eds.), New York, NY: Routledge, pp. 30–66.

Wynter, S. (2003). Unsettling the coloniality of being/power/truth/freedom: Towards the human, after man, its overrepresentation—An argument. *CR: The New Centennial Review*, 3(3), 257–337.

PART 1

Human Evolution, Physiological Processes, and Participation in Cultural Practices

Introduction

Human learning and development unfold in complex systems and ecologies. Human learning and development are outgrowths of the intertwining of dispositions and competencies we inherit from our evolution as a species and the ways that such dispositions and competencies are taken up through relationships between physiological processes and people's participation in cultural practices. These cultural practices are ecological in that they are manifested in relationships and the social organization of settings from the micro (e.g. family, social networks in communities, institutions such as schools, churches, community organizations) to the macro (broader societal policies and institutionalized belief systems at the societal level or more broadly across societies). Social relationships, perceptions of the self and others, tasks and settings influence goals, motivation, and persistence. The nature of these contributors to human learning and development are cultural in nature and influenced by differentiation in contexts and where we are, both in the life course and where we are situated within cultural-historical time. Among the challenges with which we wrestle across the life course are our navigations with issues of power and privilege as these influence what is available to us as sources of risk and resilience.

The chapters in this section individually and collectively wrestle with these complexities, interrogating relevant empirical, historical, and anthropological evidence from across disciplines. Packer and Cole examine evolutionary processes that have shaped the unfolding of human learning and possibility. Specifically, they examine how the processes of socialization through kinship groups organize social niches to support the development of children who can adapt to the demands of the social niche and the institutions that organize activity. They further examine the impacts of these socialization practices on neurological processing. Lee, Meltzoff, and Kuhl examine foundational human dispositions that undergird learning and development as they are evident in the learning and development of young children. They also consider the implications of these dispositions for the design of learning environments for young and older children, including implications for learning in the academic disciplines. Spencer, Offidani-Bertrand, Harris, and Velez examine learning and development through the lens of ecological systems and phenomenological meaning making, specifically drawing from research in Phenomenological Variant Ecologies Systems Theory (PVEST) to study how risk and resilience are an outgrowth of relationships between objective risks and the nature of supports available. The chapter addresses how vulnerabilities associated with racial positioning, poverty, and political disenfranchisement have been moderated and resulted in resilience because of adaptive supports. Rogers, Rosario, and Cielto address issues of risk and

Human Evolution, Physiological Processes, and Participation in Cultural Practices

resilience in human development associated with societal positioning with regard to race/ethnicity and class. They review research on risks associated with stereotype threat, but equally the buffering role of meaning making processes associated with racial identity. Rosado-May, Urrieta, Dayton, and Rogoff examine human socialization through indigenous knowledge systems. They document learning by observing and pitching in (LOPI) to family and community endeavors, anchored in a specific case of the Yucatec Maya system for passing on and creating knowledge. LOPI's strength in many Indigenous communities of the Americas provides a model of how such learning can be organized as a coherent, multifaceted way of supporting learning.

1

THE INSTITUTIONAL FOUNDATIONS OF HUMAN EVOLUTION, ONTOGENESIS, AND LEARNING

Martin Packer and Michael Cole

There is increasing agreement among developmental scientists that human psychological functioning and children's learning and development should be considered in their cultural context. Our work has explored a "bio-cultural-historical" approach to the study of children's development (e.g., Cole & Packer, 2016) and our goal in this chapter is to explore the consequences of attending not only to culture but also to human evolution. We have recently focused on how the ubiquitous phenomenon of niche construction offers a way to think about the role of culture in how humans have evolved, and how human children learn and develop (Packer & Cole, 2019).

In this chapter, then, we explore the evolutionary roots of children's learning and development. Perhaps surprisingly, given our interest in culture, our line of reasoning takes us in a different direction from the view that is popular today, that humans are involved in a special kind of "cultural evolution" which has arisen from an evolved ability for "cultural learning." Instead, we are drawn to focus on the environmental modifications that humans, like other species, make in order to exist.

It is surely an undeniable fact that humans live and care for children in constructed environmental niches that are made up of entities generally called "institutions." There have indeed been speculations about the role of institutions in ontogenesis (e.g., Rakoczy & Tomasello, 2007) and in human evolution (e.g., Richerson & Boyd, 2001), but we shall argue that what is central is the way institutions define rights and responsibilities, so that a human environmental niche is a "deontic" niche in which obligations bind people's activities not only in the present but also into the future. Institutional obligations coordinate activity over multiple time scales. This conclusion provides us with the basis upon which to offer a new definition of culture.

We then explore how children's learning and development today depend upon this distinctive kind of environmental niche. Human ontogenesis has a unique character, reflecting a uniquely human mode of reproduction. We propose that "kinship" in hunter-gatherer bands and tribes amounted to the first institution, and permitted a mode of reproduction that supported the extended and costly ontogenesis which still characterizes humans today.

Ontogenesis today occurs, then, in a complex and dynamic environment of obligatory collaboration, which caregivers modify to meet children's needs and to define a developmental pathway. In addition, children's learning and development today have been further institutionalized. Schooling is a modification of the deontic niche that defines an ontogenetic pathway that leads towards literacy, a capacity that did not exist 10,000 years ago but has become a necessity in many societies today.

A New Understanding of Evolution

In psychology today evolution is often assumed to be a slow, continuous process of random variation (genetic mutation and recombination) and invariant inheritance (replication). The ontogenesis of an individual organism is assumed to be programed by these genes, which contain the plans or instructions for the organism's development. Biologist Ernst Mayr put this point succinctly, "All of the directions, controls and constraints of the developmental machinery are laid down in the blueprint of the DNA genotype as instructions or potentialities" (Mayr, 1984, p. 1262). From this point of view, since ontogenesis involves no genetic change it has no influence on evolution (Walsh, 2014).

This was indeed how evolution was viewed by biologists during the second half of the twentieth century, in what became known as the "Modern Synthesis" (Huxley, 1942; Scott-Phillips et al., 2014). Since then, however, the key assumptions of this view have been challenged by new evidence showing that biological evolution involves more than chance and necessity (e.g., Keller, 2014; Jablonka & Lamb, 2005; Oyama, Griffiths, & Gray, 2003). It is evident that inheritance of genetic material is not the core process in evolution, and that genes are not the only kind of information guiding ontogenesis. It is becoming clear that the focus should be not only on genes but on whole organisms, or on organisms and their environments as a unity. In addition, it is apparent that changes undergone by organisms during their lifetime—results of learning and development— influence evolutionary outcomes.

The Extended Evolutionary Synthesis

An "Extended Evolutionary Synthesis" (EES) has been proposed as an extension of the Modern Synthesis (Odling-Smee et al., 2003; Pigliucci & Müller, 2010; Laland et al., 2015). The EES centers around three basic ideas:

The Active Organism in a Constructed Niche

First, organisms play an active part in their own survival and reproduction, and hence in the evolution of their species. Organisms do not merely adapt to existing conditions, they select and modify their circumstances to create an environmental niche in which they, and their offspring, are more likely to thrive. Consequently, "niche construction theory" (NCT) is a central component of the EES (Odling-Smee, 1988; Laland, Odling-Smee, & Feldman, 2000; Odling-Smee, Laland, & Feldman, 2003; Laland & Sterelny, 2006). Survival is a consequence of the organism's ongoing activity in a dynamic environment. One result is that evolutionary change can be rapid and abrupt. Biologist Kevin Laland and philosopher Kim Sterelny put the matter in these terms:

> Evolution is based on networks of causation and feedback in which organisms drive environmental change and organism-modified environments subsequently select organisms.
>
> *(Laland & Sterelny, 2006, p. 1751)*

Multiple Inheritances

The second idea is that genetic inheritance is only one of several kinds of inheritance, including epigenetic inheritance (passage of information from one generation to the next through changes in how genes are expressed; Jablonka & Raz, 2009), ecological inheritance (inheritance of the niche; Odling-Smee, 1988), and cultural inheritance (which the EES generally views as "high-fidelity transmission"; Laland, 2017).

Constructive Ontogenesis

Third, ontogenesis is a process of "constructive development." A phenotype is not simply pre-programed by the inherited genotype, it is the constructed outcome of the organism's ongoing interaction with its environment.

Evolution as an Aspect of Ontogenesis

In our opinion, the EES makes an important contribution to understanding the general process of evolution, including its relationship to ontogenesis. However, as we explored the debate between proponents of the EES and defenders of the MS we encountered the work of biologists and philosophers of biology who, though generally sympathetic to the EES, have conducted further work on each of its three central ideas. Their proposals are important to our account in this chapter.

Focus on Reproduction

First is the suggestion that reproduction is the key process in evolution. Every theory of evolution has to grapple with the link between generations, and the EES views this link as composed of inheritance of multiple kinds, of which genetic inheritance is only one. However, philosopher of biology James Griesemer emphasizes that the fundamental problem facing every living being is its mortality: the individual organism cannot live indefinitely. The solution, which species have implemented in diverse ways, is reproduction. Inheritance, Griesemer points out, is only one aspect of reproduction (Griesemer, 2016). For example, although a new organism inherits genetic material from parents, it is formed from an egg cell that was initially part of the mother's body. Development of the organism requires this cell's metabolic mechanisms, a uterine environment, and maternal provisioning, all in addition to genetic inheritance. Reproduction has itself evolved (for example, sexual reproduction appeared 1.2 billion years ago), but modes of reproduction are hard to appreciate when only inheritance is studied.

The Extended Organism

Second is the proposal that organism and environment are constituents of an indivisible whole, and that it is this which must reproduce. The EES highlights "reciprocal causation" between an organism and its environment, but this formulation suggests that organism and environment are separate entities acting causally on one another. Several researchers have proposed instead that one should think of an "organism-environment system" (Oyama, 2000; Palmer, 2004; Keller, 2014). Biologist J. Scott Turner calls this system the "extended organism" (Turner, 2000; cf. Laland, Odling-Smee, & Turner, 2014). The difference between independent entities with reciprocal causation and an inclusive system with constituents is illustrated by physiological processes such as respiration and ingestion, in which organism and environment are clearly "entangled," and their boundary is "fuzzy." Viewed this way, construction of a niche creates "distributed" functions which belong to *both* organism *and* environment. For example, the earthworm, whose ancestors lived in fresh water, transforms its environment by constructing tunnels which function as accessory kidneys, and in doing so it alters the chemical composition of the soil and the environment of future generations.

Ontogenesis Is Constitution

These two proposals lead to the third: that ontogenesis is a process not merely of construction but of "constitution." The EES proposal that ontogenesis is not programmed by the genes but is constructive implies something that is stated explicitly by "developmental systems theory", which is that ontogenesis is a process in which new properties or capabilities can emerge:

individual development is characterized by an increase in novelty and complexity of organization over time—the sequential emergence of new structural and functional properties and competencies—at all levels of analysis as a consequence of horizontal and vertical coactions among its parts, including organism-environment coactions.

(Gottlieb, Wahlsten, & Lickliter, 1998, p. 211)

An example of constitution is the emergence of the competencies needed for reproduction, which requires that specific constituents be brought together. Such emergence is not predictable, though it is explainable in retrospect as a consequence of rearrangement of constituents of the system to gain capacities previously lacking. Later in this chapter we emphasize that literacy—learning to read and write—is an emergent ability in human ontogenesis.

To summarize, where the MS viewed evolutionary change as the result of natural selection operating on genetic inheritance with random variation, the EES emphasizes the role in evolution of multiple inheritances, the reciprocal causation between organism and constructed environmental niche, and constructive ontogenesis. In addition, the work we have just summarized takes a step further by positing: (1) a process of reproduction, of which inheritance is only one aspect, (2) of an organism-environment system in which key functions are distributed, (3) whose ontogenesis is the constitution of emergent characteristics and capabilities, central among which is the capacity for reproduction (Figure 1.1).

Such a view of evolution has important implications for how ontogenesis should be viewed. The capacity for reproduction is not merely an ontogenetic achievement that marks maturity: reproduction and ontogenesis are mutually entwined, which puts ontogenesis at "the very heart of evolutionary biology" (Oyama, 2000, p. 62):

On traditional views of organism life cycles, development and reproduction are phases of life trajectories culminating in the generation of offspring, which initiate new life trajectories…. On the account of reproduction I favor, development is not a life cycle phase preceding reproduction; rather, developmental and reproduction processes are mutually embedding, entwined aspects of life made coherent by their intertwining.

(Griesemer, 2016, pp. 803, 805–806)

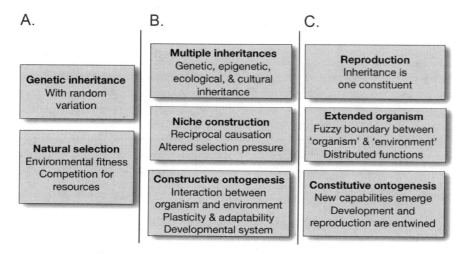

Figure 1.1 Components of evolution in (a) the Modern Synthesis, (b) the Extended Evolutionary Synthesis, and (c) an approach that emphasizes reproduction

Because evolutionary change is a consequence of the process of reproduction, it is also a consequence of ontogenesis. Rather than seeing ontogenesis as a result of evolution, one might just as easily see evolution as an aspect of ontogenesis (Griesemer, 2000a; cf. Witherington & Lickliter, 2016).

Human Evolution and Modes of Reproduction

With this understanding of evolutionary change, we can turn to the particular case of human evolution. Psychologists have offered various reconstructions of the evolution of *homo sapiens*. Evolutionary psychology, for example, maintains that human mental functioning today reflects solutions to the problems of survival in an ancient "environment of evolutionary adaptation" (Tooby & Cosmides, 1990). It assumes, like the Modern Synthesis, that evolution is slow genetic change, inherited by each new generation. Cultural evolution theory (Boyd & Richerson, 1985; 2005) posits a second mechanism of "cultural evolution" in which information is transferred from one individual to another, and so offers a "'dual inheritance theory' of the human evolutionary process" (Boyd & Richerson, 1985, p. 2). Here, both genetic inheritance and cultural inheritance are assumed to be "conventional neo-Darwinian processes" (p. 2), and culture is defined as "the transmission from one generation to the next, via teaching and imitation, of knowledge, values, and other factors that influence behavior" (p. 2).

Rather than pursue these approaches, both of which focus on transmission and inheritance, we ask what would stand out if one focused on constitution and reproduction? We sketch a brief account of two points in hominin evolution—our first hominin ancestors and Paleolithic hunter-gatherers—that is focused on the mode of reproduction that appears to have been characteristic of each.

Chimpanzees: Serial Reproduction by Single Mothers

For some time after the split between humans and chimpanzees, around 6 mya, our hominid ancestors probably lived in a manner similar to that of wild chimpanzees today. It is common to say that chimps have "family" or "kin," but this is misleading; the organization of chimpanzee reproduction and ontogenesis does not permit recognition of more than a few biological relationships. Careful observation of wild chimpanzees discloses that females usually move spontaneously to another group at puberty (around 8 years of age) to procreate and raise offspring there, so incestuous breeding is rare.

Once in the new group, mating is promiscuous and bonds are fleeting, so that chimp offspring have very limited opportunity to recognize their biological relatives. Neither mother nor baby knows who the father is, and other biologically-related individuals are unknown: the maternal grandmother, for example, was left behind in the natal group. The baby becomes familiar only with the mother and perhaps one or two sibs (Chapais, 2009).

The reproduction over time of a chimpanzee group depends on the reproduction of its individual members. However, the group contributes only minimally to individual reproduction. A chimp mother will raise one offspring at a time, which will be clinging to her or close by until weaned at about 5 years of age (Kaplan et al., 2000). The bond between mother and offspring is strong, and alloparenting is rare in chimps. Once weaned, however, offspring must fend for themselves, and many die. Furthermore, skills are not deliberately passed to offspring; young chimps must learn by observing how adults use tools and interact with other members of the group. Then, as noted, once a juvenile female reaches puberty she leaves mother and sibs to move to another group, starting the pattern over again.

Care for offspring, then, is almost entirely in the hands of the mother, who can handle only one offspring at a time, in what is called a mode of "serial reproduction." This mode is very fragile: a wild chimp group barely has sufficient live births to maintain its numbers. Chimp life expectancy at birth is less than 15 years, infant mortality is 20% in the first year, and only 50% survive to 5 years of age (Hill et al., 2001).

Hunter-Gatherers: Parallel Reproduction with Kinship Obligations

The situation around 120,000 years ago was very different. *H. sapiens* were migrating out of Africa and starting to disperse around the planet (Bae, Douka, & Petraglia, 2017). Throughout the rest of the Paleolithic they lived as hunter-gatherers, tracking and killing animals and gathering fruits, vegetables, and other foods. Hunter-gatherers today show remarkable diversity in their lifestyle, able to live in deserts, forests, and jungles, and even on the ocean. However, they share a characteristic mode of reproduction.

Hunter-gatherers today, and in all likelihood in the past, have a strikingly high fertility rate: the average number of births per woman is as high as seven or eight. They also have a low infant mortality rate, and an early adult mortality rate of only 1.2% per year (that of chimpanzees is estimated to be 4% per year; Hill et al., 2001, p. 446). Such fertility could double a community in size every 25 years (Pennington, 2001); various practices must be employed to control fertility.

A typical young woman in a hunter-gatherer band is married by puberty to a man around ten years older, and she will have a child within a few years (Konner, 2010). Like all children today, hunter-gatherer children have a short infancy followed by a childhood stage when their food is still prepared for them, then a juvenile stage which ends with a comparatively late puberty, marked by a spurt in growth. An adult female will often be nursing an infant while she has a toddler in tow, perhaps two, along with an older child.

This "parallel reproduction" is a more complex mode than the serial reproduction of chimpanzees, and it involves a long and demanding ontogenesis that requires considerable investments of time and energy by caregivers. What makes possible this mode of reproduction is that every child in a hunter-gatherer community is born into a web of reciprocal obligations. For example, among the Aché:

> The child will be held immediately after birth by a "godmother" that is responsible for washing and caring for the infant during the first few days after birth while mother rests. The child and godmother adopt ritual terms for each other, and the child can expect food, help and support from its godmother throughout its life.... Men who have provided the mother with game during her pregnancy also take on a ritual obligation to the child, and so do all the band members who hold the child and wash it soon after birth. The obligations through the life course are reciprocal such that the child is cared for by ritual 'godparents' when young and later cares for them in turn when they become elderly.
>
> *(Hill, 2008)*

These intergenerational obligations ensure successful distributed caregiving, and they reflect the way that hunter-gatherers value sharing, egalitarianism, and responsibility. Rights and responsibilities bind together not only biological relatives but the whole community. It is accepted that food ought to be shared freely, so food and care are provided to children by community members who are not their biological relatives. In fact, neither grandmothers nor fathers are particularly prominent care providers (Hurtado, 2000).

These cooperative child rearing practices have been noted by many. What has not been remarked upon, to our knowledge, is the fact that they are based upon the reciprocal obligations defined by a specific institution. This institution has been named "kinship" by ethnographers, though this label is misleading if "kin" are assumed to include only biological relatives. Hunter-gatherers, because they form stable pairs, are able to recognize multiple biological relations, but they use kin terms flexibly, not just for biological relatives. Kin terms are a resource for assigning and negotiating reciprocal obligations to bind together not just family but all members of the band. In fact, genetic analysis shows that members of a hunter-gatherer band are usually not closely related: a band is not a "family group" (Hill et al., 2011).

Kinship for hunter-gatherers, then, is not blood tie, but nor is it rigid moral obligation. It is a resource to negotiate the immediacy of face-to-face interaction (Bird-David, 1995; Schneider, 1984), providing a spontaneous, informal, and flexible way of defining relationships among people and with the environment. For example, various kin terms may be used for the same person, to trace connections through alternate routes.

In addition, hunter-gatherer kinship extends beyond relations among humans and "glues together" the world as a cosmos of interrelated entities. Hunter-gatherers do not believe that they possess their land; they understand that the land possesses them. Just as they draw no simple distinction between family and non-family, they draw none between nature and culture, or between human and animal. Persons, places, animals, and "meta-human persons" (Graeber & Sahlins, 2017) all count as kin. Hunting, for example, "is more appropriately viewed as a long-term relationship of reciprocal exchange between animals and the humans who hunt them." Hunted animals offer themselves, and "[b]y accepting such gifts from their animal benefactors, hunters incur a debt that must be repaid" (Nadasdy, 2014, p. 27).

It is likely, then, that the web of obligations of Paleolithic hunter-gatherer kinship supported a new mode of reproduction which involved *all* the community in the care and raising of children. Consequently, although ontogenesis for hunter-gatherers was more complex and costly than it had been for chimpanzees and previous hominins, their mode of reproduction was sufficiently prolific and coordinated that hunter-gatherer bands—very small by today's standards but large and complex compared with predecessors—could reproduce themselves for more than 100,000 years.

Notice that there has been no need to introduce a second evolutionary process in which only humans are involved. Humans, like every other species, construct an environmental niche, and they adapt both behaviorally and genetically to that niche, so that there is a "fuzzy boundary" between humans and their constructed niche, like other species. The key innovation, we propose, was that the hunter-gatherer niche involved, for the first time, an institution, that of kinship (Turner, 2004; Powers, van Schaik, & Lehmann, 2016). As a consequence, the environmental niche of hunter-gatherers was strikingly different from anything that had come before: it was an "institutional reality" (Searle, 2009). Nonetheless, human evolution involves all the components of evolution in general.

In the transition to the Holocene, human settlement brought further changes to human reproduction, though collaborative childrearing and its institutional setting continued. Below, we will trace the emergence of one institution that became dedicated to the preparation of children for adult life. First, though, we provide more detail on the notion of institutional reality and explain what it contributes to a new perspective on human learning and development.

Institutional Reality: A Deontic Niche

We have proposed that kinship was the first institution, defining reciprocal obligations among the members of a community within their environmental niche. More broadly, institutions are human structurings of the community-environment system that serve to stabilize both individual psychology and interpersonal interaction: they "channel and direct the thinking of the human beings who are assigned to fulfill institutionalized roles" (David, 1994, p. 218). The obligations inherent in an institution provide temporal stability to human activity and to human psychology. Consequently, institutions maintain an enduring influence: while the individuals who assume roles come and go, the institution itself persists. This is not to say that institutions never change, but they usually do so over a much longer time scale than a human lifetime.

We are certainly not the first to notice that human societies contain institutions. For example, dual-evolution theorists have argued that:

The most important cultural innovations required to support complex societies are command and control institutions that can systematically organize co-operation, co-ordination, and a division of labour in societies consisting of hundreds of thousands to hundreds of millions of people.

(Richerson & Boyd, 2001, p. 208)

Richerson and Boyd define institutions as "customary rules of behaviour that have the effect of creating sociopolitical structures serving collective functions" (Richerson & Boyd, 2001, p. 202). They follow Gintis (2009) in adopting a game-theory account of institutions as consisting of the rules that individuals employ to maximize payoff in interaction with competitors.

In contrast, we wish to emphasize that institutions—as much today as in the Pleistocene—involve a unique kind of normativity: *obligations*—rights and responsibilities—that bind people's future actions to one another. This was the insight of philosopher John Searle, who proposed that institutions are constituted by *deontic powers*. Searle suggests that every human community is an "institutional reality"; a "huge, invisible ontology" (Searle, 1995, p. 3), "invisible" because it is taken for granted as the background to everyday life, as well as to social scientific investigation. An institutional reality is made up of "institutional facts": entities—such as money, presidents, private property, parents, and degrees—which "can only exist given certain human institutions" (Searle, 2005, p. 3). Searle insists that:

The essential role of human institutions and the purpose of having institutions is not to constrain people as such, but, rather, to create new sorts of power relationships. Human institutions are, above all, *enabling*, because they create power, but it is a special kind of power. It is the power that is marked by such terms as: rights, duties, obligations, authorizations, permissions, empowerments, requirements, and certifications. I call all of these *deontic powers*.

(Searle, 2005, p. 10)

This *deontology* of institutional reality—the rights and responsibilities of participants—creates "desire-independent reasons for action," which may or may not be aligned with people's personal inclinations and desires. For example, a driver stops at a red light even though in a hurry and there is no cross-traffic.

Institutions cannot be reduced to rules that regulate interactions among rational individuals, as game theorists propose, for they define not simply rules but the powers of the players, along with deeply felt obligations among them. Furthermore, Searle's analysis implies that institutional reality is more than a matter of "customs" or "traditions." Those are conventional ways things have been done in the past (e.g., Clegg & Legare, 2016). A deontology, in contrast, is a kind of normativity that *binds* people, including those not yet born, with respect to not only their actions in the present but also their *future* actions. To assume an institutional role as professor, for example, is to acknowledge the university's rules and regulations. This ability to define a future "ought to be" is unique to humans (Peregrin, 2014); great apes, even when raised by humans, are able to cooperate and collaborate but unable to learn the force of binding obligations (Tomasello & Vaish, 2013).

It is because of this future-binding character that institutions serve human reproduction. They enable caregivers, and society in general, to make arrangements for children that extend into the future, even beyond death. Of course, *literal* kinds of inheritance are institutional obligations: inheritance of status, property, and territory after a testator's death. But institutions also ensure provisions for the future that take effect earlier in development, such as signing a contract to enroll a newborn in an exclusive school which they will attend years later. Institutions are proleptic, bringing the imagined future into a child's present, to ensure the continuity of a family and its territory. Key aspects of human reproduction are managed in a single, complexly organized process of inhabiting and reproducing an environmental niche.

In short, institutions are key to the kind of environmental niche that humans construct and crucial to the survival, reproduction, and ontogeny of a human community:

> Without institutions, humans do not survive, and societies do not exist. Institutions are thus fundamental to the viability of humans as a species.
>
> *(Turner, 2004, p. 2)*

Human viability depends on the deontic powers of institutional facts: "the glue that holds human civilization together" (Searle, 2009, p. 9). The human constructed environmental niche, the institutional reality of a human community, is a *deontic* niche.

Redefining Culture

Every definition rests on assumptions, and most definitions of culture treat it as inheritance, sometimes explicitly (as in the case of cultural evolution theory), but more often implicitly. Certainly the term "culture" has been used in a variety of informal and undefined ways, and has proved remarkably difficult to define (Kroeber & Kluckhohn, 1952; Baldwin et al., 2006). A recent survey of the members of the Cultural Evolution Society found that their principal concern is the lack of a broadly accepted definition of culture (Brewer et al., 2017). After the cognitive revolution of the 1950s it became popular to define culture as the knowledge, skills, and values possessed by individual members of a community and passed to the next generation. Many proponents of the idea that humans are involved in a second evolutionary process of cultural learning have adopted a definition of precisely this type: culture is "information stored in brains, rather than genes" (Mesoudi, 2016, p. 17). Others have adopted a broader view, such as the editors of a collection of essays on cultural evolution: "we define culture as the ideas, skills, attitudes, and norms that people acquire by teaching, imitation, and/or other kinds of learning from other people" (Richerson & Christiansen, 2013, p. 3). Defining culture this way, in terms of inheritance, was intended to identify something unique to humans. However, social transmission has been documented not only in our close cousins the other primates but also in whales, dolphins, and rats, and it seems that more species are added to the list every year.

Once one shifts focus from inheritance to reproduction it becomes evident that there is a way to define culture that does justice to both what is unique to humans and to our continuity with other species. The authors have argued that culture should be conceptualized as the "medium" in which humans live and develop and that, more specifically, culture should be defined in terms of the artifacts which *mediate* human activity (Cole, 1996; Cole & Packer, 2011; Packer & Goicoechea, 2000). Every artifact is an aspect of the material world that has been modified over the history of its incorporation into goal-directed practical activity, and human artifacts include not only simple everyday tools and signs but also more complex material representations, including speech, texts, and works of art. These are what Herskovits (1948) famously referred to as "the man (sic) made part of the environment." Through the construction of artifacts the circumstances of each human generation are conditioned by the residue of prior generations.

However, there is evidently considerable *continuity* between humans and other species in the construction of specialized environments. Although much is made of the impact humans are having on the Earth, other species have had an equal or greater impact. Darwin's final book celebrated the transformative power of earthworms: "long before [humans] existed the land was in fact regularly ploughed, and still continues to be thus ploughed by earth-worms. It may be doubted whether there are many other animals which have played so important a part in the history of the world, as have these lowly organised creatures" (Darwin, 1985/1881, p. 313).

The transformations that worms and other species produce should be considered artifacts that are necessary for their existence (Turner, 2003). Consequently, if we want to call *culture* this residue of activity that acts as the medium for subsequent generations, then many species other than humans have created culture. Let us, then, use "Culture" with a capital-C for this broad sense of the term. In this sense, "gene-Culture co-evolution" is not unique to humans (Feldman & Laland, 1996), but has occurred for many millions of years.

Consequently, if there is something unique to human culture it cannot be identified either with the information inherited by one individual from another, or with the production of environmental modifications conceived of as artifacts. Where then, should one locate the undeniable difference between humans and other species? From our current perspective, our previous approach was one-sidedly characterizing human culture in terms of the *means* of activity. We acknowledged the importance of a cultural group's norms and values only in asserting the fundamental "goal-directedness" of human action, into which artifacts are incorporated. We did not, however, explore the source of these goals.

Now, however, we would emphasize that the artifacts of a human society, as distinct from those of other species, are institutional facts with deontic powers. Analysis of the human niche in terms of the deontology (the *ought*) and the ontology (the *is*) of these institutional facts provides the basis for a definition of the kind of culture that is unique to humans: let us call it culture with a small "c." This definition maintains our prior emphasis on artifacts and the practices which they mediate, while placing them in the larger context of the institutional character of human society. Institutional facts mediate human activity owing simultaneously to their physical affordances and their deontic powers: the various kinds of obligation associated with their use; the duties, rights, authorizations, and laws according to which they can be employed. In the institutional reality of a university, a dean *could* vacuum the carpet of her office, but what she is *obliged* to do is attend to student well being. Students, equally, *could* cut class, but they are *obliged* to take the final exam. Human culture is this fusion of deontology and ontology, embodied in the materially constituted institutional reality that functions to bind together a human community.

This approach emphasizes that culture is a key characteristic of the human niche, rather than a characteristic of the human mind. We want to avoid the common assumption that culture is an interpretation, a mental representation, that is superimposed on biology and nature. On the contrary, culture is the "ought" and "is" of the material arrangements of the institutional reality of a human community. For members of the community, these objects and obligations are central aspects of daily experience. However, because institutional reality has been, as Searle put it, a "huge, invisible ontology" it has been difficult to articulate a clear definition of the concept of culture.

Human Ontogenesis in an Institutional Reality: An Extended Ontogenetic System

To review, we began by sketching a view of evolution that focuses on reproduction, sees organism and environment as an extended system, and emphasizes that ontogenesis is not preprogramed maturation but the constitution of emergent abilities. Then we suggested that when humans lived as hunter-gatherers a complex and costly ontogenesis became both necessary and possible. It became *possible* because the first institution, kinship, defined reciprocal obligations—future-binding rights and responsibilities—that guaranteed the investment of time and care required to support this new mode of reproduction. Human ontogenesis became a collaborative enterprise in which institutions played a key part, entangled with biological processes that had evolved to be tuned to the environment. This complex and costly ontogenesis became *necessary* because children had more to learn than their hominin predecessors—not only the use of tools and a native language or proto-language, but also the ability to live in an institutional reality that defined what persons, animals, events, and entities "counted as," and what they ought to do.

We turn now to the implications of the institutional character of human life for human ontogenesis today. Children are born into, and develop within, environments whose character, complexity, and dynamism have only recently been recognized by developmental science. A central ontogenetic task for all children is to acquire an understanding of this deontic niche in which they live. This understanding, we believe, is relatively slow and difficult to achieve, but it is essential for the continued existence—the reproduction—of every human community, and for children's reproduction as individuals.

Key human developmental phenomena are themselves institutional facts. For example, when conception occurs, the processes leading to and following from this critical event are woven into the deontic niche, whose rights and responsibilities specify, among other matters, who ought and who ought not to have a baby. Conception is an institutional fact, not solely a biological event. Similarly, every child is born a member of a family and a citizen of a state, so that a newborn baby has "unchosen institutional obligations" which must be recognized, understood, and fulfilled when the time comes (Hardimon, 1994). Indeed, "[t]he duties and rights of the adult are the reciprocal of the duties and rights of the child. At each age the duties and rights of adults and children differ, finally approximating the balance which characterizes adult relations" (Baumrind, 1974, p. 78).

Children's extended dependence on caregivers means that physiological and psychological functions are distributed between child and adults. The newborn, for example, depends upon caregivers to feed her, move her, and change her. Processes, capabilities, and resources that are often assumed to be located in the individual child are better viewed as properties of an extended system. For example, the components of emotion—physiological changes, evaluation, appraisal, action— are distributed among infant and caregivers: an infant makes rapid intuitive evaluations, while the action in response to these evaluations is provided by caregivers, who do so in terms of their rights and responsibilities.

Consequently, from conception onwards every child is *already* participating in an institutional reality although, of course, only coming to understand this gradually. When, for example, a toddler is taken to the grocery store and picks out candy she participates in intricate institutional systems of production and exchange. It would be inaccurate to think that ontogenesis is a matter of socialization or enculturation if by this one meant that a child were born outside culture, someone lacking its norms. On the contrary, adults make adjustments to ensure that children are always participating, within the limits of their capabilities.

In addition, adult caregivers in many species make local adjustments to their niche to meet the needs of offspring. The results have been called "ontogenetic niches" (West & King, 1987) and "developmental niches" (Harkness & Super, 1994). The human developmental niche is, however, more than the physical arrangements caregivers make, or their tacit theories of child development, because it is characterized by modifications of institutional reality to foster a child's survival and development. It is helpful to think of child, caregivers, and developmental niche as forming a dynamic system of obligatory collaboration; an "extended ontogenetic system" which developmental scientists need to study as a whole (Packer & Cole, 2019).

One could say, then, that children develop within a web of "deontic affordances" which provides both resources and constraints for learning and development (Kaufmann & Clément, 2007). Primates and monkeys are capable of in-the-moment normativity in face-to-face-interactions (de Waal, 2014), but only human children live within, and come to understand, the complex deontology of institutions such as law, finance, science, and education.

Growing up within an institutional reality, children learn not only what they can and cannot do—their physical possibilities and limitations—but also what they *ought* and *ought not* do. This aspect of human ontogenesis is invisible, or taken for granted, by cultural learning theory, which maintains that social norms are inherited by children from adults in a uniquely human transmission process parallel to genetic inheritance in biological evolution. That theory assumes that social norms and values exist only in the brains of individuals and so are invisible to the developing child. If one starts from this assumption, the only mechanism by which children could acquire the normativity of their community is indeed through transfer from brain to brain. However, since the human niche is made up of institutions, the deontology of a community is not invisible at all: it is evident in the patterns of people's interactions and in the arrangement of the child's surroundings.

Indeed, much of the information that current theories of cultural learning assume is transmitted from one person to another is in fact located in the community's persisting deontic niche. Of course children do imitate, and human caregivers do instruct in ways that other species cannot, but an account of children's development only in terms of these processes would be grossly incomplete. Equally, human ontogenesis is not simply the result of past adaptations to a lost environment, adaptations which were captured in the genes and are now programed to appear. Ontogenesis involves adaptation to the present; during an extended period of dependence and neurological plasticity human children have intimate contact and interaction with caretakers while they are highly sensitive to learning from such experiences, and while caregivers are bound by the obligations of the various institutions of the community in which they live.

Of course, children's institutional rights and responsibilities and those of their caregivers vary from one community to another, depending on the particular configuration of the family and how it relates to the deontic niche of the community as a whole. Caregivers' obligations define a caregiving style, which in turn defines a pathway of ontogenesis, as the research of Keller and colleagues shows (e.g., Keller et al., 2004). Consequently, while children's developmental task of grasping institutional reality is universal, its outcome varies across cultures as ontogenesis leads to different ways of being a person across the planet.

Furthermore, the family is not the only institution that creates an extended ontogenetic system and defines a pathway of development. Arguably, the institution that today has the greatest influence on children's learning and development is the school.

The Institutionalization of Learning

Although adults have always organized the conditions of children's learning, the particular kind of organization called schooling has been so pervasive across so much of the world's population for so many generations that it can be difficult to keep in mind that it is an institution, not a natural setting. Even today, however, a great many of the world's children have little or no direct experience of schooling, and a vast majority have not mastered the basics of an elementary school education by current educational standards. Nonetheless, to a greater or lesser extent in different times and places, schooling has become central to a human niche organized around technologies and forms of knowledge directed towards the questionable goal of seeking mastery of both the human community and the natural world.

Schooling is of particular interest to those studying ontogeny and evolution, beyond its obvious relevance to the topics of learning and development, because schooling has a long history and has been an object of intense interest to social scientists for more than a century. Moreover, with the advent of new technologies for analysis of neurological processes, schooling serves as a rich illustration of the ways evolutionary history, sociocultural history, and proximal environmental circumstances combine to create developmental pathways consistent with community reproduction.

The Origins of Schooling

For all of human history, children have learned skills necessary for successful reproduction through participation with older children and adults in the everyday activities required to provide food and shelter. Among early humans, learning was part of daily life, as adults adjusted their activities to accommodate the presence of children in the community while maintaining their well being (de Haan, 1999). This multigenerational, participatory organization of children's learning sufficed for the reproduction of both hunter-gatherer bands and, after the emergence of settlement, of small farming communities engaged in agriculture. Over time, however, as new technologies appeared, such as pottery and weaving, and new and more elaborate divisions of labor emerged to support increasing populations, the necessity arose to keep track of the rapidly expanding amount and variety of goods exchanged between increasingly large and complex cities and the surrounding rural areas. Over the centuries, as agriculture spread there were more goods to exchange and trade with more distant communities. The need to remember who was obligated to whom for what began to exceed the capacity of oral memory. Inscriptions, marks on a material surface such as an animal bone or a cave wall, date back at least 17,000 years in the form of lunar calendars and the like. However, in Sumeria around 6,000 ya inscriptions began to be used to mediate these economic exchanges. This became one of at least five independent inventions of written language. In the Sumerian case, tokens were inscribed with marks indicating small quantities and kinds of exchanged goods such as grain and animals. These inscriptions were simultaneously a new way of remembering, a new medium of exchange (in time to become money), and the precursor of both literacy and numeracy (Schmandt-Besserat, 1992).

As social grouping increased in size and complexity the token system also developed, now a vital constituent of the environmental niche of a way of life today called the Bronze Age (Olson, 1994). In place of networks of small towns and villages distributed among farms, cities grew, supporting populations as large as 50–80,000 people. Tokens were incorporated into a larger and more complex system of cuneiform writing: the creation of wedge-shaped inscriptions on clay tablets. This was part of an overall reconfiguration of society which included new technologies for smelting ore into swords and plowshares, a hierarchical social structure with a king, organized religion, extensive networks of high volume trade, and increasing warfare between competing city states (Adams, 1981).

Written language and numbers were by then essential technologies of record keeping, supporting the multiplying exchange processes and the mutual obligations of people to adhere to norms of reciprocity. This meant that scribes and accountants were needed, but the new system of record-keeping required years to master. It was under these conditions that the first formal schools appeared.

Institutionalized Public Basic Schooling

Even such a brief examination of the origins of schooling and its relationship to the growth of societies makes it clear that schooling has been an institutional constituent in the process of human evolution for at least 4,000 years. It has become increasingly central, and it is on this institutionalization of children's learning that we now focus. School, like learning alongside adults, involved an adaptation of children's circumstances in order to foster ontogenesis, but this time in service of a particular, specialized ability, hitherto unknown in the history of the human species. Those first schools—in which children and youth were separated from their family obligations for at least part of each day to be instructed in the mastery of specific techniques by adults who were typically not kin—show some remarkable similarities to aspects of classroom-based schooling today: an instructor stood in front of a group of students who wrote their exercises on clay tablets to master the form, content, and uses of writing and mathematics.

That is to say, the specialized ability that schools were created to inculcate was the ability to read and write words and numbers. As we shall describe below, becoming literate requires many hours of deliberate instruction and extensive practice that result in a profound reorganization of brain structure and function. School amounted to a completely new environment which, as it spread worldwide, placed strong selective pressure on children. The earliest schools were restricted to the training of an essential group of elite specialists. Today, in contrast, attending school has become universal and compulsory in many parts of the world. This fact reflects the way that literacy has become an essential ability for adults in most societies. Literacy has gone from being an elite skill to becoming a universal requirement. Yet schooling continues to respond to the demands of the state, the economy, and the organization of daily life by providing a constant supply of individuals with a great range and depth of literacy/numeracy skills essential for the reproduction of society.

Over the last 150 years there has been a remarkable spread of a particular standardized model of schooling which has been called "Institutionalized Public Basic Schooling" (IPBS) (Serpell & Hitano, 1997). The avowed aim of IPBS is to prepare every child for the modern world by bringing them to at least a minimal level of literacy and numeracy. It ostensibly seeks to provide equal access to education to all children, no matter what their social class, gender, or ethnicity. It does so through learning which centers around the role of "teachers" whose responsibility it is to instruct "students" through a sequence of homogenous-age grades. Typically, IPBS involves coeducation, individual work, authorized competence, and standardized evaluation. Although many of these practices are "at best extrinsic to the principal goals of basic education, and may often serve to obstruct those goals" (Serpell & Hitano, 1997, p. 369), they have become second nature to many of us.

Extensive data on the consequences of spending many thousands of hours promoting children's literacy/numeracy skills and the domains of knowledge these underpin have been collected on levels of analysis ranging from changes in the social organization of society to the organization of specialized functional systems in the brain.

Sociological studies have emphasized the way schools build human capital and sort students into levels of ability. Psychological studies have documented a shift from a syntagmatic, event-oriented mode of categories to paradigmatic, logic-based categories, and the use of such categories in remembering, verbal problem solving, etc.

Time and again, research on the influence of schooling on cognitive processes as diverse as syllogistic reasoning, sorting sets of pictures into categories, and memory for various kinds of material, points to the centrality of special forms of language use (Cole & Packer, 2016). In seeking an explanation of the way a shift in use of language is implicated in children's cognition, it has been noted that learning in school is distinct as a consequence of the fact that school children are expected to acquire knowledge not only from personal experience nor from being told by an authority; instead, they must also extract knowledge from written and printed signs. Children must decode these inscriptions to identify the words and numbers they represent, and so obtain the meaning of a text. That is to say, the curriculum of schooling today, like its counterpart in the ancient Middle East, takes as its central task instruction in literacy: reading/writing and numeracy. In every lesson, interaction between teacher and students is mediated through an artificial system of inscribed signs.

The Gateway to School Knowledge

In order to succeed in school, children must draw upon their skills with spoken language to figure out how unfamiliar inscriptions can provide access to the knowledge they are supposed to be acquiring. They must grasp the way that letters and words (graphemes) represent the sounds (the phonemes) of spoken language: the "alphabetic principle" (Liberman, Shankweiler, & Liberman, 1989). The connection between graphemes and phonemes is conventional and arbitrary, as demonstrated by the variety of writing systems around the world. Consequently, no child could discover this connection unaided. Adults—teachers and caregivers—have to provide the connection by engaging with child and text and helping convert the graphemes into sound and meaning.

Furthermore, a simple ability to sound out the parts of each written word is insufficient. Children must be able to infer the meaning of a text as a whole. As they advance through the curriculum children need to constantly increase the speed at which they are able to scan words and phrases and understand their meaning. In the USA, a student in first grade is expected to read around 23 words per minute (wpm). In second grade this should have increased to 70 wpm, and by grade three to 90 wpm. Highly literate adults can read on average 200 to 250 wpm.

Becoming literate, then, requires instruction, but once literacy is achieved it becomes the basis for further instruction. Literacy is a "gateway" to school knowledge, and success in the school's text-based curriculum is subsequently a gateway to a career and economic advancement. The level of school attendance in a country is taken as a measure of its social capital, and levels of schooling are indeed correlated with economic development, energy consumption, et cetera. Schooling is viewed as an investment in children, who will in turn become productive members of society.

In part, however, this link between school success and societal advancement is due to the fact that "school knowledge" is simply attributed greater value and status than vocational and pragmatic knowledge and skills. Schools valorize the everyday knowledge of the economically advantaged, while they stigmatize and ignore the everyday knowledge of others. Indeed, the everyday knowledge of manual workers is often treated as so deficient in comparison with that of the middle and upper classes that working class children are simply assumed to be unsuited to institutionalized schooling. This "binary conceptualization" of two kinds of knowledge (Mutemeri, 2013) reinforces existing tensions between manual workers and middle class professionals, and creates a barrier to school success for children from working class backgrounds.

In addition, as many as one child in five will have difficulty learning to read. Those who have books at home and caregivers who read to them will have an easier time. Consequently, it is the children with fewer economic resources, both in school and at home, who will have more trouble passing through the gateway of literacy to gain access to textual knowledge. In addition, the oral language of classroom instruction is often an unfamiliar dialect, and in extreme cases is not even the children's native language. Access to the text-based curriculum is not equal for all children. Working class children are unable to draw upon their everyday experiences in order to succeed in school, and are equally unable to apply what they learn in school in their everyday activities. For many children, school and home become pitted against each other.

Adding to the challenges, success in school tasks is usually interpreted not as a consequence of prior knowledge or alignment with the values of institutionalized schooling, but as an indication of innate "ability," and it often then comes to be understood in this way by the children themselves (Parsons, 1959). School encourages and perpetuates stereotypes about innate capacity.

The recognition that school is an institution brings into sight the fact that alongside its official curriculum is a "hidden curriculum." The "institutional regulations and routines" of school include "the standardization of the school environment, and the compulsory quality of daily attendence [sic]" (Jackson, 1968, p. 35, p. 5). Hence, it is in school that the young child "comes to grips with the facts of institutional life" (p. vii), and often these facts clash harshly with family practices and values (Cf. Hedegaard & Fleer, 2019).

Consequently, institutionalized schooling routinely falls short of its aspirations. For a few children it is a stepping stone to higher education and a professional career; for many it provides merely preparation for and access to low paying work that offers few opportunities. Those who fail in school will encounter extremely limited employment possibilities. By defining a sequence of gateways through which fewer and fewer children can pass, schooling perpetuates and legitimates economic inequalities. In separating children from the work and customs of the family, which often depends on children's work and which provides them with skills and a sense of identity, it undercuts traditional and minority ways of life.

Once these aspects of the IPBS have been recognized, it is no great surprise to learn that it has been a powerful instrument of colonialism. The anthropologist Claude Lévi-Strauss pointed out that:

> the European-wide movement towards compulsory education in the nineteenth century went hand in hand with the extension of military service and the systematization of the

proletariat. The struggle against illiteracy is indistinguishable, at times, from the increased powers exerted over the individual citizen by the central authority.

(Lévi-Strauss, 1961/1955, p. 293)

The issue that confronts educational professionals has always been "how to manage planfully the process of human development to conform with the economic goals and cultural values of a society" (Serpell & Hitano, 1997, p. 341). School as an institution has a key role in the reproduction—or transformation—of modern society, and it fulfills this role through its influence on human ontogeny.

Literacy and the Brain

The profundity of this influence has become evident in recent neuroscience research. We have noted that not all children are successful in learning to read and write in school. However, what is more surprising is that any children are able to do so. If human psychological functioning consisted of mental modules that evolved to solve problems of life in the Pleistocene era and have changed little since, reading and writing would presumably be impossible; there has seemingly been insufficient evolutionary time for the human brain to adapt to the invention of writing systems. The real question is, then, how do children become literate at all?

Neurological research offers an answer to that question by providing clear evidence that learning to read and write requires the development of a specialized functional brain system that enables rapid decoding of the graphic signs that are the letters of a writing system. The child's brain changes, structurally and functionally, as the connection is made between graphemes and phonemes (Dehaene et al., 2015).

A key neurological change occurs in the left ventral occipitotemporal cortex, which in non-literate persons is involved in the recognition of faces. This area starts to become specialized in the increasingly rapid recognition of strings of letters and their translation into sequences of sounds. It becomes a "visual word form area" (VWFA). Remarkably, the recognition of faces is now displaced to the other hemisphere. A direct anatomical connection forms between Broca's area (which undergirds oral language) and an area in the occipital (visual) cortex that is specialized for the perception of graphic inscriptions of the sort involved in letter recognition (or the equivalent). At the same time, other nearby brain regions are drawn into this developing network (Dehaene et al., 2015). Strikingly, as the anatomical and functional links between graphemic and phonemic representations are strengthened, the left-hemisphere network that processes speech becomes activated by the sight of printed text. The new functional system also modifies the neurological coding of phonemes: that is to say, becoming literate changes the way that *oral* language is processed in the brain.

In short, the activity of reading makes new use of cortical circuits that are universal, especially circuits for visual recognition and face processing. It reworks and rewires these circuits, "recycling" them for the new task. The result is that reading can become as fast and effortless as speaking, even though reading is a very new ability for our species and speaking a very old one. The neurological evidence reflects the fact that the human brain is unusually plastic and flexible, and it would be a mistake to assume that the abilities of children today—whether learned in school or elsewhere in the community—are in any simple sense defined by adaptations that occurred 100,000 years ago. Schooling exploits the emergent character of human ontogenesis: completely new capabilities can emerge if the appropriate constituents are assembled. Literacy is a truly emergent competence in human ontogenesis; studying a child's genes would give no clue that it could be possible. But when the constituents—a plastic brain, a text, a literate adult—are brought together, this remarkable competence is the result.

Conclusions

We have offered an account of the complex relationships between evolution in general, human evolution in particular, and children's psychological development and learning. We have suggested that, in the light of new ideas about the evolutionary process, an evolutionary perspective in developmental science should pay attention to reproduction (of both individuals and communities), to the ways that organisms are extended into an environment that often they, or their ancestors, have constructed, and to ontogenesis as a process that is constitutive and emergent.

We have proposed that what was unique in human evolution was the emergence of a new mode of reproduction, supported by the obligations of kinship, the first institution. The human niche became, and has remained, an institutional reality and a deontic niche. The new mode of reproduction involved an extended and expensive ontogenesis in which brains grew larger post-utero, with resulting flexibility and plasticity. In addition, humans, like other species, modify their niche to accommodate their offspring. The human ontogenetic niche forms, we have suggested, an extended ontogenetic system, in which psychological functions are distributed, ontogenesis leads to emergence of capabilities that are not predictable from the genotype alone, and in which the need to reproduce the institutional reality of a community defines key developmental tasks.

School is a particular case of a modification to the human niche which aims to ensure that children acquire specific abilities. We have pointed to the ways, both positive and negative, in which schooling contributes to the reproduction of society, and also to the future well being and reproductive success or ill health and disadvantage of individuals, over multiple generations. For example, young women living in poverty who attend school become better able to deal with bureaucracies, and their children subsequently benefit from this ability (Levine et al., 2012). At the same time, these children are seldom able to escape the poverty of their circumstances. The phenomenon of schooling illustrates the ways an institution can sustain the organization of society by defining ontogenetic pathways so as to ensure its reproduction.

Learning to read and write is the gateway to academic achievement, which in turn opens the door to better paying jobs, greater wealth, and involvement in the global system of consumer capitalism. At the same time, by tending to select and certify children who are already economically advantaged, institutional schooling plays a significant role in perpetuating and legitimating cycles of inequality and ill health. The institution of school literally shapes "human nature" to create kinds of people who, by and large, take for granted the institutions of today's "developed" nationstate, unsustainable though these may well be in the long run.

School literacy is a particularly clear example, then, of the interweaving of ontogenesis, societal change, and evolutionary change, and of the emergent character of ontogenesis. Literacy emerges in a child's development not because of an ancestral adaptation in distant times but because, despite the fact that all humans lacked the ability merely 4,000 years ago, it becomes possible when the appropriate conditions are assembled. Reading must be first distributed among child, text, and adult before it subsequently becomes an ability that a child applies to a text without adult involvement.

Becoming literate literally rewires the brain. Grasping the link between the visual (written or printed inscriptions) and the auditory (the sounds of words) involves a transformation from the indirect—practice with books and conversation with a literate adult—to the direct—a neural pathway between visual and auditory cortices so as to create a new functional neurological system. This neurological transformation can occur only within the extended ontogenetic system, which in turn it reorganizes.

If literacy is emergent in ontogenesis, clearly not a result of either maturation or individual construction, might it not be the case that other important abilities in ontogenesis are also emergent? Theory of mind, for example, or "we intentionality" (Tomasello, 2019)? After all, there is no reason to think that the kind of transformation that results from participation in institutionalized schooling is unique to this institution. Without doubt participation in other institutions invites similar changes in brain and body. There are in fact now multiple examples, among them structural brain changes in people training to become London taxi drivers (Woollett & Maguire, 2011); becoming chefs (Cerasa et al., 2017); and becoming divers (Liu et al., 2017). It seems indubitable that humans are transformed by their participation in each of the institutions in which they live and work, and these transformations undoubtedly feed back into the process of human evolution, in the ways we sketched at the beginning of this chapter.

Human ontogenesis, then, is not solely a result of cultural transmission, nor is it an individual construction, nor is it maturation programmed by ancient adaptations that were captured in the genes. Humans share with other organisms the ability, indeed the necessity, to construct an environment in which to live, though the human environment is unique in being a deontic niche. Human children grow and develop in complex and diverse environments which distribute their physiological and psychological functions by defining future-binding rights and responsibilities. Children's learning and development today, moreover, must be seen against the backdrop of the fundamental process of reproduction, in which individual human organisms are entangled and embedded with one another, with their community and its technology, language, and institutions, and ultimately with the planet.

References

Adams, R. McC. (1981). *Heartland of Cities: Surveys of Ancient Settlement and Land Use on the Central Floodplain of the Euphrates*. Chicago, IL: University of Chicago Press.

Bae, C. J., Douka, K., & Petraglia, M. D. (2017). On the origin of modern humans: Asian perspectives. *Science, 358*(6368), eaai9067.

Baldwin, J. R., Faulkner, S. L., Hecht, M. L., & Lindsley, S. L. (Eds.) (2006). *Redefining Culture: Perspectives across the Disciplines*. Hillsdale, NJ: Erlbaum.

Baumrind, D. (1974). Coleman II: Utopian fantasy and sound social innovation. *The School Review, 83*(1), 69–84.

Bird-David, N. (1995). Hunter-gatherers' kinship organization: Implicit roles and rules. In: E. N. Goody (Ed.), *Social Intelligence and Interaction: Expressions and Implications of the Social Bias in Human Intelligence* (pp. 68–84). Cambridge, UK: Cambridge University Press.

Boyd, R., & Richerson, P. J. (1985). *Culture and the Evolutionary Process*. Chicago, IL: University of Chicago Press.

Boyd, R., & Richerson, P. J. (2005). *The Origin and Evolution of Cultures*. New York, NY: Oxford University Press.

Brewer, J., Gelfand, M., Jackson, J. C., MacDonald, I. F., Peregrine, P. N., Richerson, P. J. et al. (2017). Grand challenges for the study of cultural evolution. *Nature Ecology and Evolution, 1*(3), 1–3.

Cerasa, A., Sarica, A., Martino, I., Fabbricatore, C., Tomaiuolo, F., Rocca, F. et al. (2017). Increased cerebellar gray matter volume in head chefs. *PloS One, 12*(2), e0171457.

Chapais, B. (2009). *Primeval Kinship: How Pair-Bonding Gave Birth to Human Society*. Cambridge, MA: Harvard University Press.

Clegg, J. M., & Legare, C. H. (2016). Instrumental and conventional interpretations of behavior are associated with distinct outcomes in early childhood. *Child Development, 87*(2), 527–542.

Cole, M. (1996). *Cultural Psychology: A Once and Future Discipline*. Cambridge, MA: Harvard University Press.

Cole, M., & Packer, M. (2011). Culture in development. In: M. H. Bornstein & M. E. Lamb (Eds.), *Developmental Science: An Advanced Textbook* (6th ed., pp. 51–107). Hillsdale; New Jersey; New York, NY & London: Psychology Press; Taylor & Francis.

Cole, M., & Packer, M. (2016). A bio-cultural–historical approach to the study of development. In: M. J. Gelfand, C.-y. Chiu & Y.-y. Hong (Eds.), *Handbook of Advances in Culture and Psychology* (Vol. 6, pp. 1–75). Oxford: Oxford University Press.

Darwin, C. (1985). *The Formation of Vegetable Mould, through the Action of Earth Worms, with Observations on Their Habits*. London: John Murray. (Original work published 1881).

David, P. A. (1994). Why are institutions the 'carriers of history'?: Path dependence and the evolution of conventions, organizations and institutions. *Structural Change and Economic Dynamics, 5*(2), 205–220.

de Haan, M. (1999). *Learning as Cultural Practice: How Children Learn in a Mexican Mazahua Community*. Amsterdam: Thela Thesis.

de Waal, F. B. M. (2014). Natural normativity: The 'is' and 'ought' of animal behavior. *Behaviour*, *151*(2–3), 185–204.

Dehaene, S., Cohen, L., Morais, J., & Kolinsky, R. (2015). Illiterate to literate: Behavioural and cerebral changes induced by reading acquisition. *Nature Reviews: Neuroscience*, *16*(4), 234–244.

Feldman, M. W., & Laland, K. N. (1996). Gene-culture coevolutionary theory. *Trends in Ecology & Evolution*, *11*(11), 453–457.

Gintis, H. (2009). *The Bounds of Reason: Game Theory and the Unification of the Behavioral Sciences*. Princeton, NJ: Princeton University Press.

Gottlieb, G., Wahlsten, D., & Lickliter, R. (1998). The significance of biology for human development: A developmental psychobiological systems view. In: W. Damon & R. M. Lerner (Eds.), *Handbook of Child Psychology* (pp. 210–257). Hoboken, NJ: Wiley Online Library.

Graeber, D., & Sahlins, M. (2017). *On Kings*. Chicago, IL: HAU Books.

Griesemer, J. R. (2000). Reproduction and the reduction of genetics. In: P. J. Burton, R. Falk & H.-J. Rheinberger (Eds.), *The Concept of the Gene in Development and Evolution: Historical and Epistemological Perspectives* (pp. 240–285). New York, NY: Cambridge University Press.

Griesemer, J. R. (2016). Reproduction in complex life cycles: Toward a developmental reaction norms perspective. *Philosophy of Science*, *83*(5), 803–815.

Hardimon, M. O. (1994). Role obligations. *The Journal of Philosophy*, *91*(7), 333–363.

Harkness, S., & Super, C. M. (1994). The developmental niche: A theoretical framework for analyzing the household production of health. *Social Science and Medicine*, *38*(2), 217–226.

Hedegaard, M., & Fleer, M. (Eds.). (2019). *Children's Transitions in Everyday Life and Institutions*. London: Bloomsbury Publishing.

Herskovits, M. J. (1948). *Man and His Works: The Science of Cultural Anthropology*. New York, NY: Knopf.

Hill, K. R. (2008, August). Aché. Retrieved from www.public.asu.edu/~krhill3/Ache.html.

Hill, K., Boesch, C., Goodall, J., Pusey, A., Williams, J., & Wrangham, R. (2001). Mortality rates among wild chimpanzees. *Journal of Human Evolution*, *40*(5), 437–450.

Hill, K. R., Walker, R. S., Bozicević, M., Eder, J., Headland, T., Hewlett, B. et al. (2011). Co-residence patterns in hunter-gatherer societies show unique human social structure. *Science*, *331*(6022), 1286–1289.

Hurtado, A. M. (2000). ANTHROPOLOGY: Origins of trade-offs in maternal care. *Science*, *287*(5452), 433–434.

Huxley, J. (1942). *Evolution: The Modern Synthesis*. London: Allen & Unwin.

Jablonka, E., & Lamb, M. J. (2005). *Evolution in Four Dimensions: Genetic, Epigenetic, Behavioral, and Symbolic Variation in the History of Life*. Cambridge, MA: MIT Press.

Jablonka, E., & Raz, G. (2009). Transgenerational epigenetic inheritance: Prevalence, mechanisms, and implications for the study of heredity and evolution. *The Quarterly Review of Biology*, *84*(2), 131–176.

Jackson, P. W. (1968). *Life in Classrooms*. New York, NY: Holt, Rinehart and Winston.

Kaplan, H., Hill, K., Lancaster, J., & Hurtado, A. M. (2000). A theory of human life history evolution: Diet, intelligence, and longevity. *Evolutionary Anthropology: Issues, News and Reviews*, *9*(4), 156–185.

Kaufmann, L., & Clément, F. (2007). How culture comes to mind: From social affordances to cultural analogies. *Intellectica*, *46*(47), 221–250.

Keller, E. F. (2014). From gene action to reactive genomes. *The Journal of Physiology*, *592*(11), 2423–2429.

Keller, H., Yovsi, R., Borke, J., Kärtner, J., Jensen, H., & Papaligoura, Z. (2004). Developmental consequences of early parenting experiences: Self-recognition and self-regulation in three cultural communities. *Child Development*, *75*(6), 1745–1760.

Konner, M. (2010). *The Evolution of Childhood: Relationships, Emotion, Mind*. Cambridge, MA: Harvard University Press.

Kroeber, A. L., & Kluckhohn, C. (1952). *Culture: A Critical Review of Concepts and Definitions*. Cambridge, MA: Peabody Museum.

Laland, K. N. (2017). *Darwin's Unfinished Symphony: How Culture Made the Human Mind*. Princeton, NJ: Princeton University Press.

Laland, K. N., Odling-Smee, J., & Feldman, M. W. (2000). Niche construction, biological evolution, and cultural change. *The Behavioral and Brain Sciences*, *23*(1), 131–175.

Laland, K. N., Odling-Smee, J., & Turner, S. (2014). The role of internal and external constructive processes in evolution. *The Journal of Physiology*, *592*(11), 2413–2422.

Laland, K. N., & Sterelny, K. (2006). Seven reasons (not) to neglect niche construction. *Evolution*, *60*(9), 1751–1762.

Laland, K. N., Uller, T., Feldman, M. W., Sterelny, K., Müller, G. B., Moczek, A. et al. (2015). The extended evolutionary synthesis: Its structure, assumptions and predictions. *Proceedings of the Royal Society B*, *282*(1813), 1–14.

Lévi-Strauss, C. (1961). *Tristes Tropiques*. London: Hutchinson. (Original work published 1955).

Levine, R. A., Levine, S., Schnell-Anzola, B., Rowe, M. L., & Dexter, E. (2012). *Literacy and Mothering: How Women's Schooling Changes the Lives of the World's Children*. New York, NY: Oxford University Press.

Liberman, I. Y., Shankweiler, D., & Liberman, A. M. (1989). The alphabetic principle and learning to read. In: D. Shankweiler & I. Y. Liberman (Eds.), *International Academy for Research in Learning Disabilities Monograph Series, No. 6. Phonology and Reading Disability: Solving the Reading Puzzle* (pp. 1–33). Ann Arbor, MI: The University of Michigan Press.

Liu, Z., Zhang, M., Xu, G., Huo, C., Tan, Q., Li, Z., & Yuan, Q. (2017). Effective connectivity analysis of the brain network in drivers during actual driving using near-infrared spectroscopy. *Frontiers in Behavioral Neuroscience*, *11*, 211.

Mayr, E. (1984). The triumph of evolutionary synthesis. *The Times Literary Supplement*, *2*, 1261–1262.

Mesoudi, A. (2016). Cultural evolution: Integrating psychology, evolution and culture. *Current Opinion in Psychology*, 7, 17–22.

Mutemeri, J. (2013). School knowledge and everyday knowledge: Why the binary conceptualization? *The Journal of Pan African Studies*, *6*, 86–99.

Nadasdy, P. (2014). The gift in the animal: The ontology of hunting and human-animal sociality. *American Ethnologist*, *34*(1), 25–43.

Odling-Smee, F. J. (1988). Niche constructing phenotypes. In: H. C. Plotkin (Ed.), *The Role of Behavior in Evolution* (pp. 73–132). Cambridge, MA: MIT Press.

Odling-Smee, F. J., Laland, K. N., & Feldman, M. W. (2003). *Niche Construction: The Neglected Process in Evolution*. Princeton, NJ: Princeton University Press.

Olson, D. R. (1994). *The World on Paper: The Conceptual and Cognitive Implications of Writing and Reading*. Cambridge, UK: Cambridge University Press.

Oyama, S. (2000). *Evolution's Eye: A Systems View of the Biology-Culture Divide*. Durham, NC: Duke University Press.

Oyama, S., Griffiths, P. E., & Gray, R. D. (2003). *Cycles of Contingency: Developmental Systems and Evolution*. Cambridge, MA: MIT Press.

Packer, M. J., & Cole, M. (2019). Evolution and ontogenesis: The deontic niche of human development. *Human Development*, *62*(4), 175–211.

Packer, M. J., & Goicoechea, J. (2000). Sociocultural and constructivist theories of learning: Ontology, not just epistemology. *Educational Psychologist*, *35*(4), 227–241.

Palmer, D. K. (2004). On the organism-environment distinction in psychology. *Behavior and Philosophy*, *32*, 317–347.

Parsons, T. (1959). The school class as a social system: Some of its functions in American society. *Harvard Educational Review*, *29*, 297–318.

Pennington, R. (2001). Hunter-gatherer demography. In: C. Panter-Brick, R. H. Layton & P. Rowley-Conwy (Eds.), *Hunter-Gatherers: An Interdisciplinary Perspective* (pp. 170–204). Cambridge: Cambridge University Press.

Peregrin, J. (2014). Rules as the impetus of cultural evolution. *Topoi*, *33*(2), 531–545.

Pigliucci, M., & Müller, G. B. (2010). Elements of an extended evolutionary synthesis. In: M. Pigliucci & G. B. Müller (Eds.), *Evolution—The Extended Synthesis* (pp. 3–18). Cambridge, MA: MIT Press.

Powers, S. T., van Schaik, C. P., & Lehmann, L. (2016). How institutions shaped the last major evolutionary transition to large-scale human societies. *Philosophical Transactions of the Royal Society of London Series B: Biological Sciences*, *371*(1687), 20150098.

Rakoczy, H., & Tomasello, M. (2007). The ontogeny of social ontology: Steps to shared intentionality and status functions. In: S. L. Tsohatzidis (Ed.), *Intentional Acts and Institutional Facts: Essays on John Searle's Social Ontology* (pp. 113–137). Berlin: Springer Verlag.

Richerson, P. J., & Boyd, R. (2001). Institutional evolution in the Holocene: The rise of complex societies. In: W. G. Runciman (Ed.), *The Origin of Human Social Institutions* (pp. 197–234). Oxford: Oxford University Press.

Richerson, P. J., & Christiansen, M. H. (2013). Introduction. In: P. J. Richerson & M. H. Christiansen (Eds.), *Cultural Evolution: Society, Technology, Language, and Religion* (pp. 1–21). Cambridge, MA: MIT Press.

Schmandt-Besserat, D. (1992). *Before Writing. Vol. 1: From Counting to Cuneiform*. Austin, TX: University of Texas Press.

Schneider, D. M. (1984). *A Critique of the Study of Kinship*. Ann Arbor, MI: University of Michigan Press.

Scott-Phillips, T. C., Laland, K. N., Shuker, D. M., Dickins, T. E., & West, S. A. (2014). The niche construction perspective: A critical appraisal. *Evolution; International Journal of Organic Evolution*, *68*(5), 1231–1243.

Searle, J. R. (1995). *The Construction of Social Reality*. New York, NY: Simon and Schuster.

Searle, J. R. (2005). What is an institution? *Journal of Institutional Economics*, *1*(1), 1–22.

Searle, J. R. (2009). *Making the Social World: The Structure of Human Civilization*. New York, NY: Oxford University Press.

Serpell, R., & Hatano, G. (1997). Education, schooling, and literacy. In: J. W. Berry, P. R. Dasen & T. S. Saraswarthi (Eds.), *Handbook of Cross-Cultural Psychology. Vol. 2: Basic Processes and Human Development* (2nd ed., pp. 339–376). Boston, MA: Allyn and Bacon.

Tomasello, M., & Vaish, A. (2013). Origins of human cooperation and morality. *Annual Review of Psychology, 64*, 231–255.

Tomasello, M. (2019). *Becoming Human: A Theory of Ontogeny*. Cambridge, MA: Harvard University Press.

Tooby, J., & Cosmides, L. (1990). The past explains the present: Emotional adaptations and the structure of ancestral environments. *Ethology and Sociobiology, 11*(4–5), 375–424.

Turner, J. S. (2000). *The Extended Organism: The Physiology of Animal-Built Structures*. Cambridge, MA: Harvard University Press.

Turner, J. S. (2003). Trace fossils and extended organisms: A physiological perspective. *Palaeogeography, Palaeoclimatology, Palaeoecology, 192*(1), 15–31.

Turner, J. H. (2004). *Human Institutions: A Theory of Societal Evolution*. London: Rowman & Littlefield.

Walsh, D. M. (2014). The negotiated organism: Inheritance, development, and the method of difference. *Biological Journal of the Linnean Society, 112*(2), 295–305.

West, M. J., & King, A. P. (1987). Settling nature and nurture into an ontogenetic niche. *Developmental Psychobiology, 20*(5), 549–562.

Witherington, D. C., & Lickliter, R. (2016). Integrating development and evolution in psychological science: Evolutionary developmental psychology, developmental systems, and explanatory pluralism. *Human Development, 59*(4), 200–234.

Woollett, K., & Maguire, E. (2011). Acquiring "the Knowledge" of London's layout drives structural brain changes. *Current Biology, 21*(24), 2109–2114.

2

THE BRAID OF HUMAN LEARNING AND DEVELOPMENT

Neuro-Physiological Processes and Participation in Cultural Practices

Carol D. Lee, Andrew N. Meltzoff, and Patricia K. Kuhl

We offer a framework for understanding human learning and psychological development as situated within a system that entails dynamic interplay between neurobiological processes and people's participation in cultural practices. We draw from multiple disciplines, including evolutionary biology, neuroscience, human development, anthropology, cognitive science, cultural and social psychology, and the learning sciences.

Human development is a complex interchange that includes neurobiological processes, evolved over many millennia (Quartz & Sejnowski, 2002; Tomasello, 2019) that now get taken up and adapted as people engage in cultural practices, which themselves vary over communities and historical time (Rogoff, 2003; Saxe & Esmonde, 2012). We highlight *intersections* between neurobiological processes and people's participation in cultural practices. These intersections shape human sense-making, which in turn influences people's goals, effort, and persistence—what people do and why. We also consider "time" as a key factor (Bronfenbrenner & Morris, 1998). A comprehensive theory of human development and learning must account for when in the life course we have experiences (age matters), when in cultural-historical time learner experiences occur (e.g. The Great Depression), as well as how micro-level interactions unfold in moment-to-moment activity.

We underscore the historical context of our proposals. We fully recognize that some readers may question elevating the relevance of neurobiology and evolution in human development and learning. For this reason, we wish to differentiate ourselves from certain ill-conceived theorizing in this vein. Hypothesizing about how biology and evolution influence psychology and sociology has been misused going back to Herbert Spencer's use of "social Darwinism" to argue for hierarchies of human communities, positioning those of European ancestry, constructed as "white," as superior to other human communities (Gould, 1981; Jackson & Weidman, 2004). In the nineteenth century, craniology—the study of brain size and shape—was also used to argue for natural human hierarchies. These views were used to advance the eugenics movement, which argued for inherited deficits within certain human communities; eugenics itself was taken up to support social policies and practices such as forced sterilizations to minimize the presence and impacts of those believed inferior. These accounts were used not only to distinguish Europeans from others (e.g. Africans, Asians, indigenous populations in the Americas, Australia, New Zealand), but also, at points, to distinguish northern European "Nordics" from southern European "Mediterraneans." These deficit orientations came to include not only biological accounts but cultural accounts of "deficits" in terms of presumed hierarchies (from superior to inferior) of cultural practices across communities associated with race/ethnicity, class, and religion. More recently, arguments for a presumed "culture of poverty" have arisen.

We reject these views, and want to articulate a new way of integrating evolution, neuro-biology, and human development. The modern study of brain science is not focused on "fixed traits" that are hardwired into the brain and immutable (and certainly not hardwired in ways correlated with the constructs of "race" or ethnicity). Modern brain science instead emphasizes the human brain's flexibility and adaptiveness. It celebrates "neuroplasticity" (studies of how experiences change the brain itself) in all humans. Modern neurobiologists focus on understanding how the brain learns socially in cultural contexts. It is this new convergence we wish to codify and amplify. We explore these ideas to see what we can learn from emerging findings in the neurosciences and the convergence of these ideas in other areas of study, including human development, studies of cognition-in-context, and studies of the socio-emotional consequences of participation in cultural practices.

Theory: Six Overarching Propositions Linking Biology, Psychology, and Culture

We offer six overarching propositions emerging across diverse fields that converge on a new conceptualization of the relations among brain science, psychology, and culture.

Proposition 1: Biology does not determine the endpoint of human ontogeny. Renewed attention to biological processes is important because such processes are largely driven by our evolution as a species and are compelling drivers of human behavior. Yet understanding how such processes influence behavior in modern humans is complex. Among the important takeaways of our current understanding is that biological processes are *not* deterministic, and that the ways such processes unfold within an individual is intertwined with people's participation in cultural practices (Cole, 1996). A central tenet of modern neuroscience is that the brain is not fixed nor finished developing at birth—the brain itself changes postnatally due to experience. One of the most rapidly growing aspects of brain science is the neuroscience of learning. Biology is therefore not personal destiny: In seeking to understand complex human behavior, it is not genetics but *epigenetics* that holds the most promise. Waddington (1942) initially coined the term epigenetics, which heavily influenced Piaget's (1971) views on human development and constructivist psychology. Epigenetic studies document how experience shapes the expression of genetic factors. Meaney's (2001) work on epigenetics continues to influence neuroscientific studies.

Proposition 2: The primacy of learning from, with, and through others. There are foundational aspects of psychological functioning shared among all human beings, but these are displayed in myriad ways because of our participation in different cultural practices. These foundational elements include, but are not limited to: (a) a focus on understanding the internal states of other people (Flavell & Miller, 1998); (b) taking in and adapting to experiences—not simply reacting to perceptions given via physical senses, but responding to our *interpretations* of events based on our life histories (Bruner, 1990; Spencer, 2006); (c) the importance of emotions in human functioning (Adam, 2012; Damasio, 1995); (d) our need to satisfy a sense of "belonging" to social groups; (e) how we interpret ongoing social interactions in terms of safety/threat and relevance to our goals (Maslow, 1943); and (f) the salience we attribute to our sense of agency and efficacy and how experiences relate to our ego-focused goals (Bandura, 1993). Moreover, our social brain has evolved in part because of our interactions with others, and human adults and children experience a basic motivation to interact socially, including the powerful activation of our "neural reward system" by social signals such as faces (Stavropoulous & Carver, 2014). A comprehensive theory of human development must take into account basic motivations for learning from, through, and in relationships with social others.

Proposition 3: Diversity in developmental pathways is core to realistic accounts of human development. A diversity in pathways of development is essential to the survival of our species. The human species occupies more diverse niches—from the poles to the equator—than most other species, which demands flexibility. Across cultural-historical time the tools we create are embedded in increasingly complex forms of social interaction and institutional configurations, requiring adaptability that is enhanced by diversity of pathways (Cole, 2007; Rogoff & Chavajay, 1995).

Indeed, humans also exhibit flexibility in the face of basic sensory losses, showing that our brain can creatively adapt to atypical input in its quest to make meaning. Many blind adults navigate the world through taps and clicks, using echolocation to sense obstacles and navigate the world. Scientists have built tools to translate light into tactile information projected onto the tongue's surface so that the blind can "see" with their tongue (Bach-y-Rita, Kaczmarek, Tyler, & Garcia-Lara, 1998). Deaf infants have advanced responses to *visual* communicative signals and exhibit enhanced gaze-following behavior compared to hearing infants—countering "deficit models" (Brooks et al., 2020). Humans can cope and even thrive with the loss of multiple sensory channels (viz. Hellen Keller), in part because we don't actually perceive with our eyes or ears alone, but rather with our brains, and our brains are flexible enough to interpret the patterns that typically come through one sense in new modalities in the quest to make meaning.

One of the most unique aspects of the human species is our cultural diversity. Here, we can refer to the film *Babies*, a documentary about babies born in San Francisco, Tokyo, Namibia, and Mongolia. What one sees in this film is each child actively seeking to develop the competencies of the first year of life, but diversely. Children are socialized through different cultural practices, deploy normative competencies toward different social goals, and learn to use different cultural tools.

Proposition 4: Individuals belong to multiple, not single, cultural groups—"intersectionality." People belong to many cultural communities, and are not limited or wholly defined by any single one. One common meta-narrative and conceptualization about "culture" suffers from what Gutiérrez and Rogoff (2003) call "the box problem": Assuming people belong to a *single* cultural community associated with race and ethnicity, especially as pan-ethnic groups (e.g., African American, Latinx, Asian American, and "White").

In this chapter, we recognize that people belong to multiple cultural communities, known as "intersectionality" (Carbado et al., 2013). Some communities—such as those associated with ethnic and in some cases with pan-ethnic communities—have inter-generational longevity that persists even when national borders change. But even with such longstanding communities, we find both stability and change. Irish communities in the USA may celebrate St Patrick's Day, but the USA celebrations look quite different from Ireland's celebrations. In African-descent communities across the diaspora, one will find commonalities concerning reverence of ancestors, respect for elders, and the centrality of the drum and rhythm. Yet, these practices also differ by time and place (Asante & Asante, 1990). In addition, people also belong to communities bound by cultural-historical periods: Video game aficionados, readers of Harry Potter novels, lovers and practitioners of particular sports, etc. Through participation in diverse cultural communities ("communities of practice"), people develop different repertoires (skills, habits, ways of using language, use of particular tools) and different identities or self-representations (e.g., ego-related goals, sense of belonging, sense of efficacy). In our efforts to understand and influence human learning and education, an essential question is what we make of such repertoires in relation to some targeted learning goals.

Proposition 5: The social brain "expects" and is modified by social interactions. Humans have evolved to be a hyper-social species. We interact with other human beings, using tools (physical and conceptual) created by humans to interrogate our experiences. Crucially, even if we are engaging in an activity without another person present, we often are still engaging with tools developed by others. We are never truly alone, devoid of all perceptions, thoughts, memories, or tools made by others.

Research has shown that young babies pay more attention to other human beings than to physical objects, but this is simply the kickoff of our path of social interaction with others. Social cognition researchers examine how the capacities for interrogating the internal states of self and others shift over the life course, and illuminate the complexities that arise in such efforts. Modern studies of the brain have widened their lens from sensory processes to investigating social understanding and social interaction. This new field is called *developmental social neuroscience* (Ward, 2012). The goal is not to usurp or replace the field of human development, but rather to provide an additional, complementary "level of analysis." The tools of modern neuroscience now allow us to begin, for the first time in history, to examine what's going on in children's brains as they learn, and how this changes with experience, development, context, and life history (Meltzoff et al., 2009).

Proposition 6: The power and pervasiveness of implicit and observational learning. We learn through explicit verbal instruction and intentional guidance from others, but we also learn more implicitly through simply observing the practices of other people (Bransford et al., 2006; Meltzoff et al., 2009). We form long-lasting representations of the behaviors we witness. These internalized representations are then used to organize our subsequent actions and color our world views. People become role models for us, and role models influence us even when they are absent or dead, or para-social as in media characters. Some of the most powerful influences of role models derive from information implicitly picked up, despite the role mentor's lack of intention to convey it.

Observational learning and implicit learning are especially powerful channels for learning prior to formal schooling. Children learn about the social world both through interactions with others and also from third-party "eavesdropping" on the interactions they observe between others. Children abstract skills, customs, norms, from such everyday implicit social learning. Many of life's most important lessons and practices are learned through merely observing others' behaviors , not through explicit, intentional instruction.

Summary of 6 propositions and organization of the chapter. What we internalize from our participation in diverse, social communities of practice is an outgrowth of the complex relations between (a) biological processes inherited as a species for taking in physical inputs from the environment (e.g., what we see, hear, taste, feel, smell), and (b) the translation of those inputs into psychological representations that embody meaning for us. The schemas and mental models we encode as filters for attributing significance and meaning to our perceptions of the world are inherently social, outgrowths of shared cultural practices among communities of humans. Because all humans, by evolutionary design, are born with an immature brain that is wired postnatally in a social context, we are socially attuned to others starting from our earliest years, months, and days of life (Kuhl, 2007; Meltzoff & Marshall, 2018). Being nurtured is part of our nature. The human brain is "prepared" to encounter and learn from others; those social interactions in turn wire and remodel the brain, starting at birth and throughout the lifespan.

We next describe new empirical work that illustrates and amplifies our six propositions. The empirical examples discussed will be drawn from educational research, and also draw heavily on our own research in early childhood. We use these examples to put empirical meat on the six skeletal propositions we have put forward. In the final section of the chapter we consider the broader implications of the six propositions and the empirical work for our understanding of how people learn in both formal and informal settings. In sum, we hope to sketch a broad arc that extends from evolution and neurobiology through developmental science to education.

Childhood Social Learning and Imitation: Where Biology First Meets Culture

Humans are unique learners. It is not that we learn faster, learn earlier, or remember our learned experiences longer. We learn differently. Human beings have evolved a distinctive type of social learning—a generative capacity for imitation (Meltzoff & Marshall, 2018). We are imitative generalists (Meltzoff, 1988b) and seamlessly intermix imitation and innovation.

In this chapter, we are using the word "imitation" in a generic way to mean copying the acts of others. More technically, there can be a distinction between copying the *way* people do things (sometimes called "imitation") and copying the *ends or goals* they achieve (sometimes called "emulation"). Many animals are restricted almost entirely to emulation (Tomasello, 2019). Human infants have the capacity for *both* imitation and emulation—they are "imitative generalists." Thus, in this chapter we use the word imitation as a superordinate term, as in everyday language, to encompass both children's imitation and their emulation of others.

The capacity for generative imitation allows infants to imitate postures, actions, vocalizations, tool use, and novel goal-directed acts. Imitation is also a mechanism for the intergenerational transfer of cultural practices prior to language, and is an avenue for learning the diverse customs, rituals, and norms that sustain social cohesion among group members. Next, we examine the roots of human imitation using empirical work to flesh out propositions 2, 5, and 6. This empirical work serves to illustrate how strikingly early in development humans start to pick up the ways of their culture.

Transfer and Generalization of Imitative Learning Is Basic to Humans: Propositions 2 and 6

For imitation to serve cultural learning, two cognitive competencies are required—deferred imitation (imitation from memory) and imitation after a change in context (generalization). Both of these capacities have been demonstrated in young children and infants. They allow children to learn from observation and to transfer their learning across time and space, and also support the early formation of "communities of practice" in the ways articulated below.

One warrant for these claims derives from a study of 14-month-old infants, who saw an adult perform an unusual act, one with no evolutionary significance and one not previously seen or performed by the child. The adult demonstrated using his head to activate a light by leaning forward and tapping a panel with his forehead. Infants simply observed the adult's odd behavior. When re-presented with the panel after a 1-week delay, infants imitated the novel head-touch act based on recall memory (Meltzoff, 1988a). The imitation of novel acts has been replicated and extended across several cultures, from infancy through the preschool period and beyond (Legare et al., 2015; Tomasello, 2019; Wang et al., 2015).

The demonstration of head-touch imitation speaks to several of our propositions. First, young children can learn new and unusual acts implicitly, based on the mere observation of other people (proposition 6). Second, imitation of novelty occurs without food inducement (imitation in non-human primates often revolves around food). For humans, imitation is its own reward—infants are intrinsically motivated to become "like others" in their group (proposition 2). Third, infants imitate using the same body part (or *means*) adopted by the adult, and do not simply duplicate the same result (or *ends*). Infants re-enact *what* the adult does and *how* he does it (a head-touch), rather than only doing the more practiced act of hand-touch to reach the goal. This is important, because it verifies that infants imitate novel acts used by members of the culture with high fidelity, which can be used for learning diverse cultural practices and customs.

Young children also demonstrate transfer of learning to new settings. In one study, infants were shown what to do with objects in a laboratory environment and later given the objects at home after a delay. We found that infants imitated across the context change (Klein & Meltzoff, 1999). Infants also rapidly learn from peers. Researchers taught an "expert infant" what to do with novel objects. The expert was then brought to daycare centers where he/she encountered "naïve infants" who watched them deftly handle the toys. Researchers subsequently visited the homes of the naïve infants, gave them the relevant objects. The naïve infants duplicated the behaviors they had seen the expert peer do two days earlier (Hanna & Meltzoff, 1993). This shows that infant learning is not place bound; they remember what they observe others do and productively use these actions across changes in space and time. This is fertile ground for young children learning the social practices they observe and becoming full-fledged members of the diverse cultures in which they are raised.

The convergence between these laboratory studies and the field studies done cross-culturally (e.g., Rogoff, 2003) lends confidence to these theoretical inferences. It helps us to understand the rapid nonverbal diffusion of skills among children, and shows that the capacities needed to form "communities of practice" is so deeply embedded in the human species as to be present in infancy, before children utter their first sentences.

Learning to Use Tools (Proposition 5)

Observational learning and imitation play a significant role in humans' learning how to use tools. If you give a nonhuman primate an instrument, it can often use trial-and-error to work out how to use the instrument to achieve an end. An important characteristic of human children is that they learn to use tools through the imitation of social others (Meltzoff, 2007; Tomasello, 2019).

Vygotsky (1978) presciently argued that tools extend and augment human capacities. Modern research shows that this begins early. Infants covet their mother's lipstick and keys because they have seen her use them; they hold mobile phones to their ears because they witness adults so use the devices; and they learn to type on screens partly by imitating others. And preschool children are beginning to use computers, smartphones, and tablets as vehicles for learning and communication with parents and grandparents. The use of amplifying tools is not learned solely through independent invention, trial-and-error learning, or linguistic instruction. Young humans get a jump start on enculturation because of a fundamental pre-existing capacity for social imitation. Vygotsky (1978) noted the role for imitation in his concept of the zone of proximal development. We wish to move the starting point for Vygotskyian processes from preschool to infancy, because laboratory research shows that imitative processes begin even before Vygotsky had surmised.

Emotions and Selective Imitation: A Choice, Not an Echo (Propositions 2 and 5)

Infants do not automatically imitate everything they see. Emotions play a major role in regulating imitation, as discovered in research where infants were shown what to do with an object by a "Demonstrator," but another adult ("Emoter") became angry at the Demonstrator for performing the act (Repacholi & Meltzoff, 2007). The Emoter then adopted a neutral face, and the infant was handed the object to see whether he/she would imitate. The study varied whether the Emoter did or did not watch the infant's behavior. Results showed that infants were more likely to imitate the Demonstrator's act when the (previously angry) Emoter did not watch the infants' imitation.

These results are not reducible to simple emotional contagion, because the same Emoter showed the same amount of anger across cases. The authors hypothesized that infants *keep track of the emotional history* of people. Infants then regulate their imitation depending on who is watching them, because they do not want to become a target of the Emoter's anger by duplicating the act that had made that person angry in the past (Repacholi, Meltzoff, Toub, & Ruba, 2016), (relevant to proposition 2's discussion of emotions and the role of threats to the self in learning).

These findings are important for three reasons. First, they suggest infants are capable of a primitive form of self-control prior to language (recalling Luria and Vygotsky's ideas about "executive function"). Second, they show infants do not need direct involvement but learn from "eavesdropping" on interactions between other people. Infants learned about the Emoter's tendencies from watching her interaction with someone else. Third, the work indicates that anger is a powerful emotion in the world of young children, and that they take action to avoid a personal threat.

Imitation is also modulated by other social factors. For example, young children preferentially duplicate intentional rather than accidental acts, ingroup versus outgroup members, models who seem more efficient and competent, and models who receive favored treatment by others (Meltzoff & Marshall, 2018; Skinner, Olson, & Meltzoff, 2019). In sum, imitation is not compulsory; it is a choice, not an echo. Young children flexibly choose what, when, and who to imitate. In a sense they choose their teachers and thus participate in their own learning and social development, starting from infancy.

Newborns: In the Beginning There Was Imitation (Proposition 6)

A primitive form of human imitation exists at birth, particularly the matching of simple facial and manual acts such as tongue protrusion or moving the fingers (Meltzoff & Moore, 1977, 1983). This discovery came as a surprise, because Piagetian theory had considered it a landmark milestone achieved later in infancy. The existence of early imitation has now been replicated in more than two dozen experiments from independent labs (reviewed by Meltzoff & Moore, 1997, also see recent replications by Heimann & Tjus, 2019; Nagy, Pal, & Orvos, 2014). One simplistic idea was that it is an arousal effect activated by seeing moving faces or fingers; however, this has now been ruled out by experiments that used other dynamic movements as controls.

The leading model explaining early infant imitation is the "active intermodal mapping" (AIM) account (Meltzoff & Moore, 1997), which emphasizes the infant's own agency. The central notion of AIM is that imitation is a cross-modal matching process involving an *active comparison* between the acts of self and other. According to AIM, infants' movements yield proprioceptive feedback that is used to correct imitative efforts so that they correspond to the visual target.

Based on this and other work, Meltzoff (2007, 2013) offered the "Like-Me" social-developmental framework. It holds that newborns are not born social isolates, monads, devoid of all connections to social others. The baby is born into a social community and immediately recognizes similarities between their own bodily actions and those they see. This is the starting state for interpersonal engagement, not an end-state achieved after years of development. Of course, newborn social cognition is primitive. For example, they are limited to matching bodily actions and are too young to use tools or to assimilate cultural norms. But the initial state is a launchpad for the further social learning and development. It is a foundational launchpad because infants grasp a primordial, nonverbal connection between self and other. Infants are born learning socially. Through observations of others and social interactions, they construct more complex beliefs, desires, intentions, and values.

What's the Brain Got to Do With It? (Proposition 5)

The neurobiology of social learning and imitation has been illuminated by using the modern tools of brain science with infants and young children.

Connecting Perception and Action

One new line of studies on social learning used electroencephalography (EEG) techniques. These studies discovered significant changes in neural oscillations ("brain waves") that occur between 6–9 times a second (the "mu rhythm"), both when a baby performed an action (such as pushing a button), and also when they simply watched someone else do the same action (Marshall & Meltzoff, 2014).

In other EEG work, researchers tested infants' brain reactions to social games. Infants played a mutual imitation game with an adult while infants' brain waves were measured (Saby, Marshall, & Meltzoff, 2012). Results showed significant changes in mu rhythm when the adult imitated the infant compared to when the adult did not. There are special neural signatures associated with being "in synch" with another person and having them imitate your behavior. Mother-infant dyads commonly play mutual pat-a-cake and mutual rattle shaking games, often to peals of laughter. Babies—like marital partners and psychotherapy patients—like to be "matched," because it is a form of nonlinguistic communication and an embodiment of "being in synch" with one's interactive partner.

Infant Embodiment: What the Infant Body Tells the Infant Brain

Further work has zeroed in on similarities between the bodies of self and other: My hand is like your hand; my lips are like your lips. The way these studies worked was to touch different parts of the infant's body and to measure brain responses. Scientists have been able to localize the infant's body in the infant's brain with enough precision to identify the "hand area," "foot area," and "lip area" in the infant brain (Meltzoff, Saby, & Marshall, 2019). The crucial findings involved having infants observe *another person's* body being touched without the infant being touched themselves. The results showed activity in the infant's *own hand* area when they saw *another person's* hand being touched (Meltzoff et al., 2018). The infant brain uses some of the same neural machinery to process both self and other, emphasizing a fundamental social connectivity from a young age.

Theoretical Synthesis: Brain, Body, and Roots of Social Understanding

These brain studies inform theories about the neural underpinnings of imitation, perspective-taking, and empathy. To imitate, infants need to know what part of their body corresponds to yours. Empathy also depends on recognizing the other as "Like-Me"—at first at a bodily level (Meltzoff, 2013). Of course, young children do not construe self-other similarities in the sophisticated ways that adults do. This will come through social interactions with others. But by the same token, infants are not born blank slates. They are deeply connected to other people through their body and actions even before they can talk, and this launches them on the stormy path of navigating the similarities and differences between self and other.

We now turn to how infants' build on these foundational social capacities to acquire language, which in turn transforms their understanding of people, things, and events.

Language, Brain, and Culture: Rethinking Language Through a Sociocultural Lens

Language acquisition presents a cardinal case of culture influencing the mind (Bruner, 1983; Vygotsky, 1962). Children's acquisition of a culture's unique coding of meaning, and its distinctive sound patterns and gestures, represents a powerful case in which infants rapidly and effortlessly construct a highly complex system that allows them to communicate effectively with other members of their social group—and the language(s) they learn influence cognition.

Theories of language acquisition have been transformed over the last half-century from being linked primarily to biology to theories in which biology and culture are inextricably intertwined. Chomsky's (1957) view of the child's innate universal grammar downplayed the role of learning. Culture's contribution was minimal in that the language a child heard simply served to "trigger" the appropriate innately specified parameters, which then generated a specific language. Fodor's (1983) *Modularity of Mind* characterized language as an innately specified "module" that was cognitively impenetrable and informationally encapsulated—an entity separate from other higher-order cognitive processes, and immune to sociocultural influences. The opposing view of language acquisition offered by Skinner (1957) was a learning account, but highly reductionist, suggesting that language acquisition required explicit reinforcement on the part of parents to "shape" specific verbal behaviors. These views deeply underestimated the role of social, cultural, and cognitive influences in the child's acquisition of language (Kuhl & Meltzoff, 1997), but they dominated the study of language for decades.

A newer view emerged from a variety of scholars who studied the earliest forms of language learning in flesh-and-blood contexts, in the crib. Breakthrough diary studies conducted by Brown (1973), Bloom (1973), and Bates (1976) chronicled children's words and grammatical utterances from the beginning, in actual settings, emphasizing the complexity of children's constructions of meaning and the role of prior cognitive and social development on the language learning process. Similarly, Tomasello (2003) argued that children learn language through social-cognitive processes that allow young children to read the intentions of others and find patterns in their social discourse interactions with others. It was shown that children's early language learning critically depends on social interactions with others during infancy (Kuhl et al., 2003).

Current views of language acquisition embrace the child's natural drive to learn from and with other members of a culture, and the way in which the construction of language occurs in the brain through social interaction within a particular cultural community. The details of how language is expressed in a particular culture—whether signed or spoken language and whether one or three languages are mastered—are viewed as diverse routes for children engaging through social interaction with members of their community and learning to communicate. On this emerging view, biology's contribution is the extraordinary adaptability and neuroplasticity of the child. Our six propositions help illuminate language acquisition in interesting ways.

Young Children Learn Language Implicitly (Proposition 6)

It doesn't require a scientist to see that young infants absorb language by being bathed in the world of words and sounds (or signs) that characterize a particular culture. By ten months of age, the babbling of a baby raised in France will sound "French," a baby in Rome will babble in Italian, and a baby in Beijing will sound distinctly Chinese. The infants already are conforming to their cultural milieu through vocal learning and imitation (Kuhl & Meltzoff, 1996). By 12–15 months, these same infants will harness their language-specific babbling to create words in their mother tongue as they become more formal French, Italian, or Mandarin speakers.

Studies of young children show they are implicit learning masters. Learning occurs unconsciously as infants experience the patterns in auditory (speech) or visual (sign) input. A specific form of implicit learning, referred to as "statistical learning," helps explain how young children begin to master the sound structure and words of a language. This is easily illustrated by examining the earliest learning infants accomplish, learning which phonetic units (the consonants and vowels that make up words) are used in their mother tongue. Prior to six months of age, infants accomplish a feat that no adult can achieve. Under the age of six months, infants from all cultures can hear the sound differences used to differentiate words (like the 'r' vs. 'l' difference that distinguishes 'read' from 'lead') in *all languages of the world*, something adults cannot do. Each language employs a distinct set of these phonetic distinctions, and 6-month-olds discriminate between them all. Yet six months later, perception for all infants has narrowed. The universal differences 6-month-old infants once were able to hear in foreign languages can no longer be discerned by the 12-month-old, and only the sounds used in the language(s) spoken by their caretakers and surrounding community can be distinguished. Despite rapid and impressive advances in AI, no current computer in the world can glean the sound structure of a language from language input, yet all infants across the world do so with ease, whether reared in Western society or in a non-industrialized culture.

What kind of learning allows the child to construct a linguistic system that contains certain sounds, words, and grammatical constructions by listening to us speak? It turns out that unlike the learning theory held by Skinner, in which young children learn through structured reinforcement, children can learn simply by listening and detecting the stochastic patterns in language input (Kuhl et al., 1992; Saffran et al., 1996). This "observational" learning in language is not unrelated to the observational learning in actions described in the previous section (Meltzoff et al., 2009). During an early "sensitive period" between 6 and 12 months of age, infants are particularly sensitive to the distributional frequency of phonetic patterns in language they hear (Kuhl et al., 2006).

Children's early word learning similarly exploits the stochastic properties in language input. Experiments have shown that when 8-month-old infants are presented with a 2-minute long uninterrupted sequence of syllables with no discernable breaks (e.g., the string of syllables *pigudofadimepigulatu* spoken in a monotone voice) the transitional probability that one syllable will follow another affects children's detection of likely words even before they know words exist. In the example above, the sequence 'pigu' appears twice in the string. After two minutes of listening, young children treat sequences of syllables that always follow one another as units ('pigu' in the string), as "words" (Saffran et al., 1996). They remember these units and easily link them to a new object they have not seen before. These findings emphasize infant learning and show that infants learn in unsuspected ways from cultural experience, and in ways that allow them to structure and interpret the input they hear.

Two additional notes about implicit learning are important. The first is that the *timing* matters. The period between 6 and 12 months of age constitutes a sensitive period in human phonetic learning (Kuhl et al., 2006), and infants' statistical learning of likely "words" is particularly keen at the end of the first year when infants' cognitive and social capacities increase and word learning begins. The second is that statistical learning is a *cross-domain* skill, a cognitive skill on which language capitalizes mightily.

Cross-cultural studies designed to test across diverse cultures and languages have shown that children throughout the world exhibit this capacity to learn from language experience, regardless of the culture, language, or socio-economic status (SES) of their parents. The emerging model thus depends heavily on learning, but learning of a type that differs fundamentally from the classic Skinnerian learning, and also offers more details and mechanisms for language acquisition than described by Piaget (1962) and Vygotsky (1962, 1978).

Early Learning of Language is Driven by Social Interaction (Propositions 2 and 5)

A key component of the transformation in language acquisition theory is the requirement that infants' early learning of language mandates a social context. The critical nature of social interaction in early second-language learning was demonstrated experimentally in studies in which language learning through social interaction was compared to learning from a disembodied source (a video) at nine months of age (Kuhl, 2007). Infants were given the exact same language material, in the same setting, with the same frequency; the only difference was whether infants experienced live speakers interacting with them or the identical input delivered via video (Kuhl et al., 2003). Results showed that the *live* social interaction resulted in rapid and robust learning of sounds and words from the new language. However, exposure via video yielded no language learning whatsoever. Additional studies revealed that infants in the live sessions used tutors' social (eye gaze) patterns to learn, and that infants' attention in the live, interactive social settings is significantly higher than when watching the same material via video (Conboy et al., 2015). The idea that infants' social motivation and their early abilities to detect intentionality in human actions is a key driver of language acquisition has also been discussed by Tomasello (2019) who theorizes that the origins of human language emerged from the drive to cooperate socially.

Parents in cultures around the world adapt the type of language used when speaking to their infants and young children—often termed "motherese" or "parentese." Parentese is inherently social and engages children, fostering turn-taking conversations (Kuhl & Ferjan Ramírez, 2019). Parentese was first discovered by anthropologists and linguists documenting languages in the 1960s and was later revealed to be nearly universal in the world's languages, although some cultures rely on it more than others (e.g., Ferguson, 1964). It has a simpler grammar and lexicon, a slower tempo, and it exaggerates the relevant acoustic differences in speech. Infants given a choice choose to listen to parentese over standard speech, and its use has been shown to be linked to advanced language development.

Parents' social reactions to children's vocalizations increase the complexity of children's vocalizations. It's as though having a social audience motivates young children to display their best and most complex linguistic abilities (Sundara et al., 2020). Once again, the social exchange is critical to this kind of developmental advance. Through back and forth exchanges, parents provide feedback that is constantly adjusted to their child's linguistic needs, and children, in turn, adjust their vocalizations in response to parental reactions. Communicative turn-taking between parents and infants is prevalent long before infants utter their first words and may have been essential for the evolution of language.

In short, historically, the role of the "social" brain and the sociocultural context has been under-appreciated by language theorists. On the one hand, the profound impact of the social context was not predicted by nativists (Chomsky, Fodor) or learning theorists (Skinner). On the other hand, social-developmental theories duly discussed the importance of social interaction for language (Bruner, Vygotsky), and research amply demonstrated that language acquisition is assisted by children's grasp of communicative intentions, and their sensitivity to joint visual attention and goals (Brooks & Meltzoff, 2008; Kuhl, 2007; Tomasello, 2019). However, the new data demonstrating that babies need social contexts to learn even the earliest aspects of language, phonetic units—the essential building blocks of language—was not expected. It suggests that language, social evolution, and social learning contexts are entwined from the earliest phases.

Diversity of Pathways Toward Language (Propositions 3 and 4)

Culture provides a social context and engaging speakers that stimulate the young brain. In children born unable to hear, language input comes from culturally-invented visual sign languages that differ across countries like oral languages do. Deaf infants exposed to natural sign language (such as ASL) acquire language through the visual-manual pathway following many of the same principles and same developmental timeline as infants acquiring oral language. There is evidence that experience with sign language in deaf speakers activates the same brain tissue as spoken language in hearing speakers (Petitto et al., 2001). Moreover, the "deficit model" of deafness has been overturned. Deaf children who experience visual sign language from birth show certain social-cognitive strengths. They show *accelerated* gaze following of others, illustrating the neuroplasticity of infants, and a strong capacity to become well-adapted to their particular sociocultural and linguistic ecologies (Brooks et al., 2020). In other words, there is no one pathway to language.

Multilingualism also provides an example of a pathway that differs from what is typical in the United States (though it is common worldwide). In the USA, some politicians and pundits speculated that hearing multiple languages could overwhelm the infant brain and lead to deficits in learning. This pernicious and inaccurate view of bilingual learning has been disproven, and indeed additional evidence indicates *benefits* of bilingualism in certain domains.

Taking a step back, the original claims were that bilingual children were slower to develop vocabulary when compared to their monolingual peers, but more recent studies by Hoff and colleagues (2012) showed that when young bilingual learners are given credit for each conceptual vocabulary item that they know (from either of their two languages) bilingual children's total vocabulary skills either equal or exceed those of their monolingual peers. Behavioral and brain-imaging studies comparing monolingual and bilingual infants confirm that bilingual infants are on the same timetable with regard to mastery of the sound systems of their two languages when compared to monolingual infants who master only one language (Ferjan Ramírez et al., 2017). In other words, bilingual infants and children do not lag behind their monolingual peers in either behavioral or brain measures of learning.

More strikingly, bilingual infants show cognitive advantages. Bilingual infants learn novel speech structures faster, and exhibit a more prolonged period of flexibility in their interpretation of potential words. Bilingual children also show advantages on cognitive "executive function" tasks that involve task switching or inhibitory control tasks; and there is evidence of a protective effect against cognitive decline with aging in bilingual adults (Bialystok, 2011). In translational science work taking place in Madrid, Spain, results show that a *Bilingual Baby* curriculum based on language learning principles uncovered in the laboratory can be used to ignite infant bilingual learning at rates about five times faster than ordinary community bilingual programs that are not evidence based (Kuhl & Ferjan Ramírez, 2019; Ferjan Ramírez & Kuhl, 2000).

Deafness and bilingualism provide evidence that all young brains are malleable—open to the right experience at the right time—rather than fixed at birth. They are not rigidly fixed either with regard to the modality thorough which they learn language, nor the number of languages that they learn. In a world in which communication, flexibility, and understanding of cultural differences and values are of vital importance, understanding the nature of human brain flexibility and the positive effects of diversity would appear to be a rich vein of scientific research with potential educational and policy implications. The fact that human brain plasticity and flexibility are fundamental characteristics of our species means that infants' brains expect and are prepared for cultural diversity—and all the advantages cultural diversity provides.

What's Biology Got to Do With It? (Proposition 1)

The baby brain begins with all of the brain areas necessary for processing sights, sounds, touch, smells, and taste. At birth, sound activates the baby's auditory brain areas, the sight of an object or person activates the visual brain centers, and touch activates the somatosensory cortex. In short, the infant brain comes into the world remarkably well organized. However, the cultural information coded by neurons in those brain areas—the cells that will eventually allow us to detect individual faces, people's voices, human actions, and, importantly, the *neural pathways that connect* brain areas to one another to process a "whole" person or event—require experience. In other words, although the baby brain begins with all of the brain areas necessary for processing auditory, visual, somatosensory, and motor information, the development of neurons that code specific culturally-valued information, and the architecture of neuronal networks that connect brain areas, requires cultural experience. Brains begin life ready to learn, but experience is necessary to construct the infant brain with all its culturally-dependent processing networks. The baby brain comes ready to be mapped by cultural experience.

Multiple genes play a role in this developmental unfolding, but they are *not* deterministic. As Gottlieb (2007), Meaney (2001), and others have elegantly described, extragenetic factors modify the expression of genes during development (Waddington's "epigenetics"). The earlier orthodox view that our genes determine development no longer predominates, and the debates about nature *or* nurture have given way to nature *and* nurture and a more nuanced understanding about how culture and biology interact.

Recent neuroscience studies suggest that the infant brain "expects" experience, and that without it, the brain does not develop normally. Experience maps the neurons and networks as infants interact in the world, and the infant brain begins to construct internal representations of culturally valued information. As infants' brains develop internal representations of the world, and the brain's neural networks become tuned to the categories and constructs embodied in their cultural environments, children's brains begin to act as "filters" on new incoming information. It is as though a child's new experiences are processed through the lenses formed by cultural experience, amplifying a particular way of perceiving the world. In the field of language, these "filters" are the phonetic structure of the learned language, the words and concepts we understand, and the grammar of the language(s) we know. The child's construction of these filters, based on experience, is the primary reason why learning a second language later in life is so difficult. The second language does not fit the filters established by the first.

Studies of children's brains can now use sophisticated brain-imaging technologies such as magnetoencephalography (MEG), which provides a movie of brain activity as the infant listens to speech or sees a person. Another technology, magnetic resonance imaging (MRI), can be used to track the growth of individual brain areas and the connections linking them, and allows us to measure how experience alters the anatomy of the brain. Studies using these technologies are now beginning to reveal how closely the social areas of the brain are linked to the language networks (e.g., Kuhl et al., 2014). Eventually, we believe that studies of the child's brain in action may reveal neural mechanisms by which the child constructs not only a language, but behavioral patterns, values, and beliefs (Meltzoff & Marshall, 2018) that reflect a particular human environment. Of course, brain studies will need to be done in conjunction with psychological and sociological studies, both within and across cultures, and across developmental time periods, in order to construct a comprehensive theory of how culture affects biology and vice versa.

Implications

In this chapter we have articulated several synthetic ideas about human learning and development starting from birth: (a) human functioning is an outgrowth of neurophysiological and psychologically linked capacities that have emerged over evolutionary history, but that are taken up and shaped by people's participation within and across a diverse array of cultural practices; (b) these neurophysiological-psychological relationships create representations in the brain subject to immense plasticity over the life course; (c) from a young age, humans seek to read the internal states of others, and in so doing to engage in social interactions with people and tools (physical, conceptual, ideological) embedded in the activities and settings in which they engage; in the earliest years, humans chiefly learn in informal settings, often through observation and imitation of others, and during the K-college years this is supplemented with explicit verbal instruction in formal learning institutions such as schools; (d) our social experiences (and even basic perceptions) are threaded through our emotional reactions, feelings of safety/threat, and weighed for relevance, in the human striving to feel efficacious, agentive, and a sense of belonging; (e) the diversity in pathways through which human learning and development unfold is essential to the human species; (f) all people participate in multiple cultural communities.

We have sought to illustrate these principles as they unfold in infancy and early childhood, as demonstrated by empirical studies. We have focused on infancy and early childhood because the evidence for the existence of these foundational principles during these early phases is so dramatic and often unexpected. These principles are operative even before children receive formal training, during the earliest years of brain and body development, and before the development of complex linguistic communication. This primacy supports the idea that these dispositions and competencies are an outgrowth of natural processes—where "natural" still means a combination of biology and culture.

In this section we want to draw out the implications of these foundational propositions for learning in later childhood and adolescence, and in particular the implications they have for the intentional design of robust learning environments that productively take up these foundational ideas (Lee, 2005, 2010, 2017). We can think about what it means to take seriously the importance of perceptions of safety, efficacy, and relevance, the importance of emotional salience, the kinds of knowledge we develop as we grow and experience the social and physical world, and the relevance of such prior knowledge for our choices to engage in tasks and challenges.

In many respects, parents and other early caregivers have an intuitive sense of the relevance of these ideas for how we interact with infants and young children. Yet we have greater challenges in translating these ideas with older children and adolescents. And even here, we are more efficacious in thinking about these ideas in non-formal settings, where youth elect to participate, than in formal schooling where children are forced to attend (Barron, 2006; Master & Meltzoff, 2020).

With this challenge in mind, we examine the implications and applications of our six theoretical propositions to older children and adolescents. We do so through examining the role of everyday knowledge for youth within and across diverse communities. We particularly focus on the work of learning in academic disciplines and on examining the design of robust learning environments that explicitly address relationship building, self-efficacy, and socio-emotional well-being.

Everyday Knowledge and the Academic Disciplines

One fundamental idea from studies of human cognition is the importance of prior knowledge to new learning (Bransford, Brown, & Cocking, 1999; National Academies of Sciences, Engineering,

& Medicine, 2018; Piaget, 1952; see also our six propositions). For example, studies have documented how young children develop competencies about numeracy and narrative prior to explicit formal training, and supported by social interactions and observation of the physical world that are primed by our evolutionary roots. Infants are able to distinguish between what is more and what is less (Starkey & Gelman, 1982; Wynn, 1992). Bruner (1990), Pinker (2007) and others (Mandler, 1984, 1987) have argued that narrative is a form of sense-making endemic to humans. Research on what is called story grammar (Applebee, 1978; Stein & Glenn, 1979; Trabasso & van den Broek, 1985) documents that even young children intuitively understand that stories involve agents with internal states that inform their goals, who engage in actions chronologically and logically connected, toward some broader goal or coda. We have shown in earlier sections how intuitively children learn the nuances of the languages they routinely hear. There is also research on how children intuit naive concepts about biology and physics (Carey, 2009; diSessa, 1982), again from observations in the world and building upon prior knowledge they bring to those observations. These well-established findings open up questions about their implications for learning beyond early childhood. They raise questions about how academic disciplinary knowledge is connected to everyday practices, and how the diversity of related everyday practices may inform the design of formal teaching practices.

The field of ethno-mathematics (Ascher, 1991; Saxe, 1991) takes up this issue by documenting the range of ways that cultural communities now and historically have created mathematical representations and forms of reasoning. Saxe's (1988a, 1988b) research on the mathematical problem solving of child street vendors in Brazil, as well as his longitudinal studies of the changes in mathematical representations among the Oksapmin of Papua New Guinea (Saxe, 1981; Saxe & Esmonde, 2005), contribute to our understandings of relations between everyday and academic knowledge in mathematics. Nasir (2005) and colleagues have analyzed the mathematical reasoning of children who routinely learn to play dominoes, including the nature of the social supports that surround the practice, socializing a sense of self-efficacy. Similarly, she has analyzed statistical reasoning used in everyday life among adolescent basketball players (Nasir, 2000). Taylor (2009) has documented how young African American children living in poverty develop arithmetic problem solving through the social practices surrounding purchasing activities after school at the local liquor store.

Other research has examined how language repertoires from everyday experiences, especially of youth from minoritized communities, can scaffold disciplinary literacies. Lee's (1995, 2007, 2014) research in Cultural Modeling empirically documented the affordances of supporting students in making public and explicit tacit strategies they employ in examining everyday texts (music lyrics, oral figurative language use, visual media) as heuristics in interpreting literature. Orellana (2009; Orellana & Reynolds, 2008), Valdés (1996, 2003) and others have examined the meta-linguistic knowledge that children who act as translators for their families develop as bilinguals. Levine and Horton (2013) have examined how the basic dispositions to attend to the salience of emotions can serve as a resource for detecting interpretive problems in literature. Champion (1998, 2003) has documented the range of oral storytelling styles among children who are speakers of African American English, and Gee (1989) has examined relations between these storytelling styles and more complex literary narratives.

The Salience of the Social Organization of Learning Environments

Among the big ideas we have attempted to convey is the importance of how learning environments are organized to optimize engagement, rooted in understanding the importance of social relationships, and of emotional attributions in signaling opportunities for self-efficacy and a sense of belonging. These principles are well demonstrated in the infant studies, which shows how fundamental they are to human beings. At the same time, studies of robust learning in everyday settings exemplify how learning across the life-span is also an outgrowth of distributed sources of support. Scribner's (1984, 1985) studies of dairy factory workers document how reasoning is socially distributed across people, objects, and tools, and that the knowledge being deployed embodies rich mathematical problem solving. Rose's (2001) examination of the social organization of learning in waitressing illustrates the distribution of supports, but equally the multi-dimensional nature of the knowledge being deployed and the ways the efficiencies (e.g., on deploying limited working memory) are distributed.

Other studies integrate cognitive, social, and phenomenological goals in designed learning environments. Gutiérrez's (Gutiérrez et al., 2009) longitudinal Migrant Student Project worked with high school students from migrant families in California during summer months across years on the UCLA campus, supporting students in seeing the campus as accessible to them, and that they belong. Students examined sociological texts interrogating political, ideological, and economic conundrums that impacted their lives through community cultural practices such as teatro (writing and enacting testimonials based on their work together and their readings). A striking outcome was that the students were overwhelmingly accepted into UC system colleges.

Cole and colleagues, across multiple sites of the 5th Dimension Project (Cole & Consortium, 2006; Vásquez, 2003), recruited cultural resources of elementary school children from non-dominant groups in a modest digital environment of game playing. The program also recruited college students as mentors, who came to learn directly about the language and intellective resources these children brought to problem solving. Relationship building, supports for self-efficacy, and the recruitment of students' cultural repertoires were central to program success. The research found strong impacts across sites on literacy development in the schools students attended, although the project did not work directly in them. Winn (2010) has documented restorative justice practices, including in sites with pre-incarceration adolescent girls, where literacy practices were employed to facilitate relationship building and identity wrestling, again recruiting everyday knowledge and repertoires of youth from minoritized communities.

Collectively, these studies illustrate how attention to relationship building, socializing efficacious identities, recruiting prior repertoires of knowledge and language, especially among youth and adults from minoritized communities, have achieved positive academic and psycho-social outcomes. They illustrate further how knowledge development unfolds in diverse environments that were designed to recruit repertoires of prior knowledge.

Re-visiting Our Understanding of Culture

All of these programs of research illustrating the recruitment of everyday repertoires take place in communities that represent what some call non-dominant communities. They serve well as exemplars because they help us interrogate one of the conundrums around how research communities, and other institutions of power, conceptualize the affordances of different cultural practices. The history of scientific racism that we briefly discussed in the Introduction typically used biological explanations to justify assumptions about hierarchies of human communities. Those historical efforts have been followed by "deficit theories" based on deficit attributions ascribed to practices associated with minoritized communities and those living in poverty (Bereiter & Engelmann, 1966; Herrnstein & Murray, 1994; Payne, 1999). Yet, diversity of pathways of human development is one of the powerful insights we gather from examining more modern studies of brain science and human evolution. Diversity of pathways is normal and indeed generative. Moreover, people belong always to multiple cultural communities, each with different affordances and different meanings and significance for the individual. Lamination is a useful metaphor for thinking about the ways that cultural practices and beliefs disperse across contexts (e.g. Alim's, 2009, examination of rap in the USA, China, South Africa).

Conclusions

We have argued for the need to understand the complex interactions among biological processes (including neuro-physiological processes) derived from our evolutionary roots as these are taken up, adapted, and transformed through people's participation in different cultural practices, within and across time periods. We have shown that these processes are so fundamental to human beings that they are already evident in infancy. We offer the metaphor of the braid of human development to capture these intricate and complex intertwinings. There is still much to be learned about how these processes operate, including a deeper understanding of the important function(s) that the diversity of culture and environments have in human development. This challenge cannot, however, be taken up without first acknowledging that a key feature of human uniqueness, and a source of strength of the human species, is simply this: Our development across the lifespan, and our past and future survival, are centrally connected to our participation in diverse cultural practices.

References

Adam, E. K. (2012). Emotion—Cortisol transactions occur over multiple time scales in development: Implications for research on emotion and the development of emotional disorders. *Monographs of the Society for Research in Child Development, 77*(2), 17–27.

Alim, H. S. (2009). Hip hop nation language. In: A. Duranti (Ed.), *Linguistic Anthropology: A Reader* (pp. 272–289). Malden, MA: Wiley-Blackwell.

Applebee, A. N. (1978). *The Child's Concept of Story: Ages Two to Seventeen.* Chicago, IL: University of Chicago Press.

Asante, M. K., & Asante, K. W. (1990). *African Culture: The Rhythms of Unity.* Trenton, NJ: Africa World Press.

Ascher, M. (1991). *Ethnomathematics: A Multicultural View of Mathematical Ideas.* Pacific Grove, CA: Brooks/Cole.

Bach-y-Rita, P., Kaczmarek, K. A., Tyler, M. E., & Garcia-Lara, J. (1998). Form perception with a 49-point electrotactile stimulus array on the tongue: A technical note. *Journal of Rehabilitation Research and Development, 35*(4), 427–430.

Bandura, A. (1993). Perceived self-efficacy in cognitive development and functioning. *Educational Psychologist, 28*(2), 117–148.

Barron, B. (2006). Interest and self-sustained learning as catalysts of development: A learning ecology perspective. *Human Development, 49*(4), 193–224.

Bates, E. (1976). *Language and Context: The Acquisition of Pragmatics.* New York, NY: Academic Press.

Bereiter, C., & Engelmann, S. (1966). *Teaching Disadvantaged Children in Preschool.* Englewood Cliffs, NJ: Prentice-Hall.

Bialystok, E. (2011). Reshaping the mind: The benefits of bilingualism. *Canadian Journal of Experimental Psychology, 65*(4), 229–235.

Bloom, L. (1973). *One Word at a Time: The Use of Single Word Utterances before Syntax.* The Hague: Mouton.

Bransford, J. D., Brown, A. L., & Cocking, R. R. (Eds.) (1999). *How People Learn: Brain, Mind, Experience and School.* Washington, DC: National Academy Press.

Bransford, J., Stevens, R., Schwartz, D., Meltzoff, A. N., Pea, R. D., Roschelle, J., … Sabelli, N. (2006). Learning theories and education: Toward a decade of synergy. In: P. A. Alexander & P. H. Winne (Eds.), *Handbook of Educational Psychology* (pp. 209–244). Mahwah, NJ: Erlbaum.

Bronfenbrenner, U., & Morris, P. A. (1998). The ecology of developmental processes. In: W. Damon & R. M. Lerner (Eds.), *Handbook of Child Psychology: Theoretical Models of Human Development* (5th ed., Vol. 1, pp. 993–1028). New York, NY: Wiley.

Brooks, R., & Meltzoff, A. N. (2008). Infant gaze following and pointing predict accelerated vocabulary growth through two years of age: A longitudinal, growth curve modeling study. *Journal of Child Language, 35*(1), 207–220.

Brooks, R., Singleton, J. L., & Meltzoff, A. N. (2020). Enhanced gaze-following behavior in Deaf infants of Deaf parents. *Developmental Science, 23*(2), e12900.

Brown, R. (1973). *A First Language: The Early Stages.* Cambridge, MA: Harvard University Press.

Bruner, J. (1983). *Child's Talk: Learning to Use Language.* New York, NY: Norton.

Bruner, J. (1990). *Acts of Meaning.* Cambridge, MA: Harvard University Press.

Carbado, D. W., Crenshaw, K. W., Mays, V. M., & Tomlinson, B. (2013). Intersectionality: Mapping the movements of a theory. *Du Bois Review: Social Science Research on Race, 10*(2), 303–312.

Carey, S. (2009). *The Origins of Concepts*. New York, NY: Oxford University Press.

Champion, T. B. (1998). "Tell me somethin' good": A description of narrative structures among African American children. *Linguistics and Education, 9*(3), 251–286.

Champion, T. B. (2003). *Understanding Storytelling among African American Children: A Journey from Africa to America*. Mahwah, NJ: Erlbaum.

Chomsky, N. (1957). *Syntactic Structures*. The Hague: Mouton.

Cole, M. (1996). *Cultural Psychology, A Once and Future Discipline*. Cambridge, MA: Harvard University Press.

Cole, M. (2007). Phylogeny and cultural history in ontogeny. *Journal of Physiology - Paris, 101*(4–6), 236–246.

Cole, M., & Consortium, D. L. (2006). *The Fifth Dimension: An After-School Program Built on Diversity*. New York, NY: Russell Sage Foundation.

Conboy, B. T., Brooks, R., Meltzoff, A. N., & Kuhl, P. K. (2015). Social interaction in infants' learning of second-language phonetics: An exploration of brain–behavior relations. *Developmental Neuropsychology, 40*(4), 216–229.

Damasio, A. R. (1995). Toward a neurobiology of emotion and feeling: Operational concepts and hypotheses. *Neuroscientist, 1*(1), 19–25.

diSessa, A. A. (1982). Unlearning Aristotelian physics: A study of knowledge-based learning. *Cognitive Science, 6*(1), 37–75.

Ferguson, C. A. (1964). Baby talk in six languages. *American Anthropologist, 66*(6), 103–114.

Ferjan Ramírez, N., Ramírez, R. R., Clarke, M., Taulu, S., & Kuhl, P. K. (2017). Speech discrimination in 11-month-old bilingual and monolingual infants: A magnetoencephalography study. *Developmental Science, 20*(1), e12427.

Ferjan Ramirez, N., & Kuhl, P. K. (2020). Early second language learning through SparkLing™: Scaling up a language intervention in infant education centers. *Mind, Brain, and Education*. [Epub ahead of print]

Flavell, J. H., & Miller, P. H. (1998). Social cognition. In: D. Kuhn & R. Siegler (Eds.), *Handbook of Child Psychology* (5th ed., Vol. 2, pp. 851–898). New York, NY: Wiley.

Fodor, J. A. (1983). *The Modularity of Mind: An Essay on Faculty Psychology*. Cambridge, MA: MIT Press.

Gee, J. P. (1989). The narrativization of experience in the oral style. *Journal of Education, 171*(1), 75–96.

Gottlieb, G. (2007). Probabilistic epigenesis. *Developmental Science, 10*(1), 1–11.

Gould, S. J. (1981). *The Mismeasure of Man*. New York, NY: Norton.

Gutiérrez, K. D., Morales, P. Z., & Martinez, D. C. (2009). Re-mediating literacy: Culture, difference, and learning for students from non-dominant communities. *Review of Research in Education, 33*(1), 212–245.

Gutiérrez, K. D., & Rogoff, B. (2003). Cultural ways of learning: Individual traits or repertoires of practice. *Educational Researcher, 32*(5), 19–25.

Hanna, E., & Meltzoff, A. N. (1993). Peer imitation by toddlers in laboratory, home, and day-care contexts: Implications for social learning and memory. *Developmental Psychology, 29*(4), 701–710.

Heimann, M., & Tjus, T. (2019). Neonatal imitation: Temporal characteristics in imitative response patterns. *Infancy, 24*(5), 674–692.

Herrnstein, R. J., & Murray, C. (1994). *The Bell Curve: Intelligence and Class Structure in American Life*. New York, NY: Free Press.

Hoff, E., Core, C., Place, S., Rumiche, R., Señor, M., & Parra, M. (2012). Dual language exposure and early bilingual development. *Journal of Child Language, 39*(1), 1–27.

Jackson, J. P., & Weidman, N. M. (2004). *Race, Racism, and Science: Social Impact and Interaction*. New Brunswick, NJ: Rutgers University Press.

Klein, P. J., & Meltzoff, A. N. (1999). Long-term memory, forgetting, and deferred imitation in 12-month-old infants. *Developmental Science, 2*(1), 102–113.

Kuhl, P. K. (2007). Is speech learning 'gated' by the social brain? *Developmental Science, 10*(1), 110–120.

Kuhl, P. K., & Ferjan Ramírez, N. (2019). Neuroscience and education: How early brain development affects school. In: P. K. Kuhl, S.-S. Lim, S. Guerriero & D. van Damme (Eds.), *Developing Minds in the Digital Age: Towards a Science of Learning for 21st Century Education* (pp. 25–36). Paris, France: OECD Publishing.

Kuhl, P. K., & Meltzoff, A. N. (1996). Infant vocalizations in response to speech: Vocal imitation and developmental change. *Journal of the Acoustical Society of America, 100*(4), 2425–2438.

Kuhl, P. K., & Meltzoff, A. N. (1997). Evolution, nativism, and learning in the development of language and speech. In: M. Gopnik (Ed.), *The Inheritance and Innateness of Grammars* (pp. 7–44). New York, NY: Oxford University Press.

Kuhl, P. K., Ramírez, R. R., Bosseler, A., Lin, J.-F. L., & Imada, T. (2014). Infants' brain responses to speech suggest analysis by synthesis. *Proceedings of the National Academy of Sciences of the United States of America, 111*(31), 11238–11245.

Kuhl, P. K., Stevens, E., Hayashi, A., Deguchi, T., Kiritani, S., & Iverson, P. (2006). Infants show a facilitation effect for native language phonetic perception between 6 and 12 months. *Developmental Science, 9*(2), F13–F21.

Kuhl, P. K., Tsao, F.-M., & Liu, H.-M. (2003). Foreign-language experience in infancy: Effects of short-term exposure and social interaction on phonetic learning. *Proceedings of the National Academy of Sciences, 100*(15), 9096–9101.

Kuhl, P. K., Williams, K. A., Lacerda, F., Stevens, K. N., & Lindblom, B. (1992). Linguistic experience alters phonetic perception in infants by 6 months of age. *Science, 255*(5044), 606–608.

Lee, C. D. (1995). A culturally based cognitive apprenticeship: Teaching African American high school students skills in literary interpretation. *Reading Research Quarterly, 30*(4), 608–630.

Lee, C. D. (2005). Intervention research based on current views of cognition & learning. In: J. E. King (Ed.), *Black Education: A Transformative Research and Action Agenda for the New Century* (pp. 73–114). Mahwah, NJ: Erlbaum (joint publication with the American Educational Research Association).

Lee, C. D. (2007). *Culture, Literacy and Learning: Taking Bloom in the Midst of the Whirlwind.* New York, NY: Teachers College Press.

Lee, C. D. (2010). Soaring above the clouds, delving the ocean's depths: Understanding the ecologies of human learning and the challenge for education science. *Educational Researcher, 39*(9), 643–655.

Lee, C. D. (2014). A multi-dimensional cultural modeling framework for the design of robust literacy instruction. In: P. J. Dunston, S. K. Fullerton, M. W. Cole, D. Herro, J. A. Malloy, P. M. Wilder, & K. N. Headley (Eds.), *63rd Yearbook of the Literacy Research Association* (pp. 78–85). Altamonte Springs, FL: Literacy Research Association.

Lee, C. D. (2017). Integrating research on how people learn and learning across settings as a window of opportunity to address inequality in educational processes and outcomes. *Review of Research in Education, 41*(1), 88–111.

Legare, C. H., Wen, N. J., Herrmann, P. A., & Whitehouse, H. (2015). Imitative flexibility and the development of cultural learning. *Cognition, 142*, 351–361.

Levine, S., & Horton, W. S. (2013). Using affective appraisal to help readers construct literary interpretations. *Scientific Study of Literature, 3*(1), 105–136.

Mandler, J. (1984). *Stories, Scripts, and Scenes: Aspects of Schema Theory.* Hillsdale, NJ: Erlbaum.

Mandler, J. (1987). On the psychological reality of story structure. *Discourse Processes, 10*(1), 1–29.

Marshall, P. J., & Meltzoff, A. N. (2014). Neural mirroring mechanisms and imitation in human infants. *Philosophical Transactions of the Royal Society Series B: Biological Sciences, 369*(1644), 20130620.

Maslow, A. H. (1943). A theory of human motivation. *Psychological Review, 50*(4), 370–396.

Master, A. H., & Meltzoff, A. N. (2020). Cultural stereotypes and sense of belonging contribute to gender gaps in STEM. *International Journal of Gender, Science and Technology.* [Epub ahead of print].

Meaney, M. J. (2001). Maternal care, gene expression, and the transmission of individual differences in stress reactivity across generations. *Annual Review of Neuroscience, 24*(1), 1161–1192.

Meltzoff, A. N. (1988a). Infant imitation after a 1-week delay: Long-term memory for novel acts and multiple stimuli. *Developmental Psychology, 24*(4), 470–476.

Meltzoff, A. N. (1988b). The human infant as *Homo imitans*. In: T. R. Zentall & B. G. Galef (Eds.), *Social Learning: Psychological and Biological Perspectives* (pp. 319–341). Hillsdale, NJ: Erlbaum.

Meltzoff, A. N. (2007). The 'like me' framework for recognizing and becoming an intentional agent. *Acta Psychologica, 124*(1), 26–43.

Meltzoff, A. N. (2013). Origins of social cognition: Bidirectional self-other mapping and the "Like-Me" hypothesis. In: M. R. Banaji & S. A. Gelman (Eds.), *Navigating the Social World: What Infants, Children, and Other Species Can Teach Us* (pp. 139–144). New York, NY: Oxford University Press.

Meltzoff, A. N., Kuhl, P. K., Movellan, J., & Sejnowski, T. J. (2009). Foundations for a new science of learning. *Science, 325*(5938), 284–288.

Meltzoff, A. N., & Marshall, P. J. (2018). Human infant imitation as a social survival circuit. *Current Opinion in Behavioral Sciences, 24*, 130–136.

Meltzoff, A. N., & Moore, M. K. (1977). Imitation of facial and manual gestures by human neonates. *Science, 198*(4312), 75–78.

Meltzoff, A. N., & Moore, M. K. (1983). Newborn infants imitate adult facial gestures. *Child Development, 54*(3), 702–709.

Meltzoff, A. N., & Moore, M. K. (1997). Explaining facial imitation: A theoretical model. *Early Development and Parenting, 6*(3–4), 179–192.

Meltzoff, A. N., Ramírez, R. R., Saby, J. N., Larson, E., Taulu, S., & Marshall, P. J. (2018). Infant brain responses to felt and observed touch of hands and feet: An MEG study. *Developmental Science, 21*(5), e12651.

Meltzoff, A. N., Saby, J. N., & Marshall, P. J. (2019). Neural representations of the body in 60-day-old human infants. *Developmental Science, 22*(1), e12698.

Nagy, E., Pal, A., & Orvos, H. (2014). Learning to imitate individual finger movements by the human neonate. *Developmental Science, 17*(6), 841–857.

Nasir, N. S. (2000). "Points ain't everything": Emergent goals and average and percent understandings in the play of basketball among African American students. *Anthropology & Education Quarterly*, *31*(3), 283–305.

Nasir, N. S. (2005). Individual cognitive structuring and the sociocultural context: Strategy shifts in the game of dominoes. *Journal of the Learning Sciences*, *14*(1), 5–34.

National Academies of Sciences, Engineering, & Medicine. (2018). *How People Learn II: Learners, Contexts, and Cultures*. Washington, DC: National Academies Press.

Orellana, M. F. (2009). *Translating Childhoods: Immigrant Youth, Language, and Culture*. New Brunswick, NJ: Rutgers University Press.

Orellana, M. F., & Reynolds, J. F. (2008). Cultural modeling: Leveraging bilingual skills for school paraphrasing tasks. *Reading Research Quarterly*, *43*(1), 48–65.

Payne, R. K. (1999). *A Framework for Understanding and Working with Students and Adults from Poverty*. Baytown, TX: RFT Publishing.

Petitto, L. A., Zatorre, R. J., Gauana, K., Nikelski, E. J., Dostie, D., & Evans, A. C. (2000). Speech-like cerebral activity in profoundly deaf people processing signed languages: Implications for the neural basis of human language. *Proceedings of the National Academy of Sciences*, *97*(25), 13961–13966.

Piaget, J. (1952). *The Origins of Intelligence in Children* (M. Cook, Trans.). New York, NY: International Universities Press.

Piaget, J. (1962). *Play, Dreams and Imitation in Childhood* (C. Gattegno & F. M. Hodgson, Trans). New York, NY: Norton.

Piaget, J. (1971). *Biology and Knowledge: An Essay on the Relations between Organic Regulations and Cognitive Processes*. Chicago, IL: University of Chicago Press.

Pinker, S. (2007). *The Stuff of Thought: Language as a Window into Human Nature*. New York, NY: Viking.

Quartz, S. R., & Sejnowski, T. J. (2002). *Liars, Lovers, and Heroes: What the New Brain Science Reveals about How We Become Who We Are*. New York, NY: William Morrow.

Repacholi, B. M., & Meltzoff, A. N. (2007). Emotional eavesdropping: Infants selectively respond to indirect emotional signals. *Child Development*, *78*(2), 503–521.

Repacholi, B. M., Meltzoff, A. N., Toub, T. S., & Ruba, A. L. (2016). Infants' generalizations about other people's emotions: Foundations for trait-like attributions. *Developmental Psychology*, *52*(3), 364–378.

Rogoff, B. (2003). *The Cultural Nature of Human Development*. New York, NY: Oxford University Press.

Rogoff, B., & Chavajay, P. (1995). What's become of research on the cultural basis of cognitive development? *American Psychologist*, *50*(10), 859–877.

Rose, M. (2001). The working life of a waitress. *Mind, Culture, and Activity*, *8*(1), 3–27.

Saby, J. N., Marshall, P. J., & Meltzoff, A. N. (2012). Neural correlates of being imitated: An EEG study in pre-verbal infants. *Social Neuroscience*, *7*(6), 650–661.

Saffran, J. R., Aslin, R. N., & Newport, E. L. (1996). Statistical learning by 8-month-old infants. *Science*, *274*(5294), 1926–1928.

Saxe, G. B. (1981). Body parts as numerals: A developmental analysis of numeration among the Oksapmin in Papua New Guinea. *Child Development*, *52*(1), 306–316.

Saxe, G. B. (1988a). Candy selling and math learning. *Educational Researcher*, *17*(6), 14–21.

Saxe, G. B. (1988b). The mathematics of child street vendors. *Child Development*, *59*(5), 1415–1425.

Saxe, G. B. (1991). *Culture and Cognitive Development: Studies in Mathematical Understanding*. Hillsdale, NJ: Erlbaum.

Saxe, G. B., & Esmonde, I. (2005). Studying cognition in flux: A historical treatment of Fu in the shifting structure of Oksapmin mathematics. *Mind, Culture, and Activity*, *12*(3–4), 171–225.

Saxe, G. B., & Esmonde, I. (2012). *Cultural Development of Mathematical Ideas: Papua New Guinea Studies*. New York, NY: Cambridge University Press.

Scribner, S. (1984). Studying working intelligence. In: B. Rogoff & J. Lave (Eds.), *Everyday Cognition: Its Development in Social Context* (pp. 9–40). Cambridge, MA: Harvard University Press.

Scribner, S. (1985). Knowledge at work. *Anthropology and Education Quarterly*, *16*(3), 199–206.

Skinner, A. L., Olson, K. R., & Meltzoff, A. N. (2019). Acquiring group bias: Observing other people's nonverbal signals can create social group biases. *Journal of Personality and Social Psychology*. doi:10.1037/pspi0000218. [Epub ahead of print].

Skinner, B. F. (1957). *Verbal Behavior*. New York, NY: Appleton-Century-Crofts.

Spencer, M. B. (2006). Phenomenology and ecological systems theory: Development of diverse groups. In: W. Damon & R. M. Lerner (Eds.), *Handbook of Child Psychology* (6th ed., Vol. 1, pp. 829–893). Hoboken, NJ: Wiley.

Starkey, P., & Gelman, R. (1982). The development of addition and subtraction abilities prior to formal schooling in arithmetic. In: T. P. Carpenter, J. M. Moser & T. A. Romberg (Eds.), *Addition and Subtraction: A Cognitive Perspective* (pp. 99–116). Hillsdale, NJ: Erlbaum.

Stavropoulos, K. K. M., & Carver, L. J. (2014). Reward sensitivity to faces versus objects in children: An ERP study. *Social Cognitive and Affective Neuroscience, 9*(10), 1569–1575.

Stein, N. L., & Glenn, C. G. (1979). An analysis of story comprehension in elementary school children: A test of a schema. In R. O. Freedle (Ed.), *New Directions in Discourse Processing*, (Vol. 2, pp. 53–120). Norwood, NJ: Ablex.

Sundara, M., Ward, N., Conboy, B., & Kuhl, P. K. (2020). Exposure to a second language in infancy alters speech production. *Bilingualism: Language and Cognition*, 1–14. [Epub ahead of print].

Taylor, E. V. (2009). The purchasing practice of low-income students: The relationship to mathematical development. *Journal of the Learning Sciences, 18*(3), 370–415.

Tomasello, M. (2003). *Constructing a Language: A Usage-Based Theory of Language Acquisition*. Cambridge, MA: Harvard University Press.

Tomasello, M. (2019). *Becoming Human: A Theory of Ontogeny*. Cambridge, MA: Harvard University Press.

Trabasso, T., & van den Broek, P. (1985). Causal thinking and the representation of narrative events. *Journal of Memory and Language, 24*(5), 612–630.

Valdés, G. (1996). *Con Respeto: Bridging the Distances between Culturally Diverse Families and Schools*. New York, NY: Teachers College Press.

Valdés, G. (2003). *Expanding Definitions of Giftedness: The Case of Young Interpreters from Immigrant Communities*. Mahwah, NJ: Erlbaum.

Vásquez, O. A. (2003). *La Clase Mágica: Imagining Optimal Possibilities in a Bilingual Community of Learners*. Mahwah, NJ: Erlbaum .

Vygotsky, L. S. (1962). *Thought and Language* (E. Hanfmann & G. Vakar, Trans.). Cambridge, MA: MIT Press (Original work published 1934).

Vygotsky, L. S. (1978). *Mind in Society: The Development of Higher Psychological Processes*. Cambridge, MA: Harvard University Press.

Waddington, C. H. (1942). The epigenotype. *Endeavour, 1*, 18–20.

Wang, Z., Williamson, R. A., & Meltzoff, A. N. (2015). Imitation as a mechanism in cognitive development: A cross-cultural investigation of 4-year-old children's rule learning. *Frontiers in Psychology, 6*, 562.

Ward, J. (2012). *The Student's Guide to Social Neuroscience*. New York, NY: Psychology Press.

Winn, M. T. (2010). 'Our side of the story': Moving incarcerated youth voices from margins to center. *Race, Ethnicity and Education, 13*(3), 313–325.

Wynn, K. (1992). Addition and subtraction by human infants. *Nature, 358*(6389), 749–750.

3

EXAMINING LINKS BETWEEN CULTURE, IDENTITY, AND LEARNING

Margaret Beale Spencer, Carly Offidani-Bertrand, Keshia Harris, and Gabriel Velez

Learning as a cultural process is deeply rooted in our biology and in our evolutionary history. Prior generational intrusions and major events have implications for patterned interactions, processes, and outcomes for subsequent cohorts. Elder's "Children of the Great Depression: Social Change in Life Experience" (1974) provides an illustration determined by a major socioeconomic fluctuation. Specifically, his description of the long-term impacts of the early 20th century economic depression on youth as observed across time are parallel to current 21st century observations of developmental expressions of cultural processes having under-acknowledged foundations (Davis, Burleigh, & Gardner, 1941; Davis & Havighurst, 1946; Franklin V.P., 1979; Havighurst & Davis, 1943; Siddle-Walker, 2013). The impact of the latter temporal interval on social science conceptual leanings, particularly with reference to youth of color, was made worse for current analyses due to the penchant to ignore or "problematize" developmental expressions of *humanity in context*. Varied cultural expressions of learning have been devalued or "othered" as compared against a particular privileged standard (e.g., see Spencer, 2019; Spencer et al., 2019; Spencer & Dowd, upcoming).

Alternatively, we put forward a viewpoint which recognizes *not simply that culture impacts development. Moreover, we posit that the* **expression** *of intergenerationally determined patterns of development and social experience may be cultural in nature* given significant fluctuations or social disruptions associated with prior generations. Particularly significant to contemporary life, there are *few 18th through 20th century* **contexts serving as conduits** for interpreting and reacting to *learning patterns as cultural expressions*, other than schools (i.e., both as the context of student learning and the institutions serving as the producers of knowledge utilized for teaching and socialization). The early observations by Havighurst and Davis in "Child Socialization and the School" illustrate the perspective emphasized in this section:

> Educators and other students of human development increasingly are viewing human learning as a function of the total biological and social history of the learner. It seems clear also that all new learning involves the changing of previously learned behavior. Since social behavior is learned, these principles indicate that what the child learns in his school culture is influenced by what he learns in his social life outside of school and what he has learned before he entered school....His socialization in these groups largely determines what aspects of the school culture are experienced by him as either punishing or rewarding.
>
> *(Havighurst & Davis, 1943, p. 29)*

Introduction

Development (and learning) is constituted by social and cultural processes as individuals develop through their participation in cultural practices. The perspective argues that individuals navigate diverse spaces and places, make attendant meanings about, and engage in, culturally mediated interactional processes. Accordingly, development occurs as individuals engage in and make meanings of cultural learning and opportunities. Both for self and as group members, particularly structured social pathways are navigated. As socialization experiences, members respond to the requirements of developmental tasks through youthful participation in cultural practices and culturally mediated interactional processes.

As a cultural tradition particularly in the social sciences, we refer to the longstanding penchant to characterize *cultural variation and social differences from a designated norm as "less than" an assumed performance standard and, thus, presumed to be deficit, deficient and/or deviant* (Allen, 1985; Epps, 1985; Fisher, Hoagwood, Boyce, Duster et al., 2002; Guthrie, 1976); Pierce, 1985; Spencer, 2019; Spencer et al., 2019). This perspective assumes that only those considered "the other" represent and have culture and that the group "having power to define" represents the *privileged **performance standard***.

Developmental outcomes as cultural products of coping and adaptation—given stage specific developmental tasks including learning—produce particularly patterned findings. As a consequence of context-imbued conditions of inequality, outcomes frequently stray from those considered "the societal norm." The situation generates values-specific complexities (i.e., patterned processes and outcomes) observed for privileged members of society who demonstrate unparalleled access to awards and supports and thus are viewed as the expected norm without regard for the benefits associated with whiteness, privilege, and power (Spencer, 2019; Spencer et al., 2019). Adding further convolution, developmentally linked meanings are made of observed outcome differences between cultural communities. The particular cultural adaptations enacted by individuals within socially constructed systems of high risk may communicate meanings associated with particular under-valued cultural products. Also possible—as well—*are under-acknowledged access to effective but novel supports and resources* functioning as impactful protective factors (McGee & Spencer, 2013, 2015; Rious, Cunningham & Spencer, 2019). These might include cultural models generally not considered, as such, for privileged groups; thus, the latter might comprise cultural socialization resources, racial identity formation processes and culturally relevant achievement models which serve as supports. As community and/or family relevant protective factors and supports, such resources may increase engagement and psychological well-being (McGee & Spencer, 2013, 2015; Rious, Cunningham, & Spencer, 2019; Spencer et al., 2019).

Affectivity and cognition intersect and interact across the life course *and produce context linked cultural practices contributing to meaning making variation* (Spencer 1995, 2006, and 2008; Spencer et al., 2006). Particularly relevant to learning experiences are those associated with the various features of the *ecology of human development including historical factors* referred to by Bronfenbrenner (1979) as the chronosystem, and which are broadly disseminated by education researchers and historians (e.g., see Franklin, J. H., 1967, 1993; Franklin, V. P. 1979; Siddle-Walker, 2013). When phenomenological processes as development specific "meaning making" are added as impactful factors determinative to how individuals make interpretations about their world, *stable outcomes are observed as a result*. Produced are patterned responses to structured conditions and interactions. Thus, the process results in psychosocial outcomes that are specific to development (e.g., sense of self as a learner, as a valued member of society, and an esteemed member of a cultural community). Although copious identity research and theorizing have occurred over the prior fifty years, nonetheless, fundamental aspects of Eriksonian (1964) theorizing along with others remain cogent for delineating the process.

An identity focused cultural- and ecology-emphasizing framework has been helpful in describing the process (see phenomenological variant of ecological systems theory [PVEST: Spencer,

1995, 2006, 2008]). It provides a social-justice-relevant and equity-sensitive conceptual base for understanding the "how" and "why" of the patterned and context linked process and outcomes. Specifically, phenomenological variant of ecological systems theory (PVEST) explains how patterned and episodic physical conditions and psychological processes as cultural practices and context relevant traditions unavoidably shape the nature of mediating cultural processes and products of development (Spencer 1995, 2006, 2008). Accordingly, our strategy for linking culture, identity, and learning suggests a particular chapter organization.

Following the paper's introduction, we first provide *historical contributions* which aid obtaining insights for appreciating the power and nature of contexts of human development. Our paper makes use of research perspectives designed primarily from adolescent research in the United States (i.e., both minority youth of color and white, non-minority privileged adolescents). Following the historical framing, we present phenomenological variant of ecological systems theory in order to articulate the ways by which historical circumstances, the biology-based maturation of individuals and brain changes—particularly at adolescence—are linked with context features. And as a demonstration, we provide studies conducted in unique cultural communities around the globe for demonstrating the efficacy of the conceptual strategy for understanding (and ultimately decreasing) human vulnerability and increasing resiliency. In the paper's third section, we describe brain science's contributions and challenges via interpreting cultural influences and impacts on development in order to delineate the role of biology in the cultural process of learning.

Racial/Ethnic and Cultural Context of Learning: Historical Factors Acknowledged from a PVEST Perspective

Although discussions of reparations have continued to resurface over the last two decades (see e.g., Coates, 2014; Robinson, 2001), and although they formally ended over 150 years ago, the residual impact between and within racial group relationships continues to rage, albeit under-acknowledged by many non-minority United States citizens. The history of North American slavery is generally viewed as a period having no relevance for 21st century United States politics and everyday cultural practices. North America's economic interests and evolved cultural traditions have remained generally under-addressed in the scientific literature though, of course, there are exceptions (e.g., see Roediger, 1991). But the 21st century—as particularly evidenced in developmental science—is depicted without attention to the role of slavery, a persistently under-acknowledged source of impact on human development and everyday cultural practices. It too frequently remains invisible as a source of social class and ethnicity/caste contributors to human development.

Reciprocally, the various developmental requirements for health, well-being and myriad types of learning relevant competencies are important. Considered at either the group or individual level, in response to specific *risks and challenges* as well as seamlessly accessed *protective factors and supports* associated with *contextual conditions of stress and trauma*, phenomenological variant of ecological systems theory (PVEST) posits that **coping is required**. It is our perspective that the responses produced, considered jointly or as collective responses, *include particularly patterned cultural practices*. The alluded-to behavioral traditions are characterized—too frequently—as devalued and functionally destabilizing stereotypes. The behavioral responses to particular reinforcement conditions (e.g., the benefits or "wages of whiteness"), as described by Roediger (1991) and others, give rise to stable conditions of bias. Stereotyping sets of historical conditions include unavoidable associations with power. Consequent responsive behavioral characterizations of others precipitate societal cultural practices requiring coping processes (i.e., both those which are "reactive" and manifested in the moment as well as those that are internalized given redundancies and then "internalized" as more stable identity processes, thus, observed over time). The viewpoint is consistent with the cultural meanings suggested by the volume's editors and certainly referenced as the chronosystem by Bronfenbrenner (1979) and suggests the utility of an identity focused cultural ecological perspective represented by the PVEST developmental perspective (Spencer, 1995, 2006).

As a function of the problem of racism and other forms of institutionalized bias, there has been a history of resistance concerning to whom a normal *human development* perspective has been applied, and those individuals and groups who have been historically excluded (Spencer et al., 2019). Acknowledging "the challenge" concerning whose humanity is recognized in the literature has been only very recently addressed in developmental science. Other interdisciplinary fields such as education may have "pushed the perspective" (e.g., see Franklin, 1979; Siddle-Walker, 2013). However, the more recent focus on trauma has helped to articulate the sources and varied impacts of trauma on development, thus representing a particular responsive orientation as a cultural practice, both for those serving as sources of trauma and those providing cultural responses.

Racial/Ethnic Trauma as Context for Learning: PVEST and Marginalized Youth

Salient to acknowledge is that the formal study of trauma as an aspect of the standard contextual experiences over time for particular citizens is no less complex than the prior conundrum concerning whose humanity is assumed in programs of research. The study of racial trauma reveals several obstacles to incorporating it into an acknowledged clinical category as a consideration for effective programing and policy decisions. Jernigan and Daniel (2014) point out that definitions of trauma are limited to physical incidents as defined by the DSM-IV. Additional challenges include a lack of conceptualization of racial trauma and fears of diluting the meaning of "legitimate" (i.e., physical trauma). They note that additional work is needed to better highlight racial incidents as trauma as opposed to mere stressors (Bryant-Davis & Ocampo, 2005). Some have sought to broaden the definition of trauma as a "deeper psychological harm arising from a wide array of events and experiences that interact with development over time and exist in a cultural context" (Graves, Kaslow, & Frabutt, 2010; Danzer, Rieger, Schubmehl, & Cort, 2016).

Particularly relevant to the institution of American slavery, intergenerational transmission of trauma (ITT) consists of the effect of parental trauma adversely affecting their descendants (immediate and future generations). This has led to increased traumatic symptoms and the increased vulnerability to later psychopathology (Braveheart, 2011; Sirikantraporn & Green, 2016). This model draws from our understanding of Post-Traumatic Stress Disorder (Sotero, 2006) as a model which references three frameworks: (1) psychosocial theory where traumatic stressors can increase susceptibility to disease and have other negative influences on human physiology; (2) political–economic theory, which looks at the impact of political, economic, and structural inequalities on the individual; and (3) social–ecological systems theory, which examines dynamics and interdependences between the past and present life course development factors that influence susceptibility to disease (Danzer, Rieger, Schubmehl, & Cort, 2016).

Given the physiological manifestations of persistent stress, discrimination from law enforcement is known to have contributed to trauma in its immediate effects of PTSD and, as some have speculated, that subsequent delinquent behavior might stem from the initial interaction (Kang & Burton, 2014). "In lower income, urban African American neighborhoods, police tend to over patrol and counterproductively treat African American males with suspicion" (Kang & Burton, 2014). Additionally, "racist events exacerbate preexisting racial tensions and lead to widespread reluctance to seek protection from the police and other institutions that have historically safeguarded Whites" (Graves et al., 2010).

African American women are at a greater risk of being traumatized multiple times and are less likely to seek mental health services than white women (Osobor, 2009; Graves, Kaslow, & Frabutt, 2010; Danzer, Rieger, Schubmehl, & Cort, 2016). It has been shown that this results from fears concerning what might happen to the perpetrator, particularly if that person is also African American. Some have pointed out that this reflects the notion that an attack on one is an attack on all (Parham, White, & Ajamu, 1999; Graves, Kaslow, & Frabutt, 2010; Danzer, Rieger, Schubmehl, & Cort, 2016). It is also noted, ironically, that despite being raised to be fiercely independent and willing to help others (often at their own expense), being a black woman can furthermore exacerbate symptoms of trauma (Stevens-Watkins et al., 2014).

One area where symptoms of trauma have brain relevant implications is when delineating how it can impact long-term outcomes (e.g., in higher education) (Boyraz et al., 2013). For trauma-exposed females, PTSD symptomatology in the first semester of college was associated with an increased likelihood of not completing college. This was not significantly associated with academic achievement or persistence for males. For trauma-exposed females, in addition to PTSD symptomatology, being a student at a predominantly white institution and entering college with a low high school GPA were identified as risk factors for low academic achievement and college dropout. They also found that involvement in on-campus activities and higher levels of perceived academic integration by the first semester were associated with a higher first-year GPA as well as increased likelihood of remaining in college (Boyraz et al., 2013).

There has been some work on the implications for psychologists and therapists in dealing with racial and generational trauma. One interesting item of note is the value of ethnic matching. African American patients generally prefer to be matched with a mental health care professional who is of the same race/ethnicity. This has been seen in the study of African American college students in particular. They have observed that up to 50% of African Americans who see a White practitioner will drop out after a single session. It is noted that it is usually because of their own reported feelings of not being understood or connected with (Duncan & Johnson, 2007; Parham et al., 1999; African American Psychologist, 2008; Graves, Kaslow, & Frabutt, 2010; Danzer, Rieger, Schubmehl, & Cort, 2016).

As reported nearly forty years ago by Allen, Spencer, and Brookins (1985), unfortunately, *developmental science* has contributed to a history of reserving analyses concerning *developmental processes*, and attendant considerations and implications about same, as reserved for non-minorities; thus, it has not been a conceptual and research orientation inclusive of all learners. As noted previously, *culture* has been treated generally as meaning "others" not of Euro-American ancestry. The penchant for a less than "humanity equivalent" conceptual strategy is highly salient. It is a critically important conceptual challenge to acknowledge when referencing anything having to do with 21st century developmental science (see Spencer, 1985; Spencer et al., 2019).

Consistent with a PVEST systems theoretical perspective (Spencer, 1995, 2006) young people of various nationalities, genders, racial backgrounds and ethnic groups engage in adaptive and/or maladaptive processes as they negotiate the complex implications of their particular social positions, including learning how they fit into their culturally specific social groups (e.g., Thompson, Harris, & Clauss-Ehlers, 2013). Such entities comprise multiple culturally specific and culturally overlapping groups. This chapter employs an ecological perspective in examining how young people interact with and internalize aspects of their cultural context in psycho-biologically relevant ways as they learn to adapt their unique selves to the various social roles that are a necessary part of their multiple cultural communities.

International Exemplars and Contributions of a PVEST Perspective: Three Case Studies

Thus far, our conceptual orientation focuses on the overlap between *culture, learning, and identity* by making use of the phenomenological variant of ecological systems theory (PVEST) to understand identity formation in adolescence as identity relevant processes of culturally situated learning (Spencer, 1995, 2006). Of course, it is critical to acknowledge that frequently—as a methodological failure—sample descriptions fail to delineate and report distinctiveness within unique cultural communities of adolescents

The PVEST framework was integrated throughout the preceding sections. Accordingly, as the third section following the introduction, the current segment uses the framework with multiple international data sources to demonstrate the dialectical relationship between culture and identity as a culturally mediated learning process. We frame these examples with an identity-focused cultural ecological perspective (i.e., PVEST) to demonstrate how these groups of young people come to identify with and learn strategies to fulfill culturally specific social roles which, in turn, are internalized in the form of *social-class identity, civic identity, and occupational identity*.

We present our work from three different contexts in Latin America to demonstrate this perspective about learning processes as representative of broader identity processes influenced by different cultural contexts. The three specific cases—Argentina, Peru, and Brazil—were chosen because they draw on our own work to cover a range of contexts and identity domains. The individuals in each study are developing within particular national and local histories, racial and ethnic dynamics, and social roles and expectations. Therefore, important factors like race or socioeconomic status play different roles in each case, and our empirical support focuses on particularly salient cultural aspects of the specific case, rather than comparing across the contexts. We support our argument—that learning can be understood as an element of identity development through the processing of and response to environmental contexts— and make use of the PVEST theoretical framework to demonstrate its utility for researchers in deepening understandings of learning as a process shaping civic, occupational, and social identities that are situated within cultural contexts and frames.

Argentina Youth

In keeping with the idea that individual coping behaviors are learned in dialogic interaction with their sociocultural context, our conceptual strategy examines how cultural patterns of behavior and thought are taken up by individuals, and employed as they make meaning of their experiences. Individuals form and test their own values and actions based upon personal experiences as well as collective and cultural narratives about their community's history. How youth learn to manage possibilities and constraints and to navigate their environment as agents have implications both for their identities and their life course outcomes. Learning as conceptualized through PVEST can be understood as learning to be agents, as individuals come to test their own capabilities as they face different stressors and engage in reactive coping strategies. This section provides a case study that examines the influence of culture and class in shaping how highly vulnerable Argentine youth develop agency.

Though the self is often privileged in discussions of agency, the locus of agency is not exclusively situated within the self (Strathern, 1988). In many ways action is motivated by external conditions, suggesting that agency is better defined in relation to "systems of objective potentialities inscribed in the present" (Bourdieu, 1977, p.77). Individuals must learn to both exercise their agentive capacity and from these experiences form an understanding of their agency, and we argue that experiences of economic precarity and social exclusion can shape the way that youth come to understand their agentive power. By examining different individual and collective narratives about agency, we can explore how agency is defined by different actors, and how it is individuals come to learn their agentive capabilities in response to challenges they face.

We will take as a case study an educational program meant to facilitate social mobility for homeless youth in Argentina. This program focuses on the promotion of agentive capacity among young adults with highly constrained structural resources at their disposal—due to their homelessness—and thus serves as a context in which narratives of agency were particularly salient. After a period of severe economic and social instability, the government of Buenos Aires began to implement programs focusing on the importance of preparing young people to construct new forms of democratic citizenship in order to facilitate upward social mobility for impoverished groups. These intervention programs aimed to promote the well-being of youth, but our analysis reveals that these programs also promote a particular representation of agentive capacity that sometimes conflicts with their participants' experientially learned sense of agency. This section will present conclusions based on the analysis of qualitative interview and ethnographic data taken from one particular intervention program, *El Hogar de los Jóvenes.*[1]

Dominant Narrative of Internal Agency

The intervention intends to teach youth to process and respond to their environmental context as agents capable of creating change in their environment. Underlying this interventional strategy lies a particular narrative emphasizing the value of learning future-oriented habits so that youth can direct their own paths towards adulthood. One employee described the process through which they begin to shape youth's agency:

> We go accompanying them in the process to get their national ID, their documents, to improve their health, things they need, and to deepen a bond with them through the cultural workshops, they are all excuses to develop a link with the kid, to accompany them in their track, to generate strategies oriented towards the future, to generate their potential towards solutions.

By getting their first legal ID, the adolescent gains both legal and symbolic proof of social belonging which is intended to facilitate their confidence as agents of change in their own life.

Individual Narratives of External Agency

While program staff focused on teaching youth to exercise their agentic capacity in planning towards long-term goals, youth shared how they had learned to consider their agentive capacity as embedded within and dependent upon situational contingencies. Melina describes:

> How can a person get a job if they say 'no, I'm in front of a pharmacy, sleeping in the streets?' They can't say that. Because society is created like that, you get it?…It's all a chain. If I have a house and food, I can go to school, or work. But if you have nothing, what do you do? I can come here and make art, play for a while, but after that? Because life is a chain, it's all a chain.

Homeless youth in Buenos Aires experience vastly different forms of daily existence than other citizens, and many youth feel unable to take control of their lives due to a lack of access to the "chain" of resources needed to meet institutional expectations for belonging. Often these youth describe their actions as dependent upon shifting sets of contingencies; to survive, they must react to fleeting opportunities or sudden risks. Drawing on PVEST, we can understand their actions as reactive coping as they learn to adapt to their precarious circumstances. Julian explains his strategy: "You move it around, tac, tac, looking for the right path, and you go molding. You can't be very rigid because if you're too straight the unexpected will roll right over you. So you have to live every day like it's your last." It is important that youth don't let life take them by surprise, as Julian shares, so they deny expectations and live in the moment. This can often lead to actions that provide short-term rewards, but are detrimental in the long-term. Alejo describes an incident in which "the urge to do bad" struck him:

> I'm impulsive. I can't control myself. Today the urge to do bad struck me, I crossed paths with someone selling weed and then I went out all night. I knew what was going to happen when I was there, but I couldn't not do it…You understand that you don't want this…But, being a kid of the street, you light a fire and say 'My errors die here', and go forward.

Alejo characterizes his behavior as contingent upon impulses that are activated by his environment, and beyond his control. He recognizes that his actions are not strategic, but narrates agency as a force embedded within his circumstances, and depicts himself as lacking the power to control his own behavior. Ultimately, he has learned to conceive of his own agency as being that of contingent reaction, propelled by his context, rather than from internal motivations.

Alejo's expression of agency echoes Dewey's (1922) notion that motives do not exist prior to an act and produce it, but rather that action and the idea are imbricated completely. Because routine habits are only useful where conditions recur in uniform ways, they do not fit the unpredictable circumstances that characterize the lives of street youth. Street youth instead learn to respond to their environment through instinctive reactions, in order to respond to shifts in their surroundings. However, because the youth conceive of their own agency as reactive and motivated by contingencies within their environment, my participants felt unable to adopt routine behaviors that fit more predictable environments. They felt incapable of maintaining future-oriented action, which the dominant narrative portrays as desirable for young agents.

The PVEST framework emphasizes the centrality of meaning-making processes in considering how individuals understand and respond to their experiences. If social supports or learning opportunities are not perceived as such, or are not interpreted by young people as they might have been intended, they can in fact serve as additional challenges to young people's development. The homeless youth develop reactive coping strategies to accommodate the constant transitions associated with their uncertain living situations. However, they begin to solidify both reactive coping as a lifestyle (i.e., using both positive and negative strategies) and this frequently impedes their ability to plan long-term. As they develop these patterns of reactive coping, they might interpret intended supports as frustrating or threatening; for example, the feeling of frustration as one attempts to learn a difficult concept in school might motivate them to abandon the pursuit, rather than persist. This emotional dilemma, in fact, can add to the inherent challenges of their situation, which makes it difficult for them to maintain the consistent habits that adults insist upon, or understand why it is that adults expect them to behave in a particular way. While the intervention program of *El Hogar* did provide social supports to young people in their time of need, the conceptions of agency embedded within the intervention program were not aligned with the ways participants learned to view themselves as agentic subjects. Using the PVEST framework, we can see that these coping strategies are part of the process of identity formation for these young people, and that the ways youth come to understand their role and capacity as agents matters in determining how they interpret and ultimately make use of the resources provided by the intervention program.

Peru Youth

An effective democracy depends on active citizenry, which includes young people (Almond & Verba, 1963). Youth receive explicit and implicit lessons about civic structures and norms in many settings (e.g., home, school), but are not passive receptacles of political socialization (Flanagan, 2003; Hope & Spencer, 2017). Instead, they learn to be citizens by an iterative process of interpretation and response to norms and expectations inherently related to collective historical positionings with regard to ethnicity, race, and class. Within these contexts, individuals make meaning of social ecologies and their own social positions as they develop civic behaviors, attitudes, and identities (Sherrod, 2003).

In this section, *we argue that civic identity development can be understood as a learning process involving interpretation, response, and identification within cultural contexts*. Cultural contexts are nuanced and include civic meanings, expectations, and practices. We illustrate the robustness of our theoretical frame by applying it to post-conflict contexts and our study with youth from Tacna, Peru. By offering this comparative perspective, we highlight that across varied contexts, the formation of youth civic identity can be understood as a learning process of development in relation to their ecological contexts.

Civic Identity as Contextualized Learning in Peru

Previous research highlights developmental and contextually embedded processes underlying how youth build ideas about who they are as citizens. Adult civic outcomes like voting behaviors and community involvement are linked to experiences and attitudes in early adolescence (Pancer, 2014). Adolescents can be understood as emergent participatory citizens because of a number of social and cognitive developments that mark this time in the life course: interaction with broader social networks; developing abilities to think more abstractly; increasingly understanding themselves as members in social groups and systems; and being challenged to form personal identities (Arnett, 2004; Keating, 2004; Torney-Purta & Amadeo, 2011). Expanding social interactions offer spaces to practice citizenship behaviors and attitudes (Sherrod, 2003). Youth civic engagement matters for individuals' psychological development and has been correlated with academic success (Barber, Eccles, & Stone, 2001), self-esteem (Maton, 1990) and fewer problem behaviors (e.g. Pancer, Pratt, Hunsberger, & Alisat, 2007).

Our goal in presenting this case is to demonstrate PVEST's utility in framing how post-conflict youth learn about culturally based norms and roles as they actively construct their own citizenship. We focus on how youth form these identities in response to civic culture rooted in historical legacies of conflict. Post-conflict countries are deeply marked by tension from the legacies of violence and human rights violations. Part of the transition to peaceful democracy involves rebuilding social fabric, trust, and vibrant and active citizenry (Schwartz, 2010). Positive civic attitudes and behaviors, especially among younger generations, are fundamental to stable, accountable democracies (Davies, 2004; McEvoy-Levy, 2006; Schwartz, 2010).

Peru offers a prime example of these dynamics. After an armed conflict in the 1980s and 1990s between the government and the Maoist guerrilla Shining Path, Peru underwent a process of transitional justice in the early 2000s in an attempt to address the conflict's legacies. The Peruvian government of the early 2000s openly tried to split from the past and recognize its problematic history through acknowledging the state's previous failures (Paulson, 2010). After a few years, however, political winds shifted and many reforms were never implemented. Today, the armed conflict is conspicuously absent from formal civics and history curricula, while militarized rituals, patriotic displays, and other remnants of the authoritarian government of the past are still salient in school contexts (Ministerio de Educación, 2014; Paulson, 2010).

Relatively little research in post-conflict countries has focused on how youth think about citizenship in relation to developmental processes. Our work utilizes PVEST to examine how youth in Tacna, Peru, form ideas about citizenship in relation to what they learn about local civic culture, norms, and expectations. This meaning making is part of interpretation and processing as youth form civic identities. In a mixed-methods study of 293 15-year-old adolescents, we found that respondents who demonstrated identity exploration—had actively thought about their values, beliefs, and roles in society (Marcia, 1994)—were more likely to hold nationalist feelings and beliefs that were rooted in ideas about self, as opposed to external pressures or instruction.

Respondents who demonstrated minimal identity exploration described their ideas about citizenship as coming from what they were taught either in schools or at home. For one, school was "where they teach us how to be citizens...you come to school and learn how to be a good citizen." Adolescents who demonstrated greater identity exploration reported similar attitudes, but also rooted nationalism in their own sense of self and internal values. One, for example, stated that

> being Peruvian means I identify with my country. Being Peruvian means I was born here and this is where I belong. If I see another Peruvian anywhere in the world, I identify with him because we are part of the same family that is Peru.

While a surface-level focus on outcomes might portray these attitudes as similar, there are different meaning making processes at work. For the former, civic norms and orientations are embraced

Examining Culture, Identity, and Learning

from external socialization, while for the latter these must be consonant with their own identities and identifications.

This distinction has implications for a post-conflict society where the roots and tensions of the past are still largely unaddressed. Young people learn in schools about the nationalistic expectations of Peruvian citizenship: to march and sing the national anthem regularly, to extol the virtues of Peruvian cuisine. Some have begun exploring their own sense of self in relation to these civic discourses and expectations, and ultimately have begun to internalize these concepts as part of who they are as citizens. Their civic identities are the result of internalized engagement with the civic cultures around them, rather than a simple adoption of the dominant narrative (i.e., they are socialized through schools, civic celebrations, and political discourses). The fact that these prosocial and nationalist orientations come from understandings of self may provide these youth with motivation to engage in critical civic engagement (Hope & Spencer, 2017). Their civic identities may be more robust and resilient as they become aware of complicated histories and lasting social inequities (tied to the previous conflict). The education system does not provide supports to engage and process this dissonance, and so young people who are taking on external discourses may struggle to manage the disconnect between these civic norms and discourses and their growing awareness of social positioning and historical inequality.

More broadly, post-conflict youth face complicated cultural contexts related to the past and its legacies. Their civic outcomes reflect how they process and respond to culturally salient expectations about citizenship, which have emerged in response to conflict (Davies, 2004). They develop civic identities by learning about expectations and responding with identity-based coping. Similar to minority youth in the United States, ecological context is not deterministic of civic outcomes. Young people have the potential to be active agents in processing and making sense of what they learn—explicitly or implicitly—about their social positioning and place as citizens. PVEST, with a specific focus on social ecologies as involving cultural discourses on citizenship, provides this framework for understanding how these identity-based processes involve learning, meaning making, and response as young people construct their citizenship.

Learning and Citizenship

We have argued that civic development can be understood as part of a contextualized learning process. While socialization experiences in the school, home, and peer group are spaces where civic norms and expectations are conveyed, our theoretical approach emphasizes the active role that youth take in processing this culturally embedded learning and responding by forming civic identities. Utilizing PVEST, the exploration and development of civic identity can be understood as rooted in individual interpretation and coping responses to social ecologies. To this end, youth are agents in their learning about citizenship, and not simply passive recipients of socialization. A focus on the perspective and active processing of youth also demonstrates how marginalized youth can succeed and become proactive citizens within structural inequalities and injustice. Learning involves active construction as situated within cultural and historical contexts (Haste, 2004). As young people come to form a sense of identity within their socio-cultural context, they can learn to identify themselves as agents of change and as citizens.

Brazil Youth

As discussed throughout the chapter thus far, learning is shaped and reinforced by the character of the contexts in which humans interact, providing implications for identity formation processes. This case provides an additional cultural context to which PVEST is applied in order to explore the role of social stratification on adolescent learning processes that shape occupational identities. We examined effects of social stratification on adolescent perceptions of career opportunity in Brazil to better understand variability in the learning of identity in educational experiences.

Literature on economic disparity in Brazil has frequently addressed the intersection of structural inequality and skin color identification (Htun, 2004; Marteleto, 2012; Telles, 2014). However it has not explored a considerable understanding of the complexity of self-identification and perceptions of upward mobility among adolescents. Examining identity processes of youth in Brazil provides an additional lens to conceptualize learning from cultural contexts, diverse meaning making processes and goal-oriented decision making in today's multiethnic societies.

Social Trajectory and Skin Color in Brazil

Brazil provides a rich context to discuss conceptualizations of race and identity formation as it houses the largest population of people of African descent outside of Africa (Mitchell, 2010). Researchers have indicated Brazil as one of the most racially heterogeneous countries of the world constituting a tri-hybrid population of Europeans (primarily represented by the Portuguese), Africans and Amerindians (Htun, 2004; Telles, 2014). Traditionally, the Brazilian government has condemned the racist ideologies and practices of the United States by encouraging racial mixing, described as individuals of African or Amerindian ancestry mating with a white partner. Brazilian sociologist and anthropologist, Gilberto Freyre, is viewed as the forefather of the national ideology, *democracia racial* or racial democracy (Perry, 2013).

Many researchers have challenged the validity of Brazil's racial democracy ideology by documenting the significant advantages of Brazilians with European features (i.e., light skin, straight hair) over Brazilians with African features (i.e., dark skin, curly/kinky hair), particularly in educational and labor market outcomes (Cicalo, 2012; Telles, 2014). Data from the Project on Ethnicity and Race in Latin America (PERLA) illustrates that 33.5% of light-colored respondents in Brazil had high-status non-manual occupations, while medium-colored respondents represented 22.5% of high status occupations and dark-colored respondents represented 20% (Telles, 2014). Likewise, light-skin toned respondents reported 7.9 years of schooling, medium-skin toned respondents reported 7.0 years, and dark-skin toned respondents reported 6.3 years of schooling. Despite extensive discourses of racial paradise in Brazil, structures of career and educational opportunity are linked to physical appearance.

Perceptions of Opportunity among Brazilian Adolescents

Emerging identities of ethnically diverse youth are influenced by what they learn about the history of the social positions of their ethnic group within their nations and how they experience the opportunities that are available to their groups. Adolescents negotiate their own experiences with observations of inequalities in their social environments to determine the trajectories (opportunities and challenges as framed by PVEST) of their future. This case study investigated how Brazilian adolescents aged 14–17 at two high schools (one public, one private) in Salvador, Brazil, experienced economic disparity and skin color stratification in the context of educational and occupational attainment. We administered surveys to 68 participants and conducted semi-structured interviews with 11 of the 68 participants to discern (1) the relationship between skin color identification and occupational aspirations and (2) the relationship between skin color and perceived access to upward mobility.

While regression analyses from the survey data indicated that skin color did not predict the level of prestige of occupations (i.e., physician vs. administrative assistant) that participants aspired to obtain, darker skin color categories significantly predicted perceived disadvantage in competitive labor outcomes. In other words, participants illustrated awareness of societal barriers that prohibit or support them in achieving their goals irrespective of aspirations. Additionally, skin color did not predict occupational aspirations. These survey findings were consistent with research conducted with minority youth in the United States, suggesting that adolescents' career aspirations are consistent across racial groups (Kao & Thompson, 2003). However, the interviews illustrated that the youth were aware of structural barriers that persist based on their physical features and socioeconomic status, regardless of the lightness or darkness of their skin. Thus, what they'd learned regarding socioeconomic mobility and success from social patterns within their nation was consistent despite differences among individual experiences.

Occupational Aspirations within Context

As described earlier, Freyre's romanticized portrayal of Brazil as a racial democracy encompassed a cultural emphasis of racial mixing. This cultural ideology of miscegenation represents macrosystem values that contribute to how child and adolescent racial identity is formed and later crystallized during adulthood. The means by which this contribution unfolds, however, depends on socialization patterns at the micro level such as family relationships. It is very possible for families to create socialization practices that resist the meta narratives. The values that adolescents incorporate from Brazil's national identity in addition to family heritage and peer group influence, shape their own perception of skin tone and racial identity. Barbara, a 14-year-old girl with a light brown complexion, who identified as parda (brown), described:

> I am *parda*. I'm a mixture. There are a lot of blacks in my family; whites, Spanish, and blacks. So, I feel *parda*. Truthfully, I think that's really important because a white person isn't totally white because of their parents; like my father is black. So a white person isn't totally white and a black person isn't totally black. My friends call me *amarela* (yellow/ Asian or Indigenous). For me, *amarela* is a mixture between the indigenous race and whites. There are indigenous people in my family but *pardo* means you have more black heritage. We have more blacks.

Barbara's account illustrates a nature of fluidity in identifying with a particular racial category. From her perspective, racial classification in Brazil does not exist along a black–white continuum; rather, everyone has some form of European, African or Indigenous heritage. Her position as someone whose physical appearance reflects a mixed racial heritage contributes to her perspective that a multiethnic and multiracial society is a positive aspect of Brazilian culture. Additionally, Barbara's upbringing in Bahia, a Brazilian state made up of a population that highly values African descent heritage exhibited through a plethora of public displays and festivities, situates her within an environment that very likely resists meta narratives that discourage positive portrayals of black culture in other parts of the country. Taisa, a 16-year-old medium brown skinned female, expressed a similar sense of pride in being *negra*.

> Here in Brazil it's a complicated thing because we're all mixed. We're like a fruit salad. I am black, but people will say, "no you're not black, you're 'cafe com leite'" (coffee with milk). Then they invent *pardo, moreno*. So many colors! So, I needed to study more. First, what region am I in? I am in Bahia. I am in the blackest city of Brazil. So, I can't say that I am white. I can't say that I am *parda*. Of course, I have these influences in my culture. My grandmother is Indigenous. My mom is black.

Taisa indicated that discovering her racial group was quite a difficult endeavor considering her country's history. While Barbara spoke positively about Brazil's diverse ethnic makeup, Taisa believed that the "fruit salad" of racial groups make it difficult to determine who she is and how she fits into society. Before Taisa discovered her own racial identity, she perceived that people simply stated who they wanted to be without considering their heritage. For her, learning about and acknowledging her heritage was more important than her physical appearance.

Gabriel, a 17-year-old dark brown skinned male, who identified as *negro*, illustrated his perception of present social disadvantages:

> In Brazil, whites have more opportunity and blacks have less opportunity because of racial prejudice, specifically with jobs. If you have a white person and a black person, the black person could have a great education and the white person could have nothing. Who's going to win? The white person. I've already seen this happen. And if you enter any university in Brazil, or in our case Salvador, you can go to a classroom and see that it is made up of more white people than black people. If there are blacks, the maximum amount will be three to ten whites, four to ten whites. It's always the same.

Gabriel illustrated an awareness of current inequalities between blacks and whites in higher education. According to PVEST's conceptualization of vulnerability, Gabriel indicated race as a risk factor that impacts the educational and occupational opportunities that blacks are permitted access to. The vulnerability level of PVEST consists of risk factors that create obstacles in an individual becoming mentally and physically healthy as well as economically successful, while protective factors may be positive aspects of an individual's life, such as parental support, that offset these risks. While a college education is typically perceived as a protective factor, Gabriel believes that the risk of being black outweighs the protective factor of education in Brazil's job market. Here, race represents an imbalance in vulnerability.

By applying a phenomenological perspective, we have framed racial identification and career aspirations within an ecological context in which adolescents actively negotiate their own identities with both the national ideology and economic reality of hierarchies of opportunity in their country. Youth learn what resources are available to them to achieve their long-term occupational aspirations, while the roles they take on become interconnected with social expectations of their abilities, often based on physical attributes and economic standing. The case acknowledges the complexity of racial narratives that can vary from state to state within a nation, giving Bahia a particular position of African heritage pride that illustrates a compelling influence on youth occupational aspirations.

PVEST Approach to Culture, Identity, and Learning

The specific cases illustrate examples of how societal contexts shape how adolescents come to learn their roles and culturally embedded responses as part of identity development. While our cases do not include every possible social role that young people must learn, we have particularly chosen three different aspects of identity across different cultural contexts to demonstrate the flexibility and broad applicability of this framework. Additionally, we open up the theoretical discussion to extend to broader geographical regions and contexts. Our purpose in choosing these cases is not to provide a complete summary of the possible applications of this framework or to cover identity development across Latin America. Rather—given adolescence as a period of significant and rapid biological changes and myriad context-linked life course relevant decision making points—our goal is different. We use the case studies to demonstrate the broad efficacy of the theoretical argument across diverse contexts. Accordingly, also critical to acknowledge are the specific contributions available from adolescent brain science.

Critical Issues in Adolescent Brain Research

Given the potentially significant bifurcation of experiences had by culturally diverse individuals, the early research on the adolescent brain continues to be informative. It emphasizes the heightened intensity and volatility of emotions particularly relevant to and experienced during that devel-

Examining Culture, Identity, and Learning

opmental period (Compas, Orosan, & Grant,1993; Guyer, Silk, & Nelson, 2016). The historically framed "sturm und drang" model emphasized tumultuous relationships (with peers and parents), moodiness (emotionality), and risky behavioral traits (crime, suicide), with the media reporting a generalized stereotype of adolescents—more generally—as lacking self-control due to their under-developed prefrontal cortex. This perspective was introduced at the same time that adolescence was defined as a distinct period (Hall, 1904). Critics have pointed out that their own research contradicted the idea that adolescence was inherently "stormy" (Bandura, 1964). In recent years, developments in neurobiological research and MRI brain imaging techniques has led scholars to further challenge this model. MRI brain imaging has revealed major structural changes occurring in the brains of adolescents that have particular significance for their social interactions. Well into late childhood, the prefrontal cortex continues to develop new synapses, becoming more complex and efficient. The sources of the heightened emotionality and erratic behavior are uncertain as an underdeveloped prefrontal cortex is present for younger children who do not display the same behavior, suggesting a nonlinear development. In fact, *research in the last few decades has revealed that the adolescent brain is more vulnerable to stress than children or adults.* These developments have led some to suggest that this period is better characterized as one of *increased vulnerability as well as opportunity* (Armstrong, 2016). The sensitivity of the adolescent brain is a risk factor but environmental influences can assist in mediating positive outcomes. Less frequently considered, of course, have been culturally mediated factors.

Casey and Caudle (2013) highlight *three major misconceptions about the adolescent brain and its relation to self-control and social interaction.* These include the notion that (1) adolescent behavior is irrational or deviant, (2) that adolescents are incapable of making rational decisions because of their immature prefrontal cortex, and (3) that all adolescents experience "sturm und drang." Their work suggests that *adolescents can demonstrate rational motivation and self-control, notably in emotionally neutral contexts with diminishing success in emotionally taxing ones.* Providing a neuro-biological perspective, Casey et al. (2010) found that the *increased emotionality in adolescence is the product of an imbalance in the development of subcortical limbic (e.g., amygdala) relative to prefrontal cortical regions.*

Another stereotype concerning adolescent behavior is in their capacity and tendency towards risk taking behavior. Research has revealed that adolescents are much more nuanced in their assessments of risk (Blakemore, 2018). For example, and important for cultural communities and efforts at desegregation, risks associated with social interactions are often mediated by youths' perceptions of how their peers have assessed the particular risk behavior.

Research has shown that adolescents use different parts of the brain to process information compared to adults. fMRI studies have shown that the adolescent brain is inefficient in processing inhibitory tasks. Despite great effort, it does not adequately interact with the neural structures and can result in inappropriate behavior and poor self-control compared to adults (Casey et al., 1997). Many of these studies standardly compare adolescents with adults; however, one infers an assumption of similarity across adolescence. Our treatment of contextual variation, including the experience of trauma, suggested unique mediated cultural practices and learning experiences as exposures for culturally diverse youth. One can only ask whether the brain science outcomes described between adults and youth show parallel distinctiveness within adolescence for culturally diverse youth. As reviewed under the section on trauma, the level of stress engagement is different for the learning opportunities experienced by minorities versus privileged youth. The significant challenges experienced by minority youth, particularly male youths when one considers specifically disproportionate minority contact (DMC), suggests different levels of "coping practice." The brain research reported might be the result of minority youth of color needing to cope with greater observed imbalances in the subcortical limbic region versus those who systematically enjoy myriad sources of privilege or the benefits of the "wages of whiteness" (e.g., see Roediger, 1991).

Implications and Conclusions

Lives are never risk-free nor totally without supports. Thus, all individuals experience unique combinations of strengths, challenges, and levels of vulnerability at various periods of their lives. However, these strengths and myriad challenges are not exclusively situated within the individual, but rather occur as processes of learning about contexts, expectations, supports and risks that a particular socio-cultural environment provides. How young people learn to adapt and cope with developmental challenges and utilize the resources available to them is crucially important in determining their individual long-term outcomes, as well as the health and vitality of the communities in which they reside and develop. However, the processes through which development occurs are often significantly more complex, nuanced, and difficult to address than assumed. In this chapter, we have utilized PVEST, analyzing particular aspects of identity formation to illustrate the fundamental importance of understanding cultural context as we seek to deepen our understanding of learning as a social process. Young people are not simply passive recipients of knowledge, but perceive and create meaning within their social environments as they learn how to occupy the various roles they must inhabit within their communities.

Our analysis suggests that when considering social communities, it is a flawed assumption to infer that protective factors and risks are naturally balanced. There are some who experience exceptional burdens in their daily life, and for these people, everyday developmental tasks may morph into major trials, which precipitate heightened stress. These stressors require adaptations which influence how young people learn to navigate their societies, and in turn who they are, ultimately shaping their long-term outcomes. The field of human development points to the need for coordination between sources of support to serve as protective factors for the challenges young people face as they learn their social roles. It is imperative to develop more studies that adopt conceptually and theoretically driven approaches for supporting human development under diverse and highly challenging contexts and which produce cultural patterns too frequently simplistically critiqued. Accordingly, efforts for securing equality without an appreciation for equity are inadequate given that certain situations require significantly greater, intersectionally nuanced and culturally relevant assistance(!). We seek to support the cultural uniqueness and attendant practices surrounding developing young people and thus—by acknowledging, interrogating and offsetting linked challenges—create a more just and equitable world for youth and, ultimately, their progeny.

Note

1 "The house of the young people," a community center funded by the government to promote human rights and cultural expression. We will refer to it, in short, as "El Hogar."

References

African American Psychologists. (2008, December 14). Re: African Americans and therapy [Online posting]. Retrieved from http://www.africanamericanpsychologists.com.

Allen, W. (1985). Race, income, and family dynamics: A study of adolescent male socialization processes and outcomes. In: Margaret B. Spencer, Geraldine K. Brookins & Walter R. Allen (Eds.), *Beginnings: The Social and Affective Development of Black Children*. Hillside: NJL Lawrence Erlbaum Associates.

Almond, G. A., & Verba, S. (1963). *The Civic Culture: Political Attitudes and Democracy in Five Nations*. Princeton, NJ: Princeton Univ. Press.

Armstrong, T. (2016). *The Power of the Adolescent Brain: Strategies for Teaching Middle and High School Students*. Alexandria, VA: ASCD.

Arnett, J. J. (2004). *Adolescence and Emerging Adulthood: A Cultural Approach* (2nd ed.). Upper Saddle River, NJ: Pearson Prentice Hall.

Bandura, A. (1964). The stormy decade: Fact or fiction? *Psychology in the School*, 1, 224–231.

Examining Culture, Identity, and Learning

Barber, B. L., Eccles, J. S., & Stone, M. R. (2001). Whatever happened to the jock, the brain, and the princess? Young adult pathways linked to adolescent activity involvement and social identity. *Journal of Adolescent Research*, 16(5), 429–455.

Blakemore, Sarah-Jayne. (2018). *Inventing Ourselves: The Secret Life of the Teenage Brain*. New York, NY: Public Affairs Books.

Bourdieu, Pierre. (1977) *Outline of a Theory of Practice*. Trans. Richard Nice. London: Cambridge University Press.

Boyraz, G., Horne, S., Owens, A., & Armstrong, A. (2013). Academic achievement and college persistence of African American students with trauma exposure. *Journal of Counseling Psychology*, 60(4), 582–592. doi:10.1037/a0033672.

Brave Heart, M.Y. H. (2011). Welcome to Takini's historical trauma: Historical Trauma. Retrieved from http://historicaltrauma.com/.

Bronfenbrenner, U. (1979). *The Ecology of Human Development: Experiments by Nature and Design*. Cambridge, MA: Harvard University Press.

Bryant-Davis, T., & Ocampo, C. (2005). Racist incident–based trauma. *The Counseling Psychologist*, 33(4), 479–500. doi:10.1177/0011000005276465.

Casey, B. J., & Caudle, K. (2013). The teenage brain: Self control. *Current Directions in Psychological Science*, 22(2), 82–87. doi:10.1177/0963721413480170.

Casey, B. J., Jones, R. M., Levita, L., Libby, V., Pattwell, S. S., Ruberry, E. J., Somerville, L. H. (2010). The storm and stress of adolescence: Insights from human imaging and mouse genetics. *Developmental Psychobiology*, 52(3), 225–235. doi:10.1002/dev.20447.

Casey, B. J., Trainor, R. J., Orendi, J. L., Schubert, A. B., Nystrom, L. E., Giedd, J. N., Castellanos, F. X., Haxby, J.V., Noll, D. C., Cohen, J. D., Forman, S. D., Dahl, R. E., & Rapoport, J. L. (1997). A developmental functional MRI study of prefrontal activation during performance of a Go-No-Go task. *Journal of Cognitive Neuroscience*, 9(6), 835–847.

Cicalo, A. (2012). Nerds and barbarians: Race and class encounters through affirmative action in a Brazilian university. *Journal of Latin American Studies*, 44(02), 235–260.

Coates, T. (2014). The case for reparations [Online]. *The Atlantic*. Retrieved from http://www.theatlantic.com/magazine/archive/2014/06/the-case-for-reparations/361631/ [Accessed 17 Dec. 2015].

Compas, B. E., Orosan, P. G., & Grant, K. E. (1993). Adolescent stress and coping: Implications for psychopathology during adolescence. *Journal of Adolescence*, 16(3), 331–349. doi:10.1006/jado.1993.1028.

Davies, L. (2004). *Education and Conflict: Complexity and Chaos*. London; New York, NY: Routledge Falmer.

Davis, A., Burleigh, B., & Gardner, M. (1941). *Deep South: A Social Anthroprological Study of Caste and Class*. Chicago, IL: University of Chicago.

Davis, A., & Havighurst, R. J. (1946). Social class and color differences in child rearing. *American Sociology Review*, 11(6), 698–710.

Danzer, G., Rieger, S. M., Schubmehl, S., & Cort, D. (2016). White psychologists and African Americans' historical trauma: Implications for practice. *Journal of Aggression, Maltreatment and Trauma*, 25(4), 351–370. doi:10.1080/10926771.2016.1153550.

Dewey, John. (1922). *Human Nature and Conduct*. New York, NY: Holt.

Duncan, L., & Johnson, D. (2007). Black undergraduate student's attitude toward counseling and counselor preference. *College Student Journal*, 41, 696–719.

Elder, Glen. (1974). *Children of the Great Depression: Social Change in Life Experience*. Chicago, IL: University of Chicago Press.

Epps, E. G. (1985). *Preface. Beginnings: The Social and Affective Development of Black Children*. Hillsdale, NJ: Lawrence Erlbaum Associates, Pub.

Erikson, E. H. (1964). *Insight and Responsibility*. New York, NY: Norton.

Fisher, C. B., Hoagwood, K., Boyce, C., Duster, T., Frank, D. A., Grisso, T., Levine, R. J., Macklin, R., Spencer, M. B., Takanishi, R., Trimble, J. E., & Zayas, L. H. (2002). Research ethics for mental health science involving ethnic minority children and youths. *The American Psychologist*, 57(12), 1024–1040.

Flanagan, C. (2003). Developmental roots of political engagement. *Political Science and Politics*, 36(02), 257–261.

Franklin, J. H. (1993). *Racial Equality in America*. Columbia, MO: University of Missouri Press.

Franklin, J. H. (1967). *The Negro in Twentieth Century America; a Reader on the Struggle for Civil Rights*, by John Hope Franklin & Isidore Starr. New York, NY: Vintage Books.

Franklin, V. P. (1979). *The Education of Black Philadelphia: The Social and Educational History of a Minority Community, 1900–1950*. Philadelphia, PA: University of Pennsylvania Press.

Graves, K., Kaslow, N., & Frabutt, J. (2010). A culturally-informed approach to trauma, suicidal behavior, and overt aggression in African American adolescents. *Aggression and Violet Behavior: A Review Journal*, 15(1), 36–41.

Guthrie, R. V. (1976). *Even the Rat Was White: A Historical View of Psychology*. New York, NY: Harper and Row.

Guyer, A. E., Silk, J. S., & Nelson, E. E. (2016). The neurobiology of the emotional adolescent: From the inside out. *Neuroscience and Biobehavioral Reviews*, 70, 74–85. doi:10.1016/j.neubiorev.2016.07.037.

Hall, G. S. (1904). *Adolescence: In Psychology and Its Relation to Physiology, Anthropology, Sex, Crime, Religion, and Education* (Vols. I & II). Englewood Cliffs, NJ: Prentice-Hall.

Haste, H. (2004). Constructing the citizen. *Political Psychology*, 25(3), 413–439.

Havighurst, R. J., & Davis, A. (1943). Child socialization and the school. *Review of Educational Research*, 13(1), 29–37.

Hope, E., & Spencer, M. B. (2017). Civic engagement as an adaptive coping response to conditions of inequality: An application of phenomenological variant of ecological systems theory (PVEST). In: N. Cabrera & B. Leyendecker (Eds.), *Handbook on Positive Development of Minority Children and Youth* (pp. 421–434). New York, NY: Springer.

Htun, M. (2004). From "racial democracy" to affirmative action: Changing state policy on race in Brazil. *Latin American Research Review*, 39(1), 60–89.

Jernigan, M. M., & Daniel, J. H. (2014). Racial trauma in the lives of black children and adolescents: Challenges and clinical implications. *Journal of Child and Adolescent Trauma*, 4(2), 123–141. doi:10.1080/19361521.2011.574678.

Kang, H., & Burton, D. (2014). Effects of racial discrimination, childhood trauma, and trauma symptoms on juvenile delinquency in African American incarcerated youth. *Journal of Aggression, Maltreatment and Trauma*, 23(10), 1109–1125. doi:10.1080/10926771.2014.968.

Kao, G., & Thompson, J. S. (2003). Racial and ethnic stratification in educational achievement and attainment. *Annual Review of Sociology*, 29(1), 417–442. doi:10.1146/annurev.soc.29.010202.100019.

Keating, D. P. (2004). Cognitive and brain development. In: R. M. Lerner & L. Steinberg (Eds.), *Handbook of Adolescent Psychology* (2nd ed., pp. 45–84). New York, NY: Wiley.

Marcia, J. E. (1994). The empirical study of ego identity. In: H. Bosma, T. Graafsma, H. Grotebanc & D. Delivita (Eds.), *The Identity and Development*. Newbury Park, CA: Sage.

Marteleto, L. J. (2012). Educational inequality by race in Brazil, 1982–2007: Structural changes and shifts in racial classification. *Demography*, 49(1), 337–358.

Maton, K. I. (1990). Meaningful involvement in instrumental activity and well-being: Studies of older adolescents and at risk urban teen-agers. *American Journal of Community Psychology*, 18(2), 297–320.

McEvoy-Levy, S. (Ed.) (2006). *Troublemakers or Peacemakers?: Youth and Post-Accord Peace Building*. Notre Dame, IN: University of Notre Dame Press.

McGee, E. O., & Spencer, M. B. (2013). The development of coping skills for science, technology, engineering, and mathematics students: Transitioning from minority to majority environments. In: C. C. Yeakey, V. S. Thompson & A. Wells (Eds.), *Urban Ills: Post Recession Complexities of Urban Living in the Twenty First Century* (pp. 351–378). Lanham, MD: Lexington Books.

McGee, E. O., & Spencer, M. B. (2015). Black parents as advocates, motivators, and teachers of mathematics. *The Journal of Negro Education*, 84(3), 473–490.

Ministerio de Educación [Ministry of Education]. (2014). *¿Qué y cómo aprenden nuestros adolescentes? Ejerce plenamente su ciudadanía vi ciclo* [What and how do our adolescents learn? Exercising their Citizenship vi Cycle; Fascículo 1, Rutas de Aprendizaje]. Lima, Peru: Industria Gráfica Cimagraf S.A.C.

Mitchell, G. (2010). The politics of skin color in Brazil. *The Review of Black Political Economy*, 37(1), 25–41.

Osobor, R. (2009). Prison ministry with chemically dependent African American women exposed to trauma: An interview. *Alcoholism Treatment Quarterly*, 30, 371–374. doi:10.1080/07347324.2012.691043.

Pancer, S. M. (2014). *The Psychology of Citizenship and Civic Engagement*. Oxford: Oxford University Press.

Pancer, S. M., Pratt, M., Hunsberger, B., & Alisat, S. (2007). Community and political involvement in adolescence: What distinguishes the activists from the uninvolved? *Journal of Community Psychology*, 35(6), 741–759.

Parham, T., White, J., & Ajamu, A. (1999). *The Psychology of Blacks: An African Centered Perspective* (3rd ed.). Upper Saddle River, NJ: Prentice Hall.

Paulson, Julia. (2010). 'History and hysteria': Peru's truth and reconciliation commission and conflict in the national curriculum. *International Journal for Education Law and Policy* [Special Issue], 132–146.

Perry, K.-K. Y. (2013). *Black Women against the Land Grab: The Fight for Racial Justice in Brazil*. Minneapolis, MN: The University of Minnesota Press.

Pierce, C. M. (1985). Afterword. In: M. B. Spencer, G. K. Brookins & W. R. Allen (Eds.), *Beginnings: The Social and Affective Development of Black Children* (pp. 315–316). Hillsdale, NJ: Lawrence Erlbaum Associates, Pub.

Project on ethnicity and race in Latin America. Princeton University. Retrieved from https://perla.princeton.edu/ [Accessed 16 Oct. 2019].

Rious, J. B., Cunningham, M., & Spencer, M. B. (2019). Rethinking the notion of "hostility" in African American parenting styles. *Research in Human Development*, 16(1), 35–50. doi:10.1080/15427609.2018.1541377.

Robinson, R. (2001). *The Debt: What America Owes to Blacks*. New York, NY: Plume.

Roediger, D. (1991). *The Wages of Whiteness: Race and the Making of the American Working Class*. New York, NY: Verso.

Schwartz, S. (2010). *Youth and Post-Conflict Reconstruction: Agents of Change*. Washington, DC: United States Institute of Peace Press.

Sherrod, L. R. (2003). Promoting the development of citizenship in diverse youth. *Political Science and Politics*, 36(02), 287–292.

Sirikantraporn, S., & Green, J. (2016). Special Issue Part 1 Introduction: Multicultural perspectives of intergenerational transmission of trauma. *Journal of Aggression, Maltreatment and Trauma*, 25(4), 347–350. doi:10.1080/10926771.2016.1158219.

Sotero, M. (2006). A conceptual model of historical trauma: Implications for public health practice and research. *Journal of Health Disparities Research and Practice*, 1(1), 93–108.

Spencer, M. B. (1995). Old issues and new theorizing about African American youth: A phenomenological variant of ecological systems theory. In: R. L. Taylor (Ed.), *African-American Youth: Their Social and Economic Status in the United States* (pp. 37–69). Westport, CT: Praeger.

Spencer, M. B. (2006). Phenomenology and ecological systems theory: Development of diverse groups. In: R. M. Lerner & W. Damon (Eds.), *Handbook of Child Psychology, Vol. 1: Theoretical Models of Human Development* (6th ed., pp. 829–893). New York, NY: Wiley Publishers.

Spencer, M. B. (2008). Phenomenology and ecological systems theory: Development of diverse groups. In: W. Damon & R. M. Lerner (Eds.), *Child and Adolescent Development: An Advanced Course* (pp. 696–735). New York, NY: Wiley Publishers.

Spencer, M. B. (2019). Developmental and intersectional insights about diverse children's identity. *Florida Law Review*, 71(1), 12.

Spencer, M. B., Brookins, G. K., & Allen, W. R. (Eds.) (1985). Child psychology. *Beginnings: The Social and Affective Development of Black Children*. Hillsdale, NJ: Lawrence Erlbaum Associates, Inc.

Spencer, M. B., & Dowd, N. (Upcoming). *Radical Brown*. Full Citation Pending.

Spencer, M. B., Harpalani, V., Cassidy, E., Jacobs, C., Donde, S., Goss, T. N., Muñoz-Miller, M. M., Charles, N., & Wilson, S. (2006). Understanding vulnerability and resilience from a normative development perspective: Implications for racially and ethnically diverse youth. In: D. Cicchetti & D. J. Cohen (Eds.), *Handbook of Developmental Psychopathology, Vol. 1: Theory and Method* (2nd ed., pp. 627–672). Hoboken, NJ: Wiley Publishers.

Spencer, M. B., Lodato, B. N., Spencer, C., Rich, L., Graziul, C., & English-Clarke, T. (2019). Chapter Four – Innovating resilience promotion: Integrating cultural practices, social ecologies and development-sensitive conceptual strategies for advancing child well-being. In: D. A. Henry, E. Votruba–Drzal & P. Miller (Eds.), *Advances in Child Development and Behavior* (Vol. 57, pp. 101–148). JAI. doi:10.1016/bs.acdb.2019.05.005

Stevens-Watkins, D., Sharma, S., Knighton, J., Oser, C., & Leukefeld, C. (2014). Examining cultural correlates of active coping among African American female trauma survivors. *Psychological Trauma: Theory, Research, Practice, and Policy*, 6(4), 328–336. doi:10.1037/a0034116.

Strathern, M. (1988). *The Gender of the Gift: Problems with Women and Problems with Society in Melanesia*. Berkeley, CA: University of California Press.

Telles, E. (2014). *Pigmentocracies: Ethnicity, Race, and Color in Latin America*. Chapel Hill, NC: University of North Carolina Press.

Thompson, K. V., Harris, K., & Clauss-Ehlers, C. S. (2013). The racial/ethnic identity development of tomorrow's adolescent. In: C. S. Clauss-Ehlers, Z. N. Serpell & M. D. Weist (Eds.), *Handbook of Culturally Responsive School Mental Health: Advancing Research, Training, Practice, and Policy* (pp. 157–175). New York, NY: Springer Science + Business Media. doi:10.1007/978-1-4614-4948-5_12.

Torney-Purta, J., & Amadeo, J.-A. (2011). Participatory niches for emergent citizenship in early adolescence: An international perspective. *The Annals of the American Academy of Political and Social Science*, 633(1), 180–200.

Walker, V. S. (2013). Ninth annual Brown lecture in education research black educators as educational advocates in the decades before Brown v. Board of Education. *Educational Researcher*, 42(4), 207–222. doi:10.3102/0013189X13490140.

4

THE ROLE OF STEREOTYPES
Racial Identity and Learning

Leoandra Onnie Rogers, R. Josiah Rosario, and Janene Cielto

Learning is foundational to human development and unfolds within a sociocultural system of relationships that are informed by societal values, beliefs, practices, and inequalities (Nasir & Hand, 2006; Rogers & Way, 2018). Identity is also fundamental to human development (Erikson, 1968); it is that general sense of knowing who you are, where you belong, and where you are going (Burrow & Hill, 2011; Erikson, 1968; Harter, 2012). Identity guides and motivates behavior, in part, because individuals are driven to behave in ways that are consistent with their goals, aspirations, and conceptions of the self, making it a motivational and directional force (Oyserman, 2001; Sumner, Burrow, & Hill, 2018). Our identities orient us in the world, helping us to know where to focus our attention, what to value, and who to emulate as well as what we ought to avoid. From birth, infants attune to people around them and begin to learn via modeling—mimicking the behaviors and intentions of those around them (Meltzoff & Gopnik, 1993; Bandura, 2001). But, young children do not simply mirror *any* behavior; they are selective and are more likely to imitate (and learn from) others who look like them or with whom they identify, and to engage in a behavior or to recall a piece of information if it is relevant to the self or one's social role (Bandura, 2001; Martin & Ruble, 2010; Meltzoff, 2007). In this way, identity is a pathway through which learning occurs in a variety of learning domains.

In academic domains, research on identity-based learning has shown how identification with a particular subject (i.e., being a "math person") or with academics more generally (i.e., having an "academic identity") is related to learning processes, behaviors, and outcomes, such as engagement, persistence with difficult tasks, enjoyment, and achievement (Eccles, 2009; Oyserman, Terry, & Bybee, 2002; Pizzolato, 2006; Rodgers, 2008). Thus, when a person considers an activity or behavior to be a relevant part of who they are or want to be, this identity process *facilitates* learning. Likewise, if one's identity conflicts with the task or information, it can interfere with or disrupt learning processes.

In this chapter, we look at identity as a conduit for learning because it is core to much of the theorizing and research on school-related outcomes, specifically with regard to the "achievement gap" between Black and White students in academic settings (Horvat & O'Connor, 2006). Specifically, we review three major bodies of research that have powerfully shaped the way researchers and educators have come to conceptualize the learning processes of youth of color in educational settings: (1) Stereotype Threat; (2) Ethnic-Racial Identity Development; and (3) Oppositional Identity Theory (i.e., "acting White hypothesis"). Across these substantive literatures, the role of stereotypes is a central thread. In particular, most of the research underscores how stereotypes constrain identity and learning, and emphasize the role of *accommodation*—how youth may align with or incorporate stereotypes into their own identities in ways that disrupt learning. We highlight in this chapter a line of research that also demonstrates that *resistance* to stereotypes is integral to human learning and development (Rogers & Way, 2018), a perspective that positively transforms how we interpret the learning processes and identities of youth of color (Boykin, 1986; Carter, 2008; Nasir, 2011; Spencer, 2017). Through our review and critique of the existing narratives, we keep both constraints and opportunities at the fore and discuss the role of resistance to reframe the conversation about Black youth.

Stereotypes

The role of stereotypes in human behaviors and interactions has a long history in psychology (Allport, 1954; Hilton & Von Hippel, 1996). Given the breadth of stereotype research, we first provide a general definition and brief historical outline of its conceptualization in psychological research.

Stereotypes refer to widely held societal beliefs and expectations about individuals who share a set of common physical and/or sociocultural characteristics or group memberships, such as: ethnicity, race, gender, social class, or nationality (Stangnor & Schaller, 2000). The earliest conceptualizations of stereotypes can be traced to the beginning of the 20th century when stereotypes were defined as generalizations of social groups that were *illogical* and *rigid* (Lippmann, 1922). Tajfel and colleagues later redefined stereotypes as *probabilistic generalizations* about a group or class of people according to a set of features that were characteristic of that group (Tajfel, 1969). Rather than "illogical", stereotypes were based on probabilistic observations and therefore had logical underpinnings. This reconceptualization birthed an entire generation of research on what is known as "stereotype accuracy"—or the study of how accurately stereotypes align with real-world observations and social roles (e.g., Eagly, 1987; Judd & Park, 1993; Ryan, 2003).

In the probabilistic-observation approach, and related social–cognitive perspectives, stereotypes are located in cognition, described as mental strategies or "energy-saving devices" that enable humans to catalog, retrieve, and respond efficiently to social stimuli (Macrae, Milne, & Bodenhausen, 1994; Fiske & Neuberg, 1990). Stereotypes, then, are cognitive tools, and their content is based on social experiences and interactions. For example, *social role theory* (Eagly, 1987) explains that stereotypes are built on the observation of social roles. Because individuals occupy specific social roles in society based on social group membership (gender, ethnicity, age), individuals can gather accurate probabilities from these observations (Lee & Ottati, 1995; Ryan, Park, & Judd, 1996). Therefore, women are stereotyped as nurturing, for example, because women are more likely to be in nurturing social roles in society (mothers, teachers, nurses), and Black males are stereotyped as athletic because there is a high probability of observing Black males in the role of professional athlete. In short, people form the stereotype that women are more nurturing and believe it to be true not because it is a stereotype per se, but because it is an *accurate* representation of the world they observe.

Another feature of early stereotype research was its focus on how stereotypes shape the way that individuals perceive and make judgments about *others*. It was not until about 20 years ago that scholars began to study the impacts of stereotypes on the self. For example, research on explicit self-stereotyping shows that individuals often self-ascribe stereotypes (even negative ones) to themselves as well as members of their social group (Sinclair, Hardin, & Lowery, 2006; Spears, Doosie, & Ellemers, 1997). Research on implicit processes shows similar effects such as the Implicit Associations Test (IAT; Greenwald & Banaji, 1995), which tests how quickly people associate two stimuli by measuring reaction times. Studies show that people are quicker and more accurate for stereotype-consistent stimuli than stereotype-inconsistent stimuli (Fazio & Olson, 2003). This seems to be true whether individuals are evaluating and making judgments about *other groups* or *their own group*. For example, by elementary school, children—both boys and girls—are faster to ascribe "math" qualities to boys than to girls (Cvencek, Meltzoff, & Greenwald, 2011).

In this chapter, our interest in and approach to stereotypes shifts focus from the cognition and psychology of individuals and social groups to the broader historical and ideological context

(Kteily & Richeson, 2016; Nasir, Snyder, Shah, & Ross, 2012). Specifically, we ascribe to the perspective that stereotypes are inextricable from sociopolitical power. As such, the longstanding ideologies of white supremacy and patriarchy are encased in stereotypes about gender, race, sexuality, and social class, such that stereotypes are fundamentally about who is and who is not fully human (Fiske, 2018; Rogers & Way, 2018; Way et al., 2018). From this vantage point, stereotypes are part of the context of human development and inextricable from the sociocultural context of learning (Nasir & Hand, 2006; Spencer, 2017).

The Narrative of Resistance

For centuries, the innate desire to learn has been, for Black (and Brown) people in the United States, an act of resistance (Carter, 2008; Perry, 2003). Genovese (1976) introduced the concepts of resistance and accommodation in his historical work *Roll, Jordan, Roll: The World the Slaves Made* to describe the daily lives of African slaves on the plantation. "Accommodation" referred to accepting the components of their lives they could not change (enslavement), while "resistance" referred to the fight for moral survival and preservation of personhood. These processes were joint and ongoing strategies—sometimes conscious and intentional, other times implicit and subtle—to maintain a sense of humanity in a dehumanizing context (Genovese, 1976). Developmental scholars have also adopted resistance as a narrative that acknowledges equally the oppressive power of racism *and* the agency, optimism, and curiosity of the human spirit (Hammack, 2008; Rogers & Way, 2018; Spencer, 2017; Ward, 1996). As a psychological concept, resistance refers to the ways in which humans reject cultural ideologies that are incongruent with basic human needs and desires, such as girls rejecting the constraints of gender norms (Anyon, 1984; Brown & Gilligan, 1993), or Black youth retaining their curiosity to learn in a society that devalues their humanity (Carter, 2008; Dumas & Nelson, 2016; Nasir, 2011). Margaret Spencer (1995, 2017) similarly argues that the normative development of Black youth depends on the adequate supports to develop effective "coping" strategies to negotiate the oppression they will inevitably encounter in a racist society. "Like a healthy body", Carol Gilligan (2011) writes, "a healthy psyche resists disease" (p. 32–33). In a culture where racism and dehumanizing stereotypes are a disease, resistance is a normative and necessary response for healthy human development and learning to unfold.

Robinson and Ward (1991; Ward, 1996, 2018) have outlined two forms of resistance that can be utilized to interpret the developmental experiences of youth of color. *Resistance for survival* strategies are defined as "short term solutions" to persistent oppression; this might involve dropping out of school, not because a Black adolescent does not *want* to learn or does not *value* learning but because she values her humanity more. Thus, subjecting the self to a teacher that dehumanizes her spirit and undermines her curiosity is not healthy; her healthy psyche resists this experience of oppression by dropping out (Du Bois, 1935). Of course, the act of dropping out of school simultaneously affirms a negative stereotype and sets up the adolescent for greater life adversity. The key point is that such resistance neither emerges from disengagement from or disinterest in learning, nor does it simply reflect self-stereotyping (or internalized negative beliefs about the self), despite its less-than-optimal long-term consequences. The second strategy outlined by Robinson and Ward is *resistance for liberation*. In contrast to survival, liberation strategies are "long-term" and serve to affirm the self and others. Resistance for liberation comes from a place of wholeness and calls into question negative stereotypes; rather than being subsumed by these stereotypes, one can see the self beyond them.

Without a doubt, in a racially stratified society, stereotypes can constrain and undermine identities and learning opportunities for Black youth. Yet, attending only to the ways that individuals are oppressed by or reaffirm such stereotypes perpetuates a deficit-narrative and underestimates the human desire and capacity for curiosity and learning. By framing human learning and development as a process that also involves resistance, we are better able to interpret and nurture young people's identity-relevant pathways to learning.

Stereotype Threat

Stereotype Threat (ST) is perhaps one of the most extensive literatures to examine the link between stereotypes, identity, and learning. ST is a psychological phenomenon in which the fear of confirming a negative stereotype about one's social group, such as race, ethnicity, or gender, undermines behavioral outcomes, most often the ability to perform successfully on an evaluative task (Steele, 1997, 2011).

The work on ST was pioneered by Claude Steele and Joshua Aronson who sought to understand the academic performance of Black students. Using a lab-based experimental design, Steele and Aronson (1995) showed that they could reduce, and even eliminate, the "gap" in test scores between Black and White college students with equivalent scores on the SAT college entrance exam. Students in the "stereotype threat" condition were explicitly told that the test was a measure of their intelligence while those in the control condition were told that the test was unrelated to intelligence. They found that Black students in the control condition performed at the same level as their White counterparts, but those in the threat condition (perceiving the test was evaluating their intelligence) performed significantly worse than their White peers as well as their Black counterparts in the control condition. In a second iteration of the experiment, they asked Black students to indicate their race on the test packet before the verbal SAT task; simply noting race created an identity "threat" for Black students and they performed worse than those who were not asked to indicate their race. Steele and Aronson concluded from these results that the context cues in their experiments activated age-old stereotypes about race and intelligence that undermined Black students' ability to perform successfully on the task.

The ST phenomenon has been replicated across a number of academic settings, demographic groups, and other stereotype domains, such as women in math, White men in sports, the elderly and memory, and non-native English speakers and accents (see Aronson & Rogers, 2008; Lamont, Swift, & Abrams, 2015; Quinn, Kallen, & Spencer, 2010). Research consistently shows that when stereotypes are primed, it can affect how individuals learn and perform (for a review see Steele, Spencer, & Aronson, 2002; Steele, 2011). Unlike the process of a self-fulfilling prophecy, which emphasizes that an individual *learns* to behave in ways that either confirm their own or others' social expectations (Skrypnek & Snyder, 1982), ST concerns the ways in which the *experience* of identity-threatening situations can transact specific performance-based consequences for the stereotyped individual (Steele, 1997). ST operates, in other words, through identity—one's sense of belonging to or identifying with a group that is stereotyped. Indeed, follow-up studies have shown that women who identify more strongly with their gender are particularly vulnerable to underperformance in ST conditions that prime gender (Schmader, 2002).

ST is tied to identity but its consequences seem to operate through a number of pathways, including self-handicapping and performance confidence (Stone, 2002); anxiety (Spencer, Steele, & Quinn, 1999); and academic disidentification—whereby students diminish the value placed on the stereotyped domain and thus reduce the personal threat of confirming a negative stereotype (Cokley, 2002; Osbourne, 1997) (for a review see Smith, 2004 or Pennington et al., 2016). Some newer research on ST has also explored ways to disrupt its effects. For example, Elizaga and Markman (2008) exposed female participants about to take a difficult math test to comparisons that either challenged or reified gender-math stereotypes. Comparative information that *challenged* the stereotype (i.e., "women are good at math, not men") diminished the ST effect, and comparisons that *reified* the negative stereotype enhanced its effects (Elizaga & Markman, 2008). Aronson and colleagues (2002) also implemented an intervention that was designed to target students' beliefs about the stereotyped domain itself—intelligence. The rationale was that shifting the belief that intellectual ability is a *fixed* trait (limited and determined by genetics) to a belief that it is *malleable* (grows with effort), would reduce the threat of the race-academic stereotype activated in ST studies. Their hypothesis was supported: increasing a student's belief in the malleability of intelligence increased students' performance and overall enjoyment of academic work.

Approach to Stereotypes

The content of a stereotype and its relevance to the individual's identity-group is core to ST processes. For example, in the original ST studies, White students performed equally well in both the threat and control conditions. This was not because White students are indeed smarter or do not encounter stereotypes, but because the stereotype activated in the experimental context was not a relevant identity-threat. However, placing White students in a math context in comparison to Asian students (Aronson et al., 1999), or in an athletic context in comparison to Black students (Stone, Sjomeling, & Darley, 1999), produces the ST effect. This emphasis on the content of stereotypes (and the cognitive processes that have been shown to underlie their effects) has led to a micro-level focus on specific stereotypes and proximal contexts. This has powerfully shaped how we think about youth of color in academic spaces and, in important ways, shifted how educators and institutions approach standardized tests and performance situations (Good, Aronson, & Inzlict, 2003) as well as daily classroom and teacher-student interactions (Dee, 2005).

However, an implicit assumption in this line of research is that a solution to the problem also lies within individuals or immediate contexts—students should *think* differently about testing situations, and teachers should *create* testing environments and classrooms that signal "inclusive" cultures (e.g., Cheryan, Master, & Meltzoff, 2015). These are important and practical examples that pinpoint identity-threatening context cues and ways to modify the learning environment to optimize learning opportunities for racial minority students. At the same time, the design paradigms often portray the individual as a passive recipient of oppression, and underestimate the resistance strategies that students of color develop and bring with them into learning contexts to construct identity safety for themselves. Developing contextual supports that disrupt stereotypes must happen in concert with acknowledging the larger sociopolitical hierarchy of oppression (Kteily & Richeson, 2016; Rogers & Way, 2018) as well as agency of Black students.

Ethnic-Racial Identity

A second body of literature that examines the link between identity and achievement among students of color falls under the umbrella of ethnic-racial identity (ERI; Rivas-Drake et al., 2014; Umana-Taylor et al., 2014). The premise of identity research is that a positive, strong sense of self leads to positive developmental outcomes (Erikson, 1968). Early conceptualizations of social identity, including racial identity, theorized that self-perceptions reflect or "mirror" the social context; Cooley's (1902; James, 1890) "looking glass self" (or reflected appraisal) was premised on the idea that individuals come to see themselves through the eyes of others. The identities of Black people were not a focus point in the Euro-centric mainstream psychological writings and theorizing about identity, so the "looking glass self" rationale was applied as scholars began to research the Black psyche (Clark & Clark, 1939; Cross, 1991). However, in an explicitly racialized and oppressive context, the reflected appraisal approach to social identity fails to answer some important questions: what do Black people see of themselves as reflected in the eyes of others? And, necessarily, who constitutes the "other"? Is the "other" Black people, is it the dominant society, or is it both? To draw on DuBois' notion of "double consciousness", Black individuals must respond to and make sense of dualistic reflections: that of one's in-group (other Black people) and that of the larger racist society in which they live.

Early research on racial identity framed society as the mirror in which Black people were forming a sense of self. In the 1930s, the now classic "doll studies" conducted by Kenneth and Mamie Clark (Clark & Clark, 1939) poignantly demonstrated how societal beliefs about Black people (stereotypes) affected the self-perceptions and beliefs (identities) of Black children. The Clarks interviewed a sample of Black and White preschool-aged children about their preferences for Black and White racially colored dolls. They discovered that Black (and White) children not only preferred the White dolls over the Black dolls but ascribed racial stereotypes to the dolls; the children overwhelmingly selected the White doll as "prettier", "smarter", and "nicer" than the Black doll (Clark & Clark, 1939). This landmark research played a role in the legal case Brown v. Board of Education to overturn separate—but—equal education and at the same time introduced "self-hatred" into the psychological framing of Black identity. This interpretation was aligned with reflected appraisals but went a step further to conceive of these children as passive recipients of a defective identity. The assumption is that Black people, from a young age, construe their identities on the basis of the expectations, beliefs, and values that reside *outside* of their own racial group, with Whiteness and the dominant Eurocentric society as the prime audience.

William Cross endeavored to nuance this perspective of Black racial identity. In his *Nigrescence* model, Cross proposed a set of stages to conceptualize the process of "becoming Black"—coming to the realization of racial oppression and one's worth within a racist society (Cross, 1991, 1995). In essence, he traced the pathway from viewing the self (exclusively) through the mirror of society to seeing the self as reflected in the eyes of one's own racial group/community. Cross defined racial identity as a person's self-concept derived from their personal identity and their racial group membership. In a racist society, the identity development of Black people was a process of (un) learning racial oppression, of questioning the images in the "looking glass" presented to them. The initial stage, *pre-encounter*, is defined by pro-White and anti-Black attitudes; a stage characterized by self-hatred, or a denial of race as relevant to the self. The second stage is defined by an *encounter*—a race-based experience that forces the individual to acknowledge racism, which leads to the third stage: *immersion/emersion*, which is marked by exploring one's racial history and Blackness and deeply questioning the White supremacist beliefs of society. Finally, individuals emerge from this period of learning with a clear sense of who they are and what it means to be Black in society, the stage of *internalization*.

Cross' perspective of racial identity as a developmental process that matures with age and experience is a prevalent one in the study of ERI (Cross & Fhagen-Smith, 2001; Yip, Seaton, & Sellers, 2006). Other stage-like models of ERI, namely Jean Phinney's Multiethnic Model of Ethnic Identity, and Adriana Umaña-Taylor's Ethnic-Racial Identity Development Model (Umana-Taylor et al., 2004), state that ERI begins as *unexamined* and through a period of *exploration* an individual would reach *achievement* or *resolution* status with clarity and positivity about one's culture and ethnic background. In all of these perspectives, ethnicity/race is the part of a person's larger self-concept that derives meaning from being a member of an ethnic group and includes an emotional or affective evaluation of oneself and one's group (Phinney, 1991; Tajfel & Turner, 1986). The "double consciousness" is implicit in these developmental perspectives, such that as Black individuals mature, they grapple with and must integrate dual reflections from society and from their own group in order to form a positive sense of self. And, failure to do so can help to explain negative learning and developmental outcomes. For example, in the "pre-encounter" or unexamined stages of racial identity, individuals are likely to hold more assimilation attitudes, characterized by self-hatred or miseducation, which are associated with lower psychological well-being and lower scholastic achievement (Cross, Strauss, & Fhagen-Smith, 1999; Vandiver et al., 2002; Yip et al., 2006). But, as racial identity develops, or individuals move through the stages, they are more likely to report more positive psychosocial and academic outcomes (Phinney, 1990; Rivas-Drake et al., 2014; Umana-Taylor et al., 2014).

In addition to the *process* or stages individuals moved through sequentially, Sellers and colleagues (1998) provided a model of the *content* of ERI. The Multidimensional Model of Racial Identity (MMRI) takes a social-personality perspective to describe the multiple facets of racial identity and underscore that Black people are diverse and, thus, there is no singular "positive" racial identity. In this way, MMRI diverges from previous ("mainstream") work that overemphasizes the deterministic function of oppression in Black people's conceptions of their racial identity by highlighting that individuals may differ in their attitudes about societal oppression and may come to positive self-concepts despite negative societal beliefs. Sellers and colleagues (1998) outlined four components relevant to understanding racial identity: (a) *centrality*—the subjective importance of race to the overall sense of self; (b) private and public *regard*—one's personal evaluation of race as well as how other people evaluated your racial group; (c) *salience*—the "in-the-moment" attention given to race; and (d) *ideology*—the beliefs one held about how Black people ought to behave in society and interact with other races.

Over the years and across theoretical models and approaches, the research of ERI has supported the idea that a strong, positive ERI is related to learning and achievement among students of color (Rivas-Drake et al., 2014; Umana-Taylor, 2014). For example, in stage-like models (Cross, 1991; Phinney, 1989), individuals with more developed racial and ethnic identities (those further along in the stages of ERI development) also score higher in measures of psychological health as well as indicators of academic engagement and performance (Quintana, 2007; Phinney, 1990; Sellers et al., 1998; Umaña-Taylor & Fine, 2001; Yip et al., 2006). Research using dimensional models shows similar patterns: those with a strong, positive sense of racial identity are psychologically healthy and academically successful.

The dimensional approach also complicates the story by capturing the variability of racial identity beliefs among Black students. For example, Chavous and colleagues (2003) examined over 600 Black adolescents' beliefs about race, the self, and academics. Specifically, they were interested in the complex relationships between the importance of race and the meaning ascribed to one's racial group, and ultimately how these constructs related to academic outcomes. Using a person-centered clustering approach to examine racial identity, they found that African American students whose race was important to them (high centrality), held high group pride (private regard), and perceived positive societal views of African Americans showed stronger academic beliefs, but those with negative societal views showed the highest rates of post-high school educational attainment. Furthermore, across all identity clusters, the configurations with high private regard had the most positive academic beliefs regardless of whether they held race as personally important and relevant (centrality). Lastly, the authors find that those with the lowest academic attainment held their racial group membership in a negative light, perceived society's view of their group to be negative, and did view race as important to them (Chavous et al., 2003).

Other research has focused on the interactions between racial ideology beliefs and academic outcomes, which also show considerable variability among Black students. For example, Small, White, Chavous, and Sellers (2007) study of 390 African American middle school and high school students' experiences of racial discrimination and academic engagement found that assimilationist ideological beliefs (emphasizing an ideology that Blacks should be more like Whites) were associated with lower academic curiosity or interest in new class material, lower reported persistence in classroom activities, and more school-related misbehavior (Smalls et al., 2007). In addition, they find that in the context of racial discrimination, students who endorsed an ethnic minority group status ideology (emphasizing the shared experience of oppression with other minority groups) reported being less apprehensive of being associated with academics and were more persistent during academic challenges. Altschul, Oyserman, and Bybee (2006) also demonstrated the positive influence of ERI on academic achievement for Black and Latino eighth graders using a similar multi-dimensional approach. Students who were: (a) highly *aware* of racism, (b) felt highly *connected* to their racial group, and (c) *embedded achievement* as a core characteristic of their racial identities, attained better grades across time. These findings broadly demonstrate the unique identity-related attitudes, beliefs, and ideologies that shape the girth of Black identity, and contribute to the individual differences we see therein.

The multidimensional perspective of racial identity proved critical for (re)interpreting the drop-out rates in college. In the 1990s, Tinto's (1993) landmark study on student attrition in college proposed that student departure was due to a student's inability to *integrate* themselves into the college and institutional culture. The argument was that all students, including those of color, needed to separate and depart from their previous cultural backgrounds and social environments in order to assimilate into the social structure of college to academically succeed. In other words, racial assimilationist attitudes would help Black students persist in college. Yet, Tinto's perspective failed to recognize the ways that students of color often use and understand their identities and cultural backgrounds as motivation to academically succeed (Oyserman & Lewis, 2017; Syed, Azmitia, & Cooper, 2011). In contrast to Tinto's model, ample research has shown that Black students with higher levels of racial centrality and lower assimilation beliefs have better academic outcomes (e.g., Carter, 2008; Chavous et al., 2003; Sellers, Chavous, & Cooke, 1998; Smalls et al., 2007). The notion of "embedded achievement", specifically, has been crucial in disrupting years of research that largely proposed that students of racial/ethnic minority background should assimilate into the dominant white, middle-class culture of educational spaces. Although Tinto has since responded to these critiques, his perspective of student success engendered tangible policies and practices that worked to restrict the identity development of students of color in the college context, thereby impacting learning and achievement. Collectively, this body of research underscores the relevance of ERI in the learning and achievement outcomes of racial minoritized youth, and the value of adopting a multidimensional view of Black students' racial identity development.

Approach to Stereotypes

Within the ERI literature, stereotypes are often understood to be incorporated into identity development and operate as identity-constraining messages of inferiority. The assumed influence of stereotypes is via their negatively valanced content (e.g., Black people are not smart). Most recently, however, a group of identity scholars convened the 21st Century ERI Working Group and explicitly distinguished the personal aspect of ERI from the sociohistorical context of ERI, where the former refers to the cultural experiences related to one's family and background and the latter refers to the racialized history and context of American society (Umaña-Taylor et al., 2014). Certainly, the sociocultural context in America has a long and troubled racial history. From the advent of slavery to the post-Civil Rights era, racial stratification has had a unique role in the socialization of the American people, and, more specifically, the identity development of people of color. Stereotypes, then, operate as the bridge between the macro-sociocultural contexts and micro-context of groups and personal identities.

In ERI theories, stereotypes are conceptualized as threats or barriers to positive identity formation, but their impact is somewhat isolated to a "stage" of development. For example, in the early stages of ERI, stereotypes have a negative effect because the individual is "unaware" (Cross, 1991), "unexamined" (Phinney, 1989), or in "self-denial" (Umaña-Taylor et al., 2004). In these stages, the assumption is that individuals have internalized society's messages about one's ethnic or racial group, adopting a view of the self and the group that coheres with that of the dominant society. It is assumed, at least implicitly, that individuals effectively "grow" out of this stage or develop to a level where such stereotypes are no longer significant because they have reached identity "achievement" or "resolution" in which they now hold positive views of their own group (Cross, 1991; Umaña-Taylor et al., 2014). This framing assumes, implicitly, that the stereotypes of the sociocultural context become less relevant or dismissed over time. Nonetheless, students of color exist in a web of sociohistorical and cultural influences that impact ERI in important and substantive ways across the lifespan, underscoring the importance of understanding *how* youth continually negotiate stereotypes as they learn and develop their identities.

Research on racial identity from the perspective of resistance shifts attention to explore how youth of color negotiate their ERIs and the related stereotypes in academic settings (Carter, 2006; Nasir, 2011; Rogers & Way, 2016; Way et al., 2008). Racial identity development is a process of *negotiating* these societal stereotypes and expectations, which, by definition, positions students of color as active participants (Rogers, 2018; Way et al., 2008, 2013). Similarly, Nasir and Saxe (2003) frame identity from a "cultural practice perspective" wherein students develop their identities in the moment-to-moment interactions that are simultaneously informed by history and the present moment. Rather than telling a story of negative or oppositional identities that thwart learning, these approaches ask: how do youth navigate the oppressive stereotypes and ideologies of the dominant culture?

For example, Rogers and Way (2018; Rogers, 2018) analyzed research with boys and observed patterns of resistance in their narratives about their racial and gender identities and relationships. They identified three different identity pathways in this research. Some Black boys, the "accommodators", largely adopted and incorporated racial and gender stereotypes, taking the stance of the "scary Black male" in response to society's expectations. Other boys, "the resisters", were characterized by their clear and explicit rejection of society's "Black box" of racial, gender, and sexuality stereotypes; as one Black adolescent boy, said: "I have goals to prove all those people wrong and not fit into any one of those boxes" (Rogers, 2018, p. 129). Finally, the "exceptions" were boys who formed their identities as *exceptions* to the stereotypes:

> I'm not, I'm not like the average African American; like, I'm different. I know that some of them, most of them probably like don't study or care about school, and I'm not like that. My backpack has a lot of books and you won't find a lot of African Americans reading Harry Potter.
>
> *(Way & Rogers, 2015, p. 277)*

Another Black adolescent boy (17 years old), when asked to describe himself, said:

> I'm [a] tall, Black, handsome man…I love God. I'm a positive man…Um, not like the other men on the street that would, um, go and sell drugs, get high. And do the all the ordinary stuff like, uh, like another Black man would: leave out on his wife or kids…
>
> *(Way & Rogers, 2015, p. 277).*

While both boys view themselves positively and view their race as central to their identities, they also ascribe the stereotypes to "ordinary" and "regular" Black people. In other words, they do not reject the truth of the stereotypes, but negotiated their identities by separating themselves from "other" Black people (Rogers & Way, 2016). These patterns show that youth of color both accommodate and resist ideologies pertaining to race (and gender) in dynamic ways, and these stereotypes remain integral to their ongoing development as learners, which is essential to our interpretations of the identity and learning experiences of youth of color.

Oppositional Identity Theory

Oppositional Identity Theory is a third literature and brings a sociological perspective to identity within the system of education (Ogbu, 1978; Fordham & Ogbu, 1986). The premise of this theory is that marginalized youth, specifically those who are from involuntary immigrant groups (i.e., brought to the United States as slaves), adopt an "oppositional" stance toward the dominant cultural values and norms. Whereas psychological approaches to identity are critiqued for giving too little weight to the structure and system, Oppositional Identity Theory relies heavily on systematic determinism, framing a single, unidirectional pathway from slavery to a present-day negative view of Blackness. In this frame, the only "agency" afforded to individuals is by way of accommodation to and adoption of the White-supremacist ideologies of the 'dominant' culture.

Oppositional Identity Theory employs a cultural-ecological framework which aims to identify the factors that influence minority students' learning and engagement in school. The "*ecological*" part refers to the setting (i.e., the society) and "*cultural*" refers to the minority groups' peer, family

The Role of Stereotypes

and community micro-cultures in which youth grow up and learn values and expectations (Ogbu & Simons, 1998). From its origins, this definition of "culture" misses the larger cultural ideologies, stereotypes, and oppressions embedded in the American culture. Ogbu (2004) instead described three premises as they relate to Black students and other racial minorities. The first is that racial minorities do not occupy the same statuses in American society. The second is a sociohistorical perspective that situates the lived experiences of subordinate minority groups (i.e., Black people) in a context in which their collective identity is created and maintained by White Americans, which locates agency and power outside of the minority group. The third reality is that subordinate minorities, in response, develop coping mechanisms or survival strategies to contend with systemic oppression and marginalization. From this view, Black youth "oppose" learning and education in order to define their own Blackness as separate from Whiteness. These oppositional identities are thus created and maintained, according to Ogbu, by the "culture" of Blackness—peer groups, parents, and communities.

The primary empirical evidence of "oppositional identity" was gathered by Signithia Fordham and John Ogbu in an ethnographic study of Black adolescents attending a predominantly low-income high school in Washington DC. Fordham and Ogbu found that the Black students at "Capitol High School" actively distanced themselves from what has come to be known as "acting white". According to Fordham and Ogbu (1986), in these hallways, being smart was coded not as nerdy but as "White". Equating academic success with Whiteness, Fordham and Ogbu noted, was a belief enforced by teachers and White students as well as by the Black students themselves. This, they argued, was evidence of an "oppositional identity", a survival strategy that was rooted in a history of slavery and reinforced within the culture of Black peer groups, families and communities. To explain this phenomenon, they employed the anthropological concept "fictive kinship" to describe how the whole of Black students' identities are forged in response to maltreatment by Whites (Fordham & Ogbu, 1986). Thus, by rooting negative outcomes within the Black community via "fictive kinship", this argument serves to reinforce the structures of White supremacy, anti-Blackness, and oppression. Oppositional Identity Theory clearly threads together identity and learning in school for Black students but leaves little space for self-affirmation, positive agency and healthy resistance.

Approach to Stereotypes

According to Oppositional Identity Theory, stereotypes are the mechanism through which subordination is maintained, but more importantly, they are how Black people decide which behaviors to "oppose"; that is, stereotypes are used by Black people to conceptualize boundary-maintaining behaviors and attitudes—indicators that separate them from the dominant White norm. Fordham and Ogbu (1986) concluded that part of the reason Black students underperform in school was their choice to *disidentify* with academics in order to retain "fictive kinship" with their peers— assuming that Black youth as a whole do not desire to learn. The empirical support for dis-identification is lacking (Horvat & O'Connor, 2006; Spencer, 2001), but more importantly, scholars have critiqued the interpretation of such data on the premise that the theoretical assumptions are deeply racist and deficit-orientated because it removes the context of White supremacy that shapes the learning opportunities and experiences of Black students.

A robust counter-literature has been built to identify and deconstruct the anti-Black bias inherent in Ogbu's cultural ecological theory and the related Oppositional Identity Theory as it has been taken up in popular press and within the academy. Spencer and colleagues (2001), for example, found in a sample of African American middle schoolers ($N = 562$) that students valued academic achievement and were disappointed with poor academic performance. Tyson, Darity, and Castellino (2005) conducted a multi-site, qualitative study with eight schools in North Carolina to directly assess the acting White hypothesis. Their interviews with 85 middle school and high school students (White, Black and other) revealed that none of the Black students opted out of advanced courses for fear of negative peer reactions. On the contrary, many of the Black students espoused a desire for academic success and aspired to attain a college degree. These data directly contradict the conclusions of Oppositional Identity Theory and highlight an alternative narrative and set of conclusions.

The acting White hypothesis and Oppositional Identity Theory begin with the assumption that the Black experience is always against the referent of Whiteness, framing Black youth as passive recipients of a status they did not choose and enforcers of a culture they did not create. *Beyond Acting White: Reframing the Debate on Black Student Achievement,* an edited volume by Horvat and O'Connor (2006), summarizes many of the views against Oppositional Identity Theory and the faulty assumptions that underlie it. The three major arguments of the volume are that the acting White hypothesis: (a) oversimplifies race and uses culture deterministically; (b) homogenizes the Black experience in ways that demean the impact of its intersections with class, gender and even familial socialization (Hemmings, 2006); and (c) minimizes the role of context, especially the school context, in the coproduction of race and the racialization of the Black body (Mickelson & Velasco, 2006). In other words, Black students do not report wanting to avoid Whiteness because they oppose school or learning, but rather because they oppose racism (Nasir, 2011; Spencer, 2001).

There is also research using the accommodation and resistance framework to address the link between racial identity and student achievement. For example, Carter (2008) reports in a study of high achieving Black students that their "achievement ideology integrates a sense of individual agency with an awareness and understanding of racism as a structural condition designed to impede upward mobility" (p. 478). Such awareness and agency highlights that adolescents can be aware of stereotypes without conforming to them (Nasir, McKinney d Royston, O'Connor, & Wischnia, 2017), and that they often use stereotypes to dynamically interpret what they should become in the affirmative as well as what they should reject and resist in the negative. For example, Devin, a Black adolescent male in Way and Rogers' research (2015), explained: "They say Black men probably won't make it, but I know I'm going to make it" (p. 278). Acknowledging that it is a stereotype that "they" (society) have but not necessarily one he endorses, Devin defines who he wants to be not by denying or accommodating to the stereotype, but by resisting society's negative identity expectations.

Centering resistance in a conversation dominated by accommodation also reveals the intersectionality of oppression—the interlocking systems of race, class, and gender that are relevant to learning and development (Crenshaw, 1989). While much of the prior work has focused on slices of oppression (race or gender), an intersectional approach is inextricable from a focus on the cultural context of oppression. Carter's (2006) research on the intersection of gender and race showed that gender-specific behaviors dynamically intersect with ethno-specific behaviors that students categorized as "Black" or "White". Carter found that "acting white" was not about intelligence or academic curiosity, but a term used to demarcate social groups. For example, "acting white" was a label used for certain speech codes and dress styles associated with Whites. For Black boys, these identity-threats were not necessarily tied to being smart or academically engaged but to the larger social construction of the racialized, gendered and sexualized social hierarchy. In this way, students' racial identities in academic settings are inextricable from other identities and structures that are much broader than the micro-level scale of "fictive kinship".

Rather than continue with deficit-minded perspectives, research on identity and learning requires more nuanced conceptualizations that afford students of color the same basic truths of human development: human beings are designed to learn, born with curiosity and the capacity to succeed in school and beyond. Indeed, this part of the story, based on empirical data, reads that the link between identity and learning is innately human; It is the racist stereotypes and structures that Black youth oppose, not their own identities or humanity.

Summary

Across the three literatures reviewed, stereotypes are primarily framed as constraints and racial minority youth are mostly construed as passive recipients of an oppressive culture. For example, ERI scholarship often shortchanges the sociocultural context, with measures that abstract the individual's identity from the context in which it unfolds. This abstraction can lead to (mis)interpretations of identity development that support the assumption of internalization. The powerful contribution of the multidimensional model provides an avenue to offset this view, with more nuanced measurements and interpretations, but greater attention is needed to view Black youth as active agents who possess the capacity to radically transform their identities. The stereotype threat literature also begins with a broader systemic perspective but much of the subsequent research construes Black students as the cause of their own underperformance—their anxiety, cognitive distractions, disidentifications. Certainly, the "acting white" hypothesis is problematic as it situates youth of color as reinforcers of a sociohistorical context they did not create. In sum, the role of stereotypes has focused on describing the ways Black students *accommodate* or internalize stereotypes, as a unidirectional pathway. This perspective, even if unintentional, locates the problem and the solution *within* students of color. As a result, students of color are often viewed as perpetrators of their own academic underperformance, whether by incorporating stereotypes into their identities, allowing stereotypes to hinder their performance, or choosing to disidentify with academic success as a way to defy Whiteness to their detriment in response to societal stereotypes.

The narrative of resistance in research with youth of color starts from the assumption that Black students, like *all* students, *want* to learn (Dumas & Nelson, 2016; Way et al., 2018). This basic truth shifts our attention to the barriers (the risk factors) that disrupt their abilities to do so (Spencer, 1995). It also highlights the dual realities of oppression and liberation so the question is not about specific stereotypes that operate within a specific learning environment but in cultivating within youth the "ability to reject oppressive messages" of society and remain connected to their own humanity as well as the humanity of others (Rogers & Way, 2018).

Learning and identity are normative to and inseparable from human development. Supporting the identity development and learning of students of color begins with acknowledging the oppressive culture in which they are embedded. From this critical perspective, we are better able to understand how identity develops, and its relation to learning processes and outcomes. Naming the oppressive sociocultural context does not undermine the agency or contributions of students, instead it enhances our understanding of their humanity, the way they are actively negotiating— resisting and accommodating—the intersectional stereotypes and inequalities that surround them. As researchers and educators, we are tasked with recognizing and nurturing the resistance of Black youth and creating space for them to thrive.

References

Allport, G. W. (1954). *The Nature of Prejudice*. Oxford, England: Addison-Wesley.

Altschul, I., Oyserman, D., & Bybee, D. (2006). Racial-ethnic identity in mid-adolescence: Content and change as predictors of academic achievement. *Child Development, 77*, 1155–1169.

Anyon, J. (1984). Intersections of gender and class: Accommodation and resistance by working-class and affluent females to contradictory sex role ideologies. *The Journal of Education, 166*, 25–48.

Aronson, J., Fried, C. B., & Good, C. (2002). Reducing the effects of stereotype threat on African American college students by shaping theories of intelligence. *Journal of Experimental Social Psychology, 38*(2), 113–125.

Aronson, J., Lustina, M. J., Good, C., Keough, K., Steele, C., & Brown, J. (1999). When white men can't do math: Necessary and sufficient factors in stereotype threat. *Journal of Experimental Social Psychology, 35*(1), 29–46.

Aronson, J., & Rogers, L. O. (2008). *Perspectives on Positive Psychology*, Lopez, S. (Ed.). New York, NY: Lawrence Erlbaum Associates.

Bandura, A. (2001). Social cognitive theory: An agentic perspective. *Annual Review of Psychology, 52*, 1–26.

Boykin, A. W. (1986). The triple quandary and the schooling of Afro-American children. In: U. Neisser (Ed.), *The School Achievement of Minority Children: New Perspectives*. Hillsdale, NJ: Erlbaum.

Brown, L. M., & Gilligan, C. (1993). Meeting at the crossroads: Women's psychology and girls' development. *Feminism & Psychology, 3*, 11–35.

Burrow, A. L., & Hill, P. L. (2011). Purpose as a form of identity capital for positive youth adjustment. *Developmental Psychology, 47*(4), 1196.

Carter, D. (2008). Achievement as resistance: The development of a critical race achievement ideology among Black achievers. *Harvard Educational Review, 78*, 466–497.

Carter, P. L. (2006). Straddling boundaries: Identity, culture, and school. *Sociology of Education, 79*(4), 304–328. doi:10.1177/003804070607900402.

Chavous, T., Bernat, D. H., Schmeelk-Cone, K., Caldwell, C. H., Kohn-Wood, L., & Zimmerman, M. A. (2003). Racial identity and academic attainment Among African American adolescents. *Child Development, 74*(4), 1076–1090.

Cheryan, S., Master, A., & Meltzoff, A. N. (2015). Cultural stereotypes as gatekeepers: Increasing girls' interest in computer science and engineering by diversifying stereotypes. *Frontiers in Psychology, 6*, 1–8.

Clark, K. B., & Clark, M. K. (1939). Segregation as a factor in the racial identification of Negro pre-school children: A preliminary report. *The Journal of Experimental Education, 8*, 161–163.

Cokley, K. O. (2002). Ethnicity, gender, and academic self-concept: A preliminary examination of academic disidentification and implications for psychologists. *Cultural Diversity and Ethnic Minority Psychology, 8*(4), 378–388.

Cooley, C. H. (1902). *Human Nature and the Social Order*. New York, NY: Scribner.

Crenshaw, K. (1989, July). Mapping the margins: Intersectionality, identity politics, and violence against women of color. *Stanford Law Review, 43*(6), 1241–1299.

Crocker, J., & Major, B. (1989). Social stigma and self-esteem: The self-protective properties of stigma. *Psychological Review, 96*, 608–630.

Cross, W. J. (1991). *Shades of Black: Diversity in African-American Identity*. Philadelphia, PA: Temple University Press.

Cross, W. E., Jr. (1995). The psychology of nigrescence: Revising the cross model. In: J. G. Ponterotto, J. M. Casas, L. A. Suzuki, & C. M. Alexander (Eds.), *Handbook of Multicultural Counseling* (pp. 93–122). Thousand Oaks, CA: Sage Publications, Inc.

Cross, W. E. Jr., & Fhagen-Smith, P. (2001). Patterns of African American identity development: A life span perspective. In: B. Jackson, & C. Wijeyesinghe (Eds.), *New Perspectives on Racial Identity Development: A Theoretical and Practical Anthology* (pp. 243–270). New York, NY: New York University Press.

Cross, W. E. Jr., Strauss, L., & Fhagen-Smith, P. (1999). African American identity development across the life span: Educational implications. In R. Hernandez Sheets (Ed.), *Racial and Ethnic Identity in School Practices* (1st ed., pp. 39–58). New York, NY: Routledge.

Cvencek, D., Meltzoff, A., & Greenwald, A. (2011). Math-gender stereotypes in elementary school children. *Child Development, 82*, 766–779.

Dee, T. S. (2005). A teacher like me: Does race, ethnicity, or gender matter? *American Economic Review, 95*(2), 158–165.

Du Bois, W. B. (1935). Does the Negro need separate schools?. *Journal of Negro Education*, 328–335.

Dumas, M. J., & Nelson, J. D. (2016). (Re)imagining Black boyhood: Toward a critical framework for educational research. *Harvard Educational Review, 86*(1), 27–47.

Eagly, A. (1987). *Sex Differences in Social Behavior: A Social Role Interpretation*. Hillsdale, NJ: Lawrence Erlbaum Associates.

Eccles, J. (2009). Who am I and what am I giong to do with my life? Personal and collective identities as motivators of action. *Educational Psychologist, 44*(2), 78–89.

Elizaga, R. A., & Markman, K. D. (2008). Peers and performance: How in-group and out-group comparisons moderate stereotype threat effects. *Current Psychology, 27*, 290–300.

Erikson, E. H. (1968). *Identity: Youth and Crisis*. Oxford, England: Norton & Co.

Fazio, R. H., & Olson, M. A. (2003). Attitudes: Foundations, functions, and consequences. In: M. A. Hogg, & J. Cooper (Eds.), *The Sage Handbook of Social Psychology* (pp. 139–160). London: Sage.

Fiske, S. T. (2018). Controlling other people: The impact of power on stereotyping. In S. Fiske (Ed.), *Social Cognition* (1st ed., pp. 101–115). London, England: Routledge.

Fiske, S., & Neuberg, S. (1990). A continuum of impression formation, from category-based to individuating processes: Influences of information and motivation on attention and interpretation. *Advances in Experimental Social Psychology, 23*, 1–74.

Fordham, S., & Ogbu, J. U. (1986). Black students' school success: Coping with the "burden of 'acting white'." *The Urban Review, 18*, 176–206.

Genovese, E. D. (1976). *Roll, Jordan, Roll: The World the Slaves Made*. New York, NY: Vintage Books.

Gilligan, C. (2011). *Joining the Resistance*. Malden, MA: Polity Press.

Good, C., Aronson, J., & Inzlict, M. (2003). Improving adolescents' standardized test performance: An intervention to reduce the effects of stereotype threat. *Journal of Applied Developmental Psychology, 24*, 645–662.

Greenwald, A. G., & Banaji, M. R. (1995). Implicit social cognition: Attitudes, self-esteem, and stereotypes. *Psychological Review, 102*, 4–27.

Hammack, Phillip (2008). Narrative and the cultural psychology of identity. *Personality and Social Psychology Review: An Official Journal of the Society for Personality and Social Psychology, Inc., 12*(3), 222–247. doi:10.1177/1088868308316892.

Harter, S. (2012). Emerging self-processes during childhood and adolescence. In: M. R. Leary, & J. P. Tangney (Eds.), *Handbook of Self and Identity* (pp. 680–715). New York, NY: Guilford Press.

Hemmings, A. (2006). Shifting images of blackness: Coming of age as black students in urban and suburban schools. In: E. Horvant, & C. O'Connor (Eds.), *Beyond Acting White: Reframing the Debate on Black Student Achievement* (pp. 91–110). Lanham, MD: Rowman and Littlefield, Inc.

Hilton, J. L., & Von Hippel, W. (1996). Stereotypes. *Annual Review of Psychology, 47*, 237–271.

Horvat, E. M., & O'Connor, C. (2006). *Beyond Acting White: Reframing the Debate on Black Student Achievement*. Lanham, MD: Rowman & Littlefield, Inc.

James, W. (1890). *The Principles of Psychology*. New York, NY: Holt.

Judd, C. M., & Park, B. (1993). Definition and assessment of accuracy in social stereotypes. *Psychological Review, 100*, 109–128.

Kteily, N., & Richeson, J. (2016). Perceiving the world through hierarchy-shaped glasses: On the need to embed social identity effects on perception within the broader context of intergroup hierarchy. *Psychological Inquiry, 27*, 327–334.

Lamont, R. A., Swift, H. J., & Abrams, D. (2015). A review and meta-analysis of age-based stereotype threat: Negative stereotypes, not facts, do the damage. *Psychology and Aging, 30*, 180–193.

Lee, Y.-T., & Ottati, V. (1995). Perceived in-group homogeneity as a function of group membership salience and stereotype threat. *Personality and Social Psychology Bulletin, 21*, 610–619.

Lippmann, W. (1922). *Public Opinion*. New York, NY: The Free Press.

Macrae, C. N., Milne, A. B., & Bodenhausen, G. V. (1994). Stereotypes as energy-saving devices: A peek inside the cognitive toolbox. *Journal of Personality and Social Psychology, 66*, 37–47.

Martin, C. L., & Ruble, D. N. (2010). Patterns of gender development. *Annual Review of Psychology, 61*, 353–381. doi:10.1146/annurev.psych.093008.100511.

Meltzoff, A. N. (2007). 'Like me': A foundation for social cognition. *Developmental Science, 10*, 126–134.

Meltzoff, A., & Gopnik, A. (1993). The role of imitation in understanding persons and developing a theory of mind. In: S. Baron- Cohen, H. Tager-Flusberg, & D. Cohen (Eds.), *Understanding Other Minds* (pp. 335–366). New York, NY: Oxford University Press.

Mickelson, R., & Velasco, A. (2006). Bring it on! diverse responses to "acting white" among academically Able Black adolescents. In: E. Horvat, & C. O'Connor (Eds.), *Beyond Acting White: Reframing the Debate on Black Student Achievement* (pp. 27–56). Lanham, MD: Rowmand & Littlefield.

Nasir, N. S. (2011). *Racialized Identities: Race and Achievement Among African American Youth*. Stanford, CA: Stanford University Press.

Nasir, N. I. S., & Hand, V. M. (2006). Exploring sociocultural perspectives on race, culture, and learning. *Review of Educational Research, 76*(4), 449–475.

Nasir, N. I. S., & Saxe, G. B. (2003). Ethnic and academic identities: A cultural practice perspective on emerging tensions and their management in the lives of minority students. *Educational Researcher, 32*(5), 14–18.

Nasir, N. I. S., McKinney de Royston, M., O'Connor, K., & Wischnia, S. (2017). Knowing about racial stereotypes versus believing them. *Urban Education, 52*(4), 491–524.

Nasir, N., Snyder, C., Shah, N., & Ross, K. (2012). Racial storylines and implications for learning. *Human Development, 55*, 285–301.

Ogbu, J. (1978). *Minority Education and Caste: The American System in Cross-Cultural Perspective*. New York, NY: Academic Press.

Ogbu, J. U. (2003). *Black American Students in an Affluent Suburb: A Study of Academic Disengagement*. Mahwah, NJ: Routledge.

Ogbu, J. U. (2004). Collective identity and the burden of "acting White" in Black history, community, and education. *The Urban Review, 36*, 1–35.

Ogbu, J. U., & Simons, H. D. (1998). Voluntary and involuntary minorities: A cultural-ecological theory of school performance with some implications for education. *Anthropology and Education Quarterly, 29*, 155–188.

Osbourne, J. (1997). Race and academic disidentification. *Journal of Educational Psychology, 89*, 728–735.

Oyserman, D. (2001). Self-concept and identity. In: A. Tesser, & N. Scwarz (Eds.), *The Blackwell Handbook of Social Psychology* (pp. 499–517). Malden, MA: Blackwell.

Oyserman, D., & Lewis, N. A. (2017). Seeing the destination AND the path: Using identity-based motivation to understand and reduce racial disparities in academic achievement. *Social Issues and Policy Review*, *11*(1), 159–194.

Oyserman, D., Terry, K., & Bybee, D. (2002). A possible selves intervetion to enhance school involvement. *Journal of Adolescence*, *25*(3), 313–326.

Perry, T. (2003). Achieving in post-Civil Rights America: The outline of a theory. In: T. Perry, C. Steele, & A. G. Hilliard (Eds.), *Young, Gifted, and Black: Promoting High Achievement among African-American Students* (pp. 87–108). Boston, MA: Beacon Press.

Pennington, C., Heim, D., Levy, A., & Larkin, D. (2016). Twenty years of stereotype threat research: A review of psychological mediators. *PLoS One*, *11*(1), 1–25.

Phinney, J. S. (1989). Stages of ethnic identity development in minority group adolescents. *The Journal of Early Adolescence*, *9*(1–2), 34–49. doi:10.1177/0272431689091004.

Phinney, J. S. (1990). Ethnic identity in adolescents and adults: Review of research. *Psychological Bulletin*, *108*(3), 499–514. doi:10.1037/0033-2909.108.3.499.

Phinney, J. S. (1991). Ethnic identity and self-esteem: A review and integration. *Hispanic Journal of Behavioral Sciences*, *13*(2), 193–208. doi:10.1177/07399863910132005.

Pizzolato, J. E. (2006). Achieving college student possible selves: Navigating the space between commitment and achievement of long-term identity goals. *Cultural Diversitiy and Ethnic Minority Psychology*, *12*(1), 57.

Quinn, D., Kallen, R., & Spencer, S. (2010). Stereotype threat. In: J. F. Dovidio, M. Hewstone, & P. Glick (Eds.), *The SAGE Handbook of Prejudice, Stereotyping and Discrimination* (pp. 379–394). London: SAGE Publications Ltd. doi:10.4135/9781446200919.n23.

Quintana, S. M. (2007). Racial and ethnic identity: Developmental perspectives and research. *Journal of Counseling Psychology*, *54*(3), 259.

Rivas-Drake, D., Seaton, E. K., Markstrom, C., Quintana, S., Syed, M., Lee, R. M., Schwartz, S. J., Umaña-Taylor, A. J., French, S., Yip, T., & Group, E. a. (2014). Ethnic and racial identity in adolescence: Implications for psychosocial, academic, and health outcomes. *Child Development*, *85*, 40–57.

Robinson, T., & Ward, J. V. (1991). A belief in self far greater than anyone's disbelief: Cultivating resistance Among African American female adolescents. *Women and Therapy*, *11*, 87–103.

Rodgers, K. A. (2008). Racial identity, centrality and giftedness: An expectancy-value application of motivation in gifted African American students. *Roeper Review*, *30*(2), 111–120.

Rogers, L. O. (2018). The "Black Box": Identity development and the crisis of connection among Black adolescent boys. In: N. Way, A. Ali, C. Gilligan, & P. Noguera (Eds.), *The Crisis of Connection: Its Roots, Consequences, and Solutions*. New York, NY: New York University Press.

Rogers, L. O., & Brooms, D. R. (2019). Ideology and Identity Among White Male Teachers in an All-Black, All-Male High School. *American Educational Research Journal*, *57*, 440–470.

Rogers, L. O., & Way, N. (2015). "I Have Goals to Prove All Those People Wrong and Not Fit Into Any One of Those Boxes" Paths of Resistance to Stereotypes Among Black Adolescent Males. *Journal of Adolescent Research*, *31*, 263–298.

Rogers, L. O., & Way, N. (2016). "I have goals to prove all those people wrong and not fit into any one of those boxes" paths of resistance to stereotypes among black adolescent males. *Journal of Adolescent Research*, *31*(3), 263–298.

Rogers, L. O., & Way, N. (2018). Reimagining social and emotional development: Accomodation and resistance to dominant ideologies in the identities and friendships of boys of color. *Human Development*, *6*, 1–21.

Ryan, C. (2003). Stereotype accuracy. *European Review of Social Psychology*, *13*(1), 75–109.

Ryan, C., Park, B., & Judd, C. (1996). Assessing stereotype accuracy: Implications for understanding the stereotyping process. In: C. N. Macrae, C. Stangor, & M. Hewstone (Eds.), *Stereotypes and Stereotyping* (pp. 121–157). New York: Guilford.

Schmader, T. (2002). Gender identification moderates stereotype threat effects on women's math performance. *Journal of Experimental Social Psychology*, *38*(2), 194–201.

Schmader, T., & Johns, M. (2003). Converging evidence that stereotype threat reduces working memory capacity. *Journal of Personality and Social Psychology*, *85*(3), 440–452. doi:10.1037/0022-3514.85.3.440.

Sellers, R. M., Caldwell, C. H., Schmeelk-Cone, K. H., & Zimmerman, M. A. (2003). Racial identity, racial discrimination, perceived stress, and psychological distress among African American young adults. *Journal of Health and Social Behavior*, *44*(3), 302–317.

Sellers, R. M., Chavous, T. M., & Cooke, D. Y. (1998). Racial ideology and racial centrality as Predictors of African American College Student's Academic Performance. *Journal of Black Psychology*, *24*(1), 8–27.

Sellers, R. M., Linder-Copeland, N., Martin, P., & Lewis, R. L. (2006). Racial identity matters: The relationship between racial discrimination and psychological functioning in African American adolescents. *Journal of Research on Adolescence*, *16*(2), 187–216.

Sellers, R. M., Smith, M. A., Shelton, J. N., Rowley, S. A., & Chavous, T. M. (1998). Multidimensional model of racial identity: A reconceptualization of African American racial identity. *Personality and Social Psychology Review, 2*(1), 18–39.

Sinclair, S., Hardin, C. D., & Lowery, B. S. (2006). Self-stereotyping in the context of multiple social identities. *Journal of Personality and Social Psychology, 90*, 529–542.

Skrypnek, B., & Snyder, M. (1982). On the self-perpetuating nature of stereotypes about women and men. *Journal of Experimental Social Psychology, 18*, 277–291.

Smalls, C., White, R., Chavous, T., & Sellers, R. (2007). Racial ideological beliefs and racial discrimination experiences as predictors of academic engagement among African American adolescents. *Journal of Black Psychology, 33*(3), 299–330.

Smith, J. (2004). Understanding the process of stereotype threat: A review of mediational variables and new performance goal directions. *Educational Psychology Review, 16*, 177–206.

Spears, R., Doosie, B., & Ellemers, N. (1997). Self-stereotyping in the face of threats to group status and distinctiveness: The role of group identification. *Personality and Social Psychology Bulletin, 23*(5), 538–553.

Spencer, M. B. (1995). Old and new theorizing about African American youth: A phenomenological variant of ecological systems theory. In: R. L. Taylor (Ed.), *Black Youth: Perspectives on Their Status in the United States* (pp. 37–69). Westport, CT: Praeger.

Spencer, M. B. (2001). Identity, achievement, orientation, and race: "Lessons learned" about the normative developmental experiences of African American males. In: W. Watkins, J. H. Lewis, & V. Chou (Eds.), *Race and Education: The Roles of History and Society in Educating African American Students* (pp. 100–127). Boston, MA: Allyn & Bacon.

Spencer, M. B. (2017). Privilege and critical race perspectives' intersectional contributions to a systems theory of human development. In: N. Budwig, E. Turiel, & P. David (Eds.), *New Perspectives on Human Development* (pp. 287–312). New York, NY: Cambridge University Press.

Spencer, S., Steele, C., & Quinn, D. M. (1999). Stereotype threat and women's math performance. *Journal of Experimental Social Psychology, 35*, 4–28.

Stangnor, C., & Schaller, M. (2000). Stereotypes as individual and collective representations. In: C. Stangnor (Ed.), *Stereotypes and Prejudice: Essential Readings* (pp. 64–82). Philadelphia, PA: Psychology Press.

Stangor, C. (2000). *Stereotypes and Prejudice: Essential Readings*. Philadelphia, PA: Psychology Press.

Steele, C. M. (1997). A threat in the air: How stereotypes shape intellectual identity and performance. *American Psychologist, 52*(6), 613.

Steele, C. (2011). *Whistling Vivaldi: How Stereotypes Affect Us and What We Can Do*. New York, NY: W. W. Norton & Company, Inc.

Steele, C., & Aronson, J. (1995). Stereotype threat and the intellectual test performance of African Americans. *Journal of Personality and Social Psychology, 69*(5), 797–811.

Steele, C., Spencer, S., & Aronson, J. (2002). Contending with group image: The psychology of stereotype and social identity threat. *Advances in Experimental Social Psychology, 34*, 379–440.

Stone, J. (2002). Battling doubt by avoiding practice: The effects of stereotype threat on self-handicapping in white athletes. *Personality and Social Psychology Bulletin, 28*, 1667–1678.

Stone, J., Lynch, C. I., Sjomeling, M., & Darley, J. M. (1999). Stereotype threat effects on Black and white athletic performance. *Journal of Personality and Social Psychology, 77*, 1213–1227.

Sumner, R., Burrow, A. L., & Hill, P. L. (2018). The development of purpose in life among adolescents who experience marginalization: Potential opportunities and obstacles. *American Psychologist, 73*(6), 740.

Syed, M., Azmitia, M., & Cooper, C. R. (2011). Identity and academic success among underrepresented ethnic minorities: An interdisciplinary review and integration. *Journal of Social Issues, 67*(3), 442–468.

Tajfel, H. (1969). Cognitive aspects of prejudice. *Journal of Social Issues, 1*, 79–98.

Tajfel, H., & Turner, J. C. (1986). The social identity theory of intergroup behaviour. In: S. Worchel, & W. G. Austin (Eds.), *Psychology of Intergroup Relations* (pp. 7–24). Chicago, IL: Nelson-Hall.

Tinto, V. (1993). Building community. *Liberal Education, 79*, 16–21.

Tyson, K., Darity Jr, W., & Castellino, D. R. (2005). It's not "a black thing": Understanding the burden of acting white and other dilemmas of high achievement. *American Sociological Review, 70*(4), 582–605.

Umaña-Taylor, A., & Fine, M. A. (2001). Methodological implications of grouping Latino adolescents into one collective ethnic group. *Hispanic Journal of Behavioral Sciences, 23*(4), 347–362.

Umaña-Taylor, A. J., Quintana, S. M., Lee, R. M., Cross Jr., W., Rivas-Drake, D., Schwartz, S. J., Syed, M., Yip, T., Seaton, E., & Group, E. a. (2014). Ethnic and racial identity During adolescence and into young adulthood: An integrated conceptualization. *Child Development, 85*(1), 21–39.

Umaña-Taylor, A. J., Yazedijian, A., & Bamaca-Gomez, M. Y. (2004). Developing the ethnic identity scale using Eriksonian and social identity perspectives. *Identity, 4*, 9–38.

Vandiver, B. J., Cross, W. E., Jr., Worrell, F. C., & Fhagen-Smith, P. E. (2002). Validating the cross racial identity scale. *Journal of Counseling Psychology, 49*(1), 71–85. doi:10.1037/0022-0167.49.1.71.

Ward, J. V. (1996). Raising resisters: The role of truth telling in the psychological development of African American girls. In: B. J. R. Leadbeater, & N. Way (Eds.), *Urban Girls: Resisting Stereotypes, Creating Identities* (pp. 85–99). New York, NY: New York University Press.

Ward, J. V. (2018). Staying woke: Raising Black girls to resist disconnection. In: N. Way, A. Ali, C. Gilligan, & P. A. Noquera (Eds.), *The Crisis of Connection: Its Roots, Consequences, and Solutions* (pp. 106–128). New York, NY: New York University Press.

Way, N. (2011). *Deep Secrets: The Landscape of Boys' Friendships*. Cambridge, MA: Harvard University Press.

Way, N., Gilligan, C., Noguera, P., & Ali, A. (2018). Introduction: The crisis of connection. In: N. Way, A. Ali, C. Gilligan, & P. Noguera (Eds.), *The Crisis of Connection: Its Roots, Consequences, and Solutions* (pp. 1–62). New York, NY: New York University Press.

Way, N., Hernández, M. G., Rogers, L. O., & Hughes, D. L. (2013). "I'm not going to become no rapper" stereotypes as a context of ethnic and racial identity development. *Journal of Adolescent Research, 28*(4), 407–430.

Way, N., & Rogers, L. O. (2015). "[T]hey say Black men won't make it, but I know I'm gonna make it": Identity development in the context of cultural stereotypes. In: M. Syed, & K. McLean (Eds.), *Oxford Handbook of Identity Development* (pp. 269–285). New York, NY: Oxford University Press.

Way, N., Santos, C., Niwa, E.Y., & Kim-Gervey, C. (2008). To be or not to be: An exploration of ethnic identity development in context. *New Directions for Child and Adolescent Development, 2008*, 61–79.

Yip, T., Seaton, E. K., & Sellers, R. M. (2006). African American racial identity across the lifespan: Identity status, identity content, and depressive symptoms. *Child Development, 77*, 1504–1517.

5

INNOVATION AS A KEY FEATURE OF INDIGENOUS WAYS OF LEARNING

Individuals and Communities Generating Knowledge[1]

Francisco J. Rosado-May, Luis Urrieta Jr.,
Andrew Dayton, and Barbara Rogoff

Indigenous ways of learning in the Americas have important lessons for scholars and practitioners far from Indigenous communities, in addition to their importance for ensuring that the next generations benefit from and contribute to the knowledge and worldviews of Indigenous American communities. Understanding Indigenous ways of learning can foster relations of mutuality and construction of new knowledge (Grande, 2015) in which Indigenous knowledges and ways of learning play a critical role, especially in relation to achieving sustainability worldwide (Tom, Huaman, & McCarty, 2019).

We aim to delineate the nature of some Indigenous ways of learning, the philosophies that undergird them, and how they can be used in broader communities (and schools). We also hope that making these learning processes explicit will serve Native communities, where they may be widely used but not often articulated in everyday life.

There have been some efforts to incorporate Indigenous ways of learning into schooling systems, such as in bilingual intercultural education in Mexico, Native language revitalization immersion programs in North America, and intercultural inductive education in Brazil and Mexico (da Silva, 2012; McCarty & Nicholas, 2014; Nigh & Bertely, 2018; Schmelkes del Valle, 2009). However, Western schooling in the Americas seldom meaningfully incorporates Indigenous knowledges, languages, worldviews, or ways of learning (Barnhardt & Kawagley, 2005; Battiste, 2010; Bolin, 2006; Lomawaima, 2015; Kirkness & Barnhardt, 1991; Rogoff, 2011; Schmelkes, 2012).

There are many complex reasons for the lack of inclusion of Indigenous ways of learning; one is a general misunderstanding of what Indigenous ways of learning entail (Grande, 2004). Another is the often difficult relations that many Indigenous communities have experienced between colonial/government schooling and their local ways of learning and constructing knowledge. Western schooling commonly employs a model of didactic instruction usually imposed or adopted from the United States and Western Europe, often as part of colonialism and empire-building with the goal of eradicating or changing Indigenous values and practices (Rogoff, 2003; Arenas, Reyes, & Wyman, 2009; Sandoval-Forero & Montoya-Arce, 2013). Indigenous ways of learning in the Americas rest on deep epistemological understandings that contrast with the assumptions and ways of learning that are often the basis of Western schooling (Bang, Marin, Medin, & Washinawattok, 2015; Dayton & Rogoff, 2016; Mejía-Arauz, Rogoff, Dayton, & Henne-Ochoa, 2018; Rogoff, 2016).

This article examines Indigenous ways of learning that are inherent in the Indigenous Knowledge Systems employed in the Americas. Indigenous Knowledge Systems are empirical, normative ways of knowing and ways of being in the world that guide everyday relational life between living and nonliving things and protect cultural continuance in many Indigenous communities (Barnhardt & Kawagley 2005; Bates, Chiba, Kube, & Nakashima, 2009; Battiste, 2002; Cajete, 1994; Chilisa, 2012; Lee, 2009; Little Bear, 2009; Lomawaima & McCarty, 2006; Morales Velázquez & Lepe Lira, 2013; Okakok, 1989; Teuton, 2012; Thomas, 1972; Tippeconic, 1999; Urrieta, 2015).

The ways of learning employed to pass knowledge to future generations and to ensure the continuance of Indigenous cultures are important in Indigenous Knowledge Systems. First Nations scholar Battiste (2002) described how Indigenous knowledge is conveyed across generations:

> Often oral and symbolic, it is transmitted through the structure of Indigenous languages and passed on to the next generation through modeling, practice, and animation, rather than through the written word.
>
> *(2002, p. 2)*

Scholarship regarding Indigenous Knowledge Systems highlights ways of learning that include observation, early involvement in family and community activities, responsibility, learning at an individual pace, and learning by contributing and gaining experience.

In this article, we discuss characteristics of Indigenous ways of learning in the Americas, including a framework that articulates key features of these ways of organizing learning: *Learning by Observing and Pitching In to family and community endeavors* (LOPI; Rogoff, 2014). We then expand the LOPI framework by discussing the importance of innovation as an important feature of Indigenous ways of learning. We counter the common misconception that Indigenous ways of learning only teach what is already known.

The chapter then examines a successful effort to make use of Indigenous ways of learning, through the Yucatec Maya concept of *iknal* in an intercultural university in Mexico. This case study reveals innovations resulting from combining Indigenous ways of learning with the ways of Western universities, exemplifying the co-creation of new knowledge.

What Characterizes Indigenous Ways of Learning?

Although we believe that Indigenous ways of learning have important commonalities across a wide variety of Indigenous communities of the Americas, we refer to Indigenous ways of learning in the plural, because we do not assume that these complex processes are general to all Indigenous communities. Ways of learning in Indigenous communities change over time and circumstances (Madjidi & Restoule, 2008; Rogoff, Najafi, & Mejía-Arauz, 2014). As in other communities, people mix processes deriving from their experience of a variety of models. For example, many people in Indigenous communities of the Americas now have extensive experience with the model common in Western schooling; for some of them, certain aspects of Indigenous ways of learning have become less common (Chavajay & Rogoff, 2002; Dayton & Rogoff, 2013; McCarty & Nicholas, 2014; Rogoff et al., 1993). In addition, Indigenous individuals or groups do not always *use* the community philosophies or processes that we refer to as Indigenous ways of learning; just as people do not always employ community ideals.

Nonetheless, many research observations of learning in Indigenous American communities share some features that suggest underlying precepts that may be held in common about learning and the role of children and youth in many communities. Here are some examples of such observations.

Some Research Observations of Indigenous Ways of Learning

Research indicates that Indigenous ways of learning often involve guidance using nonintrusive approaches towards children and other members of the community: Explicit focus on instructing children or youth in how to do something is rare. Rather, Indigenous ways of learning emphasize observing, listening, and contributing to activities in social and cultural context (Battiste, 2002; Chavajay & Rogoff, 1999; Correa-Chavez, Mejia-Arauz, & Rogoff, 2015; Gaskins & Paradise, 2010; Paradise & Robles, 2015; Rogoff, 2003), including through play (Lancy, 2016).

Indigenous ways of learning often flow with everyday life rather than dividing activities into isolated, sequential steps as in school-style teaching (Rogoff, 2014; Paradise et al., 2014). Learning is generally productive, for "real" purposes (Brayboy & Maughan, 2009; Fortes, 1938; Paradise & Rogoff, 2009). For example, for Hector Sueyo Yumbuyo (Sueyo, 2003), an Arakmbut man from the Peruvian Amazon, it was through going on childhood hunting trips with his father and family that he learned to recognize animal tracks, and the sounds, songs, and smells of birds and animals; he learned that not all animals can be eaten and that spirits inhabit all of the natural world.

Children and youth in a number of Indigenous communities of the Americas generally engage in household practices in holistic and purposeful ways that are integrated within family and community social, cultural, political, and economic realities (Alcalá et al., 2014; Ames, 2013). Children are generally not segregated or excluded from participation in collective events, even when that participation is intense, such as during moments of crisis, funerals, or festivities dealing with death and loss (Gutiérrez, Rosengren, & Miller, 2015; Morelli, Rogoff, & Angelillo, 2003). In such instances, Indigenous children not only learn skills, but also broader concepts about life itself and worldviews that are important in their community and in the broader contexts of Indigenous life (Chilisa, 2012). Everyone has a place in the community, including children.

Adults tend to encourage children to take initiative in mature activities. With the understanding that mistakes are steps that help children become competent and respectful members of the family and community, adults allow children to engage in most collective endeavors (Cajete, 1994; Bolin, 2006). Not-learning is generally not an option—children are expected to learn how to contribute to the family's and community's needs and they are generally interested in doing so (Alcalá et al., 2014; Coppens, Alcalá, Mejia-Arauz, & Rogoff, 2014; Paradise, 1985; Thomas, 1993; Urrieta, 2015).

All children are expected to learn, but not necessarily in the same way. The initiative and pace of learning are based on the child's, family's, and community's needs and interests, in highly specialized, meaningful, individualized learning opportunities (Battiste, 2002; Bolin, 2006). Indigenous ways of learning build on children's strengths and capacities, as children routinely take initiative in everyday activities and thereby advance their own learning as they improve their practice, with the understanding that each person eventually learns how to accomplish cultural activities in their own way (Alcalá et al., 2014; Bolin, 2006; Cajete, 1994; Scollon & Scollon, 1981; Swisher, 1990).

A Framework Building on Observations of Indigenous Ways of Learning: LOPI

A conceptual framework that articulates related precepts of Indigenous ways of learning has been developed by an international consortium of scholars living and working in Indigenous communities in many parts of the Americas. (Many members of the consortium also grew up in Indigenous American communities.) The consortium is interdisciplinary, building productive conversations across fields, including education, psychology, anthropology, linguistics, and history, to understand Indigenous ways of learning. The framework is based on the consortium's lived experience and research, responses to presentations of the framework especially by members of Indigenous communities, and published ethnographies, autobiographies, and comparative research.

Our own experience in Indigenous communities of the Americas is a part of the basis of the present article, along with our diverse disciplinary and cultural backgrounds: Rosado-May (PhD in biology) is a member of the Yucatec Maya community that receives special focus in this article; he founded the Intercultural Maya University that serves it. Urrieta (PhD in Education) is of P'uhré descent and has lived and done research for many years in the P'urhépecha community of his forebears in Mexico. Dayton (PhD expected in Developmental Psychology) is an enrolled member of the Cherokee Nation of Oklahoma and does research in his home community where he has years of involvement in immersion schooling and community leadership. Rogoff (PhD in Psychology and Social Relations) grew up in mostly European American communities, and has lived and done decades of research in a Tz'utujil Maya community of Guatemala.

The framework that attempts to articulate the defining features of a way of learning that appears to be especially prevalent in Indigenous communities of the Americas is currently known as *Learning by Observing and Pitching In to family and community endeavors* (LOPI; previously called Intent Community Participation; Paradise & Rogoff, 2009; Correa-Chávez et al, 2015; Rogoff, 2014; www.learningbyobservingandpitchingin.com).

LOPI is defined by a multidimensional prism composed of seven related features ('Facets;' Rogoff, 2014). The features of LOPI are based in a community structure in which children are included as contributors, like anyone else, in family and community endeavors (Facet 1), and are interested in doing their part (Facet 2). The organization of groups is also collaborative, with fluid coordination and initiative and leadership from children as well as adults (Facet 3). In LOPI, the goal of learning is for people to develop their skills, knowledge, and attitudes as contributors to family and community activities, with consideration and responsibility (Facet 4). Wide, keen attention and pitching in to ongoing events are key means of learning, along with guidance provided by other people and by community expectations (Facet 5), and communication is based on the shared context of the ongoing activity (Facet 6). Evaluation of learning is for the purpose of improving learners' contributions, in the ongoing context of the activity, and focuses not only on the learners' contributions but also on how guidance and supports can better foster learning and the success of the ongoing endeavor (Facet 7).

In this chapter, we extend the idea of LOPI to emphasize how Indigenous ways of learning not only assist people in gaining existing skills and knowledge, but also support their creation of new knowledge. Learning existing skills and knowledges and innovating new ones are essential for Indigenous communities' survival, sustainability, and futurities.

Innovation and Continual Change as Key Features of Indigenous Ways of Learning

Indigenous ways of learning and LOPI are not simply ways of learning what is already known, but also generative ways of advancing knowledge through innovation. Construction of new knowledge is a vital and collaborative community endeavor, developed by Indigenous communities to create the knowledge needed for life.

As indicated by Facet 4 of LOPI, a central goal of learning is the ongoing transformation of one's participation in family and community endeavors, to improve one's ability to make contributions to the family and community (Rogoff, 2014). Sharing new knowledge is an important motivation for community members. For example, to Maya peoples, and likely in other Indigenous communities of the Americas, learning by itself without a goal to serve the community makes little sense (de León, 2015; López et al., 2012). Ingenuity and innovation feed new knowledge in Indigenous communities.

The epistemologies of Indigenous knowledge systems connect learning with innovating, with the foundational assumption of continual change. Even when things appear to be static, they are part of a larger changing system. Little Bear (2000, 2011) calls this process "dynamics without motion," in which a momentary look at events makes them seem unchanging, but the moment is a part of a larger changing system, in "constant flux," forever changing. Little Bear (2011) gives

Innovation as a Feature of Indigenous Learning

this example, attributing it to a conversation about dynamics without motion he had with a Haida Native from Queen Charlotte Islands:

> Go out on the ocean in a canoe, and when you're far enough away from the land where you can't see the land and use it as a reference point, you know your canoe is moving because you're rowing it. But 360 degrees around you, you're always the same distance from the horizon…That's dynamics without motion. (2011, 28 minutes from the beginning of the video)

According to Little Bear, the flux notion in which "things are forever dissolving, reforming, transforming" is one of the most important tenets of Native paradigms.

Individuals' momentary decisions to follow customary approaches are themselves part of what maintains a community's cultural practices in a state of dynamics without motion, until an accumulation of practices and knowledge are enough to produce a more noticeable change, like the creation of a new variety of crop or a shift in medicinal practices. For example, in a Guatemalan Maya community, Marta Navichoc Cotuc observed that the maintenance of millennial knowledge of traditional midwives in her town depends on the ongoing decisions of many individuals to continue using their services (rather than relying on Western medical personnel; reported in Rogoff, 2011).

Decisions to continue with traditional practices may seem like an unchanging static situation, but viewed in the larger scheme, they are moments of apparent stability in a constantly dynamic community process. Cultural practices are constantly in motion, with moments in which an untrained eye might not see any change.

Constructing knowledge in Indigenous communities is a system of "dynamics without motion." Contact among different cultural communities often contributes both to the need for adjustment and as a basis of new knowledge. An example of innovation stemming from reconfiguration of knowledges from distinct cultural communities is provided by the case of Andy Dayton's great-grandmother, who was a Cherokee seminarian—a member of a consciously created group of female Cherokee leaders focused on mastering University education as well as maintaining Cherokee cultural continuity. She used the skills she learned in the Seminary and re-configured them to create Cherokee traditional community along matriarchal clan kinship principles that used modern "white ways" (such as legal and land dealing, negotiations with railroads and developers) to create community-based economic sustainability and renewal. All of this (along with the entire world of cattle ranching practices) was learned through LOPI by her sons, daughters, and extended clan family. They all built the Claremore, Foyil, and Chelsea Oklahoma Cherokee/Shawnee communities together, learning together as they went, and re-configuring the skills that any of them brought to the task, in order to maintain older, more "stable" cultural community values.

Such innovative approaches highlight Native communities' dynamism in knowledge co-construction, where Native wisdoms provide guidance for the future. Such ingenuity is a creative process, using pieces or parts of processes and re-configuring them to suit other, perhaps more durable culturally valued processes, such as group harmony and relational accountability, renewal and temporal cycles, and reinvigoration across generations (Dayton & Rogoff, 2013; Wilson, 2008). Learning, teaching, and creating new knowledge are all one process in this kind of ingenuity.

Innovation in Indigenous ways of learning happens in fractal form, across micro and macro scales, as argued by Dayton and Rogoff (2016), extending from tones of voice and subtle movements of the hands, head and torso, all the way to ongoing interactions between members of Indigenous communities across lifespans and generations. Learning as processes of transformation of people's participation (Rogoff, 1998, 2016) involves the mutual adjustments that occur in synchronous attunement with the relations that form the web of all life, in ensembles. For example, transformation of participation extends from the attuned movements of everyone's hands when Andy is engaged in some task with his aunties and daughters, all the way to Cherokee deliberate, careful re-configuration of conventional Western practices across generations. These are re-cycled through Cherokee communities from moment-to-moment and generation-to-generation in order to maintain harmonious relations and to ensure community renewal. Thus, Indigenous knowledges involve embodied engagement in which ongoing family and community practices bear qualitatively and quantitatively structured patterns of interaction at all temporal scales simultaneously.

Such fractal relationships are open to perennial, asymmetrical change across scales. "Noise" contributes to innovation, resulting in constant emergence of new patterns that are similar but not identical to earlier patterns (an idea that also appears in Dynamical Systems theories). The creation of Indigenous knowledge via the recreation of patterns in community resemblance, through constant, innovative change, is fundamental to the very existence, continuance, innovation, and renewal of culturally patterned behavior itself.

In Indigenous ways of learning, several features support innovation. The initiative of children as well as adult flexibility in adapting to each child's learning pace and way of learning often lead to distinct individual approaches. For example, in the community of Nocutzepo in Mexico, women claimed to have developed their "own" individual tortilla style when they were girls learning to make tortillas; they asserted that they could identify who made the tortillas by looking at their shape, size, and girth (Urrieta, 2013). The process of learning and creating knowledge includes some specialization in adulthood that tends to be appreciated and encouraged. Community members acknowledge who is a good cook, who is a skilled dressmaker, or who is the finest farmer of a given crop. The person who develops a new form of planting or dealing with insect pests, for instance, is recognized and acquires an esteemed sense of belonging in the community. These community specialists are especially respected for sharing their co-constructed knowledge, and their generosity with new knowledge reinforces and advances learning systems developed by the community over millennia.

Such community-based innovation is apparent in agroecology, for instance, where a wealth of knowledge based on cultural processes among different Indigenous groups in various parts of Mexico contributed to the origin and diversity of maize (González Jácome, 2004, 2009). Corn, an important grain for humanity, was developed out of a sophisticated process of analysis and synthesis created and modified over millennia through Indigenous ways of learning and knowledge production based on cultural values and generosity with new knowledge. According to González Jácome (2011), the cultural processes involved in the origin and diversity of corn are similar throughout the impressive array of plants grown and used by Mesoamerican Indigenous groups and eventually shared with the world (e.g., tomatoes, peppers, squashes, and pumpkins).

In Indigenous Knowledge Systems, phenomena such as the creation of a new variety of crop, a new taste in food, a new technique in hunting or construction of a house, are framed as cyclical rather than linear in progression and perennial rather than progressive in evolution. Hence, in Indigenous ways of learning, these patterns of cultural practice are not "learned" or "taught", as separate acts, but continually renewed in everyday practice from microseconds to centuries in continuous, interconnected contingency. From this perspective, learning and innovation are just something people do in the process of living in families and communities across generations.

Conflicts and Innovations in Schooling in an Indigenous Region of Mexico

In this section, we first describe the problems brought by the imposition of colonial schooling in Maya communities of the Yucatan region of Mexico. Then we turn to observations of a successful effort to include Maya ways of structuring learning, in a university program.

Schooling Imposed on the Maya of the Yucatan

Among the Yucatec Maya, Indigenous cultural ways of learning and facilitation of learning are not reflected in the official, government schooling system (Gaskins, 2003; Gaskins & Paradise, 2010). Differences in ways of structuring learning processes may help to explain Yucatec Maya people's hesitance, even today, to participate in the official school system, including in higher education.

Cultural aspects of education were a major issue discussed before the signing of the peace agreement in 1929 to end the long and brutal Casta War that the Yucatec Mayas fought against the Mexican Federal government (Reed, 2001). In the peace agreement between the Mexican government authorities and the Yucatec Maya leader, Francisco May (the first author's great grandfather), the Maya allowed schoolteachers to work in the central part of what is now the state of Quintana Roo. However, the Mayas, and Francisco May, did not follow through with the agreement (Ramos Díaz, 2001) because the government's education system, brought via the teachers, was foreign to the local system and was taught in a nonlocal language.

An important part of the resistance to the government school system was rooted in distinct concepts of education (Flores Escalante, 2010). The education system that was imposed by the government was (and is) based on a vertical unilateral approach with the teacher at the top. To the Yucatec Maya, education is based on the combined and dynamic process of both passing on knowledge and learning/constructing knowledge through everyday activities. In Yucatec Maya, the word *kaanbal* means to learn; two other words complement the process—they have the same root, *kaan*, and mean to teach: *kaans* and *kaanbes*. Both the learner and the experienced one, sharing knowledge, work in a participatory process that involves passing on knowledge and learning/constructing knowledge. Any new knowledge is thus the result of a coordinated effort; it is co-constructed, unlike the typical vertical unilateral system common to schooling.

Resistance to the government's education system was, and still is, often expressed through school absenteeism, desertion, and by low school completion rates (Everton, 2016; see also Urrieta, 2016). Nation states have not desisted from imposing conventional schooling on Indigenous communities (Mato, 2012).

The right to an education that acknowledges, values, and is consistent with local cultures and languages has been at the center of several Indigenous struggles (Urrieta, 2016). These include the 1994 Zapatista Maya rebellion in Chiapas, which set in motion political and social processes that included improvement in living conditions related to land, health, jobs, and schooling for Indigenous people. The Zapatistas sought to have a formal education suited to everyday Maya community life and they took a stance against an institutionalized system of knowledge that did not represent Indigenous precepts nor Indigenous ways of constructing knowledge (Mato, 1996; Vargas-Cetina, 1998).

The Zapatista rebellion, in part, led to the creation of public Intercultural Universities in Mexico (Ávila Romero & Ávila Romero, 2016). One of them is the Universidad Intercultural Maya de Quintana Roo (UIMQRoo, in the Yucatan Peninsula), which serves this chapter as an example of university-level institutionalization of Indigenous ways of learning. Over 90% of UIMQRoo's student population is of Maya origin, and until 2015, around 80% of students were the first in their families to achieve a university education.

Recognizing the Need for Indigenous Ways of Learning in School

The Intercultural Maya University of Quintana Roo implemented Indigenous ways of learning and construction of knowledge by means of a system known as *iknal* in Yucatec Maya communities (Rosado-May, 2012). The governing body of UIMQRoo decided to incorporate *iknal* as a basis for designing learning opportunities for Maya students to accomplish their goal of obtaining a university degree.

The need for this was recognized when, using conventional forms of university instruction, above 90% of the inaugural class of UIMQRoo students failed their first midterm exam (Fall 2007); the prognosis for successfully completing their first semester was not good (Rosado-May, 2012). Assuming that the students had hidden skills and capabilities that would allow them to successfully complete their university degree, UIMQRoo staff and faculty directed their focus towards how Maya students learn and under what community system they learn.

Thus, *Iknal* was re-cognized, recovered, re-created and introduced as a concept in UIMQRoo's structure and function that semester. As became apparent—by talking to Maya elders from different villages and closely examining how the Maya-origin faculty learned in their own communities, as well as through intensive participatory action and observation with students and communities—the university was not making use of longstanding local Maya practices in the learning process. One of the most important realizations was that the university did not even minimally approach providing students with the opportunities for assistance routinely available to them in their home communities to fulfill their goals, in *iknal*.

Iknal: A Zone for Learning

Iknal is a platform that provides the basis for a well-articulated combination of practices, where people accompany, follow up, work with, guide, help to learn and carry out duties using words as well as body language and actions, assess tasks, pass on knowledge and help to create new knowledge through innovation, and team up to accomplish a task with togetherness. Linguistically, the word *iknal* represents "someone's place" (Hanks, 1993, p. 148). For Yucatec Maya, and implicit in Hanks' linguistic work, someone's place represents a space where activities (such as accompaniment and togetherness, following up on an activity, guiding with conversations and other means of communication, and collaborating) are carried out and allow for the emergence of results needed by a community, including new knowledge.

Iknal rests on the notion that any community member, across the lifespan, can tap into the knowledge of anybody else in the community. Parents are not the only people responsible for passing on concepts, skills, responsibilities, and respect to their children; the entire community is. For instance, in a family with five children, the parents cannot provide all of the answers and skills needed by each child along their path to adulthood. Children, or anyone, can make use of the guidance of whoever else has knowledge and skill in the area they need and would like to acquire. *Iknal*, thus, is critical in the process of creating places and spaces for the exchange of knowledge, including learning, in a community. It is an efficient way to ensure continuity in the diversity of skills and expertise needed in the development of that community.

Iknal provides conditions for generating innovation across generations, whether it is for new ways of farming or hunting, better techniques for building houses or for midwifery, or new ways to cure illnesses with medicinal plants. Adults have the responsibility to further develop their learning and specialized knowledge, and to transform this into innovative knowledge, which is then passed on to new generations. In the process of creating and sharing this new knowledge, adults gain respect and recognition, and their sense of belonging is strengthened. Learning and co-construction of knowledge occur together, for the wellbeing of the community.

Learning in Indigenous communities like the Yucatec Maya means co-constructing knowledge that will be shared and perfected through strong relations and identity with the community. For example, Maya farmers in an area called Los Chunes in Quintana Roo, Mexico, developed new and more successful ways of farming dragon fruit (pitahaya), and claimed that their success resulted from the application of their own childhood learning system, especially by carefully observing the crop's response to different stimuli during its development. The process of sharing knowledge by the most successful farmers, who thereby achieved great recognition in their community, was an important aspect of their success (Cálix de Dios, Castillo Martínez, & Caamal Canché, 2014).

For the Yucatec Maya, *iknal* functions as a community platform that allows *Learning by Observing and Pitching In to family and community endeavors* to lead to Indigenous knowledge. The motivation of community members to contribute and to receive recognition based on the creation of innovated knowledge is the driving force behind the platform. *Iknal* facilitates the participation of people of different ages to support the ways of learning in childhood to continue in older ages, providing conditions for the functioning of Indigenous ways of learning articulated by LOPI.

Key Features of *Iknal* and Their Relation to LOPI

Since the institutionalization of *iknal* at UIMQRoo, observations of students and their performance have identified at least nine features in the learning of Maya young adults at UIMQRoo that relate to activities present in the place/space created by *iknal* in Maya communities (Rosado-May, 2017). Brief descriptions of the nine *iknal* features follow, organized in order of their relations with the seven defining features of LOPI. Clearly, each of these features is related to the others. The features are not separate components; rather, they are aspects of the multidimensional phenomena described as *iknal* and LOPI.

There is inclusion, not exclusion

In community activities, as well as in learning and constructing knowledge, no one is excluded; even young children contribute through helping, asking questions, or even playing. The community creates places and spaces that allow learners to tap into knowledge from anyone in the community. When new knowledge is gained, the community expects to know about it, to learn from it, and, if needed, to use it.

> This feature of *iknal* is related to LOPI's central feature, Facet 1, in which community organization includes children as contributors in families and communities' endeavors, like anyone else. (This feature of *iknal* is also related to LOPI Facet 4, which emphasizes learning to contribute with consideration and responsibility to the family and community.)

Mutual Help

The social fabric involves a web of social interactions in which community members help each other; the driving concept is cooperation rather than competition.

> This aspect of *iknal* relates to LOPI Facets 2 and 3, which explain individuals' motivation as deriving from their interest to contribute as valued family and community members, collaborating alongside other people who are trying to accomplish an activity.

Multiple Leadership and Individual Responsibility

Depending on the context and activity, different people provide leadership. One person might lead hunting, another may lead house construction, and someone else can lead community meetings. Leaders are people with recognized expertise in certain activities. In community activities, there is often little margin for error, so expertise is essential as is the need to fully rely on everybody's responsibility. For instance, when building a house, the guiding leader must be confident that the person setting the beams will do so with expertise and care. The person doing the roofing will be sure that the beams will properly support the roof, and the family living in the house will trust that the house was well built.

This feature of *iknal* relates to LOPI Facet 3, which calls attention to the collaborative social organization of groups as people coordinate fluidly with each other, with anyone taking initiative as they see a way to contribute.

Horizontal Organization

Community organization includes multiple leadership. Community leaders understand that earning and sustaining respect from their community depends on how they promote horizontal leadership and community participation in decision making.

This feature of *iknal* also relates to LOPI Facet 3.

Self-Discipline

Within community endeavors there is a high level of individual responsibility, which usually is not supervised but is guided by self-discipline, yielding achievements and success for both individual and community goals. Thus, anybody in the community can rely on and trust other community members, in reliable interdependence.

This feature of *iknal* connects with LOPI Facet 4, which points out that the goal of gaining information and skills—including learning to collaborate with consideration and responsibility—is transforming one's participation in order to better contribute and innovate for the good of the family, the community, and the broader world.

Learning by Doing

Yucatec Maya emphasize experimentation and accumulated experience. They use the same root word for looking for (or searching) and finding: *kaxan* and *kaxti*. It is a way of saying that searching is an ongoing process; even if what has been looked for is found, it is only considered temporary—the search continues. These Maya words also reflect a preference for practical experiences to build concepts, explanations, and general knowledge. There is learning in each action, whether successful or not. The phrase, *kaambal yetel kanan* means looking for and learning, which can be interpreted as experimentation and accumulation of knowledge.

Some accounts use the erroneous concept of "trial-and-error" as an explanation of creation and innovation of knowledge in Indigenous communities (e.g., Gadgil, Berkes, & Folke, 1993). The concept and words, "trial-and-error," do not exist in the Yucatec Maya language and culture when explaining knowledge creation; the words "*ma'alobi*" and "*ma'beyi*" do not mean error, they mean that something did not result as expected. In the process of *kaambal yetel kanan,* meaning "searching and learning," failed efforts are not errors; they are accumulated knowledge that supports the continuation of the process. The idea of trial-and-error implies that there is no progress in the search for new knowledge; an error leads to starting all over again. Rather than trial-and-error, the processes of co-creating knowledge in Maya communities involve experiment-and-build-on-results.

This aspect of *iknal* relates to LOPI Facet 5, which focuses on how learning occurs through wide, keen attention and contribution to endeavors, with guidance from community expectations and sometimes also from other people.

Observational Analysis

Observation is wide and holistic and remains focused. A colloquial expression to define these skills is that through complete and broad observation, people must always be ready to make sound decisions. Observation is not only based on seeing but also includes the skill of abstraction, making sense from several aspects of the social and physical context. It is a sophisticated and complex exercise of analysis and synthesis for all sorts of decisions, short- and long-term, strategic or simple.

Learning by observing is often assumed to be a passive process that results in rote learning (imitation), but in Indigenous ways of learning, observation is very active (Rogoff, 2003). In learning vicariously from the activities of other people and making sense of them and the contexts in which they are used, people learn both to apply them *and to innovate them* in small and major ways. Innovation is central to both the moment-by-moment use of observation and the use of observation in changes across years and generations.

> This feature of *iknal* also is a key feature of LOPI Facet 5.

Transparency and Accountability

Learning and evaluating learning are public, in the process of ongoing activities. People's property is not fenced or walled in to prevent the public's street view, and doors are usually open. People eat, cook, and do laundry openly where anyone can see what they are doing or eating. In this system, any wrongdoing or lack of participation in community endeavors is noticeable.

> This *iknal* feature relates to LOPI Facet 6, which focuses on the contextual basis of coordination and communication (whether verbal or nonverbal), based in participants' shared, mutual coordination of endeavors. This feature of *iknal* also relates to LOPI Facet 7.

Recognition of Extraordinary Contributions

The highest regard by a community to any of its members is when complex knowledge is transformed and shared publicly in the most understandable way so that everybody can benefit. Achieving this type of knowledge is not frequent, but the reward—community recognition—provides strong motivation to work for it. Such recognition is observed, for instance, when a new variety of corn, resistant to a highly damaging pest, or a new management technique that enhances agricultural production, is shared with the community.

> This feature of *iknal* is related to LOPI Facet 7, which points out that assessment includes appraisal of individuals' success in contributing, as well as appraisal of others' supports for individuals' contributions, with feedback available from the outcome of the efforts as contributions to the endeavor.

The collaborative process described in LOPI, and triggered by *iknal* in Yucatec Maya communities, is not visible to an untrained eye. This process can be either reinforced or destroyed by government impositions, such as schooling. Scientific research, oral tradition, and examples from many Indigenous communities support this statement (Battiste, 2010; Little Bear, 2009; Rentschler, Bridson, & Evans, 2015). The next section describes what happened when Indigenous ways of learning, including *iknal*, were applied in university instruction.

Indigenous Ways of Learning in a University

In its initial eight years, the incorporation of Indigenous ways of learning in UIMQRoo's pedagogy and university setting resulted in remarkable success with its student body of about 600,
including the following: Over 70% of the enrolled students successfully finished their university
degree (over 50% of each cohort completed all requirements for graduation within a four-year
academic program), and alumni employment was over 90%. The percentage of alumni continuing
on to graduate degree programs was the highest in the Mexican intercultural university system
(Rosado-May, 2017).

Understanding the learning process and knowledge construction in Maya communities was
critical for UIMQRoo's success, through merging aspects of both Indigenous and non-Indigenous
ways of learning. The working concept driving the institutional processes was that intercultural
education is the result of the university providing a safe space for different systems of constructing
knowledge (e.g., Western and local) to co-operate, significantly increasing opportunities for synergies to create new, intercultural knowledge (Rosado-May, 2013a, 2013b).

Important aspects of UIMQRoo's intercultural model include the use of a system resembling
the *iknal* platform of Maya communities. This involves students working in multidisciplinary teams
connected with their communities, and faculty and administrators working in a relatively horizontal and open structure that acknowledges and encourages the cooperation of different ways of
constructing knowledge (Rosado-May, 2012, 2013a, 2013b, 2018).

Starting in 2008, UIMQRoo implemented a tutorial system closely aligned to *iknal* in Yucatec
Maya communities. In addition to having an academic tutor, students also receive help from other
faculty, from fellow students, and a mentor referred to as *nool-iknal. Nool-iknal* is a community
elder (male or female) from the student's community, chosen by the student based on the elder's
reputation or expertise. The elder's role is to contribute to and follow the student's learning process,
including sharing knowledge and assessing the student's community work, the student's respect
towards community members, and use of the local language. At the end of a semester, the *nool-
iknal* would provide an important assessment about the student's community performance; this
evaluation is critical to determine whether a student with good academic performance was also
performing well at the community level, or needed to strengthen that part of their training. For
students with poor academic performance, the *nool-iknal*'s opinion would be critical in the decision
of whether to grant another opportunity or fail the student.

In addition to the tutorial system with the *nool-iknal*, UIMQRoo's bylaws were designed to
allow the hiring, as faculty, of elders who have no formal schooling but who are highly regarded in
their communities for their knowledge and their success in sharing that knowledge with the community. These faculty elders co-taught with faculty who had graduate degrees and conventional
training, in classrooms or, often, in the field.

Students thus had the benefit of learning the local knowledge, in the local language, and also of
learning Western knowledge. This provided the opportunity to create new knowledge that com-
bines both sources, for not only technical matters but also philosophical issues such as understanding social processes and developing new worldviews. For example, the Community Health students
had classes and field practice with both a professor and a *nool-iknal* at the same time. The professor,
with a graduate degree in advanced botany, taught the scientific name, physiology, anatomy, and
secondary compounds from medicinal plants; the *nool-iknal* taught them, in Maya, the local name
of the plants, how they grow, how the elders use the plant for medicinal or ceremonial purposes,
how to collect and prepare the plant for medicinal use, how to care for the plant, at what stage of
growth the plant can be used, and the like. The students then had the opportunity to discuss in the
classroom both approaches to understanding plants and human affairs. This included philosophical
topics like how both knowledges can coexist and how to create something new by combining
both visions, both knowledges. The same sort of exercise was carried out in all majors, whether

business, information technology, or politics, and resulted in publications on intercultural business and intercultural leadership.

In addition to the *nool-iknal* and elders as faculty at UIMQRoo, students had to successfully carry out a project around a subject of interest in their own community in order to complete graduation requirements. This was primarily designed to keep students from losing contact and connection with their communities. Through the years, Maya communities have witnessed the loss of young members leaving the community to pursue university degrees, losing connection with the community's ways of life.

The student projects had to be aligned with community needs, and thus negotiated with and accepted by the community. Students often worked on interdisciplinary projects in teams but with clear individual responsibility. The nature and topic of a project also depended on whether the student's interest included a professional career in academia, business, public service, or non-governmental organizations (Rosado-May & Cuevas Albarrán, 2015). Some examples of projects are the design and implementation of a workshop on natural childbirth and breast feeding; the evaluation of chile varieties; a business plan for marketing a local product; the description of local dances for religious ceremonies; and the limiting factors for amplifying the use of the Maya language in schools.

The organization of the administration and management at UIMQRoo was as horizontal as possible, not pyramidal. The basic unit of administration was the Department, with no Divisions or Schools or Colleges. Transparency, accountability, and participation were prioritized in the decision-making process and in the administration of all university assets and financial resources. Potential faculty and staff members were evaluated by hiring committees integrated by senior faculty from UIMQRoo and other universities, one or two students, and one or two community members. This participatory process assured community members that they would have the best faculty to pass on knowledge to their children, with respect for local culture.

UIMQRoo is a successful but exceptional case where Indigenous pedagogies and ways of learning are respected and implemented at a public university level in Mexico, coexisting with unavoidable government regulations and policies. There is further work to do to innovate actions and decisions at UIMQRoo, to take optimal advantage of the Indigenous ways of learning that sustain Indigenous Knowledge Systems. However, UIMQRoo's *iknal* experiment provides a powerful test of the idea that Indigenous ways of learning can benefit university instruction, and that a combination of knowledge across cultures can be fertile for innovating new knowledge.

Conclusion: Co-Constructing for Innovation Across Cultural Systems

The process of co-constructing Indigenous knowledge—even within an institutional context like UIMQRoo—may play a critical role in Indigenous peoples' continued survival as simultaneously millennial and modern communities. Combining the know-how of Indigenous ways of learning with conventional Western schooling provided positive outcomes for Indigenous students by creating conditions in which not only were their ways of learning recognized and encouraged, but the combination also allowed the emergence of skills and knowledge needed in multicultural settings.

Keeping and improving the ways knowledge is created, passed on, and innovated in Indigenous communities, throughout generations, is crucial in the cultural survival/resilience of Indigenous communities. There is a great need to understand and foster the processes for learning and creating new knowledges by Indigenous people. Evidence indicates that erosion in the creation and transmission of Indigenous knowledge can be correlated to a community's loss of well-being. Atran, Medin, and Ross (2004) argue that the extinction of experience, due to the extinction of Indigenous ways of constructing knowledge, is a devolutionary process that neglects cultural values and ecological features that directly affect a society's manner and possibility of survival.

Knowledge co-creation, involving different cultures, requires that different systems of creating knowledge and of ways of learning work together. Potential synergies in interaction across systems help to build stronger bridges of understanding among different cultures with distinct knowledge, worldviews, and ways of learning. In a world that is increasingly interconnected, it is critical to understand cultural differences in processes of learning and of constructing knowledge, for many reasons—peace being the most important. Interculturalism results from the process that emerges when different ways of supporting learning and creating knowledge work together, in a safe environment, to understand a situation or to solve a problem (Rosado-May, 2015).

Respecting and using Indigenous ways of learning and Indigenous Knowledge Systems, in conjunction with Western approaches, offer advances in learning and innovation for all communities. Indigenous Knowledge Systems have begun to be acknowledged and praised (such as in the recently released special United Nations report by the Intergovernmental Panel on Climate Change, on climate change and land, August 2019, https://ipccresponse.org/home-en).

Of course, Indigenous ways of learning are not unique to Indigenous communities. For example, *Learning by Pitching In to family and community endeavors* is likely to be practiced to some extent in all communities (such as in first language learning; Rogoff, 2014). Similar approaches to learning have also been employed in some schools, such as an innovative school in Utah, United States (Rogoff et al., 2001).

However, LOPI's strength in many Indigenous communities of the Americas provides an important model of how such learning can be organized as a coherent, multifaceted way of supporting learning. The ways of learning and of supporting learning that have been examined in this article provide guidance not only for the improvement of learning opportunities for Indigenous children and youth of the Americas, but also for advancing knowledge of instruction and learning more generally, in an iterative process involving exchange between different cultures in a context of mutual respect.

Note

1 Acknowledgments: We deeply appreciate the wisdom of the Indigenous elders, grandparents, parents, and scholars, students, and teachers who have created and sustained and continue to develop ways of learning and supporting learning that we discuss in this chapter. Development of this chapter was supported by the UCSC Foundation Professorship in Psychology, to Barbara Rogoff.

References

Alcalá, L., Rogoff, B., Mejía-Arauz, R., Coppens, A.D., & Dexter, A.L. (2014). Children's initiative in contributions to family work in Indigenous-heritage and cosmopolitan communities in Mexico. *Human Development, 57*(2–3), 96–115.

Ames, P. (2013). Niños y niñas Andinas en el Perú: Crecer en un mundo de relaciones y responsabilidades. *Bulletin de L'institut Français d'Études Andines, 42*(3), 389–409.

Arenas, A., Reyes, I., & Wyman, L. (2009). When indigenous and modern education collide. In: J. Zajda, & K. Freeman (Eds.), *Race, Ethnicity and Gender in Education*, pp. 59–84. Melbourne: Springer.

Atran, S., Medin, D., & Ross, N. (2004). Evolution and devolution of knowledge: A tale of two biologies. *Journal of Royal Anthropological Institute (N.S.), 10*(2), 395–420.

Ávila Romero, L.E., & Ávila Romero, A. (2016). Las universidades interculturales de México en la encrucijada. *Revista de Ciencias Sociales y Humanidades, 25*(50), 198–215.

Bang, M., Marin, A., Medin, D., & Washinawatok, K. (2015). Learning by observing, pitching in, and being in relations in the natural world. In: M. Correa-Chávez, R. Mejía-Arauz, & B. Rogoff (Eds.), *Children Learn by Observing and Contributing to Family and Community Endeavors. Advances in Child Development and Behavior*, vol. 49, pp. 303–313. San Diego, CA: Elsevier-Academic Press.

Barnhardt, R., & Kawagley, A.O. (2005). Indigenous knowledge systems and Alaska native ways of knowing. *Anthropology and Education Quarterly, 36*(1), 8–23.

Innovation as a Feature of Indigenous Learning

Bates, P., Chiba, M., Kube, S., & Nakashima, D. (2009). *Learning and Knowing in Indigenous Societies Today*. Paris: UNESCO.

Battiste, M. (2002, October). Indigenous knowledge and pedagogy in first Nations education. National Working Group on Education and the Minister of Indian Affairs. Indian and Northern Affairs Canada (INAC), Ottawa, Ontario, http://www.afn.ca/uploads/files/education/24._2002_oct_marie_battiste_Indigenousknowledgeandpedagogy_lit_review:for_min_working_group.pdf.

Battiste, M. (2010). Nourishing the learning spirit. *Education Canada, 50*(1), 14–18.

Bolin, I. (2006). *Growing up in a Culture of Respect: Childrearing in Highland Peru*. Austin: U of Texas Press.

Brayboy, B.M.J., & Maughan, E. (2009). Indigenous knowledges and the story of the bean. *Harvard Educational Review, 79*(1), 1–21.

Cajete, G. (1994). *Look to the Mountain: An Ecology of Indian Education*. Durango, CO: Kivaki Press.

Cálix de Dios, H., Castillo Martínez, R., & Caamal Canché, H. (2014). Caracterización de la producción de pitahaya (Hylocereos spp.) en la zona Maya de Quintana Roo, México. *Agroecología, 9*(1y2), 123–132.

Chavajay, P., & Rogoff, B. (1999). Cultural variation in management of attention by children and their caregivers. *Developmental Psychology, 35*(4), 1079–1090.

Chavajay, P., & Rogoff, B. (2002). Schooling and traditional collaborative social organization of problem solving by Mayan mothers and children. *Developmental Psychology, 38*(1), 55–66.

Chilisa, B. (2012). *Indigenous Research Methodologies*. Thousand Oaks, CA: Sage Publications.

Coppens, A.D., Alcalá, L., Mejía-Arauz, R., & Rogoff, B. (2014). Children's initiative in family household work in Mexico. *Human Development, 57*(2–3), 116–130.

Correa-Chávez, M., Mejía-Arauz, R., & Rogoff, B. (Eds.) (2015). Children learn by observing and contributing to family and community endeavors: A cultural paradigm. In: *Advances in Child Development and Behavior*, vol. 49, pp. 91–112. San Diego, CA: Elsevier-Academic Press.

da Silva, L.J. (2012). El método inductivo intercultural y el calendario sociológico como estrategias para el fortalecimiento de una formación crítica e intercultural de profesores indígenas de los estados de Minas de Gerais y Bahía, Brasil. *Revista ISEES, 10*, 79–94.

Dayton, A., & Rogoff, B. (2013). 'On Being Indigenous' as a process. *Human Development, 56*(2), 106–112.

Dayton, A., & Rogoff, B. (2016). Paradigms in arranging for children's learning. In: D.S. Guimarães (Ed.), *Amerindian Paths: Guiding Dialogues with Psychology*, pp. 133–142. Charlotte, NC: Information Age Publishing.

de León, L. (2015). Mayan children's creation of learning ecologies by initiative and cooperative action. In: M. Correa-Chávez, R. Mejía-Arauz, & B. Rogoff (Eds.), *Children Learn by Observing and Contributing to Family and Community Endeavors: A Cultural Paradigm. Advances in Child Development and Behavior*, vol. 49, pp. 153–184. San Diego, CA: Elsevier-Academic Press.

Everton, M. (2016). *Los Mayas contemporáneos. Incidencias de viaje y amistad en Yucatán*. José MA. pp. 224–253. Morelos, Quintana Roo, México: Universidad Intercultural Maya de Quintana Roo, Capítulo IV.

Flores Escalante, J.M. (2010). La resistencia Maya en las escuelas rurales en Quintana Roo, 1928–1934. *História Unisinos, 14*(2), 161–176.

Fortes, M. (1970 [1938]). Social and psychological aspects of education in Taleland. In: M. Fortes (Ed.), *Time and Social Structure*, pp. 201–250. New York, NY: University of London, The Athlone Press.

Gadgil, M., Berkes, F., & Folke, C. (1993). Indigenous knowledge for biodiversity conservation. *Ambio, 22*(2/3), 151–156.

Gaskins, S. (2003). From corn to cash: Change and continuity within Mayan families. *Ethos, 31*(2), 248–273.

Gaskins, S., & Paradise, R. (2010). Learning through observation in daily life. In: D.F. Lancy, J. Bock, & S. Gaskins (Eds.), *The Anthropology of Learning in Childhood*, pp. 100–140. Lanham, MD: Alta Mira Press.

González Jácome, A. (2004). Ambiente y cultura en la agricultura tradicional de México: Casos y perspectivas. *Ciencia Ergo Sum, Julio-Octubre, 11*(2), 153–163.

González Jácome, A. (2009). El maíz como producto cultural desde los tiempos antiguos. In: C. Morales Valderrama, y C. Rodriguez Lazcano (Coords.), *Desgranando una mazorca. Orígenes y etnografía de los maíces nativos. Diario de Campo*, Suplemento Número. 52, Enero-Febrero, pp. 40–67. Mexico, D.F.: Instituto Nacional de Antropología e Historia.

González Jácome, A. (2011). *Historias varias. Un viaje en el tiempo con los agricultores mexicanos*. México: Universidad Iberoamericana.

Grande, S. (2004). *Red Pedagogy: Native American Social and Political Thought*. Lanham, MD: Rowman & Littlefield.

Grande, S. (2015). *Red Pedagogy: Native American Social and Political Thought*. Tenth Aniversary Edition. Lanham, MD: Rowman & Littlefield.

Gutiérrez, I.T., Rosengren, K.S., & Miller, P.J. (2015). Día de los muertos: Learning about death through observing and pitching in. In: M. Correa-Chavez, R. Mejía-Arauz, & B. Rogoff (Eds.), *Children Learn by Observing and Contributing to Family and Community Endeavors: A Cultural Paradigm: Advances in Child Development and Behavior*, pp. 229–252. San Diego, CA: Elsevier.

Hanks, W.F. (1993). Metalanguage and pragmatics of deixis. In: J.A. Lucy (Ed.), *Reflexive Language: Reported Speech and Metapragmatics*, pp. 127–158. New York, NY: Cambridge University Press.

Kirkness, V.J., & Barnhardt, R. (1991). First nations and higher education: The four R's—Respect, Relevance, Reciprocity, Responsibility. *Journal of American Indian Education*, 30(3), 1–15.

Lancy, D. (2016). New studies of children's work, acquisition of critical skills, and contribution to the domestic economy. *Ethos*, 44(3), 202–222.

Lee, T. (2009). Language, identity, and power: Navajo and Pueblo young adults' perspectives and experiences with competing language ideologies. *Journal of Language, Identity and Education*, 8(5), 307–320.

Little Bear, L. (2000). Jagged worldviews colliding. In: M.A. Battiste (Ed.), *Reclaiming Indigenous Voice and Vision*, pp. 77–85. Vancouver: University of British Columbia Press.

Little Bear, L. (2009). *Naturalizing Indigenous Knowledge*, Synthesis paper. University of Saskatchewan, Aboriginal Education Research Centre, Saskatoon, Sask. and First Nations and Adult Higher Education Consortium, Calgary, Alta. Available at www.fnahec.org (Accessed September 26, 2017).

Little Bear, L. (2011). *Native Science and Western Science*. Arizona State University, ASU Library, The Library Chanel, posted on May 16, 2011. Available at: https://lib.asu.edu/librarychannel/2011/05/16/ep114_littlebear.

Lomawaima, K.T. (2015). Education. In: R. Warrior (Ed.), *The World of Indigenous North America*, pp. 365–387. New York, NY: Routledge.

Lomawaima, K.T., & McCarty, T.L. (2006). *"To Remain Indian": Lessons in Democracy from a Century of Native American Education*. New York, NY: Teacher's College Press.

López, A., Najafi, B., Rogoff, B., & Mejía-Arauz, R. (2012). Collaboration and helping as cultural practices. In: J. Valsiner (Ed.), *The Oxford Handbook of Culture and Psychology*, pp. 869–884. New York, NY: Oxford University Press.

Madjidi, K., & Restoule, J. (2008). Comparative Indigenous ways of knowing and learning. In: K. Mundy, K. Bickmore, R. Hayhoe, M. Madden, & K. Madjidi (Eds.), *Comparative and International Education: Issues for Teachers*, pp. 77–106. New York, NY: Teachers College Press.

Mato, D. (1996). The Indigenous uprising in Chiapas. *Identities*, 3(1–2), 205–217.

Mato, D. (Coord.) (2012). *Educación superior y pueblos indígenas y afrodescendientes en América Latina. Normas, y prácticas*. Caracas: IESALC/UNESCO.

McCarty, T.L., & Nicholas, S.E. (2014). Reclaiming Indigenous languages: A reconsideration of the roles and responsibilities of schools. *Review of Research in Education*, 38(1), 106–136.

Mejía-Arauz, R., Rogoff, B., Dayton, A., & Henne-Ochoa, R. (2018). Collaboration or negotiation: Two ways of interacting suggest how shared thinking develops. *Current Opinion in Psychology*, 23, 117–123.

Morales Velázquez, J.J., & Lepe Lira, L.M. (2013). Parankuecha, diálogos y aprendizajes: Las fogatas de Cherán como praxis educativa comunitaria. *International Journal of Multicultural Education*, 15(3), 61–75.

Morelli, G., Rogoff, B., & Angelillo, C. (2003). Cultural variation in young children's access to work or involvement in specialized child-focused activities. *International Journal of Behavioral Development*, 27(3), 264–274.

Nigh, R., & Bertely, M. (2018). Indigenous knowledge and education in Chiapas, Mexico: An intercultural method. *Dialogos sobre Educación, Temas Actuales en Investigación Educativa*, 9(16), 1–20.

Okakok, L. (1989). Seeing the purpose of education. *Harvard Educational Review*, 59(4), 405–422.

Paradise, R. (1985). Un análisis psicosocial de la motivación y participación emocional en un caso de aprendizaje individual. *Revista Latinoamericana de Estudios Educativos*, 15(1), 83–93.

Paradise, R., Mejía-Arauz, R., Silva, K.G., Dexter, A.L., & Rogoff, B. (2014). One, two, three, eyes on me! Adults attempting control versus guiding in support of initiative. *Human Development*, 57(2–3), 131–149.

Paradise, R., & Robles, A. (2015). Two Mazahua (Mexican) communities: Introducing a collective orientation into everyday school life. *European Journal of Psychology of Education*, 31, 61–77.

Paradise, R., & Rogoff, B. (2009). Side by side: Learning through observing and pitching in. *Ethos*, 37(1), 102–138.

Ramos Díaz, M. (2001). *Niños Mayas, maestros criollos. Rebeldía indígena y educación en los confines del trópico*. Chetumal, Quintana Roo: Universidad de Quintana Roo, México, Chapters VII & VIII.

Reed, N. (2001). *The Casta War of Yucatan*. Revised ed. Stanford, CA: Stanford University Press.

Rentschler, R., Bridson, K., & Evans, J. (2015). Civic pride and community identity. The impact of the arts in regional Australia. *Stats and Stories – Theme 4*. Australia: Deakin University. Available at: http://regionalarts.com.au/wp-content/uploads/2015/05/Stats-Stories-4-Civic-Pride.pdf.

Rogoff, B. (1998). Cognition as a collaborative process. In: D. Kuhn, & R.S. Siegler (Eds.), *Cognition, Perception and Language: Vol 2. Handbook of Child Psychology*, 5th ed, pp. 679–744. New York, NY: Wiley.

Rogoff, B. (2003). *The Cultural Nature of Human Development*. New York, NY: Oxford University Press.

Rogoff, B. (2014). Learning by observing and pitching in to family and community endeavors: An orientation. *Human Development*, 57(2–3), 69–81.

Rogoff, B. (2016). Culture and participation: A paradigm shift. *Current Opinion in Psychology*, 8, 182–189.

Rogoff, B., Goodman Turkanis, C., & Bartlett, L. (2001). *Learning Together: Children and Adults in a School Community*. New York, NY: Oxford University Press.

Rogoff, B., Mistry, J., Göncü, A., & Mosier, C. (1993). Guided participation in cultural activity by toddlers and caregivers. *Monographs of the Society for Research in Child Development*, 58(7, Serial No. 236).

Rogoff, B., Najafi, B., & Mejía-Arauz, R. (2014). Constellations of cultural practices across generations: Indigenous American heritage and Learning by Observing and Pitching In. *Human Development*, 57(2–3), 82–95.

Rogoff, B., with Pérez González, C., Chavajay Quiacaín, C., & Chavajay Quiacaín, J. (2011). *Developing Destinies: A Mayan Midwife and Town*. New York, NY: Oxford University Press.

Rosado-May, F.J. (2012). Una perspectiva intercultural al concepto de tutoría académica. El caso de la UIMQRoo. In: I. Deance, & V. Vázquez Valdés *Aulas Diversas. Experiencias sobre educación Intercultural en América*, pp. 65–90. Quito: ABYA/YALA Universidad Politécnica Salesiana, Deance-Vázquez y Universidad Intercultural Maya de Quintana Roo.

Rosado-May, F.J. (2013a). *Indigenous Education. Which Way to Go? The Intercultural Model for Higher Education Developed in Mexico*. Canada: II International Meeting Canada-Mexico On Indigenous Education, University of Lethbridge, June 22nd.

Rosado-May, F.J. (2013b). Experiencias y visión de futuro de la Universidad Intercultural Maya de Quintana Roo. Aportaciones del modelo intercultural a la sociedad. In: A. Wind (Ed.), *Experiencias y visiones para el futuro de las Universidades Indígenas en el mundo*, pp. 157–172. La Paz, Bolivia: Instituto Internacional de Integración- Convenio Andrés Bello.

Rosado-May, F.J. (2015). The intercultural origin of agroecology: Contributions from Mexico. In: V.E. Méndez, C.M. Bacon, R. Cohen, & S.R. Gliessman (Eds.), *Agroecology*, pp. 123–138. Boca Raton, MA: CRC Press/Taylor and Francis, Chapter 8.

Rosado-May, F.J. (2017). Los retos y oportunidades de guiar inteligencia con inteligencia. El modelo de educación superior intercultural en Quintana Roo. In: F. González González, F.J. Rosado-May, & G. Dietz (Coords.), *La gestión de la educación superior intercultural en México. Retos y perspectivas de las universidades interculturales*. Chilpancingo, Guerrero, México: Universidad Autónoma de Guerrero y El Colegio de Guerrero A.C.

Rosado-May, F.J. (2018). Participación comunitaria en educación superior intercultural en el contexto de la construcción de identidad en un mundo global. In: F.J. Rosado-May, M. Chan Collí, & H. Cálix de Dios (Eds.), *Sin memoria no hay historia. El Rostro humano en la creación de la Universidad Intercultural Maya de Quintana Roo*, pp. 503–522. José Ma. Morelos, Quintana Roo, México: Glocal Bej.

Rosado-May, F.J., & Cuevas Albarrán, V.B. (2015). El programa educativo "Ingeniería en Desarrollo Empresarial" de la Universidad Intercultural Maya de Quintana Roo. ¿Qué justifica su creación? In: E.E. Brito Estrella (Ed.), *Empresa, sostenibilidad y desarrollo regional*, pp. 51–53. José María Morelos, Quintana Roo, México: Universidad Intercultural Maya de Quintana Roo.

Sandoval-Forero, E.A., & Montoya-Arce, B.J. (2013). La educación indígena en el estado de México. *Papeles de Población*, 19(75), 239–266.

Schmelkes, S. (2012). Educación para un México intercultural. *Sinéctica, 40*. Recuperado de: http://www.sine ctica.iteso.mx/articulo/?id=40_educacion_para_un_mexico_intercultural.

Schmelkes del Valle, S. (2009). Interculturalidad, democracia y formación valoral en México. *Revista Electrónica de Investigación Educativa*, 11(2). Consultado el 8 de julio de 2016, en: http://redie.uabc.mx/vol11no2/contenido-schmelkes2.html.

Scollon, R., & Scollon, S. (1981). *Narrative, Literacy, and Face in Interethnic Communication*. Norwood, NJ: Ablex.

Sueyo, H. (2003). Educational biography of an Arakmbut. *Comparative Education*, 39(2), 193–197.

Swisher, K. (1990). Cooperative learning and the education of American Indian/Alaskan Native students. *Journal of American Indian Education*, 29, 36–43.

Teuton, C. (2012). *Cherokee Stories of the Turtle Island Liar's Club*. Chapel Hill, NC: University of North Carolina Press.

Thomas, R. (1972). Indians and white people. In: H. Bahr, B. Chadwick, & R. Rowe (Eds.), *Native Americans Today: Sociological Perspectives*, pp. 30–40. New York, NY: Harper and Rowe.

Thomas, R. (1993). Childhood. Unpublished chapter. *Selected Works of Robert K. Thomas*. Available at: https://works.bepress.com/robert_thomas/.

Tippeconic, J.W. III (1999). Tribal control of American Indian education. In: K.G. Swisher, & J.W. Tippeconic III (Eds.), *Next Steps: Research and Practice to Advance Indian Education*, pp. 33–52. Charleston, WV: ERIC Clearinghouse on Rural Education and Small Schools.

Tom, M.N., Huaman, E.S., & McCarty, T.L. (2019). Indigenous knowledges as vital contributions to sustainability. *International Review of Education*, 65(1), 1–18.

Urrieta, L. Jr. (2013). Familia and comunidad-based saberes: Learning in an Indigenous heritage community. *Anthropology and Education Quarterly, 44*(3), 320–335.

Urrieta, L. Jr. (2015). Learning by observing and pitching in and the connections to native and Indigenous knowledge systems. In: M. Correa-Chávez, R. Mejía-Arauz, & B. Rogoff (Eds.), *Children Learn by Observing and Contributing to Family and Community Endeavors: A Cultural Paradigm: Advances in Child Development and Behavior*, pp. 357–380. San Diego, CA: Elsevier.

Urrieta, L. Jr. (2016). Native and indigenous education in the Americas: Indigenous knowledge systems, equity, and economies. In: G. Noblit, & W. Pink (Eds.), *Education, Equity, and Economy: Crafting a New Intersection*, pp. 161–174. Switzerland: Springer International.

Vargas-Cetina, G. (1998). Uniting in difference: The movement for a new Indigenous education in the state of Chiapas, Mexico. *Urban Anthropology and Studies of Cultural Systems and World Economic Development, 27*(2), 135–164.

Wilson, S. (2008). *Research is Ceremony: Indigenous Research Methods*. Halifax, NS Canada: Fernwood.

PART 2

Discourse, Positioning, Argumentation, and Learning in Culture

Introduction

Among all species, humans uniquely interact using both their bodies and the representational systems of culture as a social process to make meaning for reproducing and innovating culture. How we communicate using diverse modes of semiotic expression—the body, spoken language, written language, symbol systems—is integral to what it means to be human and to learn. The what, how, where, when, why, and who of human learning is sculpted by the complex and consequential history of how differences have been socially constructed in discourse and experienced in society, how they relate to power and privilege, and how they have contributed to political and economic inequalities. The marking of differences by gender, class, race, language, ability, and other categorizations has consequential outcomes for learners and the learning opportunities and identities made accessible for them in their learning ecologies. These chapters address some of the ways in which learning is shaped by people's participation in cultural practices and by these markers of difference.

McDermott and Pea's chapter is about learning "how to mean"—how to construct meaningful embodied and spoken expressions—through participation in the context of cultural practices. They offer a synopsis of fundamental aspects—the expressive media of the body, of eye gaze, of bodily orientation, of gesture, and of doing things with spoken words—in how people learn how to mean and to read meanings with others in their host culture. Levine, Keifert, Marin, and Enyedy propose an alternative approach for promoting the discourses of school-based argumentation in K–12 literature and science. They create a hybrid pedagogical model to uphold the diverse and complex nature of argumentation practices encompassing everyday and academic contexts and identify six characteristics for use in designing argumentation instructional models.

Several of the chapters in this section also make visible how learning is a contested activity, involving the navigation of systems of power. Green, Brock, Baker, and Harris focus on Positioning Theory as an analytic lens and explanatory theory to show how learning, and development of identity, evolves through discourse. This theory centers on the positioning actions of teachers and students as they co-construct practices and processes in classrooms. In their chapter on Power, Language, and Bilingual Learners, Flores and Garcia examine efforts in educational linguistics to understand the relationships between language, education, and social inequalities by exposing how the marginalization of racialized bilingual communities connects to larger political and economic inequalities. They interrogate the theory of social change undergirding linguistic solutions by emphasizing they may reproduce inequality by suggesting solutions to social inequalities are achievable solely by modifying the linguistic behaviors of racialized bilingual communities rather

Discourse, Positioning, Argumentation, and Learning in Culture

than in structural transformation of the larger political and economic factors spawning their marginalization. Artiles, Rose, Bal, and Gonzales illuminate the topic of Culture in Learning Disabilities Research by providing a critical overview of research on learning disabilities (LDs), grounded in a cultural perspective of learning, as contrasted with the privileging in most LD research of the biological line of development, emphasizing cognitive dimensions of learning, and problematically using culture as a essentialized concept associated with race, ethnicity, gender, religion, geography, social class, and language. They synthesize sociocultural theory-grounded LD studies, and sketch priorities for overdue opportunities for interdisciplinary theoretical cross-fertilizations for future LD research.

6

LEARNING "HOW TO MEAN"
Embodiment in Cultural Practices

Ray McDermott and Roy Pea

Introduction

Jean Piaget and Lev Vygotsky concur that the social world's details have an enormous influence on the development and learning of children right into adulthood. Piaget frames his statement as a two-sided affair, one half biological environment, the other half the sociocultural practices of others, as in, for example:

> The human being is immersed right from birth in a social environment which affects him just as much as his physical environment.
>
> *(1973, p. 156)*

Piaget's primary emphases are on embryology and ongoing biological processes of growth as a model for all human development, but the influence of the social world in a consequential fashion does not begin until the acquisition of the semiotic function at around the age of 18 months. For Piaget, social transformations in the child's development are an add-on to all that biological adaptation has delivered in the first 18 months.

Vygotsky's focus is more comprehensively sociocultural. The change in the social structure of the child commences with birth and is then transformed again with language acquisition and a deeper appropriation of the culture.

> The path through others, through adults, is the basic path of the child's activity.
>
> *(Vygotsky, 1998, p. 215)*

For Vygotsky, following birth, the social environment becomes a central cause of developmental change. Pea and Cole (2019) offer a contemporary phrasing:

> Infants depend upon the care of social others [which] requires the coordinated activity of the social group into which they are born. That activity, in turn, is organized in terms of culturally inherited social practices…all such forms of social interaction involve mediation of infants' experiences through a wide variety of cultural artifacts and practices employed by caretakers as a technology of child care.
>
> *(p. 4)*

In Bali, observes Margaret Mead, to illustrate the child's enmeshing in cultural milieu:

> the child is fitted into a frame of behavior, of imputed speech, imputed thought and complex gesture, far beyond his skill or maturity...Where the American mother attempts to get the child to parrot simple courtesy phrases, the Balinese mother simply recites them, glibly, in the first person, and the child finally slips into speech, as into an old garment, worn before, but fitted on by another hand.
>
> *(Bateson & Mead, 1942, p. 13)*

Invigorated by Bateson and Mead, this chapter is about learning "how to mean"—how to construct meaningful embodied and spoken expressions—through embodied participation in the context of cultural practices and with the conceptual tools the cultures have developed.

Our aim is to provide a synopsis of fundamental aspects of how people learn how to mean and, correlatively, how to read meanings with others in their host culture. Anything less than this leaves the description of organism-environment relations weak on the environment side. To describe people in action, we prefer to not limit the description of the environment to our imagination, complete, as it must be, with all the biases of our present situation. We would prefer to be surprised by what real people do with each other in the press of their present. Our synopsis has two parts: first, we summarize how infants develop an attentional machinery for engaging in social life, and, second, we examine such developments in use among three adults meeting each other in an ordinary interaction in Tokyo, Japan. These fundamentals include the expressive media of the body—of eye gaze, bodily orientation, gesture, and doing things with spoken words. In 41 seconds, they start to bow five times, but only two bows reach completion (Figure 6.1). It takes a surprising amount of interactional work to reach an ending.

In combining experimental studies of Western babies and an interactional analysis of Japanese adults greeting each other, we are not trying to describe a universal ground zero of skills developed by the babies and put to use by adults everywhere, even on the other side of the world, as much as we want to provide a sense of the complex varied environments in which people have to employ whatever they might have developed in previous environments for use in new environments. This language, highlighting interactive learning in mutually constituted contextual conditions, with roots in pragmatism and phenomenology and carried forward by ethnomethodology, stresses the importance of the temporal organization of activities. We are less interested in understanding already developed skills dropped into stable, preset environments than we are in people recombining old and new skills, attitudes, plans, and hopes in newly emerging environments. People of all kinds, whether babies or adults, are more than dormant skill sets, and their situations are more than preset buckets into which people are inserted. Notes from a keyboard, words from a dictionary, isolated questions from standardized tests, commodities from their markets—each has a history that

Figure 6.1 In the midst of the two women's first bow. Preliminaries are designed to bring people to this form.

Learning "How to Mean"

Figure 6.2 Man begins to point to chair; seated woman joins in; standing woman about to point to chair.

makes a difference as they are grasped in an oncoming present and scaled into a future. So much more so when people—ever squiggly, confused, strategic, emergent people—are our most pressing environments.

Our most immediate focus is on the use of pointing as a lightning rod for sociability and attention across persons in each others' presence (Goodwin, 2007, 2017; Kendon, 2004). A woman entering a room finds two seated people directing her to a seat (Figure 6.2: see white circles). Our analysis of the expression of meaning and sense-making in this bowing episode will illustrate a variety of mechanisms of cultural learning in interactions.

The Semiotic Function and Five Building Blocks of Enculturation

We can begin with a general development that Piaget (1962) called the semiotic function, by which he meant a representational competency that enables the child to engage an object/event not present (the signified) by means of another object that is present (the signifier). For Piaget, the development of semiotic function fuses a child and the social world in a symbiotic relationship that will last a lifetime of constant renewals. If not at first, it is the eventual foundation for humor, insight, paranoia, insanity, poetry, and other sites for the integration of personal development and public enchantment (and disenchantment). Semiotic function is a powerful tool that allows people to operate on things unseen.

On the way to semiotic function, various competencies are acquired by the child for use in the production and reproduction of positions and dispositions, tensions and pretensions, and desires and grudges as sites for the study of how objects/events are made manifest in the daily round. Beneath these high-profile events are a series of deeply embodied proficiencies that allow, guide, and invite the semiotic packaging that makes possible the flow of cultural arrangements and practices. Behaviors manifesting the semiotic function in young children include utterances referring to absent objects or situations ("pussy gone", or "gone get dinner": Pea, 1980) and pretend play by which a child pretends one state of affairs and uses it to understand pretense in others. Leslie (1987) astutely argues that pretending something is the case when it is not (while knowing it is not) is a minimal example of semiotic function. As a meta-representational collusion, "acting as if" is an early manifestation of how children can understand mental states. The same is true for fully enculturated adults who embrace beliefs like, "All men are created equal" and "Every child can learn", while they work tirelessly for displays of how much they or their children are better than others. The game of semiotic function requires constant attention to the details of lives—real and imagined—in interaction.

Here are five building blocks children learn to put together on their way to semiotic function and enculturation. They all contribute to how the Japanese bow sequence develops. Without them, there would be no bow, nor any Japanese. Over the life course, these social attunement processes get deployed in the diverse configurations of people, activity settings, and cultural artifacts in which cultural learning can be achieved and sustained.

Infants follow the attention signaled by adult eye gaze. When a person looks where another person has looked, "gaze following" happens. Among adults, gaze following is an integral communicative competency—interactional gaze is so fundamental that speakers discovering they do not have the gaze of their addressee interrupt the utterance in progress. Charles Goodwin (2006, p. 99) offers an example in Figure 6.3.

In studies of gaze-following by 12-to-18-month-old infants, Brooks and Meltzoff (2002) manipulated whether an adult could see visual targets in the direction of their gaze, and found that infants grant special status to human eyes which are accompanied by head movement. In one experiment, an adult head-turned to targets with their eyes either open or closed. Infants looked at the adult's target more for adults in the open-eyes condition. In a second study, a blindfold was compared with a headband. Infants looked more at the adult's target in the headband condition, with unblocked eyes. Infants were not simply responding to adult head turning but were sensitive to the status of the adult's eyes.

Infants follow the attention signaled by adult pointing. Parents use both eye gaze and deictic gestures to signal features of the environment and establish joint visual attention with their children (Bates et al., 1989). Infants begin following adult pointing between 10 and 13 months of age (Leung & Rheingold, 1981). Groundwork for this development appears earlier. Rohlfing et al. (2012) found that a dynamic pointing gesture triggers shifts of visual attention in infants as young as 4.5 months. "Infants are prepared to orient to the distal referent of a pointing gesture which likely contributes to their learning the communicative function of pointing" (p. 426). They follow adult pointing gestures, directing their own attention in their common visual situation to the first intercept of the Euclidean line projection from the adult's pointing gesture.

Some have argued too simply that pointing is a human universal for the basic task of directing someone's attention to something. Others have more rightly emphasized the indeterminacy and multi-perspectival field of options for reference of pointing. To determine intent, said Wittgenstein (1953), the parties in a pointing interaction need to share "forms of life" to make sense of the scope and relevance of the pointing gesture.

Infants themselves point to direct attention. Werner and Kaplan (1963; also Liszkowski et al., 2004) view pointing as a referential/declarative act to share attention to events with adults ("look at that") precursory to labeling ("that's an X"). But for Vygotsky (1962), pointing is a symbolic instrument caught between reaching for X and naming X. As a developmental achievement it can become

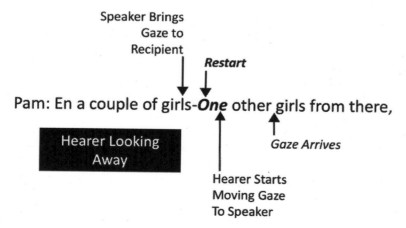

Figure 6.3 Requesting gaze of a hearer.

more imperative in meaning ("get me that"). The concomitant prototypic pointing gesture[1]—the combination of extended arm and extended index finger directed toward a target—appears in children between 12 and 14 months (Schaffer, 1984).

An important study of parent-child interaction by Bates, Camaioni, and Volterra (1975) demarcated three infant gesture types: one, "showing off" for attention; two, the *proto-imperatives* had infants using adults as a tool to get an object, for instance, pointing as a request (also DeLaguna, 1927); and three, the *proto-declaratives* when infants used an object as a tool in attempts for sharing attention to an object or event. Bates et al. argued that these triadic gestures, between infant, adult, and object, were intentionally communicative acts, evidenced in how, while gesturing, infants alternated their gaze between an adult face and an object, implying that the gesture was to influence the adult to obtain the infant's objective.

Joint attention for building common ground. In the first several years of life, as the groundwork for the semiotic function of language is being established, considerable effort is expended between a child and adults in establishing their "common ground" (Clark, 1996) for managing information concerning the referential focus of their attention, and for establishing and maintaining interpersonal affiliation (trust, intimacy) with their interlocutors (such as "social referencing" looks between infants and their parents; Feinman, 1982).

Infants share attention: joint attention as a triadic relation of self, other, object. Many developmental scientists have followed Tomasello's stringent criteria for finding a triadic relationship of joint attention:

> The fact that two individuals are simultaneously focused on the same aspect of the environment at the same time does not constitute joint attention. To qualify as joint attention, the social partners need to demonstrate awareness that they are attending to something in common.
>
> *(Tomasello, 1995, p. 106)*

> The common ground or joint attentional frame within which pointing gains its meaning is, of necessity, common or joint: We know some things or are attending to some things *together.*[2]
>
> *Tomasello et al., 2007, p. 706; their italics)*

Before joint attention appears according to the triadic definition, infants focus on either the interactional partner or an outside object/event. From 9 to 15 months, they learn to "coordinate their attention and actions on objects in their environment with the attention and actions of their social partners" (Dunham & Moore, 1995, p. 15). Neuro-imaging research reveals that 5-month-old infants are neurobiologically prepared for sharing attention with other humans (Grossman & Johnson, 2010).

The crucial difference between human cognition and that of other species is human participation with others in collaborative activities with shared goals and intentions (Tomasello et al., 2005). They conclude that participation in shared intentionality requires not only powerful forms of intention reading and cultural learning, but a unique motivation to share psychological states with others and unique forms of cognitive representation for doing so, including the creation and use of linguistic symbols, the construction of social norms and individual beliefs, and the establishment of social institutions.

By entering the meaning-saturated world of joint attentional interactions employing these five vital competencies, infants start learning with others about their environment and the cultural artifacts used by members to mediate interactions (Cole, 1998; Rogoff, 1990). Joint attention becomes a developmental crossroads, where infants meet the collective intelligence of culture, refracted through the individuals with whom they interact. We take the five social attunement mechanisms as capacities for entering the game of semiosis—meaning-making in the cultures in which children and adults imbibe. Over the lifespan, the joint attention nexus within cultural settings encompasses a significant range of activity settings and varieties of learning practice repertoires, such as eating and cooking, reading and writing, preaching and teaching, making and consuming things.

The twentieth century has produced various schools of thought with implications for theories of learning (behaviorist, gestaltist, sociocultural, cognitivist, to name only headliners), but only a few have moved beyond received categories to articulate better the lived experience of people engaging in learning activities that reproduce and innovate culture. Here we draw on the traditions that have made a difference while we work toward two goals: (1) to build two short word lists of possible service for inquiries into how people learn; and (2) to analyze a minimal sample of social interaction to see what it can reveal about the necessity and ubiquity of learning in the organization of human affairs. The joint pursuit of these intersecting goals may shed light on contrasting base metaphors for learning inquiries and their differing emphases on when learning has been or is being achieved. Temporality concerns will be consequential to the distinctions.

Two Vocabularies for Learning

We consider two short lists of words that might aid inquiries into how children and adults learn. The first is comprised of terms easy to the tongue, but likely unhelpful for understanding learning: for example, ability, knowledge, and skill. The second list offers newer terms to aid a fuller inquiry into what we do not know about learning: for example, embodied, immersed, sequentially relevant, and mutually constituted performances. The primary differences between the lists are the importance of process, timing, and temporal order. For Dewey, time:

> is the organized and organizing medium of the rhythmic ebb and flow of expectant impulse, forward and retracted movement, resistance and suspense, with fulfillment and consummation.
>
> *(1934, p. 23)*

The first list is comprised of abstractions with no direct contact with the organization of behavior. Analytically, they are theorized as sitting on a throne overseeing performances or treated as a storage bin of resources people in action might use or need. Either way, far from the fray, they keep a distance.

The second list identifies persons and things existing in a *fluxing*, peek-a-boo relation to each other across a stretch of time organized into systematically complex, multilayered sequences of *beginnings, middles,* and *ends*. Beginnings operate in anticipation of endings, endings exploit their beginnings, and together they arrange a *pulsating now* existentially dependent on edgy knowledge. They manifest a mix-and-match of hope and fear, across persons, under shifting circumstances, without any certainty of a given outcome. There is no place to stand for surety, no situation without the necessity of waiting for expected outcomes, no situation without necessary attention to what has to get learned and done differently to make one's way in the world. The very conduct of activity, like the five social attunements of infancy, is social and open to mediational means in its microgenesis. Every human interaction happens at the crossroads of human development and cultural learning. Culture is joined and made, rejoined and remade, in social interaction. This makes sense of Dewey's constant claim that education is another word for life. In a society that allows learning to be defined by the List I language of schools and their testing services, the terms on List II offer a more integral view of learning as part of wherever and whatever we are doing.[3]

> Because the need for preparation for a continually developing life is great, it is imperative that every energy should be bent to making the present experience as rich and significant as possible. Then as the present merges insensibly into the future, the future is taken care of.
>
> *(Dewey, 1916, p. 56)*

Learning "How to Mean"

Learning is a temporal phenomenon in which the connections among people and their objects of necessity, interest, and desire together undergo transformations big and small. Our first list of analytic terms cannot live up to the complex transformations at work in any setting where learning is on demand. People make do with what they have,[4] and their achievements are rarely regarded with the respect they deserve (M. Goodwin, 2006; McDermott & Raley, 2011). A mainstream education built principally on List I makes learning into a system of isolated items lifted from the knowledge closet: easy to measure, but in ways distant enough to deter learners and de-inspire teachers. List II instead treats learning as a product of co-constitutive interactions alive to possibility, fragility, and necessity with those trying to share a life.

List I holds learning to be essential, substantial, and measurable—pure knowledge inside the head—to be called on perhaps when necessary. List II, says philosopher Berel Lang (1995):

> prides itself on body and impulse…the head is sacrificed to the limbs, feeling is celebrated, and language itself is produced by touch. No mind without skin, this second view starts out, moderately enough; it ends with the mind all skin.
>
> *(1995, p. 150)*

Consider "*knowledge*": a stockpile of know-thats (declarative knowledge) and know-hows (procedural knowledge, also often called "*skills*"). These are separable topics for psychometricians. By putting them in play and on the skin, Lang speaks directly to knowledge as spatio-temporal emergent states of affairs in which people perform inquiry while fully embodied, immersed in ongoing events, mutually constituted with others, and sequentially relevant to current, future, and even past affairs. Dewey agrees:

> Knowing is itself a mode of practical action and is the way of interaction by which other natural interactions become subject to direction.
>
> *(1929, p. 86)*

Even science is unavailable without taking into account the present and its demands. We all have skin in the game.

> in the practice of science, knowledge is an affair of *making* sure, not of grasping antecedently given sureties. What is already known, what is accepted as truth, is of immense importance…but it is held subject to use, and is at the mercy of the discoveries which make it possible.
>
> *(Dewey, 1929, p. 154)*

To assert that the man pointing in the Japanese bow episode "has the skills" and "knows how to" point, that he "has the ability" to point, that he has "cognitive structures" for thinking about pointing, are claims that have kept developmental and cognitive psychologists busy for the last 150 years. Much has been learned this way, and the complexity of children (and other developing persons) has been sometimes honored by having knowledge and skills attributed to them. They have also been degraded by the absence of knowledge made apparent by what the words in List I cannot discern.

Mainstream studies of the psychology of ability, knowledge, and skills have been limited by a linear sense of time—cause/effect, pre/post, developmental levels marked by age—that leaves invisible the work people do while reflexively reorganizing a past reaching into a future. By echoing his own critique of theories of art,[5] Dewey could say about theories of learning: "by one of the ironic perversities that often attend the course of affairs", they study learning by ignoring how learning works. They try to freeze their variables and to link them mechanically as if the past is only what was and the future only what has not yet emerged. Studies based on mainstream vocabulary make learning, an "obstruction to a theory about [learning]". They leave observers with a hole in their analyses when they have to bridge the gap between the storehouses of the mind and the conditions of engagement with the world.

Our second list of words can deliver a better description of the pointing scene and the learning made manifest. The terms require we specify the spatial and temporal sequential relevancies of the activities of participants who are both co-constituting the contexts in which they operate and yielding consequences from the structures they promulgate. The pointing man is analytically no longer alone. He is with two other people who help him organize, interpret, reorganize, and reinterpret his initial pointing effort to get the walking-in woman in her seat where all three participants might have been pointing.

Like the word *knowledge*, each of the List I words can be critiqued for their pre-theoretical decision to break learning processes into isolated and measurable variables pulled from the flow of life. Similarly, all the words in List II can be praised for placing learning back in the situations that bring it forth and put it to work. We do not have the space to break each one down in the way we did for knowledge, but we can examine two words that can be found on both lists: *structure* and *context*. These words are used differently by adherents to List I and List II. *Structure* and *context* both work more in collusion with the words immediately about them than they serve any single static meaning. The same word—*context* or *structure*—can be divided by its commitment to either theorizing substantive entities that have a generalized effect on people's behavior or, quite differently, to formulating learning as a point of engagement involving many people over stretches of time. Rather than focus on the details of these variant senses of *structure* and *context* here, we offer them instead at work in the next two sections on the analysis of the pointing sequence as preliminary to two Japanese bows.

A Minimal Sample of Learning in Action

An activity-series is defined by its whence and whither…each activity-situation is a segment in a longer experience-chain.

(James, 1905, p. 39)

Our second goal is to analyze a minimal sample of social interaction to see what it can reveal about the necessity and ubiquity of learning in the organization of human affairs. We show the advantage of List II, and the disadvantage of List I, in an analysis of a simple social behavior: a grown man in the presence of two other adults points at something. The wider context is that the man is about to introduce two women, and they work attentively on bowing with each other for 18 seconds.[6] Our point: even 5 seconds of a minuscule, unremarkable, highly ritualized form of social interaction *requires ongoing learning by all involved*. They all undergo and transform the environments they make with each other, and for each other, and they have to keep track of themselves over time. Life is an endless cycle of doing and figuring, doing and figuring in interaction. It is not a credit to mainstream theories of learning that they barely acknowledge this mutually constitutive feature of people's learning. Context is not a simple variable to be manipulated. Context is not an experimental condition; contexts do not stand still. They are continually made and re-made.

Bowing is a significant part in the daily round of Japanese ritual. We estimate the adults in our video have bowed at least 100,000 times in their lives: a few times a day for formal bows with visitors and high-status others, and many quicker bows for passers-by, friends, relatives, and strangers caught momentarily in each other's orbit. So much practice should lead to a machine-like perfection. The Japanese are really good at bowing. Little children are early brought into the fold. When a visitor appears at the door, mothers grab their toddlers with one hand on the back of their neck and another hand to the stomach. With a little pressure from both hands, children conform to a bow. The basics are easy. Three Japanese people bowing with each other is the last place we should expect to find learning.

At first glance, our sample consists of one person moving his right hand across his body in the direction of something perhaps a few inches or feet away. The man is pointing at something. The conversation is in Japanese, and the pointing gesture feels Japanese. Americans tend to point by extending an index finger in the direction of something someone else should attend to.[7] Pointing in Japanese is a softer operation with the palm facing up or to the side, the thumb folded about twenty degrees into the palm, and the other fingers joined side-by-side and together leading the line of sight in a vaguely general direction. In comparison with the American finger directive, the Japanese pointing gesture feels like a suggestion.[8] That is all we have *so far*: one man moving one arm, and we observers guessing about what might develop. Not much to go on yet, but more than enough to begin.

Suddenly, there is more action. Three chairs in the room are lined up in a semi-circle suggesting a conversation. The man moving his arm sits in the middle chair, and a woman sits immediately on his right. One second after the man moves his right hand, the woman moves her left hand in the same direction. At the same time as she begins her forward movement, the man starts to pull his hand back. When their hands are near parallel to each other, he drops his hand toward his leg, and she moves her hand up. Together, they return their hands back to their bodies, he to his thigh, and she to her neck at the same time.

Something might be going on. We don't know yet, and they might not know yet, but there might be enough "interactional synchrony" (Condon & Ogston, 1966) for them to orient to, preserve, and make use of their co-presence.[9] If they continue in synchrony, we might get evidence of their expectations. Gregory Bateson once called for a psychology that would study "the reactions of individuals to the reactions of other individuals" (1936/1958, p. 175). His insight offers a general rule: what happens next might give participants—and observers—suggestions about what might be at hand.

Beyond what happens next, we have a second source of evidence co-occurring. There is a third party: the woman coming in from their right is on a path to walk in front of the two seated people.[10] She, too, cannot be sure of what will happen next. She has to learn from the others the lay of the land, and she can use what others are doing to inform herself of what she is doing.

As walking-in woman runs the semiotic gauntlet between the seated people and our camera, she gets feedback on what she is doing. She is making progress with each passing second, and so too are we, in the same way, making progress in our understanding of what she might be undergoing and overcoming. The *so far* phrase we used four paragraphs above has been enhanced: we have one man moving his arm, a nearby woman has coordinated her movements with his, and there is a third person passing by who might provide a confirming interpretation. The third person might be, Bateson again, "the pattern which connects"[11] (Bateson, 1979; Bateson & Bateson, 1927).

The woman walking in from their right does not simply walk on by. In rapid step, as she arrives where the man and woman have been sitting, she rotates the upper half of her body toward them, and, within a step, she is also raising her hands in the direction of the open chair. In joining the seated pointers, the walking woman's gestures issue a candidate "pattern which connects". It is not yet confirmed how the gestures might make sense. Our third participant *could* keep walking past the chair to the other side of the room. It would be a surprise. It would not make sense, but it is possible.[12] It would send our description begging for another angle, another explanation. Let's see if there is a connection between the gestures.

Over the next 2 seconds, the third person arrives at the side of the open chair and turns toward the two seated people. The pointing may have done its job. In reaching a possible end point—notice we do not say "the" end point—the third person completes a trajectory that had been initiated 5 seconds before. Our third *so far* had a beginning, moved quite literally through a middle, and came to a possible ending. If the problem before the entering woman is how to get a physical place in this conversation, the two seated people have supplied an answer. If the problem before the three participants is "how to make a physical shape for a conversation to occur?" the two seated people have suggested an answer, and the walking person has agreed. This is more complex than what most people can say about their own behavior. Were one to use analytic terms from List I to proclaim that each individual involved does (or does not) have the ability, knowledge, or skill to bow, the terms would be quite insufficient. Mutually constituted performances in context are the appropriate unit of assessment for such cultural competencies.

The problem writ large—*the interactional dance of cultural practice*—happens all day long, wherever people gather, in fact, and it usually gets solved well enough for everyone to accept their fate until the merry-go-round of co-constructed social events allows a move to a new place. It is rarely talked about, and it is accomplished mostly without awareness.

Our 5-second strip of "nothing going on" took careful attention by the participants while they likely had something more pressing in mind. Our brief beginning, middle, and end of *Pointing to a Seat* may well be in itself a beginning, a middle, or an end of a longer activity-series. It has "time embeddedness": the fact that all social acts are temporally fitted inside larger social acts (Lewis & Weigart, 1981, p. 437). Our strip has a whence and whither of its own. We have some hints of what they might be doing, and we can return in the next section to see what they have done with their little achievement.

Meanwhile, let's use our sample as a playground for the vocabulary needed for an appropriate and productive theory of learning. There is a *structure* to *Pointing to a Seat*. A well-structured strip of behavior is often a thing of beauty. Think of a sonnet, a sonata, or a *pas de deux*: polished performances that hide the thousands of hours that went into their production. *Pointing to a Seat* is not polished in that way. It has to get done on the spot. Each participant is on the spot. The beauty of the bow is not in its perfection, but in the work of people putting it together *in situ*. The bow as structure and the bow as an achievement of its participants are not separate phenomena. They are, in the language of List II, entwined, enmeshed, mutually designed, and so on. The minimal Japanese bow has a relatively simple structure in three parts: Gathering, Aligning, and Bowing. Each part can be thin or thick depending on circumstances. First, participants must come together for Greetings. In our sample, the Alignments took longer, because they required a pointing sequence and allowed two interruptions. The third task is to bow together once, twice, or three times before turning to a new topic. Table 6.1 shows the structure of a real bowing sequence. The three parts of the minimal Japanese bow are present, but so are two other parts added on to represent the time when the participants attended to matters not anticipated by the minimal model, for example: getting entering woman into her chair, handling the interruptions, and struggling to know when the two bows are over. Table 6.1 shows more than how any Japanese bow has to proceed; it represents the details of *how* two Japanese bows (of the five that began) are brought to fruition.

Sixty years ago, the social and behavioral sciences were dominated by a search for structures—at every level of social engagement. Think no further than Ray Birdwhistell (the raised eyebrow),

Table 6.1 Preliminaries for Two Japanese Bows*

Greetings (4 secs)	Pointing (5 secs)	Interruptions (14 secs)	Bow I (10 secs)	Bow II (8 secs)
eye contact dips, nods invitations	man points seated & arriving women also point to the chair	**Initiation 1** aborted (8 secs) **Initiation 2 (**4 secs**)** held (2 secs)	**Initiation 3 (3-sec)** bow (5 secs) **Initiation 4** (2 secs) abandoned	**Initiation 5** (5 sec) bow (3 sec)

*Note: Times approximate for current purposes

Learning "How to Mean"

Fernand Braudel (the Mediterranean), Noam Chomsky (the sentence), Roman Jakobson (the poem), Claude Lévi-Strauss (kinship systems), Talcott Parsons (patterns of modernity), and Jean Piaget (stages of child development). What treasures they brought to the fore, but by example of their success, attention to the structures underlying social life began to repress analytic consideration of people dealing with the specific circumstances of their situation. Structure was understood to determine behavior, as if people had only to follow the directions. Competence and performance were unproductively severed. So too minds and their bodies, environments and their persons. The more interesting story: structures don't come so preset they can't be resisted, reversed, and reconstructed. People have to rebuild the structures of everyday life with the materials others may have bequeathed them, but they are responsible for the yet to occur outcomes. (Karl Marx said that.)

As per Dewey's complaint about museums, the very existence of well-structured artifacts and performances can ironically become a hindrance to developing a theory about them. People don't live in or live out pre-formed structures. Rather, they build and rebuild the structures of their life together, and they do so with varying degrees of apathy, repetition, learning, creativity, mistakes, and failure. Led doubly by intelligence and ignorance, they take, retake, and mistake with the materials they are given (Klemp et al., 2016). Dewey preferred to remember the work we do, especially our work with others—my take, your take, our take, everywhere a take take—that goes into building the daily marvels of our lives. Here is Dewey's activity-driven take on structure:

> all structure is structure of something; anything defined as structure is a character *of* events, not something intrinsic and *per se.*
>
> *(1929a, p. 72)*

Every structure is an interim product of work just done and an object of work yet to be done. It constrains what can be done, but only the most current participants can take it to its latest consequences. For Dewey,

> structure is constancy of means, of things used for consequences, not of things taken by themselves or absolutely.
>
> *(1929, p. 62–63)*

The different senses of structure—*overdetermined* structure$_I$ versus *emergent* structure$_{II}$—distinguish the mainstream and alternative vocabularies (List I and II) that support theories of learning. List I key terms tell us something gets achieved because participants are capable of such a thing. List II key terms instead capture how the people achieve well-structured and recognizable activities. In the next section, similar to how we read *structure,* we find that the term *context* has both a static spatial reading, by which behavior happens inside a context, and a more complex temporal sensitivity, by which people contribute to the scene and build their own context in an ongoing manner.

Whence and Whither: What's the Point?

> It is important to see the particular utterance or action as part of the ecological subsystem called context and not as a product or effect of what remains of the context after the piece which we want to explain has been cut out from it.
>
> *(Bateson, 1972, p. 338)*

Let's see if our description (and its vocabulary) of the *Pointing* sequence can aid an account of the final 18 seconds of the two bows. At its core, a pointing gesture is a scream for whence and whither considerations. Its structure is retrospectively and prospectively organized by the cooperation of its participants. Its 5-second development calls its recipients back to the conditions inviting it, and it directs them forward to what might come of it. It can be efficient. Try pointing in public, and everyone nearby is a point of interaction and evaluation. People use pointing to direct themselves to a line of inquiry—literally a line—about the whence and the whither of what might be happening. In Charles Goodwin's (2004) conversation with Chil, a severely aphasic man with only three words, pointing became a divining rod for identifying and elaborating semantic meaning interactively, incorporating Chil's expressions of affect and prosodic contours, progressively refining the expression and recognition of Chil's intent. Goodwin would produce a sensible string of words, and Chil could re-shape them into messages. Post-severe stroke, Chil is "nonetheless able to position himself as a competent person, indeed a powerful actor, by linking his limited talk to the talk and action of others" (Goodwin, 2004, p. 151). Pointing helps people see how to look for something when the usual means have been interrupted. Context and content make each other.

Let's go first to the whither to see if it can tell us what to expect of its whence. Then we can go back to the whence to see how, with the help of our *Pointing* sequence, the whence helps to arrange for the next two or three behavioral knots (interruptions and bows) engaged in the whither. We want to know how *Pointing to a Seat* is reflexively organized back and forth in real time, mutually constituted by everyone attending and performing as expected (or unexpected, why not?), and sequentially relevant to what is going on over time.

We left the pointing scene as the entering person came to a stop at the side of the open chair. This is a possible juncture for a bow to launch. We may be observing, as conversational analysts would have it, a bow-relevant moment. Sidling up to the chair is a possible ending of the *Pointing* sequence. As the standing woman turns her gaze to the sitting couple, the man begins to raise his hand and says the Japanese equivalent of "well uh" ("ano"). If this is the beginning of the bow, it is quickly aborted when standing woman points to the microphone on the table and asks whether it is recording. Her question is answered, and the sitting woman adds a follow-up question that also gets answered. The first interruption takes about 8 seconds before it gives way to a new bow-relevant bid and another question; this second interruption takes about 4 seconds, during which time the man holds his hand to the side of his head.

How can we tell one initiation from another? The general answer is always the same. As Bateson said, it's in "the reactions of people to the reactions of people". More specific answers require closer looking (McDermott & Raley, 2011). A bow can be called for, but the context can change. A bow-relevant moment can be interrupted, even erased. Remember, when the first interruption begins, the man allows his hand to fall back onto his leg. The initial hand raising had been momentarily canceled. We can say "momentarily", because 8 seconds later the interruption comes to a halt, as the man raises his hand again. The term "interruption" describes a shift in topic and the attentional focus of the two women talking about the microphone; it also describes the behavior of the man's hand, which is now in abeyance—poised for whatever next circumstances might develop.

Once the second interruption is over, the man removes his hand from his head and begins the third initiation of the first bow. Over the next 20 seconds, the two women become introduced. The participants now know that the *Pointing* sequence was simply the beginning of a bowing sequence. Instead of all else that could have happened or would have happened if only a few behaviors were altered, the *Pointing* sequence helped get the entering woman into her seat, and the man's three bow initiation efforts at last resulted in the women being introduced to each other. In this brief analysis of the course of a 5-second *Pointing* sequence getting everyone into place,[13] we can see that the world is a busy place, and that learning is a constant necessity in doing pretty much anything with any others. More specifically, the 5-second strip can reveal a way to read the final 18 seconds; the 5-second strip can provide the materials participants used to help each other define the context as the beginning of a Japanese bow.

Now the whither comes into view. A man started to point to something, two others joined him, and 38 seconds later, the participants have been introduced and squared away enough to begin talking about their plans for the coming year. This is a great deal of culture for 38 seconds. Two of the

Learning "How to Mean"

people had never seen each other before, and off they go. With gusto, Franz Kafka characterized the place where every interaction has to get its start:

> Abraham falls victim to the following illusion: he cannot stand the uniformity of this world. Now the world is known, however, to be uncommonly various, which can be verified at any time by taking a handful of world and looking at it closely...this complaint at the uniformity of the world is really a complaint at not having been mixed profoundly enough with the diversity of the world.[14]
>
> *(1935, p. 21)*

Looking closely at a handful of the world shows how much a person must engage to get through a few seconds of life. The cultural world is filled with instruction and pedagogy in these nexus moments of pulsing tentativity. We are teaching and learning all the time. Kafka's "uncommonly various" world is not made of chaos and mayhem. It is far more productively filled with suggestions and guides about what to do next—co-constructing structures and contexts. This does not make life easy, but it does make life possible. We are all providing contexts for each other, with each other, and that in an endless line of reshaping events before and after. Whence and whither here, whence and whither there. In a nice twist on Heraclitus, Bateson defined the field of play:

> "Into the same river no man can step twice," not because the universe is in flux, but because it is organized and integrated.
>
> *(1991, p. 73)*

There is more to say about how the *Pointing* sequence is grown into a *Bowing* sequence. We can return to it after one more interruption of the linear account of beginning, middle, and end. Just as the beginning of the bow allows us to locate—to pinpoint—the end of the *Pointing* sequence, the ending might aid an appreciation of the whence. The beginning can help us discover what an account of the ending might tell us.

In the 4 seconds prior to the *Pointing*, from the sound of the closing door to the man starting to move his right hand in the direction of the empty chair, the two seated people turn their heads in the direction of the opening door (Figure 6.4).

The man seated in the middle has to move his head ~30 degrees for his line of sight to land on the entering woman. The woman on his right has to turn ~75 degrees to the same end. The two seated persons invite the entering person to a series of moves that end with the *Pointing* sequence: the man moves his hand in the direction of the entering woman and says, "Welcome" ("doozo"); seated woman moves forward into a dip,[15] then straightens her posture in preparation for a proper bow, and nods her head while saying, "Good afternoon" ("konichi wa"). Before the seated man begins to point to the empty chair (Figure 6.5, same as Figure 6.2), by their coordinated bodily

Figure 6.4 Two seated people look up to find entering woman.

Figure 6.5 Man begins to point to chair; seated woman has joined in; standing woman about to point to chair (same as Figure 6.2).

orientation and eye gaze, our three participants have created an interactional space for the organization and interpretation of any next behavior. By their attention to each other, they have created a specific "here" directed to a possible "there" that might help us to make sense of the pointing behavior about to occur (Table 6.2).

So far, we have examined the 5-second *Pointing* sequence with people directing each other to next steps in the interaction. Then we returned to the *Greetings* sequence and found the two seated people performing an elaborate 4-second dance welcoming their third party before directing her to a seat. Nothing feels out of place. All three participants appear hell-bent on getting arriving woman to her seat. The work of everything going smoothly is no less real for its being hard to see at first. Contrary to how mainstream educators think about learning in school, even a ritual performed many times a day requires constant and careful attention to the fragile and edgy contexts people are trying to live by. Any hitch, interruption, mistake, or malfeasance can bring background expectations into high relief where people can learn from them (Figure 6.6).

As arriving woman gets to the chair, she goes to its side, turns to the two seated persons, straightens up, and makes herself symmetrical (Figure 6.7). She has reached a possible bow place, but is it the right place? Perhaps not. Perhaps she had been directed to the chair front. Or perhaps she should sit down in the chair before initiating a bow.

The *Pointing* sequence got her to the chair, but then what? She aligns herself next to the chair, and the man starts to initiate an introduction-and-bow sequence, until he loses his partners. The standing woman points to a microphone on a nearby table and asks if it is on. This gets a follow-up question from the seated woman. The seated man answers both questions and organizes his body again to initiate a bow. Again, sitting man is left holding the lead with no one to lend a hand. In the 8 seconds after the man's first effort to initiate a bow, standing woman glides to the front of the chair and makes herself more obviously ready to bow (Figure 6.8).

Her hands go to the inside of her thighs, and she leans into a dip. With a second question from seated woman, standing woman, now at the front of her chair, begins to sit down. The man has to hold his hand to his head about 2 seconds, until she is almost properly seated, and then he initiates the first bow for a third time (Figure 6.9). What started with the man pointing 20 seconds before had, by recipient design and much attention to sequential relevance, reached its goal. Entering woman was seated in a chair and about to be introduced to the other woman. Bowing would be required.

Summary and Conclusion

We said this chapter would be about learning "how to mean"—constructing meaningful embodied and spoken expressions—through participation in the context of cultural practices and with the conceptual tools cultures have developed. We first summarized how infants develop an attentional machinery for engaging in social life, with five building blocks for becoming enmeshed in cultural practices. The leitmotif for the building blocks is that babies and their adults use the attentional

Learning "How to Mean"

Table 6.2 Chronology of a Bow Sequence Beginning (in ~41 seconds*)

Greetings (~4 seconds)

00:52	two seated people look up to find the entering woman (*Figure 6.4*).
00:54	man says, "Doozo" (please), and raises arm toward entering woman; seated woman performs a dip (an abbreviated anticipatory bow).
00:55	seated woman pulls torso up, nods her head, and says, "Konnichi wa" (Good afternoon).

The Pointing Sequence (~5 seconds)

00:56	man nods to entering woman, then thrusts his right arm to his left, developing an arched trajectory on the way to the empty chair. He then pulls his arm back, and then drops his hand onto his leg (*Figure 6.5, also used as Figure 6.2*).
00:57	woman points left hand forward (not as far as the man), pulls back, and raises her hand up as the man allows his hand to drop down.
00:59	man's hand arrives on his thigh as seated woman's hand arrives on her neck; walking woman turns partially to sitting pair and points to right (toward empty chair).

The Interruptions (~14 seconds)

00:00	arriving woman gets to the side of the chair; man initiates a first bow for the first time (**Initiation 1**; aborted); he drops his hand onto his leg (*Figure 6.7*).
01:06	arriving woman glides from the side to the front of the chair for a second possible bow–relevant moment.
01:08	arriving woman moves into dip position and raises a side question (*Figure 6.8*).
01:09	man initiates the first bow for a second time (**Initiation 2**; held in abeyance); arriving woman raises a side question; man answers.
01:12	arriving woman moves from a dip position and begins to sit down; man holds his initiation pose until she is mostly seated.

Bow I (~10 seconds)

01:14	man initiates first bow for the third time (**Initiation 3**; *Figure 6.9*); it will go to completion.
01:18	the two women bow (*Figure 6.6*) at the end of which it takes 18 moves across the two women to rise up in a co-ordinated ending.
00:22	first bow ends; man initiates a second round of the first bow for sharing first names (**Initiation 4**); women abandon the initiation of a second part of the first bow.

Bow II (~8 seconds)

00:24	man initiates a second bow (**Initiation 5**).
00:30	second bow begins.
01:33	bowing sequence is over.

* Times approximate for current purposes.

113

Figure 6.6 In the midst of the two women's first bow. Preliminaries are designed to bring people to this form, after which it takes work (18 moves across the women) to co-ordinate an exit (same as Figure 6.1).

Figure 6.7 Woman arrives chair side; man raises hand to initiate first bow first time.

Figure 6.8 Standing woman has glided to the front of her chair for a second bow-relevant moment; man initiates first bow for second time.

Figure 6.9 Standing woman holds dip into bow, begins to sit down; man initiates first bow for third time; it will go to completion.

Learning "How to Mean"

arrangements available to build situated versions of triadic relations of self, other, and object. By 18 months, says Piaget (1962), they develop the "semiotic function" by which a child can engage an object/event not present (the signified) by means of another object that is present (the signifier).

In analyzing a minimal sample of learning in action—41 seconds in which three people convene, look, point, move, and bow—we sought to reveal the necessity and ubiquity of learning in the organization of human affairs. Even a simple behavior can occasion a complex attentional game about who the people are and how they are to proceed with each other. In Japan, introductions are an occasion for bowing. Although mundane and highly ritualized, bowing entails ongoing learning by all participants—they undergo and transform the environments they make with each other.

We also sought to differentiate two vocabularies for considering the learning embodied in social interaction. The first is common to educational research on learning: ability, knowledge, skill—each one a substantial and measurable entity operating on its own inside the organization of people's behavior. The second list offers terms for a fuller inquiry into what we do not know about learning: embodied, immersed, sequentially relevant, and mutually constituted performances—each one a series of activities across persons over time. Recall Goodwin's conversations with an aphasic man. Subject to questions about the man's ability, knowledge, and skill, he would appear unable. When approached with Goodwin's analytic vocabulary, like our List II, the same man would seem inventively able; he could do more with others than he could by himself. When we used these distinctions to analyze the various meanings of "structure" and "context" in Japanese bows, the same complexity and learning come to the fore.

The primary distinction between the lists is the importance of process, timing, temporal order, and sequential relevance in the second. We find favor in centering the complex and nuanced temporal organization of experience rather than the entity emphasis of List I. A temporal focus identifies persons and things in a fluxing relation to each other across time organized into systematic multilayered sequences of beginnings, middles, and ends. A temporal focus shows that learning is always necessary. It's a by-product of co-constitutive interactions alive to could-bes, might-nots, and must-dos. Educators have mistakenly focused on sorting students with the most ability, knowledge, or skill. Their job should be building the most productive environments for everyone to learn the best stuff.

David Plath's beautiful cultural analysis of life-long learning shares a starting point with how we have analyzed bowing. He likens culture to a "parliament of prodigals": a seemingly stable setting ironically the product of fluxing compromises for all involved. Across 41 years or 41 seconds, everyone is half-in, half-out, and attending to each other for guidance on how to proceed. We are all, says Plath, "a collective product. We all must 'author' our own biographies, using the idioms of our heritage, but our biographies must be 'authorized' by those who live them with us" (1980, p. 9). No wonder people need a well-structured context—a bow, a family, a classroom, a computer network—to hold them together. No wonder also that a bow, or any social arrangement, demands such hard work. Ongoing learning by participants in interaction should be an ongoing priority in our studies of learning here, there, anywhere.

Notes

1 Other cultures use deictic gestures beyond prototypic extended arm and index finger to procure joint attention: (1) *nose-pointing* among Papua New Guinea's Yupno (Cooperrider & Núñez, 2012); (2) *head-pointing*, beyond common head uses to point when the hands are occupied, in which a speaker orients her head to a particular place in the gesture space when referring to a specific person or entity not physically present. The speaker reorients to the same space with each subsequent mention (McClave et al., 2007); and (3) *lip-pointing* also occurs—one or both lips are protruded, sometimes with and sometimes without the lips parted, together with head tilting or "tossing"—practiced among Panama's San Blas Cuna (Sherzer, 1972) and by Laos' Yupno speakers (Enfield, 2001). Developmental studies of such deictic gesture diversity have had little attention. For prototypical manual European pointing, Kendon (2004) identified morphological variation in manual pointing among Italian and British speakers; different handshapes and palm orientations reflected distinctive discourse functions.

2 It is noteworthy that communicative interactions during periods of joint attentional engagement appear to facilitate the infant's emerging understanding of words. A positive relationship between joint attention and early word learning has been evidenced in studies across labs and homes (Brooks & Meltzoff, 2005; Smith, Adamson, & Bakeman, 1988).

3 *A Note on Sources*: Both List II and the analysis of the bow are heavily dependent on ethnomethodology (Garfinkel), conversational analysis (Sacks, C. Goodwin, M. Goodwin), and the study of body movement as communication (Kendon). We have relied deeply on two earlier traditions: Dewey's pragmatism and Bateson's natural history of mind. List I is the official language of American schooling; it dominates the interpretation of children in the popular mind. New advances in the social sciences can take us beyond List I, but so can earlier advances. The terms in List I are arbitrary, misleading, and, worse, they have taken center stage with the forces of inequality. List II needs help from both ends of the century to build an alternative.

4 This was a frequently used phrase by Pea's father (1927–2019), whose rural Kentucky hardscrabble life, being raised in the Great Depression, left this as a motto for life, and yet also a condition to overcome.

5 The full Dewey text:

> By one of the ironic perversities that often attend the course of affairs, the existence of works of art upon which the formation of an esthetic theory depends has become an obstruction to theory about them. For one reason, it is a product that exists externally and physically. In common conception, the work of art is identified with the building, book, painting, or statue in its existence apart from human experience. Since the actual work of art is what the product does with and in experience, the result is not favorable to understanding.
>
> (1934, p. 3)

6 Forty years ago, Harumi Befu and McDermott looked for six weeks at 41 seconds of the Bow Tape: from the head nod acknowledgement of each other's presence to the end of the second bow. Although this paper uses only the 5 seconds of the pointing sequence and its most immediate connections that stage the bows, the fuller analysis informs our remarks. It hurts to leave such detail behind, but fun to constrain our conclusions to fit the looser—half-second by half-second—narrative of this paper. We wish Harumi could have joined us this time.

7 For cultural variation in the index finger pointing gesture, see Note 1.

8 The Japanese do have an index finger gesture. With hand at chin height and its index finger raised to the sky, the hand goes back and forth: right, left, right, left. The message: stop doing what you are doing.

9 We use the term interactional synchrony (Condon & Ogston, 1966) for its evocative powers. We are aware that Condon and Ogston's analyses—at 96 film frames/second—operate at a level of detail far tighter than we can deliver at 30 video frames/second. In this retelling of the bow sequence, we are proceeding at approximately half-second chunks. This paper offers no technical achievement, only a story told more carefully than most stories about learning, enough, perhaps, to make our point about the importance of temporal complexities in both the organization of behavior and theories about learning.

10 The cameraman is a fourth person in the room. We cannot see him, and he does not figure in the analysis. The camera itself can be treated as a fifth participant, but we have paid little attention to it.

11 In Bateson and Bateson (1927), Gregory and his father described two birds similar enough to be of the same species and different enough to be of different species. When they obtained a third bird, it was enough like the other two birds that it made sense of the differences as variants of what made them the same. The third bird was the "pattern which connects".

12 Some schools of ethnography are unimpressed by prediction of what will happen next; they are more excited about knowing what people might do when the expected does not happen (Frake, 1980).

13 This phrasing relies on Harvey Sacks's title, "An analysis of the course of a joke's telling" (1974).

14 Harvey Sacks cited the middle line in an early publication (1963, p. 16 footnote). Kafka alerts us to why studying ordinary activity is valuable and can be subversive.

15 A full bow movement is generated from the hips. The dip is a partial bow generated from the shoulders. A nod generates movement from the neck; it occurs often in bow-possible situations but has a wider range of uses in partial performances. Goffman (1976) calls partial performances 'displays'.

References

Bates, E., Camaioni, L., & Volterra, V. (1975). The acquisition of performatives prior to speech. *Merrill-Palmer Quarterly*, 21, 205–226.

Bates, E., Thal, D., Whitesell, K., Fenson, L., & Oakes, L. (1989). Integrating language and gesture in infancy. *Developmental Psychology*, 25(6), 1004–1019.

Learning "How to Mean"

Bateson, G. (1936/1958). *Naven: A Survey of the Problems Suggested by a Composite Picture of a New Guinea Tribe.* Stanford: Stanford University Press.

Bateson, G. (1972). *Steps to an Ecology of Mind.* New York, NY: Ballantine.

Bateson, G. (1991). *Sacred Unity: Further Steps to an Ecology of Mind.* New York, NY: Harper Collins.

Bateson, W., & Bateson, G. (1927). On certain aberrations of the red-legged Partridges *Alectoris* and *saxatilis*. *Journal of Genetics*, 16, 101–123.

Bateson, G., & Mead, M. (1942). *Balinese Character: A Photographic Analysis* (pp. 17–92). New York, NY: New York Academy of Sciences.

Brooks, R., & Meltzoff, A. N. (2002). The importance of eyes: How infants interpret adult looking behavior. *Developmental Psychology*, 38(6), 958.

Brooks, R., & Meltzoff, A. N. (2005). The development of gaze following and its relation to language. *Developmental Science*, 8(6), 535–543.

Clark, H. H. (1996). *Using Language.* New York, NY: Cambridge University Press.

Cole, M. (1998). *Cultural Psychology.* Cambridge, MA: Harvard University Press.

Condon, W., & Ogston, W. (1966). Sound film analysis of normal and pathological behavior patterns. *The Journal of Nervous and Mental Disease*, 143(4), 338–347.

Cooperrider, K., & Núñez, R. (2012). Nose-pointing: Notes on a facial gesture of Papua New Guinea. *Gesture*, 12(2), 103–129.

DeLaguna, G. A. (1927). *Speech: Its Function and Development.* New York, NY: Yale University Press.

Dewey, J. (1916). *Democracy and Education.* New York, NY: Macmillan.

Dewey, J. (1929). *Experience and Nature.* New York, NY: Macmillan.

Dewey, J. (1934). *Art as Experience.* New York, NY: Minton Balch.

Enfield, N. J. (2001). "Lip-pointing": A discussion of form and function with reference to data from Laos. *Gesture*, 1(2), 185–211.

Feinman, S. (1982). Social referencing in infancy. *Merrill-Palmer Quarterly*, 28(4), 445–470.

Frake, C. O. (1980). *Language and Cultural Description.* Stanford: Stanford University Press.

Goffman, E. (1976). Gender advertisements. *Studies in the Anthropology of Visual Communications*, 3(2), 69–154.

Goodwin, C. (2004). A competent speaker who can't speak: The social life of aphasia. *Journal of Linguistic Anthropology*, 14(2), 151–170.

Goodwin, C. (2006). Human sociality as mutual orientation in a rich interactive environment: Multimodal utterance and pointing in aphasia. In: N. J. Enfield, & S. C. Levinson (Eds.), *Roots of Human Sociality* (pp. 97–125). Oxford: Berg.

Goodwin, C. (2007). Environmentally coupled gestures. In: S. D. Duncan, J. Cassell, & E. T. Levy (Eds.), *Gesture and the Dynamic Dimensions of Language* (pp. 195–212). Philadelphia, PA: John Benjamins Publishing.

Goodwin, C. (2017). *Co-Operative Action.* Cambridge: Cambridge University Press.

Goodwin, M. (2006). *Hidden Life of Girls: Games of Stance, Status, and Exclusion.* London: Blackwell.

James, W. (1905). The experience of activity. *Psychological Bulletin*, 2, 39–40.

Kafka, F. (1935/1958). *Parable and Paradoxes.* New York, NY: Schocken Books.

Kendon, A. (2004). *Gesture: Visible Action as Utterance.* Cambridge: Cambridge University Press.

Klemp, M., McDermott, R., Raley, J., Thibault, M., Powell, K., & Levitin, D. (2016). Plans, takes and mis-takes. *Education et Didactique*, 10(3), 106–120.

Lang, B. (1995). *Mind's Bodies: Thought in the Act.* Albany, NY: SUNY Press.

Leslie, A. M. (1987). Pretense and representation: The origins of "theory of mind". *Psychological Review*, 94(4), 412.

Leung, E. H. L., & Rheingold, H. L. (1981). Development of pointing as a social gesture. *Developmental Psychology*, 17(2), 215–220.

Lewis, J. D., & Weigert, A. J. (1981). The structures and meanings of social time. *Social Forces*, 60(2), 432–462.

Liszkowski, U., Carpenter, M., Henning, A., Striano, T., & Tomasello, M. (2004). Twelve-month-olds point to share attention and interest. *Developmental Science*, 7(3), 297–307.

McClave, E., Kim, H., Tamer, R., & Mileff, M. (2007). Head movements in the context of speech in Arabic, Bulgarian, Korean, and African-American Vernacular English. *Gesture*, 7(3), 343–390.

McDermott, R., & Raley, J. (2011). Looking closely: Toward a natural history of ingenuity. In: E. Margolis, & L. Pauwels (Eds.), *Handbook of Visual Research Methods* (pp. 272–291). London, UK: Sage.

Pea, R. D. (1980). The development of negation in early child language. In: D. R. Olson (Ed.), *The Social Foundations of Language and Thought* (pp. 156–186). New York, NY: W. W. Norton.

Pea, R., & Cole, M. (2019). The living hand of the past: The role of technology in development. *Human Development*, 62(1–2), 14–39.

Piaget, J. (1962). *Play, Dreams and Imitation in Childhood.* New York, NY: Norton.

Piaget, J. (1973). *To Understand Is to Invent.* New York, NY: Viking Press.

Plath, D. (1980). *Long Engagements*. Stanford: Stanford University Press.

Rogoff, B. (1990). *Apprenticeship in Thinking*. Oxford: Oxford University Press.

Rohlfing, K. J., Longo, M. R., & Bertenthal, B. I. (2012). Dynamic pointing triggers shifts of visual attention in young infants. *Developmental Science*, 15(3), 426–435.

Sacks, H. (1963). Sociological description. *Berkeley Journal of Sociology*, 8, 1–16.

Sacks, H. (1974). An analysis of the course of a joke's telling. In: R. Bauman, & J. Sherzer (Eds.), *Explorations in the Ethnography of Speaking* (pp. 337–353). Cambridge: Cambridge University Press.

Schaffer, H. R. (1984). *The Child's Entry into a Social World*. London: Academic Press.

Sherzer, J. (1972). Verbal and nonverbal deixis: The pointed lip gesture among the San Blas Cuna. *Language in Society*, 2(1), 117–131.

Smith, C. B., Adamson, L. B., & Bakeman, R. (1988). Interactional predictors of early language. *First Language*, 8(23), 143–156.

Tomasello, M. (1995). Joint attention as social cognition. In: C. Moore, & P. J. Dunham (Eds.), *Joint Attention* (pp. 103–130). Hillsdale, NJ: Erlbaum.

Tomasello, M., Carpenter, M., Call, J., Behne, T., & Moll, H. (2005). Understanding and sharing intentions. *The Behavioral and Brain Sciences*, 28(5), 675–691.

Tomasello, M., Carpenter, M., & Liszkowski, U. (2007). A new look at infant pointing. *Child Development*, 78(3), 705–722.

Vygotsky, L. S. (1962). *Thought and Language*. Cambridge, MA: MIT Press.

Vygotsky, L. S. (1998). *The Collected Works of L. S. Vygotsky, Volume 5, Child Psychology, Part 2: Problems of Child (Developmental) Psychology* (pp. 187–296). R. W. Rieber (Ed.), New York, NY: Plenum.

Werner, H., & Kaplan, B. (1963). *Symbol Formation*. New York, NY: John Wiley.

Wittgenstein, L. (1953). *Philosophical Investigations* (trans. G. E. M. Anscombe). Oxford: Blackwell.

7

POSITIONING THEORY AND DISCOURSE ANALYSIS

An Explanatory Theory and Analytic Lens

Judith L. Green, Cynthia Brock, W. Douglas Baker, and Pauline Harris

Positioning Theory was originally developed three decades ago by Davies and Harré (1990) at the intersection of social and discursive psychology and feminist theories in education. It was developed as an *analytic lens* and *explanatory theory* to show how learning, and development of identity, evolves through discourse. When used as an *analytic lens* in education, Positioning Theory focuses researchers on examining the in time and over time construction of positioning actions of teachers and students in developing episodes for learning and participating in classrooms. As an *explanatory theory*, Positioning Theory serves as a set of guiding principles for investigating the consequences of the discourse and the interactions of, and with, particular students and groups of students as they assume or reject particular positions or acts of positioning. Thus, Positioning Theory frames ways of examining position-positioning relationships as dynamic and developing within and across time, events/episodes, and configurations of actors, within and across social spaces in classrooms and other social contexts.

The goals of this chapter are presented in two parts. The first section presents the history and development of Positioning Theory as an explanatory theory that has evolved as it has been taken up by different disciplines to examine issues of identity within particular contexts (e.g., in social and discursive psychology, management studies, nursing, and education, among others). In the second section, we present two *telling case studies* (Mitchell, 1984; defined later) that make transparent[1] how Positioning Theory served as an analytic lens to guide two of the co-authors of this chapter, Harris and Baker, in (re)analyzing archived records from their original longitudinal research studies to explore position-positioning relationships. The goal of these (re)analyses was to explore how Positioning Theory made visible previously unexamined processes that framed the *identity potentials* and *performance styles* of students in each site: first grade students in literacy events in Harris' (1989) study and two first-year seniors in performing public critique in an intergenerational (Grades 9–12) high school Advanced Placement studio art program (Baker, 2001).

Positioning Theory: Its Origins, Definition, and Directions in Education

The origins of Positioning Theory rest largely with the discursive turn in the social sciences, in general, and psychology in particular (Harré & Gillett, 1994; Harré & Moghaddam, 2003). We begin this section with an overview of the key historical developments within the field of psychology that led Harré, the principal architect of Positioning Theory (Kayi-Aydar, 2019), and his international and interdisciplinary group of colleagues (e.g., Davies & Harré, 1990; Harré & van Langenhove, 1999) to the discursive turn and the creation of Positioning Theory.

Experimental Psychology: A Brief Overview of Harré's Growing Concerns

Since the beginning of psychology in the late 1800s, one dominant area in the field of psychology—especially in the U.S.—focused on psychology as a laboratory-based experimental science. Harré and Moghaddam (2003) argue that psychologists focusing on a laboratory-based experimental science are concerned primarily with *performance capacity*, or individuals' behaviors as they perform specific tasks, and not with the cultural, social, and discursive foundations of human performance. Although understanding behavior is important, as Harré argued early in his career, this approach alone does not provide a thorough analysis of human learning and development; it neglects meaning-making in shaping human thinking and learning (Harré & Moghaddam, 2003).

The First and Second Cognitive Revolutions: Movement Towards Positioning Theory

In the 1950s and 60s in the U.S., a focus on cognition (rather than primarily on observable behaviors) began to gain a foothold in psychology. Harré and Gillett (1994) attribute the work of psychologists in the Center for Cognitive Studies at Harvard in 1950s and 1960s as being central to this shift—often referred to as the first cognitive revolution. Harré and Moghaddam (2003) suggest that whereas attention to cognition was brought forth as a result of the first cognitive revolution, scholars who advocated for this shift argued for a representational view of mind. For Harré and Gillett (1994, p. 18), a representational view of mind functions as follows: individuals build mental pictures of the world from their contact with it; these pictures are derived from features of reality in the world; individuals then perform "logical operations on the resulting (pictured) combinations of these features."

As the initial cognitive revolution unfolded across time, however, a group of scholars including Harré and Gillett (1994)—drawing largely on the later work of Wittgenstein (1953)—argued for a second cognitive revolution that focused on *meaning* rather than *representation*. As articulated by Wittgenstein (1953) and Harré and Gillett (1994), there are at least two central problems with a representational view of mind: it views mental activity as a set of internal processes, and it does not account for the process of coming-to-understand during the meaning-making process. Rather, Harré and Gillett (1994, p. 19, emphasis added), argued that:

> understanding and the phenomena of meaning or intentionality, in general, could only be approached by looking at what people actually do with word patterns and other sign systems....[In short,] *meaning is the use to which we put our signs.*

Moreover, they argued that signs are used differently in different social and cultural groups of people who establish—often in a fluid manner—the norms and rules for the use of signs within their groups. This movement towards meaning drew attention to a different conception of human performance called *performance style*; Harré and Moghaddam (2003, p. 3) argue that performance style, refers to the "way people [individuals and the groups of which they are a part] do things and the meanings ascribed to what they do."

Thus, the shift from a representational view of human learning and development to a meaning-focused view of human learning and development draws attention to language-in-use in specific social and cultural contexts and foregrounds the central role of discourse (i.e., the discursive turn) in understanding mind and meaning-making (Davies & Davies, 2007). Whereas the discursive turn emphasizes *that* discourse is central to human learning and development, Davies and Harré

(1990) developed Positioning Theory as an explanatory tool (their term) to construct theoretical understandings of *how* the process of meaning construction through discourse is constructed in unique cultural and social contexts. Thus, since its inception, Positioning Theory has—and continues to—provided researchers with an *analytic lens* to study how human learning and development is constructed through discourse. Although Positioning Theory is an evolving theory, there are three key tenets to Positioning Theory, which we explain in the following subsection, and which we draw on in the two telling case studies in the second part of this chapter.

Positioning Theory Briefly Defined

Over the last three decades, Positioning Theory has evolved as a framework for exploring and explaining how people construct themselves and their worlds—and are constructed—through discourse (Davies & Harré, 1990; Harré & van Langenhove, 1999). The following quote by Harré (2011, p. ix) provides a brief definition of Positioning Theory:

> A cluster of rights and duties recognized in a certain social milieu has been called a *position*. The corresponding act by which a person claims certain rights and opts for certain duties, or has them thrust on a certain social actor is the act of *positioning*. Sometimes, positioning is a deliberate act of which the actors are aware—more often it *crystallizes* out of the background of social practices within which people are embedded. The system of concepts and hypotheses as to the principle with which they are applied is known as *Positioning Theory*.

This quote draws attention to three long-standing precepts of Positioning Theory: *positions*, *acts*, and *storylines* (Davies & Harré, 1990; Harré & van Langenhove, 1999). Storylines—described above as social and discursive practices within which people are embedded that inform actions—are ways in which social processes are typically enacted in different cultural contexts.

From this perpective, actors in *storylines* can discursively and interactionally position themselves and/or others, as well as be positioned by others. For example, consider the "typical" Cinderella storyline. A handsome prince meets a beautiful damsel in distress, he saves the day, and the prince marries the damsel. Davies (1993) shared the book *The Paper Bag Princess* (Munsch, 1981) with a group of elementary children in Australia. This children's book disrupts typical princess/prince gendered storylines positioning the princess in the story as agentive and the prince as fickle. Some children with whom Davies (1993) shared the story rejected the story because it did not "fit" with their conceptions of the typical prince/princess storyline (see also Davies & Harré, 1990).

Positions—as described above—are dynamic and evolving clusters of *norms* and *expectations* that people in particular developing storylines perform (or reject) in varied and unique ways. For example, in education, institutionally defined positions might include "student" and "teacher." However, how people assume (or reject), situationally constructed and enacted positions varies with each unique actor and her/his background, experiences, and goals in developing episodes of classroom life (see Telling Case Studies 1 and 2.) Thus, *positions* are fluid, dynamic, and always in the process of being constructed in particular contexts.

Finally, *acts* refer to the social meaning of actions attributed to particular actors in developing storylines that shape who can say or do what, in what ways, to and with whom, when and where, and under what conditions, drawing on what material and social resources (past, present, and implicated for future). As Telling Case Studies 1 and 2 in this chapter will demonstrate, these contextual dimensions of developing storylines define *what counts* (Heap, 1991) as socially, academically, personally, and interpersonally significant as participants engage in discursively constructing opportunities for learning with particular teachers and students in particular educational contexts (Bloome, Carter, Christian, Otto, & Shuart-Faris, 2005).

Positioning Theory: Its Directions, Appeal, and Uses in Education[2]

Through an analysis of studies published in research volumes and peer-reviewed journals focusing on Positioning Theory in education, we identified ways Positioning Theory has informed research in education as well as how it is being shaped by research in education. This review led to the identification of studies that span a wide range of ages of participants, disciplines, and phenomena within education, undertaken over the past several decades. Illustrative examples include *STEM* (e.g., Herbel-Eisenman, Wagner, Johnson, Suh, & Figueras, 2015; Redman, 2013; Yamakawa, Forman, & Ansell, 2009), *literacy* (e.g., Barone, 2001; Bomer & Laman, 2004; Frankel, 2016), *teacher education* (e.g., Bullough & Draper, 2004; McVee, Baldassarre, & Bailey, 2004), and *teacher professional development* (e.g., Brock, Robertson, Borti, & Gillis, 2019).

As indicated above, there is a growing body of diverse lines of research guided by Positioning Theory. Given that a comprehensive analysis of these lines of inquiry is beyond the scope of this chapter, to illustrate its potential, we now present a set of illustrative examples of different ways a key dimension of Positioning Theory, *modes of positioning,* have informed studies of equity of access to learning. Harré and van Langenhove (1991) introduced the notion of modes of positioning the year after Positioning Theory was initially developed by Davies and Harré (1990). Modes of positioning include examples of "possible forms in which positioning can occur as a discursive practice" (Harré & van Langenhove, 1999, p.20).

Whereas Harré and van Langenhove (1999) have introduced many different possible *modes of positioning,* and this work has been elaborated upon across time (cf., Brock et al., 2019; McVee et al., 2004), to illustrate the potential of this aspect of Positioning Theory, we present illustrative studies that relate most closely to the modes of positioning discussed by Harris and Baker later in this chapter. These studies have examined two central modes of positioning discussed by Harré and van Langenhove (1999, p. 22)—*self* and *other positioning*:

> whenever somebody positions him/herself, this discursive act always implies a positioning of the one to whom it is addressed. And similarly, when somebody positions somebody else, that always implies a positioning of the person him/herself.

The examples of *modes of positioning* that follow demonstrate how *self-other positioning modes* have provided theoretical understandings of the dynamic and fluid manner in which a teacher positions a student and groups (i.e., other positioning), and how these *acts of positioning* impact the student's/students' subsequent uptake (or not) of that positioning (i.e., self-positioning), which, in turn, can influence a student's learning opportunities in his classroom, as will be demonstrated in Telling Case Study 1 by Harris.

The set of illustrative studies of *modes of positioning* was drawn from an edited volume, *Sociocultural Positioning in Literacy: Exploring Culture, Discourse, Narrative, and Power in Diverse Educational Contexts* (McVee,[3] Brock, & Glazier, 2011). This volume addresses a broad range of areas in literacy education that Positioning Theory has informed both as an *analytic lens* and *explanatory theory*, and also includes a Foreword written by Harré. For example, one set of chapters draws on Positioning Theory to explore *reflexivity* as a critical process in studying educational settings. Barone's (2011) chapter was selected as an illustrative case given that she focuses on Positioning Theory affordances and constraints of her role as a researcher in her original study. Given that AERA has called for transparency in reporting the logic-of-inquiry guiding research, Barone's (re)analysis of records in an earlier study (Barone, 2001) lays a foundation for the two telling case studies undertaken for this chapter. Her study raises issues about the researcher-as-analyst and how Positioning Theory is relevant to understanding this process.

Two additional sets of studies are presented to illustrate how Positioning Theory provided new ways of understanding ways in which discourse processes shaped different aspects of equity and

Positioning Theory and Discourse Analysis

literacy practices co-constructed by teachers with students and students with others. For example, Evans (2011) drew on *modes of positioning* as an *analytic lens* to trace the consequences of what students and teacher defined as inappropriate engagement during a peer-led discussion group in a fifth-grade classroom (e.g., making fun of others). Brock and Raphael (2011), in contrast, drew on *modes of positioning* to (re)analyze records to identify how, when, and under what conditions a multilingual student (Hmong, Thai, Lao, & English) engaged in literacy learning opportunities that were co-constructed with different configurations of participants (e.g., peer-led discussion groups; whole class). These studies and others in the volume also contributed to commentaries that explore Positioning Theory as an *explanatory theory* (e.g., Glazier, 2011).

The McVee, Brock & Glazier (2011) volume, therefore, demonstrates how researchers engaged in a range of contexts drawing on Positioning Theory to investigate: *reflexivity and repositioning, identity development, culture-in-the-making, shifting* and *evolving positions*, and *issues of equity and power*. These issues have been, and continue to be, areas critical for understanding what constitutes equity of access by diverse students and their teachers in the changing world of education in the 21st century.

One final illustrative example central to understanding contributions of Positioning Theory as an analytic lens is captured in the methodological issues raised by Anderson (2009). These issues are represented in the following question: *What levels of analytic scale are crucial to identifying supports and/ or constraints on opportunities for learning and positioning processes co-constructed by students with teachers and others in classrooms?* Using an empirical example, Anderson explores layers of participation across teachers' objectives and goals for classroom activities, students' participation practices, and students' evaluations of their participation in those practices.

Anderson's analytic framework provides a process for examining empirically how learning and identity are mediated across fluid and variable micro (i.e., face-to-face), meso (i.e., institutional categories), and macro (broader social/cultural categories) scales of social life. This argument will be explored further through the telling case studies in the next section as Harris and Baker (re) analyze interdependent levels of scale that were central to understanding positioning as a dynamic and developing process.

Telling Cases of Positioning Theory as an Analytic Lens

The concept of telling case studies is grounded in work on the *reflexive turn* in social sciences reflected in the book on ethnographic research with UK anthropologists by R.F. Ellen (1984). Mitchell (1984), in the chapter on *producing data* in Ellen's book, argues that the size of the social group studied is not the issue; rather telling case studies are:

> the detailed presentation of ethnographic data related to some sequence of events from which the analyst seeks to make some theoretical inference. The events themselves may relate to any level of social organization: a whole society, some section of a community, a family or an individual.
>
> *(p. 238)*

At the center of this argument is Mitchell's conceptualization of this process as *analytic induction* through which the researcher seeks to analyze and theorize local and situated social and cultural processes being undertaken and experienced by those whose lived experiences the ethnographer-as-learner (Heath & Street, 2008) is exploring in and across times, events, and configurations of participants (Smith, 1978).

Building on this argument, we present the *logics-of-analysis* that Harris and Baker constructed as they sought to examine how Positioning Theory provides an *analytic lens* for *constructing* and *(re)analyzing data* (cf., Barone, 2011) from their extensive archives of classroom life. Through these telling case studies, therefore, we make transparent how Positioning Theory supported these researchers in tracing the complex and dynamic history of *position-positioning processes* being constructed in, and taken up (or rejected) by particular students in the developing events in classrooms.

Additionally, these telling case studies demonstrate how micro-meso-macro level (re)analyses of records from the original studies (Harris, 1989; Baker, 2001) led to new theoretical understandings of the nature of positions and positioning actions for, and by, particular students in each class. By selecting these contrasting educational contexts, we demonstrate how Positioning Theory provides a basis for constructing a more general, not generalizable, theory of positions, and the acts of (re) positioning as ongoing constructed in and through the discourse and social actions in particular classes at different levels of education systems.

Telling Case Study 1: Charlie Becoming a Reader in First Grade

In this telling case study, Harris undertook a series of non-linear steps guided by an iterative, recursive, and abductive logic (Agar, 2006), as shown in Figure 7.1. Harris unfolds her steps and the theoretical decisions that constitute her logic-of-analysis and how Positioning Theory added depth to her original analysis of Charlie's processes and practices to reveal how positioning enabled and constrained opportunities for Charlie to reveal and enact his reader identity and agency. She also demonstrates how Charlie's rejection of the choices for selecting a text assigned by the teacher in a reading station led to further analyses to examine issues of positioning at micro, meso, and macro levels of analyses.

Step 1

The original study (Harris, 1989), overviewed in Figure 7.2, was undertaken in an urban town in California. It was framed by Erickson's (1982) conceptualization of learners' functioning in pedagogic encounters that is shaped by an encounter's academic and social content and structures. Of interest was how children interpreted and enacted these dimensions of literacy task encounters in their classrooms, as evidenced in children's interactions and actions with one another during teacher-assigned literacy tasks.

To consider children's enactments in the original study, Harris also drew on Gearing's notion of *agenda* (1984), defined as:

> an expectation as to how the encounter promises or threatens to unfold…the anticipated positioning of self, each party in respect to the other…Agenda is the dimension of personal operationalization: What do I want? How important is that to me? What does he want and how badly?…Such positioning efforts…constitute one of the messages, and are often the principal message, whatever the interchange nominally may be about.
>
> *(p. 30–32)*

Charlie, the *tracer unit* of this (re)analysis, was one of the study's five focal children. Harris connected with Charlie in his fifth month of first grade, when he took Harris on a guided tour of his California classroom before school. He recognized Harris' accent as Australian, and he talked accurately, and at length, about the geography and fauna of Australia (from whence Harris comes). Keenly interested in dinosaurs and the natural world, he told Harris, "I want to be a paleontologist when I grow up." He explained he gathered what proved to be a considerable general knowledge through reading information books and watching television documentaries. Yet Charlie was positioned through school assessments as a "remedial reader," not performing to his potential, and was described as "disruptive" in class by his teacher.

Harris focused on Charlie in her original study (Harris, 1989), to understand how his classroom welcomed him (or not) as a literate person—and in these circumstances, how he enacted the literacy encounters on offer in his classroom.

Positioning Theory and Discourse Analysis

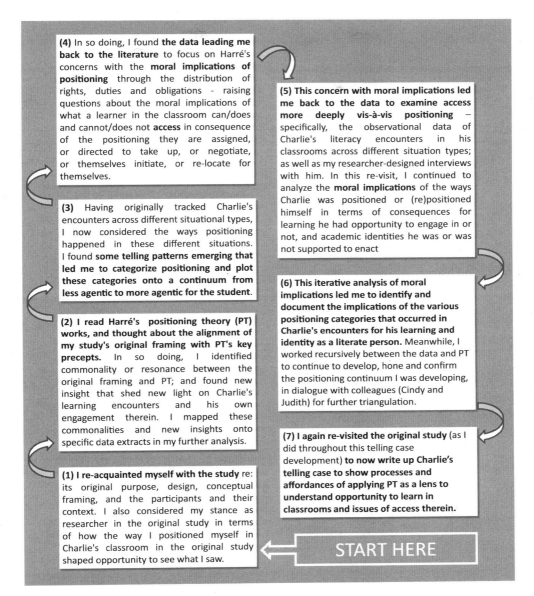

Figure 7.1 Steps Pauline took to develop Charlie's telling case.

Through methods shown in Figure 7.3, Harris *positioned herself* to focus on children's transactions with teacher-assigned literacy tasks at "Station Three", one of five rotating learning centers that ran each morning. There, mixed ability groups of six children called "teams" engaged with open-ended literacy tasks. Harris situated the children's transactions at Station Three in the bigger picture of children's literacy participation in other experiences in the classroom. In so doing, she extrapolated children's *agendas* and *subsequent positioning* in and across these experiences—ultimately to examine consequences for children's literacy learning and engagement.

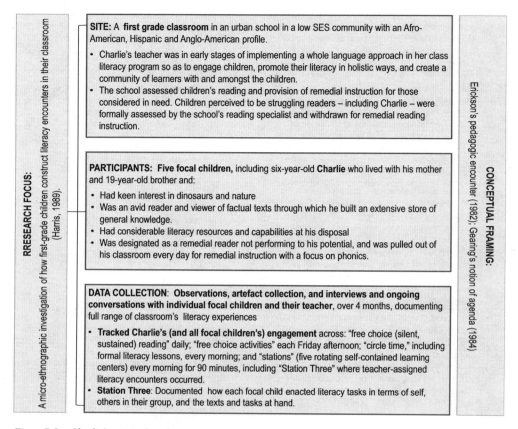

Figure 7.2 Charlie's original study.

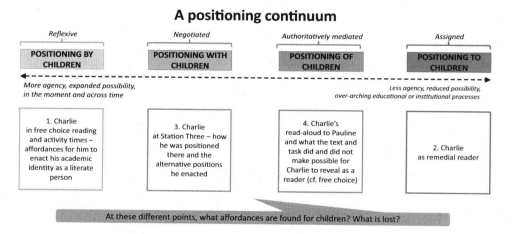

Figure 7.3 Pauline's positioning continuum developed from TCS 1.

Positioning Theory and Discourse Analysis

Step 2

This step explored how the study's original framing by Gearing's "agenda" resonates with Positioning Theory. While Positioning Theory yields new insights that concern rights, duties, and obligations, "not everyone…has equal access…to perform particular kinds of meaningful actions at that moment and with those people" (Harré, 2012, p. 193). From this perspective, in classrooms, rights, duties (norms and expectations), and obligations make up a *moral order* wherein children's positioning is constructed and through which it is possible to explore how and in what ways children comply or dispute and/or struggle with the *moral order* in a range of positions. This process is explored below through Charlie's lens in Step 3.

Step 3

A range of positioning categories were identified by tracing students' engagement across different literacy situations in Charlie's classroom. These categories were informed by Davies and Harré's (1999) notions of *interactive positioning* (where one person positions another) and *reflexive positioning* (where one positions oneself). However, other categories emerged through this telling case study, as indicated below. Harris plotted these categories along a *continuum* shown in Figure 7.3.

The categories are:

1. **Positioning that is reflexively determined by students**. For example, during "free reading," Charlie positioned himself as a fully engaged, meaning-making reader. He engrossed himself in sophisticated information books deemed by his school assessment to be well above his reading level. He displayed a range of reading strategies as he read and quietly vocalized to himself about what he was noticing and learning as he read. He skimmed and scanned; he sampled text that caught his interest; he worked to decode unknown and quite technical words; and he read and interpreted images and graphics and their captions.

   Charlie told Harris he enjoyed reading because "I think it's nice to hear new ideas that other people have in their brains and nice to know new friends…It's easy to read on your own. You have to think and concentrate and use your brain. That's what you have to do, and look at the letters and not space out." Charlie similarly engaged as an intent, focused learner during "free activities time." For example, he spent a solid half-hour meticulously sketching a stegosaurus from a 3D model, erasing and fine-tuning details as he went.

2. **Positioning that is interactively negotiated with students in open-ended learning encounters with scope for student choice**. For example, open-ended literacy tasks at "Station Three" were based on children's literature and author studies, such as the picture book author and illustrator, Pat Hutchins, whose books the teacher introduced to students. Each team had a "team captain," "floor monitor" and "marker pen monitor" assigned by the teacher. "Points" were awarded at the end of each rotation for a clean, tidy table, ready for the next group to pass through. As evidenced in his interactions, Charlie positioned himself at Station Three vis-à-vis social concerns he harbored in the classroom that overrode his academic identity as a reader and literate person by:

   - *Resisting the range of texts on offer*—e.g., "I hope we don't have to do silly Pat Hutchins again!"
   - *Asserting and disputing rights and duties* vis-à-vis Station Three's points system and monitor roles—e.g., creating his own 'Lego monitor" role, which his peers rejected; casting aspersions on group peers for not fulfilling their obligations for taking care of marker pens; and trying to pack up his group before finish time to ensure points for a tidy table.
   - *Re-defining teacher-assigned tasks*—e.g., when asked to draw "an elf-like miniature picture on a tiny square of paper" of his "favorite Pat Hutchins story" and write a caption explaining his choice, to contribute to a class survey graph, Charlie continued to re-state his

intense dislike of Hutchins' books as he arrived at Station Three. After being re-directed by his teacher to the task, he took a thick black marker pen and quickly drew a heavy illustration of Hutchins' character, One-Eyed Jake, expressively repeating the text's description of Jake as he drew, "One-Eyed Jake had a TELLLL-I-BLLLLLE temper!!!!!!" He subsequently wrote these words as his caption for his image in his thick pen on the small strip of paper provided.

- *Insisting on due process in collaborative tasks*—e.g., on being assigned the task to construct a collaborative story map of one of Pat Hutchins' stories, which they were asked to "choose as a group," Charlie demonstrated his willingness to "compromise" and "co-operate." However, Charlie perceived the cards were stacked against him when two close friends in his group held sway over the choice of book. Charlie disputed the process and its outcomes and insisted on fair voting, which the group subsequently enacted as a ballot system.

3. **Positioning of students that is authoritatively mediated by the teacher or a teacher-designed protocol imbued with performative expectations**. For example, when Harris invited Charlie to read to her, he initially chose a book about penguins and polar bears. Then saying, "Oh, I have to read this to you," he replaced his choice of book with a simple basal reader. It appeared that the *performative protocol* of reading aloud in his classroom shaped his change of mind about the book and how he read it to Harris with attention to accuracy and fluency. Yet in free choice reading, Charlie read this penguins and polar bears book and other such books with enthusiasm and meaning (as seen above).

4. **Positioning that is institutionally assigned to students**. For example, Charlie was positioned by his school as a designated remedial reader and was consequently withdrawn daily for remedial instruction, with a particular focus on phonics. This remedial emphasis was reflected in Charlie's reply when Harris asked him what he does when he comes to a word he does not know—"I sound it out." When asked what he does if that doesn't work, he said, "I put two sounds together and make a blend." When asked what he does if that still doesn't work, he looked aghast and replied, "There's not much to do but have a friend sound it out." Anticipating a further prompt, he quickly added, "And if that doesn't work, there's nothing to do but get another book!" Yet, in free choice reading, he did in fact apply many more strategies (as seen above) that he did not articulate here.

As Harré and van Langenhove (1999, p. 1–2) have argued, "people can and sometimes are offered the opportunity to acquiesce [to their positioning], contest it or subvert it." Charlie discursively positioned himself and complied with some positions while patently contesting his positioning at Station Three—for, as Moghaddam and Harré (2010, p. 3) argue "it is with words that we ascribe rights and claim them for ourselves and place duties on others."

Clearly, positioning is not fixed in classrooms, as Charlie's telling case study reveals. Positioning varies not just from moment to moment and across time, but also across situations. *Context* is everything, and in classrooms, it is the social as much as the academic content of learning (as construed by Erickson 1982, for example) to which we need to pay attention if we are to understand positioning and its influences and consequences for children's learning. In paying attention to Charlie's telling case, the question that now arises is, *What are the moral implications for opportunities to learn that are created or lost through these various positionings?*

Step 4

This question directly led Harris to review again Harré's concerns with the moral implications of positioning, "such as some person or group being located as 'trusted' or 'distrusted', 'with us' or 'against us', 'to be saved' or 'to be wiped out'" (Moghaddam & Harré, 2010, p. 2)—or in the case

Positioning Theory and Discourse Analysis

of Charlie, as someone "to be remediated," which wrought moral implications for opportunities Charlie was *not* afforded in his classroom. These implications may or may not be long-lasting, for as Davies and Harré (1999) note:

> An individual emerges through the processes of social interaction, not as a relatively fixed end product but as one who is constituted and reconstituted through the various discursive practices in which they participate…Once having taken up a particular position as one's own, a person inevitably sees the world from the vantage point of that position.
>
> *(p. 35).*

Interrogating this implication further, what did Charlie see as his classroom literacy world from the positions he was given, adopted, or contested? And what opportunities did these positions provide for him to view his place in this world as an agentic reader and literate person?

Steps 5 and 6

These questions took Harris back into the data to interrogate specific moral implications for Charlie's academic identity as a literate person and opportunities to learn that are created or lost through various positionings. These implications were found to concern:

- what Charlie demonstrated and learned in the *opportunities made available to him*
- what was and was not made possible for Charlie to *reveal about himself as a reader*
- affordances for Charlie to *enact and grow his academic identity as a literate person.*

The key point from Positioning Theory here is that positioning "impinges on the possibilities of interpersonal, intergroup and even intrapersonal action through some assignment of such rights, duties and obligations to an individual" (Harré & van Langenhove, 1999, p. 1). For example, Charlie was institutionally positioned as an under-performing reader who required remedial reading instruction and was thus withdrawn from his classroom every day for this instruction—thereby not according Charlie the *right to participate* in classroom literacy experiences that occurred at the time he was in remedial instruction, or to experience these classroom literacy experiences as an uninterrupted flow of events.

More profoundly, Charlie was not accorded the *right to be recognized and validated as a competent reader*, or to have his reader identity and capabilities validated for what they were and what they were observed to be in less official situations such as free choice reading and free choice activity times. For example, at Station Three, a different identity and positioning emerged whereby Charlie endeavored to assert his own power in demanding his peers comply with his sense of order (as previously illustrated). Charlie thereby re-positioned himself and endeavored to position his group peers in an act of what is called *metapositioning* in Positioning Theory:

> To engage in repositioning oneself or others is to claim a right or a duty to adjust what an actor has taken to be the first order positioning that is dominating the unfolding of events. These rights may be challenged too. To challenge a position may involve rights at two levels. Since a position is a cluster of rights and duties, to deny someone a right or to refuse a duty is an act of resistance to a certain positioning. However, one might challenge the right of someone to assign positions.
>
> *(Harré & Moghaddam, 2003, p. 7)*

It was precisely these processes of assertion and challenge that Charlie repeatedly initiated at Station Three. His re-positioning was opposed, in turn, by his peers, leading to group conflict and at times the breakdown of the task encounter. This difficulty would require teacher intervention to bring the encounter back on track—thereby potentially reinforcing the teacher's designation and subsequent positioning of Charlie not only as "remedial" but also "disruptive."

Step 7

In bringing this telling case together, and shuttling between data and theory to do so, we can conclude that positioning in classrooms carries moral implications for:

- what children can and do demonstrate and learn in the opportunities made available to them
- what is and was not made possible for them to reveal about themselves as literate people and learners in and through their discourse about themselves and others
- affordances for children to enact and grow their academic identities as literate people.

We can further conclude that early grade classrooms provide literacy worlds in which children are positioned and position themselves to greater or lesser degree of benefit to the enactment and growth of their learning and literate identities. The classroom literacy world, as Charlie saw it in first grade, was a world where he could and did position himself as an engaged, competent literacy learner with the kinds of reading and writing he enjoyed. However, his classroom was also a world where his preferred literacy choices did not count for much—unlike the official teacher-assigned texts and tasks at Station Three, and unlike school designation and instruction of Charlie as a remedial reader.

This step in the (re)analysis showed that children might be seen to be disruptive, when in actual fact they are contending with responsibilities within the classroom's moral order as they see it. Charlie was aware of his responsibilities to engage in his classroom's texts and tasks as best he could. In conversation with Harris, he said he did not mind, and in fact quite enjoyed, what he called "a hard assignment"; and expressed concerns with disruption other children caused when "they goof off." He was aware that reading and writing are effortful. He was happy to exert that effort but was not happy when other children's behavior disrupted his efforts. Clearly, opportunity to learn and engage was important to Charlie. He positioned himself to enact that agenda where he felt he could, but railed against forces he saw get in his way at Station Three. At Station Three, literacy encounters pushed him beyond his endurance and he subsequently pushed back—*re-positioning* himself in ways that unintentionally masked his literate identity, obscured his learning and engagement, and brought him into direct conflict with his teacher and peers.

Positioning Theory, as framed in this *telling case study,* provides critical tools for (re)theorizing how to understand children like Charlie as literate people and learners in their classrooms—noting that Positioning Theory is a *lens*, not a prescriptive theory of what should be or does happen. Charlie's telling case raises critical questions when engaging students with particular texts and tasks, about how to understand their responses—behooving teachers to pay heed to the moral implications of how they, and others in the school district, position children and children position themselves in classrooms; and to reflect upon how teachers might instead recognize and optimize students' positioning for effective opportunities to learn in classrooms.

Telling Case Study 2: (Re)Analyzing Contrastive Performances of Public Critique in Studio Art

The next telling case study provides a foundation for examining how and in what ways Positioning Theory contributed theoretical and educational insights for Baker and our author team into the ways in which a secondary school visual arts teacher created opportunities for students to learn "what it means to live the creative life" (transcript from first day of class, September 2) and to

Positioning Theory and Discourse Analysis

become artists in her intergenerational studio art class and program (grades 9–12). The basis for this exploration of Positioning Theory is a two-year interactional ethnographic study undertaken by Baker (2001) with the teacher and her students to gain understanding of how she positioned and engaged students as artists through local, discipline-based processes and practices (e.g., "public critique"). Thus, similar to Harris (this chapter), and Barone (2011), Baker engaged in a process of reanalyzing previous records to create new forms of data "to problematize a portion of it to gain more complex understandings of a participant and herself [himself] as a participant" (Barone, p. 50).

For the purposes of this telling case, Baker elected to revisit previously analyzed patterns of discourse and interaction during an iteration of an event in the third month (November) of the class. The event, *public critique*, a discipline-based, classroom practice, provided students with opportunities to present artifacts to the teacher and their peers, who would respond as part of a public conversation about the displayed artifacts and stated or implied artistic processes and practices.

The selection of the event was purposeful for three main reasons: (1) the teacher identified as an artist and consistently positioned students as artists, including engaging them in discourse and actions practiced in professional art schools ("that's what this is/art school in high school," the teacher stated on the first day (lines 1085–1086); (2) the event, the third iteration of public critique (in the third month) of the school year, had provided Baker with an opportunity to examine students' potential development through multiple levels of analytic scale; and, (3) public performances of two of the observed students, Maya and James, provided a further opportunity to explore the original contrastive analysis through a lens of Positioning Theory. To guide his (re)analysis process, Baker formulated the following question: *What positioning processes and actions were provided by the teacher to students as opportunities to develop as artists?*

Negotiating the Position of Ethnographer as Learner

Baker's original study grew from informal discussions with the teacher during a professional development program (National Writing Project) in which she was a guest presenter. Through initial conversations and a series of dialogues, Baker (2001) and the teacher identified common interests that led to her agreement for him to engage in an interactional ethnographic study[4] of her intergenerational, Advanced Placement Studio Art class with the students, who, through a process, self-selected into the course. In part of the original study, Baker examined the performances and classroom interactions of two students, Maya and James, both seniors and in their first year of the visual arts program and studio art class (i.e., "first-year seniors"), and he observed apparent, *unexpected* differences in their discourse.

For the purposes of this telling case study, Baker (re)constructed iterative, recursive and abductive processes of (re)analysis (Agar, 2006) and makes transparent how Positioning Theory served as an *analytic lens* and explanatory theory (Davies & Harré, 1990; Harré, 2011) that, when integrated with Baker's interactional ethnographic logic-of-inquiry (e.g., Baker & Green, 2007; Baker, Green, & Skukauskaite, 2008; Baker & Däumer, 2015;), supported a theoretically grounded process of (re)analysis. By (re)presenting his process of (re)analysis of the roots and moments of development of the deep critique event, Baker makes transparent, as did Harris (Telling Case Study 1), how multiple layers of analysis were critical to examining the ways the teacher engaged in *acts of positioning* for individuals and for the intergenerational group of students.

In (re)constructing selected analyses of the event (or *episode*, in terms of Positioning Theory), the third iteration of public critique, Baker presents a *logic-of-analysis* of discourse processes as a basis for examining how the teacher *signaled to* participants (including Baker as an observer participant) particular positions and how these *acts of positioning* reveal her knowledge of the differential experiential levels of students—in particular, Maya's. As the following analysis will show, this process was part of the teacher's approach to (re)framing local processes of a discipline-based practice and of orienting participants—with different levels of experience in this program (1–4 years)—to what *counted* as performing this iteration of public critique, which she labeled *deep critique*. Through this (re)analysis, Baker will show how the teacher supported students in the discursive construction of identities as speakers and audience participants through positioning acts (Davies & Harré, 1990; 1999).

As indicated, the selection of this developing event (episode) for analysis of actions of positioning was grounded in observed differences in performances by Maya and James in Baker's earlier study (Baker, 2001). In that study, as an observer participant of the event (Spradley, 1980/2016),[5] Baker identified content differences between the two performances, represented in Table 7.1 (adapted from Baker, Green, & Skukauskaite, 2008).

Table 7.1 represents excerpts of Maya's and James's discourse (columns 2 and 5, respectively) from their descriptions of their series of drawings. Based on Baker's analysis, column 1 shows three types of constructs students would presumably mention in some way during their public discussion of their artifacts: *elements of the rubric*, which the teacher provided the day prior to the first day of deep critiques to guide students in their preparation for the event; *creative processes* and *drawing practices* taught during the figure drawing unit ("Bug Art"). Column 3 makes visible *rubric elements, processes, or practices* mentioned by Maya; column 4 *reflects what James addressed.*

As indicated in Table 7.1, Baker identified how Maya's references differed from James', particularly the drawing practices, because—as Baker discovered—she missed these opportunities because she entered the class on October 11, over one month after the beginning of school (September 2). The observed differences led Baker to return to the archive to *trace the roots* and *developments of the expected discipline-based processes and practices* as they were being constructed by members of the class, beginning with the first day and across particular *cycles of activity*—a theoretical term (Green & Meyer, 1991) and local, "folk" term used by the teacher (the figure drawing unit is an example). The current analysis, undertaken to examine how the teacher positioned students as studio artists and how students *took up* and *oriented to* this process of positioning, forms two levels of analysis, framing potential areas to consider from a Positioning Theory perspective.

Tracing the Roots of Deep Critique: Exploring the Discursive Construction of Studio Artists

By tracing the roots of Maya's and James' histories in the class, Baker (2001) identified sources of influence that contributed to what Maya and James included in constructing figure drawings and in representing their rationale for the series of drawings and embedded processes and practices during the culminating event of the "Bug Art" cycle of activity, *deep critique*. In Figure 7.4, Baker represents relevant histories for Maya and James—and for Baker, as the researcher—through four levels of analytic scale, or *laminated histories*. The first (top) timeline shows the years of experience in the Visual Arts program of participants; the second timeline represents the two years of Baker's ethnographic study. In the third, a record of events on the first day of class are (re)presented based on a *running record* (i.e., an initial transcription of the class period) of the teacher's actions with students, suggesting ways she positioned them through her discursive actions as members of the class, of the program, and of its history.

Further, she frames literacy processes and practices that would become ordinary actions within this class (e.g., writing, observing videos, describing links among artifacts and actions, making connections, exploring art resources, and reflecting on past events and preparing for future art events). Importantly, the teacher created a *verbal boundary* of an activity, one that would foreshadow public critique, through announcing students would engage in "a creative activity" "tomorrow" (lines 332–334), the second day of class. *Friendly sharing* (i.e., students sharing artifacts with each other) would initiate *cycles of critique*.

In terms of positioning, the teacher purposely used pronouns (particularly "I," "you," and "we") to *signal* three types of positionings: (1) her (the "I") history with the class and program, and as a

Table 7.1 Contrastive analysis of Maya and James.

Column 1 Rubric Elements, Processes, & Practices	Column 2 Maya's Discourse	Column 3 Maya's References	Column 4 James' References	Column 5 James' Discourse
Rubric Elements:	*Transcript Excerpt*	*Rubric Elements Referenced*		*Transcript Excerpt*
Purpose/Questions	I guess my drawings will help me with shape and color (483–86).	X	X	I wanted to like express/how life is everywhere (1075–76).
Approach/Selection	[selected idea:] the beast in *Lord of the Flies* (497).	X	X	I wanted to look at the whole (1091).
Evolution/Process	[implicit, although does not mention *process*]	X	X	It's a long process/like I worked.../five/six/ seven days straight (1128–32).
Technique	I just practiced with/like dark lines/and shading/ (508–11).	X	X	I started out/like with just ink/just black ink (1077–79).
Outcome/Presentation	I don't know if I/succeeded...but I tried ...who's to say (574–95).	X	X	[the daily work and details] all adds up at the end (1142).
Processes Taught:		*Processes referenced*		
Processes for developing ideas	my first thought/when I got this idea (488-89); I don't know if I succeeded (575–77).	X	X	I wanted to like express/how life is everywhere (1075-76); long process (1128).
Process: Technique	I just practiced with/like dark lines/and shading/...(508–11).	X	X	You can't just draw the whole thing all at once (1102).
Time required: developing idea	[implicit: M states that she began with an idea and explains evolution of it]	X	X	It's a long process/like I worked.../five/six/ seven days straight (1128–32).
Practices Taught: "Seeing" (9/30–10/1)		*Drawing Practices Referenced*	X	You need to examine every single part and see how they relate/to each other (1099–00)
Layering sequence (10/5–8)			X	You can't just draw the whole thing all at once (1102).
Continuous line			X	I started out/like with just ink/.../and drew the whole butterfly (1077–80).
Texture			X	But it doesn't look/like textured (1108–09).

Disney award winning teacher; (2) the students' (the "you") role as artists; and, (3) former students ("he" or "she") as examples of young artists who learned processes and practices through the class, and struggled at times as part of their development. The teacher also positioned students by their year in the program and grade level (e.g., "first-year, senior," as Maya and James both were); and the teacher positioned the students as members of a larger program through reflections on historical events and announcements of future events.

As indicated in the fourth timeline, by moving to a meso level of analysis, Baker situated the three-month context (September through November) of the *deep critique* event, the anchor for this telling case study, by locating dates of three key cycles of critique ("Public Sharing," "Gentle Critique," and "Deep Critique"). It also situates the entry of James (Day 1) and Maya (October 11), thus providing a *warrant* to understand Maya's position in the class as a "first-year senior" who was new to public critique.

Through tracing the history of Maya and James as they engaged in cycles of activity prior to "Bug Art," Baker particularly developed warranted accounts (Heap, 1995) of the sources that Maya drew on and those she failed to display, or *include* (not reject), in her public discourse during deep critique. Furthermore, through an iterative and recursive process of (re)analysis of these historical contexts, the roots of deep critique, including embedded epistemological assumptions and local, discipline-based processes and practices, Baker sought to (re)examine how the teacher's discourse positioned students as:

- studio artists within a studio art class and visual arts program;
- as students and artists with differential experiences with art;
- an intergenerational community of artists;
- potential professional artists, or who will learn more about what it means to "live the creative life."

Therefore, Figure 7.4 also (re)presents how each layer of *analytic scale* is designed to bring to the fore particular positions of the teacher and students at macro, meso, and micro levels (cf., Anderson, 2009) bounding different levels of analytic scale. In the next section we (re)present an excerpt of the public interaction between the teacher and Maya to demonstrate a micro level of analysis of how the teacher verbally positioned Maya as inexperienced (compared to the other students) and members of the class as an intergenerational community of artists.

(Re)Analysis "Deep Critique": Exploring Position-Positioning Act Relationships

In this section, we present Baker's conceptual analysis of three developing segments (sequence units of analysis) of Maya's performance to examine how the teacher positioned Maya in relationship to other students in the class, given that she was the first to perform a critique during the developing event of public critique. Tracing these multiple levels of analytic units[6] made possible analysis of the teacher's positioning of Maya and the other students, as presented in Figure 7.5.

As indicated in Figure 7.5, during the first interaction unit, the teacher discursively positions Maya as the "new girl" (line 457), a term that becomes an *indexical*, or *a way of indexing* (Blommaert, 2007) Maya's inexperience with the class, and members' learned assumptions about particular processes and practices (e.g., public critique). This positioning alerted students, who had been encouraged by the teacher to raise questions and make observations about the artifacts, that they would need to consider Maya's inexperience when offering observations or raising questions about her presentation and artifacts.

After Maya presents her drawings, revealing how she addressed elements of the rubric, the teacher signals that Maya has finished her self-critique. However, instead of students being first to offer observations or raise questions, as was the pattern (the norm) in other critiques (Baker, 2001), the teacher once again positions Maya as inexperienced, *indexing* her inexperience through

(1) LIFE HISTORY OF CLASS: TIMELINE OF INTERGENERATIONAL STUDIO ART CLASS (1997-2000)				
Teacher – 29 years of teaching	1996-1997 (5% of students enter)	1997-1998 (12% of students enter)	1998-1999 (35% of students enter)	1999-2000 (53% of students enter)

(2) ENTERING THE FIELD: TIMELINE OF THE ETHNOGRAPHY in Academic Year 2	
Academic Year One (1998-1999)	Academic Year Two (1999-2000)

(3) FIRST DAY OF SCHOOL, Sept. 2 (Year 2 of Ethnography): INITIATING CYCLES

Clock Time (Videotape time)	Running Record of Phases (phase numbers on left)		Running Record of Events (transcript line numbers)
9:09-9:18 (00:00:01-00:10:01)	1. T preparing (talks to researcher) 2. T explaining letters from past students to present students		1. T preparing before students arrive (1-79)
9:18-9:22 (00:10:02-00:13:56)	1. T talking about class preparation 2. T instructing students to pick up two index cards and select a workbench		2. Students arriving; T greeting students at door (80-134)
(9:22-9:30) (00:13:57-00:21:04)	1. Students writing two questions, etc. 2. T giving each student an envelope 3. Students passing back index cards		3. T taking roll and initiating "index card activity" (134-235)
(9:30-9:44) (00:22:32-00:36:14)	1. *T presenting overview day and program 2. Introducing Disney award & video 3. Playing Disney video 4. Explaining links with video	*T initiates cycles of friendly sharing: "tomorrow I'll have a short activity that's kind of a creative activity" (lines 332-334) (occurs on 9/3)	4. T welcoming, presenting agenda and introducing self and program (236-686) *4a. Disney video (442-621), 6 minutes*
9:44-9:55 (00:36:15-00:47:24)	1. T reading letters from: D, M, A, C 2. T explaining connections		5. T reading and commenting on excerpts from letters of past students (687-1063)
9:55-10:00 (00:47:26-53:01)	1. T assigning letter of intent 2. Handout; quoting Z. Hurston 3. "Student agendas"		6. T assigning: Read letter from past student and write letter of intent (1064-1243)
10:00-10:09 (00:53:03-01:01:40)	1. T introducing sketchbooks 2. Notebooks: connection to AP and areas of concentration 3. Folders: Value of handouts 4. Fee: Cost of some of the materials		7. T presenting four needs for class (1234-1568)
10:09-10:15 (01:02:04-01:08:18)	1. Discussion of multiple events (e.g., Mini-chalk festival, "Film Festival"; "Breakfast Club"; "Fashion Show")		8. T discussing "Highlights" of upcoming year (1569-1792)

(4) CYCLES OF CRITIQUE

Framing class 9/2: James enters	*Friendly Sharing 9/10, 13*	*Gentle Critique 9/22-24*	Maya enters 10/11	*Deep Critique 11/16-19*

Figure 7.4 History of studio art class at multiple levels of scale.

Green et al.

Line	Speaker	Classroom Talk	Notes
634	T to M	why do you ⟶	To Maya
635		uh	*Hesitates, signaling she is deciding on next step.*
636		couple of questions	States actions to Maya
637		one	
638		uh	
639		you were talking about	
640		during your warm ups series	
641		you had already started to think about the [the novel] *Lord of the Flies*	Cf. lines: 491-497; the novel written by William Golding.
642	T	so	"So," an indexical, indexing a word signaling a lesson, or the "so what" of what came before.
643	F Student	*oh I=*	*Female student (third-year student) begins to say something in agreement with the teacher*
644	T	*=so during the warmup ⟶*	Looking at Maya
645		*were you wondering that too? ⟵*	Turns back to Female student
646	F Student	*yeah*	i.e., on her notes
647		*I wrote Lord of the Flies*	Acknowledges FS
648		*yeah*	
649	T to M	during the warmup series ⟶	Turns back to Maya
650		you mentioned	
651		uh	
652		you were	
653		practicing	
654		um	
655		'thick lines'	Cf. lines 508-509 (refers back to earlier references)
656		and 'dark shading'	Cf. line 510 (refers back to earlier references)
657		because	
658		you were already thinking about	
659		*The Lord of the Flies=*	
660	M	*=yeah*	
661	T	so ⟶	Turns to audience -- Again, "so" indexes the teacher pointing to a lesson from Maya's talk.
662		the ideas started to percolate	Part of the "creative process" mentioned earlier in the semester.
663		even before you knew	
664		there would be a final	i.e., a final drawing
665	M	yeah	
666	T-M & Audience	so something started ⟶	To audience and Maya --"So," indexical, signaling the "so what" or lesson to an observation.
667		to already generate	
668		from the work with the bugs	
669	M	yeah	
670	T	good	
671	T	um	
672		[pause]	*Pause and transitions signaled*
673-731	T/M	[Teacher asks M more about where the idea for the final drawing came from; Maya states, from her imagination about nightmares.]	
732	T to audience	*she said something very interesting ⟶*	Key: T shifts to the third person and addresses audience as she verbally repositions M as an example artist, or, at least, refers to M's discourse for purposes of proposing processes inferred from M's discourse.
733		*about the beast*	
734		*does anybody remember what she said*	
735		*it was the most real character in the book*	Cf. lines 571-573 (barely audible)
736	FS	*yeah*	*Spontaneous comment by female student confirms teacher's statements about what Maya said*
737	T	*that was one thing she said*	
738		*'it was the most real character in the book'*	Restates Maya's discourse, or engages in a "say back," a practice expected by the teacher of the students during critique.
739-852	T	[T goes on to "say back" examples of what M said and propose processes inferred from M's presentation. Two experienced students publicly engage with the teacher. Note: Lines 810-812: T asks M a clarifying question, which M answers ("in the end I did"). For the last two message units of this part (851-852), T says to M: "do you see that/that you described rather well."]	

Figure 7.5   Public interaction between teacher and Maya.

acknowledging Maya had never "critiqued with us before" (line 628). (Technically, the teacher does permit an initial student question; however, the question is irrelevant to critique—the student questioned the origin of Maya's name.)

The teacher's positioning of Maya sets up interaction three, which provides a different type of positioning by the teacher. The teacher follows the expected pattern of "saying back" to the artist something participants heard during the presentation. The "say back" serves to *ground observations in the artist's*

Positioning Theory and Discourse Analysis

discourse, a way of providing evidence for the observation or as a springboard for a particular question. The teacher also *revoices* (O'Connor & Michaels, 2019) Maya's description of her attempt at using "thick lines" and "dark shading" to make the metaphoric monster in the novel *The Lord of the Flies* "scary."

However, the teacher's response expands the general purpose of "*saying back*" to Maya: the word "so" (lines 642, 644, 661, and 666) becomes another *indexical* that parallels the teacher's positioning of Maya as inexperienced. After the teacher confirms Maya's attempt at using "thick lines" and "dark shading," she says "*so* [as in, therefore, what follows] the ideas started to percolate/even before you knew/there would be a final [drawing]" (lines 661–664). The teacher's response becomes a way of modeling for Maya (and, by implication, for other inexperienced students) how to observe and describe an initial part of the creative process that led to the series of drawings presented by the person assuming the position of artist performing critique.

This modeling for, and with, Maya becomes more obvious with the teacher's *shift from second to third person* (line 732). From line 732 through to the end of the critique (line 852), the teacher talks about Maya's discourse and drawings in the *third person*—with the exception of a brief question to Maya to clarify a point (lines 810–813). Through this *discursive process*, the teacher positions Maya as an example of an artist whose work the group can learn from, even if the artist is inexperienced in describing her process or using expected discourse—including allusions to drawing processes and practices, some of which Maya had missed given her point of entry into the class.

By *adopting Maya's discourse*, the teacher makes visible inferences about process and about how inexperience with "materials" and techniques may lead an artist to a different place than planned. Again, the teacher positions Maya as inexperienced when describing the process visible in Maya's talk: "she [Maya] starts with/an idea/about a story/that she's connected to/…/but/just because/ we're young in manipulating materials/and they don't always manipulate/the way we want them to/so something/else happens" (lines 815–835).[7] In other words, Maya planned to represent the monster in one way but being "young in manipulating materials" led her to "something/else."

In this telling case study, Baker showed how the teacher positioned Maya in different ways for different purposes. By discursively positioning Maya as inexperienced as an artist in this class and "never having critiqued with us before," the teacher acknowledged to other students that Maya's critique would be different than expected. That is, she introduced the possibility that Maya might not use the *expected discourse* and that she might frame or understand the creative process differently than was proposed to the class from the first day of class. By "saying back" to Maya what she heard during the self-critique, the teacher composed an inferred process and signaled the *lesson learned* to students through the *indexical* "*so*." Therefore, as the teacher had offered to students on day one, Maya becomes an example art student who continues to develop and, at times, struggle, which is part of the learning process. Importantly for this chapter, Positioning Theory provided Baker with a way of expanding the possible interpretations of the teacher's discourse and her purposes for her discursive moves, especially as she sought to support a beginning student and to model expected processes for other students.

A Closing and an Opening

In this section, we provide closing comments about the lessons learned from the telling case studies and open the potential for further research grounded in the conceptual developments critical to adopting and/or adapting Positioning Theory as an analytic lens for designing studies (See Anderson, 2009; McVee et al., 2011; 2019) and as an *analytic theory* for (re)analyzing existing archives of classroom records (cf., Barone, 2011; and Harris and Baker's telling cases presented in the sections above). Through these telling case studies of how Positioning Theory provided a conceptually driven approach to exploring previously unexamined dimensions of classroom life in these two educational contexts, a series of conceptual, methodological, and theoretical issues were identified that are critical to understanding the consequential nature of classroom life for students (and their teachers).

The inclusion of the core principles of Positioning Theory, with the theories guiding the original studies, provided evidence of how Positioning Theory is a dynamic and developing *analytic lens*, not a static or predefined theoretical perspective. By examining the iterative, recursive, and abductive processes undertaken by both Harris and Baker in their telling case studies in classes at different levels of education, this chapter provided evidence of the need to examine the laminated nature of classroom life and to trace the histories of particular participants as well as the developing group across times, events (episodes), and configurations of participants.

Together, these telling case studies, although in different educational contexts and at different levels of school, framed the importance of exploring the inter-relationships of micro–meso–macro levels of decisions, actions, and provision of resources for the teacher and his/her students. Future research will want to consider these conceptual arguments in both the design of primary research and in the (re)analysis of existing archived data to contribute further understandings about the consequential and dynamic nature or position-positioning relationships for students' construction of academic identities as well as access to opportunities for learning complex academic processes and practices of 21st century education.

Notes

1 See Standards for Reporting on Empirical Social Science Research of the American Educational Research Association (2006).
2 According to Moghaddam (personal communication, August 16, 2019), a publication by Harré and colleagues (i.e., Harré, Moghaddam, Cairnie, Rothbart, & Sabat, 2009) offers those interested in Positioning Theory important extensions of the theory as it has evolved across time. The authors would like to acknowledge Professor Fathali Moghaddam for his thoughtful feedback on the history of Positioning Theory section of the chapter.
3 See McVee, Silvestri, Barrett, & Haq (2019) for a seminal in-depth analysis of Positioning Theory and its application to literacy and language research, which also includes details of the expansion of Positioning Theory since its creation in 1990.
4 See Castanheira, Crawford, Green, and Dixon (2001) and Green and Bridges (2017) for descriptions of the Interactional Ethnographic logic-of-inquiry.
5 Spradley frames multiple ways that ethnographers engage in participant observation: at one end of the continuum is a passive role of observer participant while at the other end is the role of full participant. In this class, Baker undertook the position as observer participant except in moments in which the students, such as the fourth year student, engaged directly with him, or in instances in which he engaged the teacher after class in discussions of his interpretation of observed phenomena to explore *his limits to certainty* about how a student was undertaking a particular process during critique (Baker & Green, 2007).
6 The transcript approach in this table is framed by Green and Wallat, 1981, and reflects a process of mapping the developing construction of the social and discursive processes that orient students to and hold them accountable for particular academic as well as social processes. A full description of this process is present in the appendix in Kelly and Green (2019). This approach differs from conversation analysis in that its focus is on mapping the developing academic and social processes and texts being proposed, recognized, and acknowledged and interactionally accomplished, which are academically, socially, interpersonally, and intrapersonally significant in local and intertextually tied cycles of activity (cf., Green & Wallat, 1981; Bloome et al., 2005; Green et al., 2012).
7 In this (re)presentation of the talk listed by line numbers in Figure 5, Baker creates a narrative version of the developing text guided by the process described in Endnote 4. This process differs from conversational analysis in that it focuses on *message units*, bits of talk whose boundaries are marked by contextualization cues (e.g., pitch, stress, intonation, pause, juncture, kinesics, proxemics, gesture, eye gaze, and grammar and lexicon) (cf., Gumperz & Herasimchuk, 1973; Green, 1977).

References

Agar, M. (2006). An ethnography by any other name. *Forum: Qualitative Social Science Research*, 7(4), Art. 36.
American Educational Research Association. (2006). Standards for reporting on empirical social science research in AERA publications. *Educational Researcher*, 35(6), 33–40.

Anderson, K. (2009). Applying positioning theory to the analysis of classroom interactions: Mediating micro-identities, macro-kinds, and ideologies of knowing. *Linguistics and Education, 20*(4), 291–310.

Baker, W.D. (2001). *Artists in the Making: An Ethnographic Investigation of Discourse and Literate Practices as Disciplinary Processes in a High School Advanced Placement Studio Art Classroom.* Unpublished dissertation. University of California, Santa Barbara, CA.

Baker, W.D., & Däumer, E. (2015). Designing interdisciplinary instruction: Exploring disciplinary and conceptual differences as a resource. *Pedagogies: An International Journal, 10*(1), 38–53.

Baker, W.D., & Green, J.L. (2007). Limits to certainty in interpreting video data: Interactional ethnography and disciplinary knowledge. *Pedagogies: An International Journal, 2*(3), 191–204.

Baker, W.D., Green, J.L., & Skukauskaite, A. (2008). Video-enabled ethnographic research: A mircroethnographic perspective. In: G. Walford (Ed.), *How to Do Educational Ethnography* (pp. 77–114). London: Tufnell.

Bakhtin, M.M. (1986). *Speech Genres and Other Late Essays.* Austin, TX: University of Texas Press.

Barone, D. (2001). Revisioning: Positioning of a parent, student, and researcher in response to classroom context. *Reading Research and Instruction, 40*(2), 101–120.

Barone, D. (2011). Revisioning: New perspectives of literacy with positioning theory. In: C. Brock, M. McVee, & J. Glazier (Eds.), *Sociocultural Positioning in Literacy: Exploring Culture, Discourse, Narrative and Power in Diverse Educational Contexts* (pp. 49–72). Cresskill, NJ: Hampton Press.

Blommaert, J. (2007). Sociolinguitics and discourse analysis: Orders of indexicality and polycentricity. *Journal of Multicultural Discourses, 2*(2), 115–130.

Bomer, R., & Laman, T. (2004). Positioning in a primary writing workshop: Joint action in the discursive production of writing subjects. *Research in the Teaching of English, 38*(4), 420–466.

Brock, C.H., & Raphael, T.E. (2011). Repositioning our understanding of Deng's literacy learning opportunities. In: C. Brock, M. McVee, & J. Glazier (Eds.), *Sociocultural Positioning in Literacy: Exploring Culture, Discourse, Narrative and Power in Diverse Educational Contexts* (pp. 223–242). Cresskill, NJ: Hampton Press.

Brock, C., Robertson, D., Borti, A., & Gillis, V. (2019, published online). Evolving identities: Exploring leaders' positioning in the birth of a professional literacy collaboration. *Professional Development in Education.* DOI: 10.1080/19415257.2019.1647551

Bullough, R., & Draper, R.J. (2004). Making sense of a failed triad mentors, university supervisors, and positioning theory. *Journal of Teacher Education, 55*(5), 407–420.

Castanheira, M.L., Crawford, T., Dixon, C., & Green, J.L. (2001). Interactional ethnography: An approach to studying the social construction of literate practices. *Linguistics and Education, 11*(4), 353–400.

Davies, B. (1993). *Shards of Glass: Children Reading and Writing Beyond Gendered Identities.* New York, NY: Hampton Press.

Davies, B., & Davies, C. (2007). Having, and being had by, "experience": Or, "experience" in the social sciences after the discursive/poststructuralist turn. *Qualitative Inquiry, 13*(8), 1139–1159.

Davies, B., & Harré, R. (1990). Positioning: The discursive production of selves. *Journal for the Theory of Social Behaviour, 20*(1), 43–63.

Davies, B., and Harré, R. (1999). Positioning and personhood. In R. Harré and L. van Langenhove (Eds.), *Positioning Theory* (pp. 32–52). Malden, MA: Blackwell Publishers Ltd.

Ellen, R.F. (1984). *Ethnographic Research: A Guide to General Conduct.* New York, NY: Academic Press.

Erickson, F. (1982). Taught cognitive learning in its immediate environments: A neglected topic in the Anthropology of Education. *Anthropology and Education Quarterly, 13*(2), 149–180.

Evans, K. (2011). Creating spaces for equity? The role of positioning in peer-led literature discussions. In: C. Brock, M. McVee, & J. Glazier (Eds.), *Sociocultural Positioning in Literacy: Exploring Culture, Discourse, Narrative and Power in Diverse Educational Contexts* (pp. 205–223). Cresskill, NJ: Hampton Press.

Frankel, K. (2016). The intersection of reading and identity in high school literacy intervention classes. *Research in the Teaching of English, 51*(1), 37–59.

Gearing, F.O. (1984). Toward a general theory of cultural transmission. *Anthropology and Education Quarterly, 15*(1), 29–37.

Glazier, J.A. (2011). The power in and around positioning. In: C. Brock, M. McVee, & J. Glazier (Eds.), *Sociocultural Positioning in Literacy: Exploring Culture, Discourse, Narrative and Power in Diverse Educational Contexts* (pp. 251–261). Cresskill, NJ: Hampton Press.

Green, J. & Meyer, L. (1991). The embeddedness of reading in classroom life: Reading as a situated process. In: C. Baker & A. Luke (Eds.), *Towards a Critical Sociology of Reading Pedagogy* (pp. 141–160). Philadelphia: John Benjamins Publishing.

Green, J.L., Skukauskaite, A., & Baker, W.D. (2012). Ethnography as epistemology: An introduction to educational ethnography. In: J. Arthur, M. Waring, R. Coe, & L.V. Hedges (Eds.), *Research Methodologies and Methods in Education* (pp. 309–321). London: SAGE.

Green, J.L., & Wallat (1981). Mapping instructional conversations. In: J. Green, & C. Wallet (Eds.), *Ethnography and Language in Educational Settings* (pp. 161–195). Norwood, NJ: Ablex/ABC-CLIO. Norwood, NJ/Santa Barbara, CA.

Gumperz, J., & Herasimchuk, E. (1972). Conversational analysis of social meaning. In: R. Shuy (Ed.), *Sociolinguistics: Current Trends and Prospects*, Georgetown University Monographs in Languages and Linguistics (pp. 1–21). Georgetown, WA: Georgetown University Press.

Harré, R. (2011). Foreword. In: M.B. McVee, C.H. Brock, & J.A. Glazier (Eds.), *Sociocultural Positioning in Literacy* (pp. ix–xi). Cresskill, NJ: Hampton Press.

Harré, R. (2012). Social construction and consciousness. *Discusiones Filosóficas*, *13*(20), 13–36.

Harré, R., & Moghaddam, F. (2003). The self and others in traditional psychology and in positioning theory. In: R. Harré, & F. Moghaddam (Eds.), *The Self and Others: Positioning Individuals and Groups in Personal, Political, and Cultural Contexts* (pp. 1–11). London: Praeger.

Harré, R., Moghaddam, F.M., Cairnie, T.P., Rothbart, D., & Sabat, S.R. (2009). Recent advances in positioning theory. *Theory and Psychology*, *19*(5), 5–31.

Harré, R., & van Langenhove, L. (1991). Varieties of positioning. *Journal for the Theory of Social Behavior*, *21*(4), 393–407.

Harré, R. and Gillett, G. (1994). *The Discursive Mind*. Thousand Oaks, CA: Sage Publications.

Harré, R. (2011). Social construction and conscientiousness. *Discusiones Filosóficas*. Año 13 No 20, enero – junio, 2012. pp. 13–36.

Harré, R., & van Langenhove, L. (1999). *Positioning Theory: Moral Contexts of Intentional Action*. Oxford: Blackwell.

Harris, P. (1989). *First Grade Children's Constructs of Teacher-Assigned Reading Tasks in a Whole Language Classroom*. Doctoral dissertation. University of California, Berkeley, CA.

Heap, J. (1985). What counts as reading? Limits to certainty in assessment. *Curriculum Inquiry*, *10*(3), 265–292.

Heap, J. (1991). Ethnomethodology, cultural phenomenology, and literacy activities. *Curriculum Inquiry*, *21*(1), 109–117.

Heap, J. (1995). The status of claims in "qualitative" educational research. *Curriculum Inquiry*, *25*(3), 271–292.

Heath, S. & Street, B. (2008). *On Ethnography: Approaches to Language and Literacy Research*. New York: Teachers College Press.

Herbal-Eisenman, B., Wagner, D., Johnson, K.R., Suh, H., & Figueras, H. (2015). Positioning in mathematics education: Revelations on an imported theory. *Educational Studies in Mathematics*, *89*(2), 185–204.

Kayi-Aydar, H. (2019). *Positioning Theory in Applied Linguistics: Research Design and Applications*. Cham, Switzerland: Palgrave Macmillan/Springer Nature Switzerland AG.

Kelly, G., & Green, J. (2019). *Theory and Methods for Sociocultural Research in Science and Engineering Education*. New York, NY: Routledge.

McVee, M.B., Brock, C.H., & Glazier, J.A. (Eds.) (2011). *Sociocultural Positioning in Literacy: Exploring Culture, Discourse, Narrative, and Power in Diverse Educational Contexts*. Cresskill, NJ: Hampton Press.

McVee, M., Baldassarre, M., & Bailey, N. (2004). Positioning theory as lens to explore teachers' beliefs about literacy and culture. In: C.M., Fairbanks, J. Worthy, B. Maloch, J.V. Hoffman, & D.L Schallert (Eds.), *53rd National Reading Conference Yearbook* (pp. 281–295). Oak Creek, WI: National Reading Conference.

McVee, M.B., Silvestri, K.N., Barrett, S., & Haq, K.S. (2019). Positioning theory. In: D.E. Alvermann, N.J. Unrau, M. Sailors, & R.B. Ruddell (Eds.), *Theoretical Models and Processes of Literacy* (pp. 381–400). New York, NY: Routledge.

Mitchell, C.J. (1984). Typicality and the case study. In: R.F. Ellens (Ed.), *Ethnographic Research: A Guide to General Conduct* (pp. 238–241). New York, NY: Academic Press.

Moghaddam, F., & Harré, R. (2010). Words, conflicts and political processes. In: F. Moghaddam, & R. Harré (Eds.), *Words of Conflict, Words of War: How the Language We Use in Political Processes Sparks Fighting* (pp. 1–30). Santa Barbara, CA: Praeger.

O'Connor, C., & Michaels, S. (2019). Supporting teachers in taking up productive talk moves: The long road to professional learning at scale. *International Journal of Education Research*, *97*, 166–175.

Redman, C. (2013). Agentive roles, rights and duties in a technological era. In: R. Harré, & F. Moghadamn (Eds.), *The Psychology of Friendship and Enmity: Relationships in Love, Work, Politics, and War* (pp. 109–128). Santa Barbra, CA: ABC-CLIO, LLC.

Smith, L.M. (1978). An evolving logic of participant observation, educational ethnography, and other case studies. *Review of Research in Education*, *6*(1), 316–377.

Spradley, J. (1980/2016). *Participant Observation*. Long Grove, Illinois: Waveland Press.

Wittgenstein, L. (1953). *Philosophical Investigations*. Oxford: Blackwell.

Yamakawa, Y., Forman, E., & Ansell, E. (2009). Role of positioning: The role of positioning in constructing an identity in a third-grade mathematics classroom. In: K. Kumpulainen, C.E. Hmelo-Silver, & M. César (Eds.). *Investigating Classroom Interation: Methodologies in Action* (pp. 179–202). Rotterdam, the Netherlands: Sense.

8

HYBRID ARGUMENTATION IN LITERATURE AND SCIENCE FOR K–12 CLASSROOMS

Sarah Levine, Danielle Keifert, Ananda Marin, and Noel Enyedy

We—Sarah Levine, Danielle Keifert, Ananda Marin, and Noel Enyedy—come to this chapter as learning scientists who study teaching, learning, and development in two different disciplines: literature and science. We have a common concern: In the United States, discourses of the K–12 classroom, and particularly the discourses of school-based argumentation, have socialized students into diminished understandings and experiences of our disciplines. In both literature and the sciences, a continuous challenge for education researchers is to develop instructional models that uphold the diverse and complex nature of argumentation practices from across everyday and academic contexts. These models can equip young people and teachers with skills to participate in communities in ways that promote well-being, social justice, and thriving futures. To support educators in these efforts, we identified six characteristics that might be of use in the design of diverse instructional models for argumentation.

For clarity, we begin by defining two key concepts. As we understand it, argumentation is a cultural process of engaging in reasoning and dialogue for the purposes of developing an agreed-upon understanding of a phenomenon. An argument, on the other hand, can be defined as a product, and "reasons, evidence, and justifications are the material that substantiates that product" (Bricker & Bell, 2012, p. 119). Our primary interest in this chapter is on practices of argumentation.

Our approach to identifying characteristics of argumentation practices is hybrid, or syncretic. Gutiérrez, Ali, and Henríquez (2009) describe syncretism as bringing together the "seemingly dissonant genres" of everyday practice and disciplinary practice (p. 336). They offer the example of activities in which students combined the everyday practice of the oral *testimonio* and the academic genre of the extended definition to create stories about border crossings. In this hybrid activity, students shared their stories in powerful ways while exploring a new form. Similarly, Bricker and Bell (2012) emphasize the need to create opportunities for students to engage in everyday argumentation practices as part of learning to engage in argumentation in ways similar to the practices of academic scientists.

We created a set of hybrid argumentation characteristics by looking across everyday argumentation practices in the sciences and literature, as well as the argumentation practices of academic literary critics and scientists. We took a hybrid approach to represent aspects of argumentation that we think are under-emphasized in current education traditions. These hybrid characteristics include:

1. Building relationships
2. Attending to curiosity

3. Disrupting normative assumptions and taking multiple perspectives about how the world works
4. Appropriating and adapting tools
5. Engaging in playful and imaginative ways
6. Creating narratives

These characteristics address the "how" and "why" of argumentation and illustrate productive, engaging, and rewarding aspects of argumentation in literature and the sciences.

Before discussing these characteristics in more depth, we address how argumentation, like all practice, is situated within particular histories and communities. We first explore the cultural nature of argumentation by looking at different conceptualizations of argumentation. Then we look at the cultural nature of the study of argumentation by examining two analytical frameworks. We then shift our focus to K–12 classrooms, their histories of power and assimilation, the tendency of classrooms to present ready-made argumentation, and past attempts to broaden disciplinary engagement. Finally, we highlight six aspects of argumentation practice encompassing everyday and academic disciplinary engagement to expand understanding of argumentation.

Argumentation Is Cultural, Situated, and Bound in Issues of Power

In this volume, Nasir, Lee, Pea, and Royston define culture as the "routines and practices of social/ collective life." In their definitions, along with many others (Gutiérrez, 2002; Nasir, Rosebery, Warren, & Lee, 2006; Rogoff, 2003), cultural practices are both what people learn (a particular argument) and the means by which they learn (engaging in argumentation). In this chapter, we take the position that argumentation, or the process of reasoning about phenomena to develop explanations about the "what," "how," and "why" of things, is a cultural practice (Bricker & Bell, 2012; Majors, 2015). The processes that support argumentation develop within communities with sets of shared histories and practices for being, doing, and knowing. From this perspective, argumentation occurs within complex and overlapping activity systems where people navigate their roles and relations, norms for participation, ideational tools, material artifacts, and goals.

Argumentation involves relations with critical power dynamics, including those rooted in structures of oppression that by design hierarchically assign value to particular categories of social membership, as well as those rooted in relations of personal empowerment (Kimmerer, 2013; Nasir & Hand, 2006). For example, literary artists and scientists have for centuries crafted arguments or stories about how the world works. In doing so, they claimed territory over who counts as a full human being. Moreover, the disciplines themselves are cultural and thus, so are disciplinary arguments. For instance, Joseph Conrad's 1902 novel *Heart of Darkness,* which is told from the perspective of a Western white man, portrays black Africans as alien and savage; however, many Western critics considered it to be one of the greatest novels ever written (Guerard, 1958). The disciplines also debate what counts as argument and who gets to engage in argumentation, and these debates have consequences for participation in the disciplines. It wasn't until the 1970s that the academy saw a critical challenge to Guerard's claims. Nigerian literary scholar and author Chinua Achebe (1978) wrote that *Heart of Darkness* was intensely racist, as it "depersonalize[d] a portion of the human race." Such a novel, he argued, could not be called a great work of art. Here Achebe disrupted the accepted argument of the academic establishment, not only through his written argument but through his assertion of himself in that establishment.

The arguments about what counts as great literature highlight tension around historical and contemporary constructions of the "Other." In the United States, conceptualizations of the "Other" are bound up in logics of settler-colonialism, the history of chattel slavery, and the oppression of peoples deemed as non-white, where whiteness itself is a moving target (Harris, 1993; Wolfe, 2013). Similar dynamics are at work in the traditions of academic sciences where non-Western forms

Hybrid Argumentation in Literature and Science

of science, and in particular Indigenous knowledge systems, are dismissed as unscientific (Bang, Warren, Rosebery, & Medin, 2012; Brayboy & Castagno, 2008). These histories have explicitly promoted "distinctive structures of feeling, affective predispositions, and ways of being in the world that accompany the continuing dispossession of Native peoples" (Wolfe, 2013, p. 2–3). These histories also bind race and property together in ways that have worked to establish and maintain forms of racial dominance by white people over all others (Harris, 1993). Thus, the ways that people are positioned as having valuable contributions and arguments to make is critically linked to whether they are identified as white, black, native, settler, and/or "Other."

In this chapter, we set out to reconceptualize argumentation to push back against these histories of disempowering non-white persons living within what is now known as the United States. We do so by recognizing that all argumentation is situated, developed within particular cultural communities, and wrapped up in issues of power, race, politicized identities, white supremacy, and equity. We attempt to draw upon scholarship that shares this positioning and places the argumentation practices of multiple cultural communities, especially those communities not of European descent, on equal footing with the privileged argumentation practices of literature and sciences in the Western academy. This move does not dismantle the raced, classed, gendered, and nation-building dynamics within larger societal contexts. Nor does it disrupt ways that academic disciplines influence the structure of schooling. However, this move does allow us to characterize argumentation in ways we believe are more representative of the diversity of human practice. Attending to these characteristics could help teachers design instruction that disrupts settled expectations and creates opportunities for expansive learning (Bang, Warren, Rosebery, & Medin, 2012).

Heterogeneity in Perspectives on Argumentation

Like any cooperative human activity, argumentation requires an understanding by participants that what they are doing is engaging in argumentation together (Goodwin, 2018). Researchers have conceptualized argumentation in a number of ways. For example, Lakoff and colleagues (Lakoff & Johnson, 2003; Lakoff & Turner, 1989) contend that the actions people "perform in arguing" are influenced by conceptual metaphors, which, in many cultures, are metaphors of war: In the U.S. and other Western countries, for example, arguers attack and defend, gain and lose ground. Similarly, "chun qiang she jian"—to "cross verbal swords"—is a metaphor for argument used in China (Li, 2010). Van Eemeren and colleagues (2010) have conceptualized argumentation as cooperative search: The "rational search for the best solution to a problem through dialogue and…the search for the best available discursive means to one's desired ends" (Ellis in van Eemeren & Garssen, 2015, p. 3). Feminist scholars such as Al-Tamimi (2009) and Foss and Griffin (1995) have framed argumentation as "invitational," a call to explore and understand a topic's "subtlety, richness, and complexity" (Foss & Griffin, 1995, p. 5).

Importantly, these definitions attend to content and language, which are both necessary parts of any exchange and are both bound up in culturally informed beliefs and practices. Moreover, arguments are influenced by the grammar of the languages we speak. For example, scientists' classification of species is linked to the grammar of animacy. As explained by Robin Wall Kimmerer, a plant ecologist, professor, and enrolled member of the Citizen Potawatomi Nation, the English language is primarily comprised of nouns (about 70 percent). In contrast, about 70 percent of the Potawatomi language is verb-based, and nouns and verbs are both animate and inanimate. Kimmerer provides a narrative argument, situated in her own journey of learning the Potawatomi language, to illustrate the effect these differences have on categorizing the world:

A bay is a noun only if water is *dead*. When *bay* is a noun, it is defined by humans, trapped between its shores and contained by the word. But the verb *wiikegama*—to *be* a bay—releases the water from bondage and lets it live. "To be a bay" holds the wonder

Levine, Keifert, Marin, and Enyedy

that, for this moment, the living water has decided to shelter itself between these shores, conversing with cedar roots and a flock of baby mergansers.

…Water, land, and even a day, the language a mirror for seeing the animacy of the world, the life that pulses through all things, through pines and nuthatches and mushrooms. *This* is the language I hear in the woods, this is the language that lets us speak of what wells up all around us. And the vestiges of boarding schools, soap-wielding missionary wraiths, hang their heads in defeat.

(p. 54–55)

Scholars have also focused on the roles that individuals take on when engaging in argumentation. Hudicourt-Barnes (2003) describes how *bay odyans,* a Haitian-Creole argumentation practice, is accomplished when participants take on the theatrical roles of theoretician (maker of claims), challenger (offeror of humorous interpretations and new data to challenge the initial claim), and audience (contributors of laughter as a form of evaluation of the theatrical entertainment). A primary focus of engagement in *bay odyans* is relational. Participants focus not on winning an argument, but passing the time in an enjoyable way together with their audience. In contrast, Kuhn (1992) suggests that one person can take on multiple roles in thinking-as-argument. Kuhn sees argument as "implicated in all of the beliefs people hold, the judgments they make, and the conclusions they come to; it arises every time a significant decision must be made" (p. 122).

All these descriptions share a framing of argumentation as a negotiated process, "influenced and transformed in the course of discussion" (Leitao, 2000, p. 335), where arguers are constantly altering their stance, use of evidence, and language (Brem & Rips, 2000). As individuals participate in diverse communities of practice (e.g., family, classrooms, religious communities, peer groups, professional communities), they develop multiple repertoires of practice and perspectives (Gutiérrez & Rogoff, 2003), including expectations about when, how, and for what purpose someone might engage in argumentation. Over time, particular histories of interactions lead to the development of accumulated diversity within and across groups (Goodwin, 2018). Thus, the particular norms for engaging in any interactional practice, including argumentation, will be situated within communities.

The above conceptualizations for engaging in argumentation also highlight the role of researchers in developing or articulating those metaphors. We turn now to demonstrating how researchers are themselves situated within particular cultures in the following ways: (1) researchers' frameworks for argumentation are influenced by their participation in cultural communities; (2) frameworks are therefore cultural artifacts; (3) frameworks are put to use in particular settings in dynamic relation to race, ethnicity, class, and culture; and (4) the uses of particular frameworks have the power to shape the ways that argumentation may be taken up in designs for learning.

Cultural Frameworks for Argumentation and the Production of Arguments

The disciplines need multiple perspectives for understanding and modeling argument, drawn from diverse communities of practice, including multiple academic settings and cultural/ethnic communities. Below, we describe Stephen Toulmin's and Yolanda Majors' ideas to illustrate how models for argumentation have become increasingly accountable to culture and context over time.

Toulmin's Model

Scholars in science and language arts education continue to rely on Stephen Toulmin's model of argument, developed in the 1950s. Toulmin, a white British philosopher, developed a framework for argument arising from his participation in the legal studies community. He believed their mathematical form of argument was overly rigid (e.g., if A = B, and B = C, then A= C) and that it erroneously assumed absolute, universal truths with which all arguers would eventually have to agree. In response, Toulmin claimed truths are not always timeless, and *"the arguments that we encounter are set out at a given time and in a given situation, and when we come to assess them they have to be judged against this background"* (Toulmin 2003, p. 168–169). Essentially, Toulmin contended that arguments and argumentation are situated in what his mentor Ludwig Wittgenstein described as "forms of life," and must be evaluated by the expectations set within particular communities.

Toulmin defined argument as accepted data (for example, shared observations), grounded in a warrant (generalized rules or values that might help interpret that data), which supports a claim (an opinion about that data). His framework included other elements: Backing (explaining why a warrant is acceptable or at least plausible); qualifiers, such as "possibly" or "probably"; and attention to potential rebuttal. Various scholars of argument and culture have critiqued Toulmin's model for its relative lack of attention to the emergent nature of argumentation (Brockriede & Ehninger, 1960; Carter, 2006; Ellis, 2014). For example, Toulmin's model suggests that arguments arise in isolation as opposed to in dialogue with other claims or events. However, his work has been very valuable in reframing argumentation as a process and not just a finished product. In putting data, as opposed to claims, at the beginning of his model, Toulmin defines argumentation as in-the-making. And Toulmin's focus on the warrant makes explicit that data is interpreted, and not objective.

Majors' Framework

Yolanda Majors (2015) developed a framework for argumentation that focuses on the connection between the individual and the community, and emphasizes process and practice. Majors examines a particular genre of conversational discourse which she has come to define as Shoptalk, grounded in Majors' ethnographic work in African American hair salons. Shoptalk is a form of argumentation and problem solving that "emerges out of Black public spaces" and includes a multiplicity of modes, forms, and functions. Shoptalk occurs in "culturally shared situated sites of labor" and includes African American English discourse characteristics (e.g., call and response, alliteration, and narrative sequencing).

During Shoptalk, participants engage in multi-voiced discourse, crafting arguments through the performance of collaborative narrative texts. For example, on some occasions, people might put forward and modify claims to deliver cultural instructions; at other times, unofficial claims are engaged in order to analyze "multiple possibilities" and put forward frames for "intergenerational beliefs, values, and traditions for African American children and the reproduction of ideologies within a protected safe space" (p. 38). Majors observed that this kind of argumentation involves implicit processes where arguers employ a number of skills, including identifying the underlying meaning or intent of an utterance, engaging cultural norms for participation, identifying implied audience, claiming the floor, and using narrative to "strengthen one's own position" (p. 41).

Toulmin and Majors: A Synthesized Model

Looking across Majors' and Toulmin's studies, we have created a hybrid model of argumentation to represent the dialogic, multi-layered, and culturally situated nature of argumentation, and to recognize overlapping systems of ongoing activity and the communities in which that activity is embedded. This expanded framework shows argumentation as (1) enacting situated roles; (2) drawing upon cultural belief systems including particular skills and discourses; and (3) joining an ongoing dialogue to deliver cultural instructions and reach agreed-upon explanations (Figure 8.1).

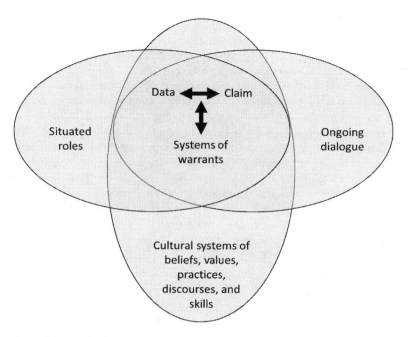

Figure 8.1 A hybrid model of argumentation.

Taking this model as our starting point, we highlight characteristics of argumentation that are underrepresented in language arts and science education argumentation literature. These characteristics describe aspects of argument that include ongoing dialogue, cultural systems, and discourses.

K–12 Classrooms: Histories and Potential Futures

Challenges in K–12 School: Histories of Power and Assimilation

The culture of schooling in the United States has historically been organized by assimilationist models of instruction, focused on learning rote skills and/or canonical texts and ideas (Rogoff, Paradise, Arauz, Correa-Chávez, & Angelillo, 2003). Here, "canonical" means a collection of texts and ideas that are valued by the culture of power. These canonical expectations were developed with respect to particular academic disciplines and arguments that claim territory about who counts as a full human being as well as how other living organisms and natural entities should be classified in relation to humans. Additionally, the structures of school are based on Western notions of division and isolation of groups of people, and the division of sets of ideas drawing upon designs that segregate by principle, such as grade bands, time periods, division of subject matters, testing, and school schedules (Stevens, Wineburg, Herrenkohl, & Bell, 2005).

These systems support the erasure of peoples categorized as the "Other" within the United States through (a) a process of bringing children into school to acculturate them into a particular set of expectations for learning based on the dominant community's values, at the cost of the children's own ways of knowing and being; (b) ideas that conceptualize the world in systematic ways that devalue certain communities while simultaneously positioning humans (primarily members of the dominant community) as having power over all aspects of the world that are not-human (e.g., other-than-human beings, land/waters); and (c) the structural constraints of school systems which prevent engagement in disciplinary practices that reflect everyday and academic communities of practice. These limitations have powerful implications for designing K–12 learning environments that empower young people and their practices.

Ready-Made Argumentation

Traditions of argumentation in both literature and science education have been implicated in this assimilationist approach. Language arts and science are still often taught with pre-cooked data, warrants, and claims prepared and presented to students, so that students do not engage in the dialogic and culturally based process of developing arguments, as they might in Shoptalk, or in one literary critic's response to another. Because argumentation is a form of sensemaking, when schools constrain students' opportunities to engage in developing arguments for themselves, they deny students opportunities for sensemaking. Borrowing from Latour (1987), this state of affairs could be called "ready-made argumentation" in the disciplines. In many cases, ready-made argumentation can narrow students' understanding of the discipline, limit opportunities for sensemaking, and constrain classrooms in ways that exclude everyday argumentation practices, thereby excluding learners' whole selves.

Ready-made Argumentation in Literature Education

In many language arts classrooms, traditional school-based discourses exert a powerful pull on interpretive discussion and argumentation. "School discourses" here are defined as the cultural, linguistic, and disciplinary expectations of the classroom (e.g., Schleppegrell, 2004), and in particular, settled practices that position dominant white middle-class culture and institutions as authoritative norms to which students should acquiesce and aspire. In general, one can see these discourses reflected in a student's tendency to speak directly to the teacher as opposed to fellow students during a discussion, or teachers' use of multiple choice questions to test student knowledge. In language arts, such discourses also tend to include a "one right answer" approach to literary interpretation, where a teacher might assume that all students must interpret a symbol in the same way, or where "finding evidence to support one claim matters more than exploring the validity of… warrants" (Weyand, Goff, & Newell, 2018, p. 111).

Studies show the constraining effects of school-based discourses on teachers and students' argumentation (Beach, 2000; Gee, 2001; Gutiérrez, Morales, & Martinez, 2009; Moje, Overby, Tysvaer, & Morris, 2008; Nasir, Snyder, Shah, & Ross, 2012). For instance, in a long-term study of three new language arts teachers, Grossman and Thompson (2008) observed that both teachers and students understood argument in terms of the school-based five-paragraph essay, "a genre that focuses more on form than on content," as opposed to seeing argument as "the unfolding of a set of ideas, or as an excursion into an author's thinking" (p. 2022). Similarly, a teacher in another study of argumentation in language arts classrooms described how his students "sort of freak[ed] out" when the teacher framed argumentation as a situated practice, focusing on audience and context, as opposed to form (Newell, Bloome, & Hirvela, 2015, p. 47).

These school-based discourses lead to a perception of literary argument as a search for a singular, often teacher-directed message or theme. One student in Wilhelm and Smith's (2016) study about the value of pleasure reading said, "When you pick up a book in school, you know that there's supposed to be something you're getting out of this, and that's all you really think about, what does the teacher want me to understand from reading this" (p. 28). Other studies find that many students do not develop opinions, concepts, and feelings in transaction with texts, but instead are trained to find and re-argue a text's single "right" message (Luttrell & Parker, 2001; Zyngier & Fialho, 2010).

The pressure for ready-made arguments in language arts classrooms derives from many cultural and historical artifacts of schooling. First, many textbooks and teaching guides ask for ready-made arguments using words like "search," "find," "message," and "lesson" when referring to thematic interpretation, suggesting there is only one message to find (e.g., Holt McDougal, 2011). Second, teachers and students may tend to see literary texts as vehicles for moral messages (Levine, 2018; Squire, 1964), which contributes to ready-made argumentation. This moralistic approach likely derives in part from Western pedagogy's historical commitment to the ennobling power of literature (e.g., Applebee, 1974).

Ready-made Argumentation in Science Education

Science has often been taught as a body of established facts about how the world works (NRC, 2012). White men are still most likely to get credit for establishing these facts, regardless of actual contributions from women or others (e.g., Lee, 2013). This approach, called ready-made science (Latour, 1987), describes knowledge produced by the scientific community after consensus has been reached (e.g., current articulations of the relationship between the earth and the sun), but erases the process of science-in-the-making (e.g., how Copernicus, Kepler, and Galileo came to understand the relationship between the earth and the sun).

Ready-made science, with its focus on memorization of facts, has failed to produce deep conceptual understandings of science ideas (Smith, diSessa, & Roschelle, 1993), help students appropriate scientific ways of reasoning (Barab & Hay 2001; Brown & Campione, 1994), or prepare students to engage in science in their everyday lives. Although "hands on science" and student "experimentation" are long-standing practices in science education designed to push back against ready-made science, those approaches are sometimes not supportive of learning (Chi, 2009) or representative of the diversity of science practice (Bell, 2004), and often cannot counteract ready-made science that expects memorization over sensemaking.

Scientific argument can also be ready-made. For instance, a teacher might divide students into teams, assign them opposing viewpoints, and give them lists of evidence they might choose to support their claims. Thus these groups may go through the motions of argumentation, assembling data that supports one side's claim and dismantling the claims of the opposing side, but the class knows that one argument is true and the other false. Berland and Hammer (2012) call this "pseudo-argumentation," saying that such practices are at odds with calls in the K–12 Framework for Science Education to engage students in the practices of science to build their own arguments (NRC, 2012), and are also at odds with understandings of young people as capable of sophisticated argumentation.

Studies of the sciences have shown that argument emerges over time from shared questions, and that in the process, multiple teams of collaborating scientists have parts of argument that get taken up and adopted as consensus (Latour, 1987). While some textbooks or videos may show scientists struggling with uncertainty, students do not necessarily have opportunities to struggle with uncertainty themselves as they engage in argumentation together. Instead, they experience scientific arguments presented to them as "truth." These ready-made argumentation discourses position teachers as authorities of science in problematic ways, leaving learners unsupported to engage in authentic argumentation practice (e.g., Sandoval, Enyedy, Redman, & Xiao, 2019). Instead, students may learn that attending to each others' ideas is potentially detrimental, as it may lead individuals away from the "truths" that teachers are attempting to impart (Berland & Reiser, 2011). Teachers certainly have understandings that are valuable for their students to learn; however, teachers also have an important contribution to make in their role of a facilitator who supports students' engagement in building their own arguments and explanations (e.g., Schwarz, Reiser, Davis, Kenyon, Acher, Fortus, Shwartz, Hug, & Krajcik, 2009). The K–12 Framework (NRC, 2012) supports drawing upon the rich practices of students as leverage for learning; however, even this framework could go further to consider how students' everyday argumentation practices are themselves valuable for learning during science-in-the-making.

Attempts to Expand Canonical Disciplinary Understanding of Argumentation

Language arts and science teachers and researchers have over time voiced concern about and made efforts to disrupt school-based discourses and canonical disciplinary understandings. In 1907, literature teachers were already voicing concern about the constraining effects of top-down mandated readings, which "seem[ed] to deaden any love for literature a pupil may have" (Tanner, 1907,

p. 37). Dewey and Rosenblatt, among others, encouraged language arts classrooms to embrace a "transactional" approach to literary reading, with a focus on the reading experience and not the information gleaned from a literary text. Teachers have recruited "everyday" texts such as songs, films, and websites as subjects of inquiry in the classroom, and adopted current events as subjects for argumentation in literature classes (e.g., Garcia, Seglem, & Share, 2013; Sosa, Hall, Goldman, & Lee, 2016).

In language arts, researchers have worked to help teachers see argumentation as situated and social (see, for example, Beach, Webb & Thein, 2015; Newell, Bloome, Hirvela, & Lin, 2019; Morrell & Duncan-Andrade, 2004; Newell, Tallman, & Letcher, 2009). Hillocks (e.g., 1975, 2011) used Toulmin's model to highlight the importance of observing and making inferences about data before constructing a claim. Newell and colleagues created guides to help teachers and students frame argument as more than a collection of claims, evidence, and warrants; they focus, for example, on argumentation as exchanges of ideas in class discussion and dialogic teacher feedback. Lee's cultural modeling framework (e.g., 2001, 2007) and Majors' Shoptalk point to the importance of drawing on students' culturally based skills when teaching students to build arguments about literary texts. Graff and Birkenstein (2018) offer sentence stems for argument about literature that also serve to remind learners that arguments emerge from ongoing dialogues, not in isolation. And other scholars have raised questions about the underlying warrants of argumentation instruction, advocating for educators to "stop treating argumentative writing as a form of cultural capital by exalting it over other forms of communication and—in doing so—being complicit in reproducing the academic and economic benefits that may come to a small number of students from learning to think, talk, and write like the well-connected and wealthy" (DeStigter, 2015, p. 28).

In science education, teachers have attempted to reframe their own understandings of students' everyday ideas about science based on students' experiences with science phenomena such as bike riding, sun sets, and trees changing color (eg. NRC, 2000; NRC, 2012; Smith, diSessa, & Roschelle, 1993). Educators have also sought to use students' everyday practices in literature and science as assets for classroom learning (Ek, 2008; Gonzales, Moll, & Amanti, 2005; Hudicourt-Barnes, 2003; Lee, 2007; Varelas, Pappas, Kane, Arsenault, Hankes, & Cowan, 2008). Their attempts have often been supported by research on the cultural nature of teaching and learning (e.g., Nasir, Warren, & Lee, 2006), as well as the standards efforts produced by the National Council of Teachers of English and the National Research Council (e.g., Next Generation Science Standards; NRC, 2012; NGSS Lead States, 2013).

While some of this research has taken up students' everyday argumentation practices as valuable for learning in its own right (e.g., Hudicourt-Barnes, 2003), perhaps too great a proportion of the research has focused on leveraging everyday practice towards engaging in forms of argumentation conceptualized by educators as scientific. The result is positioning everyday practices as indicative of only "nascent argumentation" ability (Berland & Hammer, 2012, p. 69)—a way to gain access to Western canonical understandings of highly valued science argumentation (e.g., NRC, 2012; Manz, 2015). When Western forms of argumentation are privileged as the end goal and everyday practices are positioned only as leverage towards that goal, education researchers run the risk of re-inscribing normative assumptions about teaching and learning.

Characteristics of Argumentation Across Cultural Communities That Support Expansive Sensemaking

In the remainder of this chapter, we identify a set of hybrid characteristics derived from argumentation encompassing everyday, academic sciences, and literature contexts. Although we cannot fully represent the incredible diversity of human argumentation, we present a few examples that highlight characteristics of argumentation practice that have been underrepresented in current discussions of argumentation in K–12 English language arts and science education. Each example takes up one or more aspects of our hybrid framework model for argument (Figure 8.1), positioning argumentation as part of an ongoing dialogue that draws on discourses, values, and beliefs that are embedded within and salient to particular communities at particular times. Looking across disciplines (literature and the sciences) and settings (academic and everyday), we found that arguers: build relationships; attend to their own curiosity; take multiple perspectives; appropriate and adapt tools to help build arguments of interest to them; disrupt normative assumptions about the way the world works; draw on play and imagination; and see narratives as part of argumentation.

Building Relationships

Literature

Much of everyday argument about literature grows out of and feeds into social relationships. The social nature of argumentation is particularly clear in the contexts of face-to-face book clubs and fan fiction websites. For example, Margaret Atwood defined a book club as a "graduate seminar, encounter group, and…good old fashioned village pump gossip session all rolled into one" (Slezak & Atwood, 1995, p. xi). Studies of book clubs show that when participants put forward their ideas and opinions about texts, they strengthen interpersonal bonds (Beach & Yussen, 2011; Peplow, 2016).

For instance, in a study of teenagers in an out-of-class book club (Polleck, 2010), a teenager named Gina compared herself to a fictional character who was concerned about her weight. A new kind of argument, this time about Gina, emerged between Gina and her friends:

Gina: I hate books with fat people.
Carla: You're not fat, dummy.
Gina: Yes, I am. It will happen in the book and that shit don't happen to me. I ain't got nobody coming up to me saying how beautiful I am.
Eileen: We tell you how beautiful you are.

This argument illustrates aspects of our synthesized framework of argumentation (Figure 8.1). First, Gina's claim about her own body arises out of her response to her reading (not in isolation). Second, in making their argument about Gina, her friends agreed to engage the world of the text as they would their own social world (Mar & Oatley, 2008). The underlying warrant for Gina's claim is that literary worlds are worth reflecting on, and in considering literary characters' motivations and actions, one can learn about oneself. Finally, the teens used discourses particular to their relationship and needs as they offered support to their friend.

Science

Building relationships with others—both human and more-than-human kinds—through argument is an important part of the forest walks taken by participants in Marin's (2013) study of families learning to attend and observe. For instance, an Odawa (Native American) mom, Jackie, and her two young sons, Jason and Sam, took several shared walks in an urban forest preserve. On one walk, Jackie and Jason built an argument about more-than-human kinds in relation to their own lives. Jackie noticed a plant and asked, "You think this is the beginning of a tree?" She then touched part of a tree and added, "I see these in our yard…Those are maple leaves, right?" Jason agreed, and then he and Jackie collaboratively agreed that this wasn't a bush, but a "baby, baby, baby tree." Jackie and Jason built an understanding of themselves in relationship with this "baby tree" and in relation to other trees at home. Their collaboratively developed argument about the tree being a tree (not a bush) was built on this relationship between humans (Jackie, Jason, and family) and more-than-human kinds (maple trees), a practice deeply situated within several American Indian communities and epistemologies.

Attending to Curiosity

Literature

The tendency towards ready-made arguments in school-based settings can make it difficult for teachers and students to remember that, in everyday life, many arguments arise out of curiosity. The rise of the "essential" question in units of literary instruction (e.g., "What is justice?") has helped develop inquiry-driven classrooms, but sometimes even these questions take on a rote quality. Classroom questions must be "real questions asked in the world, questions that stimulate interest and spark curiosity" (Moje, 2015). In book clubs or casual gatherings among friends discussing texts, individuals do not necessarily ask overarching thematic questions (e.g., "What is a hero? What is the author suggesting about love?") but instead often focus arguments on character motivations, specific details, and judgments (Long, 2003). For example, in a library book club for teen-aged girls (Morris, 2012, p. 83), participants zoomed in on a character's choices, asking, "Why did she do that? Why did she put up with that?"

Science

Science argumentation can arise in informal settings as people become curious about the world. For instance, in a study of young children's inquiry, four-year-old Jamie asked his mother, "What if you had a foot on the back of your head?!" Jamie's mom suggested that with only one foot, she would have to hop. Jamie then proposed having four feet, which Jamie's mom said would be confusing. Jamie responded by making a case for moving with four feet; he sat up off the ground and used his arms and legs as limbs to "show" his mother how she could do it. His mom affirmed, "Oh, you're right." Jamie's argument was built on his imagination and curiosity about human anatomy, drawing upon a form of argument—showing through embodying—that his mom accepted as adequate support for his claims (Keifert, 2015; Keifert & Stevens, 2019).

Disrupting Norms and Taking Multiple Perspectives about the Way the World Works

Literature

In the academy, Chinua Achebe's argument about the racism in Conrad's novel disrupted assumptions of the white, male-dominated world of literary criticism, as does a range of critical argument within and beyond the academy; see, for example, "The Black Guy Dies First" on blavity. com (Notez, 2017), or "What's So Cringeworthy about Long Duk Dong in *Sixteen Candles*?" (Chow, 2015). In everyday literary contexts, fanfiction writers take up multiple perspectives and disrupt social and cultural norms. In fanfiction communities, writers with an affinity to a particular fictional world (e.g., *Harry Potter*, or the television show *Empire*) create alternate characterizations, endings, spin-offs, and mash-ups to continue their experience with that world (Black, 2008; Samutina, 2017). These stories often act as arguments against accepted or canonical versions of these stories. For example, when fanfiction writers create queer romances where none previously existed (e.g., between Harry Potter and Draco Malfoy), they declare political and social ideologies, implicitly arguing for expanding the boundaries of social acceptance of sexuality and love (Tosenberger, 2008). The claim in such a piece of fiction is that queer romance does and should exist, and the evidence for that claim is in the sympathetic portrayal of the relationship.

Critical arguments about literature are popular in everyday and university contexts, and are a growing part of K–12 classroom contexts, although they have yet to be sanctioned by standardized tests that can drive language arts instruction (Levine, 2019). Fortunately, guides to critical literacy in the classroom (e.g., Appleman, 2000; Duncan-Andrade & Morrell, 2008) are supporting teachers' implementation of these argument practices in some K–12 classrooms.

Science

Perhaps the most common arguments involving science are personal and policy decisions (e.g., whether to quit smoking or whether to ban pesticides). Such decisions can potentially disrupt ongoing activities and norms. Swedish teenager Greta Thunberg became a public figure after protesting on the steps of Sweden's parliament about the human response to climate change. Thunberg (2018) argued that although the science and necessary steps for fighting climate change were established, people were not taking those steps; therefore, governmental regulation was necessary. Her argument was countered by people such as Australian columnist Andrew Bolt, who noted that Thunberg displayed tics associated with being on the autism spectrum, which, he said, illustrated she was "deeply disturbed" and "freakishly influential" and therefore should not be taken seriously (Henriques-Gomes, 2019). Thunberg responded, "When haters go after your looks and differences, it means they have nowhere left to go. And then you know you're winning," claiming too that Asperger syndrome can be a "superpower" (Twitter, 8/31/2019). Thunberg continued to build her argument about the need for change and the value of perspectives of neurodiversity in activism spaces.

In some cases, disrupting norms can take the form of simply seeing multiple perspectives on phenomena. Take for example an argument among wildlife biologists that coyote and badger, two North American carnivores and intraguild predators, compete "for limited resources on the logic that any resource removed by one species (or by one individual) reduces the amount available to others" (Ojalehto, Medin, Horton, Garcia, & Kays, 2015, p. 3). At the same time, coyotes and badgers have been observed hunting and engaging in playful behavior together. Why then did scientists' observations lead to models and arguments focused on competition? One possible explanation is that scientists' cultural models and frameworks (e.g., privileging competition over cooperation), may result in culturally inflected arguments. In this example, multiple perspectives, or seeing competition versus cooperation, led to quite different interpretations, logics, and arguments about species behavior. Taking an alternative perspective or holding both perspectives simultaneously is an act of disruption and paves the way for expanding arguments within the sciences in productive ways.

Appropriating and Adapting Tools

Literature

Across the history of literature as an academic discipline, scholars have found that their current academic tools do not suffice for the arguments they wish to make. This inadequacy is probably most obvious in the ways that scholars retool the language of the academy to serve their claims. For instance, H. Samy Alim, a hip hop and African American Studies scholar (among other things), coined the term "ill-literacies" to talk about "counter-hegemonic forms of youth literacies" (Paris & Alim, 2017, p. 10). To some degree, the lack of alignment between tool and argument lies in the lack of alignment between the cultural nature of the subject and the academic discourses used to write about it. The aptness and poetry of a term like "ill-literacies" act as an argument for expanding the cultural practices and discourses of the academy. Even the choice of an unconventional typeface or positioning of text on the page acts as an argument against conventional genres and forms (Banks, 2006).

Science

In the academic sciences, argumentation is the central method for explaining how the world works (Bricker & Bell, 2008) and includes making sense of phenomena and articulating understanding in an attempt to persuade others (Berland & Reiser, 2011). Critically, part of that work is the production of data—how samples are taken, processed, and interpreted in order to produce data that can then be analyzed to build argument (Goodwin, 2018; Latour, 1987). Thus, choices of tools are a critical part of building argument.

One study details how, in an out-of-school environmental education program, youth shaped the development of argument by adapting procedures to include new tools to explore their interests and concerns. The Chemical Oceanography Outside the Laboratory (COOL) project brought together teens from nondominant communities (youth who identified as Black, Latino, Burmese, African American, and Somali) along with learning scientists (white, Afro-Caribbean/African American), and scientists in a chemical oceanography laboratory (persons who identified as white American) (Scipio, 2015). During COOL, youth developed an interest in better understanding fish feminization in local waters. However, when collecting and analyzing data, the youth found the lab's existing plastic containers interfered with their questions about the role that chemicals in plastics or plasticizers in the water might play in fish feminization. In collaboration with lab members and mentors, the youth determined the need for new procedures and materials for the production of data that were free from contaminating substances. Students and lab members adopted these new tools to pursue students' argument about plastics and fish feminization. COOL demonstrates "students [can] have experiences in which their decision-making involves 'productively disrupting historically powered relations as part of working towards equity and forms of just democracies' (Bang & Vossoughi, 2016, p. 173)" (Keifert, Krist, Scipio, & Phillips, 2018, p. 197) as they built an argument for their community about plastics use. This experience highlights how community participants'—youth, learning scientists, and laboratory scientists—responsive practices shape opportunities for expansive learning by centering young people's interests and concerns.

Engaging in Playful and Imaginative Ways

Literature

Although writers and literary critics may be known for taking themselves too seriously, much of what they do is playful. That playfulness might be most apparent in their criticisms of their own disciplines. For instance, the following is attributed to fiction writer Flannery O'Connor: "Everywhere I go, I am asked if I think university stifles writers. My opinion is that it doesn't stifle enough of them" (Price, 2013). In book clubs, on fanfiction sites, and on cultural blogs, arguments about literature can take the form of playful teasing. Studies of fan fiction show writers using parody to argue against melodramatic plots: "He fell to his knees, now sobbing heavily…'I accidentally killed my friend! A dragon outsmarted me! Wah! My life is horrid! And to think all that was needed to save me was hot, healing sex with my one true love!'" (Barner, 2016, p. 99). Likewise, "Television Without Pity," an online site where moderators and the public joined forces to critique TV shows, made "snark" (snide, witty sarcasm) one of their identifying characteristics. Their snarky reviews included lines such as "[This show was] so bad that…other bad shows took it aside out of compassion to gently tell it how bad it was." In these cases, the claim, data, and warrants about bad argument are wrapped up in the satiric language the authors value.

Science

Scientists engage in imaginative explorations. Einstein's (1949) thinking about the Special Theory of Relativity was prompted by a thought experiment in which he imagined riding a beam of light. McClintock developed her work on genomic mechanisms by imagining herself "right down there with [the chromosomes]" (Keller, 1983, p. 117). Building on assumptions that play was a familiar practice for young children (ages 6–8), and that imaginative exploration was a productive practice within the sciences (e.g., Ochs, Gonzales, & Jacoby, 1996; Ogonowski, 2008), Danish and Enyedy designed the Science through Technology Enhanced Play (STEP) project (DeLiema, Enyedy, & Danish, 2019; Enyedy & Danish, 2015). In one iteration of STEP, first and second grade students at the UCLA Lab School (a population representative of the diversity of the state of California) engaged in imaginative explorations by embodying honeybees as they roamed fields, discovered flowers, collected nectar, and returned that nectar to the hive. Later, students acting as flowers tagged visiting honeybees with flower-specific, colored post-it note pollen, while students-as-bees spread pollen between flowers by "dropping off" post-it notes. This imaginative play supported students in building arguments about how agents within complex systems depend upon one another for survival.

Creating Narratives

Literature

Nobel laureate Toni Morrison (1988) described the writing of her novel *The Bluest Eye* as the creation of a "shattered world" that could help readers reconceive the real-world impact of things like race, power, and love. If literary texts are "world[s] created in transaction with the text" (Rosenblatt, 1982, p. 270), then much of literature is a kind of argument: a set of claims about how the world is or should be, with an entire narrative as evidence for those claims. Morrell and Duncan-Andrade (2004) give an example of this kind of reading and reconceiving in their description of a teenager building an interpretation of a rap song by Nas: "It's like society will hold you and strike like a cobra…That's the way the world is now, but that's not the way he [Nas] wants it to be" (p. 260–261).

In some schools of literary theory, the warrants for narrative arguments about the world assume that a reader will share or adopt authorial definitions and values (Rabinowitz & Smith, 1998). Thus when fanfiction writers create worlds in which Harry Potter and Draco Malfoy fall in love, they depend on sympathetic readings of the relationship in order to make an argument for a world in which such relationships can exist and thrive. Similarly, the degree to which Conrad's *Heart of Darkness* makes an argument for or against colonialism depends on the degree to which readers sympathize with his characters and Conrad's definitions. (Other schools of thought dismiss authorial expectations as irrelevant, but still attend to readers' judgments and sympathies.)

In connecting with readers' feelings, and not just their logic, literary narratives may open readers to new arguments about human nature. This perspective is supported in research on the positive relationship between empathy and the reading of fiction (e.g., Mar, Oatley, & Peterson, 2009). Similarly, Bruner (1991) and Shklovsky (1991) argue that through engaging narrative worlds, readers can construct interpretations of authorial or textual worldviews that might help clarify their own.

Science

Telling stories as a form of making an argument is a valued practice among many communities, including Indigenous families (Marin, 2019), white-American speakers of English (Ochs, Taylor, Rudolph, & Smith, 1992), and those engaged in academic science practice (e.g., McClintock telling a story to explain genomic mutations; Keller, 1983). Marin (2019) describes micro-stories—four to five sentence stories—as a form of argumentation produced by members of an Indigenous family as they walked through an urban forest preserve. A seven-year-old boy explained to his mother (an Odawa American Indian) that they were walking by a deer trail, evidenced by "deers take dis, walk like a deer, they make trails by wa, walking." He continued his story making an argument about what might have happened by imagining that one particular deer "got stuck…this must been like a long time ago when it's flooded, because look it, there's a deer trail in the river." Building the argument about a more-than-human kind—the deer—was situated within the context of exploring the path made by deer and telling a story to understand the experience of one particular deer based on their observations.

Taking up these Characteristics in K–12 Classrooms: Proposal for Hybrid Practices

This chapter's hybrid characteristics are not a checklist. Not every characteristic applies to every argument; for example, sometimes argument is deadly serious and not playful. Likewise, the same instance of argumentation can represent many characteristics; for example, imaginative argumentation may also involve taking multiple perspectives. Instead, these characteristics are interwoven in the rich argumentation practices in which youth engage every day. When contextualized within the complex dynamics of history, race, class, and gender, these characteristics can be used as guideposts in the design of expansive and transformative classroom learning experiences that critically engage cultural, social, and ideological border crossing and dismantle "settled expectations" (Bang, Warren, Rosebery, & Medin, 2012) in argumentation. We propose taking up these characteristics in designs for argumentation in school-based learning environments, not only in service of the academic pipeline, but also in the service of learners' everyday lives. Doing so acknowledges that most young people are interested in paths other than literary critic or bench scientist. Just as important, doing so values these cultural practices in their own right. By privileging a hybrid array of argumentation practices, educators can also prepare the way for young people to contribute to new kinds of arguments within the disciplines as they collaboratively create their own hybrid practices that meet their learning needs.

References

Achebe, C. (1978). An image of Africa. *Research in African Literatures, 9*(1), 1–15.

Al-Tamimi, K. (2009). Feminist alternatives to traditional argumentation. OSSA Conference Archive. Retrieved from https://scholar.uwindsor.ca/ossaarchive/OSSA8/papersandcommentaries/5.

Applebee, A. N. (1974). *Tradition and Reform in the Teaching of English: A History*. Urbana, IL: National Council of Teachers of English.

Appleman, D. (2000). *Critical Encounters in High School English: Teaching Literary Theory to Adolescents*. New York, NY: Teachers College Press.

Bang, M., & Vossoughi, S. (2016). Participatory design research and educational justice: Studying learning and relations within social change making. *Cognition and Instruction, 34*(3), 173–193.

Bang, M., Warren, B., Rosebery, A. S., & Medin, D. (2012). Desettling expectations in science education. *Human Development, 55*(5–6), 302–318. doi:10.1159/000345322.

Banks, A. J. (2006). *Race, Rhetoric, and Technology: Searching for Higher Ground*. New York, NY: Routledge.

Barab, S. A., & Hay, K. E. (2001). Doing science at the elbows of experts: Issues related to the science apprenticeship camp. *Journal of Research in Science Teaching, 38*(1), 70–102.

Barner, A. J. (2016). "I Opened a Book and in I Strode": *Fanfiction and Imaginative Reading* (Doctoral dissertation, Ohio University).

Beach, R. (2000). Critical issues: Reading and responding to literature at the level of activity. *Journal of Literacy Research, 32*(2), 237–251. doi:10.1080/10862960009548075.

Beach, R., Webb, A., & Thein, A. H. (2015). *Teaching to Exceed the English Language Arts Common Core State Standards: A Critical Inquiry Approach for 6–12 Classrooms*. New York, NY: Routledge.

Beach, R., & Yussen, S. (2011). Practices of productive adult book clubs. *Journal of Adolescent and Adult Literacy, 55*(2), 121–131. doi:10.1002/JAAL.00015.

Bell, P. (2004) *The School Science Laboratory: Considerations of Learning, Technology, and Scientific Practice*. National Academy of Sciences, High School Science Laboratories: Role and Vision.

Berland, L. K., & Hammer, D. (2012). Framing for scientific argumentation. *Journal of Research in Science Teaching, 49*(1), 68–94.

Berland, L. K., & Reiser, B. J. (2011). Classroom communities' adaptations of the practice of scientific argumentation. *Science Education, 95*(2), 191–216.

Black, R. W. (2008). *Adolescents and Online Fan Fiction*. New York, NY: Peter Lang.

Brayboy, B. M. J., & Castagno, A. E. (2008). Indigenous knowledges and native science as partners: A rejoinder. *Cultural Studies of Science Education, 3*(3), 787–791. doi:10.1007/s11422-008-9142-9.

Brem, S. K., & Rips, L. J. (2000). Explanation and evidence in informal argument. *Cognitive Science, 24*(4), 573–604.

Bricker, L. A., & Bell, P. (2008). Conceptualizations of argumentation from science studies and the learning sciences and their implications for the practices of science education. *Science Education, 92*(3), 473–498.

Bricker, L. A., & Bell, P. (2012). Argumentation and reasoning in life and in school: Implications for the design of school science learning environments. In: M. S. Khine (Ed.), *Perspectives on Scientific Argumentation: Theory, Practice and Research* (pp. 117–133). Berlin: Springer Science & Business Media. doi:10.1007/978-94-007-2470-9_7.

Brockriede, W., & Ehninger, D. (1960). Toulmin on argument: An interpretation and application. *Quarterly Journal of Speech, 46*(1), 44.

Brown, A. L., & Campione, J. C. (1994). *Guided Discovery in a Community of Learners.* Cambridge, MA: The MIT Press.

Bruner, J. (1991). The narrative construction of reality. *Critical Inquiry, 18*(1), 1–21.

Carter, P. L. (2006). Straddling boundaries: Identity, culture, and school. *Sociology of Education, 79*(4), 304.

Chow, K. (2015). What's so "cringeworthy" about Long Duk Dong in "Sixteen Candles"? Retrieved from NPR.org website https://www.npr.org/sections/codeswitch/2015/02/06/384307677/whats-so-cring e-worthy-about-long-duk-dong-in-sixteen-candles.

Chi, M. T. (2009). Active-constructive-interactive: A conceptual framework for differentiating learning activities. *Topics in Cognitive Science, 1*(1), 73–105.

Conrad, J. (1902/2007). *Heart of Darkness.* Claremont, CA: Coyote Canyon Press.

DeLiema, D., Enyedy, N., & Danish, J. A. (2019). Roles, rules, and keys: How different play configurations shape collaborative science inquiry. *Journal of the Learning Sciences, 8*(4– 5), 513–555.

DeStigter, T. (2015). On the ascendance of argument: A critique of the assumptions of academe's dominant form. *Research in the Teaching of English, 50*(1), 11–34.

Duncan-Andrade, J. M. R., & Morrell, E. (2008). *The Art of Critical Pedagogy: Possibilities for Moving from Theory to Practice in Urban Schools.* New York, NY: Peter Lang.

Einstein, A. (1949). Autobiographical notes. In: P. A. Schilpp (Ed.), *Albert Einstein: Philosopher-Scientist* (pp. 1–94). LaSalle, IL: Open Court Publishing Company.

Ek, L. D. (2008). Language and literacy in the Pentecostal church and the public high school: A case study of a Mexican ESL student. *The High School Journal, 92*(2),1–13.

Ellis, L. (2014). *The Ubiquity of the Toulmin Model In U.S. Education: Promise and Peril.* Presented at the ISSA.

Enyedy, N., & Danish, J. (2015). Learning physics through play and embodied reflection in a mixed-reality learning environment. In: V. Lee (Ed.), *Learning Technologies and the Body: Integration and Implementation* (pp. 97–111). New York, NY: Routledge.

Foss, S. K., & Griffin, C. L. (1995). Beyond persuasion: A proposal for an invitational rhetoric. *Communication Monographs, 62*(1), 2–18. doi:10.1080/03637759509376345.

Garcia, A., Seglem, R., & Share, J. (2013). Transforming teaching and learning through critical media literacy pedagogy. *Learning Landscapes, 6*(2), 109–124.

Gee, J. P. (2001). Reading as situated language: A sociocognitive perspective. *Journal of Adolescent and Adult Literacy, 44*(8), 714.

Gonzalez, N., Moll, L. C., & Amanti, C. (2005). *Funds of Knowledge: Theorizing Practices in Households, Communities, and Classrooms.* Mahwah, NJ: Erlbaum Associates.

Goodwin, C. (2018). *Co-Operative Action.* New York, NY: Cambridge University Press.

Graff, G., & Birkenstein, C. (2018). *They Say/I Say: The Moves That Matter in Academic Writing.* New York, NY: WW Norton & Company.

Grossman, P. L., & Thompson, C. (2008). Learning from curriculum materials: Scaffolds for new teachers? *Teaching and Teacher Education, 24*(8), 2014–2026. doi:10.1016/j.tate.2008.05.002.

Guerard, A. J. (1958). *Conrad the Novelist.* Cambridge, MA: Harvard University Press.

Gutiérrez, K. D. (2002). Studying cultural practices in urban learning communities. *Human Development; Basel, 45*(4), 312–321.

Gutiérrez, K. D., Ali, A., Henríquez, C., & Ali, A. (2009). Syncretism and hybridity: Schooling, language, and race and students from non-dominant communities. In: M. Apple, S. Ball, & L. Gandin (Eds.), *The Routledge International Handbook of the Sociology of Education* (pp. 376–387). New York, NY: Routledge. doi:10.4324/9780203863701-41.

Gutiérrez, K. D., Morales, P. Z., & Martinez, D. C. (2009). Re-mediating literacy: Culture, difference, and learning for students from nondominant communities. *Review of Research in Education, 33*(1), 212–245. doi:10. 3102/0091732X08328267.

Gutiérrez, K. D., & Rogoff, B. (2003). Cultural ways of learning: Individual traits or repertoires of practice. *Educational Researcher, 32*(5), 19–25. doi:10.3102/0013189X032005019.

Harris, C. I. (1993). Whiteness as property. *Harvard Law Review, 106*(8), 1707–1791. doi:10.2307/1341787.

Henriques-Gomes, L. (2019, August 2). Andrew Bolt's mocking of Greta Thunberg leaves autism advocates 'disgusted'. *The Guardian.* Retrieved from https://www.theguardian.com/media/2019/aug/02/andr ew-bolts-mocking-of-greta-thunberg-leaves-autism-advocates-disgusted.

Hillocks, G. (1975). Observing and writing. Retrieved from http://eric.ed.gov/?id=ED102574.

Hillocks, G. (2011). *Teaching Argument Writing, Grades 6–12*. Hanover, NH: Heinemann.

Holt, McDougal (2011). *Holt McDougal Literature: Teacher's Edition, Grade 10* (1st ed.). Evanston, IL: Holt McDougal.

Hudicourt-Barnes, J. (2003). The use of argumentation in Haitian Creole science classrooms. *Harvard Educational Review, 73*(1), 73–93. doi:10.17763/haer.73.1.hnq801u57400l877.

Keifert, D. (2015). *Young Children Participating in Inquiry: Moments of Joint Inquiry and Questioning Practices at Home and in School* (Doctoral dissertation, Northwestern University).

Keifert, D., Krist, C., Scipio, D. A., & Phillips, A. M. (2018). *Epistemic Agency as a Members' Experience*. London, UK: International Society of the Learning Sciences, Inc.[ISLS].

Keifert, D., & Stevens, R. (2019). Inquiry as a members' phenomenon: Young children as competent inquirers. *Journal of the Learning Sciences, 28*(2), 240–278. doi:10.1080/10508406.2018.1528448.

Keller, E. F. (1983). *A Feeling for the Organism: The Life and Work of Barbara McClintock*. New York, NY: Henry Holt & Company.

Kimmerer, R. W. (2013). The fortress, the river and the garden. In: A. Kulnieks, D. R. Longboat, & K. Young (Eds.), *Contemporary Studies in Environmental and Indigenous Pedagogies: A Curricula of Stories and Place* (pp. 49–76). Berlin: Springer Science & Business Media. doi:10.1007/978-94-6209-293-8_4.

Kuhn, D. (1992). Thinking as argument. *Harvard Educational Review, 62*(2), 155–179. doi:10.17763/haer.62.2.9r424r0113t670l1.

Lakoff, G., & Johnson, M. (2003). *Metaphors We Live By* (2nd ed.). Chicago, IL: University of Chicago Press.

Lakoff, G., & Turner, M. (1989). *More than Cool Reason: A Field Guide to Poetic Metaphor* (1st ed.). Chicago, IL: University of Chicago Press.

Latour, B. (1987). *Science in Action: How to Follow Scientists and Engineers through Society*. Cambridge, MA: Harvard University Press.

Lee, C. D. (2001). Is October Brown Chinese? A cultural modeling activity system for underachieving students. *American Educational Research Journal, 38*(1), 97–141. doi:10.3102/00028312038001097.

Lee, C. D. (2007). *Culture, Literacy, & Learning: Taking Bloom in the Midst of the Whirlwind*. New York, NY: Teachers College Press.

Lee, J. L. (2013, May 19). 6 Women scientists who were snubbed due to sexism. *National Geographic*. Retrieved from https://www.nationalgeographic.com/news/2013/5/130519-women-scientists-overlooked-dna-history-science/.

Leitao, S. (2000). The potential of argument in knowledge building. *Human Development, 43*(6), 332–360. doi:10.1159/000022695.

Levine, S. (2018). Using everyday language to support students in constructing thematic interpretations. *Journal of the Learning Sciences, 28*(1), 1–31.

Levine, S. (2019). A century of change in high school English assessments: A content analysis of 110 New York Regents Exams, 1900–2018. *Research in the Teaching of English, 54*(1), 31–57.

Li, X. (2010). Conceptual metaphor theory and teaching of English and Chinese idioms. *Journal of Language Teaching and Research, 1*(3), 206–210.

Long, E. (2003). *Book Clubs: Women and the Uses of Reading in Everyday Life*. Chicago, IL: University of Chicago Press.

Luttrell, W., & Parker, C. (2001). High school students' literacy practices and identities, and the figured world of school. *Journal of Research in Reading, 24*(3), 235–247.

Majors, Y. J. (2015). *Shoptalk: Lessons in Teaching from an African American Hair Salon*. New York, NY: Teachers College Press.

Manz, E. (2015). Representing student argumentation as functionally emergent from scientific activity. *Review of Educational Research, 85*(4), 553–590.

Mar, R. A., & Oatley, K. (2008). The function of fiction is the abstraction and simulation of social experience. *Perspectives on Psychological Science: A Journal of the Association for Psychological Science, 3*(3), 173–192.

Mar, R. A., Oatley, K., & Peterson, J. B. (2009). Exploring the link between reading fiction and empathy: Ruling out individual differences and examining outcomes. *Communications, 34*(4), 407–428.

Marin, A. M. (2013). *Learning to Attend and Observe: Parent-Child Meaning Making in the Natural World* (Unpublished doctoral dissertation). Northwestern University, Evanston, IL.

Marin, A. (2019). Seeing together: The ecological knowledge of indigenous families in Chicago urban forest walks. In: I. M. García-Sánchez, & M. Orellana (Eds.), *Everyday Learning: Leveraging Non-Dominant Youth Language and Culture in Schools* (pp. 41–58). New York, NY: Routledge.

Moje, E. B. (2015). Doing and teaching disciplinary literacy with adolescent learners: A social and cultural enterprise. *Harvard Educational Review, 85*(2), 254–278.

Moje, E. B., Overby, M., Tysvaer, N., & Morris, K. (2008). The complex world of adolescent literacy: Myths, motivations, and mysteries. *Harvard Educational Review, 78*(1), 107–154.

Morrell, E., & Duncan-Andrade, J. (2004). What they do learn in school: Hip-hop as a bridge to canonical poetry. In: J. Mahiri (Ed.), *What They Don't Learn in School: Literacy in the Lives of Urban Youth* (pp. 247–268). New York, NY: Peter Lang.

Morris, V. I. (2012). *The Readers' Advisory Guide to Street Literature*. Chicago, IL: American Library Association.

Morrison, T. (1988). *Unspeakable Things Unspoken: The Afro-American Presence in American Literature*. Lecture presented at the Tanner Lectures. Ann Arbor, MI: University of Michigan.

National Research Council. 2013. *Next Generation Science Standards: For States, By States*. Washington, DC: The National Academies Press. https://doi.org/10.17226/18290.

Nasir, N. S., & Hand, V. M. (2006). Exploring sociocultural perspectives on race, culture, and learning. *Review of Educational Research, 76*(4), 449–475. doi:10.3102/00346543076004449.

Nasir, N. S., Snyder, C. R., Shah, N., & Ross, K. M. (2012). Racial storylines and implications for learning. *Human Development, 55*(5–6), 285–301. doi:10.1159/000345318.

Nasir, Rosebery, A., Warren, B., & Lee, C. D. (2006). Learning as a cultural process: Achieving equity through diversity. In: K. Sawyer (Ed.), *The Cambridge Handbook of the Learning Sciences* (pp. 489–504). New York, NY: Cambridge University Press.

National Research Council (2000). *How People Learn: Brain, Mind, Experience, and School* (Expanded Edition). Washington, DC: The National Academies Press. doi:10.17226/9853.

National Research Council (2012). *A Framework for K–12 Science Education: Practices, Crosscutting Concepts, and Core Ideas*. Washington, DC: The National Academies Press. doi:10.17226/13165.

Newell, G. E., Bloome, D., & Hirvela, A. (2015). *Teaching and Learning Argumentative Writing in High School English Language Arts Classrooms*. New York, NY: Routledge.

Newell, G., Bloome, D., Hirvela, A. R., & Lin, T. J. (2019). *Dialogic Literary Argumentation in High School Language Arts Classrooms: A Social Perspective for Teaching, Learning, and Reading Literature*. New York, NY: Routledge.

Newell, G. E., Tallman, L., & Letcher, M. (2009). A longitudinal study of consequential transitions in the teaching of literature. *Research in the Teaching of English, 44*(1), 89–126.

Notez, C. (2017). The Black guy dies first: The importance of horror in Black culture - Blavity. Retrieved from https://blavity.com/black-guy-dies-first.

Ochs, E., Gonzales, P., & Jacoby, S. (1996). "When I come down I'm in the domain state": Grammar and graphic representation in the interpretive activity of physicists. *Studies in Interactional Sociolinguistics, 13*, 328–369.

Ochs, E., Taylor, C., Rudolph, D., & Smith, R. (1992). Storytelling as a theory-building activity. *Discourse Processes, 15*(1), 37–72. doi:10.1080/01638539209544801.

Ogonowski, M. S. (2008). Essay: Encouraging students' imagination. In: A. S. Rosebery, & B. Warren (Eds.), *Teaching Science to English Language Learners: Building on Students' Strengths*. Arlington, VA: NSTA Press.

Ojalehto, B. L., Medin, D. L., Horton, W. S., Garcia, S. G., & Kays, E. G. (2015). Seeing cooperation or competition: Ecological interactions in cultural perspectives. *Topics in Cognitive Science, 7*(4), 624–645.

Paris, D., & Alim, H. S. (Eds.) (2017). *Culturally Sustaining Pedagogies: Teaching and Learning for Justice in a Changing World*. New York, NY: Teachers College Press.

Peplow, D. (2016). *Talk about Books: A Study of Reading Groups*. New York, NY: Bloomsbury Publishing.

Polleck, J. N. (2010). Creating transformational spaces: High school book clubs with inner-city adolescent females. *The High School Journal, 93*(2), 50–68. Retrieved from JSTOR.

Price, S. D. (Ed.) (2013). *The Little Black Book of Writers' Wisdom*. New York, NY: Skyhorse Publishing.

Rabinowitz, P. J., Smith, M. W. (1998). *Authorizing Readers: Resistance and Respect in the Teaching of Literature*. New York, NY: Teachers College Press.

Rogoff, B. (2003). *The Cultural Nature of Human Development*. Oxford [UK], New York, NY: Oxford University Press.

Rogoff, B., Paradise, R., Arauz, R. M., Correa-Chávez, M., & Angelillo, C. (2003). Firsthand learning through intent participation. *Annual Review of Psychology, 54*(1), 175–203. doi:10.1146/annurev.psych.54.101601.145118.

Rosenblatt, L. M. (1982). The literary transaction: Evocation and response. *Theory into Practice, 21*(4), 268–277.

Samutina, N. (2017). Emotional landscapes of reading: Fan fiction in the context of contemporary reading practices. *International Journal of Cultural Studies, 20*(3), 253–269. doi:10.1177/1367877916628238.

Sandoval, W. A., Enyedy, N., Redman, E. H., & Xiao, S. (2019). Organising a culture of argumentation in elementary science. *International Journal of Science Education, 41*(13), 1848–1869. doi:10.1080/09500693.2019.1641856.

Schleppegrell, M. J. (2004). *The Language of Schooling: A Functional Linguistics Perspective*. New York, NY: Routledge.

Schwarz, C. V., Reiser, B. J., Davis, E. A., Kenyon, L., Acher, A., Fortus, D., Shwartz, Y., Hug, B., & Krajcik, J. (2009). Developing a learning progression for scientific modeling: Making scientific modeling accessible and meaningful for learners. *Journal of Research in Science Teaching, 46*(6), 632–654.

Scipio, D. A. (2015). *Developing Mentors: Adult Participation, Practices, and Learning in an Out-of-School Time STEM Program* (Doctoral dissertation). University of Washington, Seattle, Washington.

Shklovsky, V. (1991). *Theory of Prose*. Normal, IL: Dalkey Archive Press.

Slezak, E., & Atwood, M. (1995). *The Book Group Book: A Thoughtful Guide to Forming and Enjoying a Stimulating Book Discussion Group*. Chicago, IL: Chicago Review Press.

Smith, J. P., diSessa, A. A., & Roschelle, J. (1993). Misconceptions reconceived: A constructivist analysis of knowledge in transition. *The Journal of the Learning Sciences, 3*(2), 115–163.

Sosa, T., Hall, A. H., Goldman, S. R., & Lee, C. D. (2016). Developing symbolic interpretation through literary argumentation. *Journal of the Learning Sciences, 25*(1), 93–132.

Squire, J. R. (1964). *The Responses of Adolescents While Reading Four Short Stories* (2, pp. 1–65). Champaign, IL: National Council of Teachers of English.

Stevens, R., Wineburg, S., Herrenkohl, L. R., & Bell, P. (2005). Comparative understanding of school subjects: Past, present, and future. *Review of Educational Research, 75*(2), 125–157. doi:10.3102/00346543075002125.

Tanner, G. W. (1907). Report of the committee appointed by the English conference to inquire into the teaching of English in the high schools of the Middle West. *The School Review, 15*(1), 32–45.

Thunberg, G. (2018, November). *The Disarming Case to Act Right Now on Climate*. Video file. Retrieved from https://www.ted.com/talks/greta_thunberg_the_disarming_case_to_act_right_now:on_climate?language=en.

Tosenberger, C. (2008). Homosexuality at the online Hogwarts: Harry Potter slash fanfiction. *Children's Literature, 36*(1), 185–207. doi:10.1353/chl.0.0017.

Toulmin, S. (2003). *The Uses of Argument*. Cambridge, UK; New York, NY: Cambridge University Press.

van Eemeren, F. H. (2010). *Strategic Maneuvering in Argumentative Discourse: Extending the Pragma-Dialectical Theory of Argumentation*. Amsterdam: John Benjamins Publishing.

van Eemeren, F. H., & Garssen, B. (2015). *Scrutinizing Argumentation in Practice*. Amsterdam: John Benjamins Publishing Company.

Varelas, M., Pappas, C. C., Kane, J. M., Arsenault, A., Hankes, J., & Cowan, B. M. (2008). Urban primary-grade children think and talk science: Curricular and instructional practices that nurture participation and argumentation. *Science Education, 92*(1), 65–95.

Weyand, L., Goff, B., & Newell, G. (2018). The social construction of warranting evidence in two classrooms. *Journal of Literacy Research, 50*(1), 97–122.

Wilhelm, J. D., & Smith, M. W. (2016). The power of pleasure reading: What we can learn from the secret reading lives of teens. *English Journal, 105*, 25–30.

Wolfe, P. (2013). The settler complex: An introduction. *American Indian Culture and Research Journal, 37*(2), 1–22. doi:10.17953/aicr.37.2.c250832434701728.

Zyngier, S., & Fialho, O. (2010). Pedagogical stylistics, literary awareness and empowerment: A critical perspective. *Language and Literature, 19*(1), 13–33.

9
CULTURE AND BIOLOGY IN LEARNING DISABILITIES RESEARCH

Legacies and Possible Futures[1]

Alfredo J. Artiles, David Rose, Taucia González, and Aydin Bal

The purpose of this chapter is to provide a critical overview of research on learning disabilities (LD) with an eye on the intersections of biology and culture and offer reflections for future interdisciplinary research. We selected LD because this population represents the largest group with disabilities in the U.S.—seven million students were served in 2018 in special education programs in the U.S.; 34% had LDs (USDOE, 2018). Although the LD definition covers broader language difficulties, reading disabilities comprise the largest proportion. The percentage of students diagnosed with reading disabilities varies significantly due to variability in definitions, identification criteria, and methods (e.g., statistical cut-off scores). For these reasons, we prioritized research on reading and LDs with occasional references to dyslexia research. We also covered studies framed with a broader literacy lens.

Before we develop our arguments, a word on the uses of terms central to this chapter. There is considerable variance in the definitions and uses of these terms—most prominently "learning disabilities," "reading disabilities," and "dyslexia." For reasons explored in the text, we, like many others, have difficulties with each of these three terms. Unless otherwise noted, we will use the terms as they are used most commonly, although certainly not consistently, in the literature from the various overlapping research and clinical fields, and especially within the various research papers we will cite throughout. Thus, we will use "learning disability" as it is defined in the IDEA regulations. Please note, however, that we will argue later that the use of that term is highly problematic in its application. Second, we will use "reading disability" as it is most commonly used, as a label for the large and diverse category of students who have an "unexpected" specific difficulty in learning to read that is not a consequence primarily of ineffective or inappropriate instruction. This would ordinarily include students with the label of dyslexia, but also the full spectrum of other significant reading difficulties that range from hyperlexia to alexia. Finally, we will use "dyslexia" as defined by the International Dyslexia Association 2020:

> a specific learning disability that is neurobiological in origin. It is characterized by difficulties with accurate and/or fluent word recognition and by poor spelling and decoding abilities. These difficulties typically result from a deficit in the phonological component of language that is often unexpected in relation to other cognitive abilities and the provision of effective classroom instruction.

That is a smaller class of individuals than the much larger group of those called "reading disabled." Note, however, that we will argue, based on current research trends, that it is more accurate, and effective, to define dyslexia not as *neurobiological* but as *bio-cultural* in origin.

The charge to write a chapter on the interface of biology and culture in LD research constitutes a unique opportunity and challenge. For starters, we welcome the inclusion of this subject in the handbook because LD, and disability in general, are under-represented in most learning sciences handbooks and sociocultural learning research volumes. We deliberated about the most productive approach to build a cogent storyline. The story about biology and culture embodies tensions between *what is* the canon in LD research and *what it could be* when we consider the biology-culture interface. The normative LD perspective has emphasized the individual as the unit of analysis that foregrounds psychological factors, mainly targeting student deficits. A biological basis has been assumed throughout the history of LD, though this evidence is relatively recent and must be interpreted cautiously. Moreover, the idea of culture has been taken up in this field in problematic ways and LD researchers have not systematically examined the interdependencies of biology and culture.

We argue LD requires an interdisciplinary framing using a *bio-cultural* perspective (Cole & Packer, 2016). We define bio-culture as:

> The effects of a series of interconnected feed-downward (culture- and context-driven) and feed-upward (neurobiology driven) interactive processes and developmental plasticity at different levels (hence, cross-level) are continuously accumulated via the individual's moment-to-moment experiences (hence, dynamic) so that, together, they implement concerted biological and cultural influences (hence, biocultural coconstructivism) in tuning cognitive and behavioral development throughout the life span.
>
> *(Li, 2003, p. 171)*

We view learning as having social origins since "all higher psychological functions are internalized relationships of the social kind" (John-Steiner & Mahn, 1996, p. 192). A corollary is that people develop through "changing participation in the sociocultural activities of their communities, which also change" (Rogoff, 2003, p. 36). Therefore, goal-oriented, collective activity systems constitute the unit of analysis. A significant implication is that learning ought to be studied beyond psychological traits; that is, in the interactional contexts and institutional settings in which individuals participate. In this paradigm, LD is not located in individuals and the focus is on difference and variation rather than deficit, holding that "a child whose development is impeded by a defect is not simply a child less developed than his peers but is a child who has developed differently" (Rieber & Carton, 1993, p. 30).

A complementary tenet is that learning is *mediated* by ideal (beliefs, values, theories) and material (print, charts, lists) artifacts that have cultural origins. This means that developmental aspects regarded as universal, such as voluntary attention and attention management in mother–child interactions or learning to read and write, are considered culturally mediated (Chavajay & Rogoff, 1999). In this view, "reading text is an elaboration of the preexisting ability to 'read the world' using signs of various kinds" (Cole, 1996, p. 272). Thus, addressing learning difficulties should be framed as enabling students to *mediate* their *participation* in activities (e.g., reading text) in new ways (i.e., alternative forms of cultural re-mediation). Learning technologies can provide new kinds of options that allow and encourage greater diversity in the ways that students, especially those who have been disabled in traditional schooling environments, can re-mediate and customize their own participation. Vygotsky argued that while an impairment created social conditions that were limiting, these difficulties created alternate pathways for child development processes that compensated for the impairment (Smagorinsky, 2012). Vygotsky examined not only the performance of children with disabilities in tasks, but also how children actively modified the stimulus situations and resolved them using auxiliary artifacts or through the help of more competent others (Vygodskaya, 1999).

Thus, people with disabilities were positioned as active agents who controlled or modified both their behaviors and their immediate environment (Vygotsky, 1978).

A *situated perspective* is required to understand the cultural nature of learning in populations with disabilities. A situated research perspective is guided by questions that, "(1) do not reify culture in terms of specific behavioral or attitudinal characteristics; (2) do not isolate cultural particularities from the economic, social, political, and historical contexts in which they appear and function, but rather take these contexts into account; and (3) recognize cultural adaptation and improvisation" (Paradise, 2002, p. 230). A situated approach empowers researchers to transcend stereotypical and deficit-laden models of individual differences, including LD. It requires examining learning as mediated by the three layers of culture (Gallego et al., 2001): *what students bring* to classrooms (constituted by the cultural repertoires forged through their adaptive history of participation across settings and communities); *what is already there* (i.e., the institutional culture of schooling); and the cultural classroom practices fashioned through participation in routine interactions over time. A powerful implication is that people *use, reproduce and produce* cultural practices, which dispels deterministic views of cultural identities and communities (Artiles, 2015) and opens a theoretical space to account for individual adaptation through multiple pathways (Lee, 2010). In this regard, Lee (2017) summarized findings from cultural neuroscience by Han et al.: "categorizing people by pan ethnic identities (e.g., Chinese Americans and Chinese from the Mainland) does not account for differences in [neural] processing, suggesting rather it is the actual participation in routine practices over time that counts" (p. 101).

In order to deepen these analyses, learning is viewed as embedded in multiple time scales. Vygotsky (1978) suggested that individual development (ontogeny) is the emergent outcome of processes of phylogenetic, cultural-historical, and micro-genetic time scales. Moreover, Vygotsky theorized development occurring on two axes, one being natural, what one is born with, the other being cultural, what one learns through social practice (Kozulin & Gindis, 2007). While a child could be born with a physical or intellectual impairment (the natural axis), he/she could compensate on the cultural axis by developing higher mental functions through the appropriation of cultural tools. It is also a possibility that the cultural axis does not provide the opportunities for such a cultural appropriation of higher mental tools. For this reason, Vygotsky placed heavy emphasis on re-mediating social contexts.

This theorization of learning is aligned with contemporary neuroscience research demonstrating that the brain's potential is not simply a matter of preprogramed specialized modules, but depends crucially on culturally organized experience (Ambady & Bharucha as cited in Cole & Packer, 2016). Indeed, culture and biology are braided (Lee, 2010). Thus, we envision development as constituted by bio-cultural influences (Li, 2003). A cultural neuroscientific approach enables us to "investigate and characterize the mechanisms by which [the] hypothesized bidirectional, mutual constitution of culture, brain, and genes occurs" (Chiao & Ambady, 2007, p. 238).

We will outline our vision on the cultural foundations of learning and LD to make visible the theoretical distance between our perspective and the canonical view of LD, which we summarize in the next section. We expect this contrast will stimulate discussions about possible future research directions. We will then sketch research trends concerned with the biological substrates of LD, with an emphasis on brain research, and provide a synopsis of research grounded in the cultural foundations of learning, which we describe as a sociocultural approach. We will close with a few reflections about future research.

Setting the Context

Beneath the Skin and Between the Ears: The Limits of Traditional LD Research

The first part of this section's title is borrowed from Mehan's (1993) seminal study on LD identification. The title encapsulates persistent threads in the history of this research, namely, a concern

Culture and Biology in Learning Disabilities

with the biological substrates of this condition and the privileging of a psychological paradigm. These emphases are represented in the federal government definition of LD (USOE, 1977, p. 65083):

> a disorder in one or more of the basic psychological processes involved in understanding or in using language, spoken or written, that may manifest itself in the imperfect ability to listen, think, speak, read, write, spell, or to do mathematical calculations, including conditions such as perceptual disabilities, brain injury, minimal brain dysfunction, dyslexia, and developmental aphasia.
>
> [LD] does not include learning problems that are primarily the result of visual, hearing, or motor disabilities, of intellectual disability, of emotional disturbance, or of environmental, cultural, or economic disadvantage.

Although the term LD was coined in the 1960s, the attention to its biological underpinnings dates back to the 1800s, including research with soldiers and patients and post mortem studies mapping links between specific brain areas and language disorders (e.g., various types of aphasia). Other biological explanations included mixed brain dominance that affected reading and writing (Hallahan, Pullen, & Ward, 2013). Similarly, reading disorders have been assumed to have congenital and hereditary connections. But it was not until the last few decades that we have witnessed a systematic accumulation of evidence about biological correlates. This work, as we will explain in a subsequent section, must be assessed cautiously. LD is also considered a secondary condition—i.e., comorbid to other developmental disorders (e.g., attention deficit disorder, emotional disorders) (Grigorenko et al., 2019).

The dual attention to the brain and psychological processes has shaped the development of many interventions prescribed for this population—e.g., early approaches that prescribed learning environments with minimal simuli, sensory interventions. However, psychological processes are at the heart of LD conceptions. We should also note that the notion of LD has been contested throughout its history. The recurrent debates about the definition, identification procedures, and prevalence of LD (Hallahan et al., 2013) reflect this point. Although the discrepancy model (distance between aptitude and actual achievement) dominated for many years, definitional controversies are still visible as the field has transitioned to systemwide approaches—multi-tiered systems of support (MTSS), and response to intervention (RTI).

Cultural considerations have been present in complicated ways throughout the history of LD. At the field's official inception in the 1960s, middle-class white parents advocated for their children and secured support from the academy to name the condition, get policies approved, and obtain funding for services and research. LD represented a less stigmatizing category than intellectual disabilities, which had been historically associated with poverty and minoritized groups, particularly African Americans. Eventually, LD lost its appeal and the prevalence of this condition soared, thus getting increasingly entangled with superficial proxies of culture—race, social class, language background.

Cultural considerations are also visible in the context of equity concerns surrounding identification, specifically, racial and linguistic disparities in LD identification at the national, state, and district levels, particularly Native American and African American learners (Artiles, Dorn, & Bal, 2016). The problem is that white students with LD may benefit from academic supports and legal rights and protections that come with an LD diagnosis. On the other hand, the LD label may mean further marginalization for students from racially minoritized communities because of segregated placements, fewer related services, and reduced access to educational opportunities compared to their white counterparts with the same diagnosis (Skiba et al., 2008).

Problematic cultural considerations in LD research are reflected in the following points (Artiles et al., 2016, 2010):

1. Culture is regarded as static and group cohesion is emphasized—e.g., all Native Americans share and pass to younger generations fossilized cultural codes; African Americans have a collectivist orientation—at the expense of within-group heterogeneity. This perspective is also applied to institutions, so it is assumed that the monolithic cultures of school and home are discontinuous.
2. Socialization into a culture is emphasized in a narrow way. For instance, the cultural toolkits and repertoires that people acquire in their communities *determine* their "way of life"—i.e., what they think and do and how they feel and believe. In this view, culture is regarded as an independent variable that leads to stereotyped perceptions or is simply treated as a covariate.
3. Culture is equated with demographic markers (e.g., race, class) and it is often applied with a deficit lens that stigmatizes minoritized groups, using backward notions such as "culture of poverty." Note, however, that this perspective tends to be applied to non-white groups. Thus, some researchers have reported that the cultures of certain groups lack on various metrics— e.g., vocabulary, grammatical structures, and the like. On the one hand, LD research tends to use this deficit perspective on culture; on the other hand, the federal definition specifies that "[LD] does not include learning problems that are primarily the result of…environmental, cultural, or economic disadvantage." This apparent contradiction likely creates dilemmas for practitioners when making referral, assessment, and eligibility decisions.
4. The link between culture and learning is underspecified in most LD studies.
5. The integration of the biological and cultural lines of development is practically nonexistent in this knowledge base.

Although there has been poor integration of cultural considerations with biological dimensions, there is a growing interest in the biological turn in the LD field. Biological explanations and solutions are being sought out, but is there empirical support behind these expectations and what are we learning about the interdependencies of biology and culture?

Biology and Culture in LD research

The Changing Neuroscience of Reading and Its Disabilities

For decades researchers and practitioners have assumed that the persistent difficulties that some students experience in learning to read are neurologically based, that their difficulties in responding effectively to normal, and even intensive, instruction is the result of defects or abnormalities in their brains. As a result, they are *diagnosed* as having a specific disability, a neurological condition that, like cerebral palsy, will require different expectations and treatments than other children, even than "garden variety" poor readers.

That view received its first significant research support in the work of Galaburda and colleagues (1985). Based on a post-mortem analysis of the brains of a handful of adults with dyslexia, they reported the discovery of abnormal patterns of neuronal migration in the cortex. Since that time, hundreds of researchers have shown that, without question, the brains of individuals with dyslexia are significantly different than the brains of individuals with typical ranges of reading abilities. One key question, however, has proven challenging: While it is now clear that the brains of individuals with significant reading difficulties (i.e., those labeled as dyslexic but also the wider range of those labeled as reading disabled, see earlier) are *different* than their peers, is it correct to describe their brains as defective, damaged, abnormal? The answer to that question is often pivotal in determining policies and practices throughout the world. For several decades the defective neurology view has predominated in both theory and practice, but that is now changing.

For one thing, Galaburda et al.'s findings have recently been challenged. Using contemporary methods, more representative subjects, and a stronger research design, Guidi et.al. (2018) failed to replicate Galaburda's findings. More broadly, moreover, a recent research review concluded that "there is no evidence to support the commonly held view that there is something wrong with the brains of children who have great difficulty learning to read. We suggest that dyslexia is best viewed as one of many expressions of ordinary ubiquitous individual differences in normal developmental outcomes. Thus, terms such as 'dysfunctional' or 'abnormal' are not justified when referring to the brains of persons with dyslexia" (Protopapas & Parrila, 2018, p. 61). We should reiterate here that these conclusions are based on reviews of studies of children who have a diagnosis of reading disability or dyslexia precisely because they have had access to robust reading instruction but experienced significant difficulty or failure in learning to read nonetheless. Whether that instruction was properly differentiated to match their individual differences remains a question.

There is still some vigorous debate in response to Protopapas and Parrila's review, but both neuroscientists and reading researchers have increasingly adopted a less categorical or pathological view of reading disability in favor of one that emphasizes a normal spectrum where "there is nothing but a continuous distribution of reading skill, with an enormous range of individual differences" (Protopapas & Parrila, 2018, p. 64).

What Causes the Observed Differences in the Brains of Individuals With Reading Disabilities?

While the differences in the brains of individuals that are labeled with reading disabilities generally, or dyslexia specifically, may not be pathological, they are very significant and consequential. An important research—and pedagogical—question is: "What are the sources of those differences?"

Genetic variants that are associated with reading disability are common in the general population—many people have the gene variants who do not have a reading disability and many people who have a reading disability do not have the genetic markers. Among children with a high genetic risk for reading disability only one third to one half will actually be later diagnosed with reading disability. Bishop (2015) recently concluded: "dyslexia…appears to involve combined effects of many genes and environmental factors, each of which has a small influence…and there is no sharp dividing line between normality and abnormality. The cut-off between 'dyslexia' and normality is arbitrary" (Bishop, 2015, p. 1806).

Research in the emerging "social neurosciences" has already demonstrated the profound impacts of diverse cultural contexts on the extended ontogeny of the human brain, affecting how the brain perceives its world, responds cognitively and emotionally to it, and prioritizes its attention and effort. Certainly, one part of that cultural shaping and sculpting of the brain is the development of the "reading brain."

Post-Gutenberg humans have had to kluge together a "reading brain" from the spare parts inherited from their ancestors, most of whom had no access to, or need for, literacy until the printing press "democratized" reading by making texts more universally accessible and more essential. While there are many interconnected parts of the brain that work together for successful reading, both semiotic meaning code breaking and meaning-making beyond the printed word and text-based, it may be instructive to briefly examine the research on one critical functionality—the ability to recognize single words. The ability to recognize the "code" of written language is obviously foundational to all of the higher levels of making meaning from written texts. Many researchers have shown that one of the areas of the brain that is critical for this basic aspect of reading lies in the inferior temporal lobe and is now called the Visual Word Form Area (the VWFA Black et al., 2017). This area fails to "light up" in neuroimaging among individuals who have dyslexia-type reading disabilities. As a result, many researchers have focused on the VWFA as one of the key sources of reading disability and have discovered significant differences in its anatomy, physiology, and functionality that distinguish "good" readers from "poor" ones (Black et al., 2017; Xia, Hancock, & Hoeft, 2017). This finding is one of the most fundamental in the research on reading and its disabilities: the anatomy and physiology of this very "low-level" component of the reading brain are clearly different between those who read well and those who don't (e.g., dyslexics).

What researchers have also shown is that the VWFA is not an inherited part of our biology, but emerges and differentiates only in cultures with written forms of literacy. In the few remaining cultures that have no written language, the same area of cortex functions primarily for recognizing other highly complex visual stimuli like faces, objects, places—not words. The VWFA develops as a key part of the reading network only within cultures with written language; thus, it is as much a cultural artifact as a biological one (for full discussion, see Chyl et al., 2018; Huettig, et al., 2018; Wise Younger et al., 2017).

But for our purposes, the most important question is what happens to the VWFA when students with reading disabilities undergo successful reading interventions? Does the brain change? A considerable body of research now shows that successful interventions do indeed change the anatomy, physiology, and functionality of areas like the VWFA. For example, fMRI studies have repeatedly shown that successful interventions activate the under-activated core reading areas like the VWFA (Chyl et al., 2018; Horowitz-Kraus et al., 2014).

The VWFA is but one part of the reading brain. In fact, recent researchers have vastly extended the areas of the brain that are involved in the full spectrum of reading ability (i.e., beyond single word decoding) and thus, also in the full spectrum of reading disabilities (Edwards et al., 2018). Most importantly, recent brain studies have shown that successful interventions change both physiology and anatomy broadly throughout the extended reading networks, including the prefrontal cortex, the right hemisphere, and in medial areas (cingulate cortex and insula) as well (e.g., Barquero, Davis, & Cutting, 2014). Researchers have interpreted these changes not as "normalization" but as *compensation*—the reading disabled reader's brain is compensating for weaknesses by recruiting new areas of the brain into a different kind of reading network. This suggests there is great diversity in the parts of the brain that reading requires, and great diversity among individuals in the kinds of reading brains they develop. As a result, Pennington et al. (2012), among others, have argued that our methods of reading instruction and enculturation should be more diverse rather than standardized.

Interventions drawing from brain research such as UDL (Universal Design for Learning) are still in the early phase. Most studies focus on implementation—can teachers and learning designers effectively apply UDL principles to ensure that the full diversity of their students—including those with reading disabilities—are provided with effective alternatives to reduce the typical barriers they face in poorly designed learning environments. Several recent reviews of the research show evidence that teachers and designers are in fact able to apply the principles effectively (Seok, DaCosta, & Hodges, 2018).

For some groups of students, those who are blind or physically impaired for example, the face validity of the changed outcomes in both participation and outcomes are so striking that few research studies have been undertaken. For students with specific reading disabilities, however, there is a small number of experimental studies. For example, Hall et al. (2015) examined the effects of a UDL-designed online reading environment on both engagement (one of the principles) and comprehension scores. They found significant growth both in comprehension outcomes and engagement, and the improvements were especially large for students with reading disabilities. Of significance, students with reading disabilities reported the design features and scaffolds more helpful than their typically achieving peers. Similar findings for engagement and production have been reported for writing (Dalton & Rose, 2015).

To conclude, recent brain research with individuals who have been diagnosed with reading disabilities like dyslexia provide support for our bio-cultural perspective—i.e., cultural practices are linked to brain structures and physiology; reading interventions have an impact on brain activity

Culture and Biology in Learning Disabilities

that reflects compensatory responses to build new reading networks. Next, we shift the focus from biology to the design of learning contexts for LD students. We cover studies grounded in the cultural foundations of learning, which we describe as sociocultural LD research.

Of Mind and Social Practices: Sociocultural LD Research

The number of studies utilizing sociocultural instructional approaches stands in stark contrast with the wealth of LD intervention research that is informed by psychological (and increasingly) neuscience models of learning. Traditional reading instruction for students with LDs tends to frame learning as individual learners' performance in discrete literacy tasks such as early reading skills (e.g., decoding). However, LD research has also been conducted on reading comprehension, mathematics and writing (see Grigorenko et al., 2019 for an overview). This framing does not account for cultural aspects such as "competent" and "smart" as socially-historically-spatially constructed notions (Gresalfi et al., 2009; Hatt, 2012).

Sociocultural studies on LD constitute a heterogenous knowledge base in which the focus of analysis ranges from individual student learning processes situated in systems of participation in classrooms, to studies of students with LDs across sociocultural contexts and equity interventions to promote systemic changes in identification disability practices and educational opportunities. Thus, we group this work in terms of their foci on student learning and systemic change. Many studies use small samples and rely on qualitative methods.

Focus on Student Learning: Classroom Based Research

This work includes the design of learning environments that target either student dyads/small groups or systems of participation that apprentice learners into literacy practices. Studies draw from a broad sociocultural perspective, though they engage in disparate ways with core propositions from this approach. Peer mediated approaches, for instance, rely less on learners' repertoires of cultural practices and more on specific participation structures that stress collaboration and peer mediation.

Peer-mediated Approaches

Collaborative strategic reading (CSR) is a multi-component reading strategy that incorporates four reading comprehension strategies. Though CSR has been used in pairs, it is commonly used in small groups of students that take on different roles in order to accomplish the collaborative task of engaging in text by a) previewing and predicting, b) monitoring their comprehension during reading using a click and clunk strategy, c) identifying main ideas by providing the gist of the reading, and d) after reading summarizing key ideas (Vaughn, Klingner, & Bryant, 2001).

CSR has been used in classrooms that have diverse abilities and with Spanish-dominant Latinx students (Vaughn et al., 2001). The flexibility of this model allowed Latinx students to work together using English and Spanish as learning resources even when the grade level text was in English. Latinx middle school students showed significant comprehension gains after 15 sessions. Perhaps, just as notably, students trained in CSR were then able to teach younger students with LD on how to use comprehension strategies with minimal adult involvement. This highlights the promise of collective zones of proximal development where youth can support each other in developing comprehension strategies.

Klingner, Vaughn, and Schumm (1998) noted that fourth-grade students over-relied on initiation-response-evaluation discourse patterns, so they subsequently revised the procedures in order for students to have more opportunity to engage in high-level discussions. Although all students showed greater reading and social studies content gains than their peers in the control group after eleven sessions, the results for students with LD (n = 8) were not statistically significant, even though the LD students in the experimental group showed greater content gains compared to the control group. Small sample size and length of intervention might explain these results.

Apprenticeship Approaches

These approaches were designed to orchestrate productive ways of participation that leverage particular interactional patterns to promote student learning. One of the early literacy models was the optimal learning environment (OLE) project. The first study consisted of a year-long ethnographic study of bilingual Latinx students with LDs in urban and rural schools followed by collaborative work with teachers to learn assets-based instructional strategies (Ruiz, 1995; Ruiz & Figueroa, 1995). The OLE project relied on a social constructivist paradigm in ways that provided students with choices in learning, gave authentic opportunities to engage in literacy tasks (e.g., letter writing, book authoring), and held high expectations for what children were capable of doing. Literacy was framed first as a meaning-making process, focusing on ideas first, then mechanics. The reconfiguration of pedagogical practices demonstrated academic gains of about one grade-level for the students that had participated for a year.

In the Early Literacy Project (ELP) (Englert & Mariage, 1996), students with and without LDs in schools located in urban, low-socioeconomic communities, collaborated in meaningful literacy tasks that involved connected reading, writing, speaking, and listening through an apprenticeship model (Englert et al., 1995). Classroom discourse and social interaction were key mediational tools for learning. Curricular activities included partner reading and writing, oral storytelling, morning messages, journal writing, and sharing from the author's chair. ELP longitudinal data showed that 18 of the 19 students with LD that participated in two years of ELP instruction in primary grades maintained gains within two years of starting the program and after summer break.

These studies examined how individual learners learned through and in social contexts (Gutiérrez & Stone, 1997). Students had frequent opportunities to use new literacy tools in the context of social interactions with supports from peers and adults, and eventually appropriated the literacy tools to perform in individual tasks.

Bertrand, Durand, and González (2017) used youth participatory action research for youth with and without LDs to appropriate the tools of social scientists with the support of adult researchers in an afterschool club at a school serving predominantly Latinx youth in the Southwest. Fifteen seventh- and eighth-grade students were invited to partipate to engage in action research and pursue social change. In the re-mediated literacy space, youth were able to engage in critical fiction and non-fiction texts, redefined their roles as learners and contributors interactionally, and worked together to produce and disseminate knowedge about their school to their teachers and administrators. The researchers examined how youth (and adult) participation changed over the course of an academic year. They found that youth appropriated the literacy tools of research, not to increase achievement, but rather to challenge power structures in their school. For instance, young adult literature served as a critical tool to explore power imbalances that characters encountered, but then participants shifted focus to their own school experiences. Second, the youth began interacting in ways that voiced a vision for reorganized power relations between adults and youth.

Collins (2011; 2012) aimed to understand disability through an examination of how contexts and individuals shape each other. This multi-year study was conducted in a school with a high percentage of English learners located in a border region of the southwestern U.S. Collins supported teachers using multimodal literacy to design instruction for first through fifth graders. Focusing on a micro-genetic time scale (moment-to-moment), Collins targeted Christopher, a student with emotional disturbance and learning difficulties, to document his shifting positions and identities during literacy instruction that shaped alternative roles in the classroom learning community. Christopher's teacher attributed his learning difficulties to a possible LD. Collins documented the role of contexts in shaping academic opportunities and risks. For example, when Christopher was presented with an opportunity to engage in multimodal forms of literacy as his class prepared to perform fables, his role of costume designer allowed others to see his competence in contributing to a literacy project.

Other scholars (Lambert, 2015; McCloskey, 2005; 2012; McDermott, 1993; Varenne & McDermott, 2018) have contributed ethnographic understandings of how literacy contexts shape learning opportunities. Lambert (2015) examined how smartness in math literacy was constructed through participation, and McClosley (2012) conducted a multi-year ethnographic study that captured a student's shift to understanding literacy as a problem-solving process. McDermott and colleagues conducted 18 months of ethnographic observations of Adam, a nine-year-old with LD across multiple contexts. The researchers focused on how people across contexts organized practices in ways that made Adam's LD more or less apparent (classroom, fieldtrips, after school activities) through interpersonal choreographies and the organization of activity and resources to support students like Adam. This ethnographic work adds sociocultural texture to studies that only provide distal test scores obtained at the end of a lesson, unit, or academic year. Of significance, this research illuminates the affordances and constraints of learning environments and has the potential to inform the design of learning opportunities for students with LD.

Universal Design for Learning (UDL)

UDL is a framework for the design of learning environments that takes advantage of advances in learning sciences and modern learning technologies (Meyer, Rose, & Gordon, 2014; Rose et al., 2014). Although UDL was not conceptualized using the cultural foundations of learning, its basic tenets and practices align with a sociocultural perspective.

UDL incorporates a contemporary understanding of individual differences informed by modern neuroscience; it assumes that individuals are diverse and dynamic along many spectra or dimensions. For instance, UDL recognizes that individuals with reading disabilities display a wide spectrum of dis/abilities that range from hyperlexia (extraordinarily strong word recognition but weak comprehension) through dyslexia (weak decoding but strong language comprehension) to alexia (essentially no word recognition). Even though each falls into the category of reading disability, it seems very clear that interventions would have to be very different (Dalton & Rose, 2015; Hall et al., 2015). Often in schools they are not. Grounded in the neurosciences, UDL also takes the view that reading is much more complex than the simple dichotomy of decoding and comprehension abilities. Informed by brain research on cognition and learning, UDL uses three design principles (Meyer et al., 2014).

1. **Multiple means of representation**. There is great diversity in people's capabilities (and their underlying neurology) to take in information from the outside world and make sense of that information based on prior learning. No one would imagine that making knowledge available in one way would work equally well for a dyslexic student versus a hyperlexic one. No one would imagine that presenting information the same way for all students would be an optimal or even successful technique (the case of blind students makes this quite obvious but the same holds across all the spectra of individual differences. UDL pro-actively plans to use multiple means of representation, for equity and access to learning.

2. **Multiple means of action and expression**. No one would think that asking all students to write an essay would provide an opportunity for students with executive function weaknesses to demonstrate their knowledge equitably if planning, organizing, and producing an essay (without some kinds of scaffolds or supports) were the only ways to demonstrate their knowledge. UDL

guidelines recommend using multiple means of expression (including graduated scaffolds and supports, but also alternative media, also with scaffolding available) as important ways to ensure that the means of expression are diverse enough to accommodate all students.

3. **Multiple means of engagement**. The last decade has seen an explosion of interest by both neuroscientists and educators in the emotional and affective underpinnings of learning (Immordino-Yang, Darling-Hammond, & Krone, 2019). As a result, it is naïve to assume that all students can be engaged in the same ways. The very things that most engage students on the ADHD spectrum are threatening to students on the autism spectrum. UDL principles recommend providing not one means of engaging students but multiple means to meet the normal challenge of diversity.

UDL is a more equitable approach to educating the diversity of our children, especially those designated as disabled. UDL has made progress in emphasizing that educators should first examine whether it is the school's disabilities that are limiting a child's progress rather than the child's neurological differences. But the UDL approach has been criticized for its failure to address cultural diversity (Waitoller & Thorius, 2016). This criticism, now a focus of research and development, is what will make UDL a truly bio-cultural approach.

Changing the culture of schooling to make it more effective will require much greater individualization and customization to match the real diversity of children, including those with potential reading disabilities. That will require not only recognizing diversity—in both children and media—but encouraging and celebrating it. That is a cultural change, not a technical one.

Focus on Systemic Change: Using an Institutional Lens for Equity Purposes

We identified research that shifts the analytic focus from student learning to the transformation of school culture and systems. This body of work transcends the documentation of profiles of learners and places the notion of LD at the intersection of the technical, historical, and organizational contexts of institutions. The research is generally linked to equity concerns germane to LD identification or educational opportunity (e.g., racial disparities in identification, restrictiveness of placement, access to services, transition to college).

We characterize this scholarship as fugitive because it has been produced in the context of technical assistance (TA) centers/projects and it is often disseminated outside of research journals and academy circles. We illustrate this research strand with our work at the National Center for Culturally Responsive Educational Systems (NCCRESt) (Klingner et al., 2005) and the Learning Lab (Bal, 2018). We re-conceptualized TA as the design of mediating structures to improve the identification of students with disabilities, while being mindful of equity considerations. These initiatives share the following theoretical and methodological assumptions and approaches:

1. A cultural historical unit of analysis is used, which assumes the institutional dimension of human acting and thinking envelops individual and interpersonal layers (Cole, 1996).
2. Disability is conceptualized as a bio-cultural system that encompasses individual, institutional, and interactional planes of analysis.
3. TA and other interventions are designed as *mediating structures* in which new artifacts and practices are used to examine systematically aspects of schooling and its infrastructure that impact educational equity, such as racial disparities in LD identification.
4. Artifacts and practices were designed to re-mediate local actors' understandings of the issues they intended to change. The artifacts opened new perspectives to frame a problem and raised the need to account for social, spatial, and temporal contexts. For instance, NCCRESt provided TA and professional development to reduce the disproportionate representation of minoritized students in special education (Kozleski & Artiles, 2015). The center created

Culture and Biology in Learning Disabilities

interactive GIS national, state, and city maps by year with the distribution of LD prevalence in schools, school poverty level, enrollment by race and other cultural categories. States with sustained engagement (quarterly meetings, ongoing coaching, site visits, professional learning) pursued changes in policy, enhanced statewide professional learning, studies of change in everyday practices, and changes in monitoring and identification of disproportionality. Bal (2018) also produced comparable maps in his Learning Lab work. These artifacts represented the fluid, temporally and spatially situated nature of racial disparities in LD identification, illustrating, for instance, how certain neighborhoods with more resources had a higher probability for the racialization of disability (Artiles, 2019). Other artifacts included referral rates by grade, teacher or year, curriculum materials, school policies, classroom participation structures, assumptions about competence, and good behavior. Parents' views on opportunity and outcome disparities were also compiled.

5. The TA model as mediating structure required local actors to convene on a regular basis to analyze the target problem. These meetings entailed iterative cycles of inquiry, reflection, and action that led to systemic change, including collective expansive actions (Sannino, Engeström, & Lemos, 2016). For instance, the Learning Lab model was implemented at five public schools in Wisconsin (Bal, 2018). The project united African American, Latino, refugee and low-income parents and students, teachers, administrators, community representatives, and university-based researchers. Learning Lab members collectively examined racial disparities in disability identification, engaged in historical and empirical root cause analyses, mapped out the existing system, and designed a new schoolwide behavioral support system that was culturally responsive to diverse experiences, perspectives, and goals of the school community (Bal, 2018).

In this process, a concept, such as cultural responsiveness, helps participants mediate their understanding of the problem in a novel way and thus, expand the object of their activity system (e.g., a disabled child) and develop a new form of practice through expansive learning actions (Sannino et al., 2016). The concept (described as a germ cell) is initially generated for the resolution of a systemic contradiction in the target activity system. For instance, the contradiction that Learning Labs faced was racial disproportionality in academic and behavioral outcomes. This contradiction manifested itself in daily discourses of teachers, administrators, families, and students as dilemmas and conflicts. An African American parent's comments offer an illustration: "*My experience with Black kids at MLK was that you were fighting a beast. It was like they were in the belly of the beast and you were like 'Oh my God! You have been chewed and swallowed and I don't know how to help you'*" (Bal, Afacan, Cakir, 2018, p. 1008). Step by step, through the method of double stimulation[2] (e.g., data review, system mapping), the germ cell evolved from an ambiguous concept into a schoolwide system and a new form of practice emerged (Engeström, 2015). As participants grappled with and tested ways of solving contradictions, the Learning Lab activities built capacity, empowered stakeholders, propelled effective and just systems from the ground up, and expanded knowledge-production and decision-making processes, especially for those from historically marginalized communities.

The Learning Lab studies revealed a complex cycle of cultural re-mediation and formation of collective agency at these schools (Bal et al., 2018; Bal, Afacan, Cakir, 2019). The change cycle included six expansive learning actions: (1) questioning, (2) analyzing the existing school system, (3) modeling a new, culturally responsive (CR) system, (4) examining the CR system, (5) implementation planning, and (6) reflecting on the Learning Lab process and the new system (Bal et al., 2018). Each school's CR system was different. However, in all schools, the object of the system was expanded from "a disturbing or disabled student" to a school in need of re-mediation. The common characteristics of the new systems included preventive actions (e.g., engaging curriculum, teacher supports), restorative practices, sustained and positive family-school collaboration, enhanced communication among school staff across multiple school settings, and data collection and review for continuous improvement (Bal et al., 2019). The CR systems were informed by effective and adaptive guiding principles; for instance, in middle school, these were race consciousness and cultural responsiveness (Bal et al., 2019). High school guiding principles included school climate, family school-partnership, professional learning, and data collection (Bal et al., 2018). Learning Labs formed at the participating schools and districts an institutional memory of a productive family-school-community partnership and inclusive knowledge-production and design process (Bal et al., 2019). Of significance, the intervention contributed to transform the organizational cultures and practices of the schools and district. For instance, all schools formed and sustained inclusive design teams over the academic year. The artifacts such as system maps or school- and district-level data assemblages were adapted and used after the intervention—e.g., the state's education agency used the maps for professional learning activities. Moreover, the Learning Lab structure was infused in other key district areas, such as hiring a new principal and school-community partnerships.

The use of these artifacts afforded participants new ways to understand and explain racial disparities in special education and educational opportunities. The spatiotemporal representation of disproportionality also allowed users to develop a critical consciousness about the outcome disparities and marginalizing routine practices in classrooms, schools, and agencies. Participants engaged questions such as, what are the values, pedagogies, and tools through which different cultural communities educate individuals? What are the sources of variability in those values, pedagogies, tools, and artifacts *within* and *between* communities that will enable schools to meet the challenges and opportunities of diversity? What are the institutional barriers for students and communities "in the margins" that tend to be invisible and give advantage to certain groups, such as assumptions in the school curricula and favored ways of participation encoded in pedagogies?

The Road Ahead: LD in Worlds of Cultural Differences

We started off by pointing out the theoretical distance between our bio-cultural vision of LD and the canonical framing of this condition. Several conclusions emerged from our analysis. First, culture and biology have had complicated ties with LD; sometimes affording rights and resources, other times stratifying educational opportunity, particularly for minoritized communities (Artiles et al., 2016). Second, emerging brain research on LD is lending support to an integrated bio-cultural vision; however, research strands on the brain and sociocultural interventions have been relatively scarce and remain largely disconnected. Third, researchers have relied mostly on psychological models of learning and taken up the idea of culture in problematic ways—e.g., as orthogonal to LD, as a sign of deficits that lead to disabilities, as a demographic marker that justifies the LD label. In fewer instances, the idea of culture is used productively in LD research to design learning environments or examine equity questions. Next, we outline three themes germane to the future of LD research.

Re-framing LD: Mapping the Fluid Nature of Disability

The insights from this review open crucial opportunities to reframe the very nature of LD from a bio-cultural perspective. Schools often assume there is something defective about the brains of children with learning difficulties in ordinary classrooms. But research shows there is great diversity among children's brains within and between typical and atypical readers (Varma, McCandliss, & Schwartz, 2008). The argument that disability diagnoses are useful because they ensure attention to the special needs of some children only underscores the lack of such attention in general education pedagogical practices, and ignores the fact that minoritized groups are not always given the benefits of specialized interventions after a diagnosis (Skiba et al., 2008). Indeed, we should not ignore the historical entanglements of disability with markers such as race (Artiles, 2011).

The traditional presumption that learning difficulties are inherent in the learner is challenged by studies that illuminate how student identities and performance morph across institutional settings and participation frameworks. Disability, like race, has been theorized as a boundary object (Artiles, 2011)—i.e., disability's facade transforms over spaces and times for different purposes and consequences (McDermott, 1993). The multifaceted portraits of LD students that emerge from this standpoint compels researchers to produce situated representations of these learners, with close attention to the contingencies of context, local goals, and participation frameworks (Artiles, 2019).

Re-localizing LD: A Situated Model of Learning and Competence

Students with reading disabilities do not have general problems with *learning*—they may indeed have very high aptitudes for learning in many domains—but they have difficulty with one or more of the specific demands of text. This distinction compels researchers to reconsider where and how to locate LD. Like early neurologists who sought to *localize* functionality and dysfunctionality, many educational researchers seek to *localize* learning abilities and disabilities. A bio-cultural view recognizes the limits of localization within complex dynamic systems. The three interlocked dimensions of culture—what people bring, what is already there, and what people construct through routine interactions—attest to these complexities. We showed that even the individual vector of this framework (what people bring) constitutes complex interdependencies between biology and culture—between the great diversity in readers' neural networks and the significant heterogeneity *within* and *between* communities' everyday cultural practices.

This means future LD research needs to examine how the ever-shifting configurations of these complex dimensions mediate students' performance in school activities, including literacy learning. A situated approach will enable researchers to study these dynamic processes. The reviewed research showed learning is distributed across people, institutional tools, and interactional processes. Even the meaning of literacy is contested or multiple versions of what counts as literacy co-exist in school contexts.

Furthermore, the advent of new technologies challenges us to reconsider core ideas in LD research. In the ever-changing media world, print's limitations have become more visible and especially apparent are print's "teaching disabilities" (Meyer et al., 2014). Key barriers could conceivably be eliminated drawing from compensatory mechanisms articulated in the sociocultural tradition—e.g., students with dyslexia can use the automatic read-aloud features of digital texts to get equal access to their textbooks. Change is already in motion. The federal law titled the National Instructional Materials Accessibility Standard (NIMAS) stipulates that all children with *print disabilities* (including reading) must be provided with alternative materials that reduce or eliminate the barriers that print erects. The notion of "*print disabilities*" recognizes that abilities and disabilities are contextualized in institutional cultures, that whether someone is disabled depends not just upon their internal capabilities but upon their interaction with the cultural tools available in schools.

These contingencies make a difference in terms of who gets diagnosed with LD and who receives certain kinds of supports, how and when other boundary objects, like race, intersect with disability and become visible *and* invisible at different moments of the diagnosis maze (Artiles, 2019). A situated approach will allow research to document these contingencies generally, localized beyond children's brains or thinking processes.

Re-presenting LD: Toward a Plurality of Theory and Methods

The fluid nature of LD and the requirement for a situated approach to study it call for a plurality of theories and methodological approaches. We argue for the inclusion of the cultural foundations of learning, mainly because of its under-representation in this area of study. But we need cognitive, sociological, anthropological, philosophical, legal, neuropsychological, and many other theories and methods to generate alternative representations of LD (Artiles, 2019). Each of these threads of representation will illuminate alternative facets of this phenomenon. Each will contribute shreds of evidence to a broader interdisciplinary composite. In short, we need concerted efforts to create strategic opportunities to crosspollinate theoretical and research insights across the disciplines regarding the interdependencies of biology and culture in LD. Of significance, the insights from this approach promise to enrich the conceptualization of LD in the age of globalization and ubiquitous diversity.

Notes

1 Authors' note: Our team brought interdisciplinary expertise to this project. Three team members (Artiles, González, and Bal) ground their work in sociocultural and critical theories to understand equity issues related to disability intersections with other markers of difference, drawing largely from a Vygotskian standpoint, as well as contemporary elaborations of a sociocultural perspective of learning. In turn, the second author (Rose) is a developmental neuropsychologist. His work has focused on Universal Design for Learning, applying contemporary learning sciences and modern learning technologies to advance the inclusive education of children with disabilities.
2 In double stimulation, "the subject is put in a structured situation where a problem exists and the subject is provided with active guidance toward the construction of a new means to the end of a solution to the problem" (van der Veer & Valsiner, 1991, p. 169).

References

Artiles, A. J. (2011). Toward an interdisciplinary understanding of educational equity and difference: The case of the racialization of ability. *Educational Researcher, 40*(9), 431–445.

Artiles, A. J. (2015). Beyond responsiveness to identity badges: Future research on culture in disability and implications for RTI. *Educational Review, 67*(1), 1–22.

Artiles, A. J. (2019). Re-envisioning equity research: Disability identification disparities as a case in point. *Educational Researcher, 48*(6), 325–335.

Artiles, A. J., Dorn, S., & Bal, A. (2016). Objects of protection, enduring nodes of difference: Disability intersections with "other" differences, 1916 – 2016. *Review of Research in Education, 40*, 777–820.

Artiles, A. J., Kozleski, E., Trent, S., Osher, D., & Ortiz, A. (2010). Justifying and explaining disproportionality, 1968–2008: A critique of underlying views of culture. *Exceptional Children, 76*(3), 279–299.

Bal, A. (2018). Culturally responsive positive behavioral interventions and supports: A process-oriented framework for systemic transformation. *Review of Education, Pedagogy, and Cultural Studies, 40*(2), 144–174.

Bal, A., Afacan, K., & Cakir, H. (2018). Culturally responsive school discipline: Implementing Learning Lab at a high school for systemic transformation. *American Educational Research Journal, 55*(5), 1007–1050.

Bal, A., Afacan, K., & Cakir, H. I. (2019). Transforming schools from the ground-up with local stakeholders: Implementing Learning Lab for inclusion and systemic transformation at a middle school. *Interchange, 50*(3), 359–387.

Barquero, L. A., Davis, N., & Cutting, L. E. (2014). Neuroimaging of reading intervention: A systematic review and activation likelihood estimate meta-analysis. *PLoS ONE, 9*(1), [e83668].

Bertrand, M., Durand, E. S., & Gonzalez, T. (2017). "We're trying to take action": Transformative agency, role re-mediation, and the complexities of youth participatory action research. *Equity and Excellence in Education, 50*(2), 142–154.

Bishop, D. V. (2015). The interface between genetics and psychology: Lessons from developmental dyslexia. *Proceedings. Biological Sciences/The Royal Society, 282*(1806), 20143139. doi:10.1098/rspb.2014.3139.

Black, J. M., Xia, Z., & Hoeft, F. (2017). Neurobiological bases of reading disorder part II: The importance of developmental considerations in typical and atypical reading. *Language and Linguistics Compass, 11*(10), 1–26.

Chavajay, P., & Rogoff, B. (1999). Cultural variation in management of attention by children and their caregivers. *Developmental Psychology, 35*(4), 1079–1090.

Chiao, J. Y., & Ambady, N. (2007). Cultural neuroscience: Parsing universality and diversity across levels of analysis. In: S. Kitayama & D. Cohen (Eds.), *Handbook of Cultural Psychology* (pp. 237–254). New York, NY: Guilford.

Chyl, K., Kossowski, B., Dębska, A., Łuniewska, M., Banaszkiewicz, A., Żelechowska, A., Frost, S. J., Mencl, W. E., Wypych, M., Marchewka, A., Pugh, K. R., & Jednoróg, K. (2018). Prereader to beginning reader:

Changes induced by reading acquisition in print and speech brain networks. *Journal of Child Psychology and Psychiatry, and Allied Disciplines, 59*(1), 76–87.

Cole, M. (1996). *Cultural Psychology: A Once and Future Discipline*. Cambridge, MA: Harvard University Press.

Cole, M., & Packer, M. (2016). Design-based intervention research as the science of the doubly artificial. *Journal of the Learning Sciences, 25*(4), 503–530.

Collins, K. M. (2011). "My mom says I'm really creative!": Dis/ability, positioning, and resistance in multimodal instructional contexts. *Language Arts, 88*(6), 409–418.

Collins, K. M. (2012). *Ability Profiling and School Failure: One Child's Struggle to Be Seen as Competent*. New York: Routledge.

Dalton, B., & Rose, D. (2015). Reading digital: Designing and teaching with eBooks and digital text. In: S. R. Parris & K. Headley (Eds.), *Comprehension Instruction: Research-Based Best Practices* (3rd ed., pp. 345–355). New York, NY: Guilford Press.

Edwards, E. S., Burke, K., Booth, J. R., & McNorgan, C. (2018). Dyslexia on a continuum: A complex network approach. *PLoS ONE, 13*(12), e0208923. doi:10.1371/journal.pone.0208923.

Engeström, Y. (2015). *Learning by Expanding*. New York, NY: Cambridge University Press.

Englert, C. S., Garmon, A., Mariage, T., Rozendal, M., Tarrant, K., & Urba, J. (1995). The early literacy project: Connecting across the literacy curriculum. *Learning Disability Quarterly, 18*(4), 253–275.

Englert, C. S., & Mariage, T. V. (1996). A sociocultural perspective: Teaching ways-of-thinking and ways-of-talking in a literacy community. *Learning Disabilities Research and Practice, 11*(3), 157–167.

Galaburda, A. M., Sherman, G. F., Rosen, G. D., Aboitiz, F., & Geschwind, N. (1985). Developmental dyslexia: Four consecutive patients with cortical anomalies. *Annals of Neurology, 18*(2), 222–233.

Gallego, M. A., Cole, M. & The Laboratory of Human Cognition. (2001). Classroom cultures and cultures in the classroom. In V. Richardson (Ed.), *Handbook of Research on Teaching* (4th ed., pp. 951–997). Washington, DC: American Educational Research Association.

Gresalfi, M., Martin, T., Hand, V., & Greeno, J. (2009). Constructing competence: An analysis of student participation in the activity systems of mathematics classrooms. *Educational Studies in Mathematics, 70*(1), 49–70. doi:10.1007/s10649-008-9141-5.

Grigorenko, E.L., Compton, D.L., Fuchs, L.S., Wagner, R.K., Wilcutt, E.G., & Fletcher, J.M. (2019). Understanding, educating, and supporting children with specific learning disabilities: 50 years of science and practice. *American Psychologist, 75*, 37–51.

Guidi, L. G., Velayos-Baeza, A., Martinez-Garay, I., Monaco, A. P., Paracchini, S., Bishop, D., & Molnár, Z. (2018). The neuronal migration hypothesis of dyslexia: A critical evaluation 30 years on. *The European Journal of Neuroscience, 48*(10), 3212–3233.

Gutiérrez, K. D., & Stone, L. D. (1997). A cultural-historical view of learning and learning disabilities: Participating in a community of learners. *Learning Disabilities Research and Practice, 12*(2), 123–131.

Hall, T. E., Cohen, N., Vue, G., & Ganley, P. (2015). Addressing learning disabilities with UDL and technology: Strategic reader. *Learning Disabilities Quarterly, 38*(2), 72–83.

Hallahan, D. P., Pullen, P. C., & Ward, D. (2013). A brief history of the field of learning disabilities. In: H. L. Swanson, K. Harris & S. Graham (Eds.), Handbook of *Learning Disabilities* (pp. 15–32). New York, NY: Guilford Press.

Hatt, B. (2012). Smartness as a cultural practice in schools. *American Educational Research Journal, 49*(3), 438–460.

Horowitz-Kraus, T., Vannest, J. J., Kadis, D., Cicchino, N., Wang, Y. Y., & Holland, S. K. (2014). Reading acceleration training changes brain circuitry in children with reading difficulties. *Brain and Behavior, 4*(6), 886–902.

Huettig, F., Kolinsky, R., & Lachmann, T. (2018). The culturally co-opted brain: How literacy affects the human mind. *Language, Cognition and Neuroscience, 33*(3), 275–277. doi:10.1080/23273798.2018.1425803.

Immordino-Yang, M., Darling-Hammond, L., & Krone, C. R. (2019). Nurturing nature: How brain development is inherently social and emotional, and what this means for education. *Educational Psychologist, 54*(3), 185–204.

International Dyslexia Association. (2020, February 17). *Definition of dyslexia*. https://dyslexiaida.org/definition-of-dyslexia/.

John-Steiner, V., & Mahn, H. (1996). Sociocultural approaches to learning and development: A Vygotskian framework. *Educational Psychologist, 31*(3–4), 191–206.

Klingner, J., Artiles, A. J., Kozleski, E., Harry, B., Zion, S., Tate, W., Zamora-Durán, G., & Riley, D. (2005). Addressing the disproportionate representation of culturally and linguistically diverse students in special education through culturally responsive educational systems. *Education Policy Analysis Archives, 13*(38). http://epaa.asu.edu/epaa/v13n38/.

Klingner, J. K., Vaughn, S., & Schumm, J. S. (1998). Collaborative strategic reading during social studies in heterogeneous fourth-grade classrooms. *The Elementary School Journal, 99*(1), 3–22.

Kozleski, E. B., & Artiles, A. J. (2015). Mediating systemic change in educational systems through socio-cultural methods. In: P. Smeyers, D. Bridges, N. Burbules & M. Griffiths (Eds.), *International Handbook of Interpretation in Educational Research* (pp. 805–822). New York, NY: Springer.

Kozulin, A., & Gindis, B. (2007). Sociocultural theory and education of children with special needs: From defectology to remedial pedagogy. In: H. Daniels, M. Cole & J. Wertsch (Eds.), *The Cambridge Companion to Vygotsky* (pp. 332–362). Cambridge: Cambridge University Press.

Lambert, R. (2015). Constructing and resisting disability in mathematics classrooms: A case study exploring the impact of different pedagogies. *Educational Studies in Mathematics*, *89*(1), 1–18.

Lee, C. D. (2010). Soaring above the clouds, delving the ocean's depths: Understanding the ecologies of human learning and the challenge for education science. *Educational Researcher*, *39*(9), 643–655.

Lee, C. D. (2017). Integrating research on how people learn and learning across settings as a window of opportunity to address inequality in educational processes and outcomes. *Review of Research in Education*, *41*(1), 88–111.

Li, S. C. (2003). Biocultural orchestration of developmental plasticity across levels: The interplay of biology and culture in shaping the mind and behavior across the life span. *Psychological Bulletin*, *129*(2), 171–194.

McCloskey, E. (2005). *Taking on a Learning Disability: Negotiating Special Education and Learning to Read*. State University of New York at Albany.

McCloskey, E. (2012). *Taking on a Learning Disability: At the Crossroads of Special Education and Adolescent Literacy Learning*. Charlotte, NC: Information Age Publishing.

McDermott, R. (1993). The acquisition of a child by a learning disability. In: S. Chaiklin & J. Lave (Eds.), *Understanding Practice: Perspectives on Activity and Context* (pp. 269–305). New York, NY: Cambridge University Press.

Mehan, H. (1993). Beneath the skin and bweeen the ears: A case study in the politics of representation. In: S. Chaiklin & J. Lave (Eds.), *Understanding Practice: Perspectives on Activity and Context* (pp. 241–268). New York, NY: Routledge.

Meyer, A., Rose, D. H., & Gordon, D. (2014). *Universal Design for Learning: Theory and Practice*. Wakefield, MA: CAST.

Paradise, R. (2002). Finding ways to study culture in context. *Human Development*, *45*, 229–236.

Pennington B. F., Santerre-Lemmon L., Rosenberg J., MacDonald B., Boada R., Friend A., Leopold D. R., Samuelsson S., Byrne B., Willcutt E. G., & Olson R. K. (2012). Individual prediction of dyslexia by single versus multiple deficit models. *Journal of Abnormal Psychology*, 121, 212–224.

Protopapas, A., & Parrila, R. (2018). Is dyslexia a brain disorder? *Brain Sciences*, *8*(4), 61.

Rieber, R. W., & Carton, A. S. (Eds.) (1993). *The Collected Works of L. S. Vygotsky: The Fundamentals of Defectology (Abnormal Psychology and Learning Disabilities)*. New York, NY: Springer.

Rogoff, B. (2003). *The Cultural Nature of Human Development*. Oxford, UK: Oxford University.

Rose, D. H., Gravel, J. W., & Gordon, D. (2014). Universal design for learning. In: L. Florian (Ed.), *SAGE Handbook of Special Education* (2nd ed., pp. 475–491). London: SAGE.

Ruiz, N. T. (1995). The social construction of ability and disability. *Journal of Learning Disabilities*, *28*(8), 491–502.

Ruiz, N. T., & Figueroa, R. A. (1995). Learning-handicapped classrooms with Latino students. *Education and Urban Society*, *27*(4), 463–483.

Sannino, A., Engeström, Y., & Lemos, M. (2016). Formative interventions for expansive learning and transformative agency. *Journal of the Learning Sciences*, *25*(4), 599–633.

Seok, S., DaCosta, B., & Hodges, R. (2018). A systematic review of empirically based Universal Design for Learning: Implementation and effectiveness of universal design in education for students with and without disabilities at the Postsecondary Level. *Open Journal of Social Sciences*, *6*(05), 171–189.

Skiba, R. J., Simmons, A. D., Ritter, S., Gibb, A., Rausch, M. K., Cuadrado, J., & Chung, C. G. (2008). Achieving equity in special education: History, status, and current challenges. *Exceptional Children*, *74*(3), 264–288.

Smagorinsky, P. (2012). Vygotsky, "defectology," and the inclusion of people of difference in the broader cultural stream. *Journal of Language and Literacy Education*, *8*(1), 1–25.

U.S. Department of Education. (2018). *40th Annual Report to Congress on the Implementation of the Individuals with Disabilities Education Act*. Washington, DC: Author.

U.S. Office of Education. (1977). Assistance to states for education of handicapped children: Procedures for evaluating specific learning disabilities. *Federal Register*, *42*, 65082–65085. Washington, DC: Author.

van der Veer, R., & Valsiner, J. (1991). *Understanding Vygotsky*. Oxford, UK: Blackwell.

Varenne, H., & McDermott, R. (2018). *Successful Failure: The School America Builds*. New York, NY: Routledge.

Varma, S., McCandliss, B. D., & Schwartz, D. L. (2008). Scientific and pragmatic challenges for bridging education and neuroscience. *Educational Researcher*, *37*(3), 140–152.

Vaughn, S., Klingner, J. K., & Bryant, D. P. (2001). Collaborative strategic reading as a means to enhance peer-mediated instruction for reading comprehension and content-area learning. *Remedial and Special Education, 22*(2), 66–74.

Vygodskaya, G. L. (1999). Vygotsky and problems of special education. *Remedial and Special Education, 20*(6), 330–332.

Vygotsky, L. S. (1978). *Mind in Society*. Cambridge, MA: Harvard University.

Waitoller, F. R., & King Thorius, K. A. (2016). Cross-pollinating culturally sustaining pedagogy and universal design for learning: Toward an inclusive pedagogy that accounts for dis/ability. *Harvard Educational Review, 86*(3), 366–389.

Wise Younger, J., Tucker-Drob, E., & Booth, J. R. (2017). Longitudinal changes in reading network connectivity related to skill improvement. *NeuroImage, 158*, 90–98.

Xia, Z., Hancock, R., & Hoeft, F. (2017). Neurobiological bases of reading disorder Part I: Etiological investigations. *Language and Linguistics Compass, 11*(4), e12239. doi:10.1111/lnc3.12239.

10

POWER, LANGUAGE, AND BILINGUAL LEARNERS

Nelson Flores and Erica Saldívar García

Since its emergence as a discipline in the 1960s, educational linguistics has attempted to understand the relationship between language, education, and social inequalities (Cazden, John, & Hymes, 1972; Fishman, Ferguson, & Das Gupta, 1968; Labov, 1966). Over the past fifty years, educational linguists have exposed the ways that the marginalization of racialized[1] bilingual communities connects to larger political and economic inequalities (Arias & Wiley, 2015; García, 2009; May, 2014). Yet, the solutions most often proposed by educational linguists to challenge this marginalization address only the linguistic issues, leaving larger political and economic factors largely unaddressed. Considering that the discipline emerged as a way to develop and refine expertise in language policy, teaching, and learning, it is certainly not surprising that educational linguists have focused their efforts on providing linguistic solutions to the marginalization of racialized bilingual communities. That said, in this chapter we critically interrogate the theory of social change that undergirds these linguistic solutions. By theory of social change, we mean the assumptions pertaining to how society can become more equitable. Our assertion is that emphasizing linguistic solutions may inadvertently reproduce a theory of social change that suggests that the solution to social inequalities is rooted in modifying the linguistic behaviors of racialized bilingual communities rather than in structural transformation.

The unintended consequences of this implied theory of social change can be illustrated by a recent English as a second language (ESL) program evaluation of a small U.S. school district with a large and growing number of children of migrant farmers from Mexico. During the evaluation, which Nelson conducted along with several colleagues, educators reported to us that many of the Mexican-origin students—even those who were not officially designated as English language learners—were struggling academically. The consensus was that their academic challenge was primarily a linguistic problem. Most prominent in their discourse was the assertion that the Mexican-origin students had mastered "social language" but had failed to master the "academic language" that was needed for school success. The educators, who were predominantly monolingual and white, did not mention a myriad of other factors that may have been contributing to the academic challenges of their large and growing Mexican-origin student population, including in-school issues such as the lack of bilingual educators and support staff, or out-of-school issues such as the high poverty of migrant families that is a product of global capitalism and xenophobia. Instead, these larger sociopolitical factors were ignored in favor of a theory of social change that identified the problem as the perceived linguistic deficiencies of their Mexican-origin student population and the solution as fixing these linguistic deficiencies.

Power, Language, and Bilingual Learners

It may be tempting to dismiss this focus on linguistic issues as "folk linguistics" that has no bearing on how educational linguists understand and analyze these issues. Yet, these educators were using terms that have been developed by educational linguists—terms such as BICS (basic interpersonal communication skills) and CALP (cognitive academic language proficiency) in addition to social and academic language. It may also be tempting to say that they misunderstood these frameworks. Yet, the practitioner's views are reflective of commonly held assertions about the nature of language and language development that educational linguists have made in their attempts to advocate for racialized bilingual students within the constraints presented by school settings. Specifically, they were working under the assumption shared by many educational linguists that academic language can be "curricularized" by being broken down into discrete units, studied, learned, and assessed accurately in schools (Valdés, 2015). Both groups have typically treated this curricularization of academic language as objective, overlooking the ways that this process is co-constructed with ideologies of race and class (Valdés, 2017). These ideologies intersect and collectively influence the framing of the academic challenges confronted by students from racialized bilingual communities as primarily a linguistic issue, thereby obscuring the larger political and economic factors that lie at the root of their marginalization.

To further explore this assertion, we begin by situating notions of academic language within the larger socio-historical context that has shaped the emergence of the discursive practices that are commonly placed under this broad linguistic categorization. We then use this broader socio-historical framing as a point of entry for analyzing the conceptualization of academic language within two disciplinary strands—a cognitive strand and a functional strand (Haneda, 2014). We argue that both of these strands offer a theory of social change focused on linguistic solutions to marginalization rooted in political and economic factors produced by white supremacy and global capitalism. We end with calls for a new theory of social change in educational linguistics that moves beyond a focus on accommodating existing relations of power through the modification of the language practices of racialized bilingual communities. Instead, we argue for a theory of social change that focuses on reconfiguring these relations of power by connecting educational linguistics with broader efforts to dismantle the structural barriers that make the stigmatization of the language practices of racialized bilingual communities possible to begin with.

Nation-State/Colonial Governmentality and the Rise of Academic Language

Extending Foucault's concept of governmentality, Flores (2013) introduced the concept of *nation-state/colonial governmentality* as a general framework for analyzing the production of governable national and colonial subjects that fit the political and economic needs of modern society. At the core of nation-state/colonial governmentality were three interrelated metadiscursive regimes "that drew on assertions regarding the nature of language in regulating linguistic conduct and imbuing some ways of speaking and writing with authority while rendering other modes a powerful source of stigma and exclusion" (Bauman & Briggs, 2003, p. 32). First, at the most abstract level, nation-state/colonial governmentality is informed by a *language-as-entity paradigm* that abstracts language from the practices in which people engage into an entity that people can possess (Park & Wee, 2012). From this perspective, people "have" language rather than "do" language. Within this language-as-entity paradigm lie *monoglossic language ideologies* that position monolingualism as the norm to which all should aspire (García, 2009). The objectification of this idealized monolingualism into an entity that one could possess occurred through the standardization of national languages with those deemed to not "have" the standardized national language receiving social sanctions (Lippi-Green, 1997). From this perspective, the mixing of two or more named languages is framed as a problem that threatens the integrity of the languages and must, therefore, be eliminated (García, 2009). Finally, these monoglossic language ideologies are infused with *raciolinguistic ideologies* that co-construct language and race in ways that depict racialized communities as engaged in language practices that deviate from the monoglossic ideal. As Fanon (1967) suggested, racialized populations' subordinate positions prevented their legitimate use of standardized national languages. Here, Fanon was pointing to a catch-22 that characterizes the lives of members of many racialized communities around the world. Namely, that they are expected to adhere to monoglossic ideals even as their interlocutors rely on raciolinguistic ideologies that continue to hear them as engaging in deficient language practices that deviate from these idealized language practices (Flores & Rosa, 2015).

While educational linguists have typically focused their attention on the prescriptivist imposition of standardized national languages, another aspect of the rise of nation-state/colonial governmentality relates to the rise of the language of the human sciences (Foucault, 1970). This language of the human sciences was used to justify the marginalization of the lower classes and racialized people through supposedly objective descriptions of these communities that positioned them as lower on the evolutionary scale than the emerging European bourgeoisie (Foucault, 1978; Stoler, 1995). Bauman and Briggs (2000) specifically examined the emergence of a science of language and its connection to nationalist language ideologies. They examined the work of political theorist John Locke (1632–1704) and German nationalist Johann Gottfried Herder (1744–1803) and argued that despite superficial differences between the two thinkers' conceptions of language, their language ideologies were fundamentally the same in that they "relegate folk linguistic knowledge to or beyond the margins of linguistic inquiry" (p. 199). Both thinkers, whose ideas were emerging as part of the formation of nation-state/colonial governmentality, did not see the linguistic knowledge of lower class and racialized people as important to developing either a scientific understanding of language or a nationalist understanding of language. Language, in their view, could only be understood one step removed from the actual lived experience of people. Describing reality in a way that is removed from the actual experiences of people entailed developing new discursive practices that sought to describe the world from a distance and in seemingly objective terms. In reality, there was, and continues to be, nothing objective about these discursive practices, which serve to perpetuate colonial relations of power under the guise of disinterested knowledge production (Clough, 1998).

It is these discursive practices that educational linguistics placed under the broad umbrella of academic language in the 1970s, a period of great global upheaval. This global upheaval brought issues of education to the forefront of debates as postcolonial societies grappled with the role of colonial languages versus indigenous languages in the education of their populace and former colonial powers grappled with the increasing diversity and racial turmoil of their own societies. Educational linguists quickly positioned themselves as defenders of linguistic diversity through the promotion of bilingual education for indigenous communities in postcolonial societies and (im)migrant communities within former colonial powers (Fishman, 1976; Heath, 1976) alongside calls for pedagogical approaches that affirmed non-standardized language varieties (Labov, 1972). Yet, these educational linguists found themselves in a bind. On the hand one, they vigorously defended the legitimacy of all language varieties and celebrated linguistic diversity. On the other hand, they found themselves working to apply their theories in schools that were sites of raciolinguistic oppression. The dilemma that emerged was how to affirm the language practices of racialized communities while simultaneously accommodating the monoglossic language ideologies and raciolinguistic normativity embedded within schools as institutions. That is, how might educational linguists advocate for affirming the language practices of racialized communities within schools and a broader society that systematically pathologized these same language practices?

The primary way that educational linguists addressed this dilemma was through discussions of a linguistic and cultural mismatch between racialized communities and the language practices privileged in school settings. Heath (1983) offered a seminal study that provided the foundation for this perspective. Heath documented the different linguistic and cultural practices of two different communities—Roadville, a working class white community, and Trackton, a working class Black community. She illustrated the richness of these linguistic and cultural practices and the important role that they placed in socializing children into interacting with texts. At the same time, she pointed to the ways that these linguistic and cultural practices did not align with the linguistic and cultural practices and ways of interacting with texts privileged in school. As a result, when children from these two communities came together with children from Maintown, who were socialized at home into cultural and linguistic practices more aligned with the school expectations, they were not academically successful in the ways that children from Maintown were.

On one level, discussing linguistic and cultural mismatch appeared to address the tension by reframing discussions of racialized language practices away from deficiency and toward difference. Yet, framing challenges confronting racialized communities as an issue of cultural and linguistic mismatch obscured the racialization processes that lie at the root of the marginalization of many of these communities. Notably, the reason that Black children from Trackton were in school with white children from Roadville and Maintown was because of a desegregation order (Prendergast, 2003). While cultural and linguistic mismatch may have contributed to the marginalization of both Roadville and Trackton children, the reality was that nobody was questioning whether Roadville children should be at the school, which was not the case for Trackton children. Overlooking the racialization that lies at the core of the marginalization of Trackton children and the community where they reside, has the potential to reinforce narratives that suggest that the solution to racial inequities is simply to modify the linguistic and cultural practices of racialized communities. Within the context of the raciolinguistic ideologies that characterize modern U.S. society, it is quite easy to see how such a narrative could easily transform into the deficit ideologies utilized by the district administrators described earlier in this chapter. To be clear, we are not suggesting that educational linguists proposing a cultural and linguistic mismatch are supportive of deficit frameworks. On the contrary, these scholars have been at the forefront of challenging these frameworks. That said, what we are suggesting is that by failing to fully account for the impact of racialization, such frameworks can be taken up in unintended ways that reify rather than challenge the marginalization of racialized communities.

Below we offer dominant conceptualizations of academic language as one example of the ways that cultural and linguistic mismatch has been taken up in ways that reinforce deficit ideologies of racialized bilingual communities. The idea at the core of theorizations of academic language is that a primary rationale for the academic challenges faced by racialized bilingual communities is the mismatch between their home language practices and the academic language practices required by school, with the solution being to equip them with the skills to use academic language when appropriate. Overlooked in this framework are the ways that schools, as sites structured around a language-as-entity paradigm infused with monoglossic language ideologies, continue to reproduce raciolinguistic ideologies that frame racialized communities as perpetual outsiders to the mastery of academic language (Flores & Rosa, 2015). In the next section, we further develop the argument that notions of academic language have long been produced in ways that align with nation-state/colonial governmentality by examining two different conceptualizations of academic language—a cognitive framing and a functional framing.

The Cognitive Framing of Academic Language

The cognitive framing of academic language has its roots in research pointing to possible cognitive advantages associated with bilingualism (Peal & Lambert, 1962). This research required a reconsideration of the low academic achievement of racialized bilingual communities. After all, if bilingualism offered cognitive advantages then why did bilingual students from racialized backgrounds not seem to illustrate these advantages in their school achievement? Researchers hypothesized that this seemingly counterintuitive phenomenon could be explained by the different social statuses of white and racialized bilingual communities. White students coming from dominant backgrounds experienced *additive bilingualism*, where they were learning a second language in a context where their home language also continued to be developed because it was the dominant societal language. In contrast, racialized bilingual students experienced *subtractive bilingualism*, where they were learning a second language in a context of a language shift caused by the fact that their home language practices were heavily stigmatized by the broader society. The basic argument was that additive bilingualism led to cognitive advantages while subtractive bilingualism led to cognitive deficits (Lambert, 1975). In particular, researchers argued that subtractive bilingualism might lead to *semilingualism*, where children failed to develop full competency in either their home language or the dominant societal language (Skutnabb-Kangas & Toukomaa, 1976).

The use of the term semilingualism was immediately critiqued as coming from a deficit perspective (Brent-Palmer, 1979). Indeed scholars who proposed the concept also expressed some concern about its negative connotation (Skutnabb-Kangas, 1981). Yet, these scholars were also concerned with the possibility that these students would not receive the linguistic supports that they needed to be successful in school due to the consequences of subtractive educational programs. In response to both of these concerns, Cummins (1980) proposed the dichotomy of *Basic Interpersonal Communication Skills* (BICS) and *Cognitive Academic Language Proficiency* (CALP) as an alternative to semilingualism. He defined BICS as "the visible language proficiencies of pronunciation, vocabulary, grammar, which are manifested in everyday interpersonal communication situations" (p. 28). In contrast, he defined CALP as the proficiency "required to manipulate or reflect upon these surface features outside of immediate interpersonal contexts" (p. 28). With this framing, racialized bilingual students who were experiencing academic difficulties were no longer framed as semilingual but rather as having mastered BICS but not CALP. Cummins called for racialized bilingual students to have the opportunity to develop a strong foundation in CALP in their home language, which would then transfer to the dominant language of the society (Cummins, 1980).

Several prominent critiques of Cummins's conceptualization of CALP have emerged since the concept was introduced in the 1980s. Martin-Jones and Romaine (1986) argued that it conceptualized language as a container that can be more or less full and suggests the possibility of a complete language that one can have complete control over. They also critiqued the universalizing description Cummins proposed for CALP and pointed to the ways that what he was, in fact, describing were the culturally specific literacy practices associated with schooling. In line with this critique, Edelsky (1996) questioned whether CALP was simply measuring "test-wiseness"—the ability to do well on tests that measured specific literacy-related aspects of language privileged in school settings. Further elaborating on this point, MacSwan (2000) situated the imposition of CALP within a broader history of prescriptivism where elite language practices have been imposed on racialized bilingual communities in ways that reinforce the status quo (see also Petrovic, 2013).

Critics of CALP used these concerns as a point of entry for raising pedagogical questions related to the implications of adopting the BICS and CALP dichotomy. For example, Edelsky and colleagues (1983) worried that CALP was coming from a skills view of literacy that focused on drilling racialized bilingual students on the language privileged on school assessments. They argued that a whole-language approach to literacy that focuses on exposing racialized bilingual students to authentic literature would be more effective and empowering. In a similar vein, Martin-Jones and Romaine (1986) called for the development of language assessment procedures based on the community norms found in racialized bilingual communities. MacSwan (2000) suggested that ensuring that racialized bilingual students receive comprehensible input in school content areas would improve their academic achievement. Therefore, critics of CALP have typically expressed a similar theory of social change as its proponents, arguing that linguistically responsive pedagogical approaches will empower racialized bilingual students. The difference between these approaches

Power, Language, and Bilingual Learners

lies in what linguistically responsive pedagogy should look like rather than whether it is the solution to the challenges confronting racialized bilingual students in the classroom.

In short, both proponents and critics of the concept of CALP frame the challenges of racialized bilingual students as primarily linguistic challenges, with the solution being to affirm and build on the language practices of these students in classrooms. Uniting both ends of the debate is a consistent theory of social change that suggests that linguistically responsive approaches to the education of racialized bilingual students will empower them and provide them access to social mobility. To be clear, the affirmation of racialized bilingual students' home language practices is a laudable goal, and it is not surprising that educational linguists who dedicate their careers to the study of language in schools would make this affirmation a central part of their research and advocacy. That said, the root of the problem of the BICS and CALP dichotomy is not that it advocates a skills view of literacy—a critique that has become less relevant in recent years as the BICS and CALP theory has adopted a more explicitly social framing (Auckerman, 2007; Cummins, 2000)—but rather that it continues to conceptualize the construct of academic language as a set of objective linguistic features that can and must be mastered by racialized bilingual communities. No matter how social conceptualizations of academic language become, the very construct of academic language continues to gloss over the monoglossic and raciolinguistic ideologies that, embedded within a language-as-entity paradigm, position racialized bilingual students as deficient and in need of remediation. In order to illustrate this point, in the next section we analyze the functional perspective of academic language that originated from a social, as opposed to cognitive, view of language.

The Functional Framing of Academic Language

Functional framings of academic language have their roots in the work of British sociologist Basil Bernstein. In contrast to the cognitive approach proposed by his contemporaries, Bernstein adopted a code approach focused on the relationship between language forms and their environment (Bernstein, 1990). Yet, he still relied on a dichotomy for understanding the different types of codes that exist, arguing that the two general types of codes were *restricted codes* and *elaborated codes*. Similar to Cummins's original conceptualization of BICS, he characterized restricted codes as relying on the immediate social context in communication and simple linguistic structures. In addition, similar to Cummins's original conceptualization of CALP, he characterized elaborated codes as relying on abstraction away from the immediate social context and more complex linguistic structures.

While Cummins based his original conceptualization of BICS and CALP on the supposed differing cognitive demands of each, Bernstein connected his dichotomy to the social division of labor. He argued that the lower classes, whose lives tended to be focused on their immediate environments, relied more heavily on the use of restricted codes, while the middle and upper classes, whose lives tended to expand beyond their immediate environment, had more access to elaborated codes (Bernstein, 1990). Like Cummins, Bernstein was careful to argue that neither code was superior to the other and that restricted codes play an important role in all communities. However, he noted that elaborated codes were privileged in schools because of their role as institutions designed to socialize students into ways of communicating outside of their immediate experience.

Bernstein's code theory was taken up by Michael Halliday as part of his development of a functional approach to language that situated language practices within particular social contexts, with the language practices utilized within a specific social context referred to as *registers* (Halliday, 1978). In line with Bernstein's view of language as embedded within social relations, Halliday described the ways that registers emerge as a product of changes in the social structure of society. As Halliday and Martin (1993) described it, "certain human societies evolved along particular lines following a route from mobility to settlement; among those that settled, some evolved from agrarian to technological, and some of these again to scientific-industrial" (p. 10). They described the scientific register that emerged as a product of the shift toward a scientific-industrial society as "an elaborated register" (p. 15), arguing that this register serves the purposes required of advanced modern societies. They argued that the elaborated register of scientific language "holds reality still, to be kept under observation and experimented with; and in so doing, interprets it not as changing with time (as the grammar of clauses interprets it) but as persisting—or rather, persistence—through time, which is the mode of being of a noun" (p. 15).

Overlooked in Halliday and Martin's description of scientific language are the broader sociohistorical processes that shaped the rise of these linguistic forms. As noted above, the emergence of the language of science was not an inevitable product of the evolution of humanity to industrial society, as Halliday and Martin suggested, but rather an integral component in the production of the supposed objective scholar who possessed the only knowledge that was relevant to the understanding of the lived experiences of the lower classes and racialized people. That is, the discursive practices of the scientific register that Halliday and Martin described as functional in advanced modern societies emerged within the relations of power associated with nation-state/colonial governmentality. Therefore, mastery of the scientific register and/or other privileged registers is not empowering but is rather complicit in the production of governable subjects to fit the needs of modern society (Luke, 1997).

Rather than frame mastery of these discursive practices as part of social reproduction, scholars adopting a functional approach to academic language often frame mastery of academic registers as empowering and as essential for social transformation. For example, Hasan (1996) further developed the foundation laid by Bernstein and Halliday about differences between the language practices of different social classes in order to make the case for the importance of providing equal access to academic language and literacy practices. She argued that social change occurs when all language users "enjoy an equal opportunity for appropriating higher potential sign systems" (p. 383). This point was further elaborated on by Schleppegrell (2004), who suggested that linguistic mismatch between home and school led racialized bilingual students to be tracked "into programs that provide few opportunities for language development" (p. 39). Building on Halliday's work related to the scientific register, Schleppegrell argued for the need for racialized bilingual students to develop skills in expository writing that avoid "high involvement and emotional appeal" (p. 59) and instead rely on "arguments that are supported by evidence and presented objectively" (p. 61). In short, the burden of responsibility for gaining legitimacy in an academic setting is on the racialized bilingual writer.

Importantly, Schleppegrell did not examine the role of the reader in shaping how a text is taken up and understood. This is an important oversight since she suggested that expository writing should avoid "emotional appeal" ignoring the ways that white people often dismiss marginalized groups seeking to assert their experiences of racialization as too emotional (Calafell, 2012; Ellsworth, 1989; Gay, 2005). In addition, advanced biliteracy scholarship analyzing the writing of bilingual Latinx students has found that their writing is imbued with innovative rhetorical strategies that are uniquely informed by their multilingual and multicultural experiences (Martínez, 2007; Schwartz, 2003, 2005; Spicer-Escalante, 2005, 2007; Yanguas & Lado, 2012). Yet when these writing practices appear in school settings they meet resistance and corrective feedback that seeks to align their literacy practices with the kinds of academic language deemed necessary to participate in professional communities (Achugar & Colombi, 2008; Colombi, 2015). This resistance is, in part, based on the epistemological orientation of functional approaches to academic language that seek to explain how language works to develop and structure texts to create meaning. As such, functional approaches to academic language are less concerned with the lived experiences of individual writers and readers and the alignment of their intended or achieved meaning-making through texts. Omission of these perspectives characterizes academic writing research (Coffin & Donohue, 2012; Lillis & Scott, 2007) and has contributed to the predetermination that issues in racialized bilingual students' writing are primarily textual in nature—an assumption that is neither politically neutral nor empowering.

Power, Language, and Bilingual Learners

While functional approaches to academic language nod to the broader social processes involved in the apprenticeship of racialized bilingual students into academic language (see Coffin & Donohue, 2012; Hasan, 2005), their primary focus is on the development of linguistic solutions that focus on modifying students' language practices. In particular, the solution most often proposed is to ensure that racialized bilingual students master academic language. Hasan (1996) advocated a genre-based pedagogy that raises students' awareness of the linguistic conventions of different school-based genres while supporting students in developing "reflection literacy" that will allow them "to participate in the production of knowledge" (p. 410). In line with Hasan's pedagogical suggestions, Schleppegrell called for the adoption of an "active pedagogy" that supported racialized bilingual students in mastering the linguistic features of what she referred to as "the language of schooling." She went as far as suggesting that implementing an active pedagogy that taught racialized bilingual students "the language of schooling…can overcome the labels that separate students into different categories, and social groups and enable a focus on the common agenda of helping students gain control over the texts that have the power to shape the future that they share" (p. 161). That is, the root cause of unequal educational outcomes is presented as a linguistic issue, with questions of racial and economic inequalities presented as the byproduct of poor language education rather than its cause.

The idea that racialized bilingual students can alter their educational outcomes through the adoption of academic language as proposed by genre-based pedagogies has raised critiques focusing on the potential hegemonic and reproductive implications of adopting such approaches. Critical literacy scholars in particular have been vocal about the uncritical reproduction of texts (Pennycook, 1996) and further naturalization of the status quo (Janks, 2010) in the context of an increasingly globalized and digitally mediated world. From this perspective, overt instruction in the linguistic features of genres does not guarantee social and economic redistribution, a key theoretical component of the discourse of power of genre-based pedagogies (Luke, 1997; New London Group, 1996). In response to these concerns, scholars adopting a functional approach advocate for students and teachers to engage in broader explorations of the ideological, political, and historical features of academic texts (Gebhard & Harmon, 2011). While this critical perspective offers an important first step in connecting issues of the education of racialized bilingual students to broader political struggles, recent application of a functional approach to academic language in the United States through the Common Core State Standards illustrates the dangers of institutionalizing this approach within existing institutions. On the one hand, proponents of functional framings of academic language have been able to use the standards to support teachers in developing more functional approaches to their teaching (Moore & Schleppegrell, 2014). On the other hand, the institutionalization of a more functional approach has entailed the development of new and more challenging assessments that are meant to assess students' mastery of academic language conventions. These assessments, informed by a language-as-entity paradigm and monoglossic language ideologies, perpetuate raciolinguistic ideologies that frame racialized bilingual students as not having academic language despite evidence of their complex use of language on a daily basis (Flores & Schissel, 2014). That is, while a functional approach may offer many tools for teachers in analyzing the language of schooling, it leaves unchallenged the larger socio-historical context that shapes the emergence of the concept of academic language and emphasizes linguistic solutions to problems that require larger social transformation (Luke, 1997). In the next section, we use the newfound understanding offered by this critical reading to develop a new approach to educational linguistics that explicitly situates dominant conceptions of language within the broader political economy.

From Accommodation to Reconfiguration

Since the 1970s academic language has been a dominant concept in educational linguistics. Indeed, of all the interventions that educational linguists have sought to introduce to the education of racialized bilingual students, academic language is certainly one of the most prominent (Valdés,

2004). Unfortunately, it is also a concept that has inadvertently obscured the root causes of the marginalization of racialized bilingual students and communities. In particular, a focus on academic language has led to framing the educational challenges confronting racialized bilingual students as primarily a linguistic problem requiring linguistic solutions rather than as a political and economic problem requiring political and economic solutions. This focus on a linguistic solution to complex social problems has made its way into practitioner spaces in ways that perpetuate the marginalization of racialized bilingual students. It has provided district leaders—like the ones mentioned at the beginning of this chapter—with the tools to justify programs designed to remediate the supposed linguistic deficiencies of racialized bilingual students in ways that let the larger institutional processes of the school district off the hook. More generally, it has provided the tools for our society to perpetuate a meritocratic myth that places the burden on racialized bilingual students to overcome their political and economic marginalization while absolving the larger society from investing in the communities where these children reside.

We are not suggesting that language is unimportant. Many important contributions have been made to our understanding of the education of racialized bilingual students both within the BICS and CALP debate as well as through the development of a functional approach to the language of schooling. Conceptualizations of CALP brought attention to the inappropriate identification of racialized bilingual students for special education (Cummins, 1982) and have been connected to efforts to affirm and celebrate racialized bilingual identities (Cummins, 2014). In a similar vein, functional approaches to academic language have been used to develop concrete tools to improve the education of racialized bilingual students (Aguirre-Muñoz et al., 2009; Brisk, Hodgson-Drysdale, & O'Connor, 2010/2011; Gebhard, 2010). What we are suggesting is that language is only one piece of a much larger puzzle explaining the academic challenges confronting racialized bilingual students. Though this insight in and of itself may not seem novel, in this chapter we have sought to illustrate the disconnect between what educational linguists might understand about the complex relationship between language and other forms of social inequality and the proposed narrow linguistic solutions (Valdés, 1997). It is not enough to understand that language inequality is inextricably connected with other forms of social inequality when discussing these issues. It is also necessary to address this inextricable connection in the solutions that we propose.

The current debate about academic language is limited in its ability to make these connections because of its basis in an ideology of pragmatism that suggests that language education should focus on "getting the job done with no critical analysis of the consequences for the various parties" (Bensch, 2001, p. 27). This ideology of pragmatism leads proponents of academic language to advocate for accommodation-oriented policies that "accept the existing structure…and seek to accomplish certain goals within that structure" (Park & Wee, 2012, p. 167). These policies take for granted that there is such an entity as academic language, that this entity can be objectively identified, that all students must have mastery over this entity, and that upon mastering it they will be recognized by their interlocutors as academic. Left unaddressed are the socio-historical factors that led to the emergence of the discursive practices that many educational linguists now include under the broad umbrella of academic language, the ways that the concept of academic language has been used to pathologize the language practices of racialized bilingual students, and the ways that a focus on linguistic solutions to the marginalization of racialized bilingual students reproduces the status quo. In particular, notions of academic language place the burden on racialized bilingual students and their families to accommodate the dominant society by modifying their language practices to conform to mainstream norms while exonerating members of the dominant society from having to address the social hierarchies that have placed them in their privileged position in society to begin with.

In contrast to the accommodationist stance, Park and Wee (2012) called for a reconfiguration stance to educational linguistics. As opposed to treating academic language as an objective

Power, Language, and Bilingual Learners

categorization of language that racialized bilingual students have to master if they want to be academically successful, a reconfiguration-oriented approach would seek to connect the notion of academic language with larger issues of social inequality that have been produced as a result of the language-as-entity paradigm and the monoglossic and raciolinguistic ideologies that lie at the core of nation-state/colonial governmentality. With this in mind, a reconfiguration-oriented theory of social change would situate calls for reform in language education within calls for the improvement in the political and economic conditions of racialized bilingual communities.

A reconfiguration-oriented theory of social change would begin from the perspective that language education is not a panacea for the marginalization of racialized bilingual students. While this statement is likely one that many educational linguists would agree with, efforts to address the marginalization of racialized bilingual communities that dominate our discipline focus on linguistic solutions. In this way, there is a disconnect between what educational linguists claim to know (that language education is not a panacea) and what we propose (that linguistic solutions can empower racialized bilingual students). This is not simply a semantic issue since such an erasure serves to reify the racialization of the communities that educational linguists purportedly seek to support. This erasure can be seen in the ways that educational linguists have described the concept of academic language. Both cognitive and functional approaches suggest that providing racialized bilingual students access to academic language will empower them in ways that allow them to resist their marginalization within and outside of the classroom. This argument masks the larger political and economic factors that lie at the root of the marginalization of the language practices of racialized bilingual communities while placing the onus on racialized bilingual communities to dismantle their own oppression. In contrast, a reconfiguration-oriented theory of social change would situate advocacy for improved language education for racialized bilingual students within larger social transformation projects that address the myriad factors contributing to the marginalization of their communities. In this way, language education is not positioned as a panacea. Instead, language education becomes a small piece of a larger movement for social transformation that refuses to place the onus of academic achievement on the backs of racialized bilingual students and their families, and that refocuses attention on developing a comprehensive approach to public policy that addresses poverty, racism, and other social hierarchies.

To situate language education within the broader political and economic context does not mean that conceptualizations of language are no longer relevant. On the contrary, a reconfiguration-oriented theory of social change offers the possibility for denaturalizing the concept of academic language and reconceptualizing language in ways that resist reifying the marginalization of racialized bilingual communities. In line with the functional approach to academic language, a reconfiguration-oriented theory of social change historicizes the emergence of the discursive practices that have come to be associated with the concept of academic language. Yet, it would go further by situating the rise of these discursive practices within the broader socio-historical processes of nation-state/colonial governmentality. This denaturalization serves as a point of entry for reframing academic language away from its dominant conceptualization as an objective tool of communication toward acknowledging its association with discursive practices produced as part of broader histories of colonialism.

This denaturalization of academic language offers a point of entry for challenging the language-as-entity paradigm through the undoing of dichotomous framings of language. Both the cognitive and functional approaches to academic language rely on such dichotomous framings. While both schools of thought have been careful to insist on the legitimacy of both ends of their dichotomies, the major ways that these dichotomies have been taken up has been to value the dominant end of the dichotomy while devaluing the subordinate end of the dichotomy. In particular, mass schooling, organized around a language-as-entity paradigm, has taken up these dichotomies in ways that position students coming from dominant backgrounds as having academic language and students coming from racialized bilingual backgrounds as lacking these language practices. That is, despite the desire among educational linguists to advocate for racialized bilingual students, the concept of academic language has been taken up by schools in ways that exacerbate these students' marginalization. The development of non-dichotomous views of language that point to the complex range of language practices engaged in by all communities without dividing them a priori into separate categorizations may offer an important intervention in challenging the raciolinguistic ideologies that inform the way that the concept of academic language has been taken up in schools. In short, a reconfiguration-oriented theory of social change does not negate the important role of language in marginalizing racialized bilingual students nor does it negate the possibility that critical framings of language can serve an important role in challenging their marginalization. What it does do is take seriously the truism in educational linguistics that language education is not a panacea and ensure that this truism is reflected in the ways we discuss the role that language education can play in social transformation.

To illustrate the implications of a reconfiguration-oriented theory of social change for our scholarship and work with practitioners, let's revisit the school district mentioned at the beginning of the article. We envision working with teachers and administrators in the district to denaturalize academic language. Together, we could critically engage with the ideological assumptions that go into the discursive practices associated with academic language while examining very closely the complex language practices that the Mexican-origin children in their district engage in on a daily basis. This, in and of itself, is not necessarily novel, in that it builds on the work of many educational linguists who have sought to challenge deficit perspectives of racialized bilingual students, including many proponents of the concept of academic language.

Where a reconfiguration-oriented theory of social change differs is in its insistence that we reject dichotomous views of language that will inevitably frame the language practices of racialized bilingual students as inherently deficient. Where it also differs is in its insistence that this professional development, as important as it might be, does little to address the root cause of the marginalization of Mexican-origin students in the district. It begins from the premise that it is impossible to affirm the language practices of racialized bilingual communities within an institution such as mass schooling produced as part of nation-state/colonial governmentality. At the core of this stance is the belief that there is nothing affirming about an institution designed to prepare racialized bilingual communities for their role in a racist society. Instead, it argues that if we want to truly affirm the language practices of racialized bilingual students what we need is a fundamental transformation of school and society. That is, to truly address the root cause would require fundamental structural changes to the global political order.

Some might object that a focus on the broader political and economic context is beyond the scope of educational linguistics. This is precisely the problem that we have been pointing to throughout this chapter. By bracketing the broader political and economic issues confronting racialized bilingual communities and focusing solely on linguistic solutions, our discipline has been complicit in the production of a theory of social change that identifies the root of the challenges confronting racialized bilingual communities as linguistic and the solution as the modification of their language practices. Developing a reconfiguration-oriented theory of social change requires not only new conceptualizations of language that resist linguistic dichotomies but also a systematic incorporation of the structural barriers confronting racialized bilingual communities into the solutions we propose. In short, educational linguists must resist dichotomous framings of language that inevitably get taken up by schools in ways that perpetuate deficit perspectives while simultaneously situating this non-dichotomous framing of language within the broader political and economic processes that lie at the root of the marginalization of racialized bilingual communities. Only in this way can educational linguists truly avoid being part of the problem and instead become part of the solution to the marginalization of racialized bilingual communities.

Note

1 We use the term "racialized" as opposed to terms such as "minority" or "people of color" to emphasize that race is "a social construct rather than a description based on perceived characteristics" (Ontario Human Rights Commission, 2017, p. 15). This terminology is also in line with work in linguistic anthropology that defines racialization as "markedness…operating against an unmarked background of what social actors perceive as normative" (Uriciouli, 2011, p. E113). From this perspective, whiteness is the unmarked norm that racialized communities are marked as deviating from with material consequences.

References

Achugar, M., & Colombi, M. C. (2008). Systemic Functional Linguistic explorations into the longitudinal study of the advanced capacities: The case of Spanish Heritage Language Learners. In: L. Ortega & H. Byrnes (Eds.), *Systemic Functional Explorations* (pp. 36–57). New York, NY: Routledge.

Aguirre-Muñoz, Z., Park, J., Amabisca, A., & Boscardin, C. (2009). Developing teacher capacity for serving ELLs' writing instructional needs: A case for systemic-functional linguistics. *Bilingual Research Journal, 31*(1–2), 295–322.

Arias, B., & Wiley, T. (2015). Forty years after *Lau*: The continuing assault on educational human rights in the United States and its implications for linguistic minorities. *Language Problems and Planning, 18*, 227–244.

Auckerman, M. (2007). A culpable CALP: Rethinking the conversational/academic language proficiency distinction in early literacy instruction. *The Reading Teacher, 60*(7), 626–635.

Bauman, R., & Briggs, C. (2000). Language philosophy as language ideology: John Locke and Johann Gottfried Herder. In: P. Kroskrity (Ed.), *Regimes of Language: Ideologies, Politics, and Identities* (pp. 139–204). Santa Fe, NM: School of American Press.

Bauman, R., & Briggs, C. (2003). *Voices of Modernity: Language Ideologies and the Politics of Inequality*. Cambridge: Cambridge University Press.

Bensch, S. (2001). *Critical English for Academic Purposes: Theory, Politics and Practice*. New York, NY: Routledge.

Bernstein, B. (1990). *Class, Code and Control: Volume 4—The Structuring of Pedagogic Discourse*. New York, NY: Routledge.

Brent-Palmer, C. (1979). A sociolinguistic assessment of the notion of "immigrant semilingualism" from a social conflict perspective. *Working Papers on Bilingualism, 17*, 135–180.

Brisk, M., Hodgson-Drysdale, T., & O'Connor, C. (2010/2011). A study of a collaborative instructional project informed by systemic-functional linguistic theory: Report writing in elementary grades. *The Journal of Education, 191*(1), 1–12.

Calafell, B. (2012). Monstrous femininity: Constructions of women of color in the academy. *Journal of Communication Inquiry, 36*(2), 111–130.

Cazden, C., John, V., & Hymes, D. (Eds.) (1972). *Functions of Language in the Classroom*. New York, NY: Teachers College Press.

Clough, P. (1998). *The Ends(s) of Ethnography: From Realism to Social Criticism*. New York, NY: Peter Lang Publishing.

Coffin, C. & Donohue, J. (2012). Academic literacies and systemic functional linguistics: How do they relate? *Journal of English for Academic Purposes, 11*, 64–75.

Colombi, M. C. (2015). Academic and cultural literacy for heritage speakers of Spanish: A case study of Latin@ students in California. *Linguistics and Education, 32*, 5–15.

Cummins, J. (1980). The entry and exit fallacy in bilingual education. *NABE Journal, 4*(3), 25–59.

Cummins, J. (1982). Test, achievement and bilingual students. *Focus, 9*, 1–7.

Cummins, J. (2000). *Language, Power, and Pedagogy: Bilingual Children in the Crossfire*. Clevedon: Multilingual Matters.

Cummins, J. (2014). Beyond language: Academic communication and student success. *Linguistics and Education, 26*, 145–154.

Edelsky, C. (1996). *With Literacy and Justice for All: Rethinking the Social in Language and Education* (2nd ed.). London: Taylor and Francis.

Edelsky, C., Flores, B., Barkin, F., Altweger, B., & Jilbert, K. (1983). Semilingualism and language deficit. *Applied Linguistics, 4*(1), 1–22.

Ellsworth, E. (1989). Why doesn't this feel empowering? Working through the repressive myths of critical pedagogy. *Harvard Educational Review, 59*(3), 297–324.

Fanon, F. (1967). *Black Skin, White Masks*. London: Pluto Press.

Fishman, J. (1976). *Bilingual Education: An International Sociological Perspective*. Rowley, MA: Newbury House Publishers.

Fishman, J., Ferguson, C., & Das Gupta, J. (Eds.) (1968). *Language Problems of Developing Nations*. New York, NY: John Wiley and Sons.

Flores, N. (2013). Silencing the subaltern: Nation-state/colonial governmentality and bilingual education in the United States. *Critical Inquiry in Language Studies, 10*(4), 263–287.

Flores, N., & Rosa, J. (2015). Undoing appropriateness: Raciolinguistic ideologies and language diversity in education. *Harvard Educational Review, 85*(2), 149–171.

Flores, N., & Schissel, J. (2014). Dynamic bilingualism as the norm: Envisioning a heteroglossic approach to standards-based reform. *TESOL Quarterly, 48*(3), 454–479.

Foucault, M. (1970). *The Order of Things: An Archeology of the Human Sciences*. New York, NY: Vintage Books.

Foucault, M. (1978). *The History of Sexuality: An Introduction*. New York, NY: Vintage Books.

García, O. (2009). *Bilingual Education in the 21st Century: A Global Perspective*. Malden, MA: Wiley-Blackwell.

Gay, G. (2005). Epilogue: 'the struggle continues…'. *Counterpoints, 131*, 231–252.

Gebhard, M. (2010). Teacher education in changing times: A systemic functional linguistics (SFL) perspective. *TESOL Quarterly, 44*(4), 797–803.

Gebhard, M., & Harman, R. (2011). Reconsidering genre theory in K-12 schools: A response to school reforms in the United States. *Journal of Second Language Writing, 20*(1), 45–55.

Halliday, M. (1978). *Language as Social Semiotic: The Social Interpretation of Language and Meaning*. London: Edward Arnold Publishers.

Halliday, M., & Martin, J. (1993). *Writing Science: Literacy and Discursive Power*. Pittsburgh, PA: University of Pittsburg Press.

Haneda, M. (2014). From academic language to academic communication: Building on English learners' resources. *Linguistics and Education, 26*, 126–135.

Hasan, R. (1996). Literacy, everyday talk and society. In: R. Hasan & G. Williams (Eds.), *Literacy in Society* (pp. 377–424). New York, NY: Longman.

Hasan, R. (2005). *Language, Society and Consciousness*, Webster, J. (Ed.). London: Equinox.

Heath, S. (1976). A national language academy? Debate in a new nation. *International Journal of the Sociology of Language, 11*, 9–44.

Heath, S. (1983). *Ways with Words: Language, Life and Work in Communities and Classrooms*. New York, NY: Cambridge University Press.

Janks, H. (2010). *Literacy and Power*. New York, NY: Routledge.

Labov, W. (1966). *Some Sources of Reading Problems for Negro Speakers of Nonstandard English*. Washington, DC: ERIC Clearinghouse.

Labov, W. (1972). *Language of the Inner-City: Studies in the Black English Vernacular*. Philadelphia, PA: University of Pennsylvania Press.

Lambert, W. E. (1975). Culture and language as factors in learning and education. In: A. Wolfgang (Ed.), *Education of Immigrant Children* (pp. 55–83). Toronto: Ontario Institute for Studies in Education.

Lillis, T. & Scott, M. (2007). Defining academic literacies research: Issues of epistemology, ideology and strategy. *Journal of Applied Linguistics, 4*, 5–32.

Lippi-Green, R. (1997). *English with an Accent: Language, Ideology, and Discrimination in the United States*. London: Routledge.

Luke, A. (1997). Genres of power: Literacy education and the production of capital. In: R. Hasan & G. Williams (Eds.), *Literacy in Society* (pp. 308–338). London: Longman.

MacSwan, J. (2000). The threshold hypothesis, semilingualism, and other contributions to a deficit view of linguistic minorities. *Hispanic Journal of Behavioral Sciences, 22*(1), 3–45.

Martin-Jones, M., & Romaine, S. (1986). Semilingualism: A half-baked theory of communicative competence. *Applied Linguistics, 7*(1), 26–38.

Martínez, G. (2007). Writing back and forth: The interplay of form and situation in heritage language composition. *Language Teaching Research, 11*(1), 31–41.

May, S. (Ed.) (2014). *The Multilingual Turn: Implications for SLA, TESOL and Bilingual Education*. New York, NY: Routledge.

Moore, J., & Schleppegrell, M. (2014). Using a functional linguistics metalanguage to support academic language development in the English language arts. *Linguistics and Education, 26*, 92–105.

New London Group. (1996). A pedagogy of multiliteracies: Designing social futures. *Harvard Educational Review, 66*(1), 60–92.

Ontario Human Rights Commission (2017). *Under Suspicion: Research and Consultation Report on Racial Profiling in Ontario*. Toronto, CA: Author.

Park, J., & Wee, L. (2012). *Markets of English: Linguistic Capital and Language Policy in a Globalizing World*. New York, NY: Routledge.

Peal, E., & Lambert, W. (1962). The relation of bilingualism to intelligence. *Psychological Monographs: General and Applied, 76*(27), 1–23.

Pennycook, A. (1996). TESOL and critical literacies: Modern, post, or neo? *TESOL Quarterly, 30*(1), 163–171.

Petrovic, J. (2013). (Post)Structural analyses of deficit notions of academic language: Discourse and dialect. In: B. J. Irby, G. Brown, R. Lara-Alecio & S. Jackson (Eds.), *The Handbook of Educational Theories* (pp. 419–428). Charlotte, NC: Information Age Publishing, Inc.

Prendergast, C. (2003). *Literacy and Racial Justice: The Politics of Learning after Brown v. Board of Education.* Carbondale, IL: South Illinois University Press.

Schleppegrell, M. (2004). *The Language of Schooling: A Functional Linguistics Perspective.* New York, NY: Routledge.

Schwartz, A. M. (2003). ¡No me suena! Heritage Spanish speakers' writing strategies. In: A. Roca & M. C. Colombi (Eds.), *Mi Lengua: Spanish as a Heritage Language in the United States* (pp. 235–256). Washington, DC: Georgetown University Press.

Schwartz, A. M. (2005). Exploring differences and similarities in the writing strategies used by students in SNS courses. *Contactos y contextos: El español en los estados unidos y en contacto con otras lenguas* (pp. 323–334). Madrid, Spain: Iberomamericana.

Skutnabb-Kangas, T. (1981). *Bilingualism or Not: The Education of Minorities.* Bristol, UK: Multilingual Matters.

Skutnabb-Kangas, T., & Toukomaa, P. (1976). *Teaching Migrant Children's Mother Tongue and Learning the Language of the Host Country in the Context of the Socio-Cultural Situation of the Migrant Family.* Paris: UNESCO.

Spicer-Escalante, M. (2005). Writing in two languages/living in two worlds: Rhetorical analysis of Mexican-American written discourse. *Latino Language and Literacy in Ethnolinguistic Chicago,* 217–244.

Spicer-Escalante, M. (2007). Análisis lingüístico de la escritura bilingüe (español-inglés) de los hablantes de español como lengua hereditaria en los Estados Unidos. *Estudios de Lingüística Aplicada, 45,* 63–80.

Stoler, A. (1995). *Race and the Education of Desire: Foucault's History of Sexuality and the Colonial Order of Things.* Durham, NC: Duke University Press.

Urciuoli, B. (2011). Discussion essay: Semiotic properties of racializing discourses. *Journal of Linguistic Anthropology, 21,* E113–E122.

Valdés, G. (1997). Dual language immersion programs: A cautionary note concerning the education of language-minority students. *Harvard Educational Review, 67*(3), 391–429.

Valdés, G. (2004). Between support and marginalization: The development of academic language in linguistic minority children. *International Journal of Bilingual Education and Bilingualism, 7*(2–3), 102–132.

Valdés, G. (2015). Latin@ s and the intergenerational continuity of Spanish: The challenges of curricularizing language. *International Multilingual Research Journal, 9*(4), 253–273.

Valdés, G. (2017). From language maintenance and intergenerational transmission to language survivance: Will "heritage language" education help or hinder? *International Journal of the Sociology of Language, 2017*(243), 67–95.

Yanguas, I., & Lado, B. (2012). Is thinking aloud reactive when writing in the heritage language? *Foreign Language Annals, 45*(3), 380–399.

PART 3

Learning Across Contexts

Introduction

Learning is ubiquitous. It occurs in societies around the globe as a normal part of human activity, both in settings organized for the explicit purpose of teaching and learning (e.g. schools, apprenticeships, rites of passage), and as part of the settings and activities that make up daily life (e.g. in families, children's play, in communities, at work, in leisure activities, and on the go). Our theories of learning, then, must account for learning activity in all of its iterations and forms, and must be applicable to the full range of types of learning that occur across multiple communities and societies. Further, they must help us account for the ways that marginalization is a pervasive condition of social life, and thus, learning occurs in relation to, and sometimes in spite of, the conditions and systems of marginalization that fundamentally organize societies. In other words, at times learning is also a contested activity, involving the navigation of systems of power.

The chapters in this section take these complex concerns seriously, and work to deepen our theorization of learning. Taken together, they provide an opportunity to re-examine how we understand what learning is, how it is organized, and who does it effectively. The section begins with Nasir, McKinney de Royston, Barron, Bell, Pea, Stevens, and Goldman, who argue that we need to better understand the connection between micro-genetic moments of learning within learning settings, and the ways learning trajectories, or what they call *Learning Pathways*, take shape over the life course. They theorize the nature of these learning pathways to highlight both their local nature, the ways that they are shaped by positioning in relation to privilege and marginalization, and how they are rooted in learning that cut across formal and informal spaces. The Stevens chapter highlights a key problematic in research on children, *adultocentrism*, and posits that a strategy to avoid such adult-centric perspectives on children's activities (including learning activities), is to utilize an interaction-focused methodological approach. Peele-Eady and Moje take up the concept of "community" and explore how this notion has been conceptualized in research on learning, arguing that ideas about community have been both beneficial and harmful in research on communities, especially research with and about marginalized learners. Brice Heath, Bellino, and Winn explore how learning research has left out key populations of adult learners, arguing that adaptive learning occurs across the life course. They draw on case studies in three unconventional settings to illustrate the deep learning that occurs for adults. Alim, Paris, and Wong articulate an alternative vision for the possibility of powerful, community-centered learning that can happen in school, what they term *Culturally Sustaining Pedagogy*, and they highlight the characteristics of such an approach. In doing so, they identify school as an important site for liberatory teaching and learning. And finally, Warren, Vossoughi, Rosebery, Bang, and Taylor argue for an approach to teaching and learning that recognizes not only issues of access, but issues of epistemology—questioning whose knowledge counts as valid, and pushing us to re-imagine the possibilities for disciplinary learning in schools that encourages and supports multiple ways of learning, or epistemic heterogeneity.

11

LEARNING PATHWAYS
How Learning Is Culturally Organized

Na'ilah Suad Nasir, Maxine McKinney de Royston, Brigid Barron,
Phillip Bell, Roy Pea, Reed Stevens, and Shelley Goldman

Educational research over the past several decades has expanded our view of learning beyond the cognitive processes and psychological traits of the individual learner to consider the varied influences of local interactions with social others and with learning resources and environments. While this expanded view provides richer accounts of the social and interactional aspects of learning, the focus on *local* learning interactions has the potential to limit a deep understanding of the cultural, relational, affective, and contextual nature of learning that gets further complicated by race, gender, language, and other dynamics and systems of power (Annamma & Booker, this volume; Esmonde & Booker, 2016; Immordino-Yang, Darling-Hammond, & Krone, 2018). In part, this is because current approaches to learning often understand culture as related to learning rather than understanding learning as necessarily a cultural process (Nasir, Warren, Lee, & Rosebery, 2006; Warren, Vossoughi, Rosebery, Bang, & Taylor, this volume).

Relatedly, many accounts of learning do not attend to how it takes place as a part of an individual's longer-term trajectories of participation in a broad range of activities, across more and less formally structured learning spaces, and over longer stretches of the life span (Barron, 2006), phenomena usefully reflected in the metaphor of a "learning career" or the development of dispositions to learning for an individual over time (e.g. Bloomer & Hodkinson, 2000; Crossan, Field, Gallacher, & Merrill, 2003). Finally, few studies examine how these learning careers may be facilitated or constrained by social systems and institutions (as informed by racism, sexism, ableism, and many other isms) that differentially position individuals' access to particular resources and associated experiences that are important for future learning or engagement in learning in formal spaces.

By contrast, our approach is to examine learning across time and space—namely, how access to learning resources and experiences over time is disrupted by processes of structural inequality that get reproduced through institutions (Oakes, 2005; Warren et al., this volume). We conceptualize learning as occurring along culturally organized learning pathways—sequences of consequential participations and transitions (Beach, 1999) in learning activities that move (or do not move) one towards greater social recognition as competent in particular learning domains and situations. This framework draws attention to the resources to which learners have access over time, how learners are positioned within the broad range of learning settings in which they participate, and the roles that issues of *identity*—who one is in the process of becoming—play in learning (Nasir, 2012; Offidani-Bertand, Harris, Velez, & Spencer, this volume; Rogers, Rosario, & Cielto, this volume). It also attends to how institutions and systems structure access to and position (Green, Brock, Harris, & Baker, this volume) various types of learning and learners.

We draw on data from multiple studies of STEM learning that illustrate three key aspects of culturally organized learning pathways, namely that: (1) they are taken up in relation to identities, and have relational, affective, and motivational components; (2) they are made up of sets of cultural practices and routines, socially constructed by self and others, and they build up over multiple instances and protracted time periods; and (3) they include enactments of privilege and marginalization that occur in relation to structural constraints and supports which are experienced by learners in their families, peer relations, and institutions such as schools. A learning pathways framework is a synthetic and pluralistic approach that attends to the multi-level, longitudinal nature of how cultural processes are inherent in and intrinsic to learning.

We argue that a learning pathways framework deepens our analyses of learning by attending to how learning is fundamentally cultural (Lee, Meltzoff, & Kuhl, this volume; Rogoff, Rosado-May, Urrieta, & Dayton, this volume), and how it is shaped by structures that can empower or marginalize (Alim, Paris, & Wong, this volume; Cole & Packer, this volume). The implications of this framework extend to how we conduct research as well as how we translate research into practice. In terms of conducting research, this framework invites new empirical methods to deepen our understanding of learning as a dynamic life-long cultural process, and as an accumulation of an individual's local and longer-term interactions with differing levels of access to learning resources and opportunities. Similarly, this framework invites conversation among educational psychologists, learning scientists, and other educational researchers about how our research can translate into relevant educational interventions or designs (Greene, 2014), including how we can design learning settings that create multiple entry points and sustained opportunities for learning.

The chapter is organized into four sections. First, we review scholarship that moves towards a culturally informed learning pathways framework. In the second section we introduce three contrasting cases of student learning pathways, cases that ground the notion of pathways in the real life experiences of students and families. The third section outlines three aspects of the learning pathways framework, synthesizing the literature that elaborates each aspect of the framework and which links back to the student cases. In the fourth and final section we outline directions for future research and implications for educational practice.

Towards Culturally Informed Learning Pathways

The dictionary defines a pathway as "a route to or way of access to; way of reaching or achieving something; a trodden track or way." This metaphor implies both movement over time, and the notion that a pathway already exists from a "trodden" track—that is, pathways tend to be culturally defined and situated. Scholars concerned with the cultural contexts or ecologies relative to learning have used the metaphor of pathways to consider how developmental or learning trajectories are shaped (Greenfield, 2009; Stevens, O'Connor, Garrison, Jocuns, & Amos, 2008). For example, Greenfield (2009) provides a model to predict how changing socioeconomic demographics likewise trigger shifts in the life-long developmental pathways and outcomes of individuals and communities through changing learning environments and, at times, cultural values. Stevens et al. (2008) used pathway as a metaphor to characterize how young people "become" (or don't become) engineers over time and through experiences during their college years, with pathways rendered further into three, interrelated dimensions of change: accountable disciplinary knowledge, identity, and navigation. Each author uses the pathways metaphor differently, yet all caution that pathways are constrained and enabled by the cultural, ecological niche in which they reside.

As in the work by Greenfield and Stevens et al., our notion of a pathway reaches beyond local moments or single interactions to more fully consider how an individual's participation occurs over longer stretches within the life span and how those trajectories of participation vary with situated conditions that change at multiple time scales. Similar to Greenfield (2009), Stevens et al. (2008),

Learning Pathways

and Gallimore and Goldenberg (2001), we view individuals' pathways as being fundamentally influenced by their interaction with cultural practices and values across a range of learning environments, informal and institutional. We recognize the importance of understanding how these interactions across the institutional and the informal can be consequential for success, especially academic success within schools.

David Plath's (1985) metaphor of pathways, generated through studying a cohort of middle-aged Japanese citizens, is also useful for thinking about learning across the life span. Plath articulates life pathways as being constructed at the intersection of culture and individual choice and meaning. Pathways include routes and timetables that are associated with types of trajectories and variations in images of oneself in relation to both past and future. While culture has a heavy hand in determining the potential pathways that are made available (and to whom they are made available), constructing a pathway is more than simply choosing or following a culturally determined road. Instead, "Pathways can vary in their appeal for different persons or for the same person at different phases of life" (p. 50), which is to say that choosing a pathway involves both drawing on a frame which one uses to construct meaning and understanding that this chosen frame often implies a pathway that may be more or less desirable depending on where a person is in their life course. Moreover, although individuals have a choice of possible frames and pathways, the notion of the "trodden" track suggests that despite some agency to choose among possible frames and pathways, these pathways are not infinite and access to them is located historically, geographically and politically.

The importance of time and cohort is also expressed by Elder (1994) in his description of life course research as part of a general conceptual trend that has made time, context, and process more salient dimensions of theory and analysis. For Elder there are several guiding assumptions, including the critical role of historical times in life experience and outcomes, the way that life stage and timing matter for opportunities and ultimate outcomes, how our lives are linked in important ways to opportunities or constraints contributed by social others, and the critical role of human agency and choice in the construction of life pathways (Giele & Elder, 1998). These assumptions by Elder harken to Bronfenbrenner's (1994) notions of chronosystems, mesosystems, and microsystems where one's learning and development is influenced by and changes across time, and across the social worlds one navigates.

Two specific constructs most closely relate to our notion of learning pathways. The first one is Bloomer and Hodkinson's (2000) definition of "learning careers" which emphasizes understanding people's ways of orienting themselves to learning settings, and how these orientations or dispositions change over time. They point out that accounts of learning rarely take note of the broader social, cultural, and economic contexts within which people construct these learning careers, rendering these accounts unable to explain the complexities of how learning careers unfold. While "learning careers" broadens the conversation about learning to include external structural factors and discourses that shape young people's perceptions of learning and schooling and its role in their lives, it does not include a unit of analysis for the activities or resources we see as a crucial component for understanding learning and learning pathways. Moreover, the notion of "career" may signal attention to formal learning spaces rather than informal and life-wide experiences.

The second construct is that of "trajectories of identification" (Polman & Miller, 2010). Central to understanding these trajectories of identification is that interactions with social and cultural contexts occur in relation to perceptions of the past, present, and future—a process called *prolepsis* (Cole, 1996). Thus, trajectories of identification are shaped as people project into the future, based on the past, which structures interactions in the present. Much like the notion of pathways, Polman and Miller's (2010) trajectories of identification captures the idea that learning occurs as a part of a process that unfolds over time and consists of multiple instances of participation and positioning in multiple practices across various life spaces. Clearly, *identity* (or one's sense of one's place in the world and connection to others) has profound implications for how one engages in learning settings; conversely, the ways in which learning settings engage individuals has important implications for how they view themselves. Expanding upon Polman and Miller's notion of "trajectories of identification," our framing of learning pathways also considers how some acts or practices that position an individual may be more or less consequential for their future participation and access to learning resources and learning.

Our framing of learning pathways, like some of the constructs discussed above, relies upon some fundamental assumptions of sociocultural theories such as using the social and cultural activities that people engage in with one another towards particular shared goals as a core unit of analysis for understanding learning (Nasir, 2002; Vygotsky, 1978; Wertsch, 1991). Centering cultural activities as a unit of analysis supports an examination of individuals and their cultural and social context, especially as it is carried through social interaction and involves cultural artifacts in activity systems. Activity systems can take many forms, including that of "academic lessons" which prepare children for subsequent school-based interactions by focusing on certain content or socializing forms of discourse that are later encountered in formal education settings. Or, they may take the form of games played with parents or other caregivers that allow a child to develop familiarity with representational tools that have been developed over long periods of time, such as writing systems, maps, language, or numerical systems (Griffin, Case, & Sieger, 1994; Vygotsky, 1978).

These culturally specific patterns of interactions are driven by implicit or explicit values, and the expertise developed through them plays a role in the early learning pathways of young children, long before they enter formal schooling (Rogoff, 1990; 2003). For example, parents may evaluate their children's knowledge using question/answer/evaluation sequences that are similar to those often observed in classrooms (Mehan, 1996), or they may orchestrate dinner conversations that invite children to participate in argumentation (Ochs & Taylor, 1992). In these shared contexts, parents can express their enthusiasm, explanations can be provided spontaneously or in response to questions, and children have an opportunity to demonstrate their interest or lack of it in particular activities and content. Consider how in an ethnographic study of musical parenting, intergenerational practices of singing and music making were documented as well as reciprocal child–parent interest in listening and producing traditional, popular, and spiritual songs (Gibson, 2009). Relatedly, Goodwin (2007) described one family's "occasioned knowledge exploration" (p. 97) that routinely emerged during daily walks, dinners, car rides, or bedtime stories. Within these interactions, playful imaginative conversations were connected to prior knowledge when a child asked questions and parents provided detailed explanations. These forms of guided participation (e.g. Rogoff, 2003) take the form of co-activity and rely on joint attention as an important means of building a basis for inter-subjectivity—the shared understanding of what is happening and what will happen next.

The aforementioned scholarship suggests that the notion of a context-dependent learning trajectory may be a rich way to understand learning and variation in learning over time. Yet, we still do not have a coherent framework for studying learning that attends to the interplay between the individual, local, cultural, and institutional contexts and practices in and across time and space. Our notion of learning pathways offers such a framework and adds two important dimensions. First, our framework shifts the unit of analysis from learning outcomes to the specific and consequential learning resources or experiences that learners are able to access. These include cultural practices, activities, and events, as well as identity resources or ways in which learners are socially recognized or supported in developing positive dispositions to engage and persist in thriveful learning.

Second, although such learning resources often play out in the context of institutions, scholars who attend to the nature of these in their analyses (e.g., Mehan, 1996; Rogoff, Topping, Baker-Sennett, & Lacasa, 2002) do not systematically attend to how an individual's access to such resources (by virtue of race, class, disability status, gender, etc.) subsequently shape the learning dispositions and pathways that they form (Esmonde & Booker, 2016). By contrast, our conceptualization of pathways considers how learning pathways develop over time and across spaces, namely (1) how they are taken up in relation to identities; (2) how they are made up of cultural practices and forms of participation that are socially constructed by self and others; and (3) how they include enactments of privilege and marginalization that structure access to and position various types of learning and learners relative to dynamics of power (e.g. racialized, gendered, etc.). Below we present contrasting cases of learning pathways from three different studies. These cases illustrate the multiplicities of learning pathways individuals engage in over time, and how these unfold across formal and informal learning environments.

Contrasting Learning Pathways: The Cases of Layla, Renee, and Jill

In this section, we present the learning pathways of three students, operating within different learning contexts. These cases are all drawn from studies funded under the auspices of the Learning in Formal and Informal Environments (LIFE) Center between 2004 and 2014, involving a range of methods, including case studies, observations, and interviews. Taken together, these contrasting cases point to the limitations of notions of learning that understand learning within only one context at only one particular point in time, as well as the limitations of using constructs like identity or motivation to explain different experiences of learning and of learners devoid of a treatment of the social, cultural, institutional, and political context within which learning takes place. These cases highlight how access to learning pathways is negotiated and contested, and highlight the processes of identity and positioning that determine how one engages a particular learning context—in relation to other learning contexts, social and information networks, family life, and past interactions and access—and the kinds of dispositions towards learning they develop across time and space.

Layla's Learning Pathway in Computer Programing

Layla considers herself, and is considered by others, as a strong math learner. Layla attributes her early interest in math to her grandmother, a former math teacher, who played math games with her as a child and encouraged her. Both of her parents pursued math in their own careers, noting the strong emphasis on math and science in their country of origin, China. At age 12, Layla's initial involvement in computing activities revolved around her interest in mathematics, becoming more serious upon joining the mathematics team at her school (Barron et al., 2009), then later an online math community her mother found. After Layla began to engage in the computing community and experience success and belonging there, she became involved in other areas like programing, blogging, and discussion boards that were related to math as well as to broader social and political issues. Based on conversations with her online peers, she decided to teach herself C++ and used Google to find an online tutorial. Based on the tutorial, Layla decided to enroll in the school's programing class as a seventh grader. That course prepared Layla to teach herself a code-based 3D graphics application called POV-Ray, which she picked up as a home-based hobby.

In the online community Layla engaged with same age and older peers, as well as with adults who had expertise in mathematics. Her online peers motivated her pursuit of programing languages, and again she used her resources, in this case a course at her school, to find new ways to learn in and out of school. Since none of her local friends were interested in math, the online community was an important resource for her at that time. Later, Layla's commitment to mathematics was deepened through more local connections as she matriculated into high school and became the founder and three-year president of her school's math club.

Traditional approaches to analyzing Layla's engagement and success might highlight her individual motivation, her strong sense of identity as a computer scientist, or her diligence in seeking out opportunities in and outside of school. In noting her disposition towards engaging in and seeking out additional opportunities to learn, they might consider the important role of her family in nurturing her interest and exposing her to computer science at an early age. However, Layla's case also illustrates how learning pathways are iterative, build up over multiple instances and positionings, are often dependent upon resources one has access to and the recognition mechanisms they afford (e.g. tests, prizes, and scholarships), and are critically shaped and maintained by key social others as well as their social positions and privileges. The supports Layla had access to and experienced, repeatedly positioned her, to herself and others, as capable, and cumulatively facilitated her in assuming the role of the president of the math club, enrolling in regional and national contests, and becoming a math tutor. Taking up these roles, in turn, continued the cycle of her being recognized and positively positioned for her expertise. A learning pathways perspective thus captures Layla's agency, motivation, and identity development over time relative to computing *and* captures the repeated influence of dynamics of power, such as class, that lent access to her learning and supported her learning pathway.

Renee's Math Learning Pathway

The case of Renee similarly illustrates the role of family and the iterative layering of experiences that shapes learning pathways, but contrasts with Layla's in showing how institutions and processes of exclusion and marginalization also play into how learning experiences, and subsequently learning pathways, are constructed. Renee's family is from Mexico, and she lives with her older sister, Vivian, and her mother, Yali. The research team met the family when Renee was 14 and in the eighth grade. The team conducted a case study of the mom, Yali, and the daughters Vivian (25) and Renee (14). Yali came to the U.S. undocumented and subsequently earned an Associate of Arts degree, a Bachelor's degree, a certificate in arc welding, a California teaching credential, and is a homeowner. Daughter Vivian was a law student at Stanford University. In interviews, the three women all repeatedly said they loved math.

Renee thought of school math as the math context she dealt with most often. She was extremely proud of her achievement, yet attributed some of her success to her sister, Vivian, who helped her when she needed help. Both Yali and Vivian spent considerable time and energy clearing a learning pathway for Renee in school math, establishing regular goal-oriented routines for math study and problem-solving at home. She was two years ahead of her grade in math, taking Algebra 1 in seventh grade and Geometry in eighth grade. As she was finishing middle school, Renee asked her mom if she would pay for her to take college math classes at a local college before she finished high school, later engaging with her mom and sister in thinking about which classes to take and how to pay for them. Renee's mom, sister, and school counselors all eventually decided that she might be able to go to an early college program on the east coast, which she was later accepted into with a full scholarship. Renee struggled with her decision to skip the last year of high school to attend the program because she felt like she "was being exiled," but eventually decided to attend. Once there, she excelled and proudly posted her grade point average, her pre-med major, and her graduation picture on Facebook.

A traditional approach to understanding Renee's engagement and learning in mathematics would highlight how schools were Renee's main math context—first her high school and later the early college program—and how they supported Renee's identity and success in mathematics. It would demonstrate how Renee's teachers and other school staff, such as school counselors, supported Renee's identity formation relative to math and pushed her to engage in and benefit from additional learning opportunities such as the early college program. It might also point out how Renee's sister and mother were there to help her and how Renee herself demonstrated resilience and motivation in pursuing mathematics. Aside from the out-of-school supports that Layla had access to, a traditional analysis for Layla and Renee might present them as somewhat similar cases of highly motivated students who had very supportive families. This type of analysis may even note the differences in their profiles—e.g. the racial or class designations of their families, their documentation status, and the kinds of schools they attended. Traditional analyses, however, rarely interrogate the implications that these demographic differences and institutional configurations might have for students' access to in- or out-of-school learning opportunities and resources, the quality of these learning environments, nor the ways in which these students might differentially experience or be positioned relative to learning opportunities, resources, and environments based on societal perceptions about what these students' social demographics signify.

By contrast, a learning pathway analysis attends to Layla and Renee as contrasting cases that bring to the fore the limitations of understanding only one or two contexts—such as home and/ or school—at a time and at a particular point in time. It would examine how these various layers of experience multiplex over time in ways that can either further legitimize, marginalize, or disrupt students' engagement and identity formation. In essence, a learning pathways analysis makes visible how power operated for each of these students and points out the influential nuances that have strong implications for their participation, identification, and learning. Such an analysis might point out that Renee's family and school counselors sought out alternative learning opportunities for her beyond traditional schools. The dynamics of power and race are ever-present here as Renee may have been perceived by her teachers and peers in relation to being a Spanish-speaking, first generation Latina interested in mathematics. Thankfully, for Renee, these potential challenges were not deterministic. Renee's family supported her, making sure she had gatekeepers on her side within her school. Over time, Renee incorporated these routines and practices into her own repertoire—she internalized the social, interactional support of her math identity and competency advancement such that she was able to attend college early and become an independent math learner and user.

Jill's Learning Pathway in Engineering

The cases of Layla and Renee were illustrations of learning pathways where learners remained on the pathway. The next case, that of Jill, illustrates how a range of institutional forces can come together over time to remove a potential learner from a pathway. Pathways into the engineering profession, like in other careers, are fundamentally related to taking on a domain-specific identity, e.g. as an engineer or future engineer. Jill's story of *not* becoming an engineer illustrates the relevance of dimensions that span beyond knowledge acquisition to how identity and motivation are a core part of taking up or resisting learning pathways. It also demonstrates how institutional structures and agency work to co-construct one's pathways.

At the university that Jill attended, students needed to be admitted as engineering students after one or two years of pre-requisite coursework in cognate disciplines such as mathematics, physics, and chemistry (Stevens et al., 2008). Jill was a first-generation white college student who got very good grades in high school and initially identified herself as a future engineer. Not having clear guidance from mentors or peers, early on Jill took all the hardest classes—chemistry, physics, and higher mathematics—during the same quarter. Consequently, Jill received poor grades in each and ended her freshman year with a low GPA. Moving into her second year, when she was to apply as an engineering major, Jill became dis-identified as an engineer and lost faith in herself as a "good student" (Stevens et al., 2008). By the end of her sophomore year, Jill had left engineering but went on to successfully complete a degree in business.

A traditional approach to understanding Jill's case would highlight the role of social others at Jill's university, such as her peers and the support staff and faculty, who failed to advise Jill about appropriate course-taking patterns or to provide support to her despite her poor academic performance. They might also focus on the local learning interactions within the college classrooms she participated in and examine these learning settings and resources to understand whether they were productive for her engagement and identity development relative to engineering. This view would provide a useful account of the social and interactional aspects of learning processes that certainly influenced Jill's learning and her decision not to pursue engineering.

At the same time, analyzing Jill's case around local or specific learning interactions can limit—temporally and contextually—how we understand her shifting identification with engineering. Jill was a high achiever in high school who identified as a future engineer. Her lack of success in college—like that of many women in STEM fields—is not related to her capacity or intelligence nor her motivation or interest in identifying with engineering. Rather, like Layla and Renee, Jill's case requires examining how her learning and identification as an engineer was culturally organized along a particular pathway. For Jill, however, that pathway in high school did not evolve into a pathway in college, instead it was shut down and supplanted with another pathway. The official, non-contextual pathway into an engineering major—a high GPA—was the only one to which Jill had access and became her *only* image of a pathway into engineering. She had no exposure to other pathways into engineering or to practices that would aid her in achieving the official pathway. Perhaps not surprisingly, once Jill became a business major and a recognized member of a community of future business people, she excelled.

Jill's case shows that constructing or maintaining a positive trajectory on a learning pathway is as much about one's ability to acquire knowledge or engage in learning activities as it is about *continuing to have access to and iteratively crafting a sense of oneself as belonging on that pathway.* This sense of identity can be privileged, marginalized, disrupted, or foreclosed by prevailing ideologies about race, gender, and other dynamics of power, and the accompanying institutional norms and practices that can critically influence one's motivation to remain on a learning pathway. Jill's case demonstrates that a student's persistence and success is often a function of their access and exposure to social, cultural, and navigational capital (Yosso, 2005) that make official and alternative pathways available and that, in turn, open up opportunities for participation, recognition, and ongoing acquisition of domain-specific knowledge and identities.

These three cases, taken together, illustrate the range of forces that impact the cultural nature of learning in local learning settings, *and* how these moments and instances of learning become consequential for future participation on a pathway. They make salient the multiple layers of access, institutional positioning, and identity processes that play into sustaining one's position within, and movement along, a learning pathway. Drawing on these cases, below we highlight three key aspects of learning pathways.

Three Characteristics of Learning Pathways

The Learning Pathways framework identifies three key characteristics of learning pathways: (1) They are taken up in relation to identities, and have relational, affective, and motivational components; (2) They are made up of sets of cultural practices and routines, socially constructed by self and others, and build up over multiple instances and protracted time periods; and (3) They include enactments of privilege and marginalization that occur in relation to structural constraints and supports which are experienced by learners in their families, peer relations, and institutions such as schools.

Characteristic 1: Learning Pathways Are Taken Up in Relation to Identities, and Have a Relational, Affective, and Motivational Component

Research studies over the last decade or so highlight how identity formation processes are fundamentally related to learning (e.g. Anderson, 2009; Boaler & Greeno, 2000; Esmonde & Langer-Osuna, 2013; Lave & Wenger, 1991; Nasir, 2002, 2011; Stevens, O'Connor, & Garrison, 2005; Stevens, O'Connor, Garrison, Jocuns, & Amos, 2008; Wenger, 1998; Wortham, 2008). In her studies of learning in the practices of basketball and dominoes, Nasir (2002) demonstrates how learning and identity processes support one another, such that as one learns the skills and content in a given domain, one's identity as a learner in that domain is reinforced. Hence, the taking up of an identity as a learner in a domain supports the learning underway, and further motivates the learner for future domain-specific learning.

Likewise, Wortham (2008) makes deep connections between processes of learning and processes of identity (or identification) in his study of learning in a social studies classroom. His findings show how students drew on the material they were learning to create identity categories (e.g. the category of a social outcast, or "beast") and to position members of the class into those categories. Students who were positioned in these ways took them up as a part of their identities or resisted them with varying degrees of success.

In each line of research, the relational and affective nature of learning and identity processes is apparent. In Nasir's work on basketball and dominoes, identities as participants in these practices are supported as players are engaged in relationships with other players—as teammates, or as adversaries—and as they develop a *sense of belonging* in and to the practice. This sense of belonging (powell & Roediger, 2012) is motivational in that it increases a player's identification with the practice and is related to affective feelings of connection and responsibility to other players that enhance the players' practice-based engagement and learning. In Wortham's study, students positioned one another relationally, ultimately creating new (and marginal) identities for some students. The identity and learning processes were also affectively laden in that peer positionings eventually shaped students' modes and patterns of participation in a classroom, and their respective domain-specific learning trajectories over the course of an academic year. Hence, learning pathways get shaped, taken up, and resisted in relation to identities—the identities others perceive one to have, and the identities ascribed to oneself. As identity and identification are related to a sense of belonging, affective and relational processes are central to both identity and learning (e.g. Nasir, 2012; Spencer, 2008).

This cycle of identity as supported by access to a set of practices where one feels connected to others and has a positive affective experience that provides the intrinsic motivation for continued learning is prevalent in the research literature (e.g. Bricker & Bell, 2014; Stevens et al., 2008). These findings resonate with other in- and out-of-school studies that discuss how to support intrinsic motivation for creative contributions in corporations (e.g., Collins & Amabile, 1999) or for inducting youth into an interest in technology (e.g. Barron, Martin, Takeuchi, & Fithian, 2009). Barron et al. show how in developing technology fluency while making computational artifacts, it was common for young people to begin participating in a technology learning space (usually a class or community program) because of their relationships with other youth or with their families, and to then develop an identity as someone who "belonged" in the setting, which supported learning and continued participation.

However, these cycles can also be negative ones, in which an identity as a participant was not encouraged by others and thus learning and engagement with the learning pathway ends. Pathways are also "validated" and confirmed in relations with a person's intimates at various phases of the life course. Building on Schutz (1932/1967), Plath theorized that a person's intimate and enduring social group is deeply implicated in the pathways that are made available or abandoned. Different pathways, therefore, can circumscribe different "possible selves" (Markus & Nurius, 1986) that facilitate cultural goals and regulatory strategies (Oyserman, Bybee, Terry, & Hart-Johnson, 2004; Saxe, 1999) that people construct and that then make available particular pathways that can facilitate goal achievement. Indeed, there is a robust literature on the relationship between parental racial socialization practices (quite related to identity) and various motivational and academic outcomes, which shows that when parents support young people in developing strong racial/ethnic identities, academic and social outcomes are improved (Wang, Smith, Miller-Cotto, & Huguley, 2019).

Layla, Renee, and especially Jill's cases demonstrate how learning pathways are deeply related to identities—as to how one sees oneself and how one is viewed by others. They also demonstrate how the initiation and maintenance of these identities, and with a learning pathway more broadly, are influenced by relational, affective, and motivational factors. Learning pathways are reciprocally linked to one's access to resources of identification and to the life choices that one has and that one makes.

Characteristic 2: Learning Pathways Are Made Up of Sets of Cultural Practices and Routines, Socially Constructed by Self and Others, and Build Up over Multiple Instances and Protracted Time Periods

Characteristic 2 demonstrates how the cultivation and sustaining of learning pathways occur via culturally organized and goal-oriented practices and routines. This characteristic draws from sociocultural theorists that have focused on cultural practices and activities as important units of analysis in studying learning (Saxe, 2002; Scribner & Cole, 1981; Wertsch, 1991). These units of analysis capture the ways that learning takes place within communities, as people take part in and help reproduce culturally valued activities and practices (e.g. Greenfield, 2009; Gutierrez & Rogoff, 2003; Lee, 2007; McInerney, 2008; Saxe, 1999, 2002), and illustrate how mathematical and cultural processes interact in the context of personal and community goals (Martin, Goldman, & Jimenez, (2009). For instance, Martin et al. show how people start learning about, and over time participating in, the practice of Tanda—a rotating, community-based credit and savings practice. Mathematical work in the context of the Tanda is in service of, and intimately tied up with, familial community and cultural goals and values—for instance the goal to buy a house or pay off debt. Learning pathways thus provide a way to characterize the learning that occurs as goal driven practices and routines that do not simply occur within one activity, but accumulate over time as individuals participate in multiple activities, or multiple instances of the same activity, over time, place, context.

Such a perspective requires moving beyond an individual level of analysis to a focus on understanding individual development in the complex social and cultural ecologies where learning and development occur (e.g. Rogoff, 2003; Lee, 2010; McDermott & Pea, this volume; Moje & Peele-Eady, this volume). From this perspective, learning is understood as an ongoing, iterative project that involves complex interactions between multiple contexts (e.g. Cantor, Osher, Berg, Steyer, & Rose, 2018). Further, given that humans are naturally adaptive, it follows that learning pathways too have multiple beginning and end points (Lee, 2010; Cantor et. al., 2018). This perspective views variability as a norm, and as a strength. Further, as pathways are socially constructed and take shape over multiple instances, we must recognize that instances of learning are not isolated but occur across formal and informal settings. Developing expertise in any domain requires access to a continual cache of diverse opportunities to learn, to identify with others engaged in domain-relevant practices, to engage in deliberate practice, and to be challenged above one's current threshold of expertise (Ericsson, 2006). The metaphor of pathways honors the multiplicity of routes to become disciplinarily engaged and the multiplicity of destinations that are possible.

The metaphor of pathways also evokes longer timescales, one where parents and educators play an active role in coordinating learning opportunities *across* settings. These brokering moves involve connecting young people to experiences, people, institutions, or information sources. Brokering relies on access to the right social networks and benefits and often requires financial resources such as access to transportation. The impact of brokering roles has been made clear in studies of interest-driven learning in families with parents taking on this role (Barron, Martin, Takeuchi, & Fithian, 2009) and in community-based learning centers where adult mentors or advanced peers engage in brokering (e.g. Barron, Gomez, Pinkard, & Martin, 2014; Ching, Hoadley, Santo, & Peppler, 2015; Erstad & Sefton-Green, 2013). The moves to coordinate learning experiences help forge pathways by increasing opportunities for identity building, expertise, interests, and learning partnerships with peers (Barron & Bell, 2015).

It is equally important to understand educators and institutions as intentional or unintentional gatekeepers. In a retrospective study of the learning pathways of adults who became "naturalists," the opportunity to explore nature during childhood was critical for the interest development of all participants (Hecht, Knudson, & Crowley, 2019). However, school opportunities varied in valence and generativity—some participants were discouraged by school counselors from taking science courses and did so anyway, whereas others did not have the financial backing to complete college and their interest in taking care of the natural world was not expressed in a formal career. For others, parents and teachers played important roles as models and brokers, connecting young naturalists with formal educational opportunities or additional informal experiences that kept them engaged. This study and others foreground the distributed nature of learning (Barron, 2006) and show fluctuations in "interest episodes" as varying with the amount of support for learning and resource constraints (Azevedo, 2013). In contrast to linear perspectives on interest development, the learning biographies of naturalists suggest cycles of more and less stable interest (Hidi & Renninger, 2006) that often depend upon the opportunities available and the social or material constraints faced. In other accounts of educational journeys, we learn about the role of discipline and punitive responses to traumatized young people, in consequence removing formal schooling as an option (Annamma, 2016).

When and where a pathway is entered, and how easy it is to stay on, is highly dependent on the cultural practices and supports one grows up in, has access to, and how well others have cleared the way, left signposts, and eliminated obstructions to opportunities to learn. The cases of Layla and Renee highlight that while most parents seek out ways to develop their child's talents and interests, families vary in their access to the resources to realize such goals. Camps, lessons, and materials that sustain disciplinary engagement are expensive and beyond the reach of many families like Renee's. Social networks, like those Layla had access to online and through extracurricular activities at her school, can offer more informal learning partnerships and the distribution of adult hobbies, occupations, and interests can shape youth's learning opportunities. It is often too easy to undervalue the *readiness* of learning pathways when others have done much of the work that has ensconced future generations in privileged positions.

Learning pathways are often constructed by others—parents, teachers, peers—who offer resources for learning and make available learning opportunities for a particular practice that can get reinforced once one strongly identifies with a practice or a domain. As DiSessa (2002) notes, when learners become "committed," they seek out opportunities that increase their expertise. Indeed, as individuals move along learning pathways, they make critical choices (such as to take or not take on a course or the challenge of a team design project), and develop motivation to continue (or discontinue) participation in a practice or domain. Yet, as Jill's case demonstrates, learning pathways are not de-contextualized "tracks" to which everyone has equal access. A lack of access and support by social and institutional others can become difficult for one individual to maintain. Indeed, certain practices and routines like not seeking out an alternate advisor or not utilizing academic supports at a university, can *constrain* access to learning pathways irrespective of an individual's goal orientations. These constraints are less about an individual's disposition and goals towards learning than they are about how one has been socialized into navigating and understanding a pathway. Renee's interest in STEM, by contrast, began in relation to her sister and mother creating particular routines and practices around mathematics to support her learning. Renee took up this repertoire of practices that they developed in their household, and then used it towards her goal of learning mathematics and her and her family's goal of preparing her for college.

Characteristic 3: Learning Pathways Include Enactments of Privilege and Marginalization That Occur in Relation to Structural Constraints and Supports in Families and Institutions

So far, we've discussed the learning pathways of Layla, Renee, and Jill in relation to cultural practices and routines and to the types of disciplinary identities that have been socially constructed by themselves and others, each having been built up over multiple instances, protracted time periods, and across multiple formal and informal learning settings. These renderings of their pathways effectively shift the unit of analysis around learning from static outcomes measures or local interactional accounts to centering cultural and social activities and resources as a unit of analysis. This re-centering allows us to examine individual learners as embedded within cultural and social contexts across time and space, and leads us to understand how learning and identifications are influenced by an individual's access to, and choices around how to utilize, cultural, social, relational, affective, motivational, and identity resources and supports. This rendering of the notion of a "pathway," however, offers an incomplete analysis of the broader social systems and institutional structures within which pathways get constructed, privileged, disrupted, or foreclosed.

Consequently, the third characteristic of our learning pathways framework posits that pathways are not always infinite for every person—viz. choosing a pathway is not a matter of individual choice; instead, accessing learning pathways is located historically, geographically, and politically by virtue of race, class, disability status, documentation status, gender, etc. It is no secret that the United States is a society highly stratified by race and class with increasing wealth and opportunity gaps (Carter, 2018; Nasir, Scott, Trujillo, & Hernandez, 2016; Reardon, 2011). Black and Latinx communities have significantly less access to resources and have been systematically disenfranchised in every dimension of social life, from health, wealth, education, and exposure to the criminal justice system, to housing (Carter, 2018; Ladson-Billings, 2006; Massey & Brodman, 2014). As with other realms of society riddled with patterns of inequality (Carter, 2018; Reardon, 2011), systems and institutions often have the power to facilitate or constrain individuals' access and opportunities. In the case of education, this power frequently operates relative to particular learning pathways.

Taking up this third characteristic allows us to see how Layla benefited from enactments of privilege via her family supports and institutional supports—like her seventh grade programing class and her high school math club—that spanned across time and context to facilitate her pathway into computing. Layla, also benefitted, however perversely, from the ideological supports as a Chinese American whose interests and success profile fit within the "model minority" discourse about East Asian students. That is to say, her success in mathematics and later her learning pathway in computing, did not run up against ideological or structural roadblocks that might constrain her pathway. Renee, on the other hand, ran the risk of being stereotyped as "not being good at math" by virtue of her being a bilingual girl whose mother immigrated and at one time was undocumented. However, because of her familial supports from her mother and sister, Renee was able to navigate around stereotypes and structural constraints to, like Layla, enact institutional privilege in the form of her encouraging high school counselors. It is important to note that Renee's institutional supports actually emerge out of her mother and sister's ability to access, navigate, and exploit institutional supports on her behalf—such as when Renee's mom, sister, and school counselors decided that she might be able to go to, and find funding for, an early college program. Having been undocumented and navigated the system—likely through a variety of supports unknown to us—Renee's mom (and later Renee's sister at Stanford) had the navigational and aspirational capital to activate institutional resources for Renee in ways that many other students with Renee's background may not be able to do. We see this with Jill who, as a first-generation college student, did not have the family supports or know how to leverage institutional supports to maintain her learning pathway as an engineer in college. Despite coming from a racially more privileged background with fewer ideological and structural constraints around the possibilities for her learning pathway, Jill's case demonstrates how structural and institutional constraints are nonetheless real and may have even more tenuous implications for learning pathways in high-stakes, high-status domains like mathematics, engineering, and other STEM fields and majors.

Reflecting on the cases of Layla, Renee, and Jill makes clear that processes of learning and identification are often set within institutional contexts, such as schools, science centers, families, or community organizations, which can both constrain and support access to learning pathways. Thus, learning pathways can reinforce systems of social advantage in society, or, as the case of Renee demonstrates, they can be purposefully deconstructed or constructed to disrupt social systems of advantage.

Learning Pathways

Conclusion and Implications

We have argued in this paper that learning might be productively characterized as occurring along learning pathways (Stevens et. al., 2008) to better capture the situated, social, relational, affective, cultural, and political (in terms of power dynamics) nature of learning. Indeed, we often already think about how learning and the learning pathways within schools are socially constructed wherein learners on different tracks have very different experiences than students on other tracks in ways that often correlate with race and social class (e.g. Oakes, Lipton, Anderson, & Stillman, 2018; Wells, 2015). However, these historicized and situated conceptualizations of learning and of learning pathways can be limited to specific learning settings, types of learners (e.g. racially, linguistically, and/or gender minoritized), or points in time within a learner's broader trajectory. Instead, the framework and cases presented here have the potential to offer guidance about how positive learning pathways can be supported across time, space, and context (formal or informal) for young people while paying deep attention to the structural and ideological constraints and affordances of institutions and systems that often feed into students' experiences of privilege and marginalization. Our case descriptions and understandings of the characteristics of learning pathways, and their intersections with culture, identity, and power, gives deeper insight into how we can nurture and understand the development of interests, positive learning identities and settings, and domain expertise of learners whose stories do not mirror our own but which reflect the diversity of today's youth.

We presented several cases to illustrate the three key characteristics of learning pathways, including cases where positive learning trajectories were maintained for students and cases where accessing such learning pathways was unavailable, constrained, or where learners chose not to pursue them. Renee and Layla's cases illustrate how families make concerted efforts to support learning pathways, by supporting the creation of opportunities to engage with, in these cases, STEM learning over multiple instances and in a range of activities. These pathways are sustained and deepened over time, and further validated when they intersect with school mathematics learning pathways. In these cases, the alignment between school learning and out-of-school learning prevented marginalization in school learning, and worked to privilege the students. These pathways, too, were shaped in vital ways by families, educators, and the young people themselves and how they reified their identities as mathematics learners and doers.

While Layla and Renee's pathways demonstrate how learning trajectories can be strengthened over time through familial and institutional supports, Jill's experiences illustrate that learning pathways and the sets of practices and routines that make them up are not always accessible to every student. Renee's case suggests that not all learning settings are created equally and that despite the odds some families can and will develop their own practice-level supports and seek out additional learning environments and supports. These cases make clear that learning settings are value-laden, that processes and instances of marginalization and privilege are enacted within them, and that different forms of capital (social, cultural, navigational, etc.) often get leveraged to negotiate those processes and instances. In other words, some participants are positioned with certain kinds of privileges within learning settings, and along learning pathways, while others are positioned more marginally, with less access to particular resources and pathways (Nasir & Shah, 2011; Wenger, 1998).

There is a need for studies to utilize and further this conceptualization, such as those that take into consideration characteristics of learning pathways and intentionally design learning environments that develop and enact design principles for hubs of learning that can cross formal and informal spaces, or that take analyses of power seriously and figure out and design around what students have access to and how they have been positioned as learners over time, for instance the Culturally Sustaining Pedagogy approach described by Alim, Paris, and Wong (this volume). Beyond implications for the design of learning environments and classroom instruction, the conceptual approach presented here has implications for how we study learning, and how we think about the various intersecting effects on learning outcomes for students in and across settings. Specifically, taking the concept of learning pathways seriously would encourage learning scientists to broaden the types of data collected to reflect on learning and affective, relational, political, and motivational aspects of education. This would include collecting data that would lend itself to a deeper understanding of:

- broader notions of context and of learning settings
- the ideologies or societal discourses present in the contexts
- learning and shifts in learning participations and pathways over longer stretches of time, and over more than one environment
- the contextual and shifting nature of motivational processes, especially in relation to power, access, and marginalization
- deeper analysis of barriers and disruptions to a sustained learning pathway, including social, affective, financial, geographic and institutional factors among others

For example, combining a learning pathways approach with a geographical unit of analysis may be productive for continuing to theorize important dimensions of context and place-based learning by expanding our understanding of local settings to neighborhoods, cities, and states (Chetty, Hendren, Kline, & Saez, 2014). Likewise, from an empirical perspective, we would want methods that could capture these varied dimensions as well as capture everyday interactions and transformational moments that help us as researchers and educators to really unpack the role of resources and structural dimensions in a life history vis-a-vis a future-oriented learning pathway.

In summary, the concept of learning pathways supports a more nuanced account of learning—the settings in which it occurs, the timescales across which it occurs, and the dynamics of power by which it is shaped, taking up how recent analyses and theoretical innovations highlight power as a key focus for analyzing how race, gender, language, disability, and other dynamics become consequential in learning settings and for learners (Esmonde & Booker, 2016; Gholson & Martin, 2014; Langer-Osuna & Nasir, 2016). It also provides us with more sophisticated tools to appreciate the multiple ways that learning is socially and culturally situated, as people navigate the complex social and institutional settings, where they can be positioned—by others and themselves—in a range of more or less empowering ways. We need to better understand, research, and then design for diverse learning settings in and out of school wherein pathways of learning can be expanded out to each and every learner irrespective of their sociocultural origins, geographical location, or types of capital to which they personally have access. These processes have profound implications for *what* people come to learn and *who* is able to learn, not to mention what we understand to be consequential towards learning and towards the development of positive learning dispositions and pathways.

References

Alim, S., Paris, D., & Wong, C. (this volume). *Culturally Sustaining Pedagogy: A Critical Framework for Centering Communities.* New York, NY: Routledge.

Anderson, K. T. (2009). Applying positioning theory to the analysis of classroom interactions: Mediating micro-identities, macro-kinds, and ideologies of knowing. *Linguistics and Education, 20*(4), 291–310.

Annamma, S. (2016). Disrupting the carceral state through education journey mapping. *International Journal of Qualitative Studies in Education, 29*(9), 1210–1230. doi:10.1080/09518398.2016.1214297.

Azevedo, F. S. (2013). The tailored practice of hobbies and its implication for the design of interest-driven learning environments. *The Journal of the Learning Sciences, 22*(3), 462–510.

Barron, B. (2006). Interest and self-sustained learning as catalysts of development: A learning ecologies perspective. *Human Development, 49*(4), 193–224.

Barron, B., & Bell, P. (2015). Learning in informal and formal environments. In: L. Corno & E. Anderman (Eds.), *Handbook of Educational Psychology: 3rd Edition*, pp. 323–336. Mahwah, NJ: Erlbaum.

Barron, B., Gomez, K., Pinkard, N., & Martin, C. K. (2014). *The Digital Youth Network: Cultivating Digital Media Citizenship in Urban Communities.* Cambridge, MA: MIT Press.

Barron, B., Martin, C. K., Takeuchi, L., & Fithian, R. (2009). Parents as learning partners in the development of technological fluency. *The International Journal of Learning and Media*, 1(2), 55–77.

Beach, K. (1999). Consequential transitions: A sociocultural expedition beyond transfer in education. *Review of Research in Education*, 24(1), 101–139.

Bell, P., Bricker, L. A., Lee, T. R., Reeve, S., & Zimmerman, H. T. (2006). Understanding the cultural foundations of children's biological knowledge: Insights from everyday cognition research. In: S. A. Barab, K. E. Hay & D. Hickey (Eds.), *Proceedings of the Seventh International Conference of the Learning Sciences (ICLS)*, pp. 1029–1035. Mahwah, NJ: LEA.

Bloomer, M., & Hodkinson, P. (2000). Learning careers: Continuity and change in young people's dispositions to learning. *British Educational Research Journal*, 26(5), 583–597.

Boaler, J., & Greeno, J. (2000). Identity, agency, and knowing in mathematics world. *Multiple Perspectives on Mathematics Teaching and Learning*, 1, 171–200.

Bricker, L. A., & Bell, P. (2014). "What comes to mind when you think of science? The perfumery!": Documenting science-related cultural learning pathways across contexts and timescales. *Journal of Research in Science Teaching*, 51(3), 260–285.

Bronfenbrenner, U. (1979). *The Ecology of Human Development: Experiments by Nature and by Design.* Cambridge, MA: Harvard University Press.

Cantor, P., Osher, D., Berg, J., Steyer, L., & Rose, T. (2018). Malleability, plasticity, and individuality: How children learn and develop in context 1. *Applied Developmental Science.* doi:10.1080/10888691.2017.1398649.

Carter, P. (2018). The multidimensional problems of educational inequality require multidimensional solutions. *Educational Studies*, 54(1), 1–16.

Chetty, R., Hendren, N., Kline, P., & Saez, E. (2014). Where is the land of opportunity? The geography of intergenerational mobility in the United States. *The Quarterly Journal of Economics*, 129(4), 1553–1623.

Ching, D., Santo, R., Hoadley, C., & Peppler, K. (2015). On-ramps, lane changes, detours and destinations: Building connected learning pathways in Hive NYC through brokering future learning opportunities. Document Retrieved from: http://hivenyc. org.

Cole, M. (1996). *Cultural Psychology: A Once and Future Discipline.* Cambridge, MA: Harvard University Press.

Collins, M. A., & Amabile, T. M. (1999). Motivation and creativity. In: R. J. Sternberg (Ed.), *Handbook of Creativity*, pp. 297–312. New York: Cambridge University Press.

Crossan, B., Field, J., Gallacher, J., & Merrill, B. (2003). Understanding participation in learning for non-traditional adult learners: Learning careers and the construction of learning identities. *British Journal of Sociology of Education*, 24(1), 55–67.

DiSessa, A. (2002). Why "conceptual ecology" is a good idea. In: M. Limon and L. Mason (Eds.), *Reconsidering Conceptual Change: Issues in Theory and Practice. Part 1*, pp. 28–60. Dordrecht: Springer.

Elder, G. (1994). Time, human agency, and social change: Perspectives on the life course. *Social Psychology Quarterly*, 57(1), 4–15.

Ericsson, K. A. (2006). The influence of experience and deliberate practice on the development of superior expert performance. In: K. A. Ericcson, N. Charness, P. J. Feltovich & R. R. Hoffman (Eds.), *The Cambridge Handbook of Expertise and Expert Performance*, pp. 683–703. New York: Cambridge University Press.

Erstad, O., & Sefton-Green, J. (Eds.) (2013). *Identity, Community, and Learning Lives in the Digital Age.* Cambridge: Cambridge University Press.

Esmonde, I., & Booker, A. N. (2017). *Power and Privilege in the Learning Sciences.* New York, NY: Routledge.

Esmonde, I., & Langer-Osuna, J. M. (2013). Power in numbers: Student participation in mathematical discussions in heterogeneous spaces. *Journal for Research in Mathematics Education*, 44(1), 288–315.

Gallimore, R., & Goldenberg, C. (2001). Analyzing cultural models and settings to connect minority achievement and school improvement research. *Educational Psychologist*, 36(1), 45–56.

Gholson, M., & Martin, D. B. (2014). Smart girls, Black girls, mean girls, and bullies: At the intersection of identities and the mediating role of young girls' social network in mathematical communities of practice. *Journal of Education*, 194(1), 19–33.

Gibson, R. E. (2009). *Musical Parenting: An Ethnographic Account of Musical Interactions of Parents and Young Children.* (Unpublished doctoral disseration). Seattle, WA: University of Washington.

Goodwin, M. H. (2007). Occasioned knowledge exploration in family interaction. *Discourse & Society*, 18(1), 93–110.

Greene, J. A. (2014). Serious challenges require serious scholarship: Integrating implementation science into the scholarly discourse. *Contemporary Educational Psychology*, (40), 112–120.

Greenfield, P. (2009). Linking social change and developmental change: Shifting pathways of human development. *Developmental Psychology*, 45(2), 401.

Griffin, S. A., Case, R., & Siegler, R. S. (1994). *Rightstart: Providing the Central Conceptual Prerequisites for First Formal Learning of Arithmetic to Students at Risk for School Failure.* Cambridge, MA: MIT Press.

Gutiérrez, K., & Rogoff, B. (2003). Cultural ways of learning: Individual traits of cultural repertoires of practice. *Educational Researcher*, 32(5), 19–25.

Hecht, M., Knutson, K., & Crowley, K. (2019). Becoming a naturalist: Interest development across the learning ecology. *Science Education*, 103(3), 691–713.

Hidi, S., & Renninger, K. A. (2006). The four-phase model of interest development. *Educational Psychologist*, 41(2), 111–127.

Immordino-Yang, M. H., Darling-Hammond, L., & Krone, C. (2019). Nurturing nature: How brain development is inherently social and emotional, and what this means for education. *Educational Psychologist*, 54(3), 185–204.

Ladson-Billings, G. (2006). From the achievement gap to the education debt: Understanding achievement in US schools. *Educational Researcher*, 35(7), 3–12.

Langer-Osuna, J. M., & Nasir, N. S. (2016). Rehumanizing the "Other" race, culture, and identity in education research. *Review of Research in Education*, 40(1), 723–743.

Lave, J., & Wenger, E. (1991). *Situated Learning and Legitimate Peripheral Participation.* Cambridge: Cambridge University Press.

Lee, C. (2007). *Culture, Literacy, and Learning: Blooming in the Midst of a Whirlwind.* New York: Teachers College.

Lee, C. D. (2010). Soaring above the clouds, delving the ocean's depths: Understanding the ecologies of human learning and the challenge for education science. *Educational Researcher*, 39(9), 643–655.

Lee, C. D. (2017). Integrating research on how people learn and learning across settings as a window of opportunity to address inequality in educational processes and outcomes. *Review of Educational Research*, 41(1), 88–111.

Leonardo, Z. (2009). *Race, Whiteness, and Education.* New York, NY: Routledge.

Martin, L., Goldman, S., & Jimenez, O. (2009). The Tanda: A practice at the intersection of mathematics, culture, and financial goals. *Mind, Culture, and Activity*, 16(4), 338–352.

Markus, H., & Nurius, P. (1986). Possible selves. *American Psychologist*, 41(9), 954.

Massey, D. S., & Brodmann, S. (2014). *Spheres of Influence: The Social Ecology of Racial and Class Inequality.* New York, NY: Russell Sage Foundation.

McDermott, R., & Pea, R. (this volume). *Learning How to Mean: Embodiment in Cultural Practices.* New York, NY: Routledge.

McInerney, D. M. (2008). The motivational roles of cultural differences and cultural identity in self-regulated learning. In: D. H. Schunk & B. J. Zimmerman (Eds.), *Motivation and Self-Regulated Learning: Theory, Research, and Applications*, pp. 369–400. New York, NY: Erlbaum.

Mehan, H. (1996). *Constructing School Success: The Consequences of Untracking Low-Achieving Students.* New York: Cambridge University Press.

Nasir, N. (2002). Identity, goals, and learning: Mathematics in cultural practice. *Mathematical Thinking and Learning*, 4(2&3), 211–245.

Nasir, N. (2011). *Racialized Identities: Race and Achievement among African American Youth.* Palo Alto, CA: Stanford University Press.

Nasir, N. S., & Shah, N. (2011). On defense: African American males making sense of racialized narratives in mathematics education. *Journal of African American Males in Education*, 2(1), 24–45.

Nasir, N.S, Rosebery, A. S., Warren, B. W., & Lee, C D. (2006). Learning as a cultural process: Achieving equity through diversity. In: R. K. Sawyer (Ed.), *The Cambridge Handbook of The Learning Sciences.* New York, NY: Cambridge University Press.

Oakes, J., Lipton, M., Anderson, L., & Stillman, J. (2018). *Teaching to Change the World.* New York, NY; Routledge.

Ochs, E., & Taylor, C. (1992). Science at Dinner. In: C. Kramsch & S. McConnell-Ginet (Eds.), *Text and Context: Cross-disciplinary Perspectives on Language Study*, pp. 29–45. Lexington, MA: D.C. Heath.

Oyserman, D., Bybee, D., Terry, K., & Hart-Johnson, T. (2004). Possible selves as roadmaps. *Journal of Research in Personality*, 38(2), 130–149.

Packer, M. (2000). *Changing Classes: School Reform and the New Economy.* New York, NY: Cambridge University Press.

Plath, D. (1985). *Long Engagements: Maturity in Modern Japan.* Stanford, CA: Stanford University.

Polman, J. L., & Miller, D. (2010). Changing stories: Trajectories of identification among African American youth in a science outreach apprenticeship. *American Educational Research Journal: Teaching, Learning, and Human Development*, 583–597. doi:10.3102/0002831210367513.

Powell, J., & Roediger, D. (2012). *Racing to Justice: Transforming Our Conceptions of Self and Other to Build an Inclusive Society.* Bloomington; Indianapolis: Indiana University Press. Retrieved March 27, 2020, from www.jstor.org/stable/j.ctt16gzcpj

Reardon, S. F. (2011). The widening academic achievement gap between the rich and the poor: New evidence and possible explanations. In: G. Duncan and R. Murnane (Eds.), *Whither Opportunity? Rising Inequality, Schools, and Children's Life Chances*, pp. 91–116. New York, NY: Russell Sage Foundation.

Rogoff, B. (1990). *Apprenticeship in Thinking: Cognitive Development in Social Context*. Oxford: Oxford University Press.

Rogoff, B. (2003). *The Cultural Nature of Human Development*. New York, NY: Oxford.

Rogoff, B., Topping, J., Baker-Sennett, J., & Lacasa, P. (2002). Mutual contributions of individuals, partners, and institutions: Planning to remember in Girl Scout Cookie sales. *Social Development*, 11(2), 266–289.

Saxe, G. (1999). Cognition, development, and cultural practices. In: E. Turiel (Ed.), *Culture and Development: New Directions in Child Psychology*, pp. 19–35. San Francisco, CA: Jossey–Bass.

Saxe, G. (2002). Children's developing mathematics in collective practices: A framework for analysis. *The Journal of the Learning Sciences*, 11(2), 275–300.

Schutz, A. (1932/1967). *The Phenomenology of the Social World*. London: Heinemann.

Scribner, S., & Cole, M. (1981). *The Psychology of Literacy*. Cambridge, MA: Harvard University Press.

Spencer, M. B. (2008). Fourth annual Brown lecture in education research—Lessons learned and opportunities ignored since Brown v. Board of Education: Youth development and the myth of a color-blind society. *Educational Researcher*, 37(5), 253–266.

Stevens, R., O'Connor, K., Garrison, L., Jocuns, A., & Amos, D. (2008). Becoming an engineer: Toward a three-dimensional view of engineering learning. *Journal of Engineering Education*, 97(3), 355–368.

Vygotsky, L. (1978). *Mind in Society: The Development of Higher Psychological Processes*. Cambridge, MA: Harvard University.

Wang, M. T., Smith, L. V., Miller-Cotto, D., & Huguley, J. P. (2019). Parental ethnic-racial socialization and children of color's academic success: A meta-analytic review. *Child Development*.

Wells, A. S. (2015). *Diverse Housing, Diverse Schooling: How Policy Can Stabilize Racial Demographic Change in Cities and Suburbs*. Boulder, CO: National Education Policy Center.

Wenger, E. (1998). *Communities of Practice: Learning, Meaning, and Identity*. Cambridge: Cambridge University Press.

Wertsch, J. V. (1991). *Voices of the Mind: A Sociocultural Approach to Mediated Action*. Cambridge, MA: Harvard University Press.

Wortham, S. (2008). The objectification of identity across events. *Linguistics and Education*, 19(3), 294–311.

Yosso, T. J. (2005). Whose culture has capital? A critical race theory discussion of community cultural wealth. *Race, Ethnicity and Education*, 8(1), 69–91.

12

LOCATING CHILDREN'S INTERESTS AND CONCERNS

An Interaction-Focused Approach

Reed Stevens

Introduction

While children are ever-present in our theories and are the regular recipients of our designs, this chapter argues that we adults who study children, write about them, and design for them have a limited and potentially problematic understanding of the people we call children and their cultures. The chapter therefore presents and briefly exemplifies an approach to studying children's cultural practices that seeks to overcome these limitations. I will argue that these limitations are rather baked into the assumptions and methods of the majority of academic research disciplines that take it as their business to represent children's learning, cognition, and activity. These include developmental psychology, much of sociology, educational psychology, and the learning sciences. Each of these disciplinary perspectives represents important truths, worked out over decades, about human youth. Developmental perspectives have demonstrated that children do display age/time-sequenced changes in their biology, and some of their most basic capacities develop in parallel to that age/time-sequence (e.g. Ginsburg & Opper, 1988; Lerner and Damon, 2006). Socialization and enculturation perspectives have demonstrated that children's practices are decisively shaped by their encounters with adult caregivers and consociates such that their practices often come to closely resemble those of the adults whom they regularly encounter and live with (e.g . Grusec & Hastings, 2014; Lancy, 2014; Rogoff, 2003). In addition, learning sciences and educational psychology perspectives have demonstrated that children can and do learn the ideas and practices of school academic subjects, and that there are better and worse ways to arrange school environments that promote or impede the learning of those subjects (e.g. Bransford, Brown, & Cocking, 2000; Sawyer, 2005; Slavin, 2019). However, despite capturing important truths, I will argue that each of these perspectives is susceptible to a common critique, notwithstanding consequential differences in methods and style. That critique can be named in one word—adultocentrism (Bauman, 1982).

In recent decades research at the intersection of culture and learning has advanced rapidly. Researchers working at this intersection have offered critical correctives to two prior blind spots in the field. The first blind spot involved a near total fixation only on learning in schools, in academic subjects like mathematics, reading, and science (e.g. Bransford, Brown, & Cocking, 2000). In contrast, researchers at the nexus of culture and learning have shown that school is a fairly particular way of organizing for learning. These researchers have done so by studying learning in places other than school, within other socio-cultural arrangements in families and homes (e.g. Goodwin, 2007; Ochs, Taylor, Rudolph, & Smith, 1992; Rogoff, 2014), during out of school, youth involved activities (e.g. Heath, 1991; Leinhardt, Crowley, & Knutson, 2003; Nasir & Hand, 2008; Saxe, 1988; Stevens, Satwicz, & McCarthy, 2008), in "everyday" adult practices (e.g. De la Rocha, 1985; Lave, 1988), and in adult workplaces (e.g. Becker, 1972; Engestrom, 2004; Hall, Stevens, & Torralba, 2002; Hutchins, 1995). The second blind spot involved a similarly narrow focus on certain kinds of people, mostly Western, often Anglo-American, middle class people. This meant far too little research on learning among people from other ethnic, racial, and socio-economic backgrounds in this country and among people from non-WEIRD (Henrich, Heine, & Norenzayan, 2010) backgrounds around the world. In responding to this blind spot, researchers have dramatically expanded the diversity of people among whom learning research is conducted. They have shown how complex and variable are the ways that people from distinct cultures organize themselves to learn and that learning and teaching must be understood as cultural practices (e.g. Banks et al., 2007; Rogoff, 2003; Warren, Ballenger, Ogonowski, Rosebery, & Hudicourt-Barnes, 2001). This chapter seeks to bring into view an additional blind spot in prior research, the blind spot of adultocentrism.

The Trouble with Adultocentrism

This section presents a critique of adultocentrism that draws on disciplinary perspectives largely from outside of the learning sciences. These disciplinary perspectives include children's folklore studies, the new sociology of children, cultural studies, and conversation analytic studies of children's everyday practices. Following the presentation of this critique, I will characterize an alternative that seeks to move away from adultocentric conceptions of children and toward an approach to understanding children's "interests and concerns." I will argue that the methods of interaction analysis are particularly apt for disclosing children's interests and concerns in something as close as we adults may get to "their own terms." This will be exemplified with two brief examples of interaction analysis.

The term adultocentrism comes from folklorist Richard Bauman in an early volume exploring themes shared with this handbook on culture and learning. This volume was entitled *Ethnography and Education* (1982) and included contributions from important scholars early to questions at the intersection of culture and learning, scholars widely cited elsewhere in this handbook including Erickson, Brice-Heath, and McDermott. Bauman's contribution described folklore's approach to studying children's cultural practices and juxtaposed it with representations of children in the educational literature of the time. Bauman described children's folklore as directed toward "the traditional formalized play activities of children...that are engaged in and maintained by children themselves, within the peer group" (Bauman, 1982: 172). Bauman contrasts these studies of play with those in education that he argued "view children's play as an enculturation vehicle. The children are seen as proto-adults, learning things and acquiring competencies through play that will equip them for later, more mature stages of life beyond childhood" (p. 173). He goes on to argue that studies framed like this are attractive to educators, "because education tends overwhelmingly to be conceived...as preparing children for, and moving them along toward, adulthood" (p. 173).

Bauman introduces his critique of "adultocentrism" as a direct analog to what he calls anthropology's "cardinal sin", that of ethnocentrism. He sees the threat of adultocentrism in this way: "[r]esearch on children's folklore (culture) with an eye toward enculturation and toward the potential application of childlore to education tends to be seriously skewed by the widespread underlying attitude toward play [and by extension all children's practices] that it has to be *useful* in a moral sense, that it should contribute to 'proper' and 'productive' adult ways of behaving" (p. 173). In contrast, he argues that "one of the most fundamental commitments of ethnography, really a basic ideological principle, is to the necessity of accounting for the realities of a culture in its own terms…precisely in the manner we undertake our ethnographic investigations of other cultural systems" (pp. 173–174).

Bauman's critique resonates with another folklorist of children's play, Brian Sutton-Smith, who wrote, "[w]hat appears to have happened is that the scientists of human development have taken an adult-centered view of development within which they privilege the adult stages over the childhood ones" (Sutton-Smith, 2012: 5). Danish anthropologist Qvortrup critiqued socialization, enculturation, and developmental framings because they make it too easy to see children not as "beings but becomings" (Qvortrup, 1994), as incomplete but inevitable adults.

At this point, developmentalists might rightly bring an originator of the developmental perspective, Piaget, to the defense. Piaget after all is often viewed as getting at children's ideas in something like "their own terms" (Duveen, 2000). Piaget sought to understand how children's thought was different from adult thought, and he posed questions and tasks to children in a more extended and conversational format than is typical in other psychology-based research interviews. However, there are clear ways that Piaget's approach stands in opposition to ethnographic approaches and, on balance, his approach was clearly adultocentric. Echoing Bauman's critique of adultocentrism, Ronald Silvers argued that,

> When the child's accounts of why things happen in the way they do—for example, how a shadow is cast—depart from Piaget's commonsense or scientific explanations, he does not try to pursue *how* [emphasis added] the world could be understood their way. When the child informs him that the shadow emanates from the object, he does not inquire how it could be so, he does not pursue the poetic and practical understanding, but instead he uses the account to note its difference to a later stage which he titles, "The Correct Explanation Is Found."
>
> *(Silvers, 1975: 48)*

A second way that Piagetian clinical interviewing diverges from an ethnographic ethos is that clinical interviews are typically conducted in places of convenience to the researcher, around tasks of no particular interest to the child. These are not in any clear sense naturally occurring ordinary events in children's lives. In short, absent from the interview situation are children's everyday tasks, everyday environments, and everyday consociates (e.g. adult caregivers, siblings, and friends). The environment in which children perform tasks or answer questions in clinical interviews are constructed by adults, for their research goals. What is nearly nowhere to be found in Piaget or the multiple generations of developmental studies inspired by his approach is access to and direct analysis of children's participation in *their* everyday practices. Silvers' critique of Piaget acknowledges his goal of getting at children's understandings but ultimately Silver comes down with a more damning assessment: "For Piaget's analysis rests on an authoritative version of the world, a version that children cannot address or appeal for critical evaluation against their own version; Piaget violates the very life-world he seeks to understand; he creates a violent science for understanding children." (p. 48).

In accusing Piaget of creating a "violent science," it would be a mistake to take Silvers literally (regarding violence), but instead we should likely hear him as referring to symbolic violence (Bourdieu & Passeron, 1990). That is a non-physical form of violence that appears between members of social groups with differential power, such as adults and children. Committing symbolic violence involves representing others in ways they wouldn't understand themselves or that distorts their cultural practices, usually through acts of decontextualization (cf. Lave, 1988). Symbolic violence typically presents an image of those others as somehow incomplete or deficient. How then to represent children's cultural practices in ways that avoid adultocentrism and offer alternatives to a (symbolically) violent science for understanding children?

Locating Children's Interests and Concerns

Overcoming Adultocentrism

One way to move away from an adultocentric approach is to challenge a simple model of socialization, which to adapt a famous phrase of Garfinkel's (Garfinkel, 1967), means avoiding treating children as "developmental dopes," inexorably performing what adults intend or model for them. Alternative conceptions of the relationship between adult attempts to teach or socialize children, and what children actually learn and do, acknowledge children's agency and their creative transformation of what adults organize for them. For example, Jenkins challenges a simple socialization model in arguing that, "[a]dult institutions and practices make 'bids' on how children will understand themselves and the world around them, yet they can never be certain how children will take up and respond to those 'bids' (Jenkins, 1998: 28). Similarly, Corsaro and Fingerson (2006) propose an alternative to socialization, what they call interpretive reproduction.

> The term 'interpretive' captures the innovative and creative aspect of children's participation in society. Children produce and participate in their own unique peer cultures by creatively appropriating information from the adult world to address their own peer concerns. The term 'reproduction' captures the idea that children do not simply internalize society and culture, but also actively contribute to cultural production and change.
>
> *(Corsaro and Fingerson, 2006: 129)*

These perspectives move toward a reconceptualization of how to understand and study children's culture, but they perhaps do not go far enough. Because, while Corsaro and Fingerson acknowledge children's "unique peer cultures," they at the same time see the work that children are doing as appropriating and reproducing adult culture, albeit creatively. Scholars of children's folklore represent children quite differently. In a collected volume about children's folklore, Sutton-Smith notes that "[w]hat seems remarkable about the chapters that follow is that the children who appear in these pages are *so different* [emphasis added] from the children who appear almost everywhere else in twentieth-century social-science literature," and that in studies framed within the socialization and developmental perspectives "[w]hat we do not hear about are the many ways in which they react to or do not fit into these apparently normative schemes of socialization" (Sutton-Smith et al., 2012: 4). Sutton-Smith contrasts the "conventional psychological or sociological story of child development" with what folklorists attend to in their studies of children. This includes:

> ghosts, verbal dueling, obscenity, graffiti, parties, levitation, slang, pranks, automobile lore, autograph and yearbook verses, puns and parodies, special argots, initiation rituals, folk speech, institutional legends, urine and excrement play, toilet lore...nicknames, epithets, jeers and torments, half beliefs, calendrical customs, fortune, partisanship, ambushes, telephone jokes...mean play, Halloween and April Fool's Day, among many others. While this miscellaneous list of items hardly adds up to an alternative rhetoric of childhood, it does imply the need for a rhetoric that unites such Dionysian or irrational elements with the Apollonian conventionalities of "normal" childhood socialization theory (Spariosu, 1989).
>
> *(Sutton-Smith, 2012: 5)*

Two strong differences are of particular note in the contrast between the adultocentric approaches and the alternative represented by the folklorists and others who study children's culture ethnographically. The first is the degree to which children are seen as having their own worlds of childhood, separate from adults. This was initially recognized by Opie and Opie (1959), who noticed that a good deal of European children's wordplay in the form of rhymes, tongue-twisters, and jokes circulated only among children, out of earshot from adults, yet was transmitted from one age cohort of children to subsequent ones. (If you were an American child, you will have undoubtedly heard and learned some version of the jingle, "beans, beans, the magical fruit" from other children but not adults.) The second strong difference is the degree to which children are seen as autonomous, agentive producers of cultural practices rather than just as recipients of adult culture, regardless of whether those processes are labeled as socialization, enculturation, or teaching.

Contemporary sociologists of childhood (e.g. James, Jenks, & Prout, 1998) resonate for the most part with the folklorists in highlighting distinct activities of children and emphasizing children's agency. For example, Allison James' study "Confections, Concoctions, and Conceptions" offers a clear demonstration of differences in meanings and practices between adults and children with regard to "kets," a British term of common usage among children for an inexpensive form of "sweets" (the adult term). James argues that more than just a difference in terms, "'kets' are a very distinctive kind of confectionary, belonging exclusively to the world of children" (James, 1998: 396). This analysis resonates with related findings from Thorne (1993) about "the underground economy of food and objects" that she discovered in her ethnography of an American elementary school. That economy is called "underground," because it effectively operates outside the view and regulation of the school's adults.

Where these sociologists of childhood differ from the folklorists is that they have somewhat distanced themselves from the idea of a "separate and distinctive world of childhood" that seems premised in many folklore studies and in the early work of anthropologist Charlotte Hardman who, in calling for an anthropology of children, asked whether and answered affirmatively that "there is in childhood a self-regulating, autonomous world which does not necessarily reflect early development of adult culture" (Hardman, 1973/2001: 87). The reason why these sociologists of childhood have distanced themselves from this perspective is that they see the corrective as potentially having gone too far from the necessary recognition that children are embedded within and dependent on adult society. Nonetheless, each of these lines of scholarship share a strong critique of adultocentrism and a quest for alternative ways to see and represent children as agentive and animated by their own interests and concerns.

Among these scholars there is also significant agreement, or at least a provisional hypothesis, about one activity that is central to childhood—play. Sutton-Smith contrasts the adultocentric "rhetoric of progress" found in developmental psychology with a "rhetoric of play" found in folklore studies, asking the question, "if play is so important to children, why is it we do so much to ignore that fact?" (Sutton-Smith et al., 2012: 6–7). Similarly, James, Jenks, and Prout identify play *as* children's culture, stating succinctly that, "[p]lay it would seem, is what children do" (p. 90). While play may be an underappreciated, omnirelevant aspect of children's culture, the "cultural constraints on children's play" (Lancy, 2002)—that is, how children's play is shaped by local conditions of adult society (Roopnarine Johnson & Hooper, 1994)—will vary widely. The importance of play to children may emerge from an argument against adultocentrism, but it would surely be a hypocritical argument if it assumed a culturally normative image of play based on European and American middle class contexts, because the critique of adultocentrism is an extension of the critique of the "cardinal sin of ethnocentrism" (Bauman, 1982) as applied to children and adults. Play's meaning and availability to children in different cultural contexts remains to be much more deeply explored—for, to give one comparative example, who could doubt that the millions of children now living as refugees around the world play very differently (if circumstances allow them to play at all) from American and European middle class children?

Studying Children's Culture: Together and Apart From Adults

Having argued for a different approach to understanding children's culture that at least ameliorates the problematic biases of adultocentrism, we come then to the question of how—how should we study children's cultural practices differently? At a most basic level, the answer is ethnographi-

Locating Children's Interests and Concerns

cally. The ethnographic imperative, if elusive to achieve, is to understand the activities of those we study "in their own terms." We should study children's cultural practices amidst children's everyday activities directly, in pursuit of what Marjorie Goodwin calls "an anthropology of experience" (Goodwin, 1990: 287).

Here we can be more specific in answering the how question along two dimensions: first, when and what events should we study (a sampling question); and second, how should we capture and analyze these events (a data collection and data analysis question). In this section, I will argue that a guide to sampling can be found in Thorne's book *Gender Play* (1993). Thorne argues that research on gender should involve studying girls and boys both *together and apart*, an argument that echoes James, Jenks, and Prout who, in arguing against a separate worlds approach to studying children and adults, implicitly advocate a together–and–apart approach as well. It is far more common of course to study children with adults, whether interacting with teachers at school or other involved adults (e.g. parents or coaches) outside of school. These adult–child situations, even when studied ethnographically, are arguably highly susceptible to adultocentric biases, because it is easy to see and understand (as adults ourselves) what adults are trying to do with children and to then implicitly narrow our inquiries to whether adults are effective in achieving their socialization or teaching goals.

We have found no studies that explicitly take Thorne's systematic together-and-apart approach and extend it to studying children and adults. This is the core sampling proposal of this chapter. If we follow Thorne in this approach to sampling the activities of children with and apart from adults, there are three distinct types of situations that offer different opportunities for new understandings. First, pace Jenkins, if we take it as an assumption that adult actions are only bids for children's actions, then we are led to explore *if and how* children take up, ignore, or resist these bids. This first situation in a together-and-apart approach to studying children involves examining how adult bids are taken up among children when children are together *with* adults. Additionally, this type of situation offers an opportunity to "flip the script" and try to understand how children pursue *their* interests and concerns in interaction with adults. The second type of situation involves when children are apart from adults. In these situations when children are among themselves, we can also ask how children enact versions of the practices that adults have modeled or taught when adults are not immediately present to articulate or enforce their goals for children. This should be a basic "transfer" test of all forms of education, but it is rarely explored. The third type of situation offers perhaps the most significant opportunities for new non-adultocentric understandings of children. If we as adult analysts can analytically resist adultocentric biases through appropriate methodological approaches, we can pursue basic ethnographic questions—when children are among themselves what interests and concerns are they pursuing and how are they doing so? And we can do so with disciplined indifference to whether those practices reflect how adults want children to do things. This opportunity represents a recognition that children's culture—their interests and concerns—is yet to be significantly revealed to us as adult analysts and adults living among children, but is there to be found.

Interaction Analysis Approaches to Studying Children's Culture

If Thorne's together-and-apart approach provides guidance for a sampling strategy for studying children's interests and concerns, the second dimension involves how researchers capture and analyze interactional events selected according to this sampling strategy. Here I will argue that a certain set of methods are particularly apt for adult analysts to use in order to avoid adultocentric analyses: interaction analysis (Goodwin & Heritage, 1990; Hall & Stevens, 2015; Jordan & Henderson, 1995; Sidnell & Stivers, 2012)[1] of recorded, naturally occurring events involving children, both together with adults and apart from them, among themselves.

While it is beyond the scope of this chapter to fully represent the principles of interaction analysis, it is important to highlight some of the key principles as they relate to this chapter's themes. A key principle of interaction analysis is to recover from an interaction an understanding of the actions and meanings of that interaction for the participants, abjuring an imposition of terms from the "outside" that align with analyst's preselected categories or otherwise normative concerns. In doing interaction analysis, holistic interpretations of multi-turn interactional events are built up from a sequential analysis of successive interactional turns. This work of analyzing an interaction sequentially continues until the interaction analyst can make a claim for what is "going on" for the participants across a bounded interaction, based on what the participants themselves have built and sustained together.

It is important to note that the language of "build and sustain together" does not mean that an interaction is necessarily cooperative in the everyday sense of the word. People also build and sustain such conflictual events in interaction as "an argument" or a "relationship break up." It is also important to note that these methods allow an analyst to construct an interpretation of what is going on for participants as they build and sustain a particular mutually recognizable interaction together even when interactants are seeking to organize different kinds of interactions and pursue different agendas in interaction. For example, in a two-party interaction one interactant might be building toward making an invitation to another and the other interactant, perhaps seeing that such an invitation is coming, may work to direct the interaction toward avoiding the invitation (Schegloff, 1988). This is a particularly important category of interactions when we are studying interactions in which children participate, because a non-adultocentric approach to the analysis of children's participation in interaction must be able to discover and document how children pursue their own interests and concerns when they are with adults, however they may diverge from those of adults.

Harvey Sacks, the originator of conversation analysis (CA), made a well-known observation about just this kind of situation, one that helped set the direction for subsequent analyses involving children (Sacks, 1972). Seen against the full corpus of conversation analysis studies, CA has relatively infrequently made children the focus of its analyses (until recently, with notable exceptions, as described in what follows). Sacks however had strong interests in children's culture and in the practices of socialization, in part influenced by Opie and Opie's early, influential folklore studies of children mentioned previously (Schegloff, 1989). In his key example, Sacks began his analysis by noting that, "starting to talk to adults is for small children a rather special matter" because "kids have restricted rights to talk." Sacks noticed that kids can of course simply start talking but he asked, in what came to be a characteristic kind of CA question: when is a "start" a "proper" beginning, meaning how do children achieve a proper beginning in a conversation with adults in a way that is recognized and responded to as such by the adults. Sacks observed that the "nice solution" that small children have "evolved" to this "kid's problem" (Sacks, 1972: 343) is to use formulations like: "You know what, Daddy?" or "You know something, Mommy?" Sacks argued that the "proper and recurrent answer" from the adult is "What?" after which children have not only a right to say whatever they want, but also they have an obligation to do so, because they have been asked a question that carries with it the normative expectation of an reply.

In summarizing Sacks' early contributions, Marti Kidwell, a contemporary conversation analyst, generalized Sacks' perspective as follows, a perspective consistent with the one presented in this chapter:

> Sacks is not treating children as incomplete adults whose worlds are developmentally deficient versions of theirs; rather he treats their worlds as involving a variety of problems for them to solve, which, although not necessarily the same problems as adults', rely on similar techniques of sense-making and action that exhibit an intricacy deserving of its own study—sometimes for what this might tell us about how one becomes an adult, but also for how one goes about "doing being" a child. For Sacks and subsequent CA

researchers, this means that a concern with the interests, problems, motivations, and aims of children, as they figure into the interactional accomplishment of their everyday activities, is central.

(Kidwell, 2013: 514)

Marjorie Goodwin's book length study *He-Said-She-Said* (1990) is among the most important and earliest examples of interaction analysis being used to study children when they are mostly *apart* from adults (apart from adults except for Goodwin herself, who was filming and observing them). In this study, Goodwin spent time with, observed, and recorded African-American children in their neighborhood over a period of eighteen months. Goodwin observed many activities transacted among children themselves, including girls playing jump rope and boys building slingshots, but her analysis brought a dedicated focus to girls' interactions. In her "anthropology of experience" (Goodwin, 1990: 287), Goodwin paid attention to, recorded, and analyzed children's everyday activities—as an alternative to ethnographers primarily *only* asking research participants *about* their experiences.

In this project, Goodwin found two notable things relevant to the argument of this chapter. First, by closely examining girls' interactions, and in particular disputes that arose within those interactions, Goodwin challenged broad generalizations about girls; namely that their moral concerns were not primarily oriented to "care and responsibility," as Carol Gilligan (1982) had argued, but instead that these girls were very often oriented to "justice and rights," moral themes previously only associated with boys. The techniques of interaction analysis directed to children's everyday activities, with a focus on how children themselves displayed and enacted *their* concerns, allowed this incorrect generalization about gender to be challenged. A second important finding of this study was that the close sequential analysis of interaction among African-American children allowed Goodwin to challenge other broad, deficit generalizations about the speech of working class and African-American children: "[t]he present analysis, demonstrates that, to the contrary, the speech of children at play, in particular talk taken to be what Malinowski dismissed as "aimless activity" (Malinowski, 1959: 315), constitutes a powerful manifestation not only of linguistic competence, but of social and cultural competence as well" (Goodwin, 1990: 287).

These are illustrations of the powerful empirical and theoretical insights that a focus on children's interests and concerns amidst their everyday activities can yield. As Kidwell notes,

CA [conversation analysis] investigations of children's interactions have a potentially limitless opportunity to identify, describe, and consider the significance of all manner of interactional practices that children might be discovered—in the uniquely CA way of close and detailed examination—to employ.

(Kidwell, 2013: 532)

Two examples of these kinds of analyses follow that bring to the foreground children's interests and concerns.

Exemplifying Analyses

Study Context: Early Learning Across Contexts (ELAC)

In what follows, I offer two examples of discovering children's interests and concerns using the techniques of interaction analysis. The first involves a child interacting with an adult, thus representing what can be discovered with these methods when children and adults are *together*. The second example represents children interacting with other children, *apart* from the adults.

The data exemplars included in this chapter come from a study called "Early Learning Across Contexts." This ethnographic study involved pre-school aged children at home and at school, together with adult caregivers in both settings and "alone" with other children (see also, Kiefert & Stevens, 2019). In total, the data corpus includes about 700 hours of video recordings and associated interview and fieldnote data. Though the data are specific to a middle class community in the Western United States, I argue that the approach taken in this study—distancing the analysis from adultocentrism and focusing on children's interests and concerns through the techniques of video ethnography and interaction analysis—has general utility as an alternative to other approaches to studying children. Indeed, this approach may be even more valuable in other cultural contexts than the middle-class community from which the data exemplars are drawn, because the interests and concerns of children outside of the circumstances of middle class life and culture have been far more invisible in mainstream research. However, children—treated as agentive beings not just becomings—are far too invisible in nearly all research.

Exemplar 1: The Strum Thing (Children Together with Adults)

In the first example, a father and his three-year-old son Charlie are spending time at home together on a sunny afternoon. Where we enter the scene, both are sitting on the floor of a small playroom off their kitchen. Laying on the floor next to Charlie is a mandolin.

1   Charlie: *hitting strings on mandolin next to him* Where does the thing I tan [play it
         on, d'little [fing .hhh I ta*n* play it on?
                  [*looks at dad*
2   Dad: The [**p**ick?
              [*lifts hand with first finger and thumb pinched*
3   Charlie: yea=
4   Dad: =is that what you're- [strum?
                          [*strumming in air with right hand*
5   Charlie: ya anda for da pic**k** *pulls instrument closer to him*
6   Dad: yeah. [we don'*t-*
7   Charlie: [where da pic**k**?=
8   Dad: =I don'*t* think- do we have one for this?
9   Charlie: n:o
10 Dad: °I don't th↑ink we ↓have one° [00:42.06]
11 Charlie: Where, where is the pick? [00:44.28]
12 Dad: I don'*t* know if we have a pick, buddy.
13 Charlie: But where where where is da pick with?
14 Dad: I don't think when we bought this guitar that it came with a pick? And I don't think we we bought one.
15 Dad: [And this is more of a strum thing, you know?
         [*gestures strum with hand.*
16 Dad: we're not-(2) °° we're not really professional man[dolin players°°=
17 Charlie: [{*pluck*} ah, <uh=
18 Charlie: =where's the strum thing? *plucking strings*
19 Dad: The strum thing? Well you [strum with your f.
                              [*Gestures strumming in the air*
         strum, it's, it's a motion you make. Can you strum?
20 Charlie: No.
21 Dad: Can you strum on the guitar. Do you want Daddy to strum once and then you can try?

Here we can see—across Turns 1, 5, 7, 11, 13, and 18—Charlie's *six* different requests for "the pick" in the span of just eighteen turns. Such repetitive requests appear to be something available

Locating Children's Interests and Concerns

to young children but are a form of repetition unlikely among interacting adults. Charlie's dogged pursuit over these turns thus represents something like what Sacks described—a possible "solution" that children have evolved to get something from adult caregivers. Also, Charlie's word "choices" are interesting to note here. His initial language is functional, without naming the thing he desires. When Dad names "the pick" and Charlie confirms, he subsequently calls it the pick in four turns (5, 7, 11, and 13). In these turns we see Charlie clearly pursuing his interests in this object. And in response, we see Dad attempting to redirect Charlie, saying: he doesn't think they have one, that they didn't buy one, and that they would not have one because they are not professional mandolin players. Finally, he deflects by trying to get Charlie to perform the action of strumming with just his fingers. Even that is met with an additional creative request for the pick, as Charlie adopts Dad's language, calling the pick "the strum thing." This part of the segment ends with Dad seeming to have been successful in deflecting Charlie's relentless pursuit of the pick.

In the segment, Dad holds the mandolin in the conventional position, strums a couple times to demonstrate to Charlie and then hands it to Charlie. Charlie holds the mandolin against his body, like his father did, but it is relatively large for his body and he ends up strumming with the mandolin facing upward on his lap. Charlie "strums" a few times, though his strumming is done with clawed fingers and less gentle contact. After a few clawing strums, Charlie then holds up his left hand, looks at it and announces "I hurt myself."

41 CharlieI hurt myself. *holds up his palm and looks at it and orients toward Dad*
42 Dad: didjyou, did you hurt yourself a little bit,
        [let me see
        [*scoots toward Charlie, takes his hand and examines it*
43 Dad: mmm (1) I think you just have this, (.5) you had this spot on your hand earlier this week and I think it's a little sensitive.
44 (2) *both C and D looking closely at C's hand*
45 Charlie: What is it?
46 Dad: That's probably why we should have a **pick**, °huh?°
47 (1.5)
48 Dad: >It looks okay< (.) you didn't cut it or anything
49 Charlie: I need a **pi**- I need da **pic**[**k**, wa I ha   [dat widdle fing
                                                  [looks at hand

        wri[ght dayre
           [points to finger
        ((translation: I need a pick cause I have that little thing right there))
50 Dad: *small gentle laugh* You need that? I really don't think we have [one but let me double check, make sure I'm not crazy
        [*Dad stands up and heads to a nearby room*

In this segment, Charlie announces an injury, which draws his concerned father in for a close inspection (see Figure 12.1). Though this analysis certainly cannot attribute any manipulative or deceptive *intent* to this three-year-old, we can readily observe the *effect* of this announcement; Dad himself concludes that "that's probably why we should have the pick, huh?", which Charlie quickly affirms with an upgrade of his prior requests that matches his father's "should"—"I *need* [emphasis added] da pick" (Turn 49). Charlie also explicitly links the need for the pick to his injury as Dad had. This finally launches Dad on a search for the pick, and he goes into a nearby room for a "double check." Quite possibly—and many parents and adult caregivers of young children will recognize this moment—Dad knew all along that they had a pick, but did not want to get up and get it; only when strumming by hand caused Charlie pain, did Dad make the search.

Figure 12.1 Dad inspects Charlie's injury

After Dad leaves the room, Charlie gets up to follow Dad out of the room, meeting him in the hallway as Dad returns. The elapsed time since Dad got up and meets Charlie in the hallway, pick in hand, is only 15 seconds, leaving the impression that he went directly to it.

51   Charlie: daddy, do you have the **pick?**
52   Charlie: whad.is.d.↑pic I'm talk.ing about?
      ((translation: what is the pick I'm talking about))
     Charlie extends his hand toward Dad
52   Dad: [It is. I'm crazy. It's right there in the bookshelf
       [*Dad hands pick to Charlie. After receiving the pick Charlie pivots immediately*
        and returns to the playroom, followed by Dad.
53   Charlie: I like the pick.
54   Dad: (1 sec) hmm.
     Charlie and Dad sit down; Charlie strums with the pick
55   Dad: There you go.
56   Charlie: *holding the pick in front of himself.* I like the pick.

In turns 53 and 56, Charlie's quest has proven successful. He states twice that he likes the pick and begins to strum with it, which had been his originally stated interest in Turn 1. As in Sacks' foundational example of how very young children secure access to the conversational floor, this example shows one way that very young children can secure access to desired objects. This data corpus is overflowing with examples of how children seek to secure access to desired objects (toys, foods, etc.) from adults. This represents therefore what may be hypothesized as a general interest of small children. Here Charlie pursues his interest in the pick with repetition (seven requests in under two minutes) and upgrades to his request in ways that both echo his father and that link his interest in having the pick to his well-being—an invocable, situated motive that children likely learn early to hold adults accountable to.

Exemplar 2: The "More Bad Thing" Game

The second example involves children apart from adults, pursuing their interests and concerns among their peers. The selected event is drawn from a snack time interaction among six preschool children: Madison, Jamie, Will, Gabriel, Emily, and Zach. Although adults are nearby, they do not participate in this interaction; it is entirely sustained by the children themselves (except for one seemingly not heard but recorded utterance by the teacher). Like many of the children's interests and concerns in our broader corpus of recordings, when children are apart from adults these interests and concerns are pursued within a participation framework of some kind of play.

Locating Children's Interests and Concerns

As this segment begins, Madison brings her hands to the side of her face in a pair of pretend claws, and she makes a roar. Her body and gaze are oriented first to Gabriel across the table. He does not respond verbally but does lift his hands in what seems like a similar gesture (his back is to the camera). Then Madison sweeps her head and body to the right and offers a more extended roar to those on that side of the table. Again, there is no verbal response. She then untorques (Schegloff, 1998) her body and roars again toward Gabriel sitting across from her. He does not reply with voice or embodied action. Madison then torques her body hard to the left toward the teacher standing nearby, seeming to want to get her attention. She does not respond. While she is torqued this way, Jamie roars toward her. Hearing this, she untorques again and leans in toward Jamie at her right and makes another face with a low roar. Madison's interest here, clearly, is to initiate some kind of interaction, through her roaring and embodied animal mimicry. Jamie finally accepts Madison's invitation to whatever is to come and introduces a verbal formulation ("I'm a tiger") as a next move, and then they are off (Figure 12.2).

((Madison has just roared several times in the direction of Gabriel))
1   ((Jamie roars towards Madison))
2   ((Madison roars at Jamie)
3   Jaime: I'm a tiger.
4   Madison: I'm a ja:gu:ar.
5   Jamie: [I'm a jaguar, too=
6   Gabriel: [I'm a   =I'm a li:on.
7   Jamie: ((to Madison)) Eat the lion.
8   ((Madison makes biting motions towards Gabriel))
9   Gabriel: I am the more bad thing.

In the first part of the segment, Madison's interest in starting some kind of game has been met with a contribution by Jamie, which is then followed by a verbal formulation from Madison, who follows Jamie's tiger with a jaguar. Jamie's next turn offers a next move, saying that he too is a jaguar, but Gabriel seems to sense a different kind of move is appropriate, because, overlapping with Jamie's turn, Gabriel contributes that he is a lion. Now with three wild cats on the scene, Jamie tries to tip it in a more competitive (and mortal) direction, when he turns to Madison and instructs her to "eat the lion," which she affirms with embodied eating actions directed at Gabriel. Gabriel's next turn suggests strongly that he has picked up the emerging competitive character of the game. This is now a form of wordplay somewhat reminiscent of the African-American interaction ritual of playing the dozens (Foster, 1990), in which participants in a verbal interaction seek to outdo each other in sequential turn taking. His response, "I'm the more bad thing" might sound like an odd formulation, until one understands a key biographic detail about Gabriel. He had very recently moved to the US from Israel, where his first language was Hebrew. Though his basic English was quite fluent for a child of his age, he would have been unlikely to have in his English vocabulary specialized nouns to convey the idea of an animal more menacing than a jaguar, lion, or tiger (nouns which he most likely would have had available in Hebrew). So instead of such a concrete noun, he offers a modifier to a generic noun (thing) that accomplishes the next move ("I am the

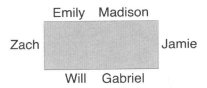

Figure 12.2 Table arrangement of children

Stevens

more bad thing"). In the next sequence, the one-upmanship of this verbal game continues, with two new children, Emily and Will, joining the interaction.

```
10   Emily:      What about I'm [a monster.
11                            [((J growls))
12   Madison:    I'm a monster to:o.
13   Jamie:          I'm a monster too [((Points to Gabriel)) You're a monster.
14   Will:                        [I'm a monster too
15   ((M growls))
16   ((Teacher is talking to Will briefly, leaning over and cutting something for him))
18   Jamie:          ((to Gabriel)) What are you::? [What are you Gabriel?
19   Teacher:                      [Madison no (      )
20   Madison:    What are you Gabriel?
21   (2.0)
22   Will:       I'm a monster=
```

In this part of the segment (Turns 10–22), it is all about monsters. First, Emily enters and offers a provisional "What about" followed by "I'm a monster." Tacitly, both Jamie and Madison accept the provisional monster as a successful move in the game, because Jamie growls (a different sound from his prior roar) and Madison states that she is a monster "too," meaning she took either Emily and/ or Jamie's turns to have established themselves as monsters. Then Jamie states he is a "monster too," which is followed by a monster growl from Madison. At this point, Jamie tries to bring Gabriel into the game with two successive direct questions, the second of which is echoed word for word by Madison ("What are you Gabriel?"). A significant pause of two seconds transpires during which Gabriel does not answer and then Will, taking his first turn, asserts that he too is a monster. But Gabriel is not done yet, offering a formulation similar to his prior, "I'm a more bad thing."

```
23   Gabriel:    =((to Madison)) I will attack to you.
24            (1.0)
25   Madison:    We can attack bigger. I'm a GI:ant.
26   Gabriel:    [I'm a tiger that goes after the giant.
27   Jamie:          [I'm a gi:ant. I-
28            I'm a gi:ant. [And I WILL EAT you::
29   Emily:              [I'm a gi:ant.
30   Will:       I'm a giant.
31   Madison:    I- I'm as big as the wor::ld. ((shakes head))
32   Zach:       [Me too
33   Gabriel:    [I'm as big as a [whale
34   Emily:                [[I fell off the [world.
35   Jamie:                          [[I'm as big as [the wor::ld.
36   Madison                        [And I'll eat you up.
37   Will:       [And I'll eat you up.
```

In this last part of the sequence, Gabriel offers, rather than a concrete noun to complete the "I'm an X" formulation, an actional statement that now seems to represent an acceptable next turn in the game, "I will attack you." Plausibly, when Gabriel did not answer the questions posed to him by Jamie and Madison (in Turns 18 and 20), he may not have known the English word "monster." Madison counters after a pause of one second, echoing Gabriel's attack by saying "we" can attack "bigger" but then she returns the game to escalating concrete nouns. She state's that "I'm a GI:ant," both stressing and stretching the noun. Gabriel still continues to play, and for the first time in a

Locating Children's Interests and Concerns

number of turns, names himself as a creature, but a creature with a consequential and well-placed difference. He claims to be a tiger (a creature that had early been surpassed by lions, monsters, and now giants) but a tiger that "goes after the Giant." At this point, Emily, Jamie, and Will are all in as giants.

Within just a few more turns this playful verbal one-upmanship game will end, and Madison may be making a move to end it with a formulation that steps away from specific creatures with a totalizing, "I'm as big as the world," which brings Zach into the interaction for the first time, as he echoes Madison that he also is as big as the world. Gabriel's last contribution directly echoes Madison's grammar, though he appears to say "whale" rather than "world," perhaps now recognizing that named creatures are appropriate and recognizing though mishearing her "world" as a very large creature he might be familiar with—a whale. There is further echoing from Emily and Jamie, with a creative twist from Emily who states that she "fell off" the world. In Madison's final turn, which can be heard as a completion of her prior "I'm as big as the world," she states definitively, looking toward Gabriel, that "I will eat you up," which is echoed by Jamie. At this point, the nearby teacher's raised voice broadcasts a question to the group about whether any need to wash their hands and a new interactional configuration is established (McDermott, Gospodinoff, & Aron, 1978), thus helping bring the verbal game to a close.

In this and many other recorded interactions in our data corpus, getting other children to play with you and sustaining a playful interaction or game is quite clearly a core interest and concern for many children. In this interaction, Madison does significant interactional and embodied work to initiate her playful game of one-upmanship. Once established, it becomes an interest of hers and Jamie's to bring Gabriel into the game, indicated both by gaze direction during their talk and their direct questions. In general, this interaction represents what Charles Goodwin exquisitely detailed in his book *Co-operative Action*—the ubiquitous, generative human practice of building new practices through repetition with transformation (Goodwin, 2018; cf. Stevens, Penney, & Mehus, 2012). In our broader data corpus, play itself is not only a core interest and concern itself, but appears to be a dominant participation framework in which children express other of their interests and concerns. This finding echoes Marjorie Goodwin's findings on how play was a participation framework for African-American girls and boys to work out arguments and disputes (Goodwin, 1990). The importance of play as a frame within which children enact other interests and concerns argues again for more research on play contexts, while also keeping in view the caveats expressed early— that play is not a culturally singular activity and will vary dramatically across cultural contexts.

The two exemplars presented show how we may discover children's interests and concerns through interaction analysis. I have sought to do so not through descriptions generated outside of naturally occurring interactions, as from interviews in which children are asked about their interests and concerns decoupled from actual situated events and motives, but from inferences generated through a direct analysis of those interactions, using the tools of interaction analysis.

Conclusions

In this chapter, I have offered an approach to studying children's culture that seeks to overcome adultocentrism, with a focus on children's interests and concerns as key constructs for this approach.

I have also argued for and exemplified the use of interaction analysis methods as useful tools for this project, methods that help us bracket adult interests and "flip the script" to see children's interests and concerns in interaction. The interests and concerns of children I have exemplified include gaining access to desired objects and initiating and sustaining a participation framework of play with other children. Using the distinction between when children are together or, alternatively, apart from adults, we can identify other interests and concerns of children from the broader data corpus. When children are together with adults, these interests and concerns include getting and holding the attention of adults, having adults answer their questions, and various issues of contested control, over their time, their bodies, and their activities. When children are apart from adults and among themselves, play is a central interest and concern of children, not only establishing and sustaining play, but also more specific problems common to preschool, such as getting into an already ongoing group play activity at school (a problem analogous to one that adults sometimes face when they enter a party where conversations are already ongoing). Preschool children also have among their interests and concerns helping their classmates and building things that others don't knock down.

These are just a few examples from one study. Here, I want to suggest that were a movement of culturally oriented researchers of children's lives and learning to pursue these analytic goals collectively, the discoveries about children's interests and concerns would multiply quickly. As argued at the beginning of the chapter, most of the established ways of studying children are adultocentric, and perhaps rightfully so. These ways of studying children do not need to be replaced, but they do need a more robust complement that spotlights children's interests and concerns and takes adultocentrism as seriously as anthropology, over its long history, has sought to take ethnocentrism seriously. The analogy is imperfect, but it is provocative and intentionally so. It is a way to start new conversations and potentially open new, fertile lines of research and design.

Ethnographic studies of children are not new, but they are also not nearly as central as they might be. This chapter is an argument that such ethnographic studies that seek to understand children's interests and concerns in something like "their own terms" can be more than illustrative complements to the more "scientific" or normative approaches to studying children, and rather should be treated as distinctive and underutilized resources for both policy and educational design. Policy and educational design that takes children's interests and concerns as a central orienting principle and starting point might yield very different forms of educational experience for children. But more importantly perhaps, the approach I have presented here is a way to better understand and live with children.

In this analysis, I have focused on short contiguous segments of interaction to make an argument for how to study children's interests and concerns, together and apart from adults. A broader program of research would explore children's interests and concerns across time and place. A focus on children's interests and concerns might also be a jarringly illuminating perspective on the place where most educational design efforts are intended for and land—school. One line of work that has explored this question is associated with the theme of 'voice and choice" (cf. Thiessen & Cook-Sather, 2007) yet broadly there are still relatively fewer studies than might be expected that seriously aim to understand how children interpret and respond to the adult-built world of school and the activities, topics, and materials that schools require of children, in something like their own terms. Alternatively, what would it mean to *start from* children's interests and concerns in the design of school-based educational experiences and continuously keep them in view?

In this chapter, "interests and concerns" has been a metonym for a broader set of possible categories in an anti-adultocentric research program organized to study children's cultures. The longer list of categories includes children's goals, their motivations, their dreams, their fears, their favorites, and their projects. We all were children once and as many traditions suggest, those children remain within us. This chapter is an appeal to understand children better so that we may take better care of them and live better among them, and support their learning in closer alignment with their interests and concerns. And, in so doing, perhaps also come to understand our adult selves better as well.

Note

1 In this chapter, I am using both the terms "interaction analysis" and "conversation analysis." These terms refer to closely related modes of inquiry; they just align with different academic disciplines. Interaction analysis (IA) is the term that has been used in the Learning Sciences since an early article in the field's

Locating Children's Interests and Concerns

primary journal (Jordan & Henderson, 1995), whereas conversation analysis (CA) has been rooted in Sociology. As Jordan and Henderson's article makes clear, most of the core ideas and research practices of IA have their roots in CA. I use the term IA, because I find it identifies the central phenomena more clearly, because "conversation" can be mistakenly understood to reference only talk and only certain kinds of talk, whereas "interaction" is a more general term and makes it easier to highlight that speech/talk is just one among the many modalities that play out in interaction (e.g. gesture, proxemics, gaze, pointing). This multi-modality of interaction is of course a central finding of conversation analytic studies (e.g. Goodwin, 2000).

References

Banks, J., Au, K., Ball, A. F., Bell, P., Gordon, E., Gutiérrez, K., Heath, S. B., Lee, C., Lee, Y., Mahiri, J., Nasir, N., Valdes, G., & Zhou, M. (2007). *Learning in and out of School in Diverse Environments: Life-Long, Life-Wide, Life-Deep*. Seattle, WA: The LIFE Center.

Bauman, R. (1982). Children's folklore. In: P. Gilmore & A. A. Glatthorn (Eds.), *Children in and out of School: Ethnography and Education. Language and Ethnography Series*, (Vol. 2, pp. 172–186). Baltimore, MD: Center for Applied Linguistics.

Becker, H. S. (1972). A school is a lousy place to learn anything in. *The American Behavioral Scientist, 16*(1), 85–105.

Bransford, J. D., Brown, A. L., & Cocking, R. R. (2000). *How People Learn*, (Vol. 11). Washington, DC: National Academy Press.

Bourdieu, P., & Passeron, J. C. (1990). *Reproduction in Education, Society and Culture*, (Vol. 4). London, UK: Sage.

Corsaro, W. A., & Fingerson, L. (2006). Development and socialization in childhood. In: J. DeLamater & A. Ward (Eds.), *Handbook of Social Psychology*, (pp. 125–155). Boston, MA: Springer.

De la Rocha, O. (1985). The reorganization of arithmetic practice in the kitchen. *Anthropology & Education Quarterly, 16*(3), 193–198.

Engeström, Y. (2004). New forms of learning in co-configuration work. *Journal of Workplace Learning, 16*, 11–21.

Foster, H. L. (1990). *Ribbin', Jivin', and playin' the Dozens: The Persistent Dilemma in Our Schools*. Foster: Herbert.

Garfinkel, H. (1967). *Studies in Ethnomethodology*. Englewood Cliffs, NJ: Prentice-Hall.

Gilmore, P., & Glatthorn, A. A. (1982). Children in and out of School: Ethnography and Education. Language and Ethnography Series, Volume 2. Colloquium on Ethnography and Education. Center for Applied Linguistics, Philadelphia, PA.

Ginsburg, Herbert P., & Opper, Sylvia (1988). *Piaget's Theory of Intellectual Development*. New York, NY: Prentice-Hall.

Goodwin, C. (2000). Action and embodiment within situated human interaction. *Journal of Pragmatics, 32*(10), 1489–1522.

Goodwin, C. (2018). *Co-Operative Action*. New York, NY: Cambridge University Press.

Goodwin, C., & Heritage, J. (1990). Conversation analysis. *Annual Review of Anthropology, 19*(1), 283–307.

Goodwin, M. H. (1990). *He-Said-She-Said: Talk as Social Organization among Black Children*, (Vol. 618). Bloomington, IN: Indiana University Press.

Goodwin, M. H. (2007). Occasioned knowledge exploration in family interaction. *Discourse and Society, 18*(1), 93–110.

Grusec, J. E., & Hastings, P. D. (Eds.) (2014). *Handbook of Socialization: Theory and Research*. New York, NY: Guilford Press.

Hall, R., & Stevens, R. (2015). Interaction analysis approaches to knowledge in use. In: A. A. DiSessa, M. Levin & N. J. S. Brown (Eds.), *Knowledge and Interaction*, (pp. 88–124). New York and London: Routledge.

Hall, R., Stevens, R., & Torralba, T. (2002). Disrupting representational infrastructure in conversations across disciplines. *Mind, Culture, and Activity, 9*(3), 179–210.

Hardman, C. (2001). Can there be an anthropology of children? *Childhood, 8*(4), 501–517.

Heath, S. B. (1991). "It's about winning!": The language of knowledge in baseball. In: L. B. Resnick, J. M. Levine, & S. D. Teasley (Eds.), *Perspectives on Socially Shared Cognition*, (pp. 101–124). Washington, DC: American Psychological Association.

Henrich, J., Heine, S. J., & Norenzayan, A. (2010). Most people are not WEIRD. *Nature, 466*(7302), 29.

Hutchins, E. (1995). *Cognition in the Wild*. Cambridge, MA: MIT Press.

James, A. (1998). Confections, concoctions, and conceptions. In: H. Jenkins (Ed.), *The Children's Culture Reader*, (pp. 394–405). New York, NY: NYU Press.

James, A., Jenks, C., & Prout, A. (1998). *Theorizing Childhood*. Cambridge, UK: Polity Press.

Jenkins, H. (1998). Introduction: Childhood innocence and other modern myths. In: H. Jenkins (Ed.), *The Children's Culture Reader*, (pp. 1–37). New York, NY: NYU Press.

Jordan, B., & Henderson, A. (1995). Interaction analysis: Foundations and practice. *The Journal of the Learning Sciences*, *4*(1), 39–103.

Keifert, D., & Stevens, R. (2019). Inquiry as a members' phenomenon: Young children as competent inquirers. *Journal of the Learning Sciences*, *28*(2), 240–278.

Kidwell, M. (2012). Interaction among children. In: J. Sidnell, , & T. Stivers, (Eds.), *The Handbook of Conversation Analysis*, (Vol. 121, pp. 511–532). West Sussex, UK: Wiley and Sons.

Lancy, D. F. (2002). Cultural constraints on children's play. *Play and Culture Studies*, *4*, 53–62.

Lancy, D. F. (2014). *The Anthropology of Childhood: Cherubs, Chattel, Changelings*. Cambridge, UK: Cambridge University Press.

Lave, J. (1988). *Cognition in Practice: Mind, Mathematics and Culture in Everyday Life*. Cambridge, UK: Cambridge University Press.

Leinhardt, G., Crowley, K., & Knutson, K. (Eds.) (2003). *Learning Conversations in Museums*. Oxfordshire, UK: Taylor & Francis.

Lerner, R. M., & Damon, W. E. (2006). *Handbook of Child Psychology: Theoretical Models of Human Development*, (Vol. 1). West Sussex, UK: John Wiley & Sons Inc.

Malinowski, B. 1959. *Methods of Study of Culture Contact in Africa*. London: Oxford UP for the International African Institute International African Institute.

McDermott, R. P., Gospodinoff, K., & Aron, J. (1978). Criteria for an ethnographically adequate description of concerted activities and their contexts. *Semiotica*, *24*(3–4), 245–276.

Nasir, N. I. S., & Hand, V. (2008). From the court to the classroom: Opportunities for engagement, learning, and identity in basketball and classroom mathematics. *The Journal of the Learning Sciences*, *17*(2), 143–179.

Nasir, N. S., Rosebery, A. S., Warren, B., & Lee, C. D. (2006). Learning as a cultural process: Achieving equity through diversity. In: R. K. Sawyer (Ed.), *The Cambridge Handbook of: The Learning Sciences*, (pp. 489–504). New York, NY: Cambridge University Press.

Ochs, E., Taylor, C., Rudolph, D., & Smith, R. (1992). Storytelling as a theory-building activity. *Discourse Processes*, *15*(1), 37–72.

Opie, I. A., & Opie, P. (1959/2001). The lore and language of schoolchildren. *New York Review of Books*.

Qvortrup, J. (1994). Childhood matters: An introduction. In: J. Qvortrup, M. Bardy, G. Sgritta, & H. Wintersberger (Eds.), *Childhood Matters: Social Theory, Practice and Politics*. Aldershot, Avebury: European Centre, Vienna.

Rogoff, B. (2003). *The Cultural Nature of Human Development*. Oxford, UK: Oxford University Press.

Rogoff, B. (2014). Learning by observing and pitching in to family and community endeavors: An orientation. *Human Development*, *57*(2–3), 69–81.

Roopnarine, J. L., Johnson, J. E., & Hooper, F. H. (Eds.), (1994). *Children's Play in Diverse Cultures*. Albany, NY: SUNY Press.

Sacks, H. (1972). On the analyzability of stories by children. In: J. J. Gumperz & D. Hymes (Eds.), *Directions in Sociolinguistics: The Ethnography of Communication*, (325–345). New York, NY: Holt, Rinehart, and Winston.

Sawyer, R. K. (Ed.) (2005). *The Cambridge Handbook of the Learning Sciences*. Cambridge, UK: Cambridge University Press.

Saxe, G. B. (1988). Candy selling and math learning. *Educational Researcher*, *17*(6), 14–21.

Schegloff, E. A. (1988). Presequences and indirection: Applying speech act theory to ordinary conversation. *Journal of Pragmatics*, *12*(1), 55–62.

Schegloff, E. A. (1989). Harvey Sacks—Lectures 1964–1965 an introduction/memoir. In: G. Jefferson (Ed.), *Harvey Sacks Lectures 1964–1965*, (pp. 3–27). Dordrecht: Springer.

Schegloff, E. A. (1998). Body torque. *Social Research*, *65*(3), 535–596.

Sefton-Green, J. (2014). Introduction: Making sense of longitudinal perspectives on literacy learning—A revisiting approach. In: J. Sefton-Green, & J. Rowsell (2015). *Learning and Literacy Over Time*, (pp. 9–23). London, UK: Routledge.

Sidnell, J., & Stivers, T. (Eds.) (2012). *The Handbook of Conversation Analysis*, (Vol. 121). Oxfordshire, UK: John Wiley & Sons.

Silvers, R. J. (1975). Discovering children's culture. *Interchange*, *6*(4), 47–52.

Slavin, R. E. (2019). *Educational Psychology: Theory and Practice*. New York, NY: Pearson North America.

Stevens, R., Penney, L., & Mehus, S. (2012). Children's imitation in its natural environments. In: *10th International Conference of the Learning Sciences: The Future of Learning, ICLS 2012*, (pp. 92–94).

Stevens, R., Satwicz, T., & McCarthy, L. (2008). In game, in room, in world: Reconnecting video game play to the rest of kids' lives. In: K. Salen (Ed.), *The Ecology of Games*, (pp. 41–66). Cambridge: MIT Press.

Sutton-Smith, B. (2012). Introduction: What is children's folklore? In: B. Sutton-Smith, J. Mechling, T. W. Johnson, & F. McMahon (Eds.), *Children's Folklore: A Sourcebook*, (pp. 3–10). Logan, UT: Utah State University Press.

Thiessen, D., & Cook-Sather, A. (Eds.) (2007). *International Handbook of Student Experience in Elementary and Secondary School.* Springer. Dordrecht: Netherlands.

Thorne, B. (1993). *Gender Play: Girls and Boys in School.* New Brunswick, NJ: Rutgers University Press.

Warren, B., Ballenger, C., Ogonowski, M., Rosebery, A. S., & Hudicourt-Barnes, J. (2001). Rethinking diversity in learning science: The logic of everyday sense-making. *Journal of Research in Science Teaching: The Official Journal of the National Association for Research in Science Teaching, 38*(5), 529–552.

13
COMMUNITIES AS CONTEXTS FOR LEARNING

Tryphenia B. Peele-Eady and Elizabeth Birr Moje

The title of our chapter may cause one to wonder what we could possibly write to add to the literature on community or contexts for learning. Indeed, we asked ourselves the same question as we began our work together. We wondered, for example, whether to focus on defining community and arguing for the application of its dimensions to classroom teaching? Should we, for instance, remind readers that learning always occurs in social and cultural contexts (Levinson et al., 2000; Levinson & Pollock, 2016) and that communities of practice (Lave & Wenger, 1991; Wenger, 1998) are some of the most productive learning spaces that people encounter in their learning lives? Or, should we complicate commonly held conceptions of community and question romanticized views that make translation of the concept into real-world learning spaces difficult? Should we critique overly essentialized notions and applications of community that reduce communities of practice to certain demographic identities? Or, should we caution those who study communities to avoid romanticizing and essentializing in their efforts to represent a given community's points of view, background, or learning experiences? Our answer to all the above, of course, is yes—we should do all these things and more.

It is the "more" that we found most interesting (and challenging) in writing this chapter. Our conception of a *learning community* is one that resists essentialized harmony and sameness and instead demands, embraces, and exploits (in a good way) *difference* in the service of generating among learners new understandings of the world, of each other, and of themselves. We argue for a view of community that centers diverse groups of people working together for a common goal—even when perceptions of that goal differ—and making the most of difference in the process. Complicated notions of community are critical to demonstrating the following: (1) why and how *diversity* in all its forms is powerful; and (2) why and how people learn in the context of community.

Overview

Why should we care about communities as contexts for learning? And, what can we learn from the ways communities come together and maintain themselves in the face of difference? To address these questions, we situate our discussion within the framework of "communities of practice," or people coming together for some shared endeavor (Lave & Wenger, 1991; Wenger, 1998).[1]

We first define community as a construct. Second, we discuss studies and theories that explicate how the construct of community works to support and/or constrain learning. Third, we critique notions of community that, although well intentioned, may essentialize or be reductionist in nature.

We then offer a view of community as purposeful gatherings of people, who embrace and exploit difference to achieve new learning, rather than as groups of the same people, who always get along, or who always hold the same values. In other words, community is a messy construct. Therefore, we advance the argument that communities are powerful learning contexts when the focus is on the goals individuals have for being and working together as much as on the identities people represent or enact. Such a conception does not assume that identities (social, cultural, linguistic, or otherwise) are irrelevant. To the contrary, they are of major interest in our own work. However, identifications based solely on race, ethnicity, gender, social class, and other related dimensions can mask and sometimes nullify intersections of identity and purpose that also matter.

Further, learning is a situated social process that occurs dynamically and progressively within a given social system (Lave & Wenger, 1991; Nasir & Hand, 2006; Wenger, 1998) and involves "shifts in sense-making, performance, or the use of tools in problem-solving" (Nasir 2012, pp. 129–130). Thus, learning and community are interdependently related in the context of shared goals, to the extent that learning is constantly happening among and between individuals and their communities of practices and within and through everyday activities of community life. Indeed, classroom communities of practice will look very different if the focus is on demanding and navigating through difference rather than on suppressing it. We conclude the chapter by offering a framework for studying communities as learning contexts comprised of individuals focused on achieving goals and embracing what members learn from working in, through, and across diversity.

Defining Communities

Understandings of community as a unit of study vary across disciplines—anthropology, education, history, psychology, and sociology. We borrow Seymour-Smith's anthropological (1986) characterization of community as "any group of persons united by a 'community of interests'...a professional group, a residential unit...a sector within such a unit or a club or voluntary association" (p. 46). At the heart of this framing of community is a shared goal, purpose, or interest. We do not mean that everyone necessarily agrees on the route to the goal or the way of pursuing the interest, but that people are coming together in both real or imagined spaces to accomplish something—whether a task with a discrete goal or simply to be part of an affinity group gathering around a shared interest, such as music or fashion. In each case, the interest or goal has brought the members together, but the members may have many other interests, beliefs, and intentions that differ. Members of the same neighborhood who, for example, may come together to protest a physical change to the space, may be alike in socioeconomic terms, but have different political views. Moreover, even groups who share broad beliefs or interests, may enact those beliefs differently. Further, a group who gathers together for political purposes, for example, might be aligned in the ultimate political goal, but have diverse beliefs about how to accomplish it. Thus, as goals shift, so do communities.

In anthropological and sociological traditions, the concept of community refers to personal relations, social networks, physical spaces, neighborhoods, or settlements, "as opposed to the more impersonal or contractual relations characteristic of modern industrial and urban society" (Seymour-Smith, 1986, p 46). The quandary presented in recognizing that communities are not necessarily places of perfect agreement is to prevent a group's work from breaking down over particularities. That recognition is especially important to considering communities as contexts for learning. Specifically, if one thinks of communities as spaces where people learn, then it is important to consider all the affordances and constraints that communities present for learning, including the fact that all members may not agree on particulars, though all members may want to learn something new. A main affordance of disagreement and difference is becoming aware of disparate views, practices, and experiences and the ways they can produce new learning and new ways of thinking.

As Place and Space

Traditional treatments of community in research have frequently associated community with place and space (Brunt, 2007; Piselli, 2007; Spindler, 1997). Classroom studies tend to follow similar patterns, often framing community in relation to "environments that foster democratic values, civic participation, and collaborative discourse with students and teachers working together" (Farmer et al., 2016). However, we argue that community encompasses not only social groups and their localities, but also other dimensions of humanity, including but not limited to emotional, spiritual, and intellectual aspects.

Several studies illustrate this point. Moje et al.'s (2004) study of Detroit-based, Latinx youth revealed their complex identity enactments and notions of community as a function of both the local spaces through which they moved daily and the national spaces they traversed over time. These youth were explicit about their identifications with many communities, routinely noting hybrid symbols, such as a Detroit Tiger baseball cap in red, white, and green, and remarking, as one young man did, "It's like it's both parts of *us*. *We* are from Mexico, but *we* are also from Detroit." It's worth noting the first person plural, indicating an identity tied to others, to a community. The localities of community, thus, were part of how these young people made sense of their everyday lives and identities.

In her profile of an independent Black institution (IBI), the New Concept Development Center (NCDC) in Chicago, Illinois, Lee (1992) positioned *community* as relational, generational, and institutionally situated. Her analysis of IBIs and African-centered education revealed a shared ethos among similar school contexts—one that reflected the "spirit of African culture" and shared understandings about what it means to be African American beyond place, space, and the school site level. Grounded in the virtues of "MAAT" or five key propositions about Black character development (p. 166), the NCDC and other IBIs exemplify a notion of community that transcends any physical building or area; family and community (and therefore, learning) are intertwined. Lee's work demonstrates connections between the broader institutional practice and shared goals of IBIs in relation to African American culture, shared history, "social relationships, belief systems, social practices, and collective responses to political and economic realities" (p. 165).

Historical accounts in the vein of Siddle Walker's (1996) ethnographic study of the Caswell County Training School (CCTS) in Caswell County, North Carolina, historicize the construct of community, rendering distinct insight into what survival looked like for Black communities in the segregated South (Anderson, 1988; Cecelski, 1994; Foster, 1997; Siddle Walker, 1996, 2000; Williams, 2005). Siddle Walker documented for example, the strength and resilience these communities demonstrated to educate African American children and provide the necessary human *and* material resources the school needed to be successful (1996, p. 5). As a context for learning, the CCTS had to reimagine and align the school with the community's local goals and practices to meet the students' needs, despite an environment that aimed to fetter their education.

Finally, Hull and Stornaiuolo's (2014) account of how young people corresponding across national boundaries via digital tools shifted their writing from writing-to-persuade to writing-for-understanding clarified both how place and space shape communities and the ways that communities are about people coming together around shared goals, purposes, or interests. Because the study participants came from different national communities with different social and cultural practices shaped by those places, they needed to understand each other and to be understood. Through their written communication, the youth built a cosmopolitan community from regional, local place-based communities. They learned not only about each other in the process of community building in a digital space, but also about themselves.

As Multidimensional

We share a few taken-for-granted assumptions about the multidimensional nature of community, based on our own research (mostly in literacy and educational anthropology) and on the literature

Communities as Contexts for Learning

theorizing community. First, we assume that communities can be both real and imagined; but, as Anderson (2006) argued, "Communities are to be distinguished, not by their falsity/genuineness, but by the style in which they are imagined" (p. 6). Even the most "real" community is also an image constructed by each member, an image that gets lived out in real ways in the real world, but is nonetheless a construction. Thus, it follows, the larger the community, the more imagined it is.

Because communities are both real and imagined, they exceed place-bound restrictions common to sociological and anthropological assumptions that often drive community-based research (Brunt, 2007). Communities can however, be located; and location can matter (Rosaldo, 1993). In reverse order, communities can also be dynamic, variable, and unstable. Thus, community is not a static phenomenon—communities are made up of real people with real lives, and as such, they are unpredictable and ever changing. Similarly, learning contexts are also plural, diverse, heterogeneous, and highly contentious—they exceed isomorphic bounds and figure prominently in broader discussions of power (Carter, 2005; Moje, 2000; Nasir, 2012; Weis & Fine, 2012; Valenzuela, 1999).

Studies of language revitalization provide a unique perspective on the relation of Indigenous knowledge systems to community and learning and power (Battiste, 2005; Warhol, 2012). Indeed, educational institutions have systematically excluded Indigenous knowledge systems and peoples (Cajete, 1995; Warhol, 2012). Battiste (2005) makes the point that traditional research on Indigenous peoples has overlooked the historical richness and fullness of Indigenous communities, failing to adequately explain (or appreciate), for example, "the holistic nature of Indigenous knowledge or its fundamental importance to Aboriginal people" (n.p.). A growing body of research has turned its attention to Indigenous language revitalization in response (McCarty & Warhol, 2016). Warhol's (2012) exploration of the "legacies" of the 1990/1992 Native American Languages Act (NALA), for instance, draws specific attention to the lasting impact that language policy and planning can have on Native communities. This research points to the ways policy practices take shape and evolve within the context of the larger power structures that created them (see also, Peele-Eady & Foster, 2018). As Warhol notes, studies of language revitalization point to "the power of traditionally disenfranchised communities to appropriate national discourses and to actively develop policies that directly impact their own language education goals and needs" (2012, pp. 71–72).

Race and ethnicity, gender, sexual orientation, religious beliefs, social class, and many other dimensions of identity also matter in making sense of community. Even as we note the role of various identities in understanding the construct of community, we also underscore our observation that communities are neither isomorphic with racial, ethnic, national, and other identities, and nor are communities independent of them. To illustrate, in as much as a group of brown-skinned people is not necessarily a "community" because of skin color, a group of women is not necessarily a community because of gender assignment. Moreover, a group of people who have experienced poverty is not necessarily a community because of the members' experiences. But, identities do matter; and they may, in fact, produce a community, even if only for a moment in time. Even when identities do not constitute a community, the identities of each individual shape how members of a given community imagine it and how its goals are lived out in practice. Community is always shaped by and rooted in histories of participation, privilege, oppression, and/or resistance, always moving forward and, to some extent, looking forward and backward. In short, as a context for learning, community is historically situated, present lived, future oriented, and power laden.

Conversely, those who study communities as contexts for learning often focus only on one aspect of the temporal life of communities, and consequently, risk missing the significance of community entailments, beliefs, or practices for studying how people learn in, with, and across communities. This temporal dimension may be one of the most understudied aspects of how communities produce, shape, mediate, or constrain learning. Longitudinal and historical studies are, thus, extremely valuable in understanding how and why communities come to be, as well as how they shift and change (e.g., Heath, 1983, 1990; Scribner & Cole, 1981; Ogbu, 2003; Valdes, 1996). Moreover, such studies are essential to understand learning, which is in effect change over time (Nasir & Hand, 2006). We can think of few studies of learning however, that examine how communities have shifted and changed *along with the learner*. Even classroom-based studies of curricula interventions rarely document how the classroom community has changed; instead, such investigations typically reduce the study of learning to change within the learner as a function of a set of activities, without examining how the learner's change functions in relation to the learning community's (i.e., the classroom) change. Consider the implications, for instance, if learning is less a function of some prescribed set of activities in a curriculum than it is a function of the ways a community (students and a teacher) shifts and changes over the course of curricular enactment.

These and many other dimensions of communities make the study of community as a context for learning more notably complex. Communities entail multidimensional relationships, identities, power dynamics, interests, behaviors, and ways of being that can be both shared and contested among the individuals comprising them. In which case, community is both physical and symbolic and expands beyond, "concrete villages or urban neighborhoods" (Brunt, 2007 p. 83); and yet, these localities (or other physical spaces) have an enormous impact on how, when, and why people see themselves (or not) as members of communities.

As Contested Terrain

Most important, communities are not always agreeable; they can be (and should be) contentious spaces. Indeed, we assert that this is one of the greatest flaws of much community-based learning work. When researchers and educators view community as an agreeable condition of sameness for everyone, they risk overlooking differences that divide. When we push to hybridity of identities, in an effort to construct a whole new person, the dominant survive and the marginalized disappear (Moje, 2013).

We see this tendency to call for sameness, for allegiance, and for homogeneity, underscored in this current 21st century climate, in political, social, and economic terms. Wanting to resist homogeneity and sameness, however, does not mean we see communities as places where people are allowed to demean, abuse, or mock others in the name of difference. Instead, we argue that masking difference, rather than embracing it, divides individuals in the long term. The purpose for coming together is what makes a community. People need to learn to talk openly and honestly about the hard topics; and we may be able to learn how to teach that open and honest talk in schools from studying how members productively navigate *difference* in communities.

Members of real communities have differences, but they work across them to achieve a common goal. And this, we think, may be the most useful dimension to explore when considering community as a context for learning. We must consider a community's diversity in different and nuanced ways, beyond fixed groupings of people, bound mostly (or exclusively) by space, or even beyond categories of difference that might bind people together. If we understand communities to be more than spaces or places and more than dimensions of phenotypic or cultural identities, then we create a pathway to examine how people, who are very different and have very different beliefs, values, identities, and experiences, nevertheless manage to work and live together for the sake of achieving a shared goal. Here we imagine some fruitful application of activity theory (Engeström, 2001; Hull & Schultz, 2001; Nussbaumer, 2012). We do so with careful attention to how power differentials and discrepancies shape the articulation of goals in a goal-directed activity and to how diverse communities can work toward something common without tamping down difference.

Ultimately, we could view communities as embedded in and productive of social practices and networks (Lave & Wenger, 1991; Latour, 2005). At a fundamental level, these systems are in constant flux as people and their tools for sense making move in, across, and out of various communities. This need to move beyond space and place, as well as beyond national, cultural, racial, and gendered identities, also requires assessing how communities define and distinguish themselves in relation to other groups. Such distinctions might present in the language, discourse, or other tools a community uses to describe the individuals who constitute it, to get things done, and to establish a legacy for their members, as they imagine and inhabit future communities.

Examining Communities as Contexts for Learning

Anthropological and sociological studies of education have long provided vivid illustrations of schooling (Carter, 2005; Casanova, 2010; DeVitis, 2016; Fine, 1991; Foley, 1990; Philips, 1983; Valenzuela, 1999; Willis, 1977; Winn, 2011; Woolley, 2012). Much of this work shows how schools function as communities and features attention to the range of interactions that happens within them, particularly in relation to language and literacy (Adger, 2003; Cazden, 2001; Dyson, 1993; Foster, 1995; Graham, 1972; Lee, 2006; Taylor & Dorsey-Gaines, 1988). In this next section, we discuss a few select studies that have explored the relationship of schooling to language and literacy practices and the unique ways these practices reflect and are shaped by culture and the broader communities they serve—locally, nationally, globally, and historically.

Studies of Language and Literacy

Studies of language in use in learning contexts have influenced the way we understand learning generally (Heath, 1983; Goodwin, 1990; Valdes, 1996; González, Moll, & Amanti, 2005). By viewing language as a social practice these studies have demonstrated that learning is grounded in community practices and understandings and is inextricably connected to community and long held cultural and historical traditions. Heath's (1983) study of two racially and culturally different and working-class communities in North Carolina—one White, which she called Roadville, and the other African American, which she called Trackton—is one example. In this seminal work, Heath shows how daily life experiences in the two community contexts shaped the ways learners engaged in language and literacy practices in school. Her study showed how differences in the children's home and community practices in relation to school could be both beneficial and disruptive to schooling for some pupils.

From research in this tradition, we have learned that local communities not only differ in the ways they socialize learners to use language and interact linguistically, but also in the ways these processes unfold, which has profound and differing consequences for learning (e.g., Adger, 2003; Foster, 2000; Heath, 1983; Peele-Eady, 2016; Philips, 1983; Schieffelin & Ochs, 1986). An important caveat is that although understandings of community are important in detailing the different ways and situations in which learning happens, what we in turn understand about the contexts embodying these processes can be misused and abused when descriptions of community fail to offer robust representations of the individuals who comprise it. Hart and Risley's (1995) well-cited claim of the limited vocabulary of African American students is one example of work that makes such broad assertions and fails to consider context.

Moll's (1992) and González, Moll, and Amanti's (2005) studies of funds of knowledge for teaching and learning in Latino households exemplify the need to look beyond the classroom and understand learning in the context of communities historically. In their work in a predominantly Mexican and working-class community of Tucson, Arizona, the authors underscore the important role that sociopolitical and economic contexts play in shaping "funds of knowledge" or, "historically developed and accumulated strategies (skills, abilities, ideas, practices) or bodies of knowledge that are essential to [participants'] functioning and well-being" (pp. 91–92). Altogether, studies of language and literacy have helped embrace a more compelling vision of community, where understandings of language are unwrapped, the possibilities of literacy are highlighted, and cultural interactions are shaped, reshaped, and facilitated.

Classrooms as Communities of Learners

Research within this tradition has also underscored contextual conceptions of the classroom as a "community of learners" that is wide in scope (Cazden, 2001; Foster & Peele, 2001; Ladson Billings, 1995; Rogoff, 1994). What students say, do, and believe in these settings "become part of the curriculum for their peers" (Cazden, 2001, p. 169). Being in community affords learners opportunity to learn about each other from each other and embrace each other's knowledge and practices in ways that broaden understandings, traverses other knowledge, and connects to the several other communities to which students belong.

In her study of African American children's storytelling practices, for example, Champion (2003) showed how language learning and use in the classroom context indexes learners' membership to and use of transnational community codes. Specifically, she found that African American children produced a repertoire of narrative structures grounded in both linear school like structures as well as West African and African American storytelling traditions (p. 86). This study illustrates the ways language embodies knowledge of the community as a phenomenon of study and at the same time bridges associations to multiple and more macro conventions. In Champion's case, students' narrative structures indexed linkages to school, neighborhood, national, and transnational communities as well. Champion's study reminds us that language and literacy practices, like the communities that give rise to them, are intertextually wide, broad in scope, and relational. As a learning community, then, the school (and classroom) needs to attend to the individual learner; provide culturally appropriate curricula; and engage students in instructional programs that consider their homes and neighborhoods as assorted spaces that matter in their lives (Graham, 1972, pp. 4–5).

This line of inquiry supports Piselli's (2007) description of community as a constellation of "social networks that interact and expand in many directions...beyond the boundaries of physical places and territories"... and "formed by ties of friendship, kinship, and acquaintance partly inherited and partly constructed by [individuals]" within it (p. 868). In this way, the individual is part of a network that is embedded within a broader context of diverse interactions (i.e., communities) that connect to and extend beyond the classroom to include global immigration, corporate industrial growth, and socioeconomic development. This connectedness strengthens and expands the social capital of both students and teachers (p. 872).

From an anthropological perspective, to the extent that schooling is a cultural practice (Spindler, 1997; Spindler & Spindler, 1997), so is learning. As such, community as a context for learning is socially constructed by cultural memberships, collective identities, and links of affection that extend and trespass the confinement of geographical boundaries. Therefore, we contend that researchers of communities must value the complexity that communities offer and consider their far-reaching connections and intertextual influences in studying them. However, research on community/ies as contexts for learning and on classrooms as learning communities has rarely focused on how difference manifests within communities or how differences are productively navigated and negotiated in the purposeful work that community members do.

It follows then, that in discussions of learning and achievement, if we neglect to identify and acknowledge the difference inherent within communities, then we risk essentializing them. More to the point, if we ignore difference in the context of community, then when learning outcomes are poor, we risk assuming it is the result of something internal to the learners, rather than the learning arrangements to which they have access (Leander, 2002; Peele-Eady, 2011; Winn, 2011). Equally important, when we overlook the complexity and difference within communities, we fall short in theorizing and studying how, and why, diversity enriches groups and leads to new understandings of the world. To ensure that education scholarship lives up to arguments about the value of diversity and the power of inclusion, education scholars need to examine how and why communities thrive across, and because of, the differences among their members.

Critiquing Communities as Places of Agreement

Instead of assuming communities are places where people come together because they agree or because they are alike, researchers should consider a conception of community that focuses on how diverse groups of people, engaged in purposeful action, manage to achieve their goals (or not) despite their differences. A focus on what happens when community members disagree and still accomplish a goal or task and remain identified with the community could teach the field a great deal about how diverse communities can come together and work through difference. What's more, if learning happens in communities of practice, and if communities are not perfectly agreeable places, then it stands to reason that learning is more likely produced in and through difference, rather than in situations of perfect agreement.

A case in point is Coffey's (2010) study of nine pre-service teachers' experiences at a summer after-school program for high school students. The program—a partnership among the local southwestern university, the Children's Defense Fund, and the Charter Freedom School—featured a service-learning component grounded in critical pedagogy perspectives. Using a narrative inquiry approach, Coffey studied the pre-service teachers' interactions with students and their parents and other members of the community (church leaders and political leaders), exploring ways to connect teaching and learning to the actual needs of the community, such as free public health care for children. The pre-service teachers not only developed a broader view of their students' community lives, they contextualized their teaching practice within their students' diverse realities.

A similar example is Marx and Pecina's (2016) study of a community immersion course offered by one educator preparation program (EPP) at a mid-western university. The course—based on critical pedagogy, experiential knowledge, funds of knowledge, culturally sustaining pedagogy, and community cultural wealth frameworks—encouraged teacher candidates to reflect on their experiences in relation to their assumptions about urban classrooms and cultural awareness of the community. Through reflection on these experiences, the teacher candidates examined their own preconceived ideas of students and their communities.

In such situations one is forced to confront other views and to integrate some new understanding of a different perspective into one's worldview. The research literature on learning in and from communities, however, has not typically recognized communities as places of difference, nor has it examined how working through differences actually produces new and powerful understandings. If we acknowledge the ways that through difference—or in contact zones (Pratt, 1991)—we make change and grow, then it makes sense that we should find the disruptions, discontinuities, and places of disagreement to examine how difference can produce new insight and knowledge.

Theory and research should also examine how and what community members learn by means of working through differences. People who come together for some reason—managing to talk, listen, and do, despite and because of their differences—can push the field to new understandings of learning, through unlikeness and struggle. It is worth questioning then, what can we learn from a close study of how people, who agree about a problem but disagree about how to solve it, learn as they work through the problem-solving process?

Research-practice Partnerships

A powerful form in education research is the research-practice partnership (RPP), in which practitioners and researchers partner to work on an issue they both agree needs attention. Several studies of such partnerships document the challenges of such work, from the fact that researchers have the luxury—and epistemological demand—to distance themselves from the common realities that produce the problem (Coburn & Stein, 2010). Practitioners have the opposite demand; they must attend to the ordinary, and consequentially, need solutions quickly. In one current research-practice partnership, Moje, university-based scholars, and school-based personnel are grappling with serious questions about the translations of theories of socially just teaching practice and curriculum into actual practice, much of which is shaped by logistical constraints (length of class periods, access to resources) and by different conceptions of what it means to teach for social justice. These conversations are producing new learning for all involved, the particulars of which take shape differently, depending on learners' experiences, identities, and intersecting communities of practice.

Apprenticeships

In now-classic studies of learning from apprenticeships (Rogoff, 1994; Lave & Wenger, 1991), scholars have theorized movement from peripheral participants (usually the young or the novice) to central participants (usually elders or experts). These apprenticing relationships, however, are filled with any number of differences, from differences in power and privilege to differences in knowledge of and skill with new and changing technologies. What could we learn that could be applied to school learning contexts?

In her study of language socialization in a Black church Sunday school community in northern California for example, Peele-Eady (2011) details how youth were socialized to membership identity development through an interactive framework of activities that centered on scholarship (explicit instruction), stewardship (guided-practice), and fellowship, which included co-practice alongside adults. This framework purposefully afforded children opportunities to take up community membership roles and responsibilities successfully and with varying levels of adult support. The high expectations that adults held for the children's success and development were deliberate and strategic. In this study, the local arrangement of activities in the church community was central in supporting the students' learning, providing a framework for constructing positive narratives of achievement and countering deficit-based constructions of African American students as learners.

Similarly, Urrieta's (2013) ethnographic study of children's learning in Nocutzepo, Mexico, underscores the role of intent community participation (ICP) in learning. Studies in the ICP tradition argue that learning occurs by observing and pitching in to family and community endeavors (LOPI) (Coppens et al., 2014). Urrieta found that when children participated in varied household and community life activities—food preparation, animal herding, and driving tractors—they did so "alongside more experienced and supportive peers and adults" and learned "indigenous heritage saberes (knowings)" (p. 321). By describing how teaching and learning happen across community contexts, these studies offer valuable insights about the potentialities of teaching and learning in school-based communities of practice.

In contemporary society, people rarely live in just one community because they have regular, even insistent access to other communities via mass and social media. As noted previously, communities of practice are not stable throughout time; they are complex and complicated—never places or groups of people with perfect agreement. In research therefore, attention to difference in communities requires a different kind of approach—one that does not portray all communities as uniform or harmonious. Peircean semiotics may offer one clue to how diverse and sometimes disagreeable communities can produce new understandings of the world.[2]

As we have argued, community entails multidimensional relationships of interdependence, membership, identity, power, interests, behaviors, and a common culture shared among the individuals that form it (Brunt, 2007). Because a community is based on symbolic assets such as culture, identity, and sentiments of loyalty and belonging, it has the potential to expand and disperse in different physical places from its original or established permanent locality. Hence, diverse communities can live in the same place whenever they respect each other's rights and comply with "local-level politics" (p. 85). It is within this space that diverse communities can experience struggles for power and resilience within a shared local context, which brings us to intersectionality.

Intersectionality

Intersectionality is an important challenge to current understandings of community as typically defined. People bring many different identities, goals, or experiences to a given social interaction. Like the communities to which they belong, human actors rarely inhabit only one set of identities, although they may enact different dimensions of their identities at different times. These differences depend on time, space, or relationships—including relationships of power—in which they find themselves (Crenshaw, 1991; Moje, 2004; Walby, Armstrong, & Strid, 2012). Thus, intersectionality is not just about the many worlds each person inhabits, but also about interlocking systems of power comprising communities and the ways people enact their various identities within and across different spaces and power relations.

People tend to experience stress and angst as they subjugate one set of values or commitments to participate in a different community of practice. These interlocking systems shape how those who are most vulnerable and marginalized in society encounter overwhelmingly positive and romantic notions of community, notions that suggest communities must have agreement and harmony to survive. From this perspective, social stratifications that exist in a community are inextricably interwoven. Intersectionality demands that researchers examine difference within communities of practice to surface the ways that communities either create new understandings as they embrace difference or subjugate some perspectives in a way that serves one part of the community's interests over another. It seems critical to distinguish between instances when community agreement is productive or generative, and when agreement is repressive or inequitable.

(Re)framing Community for Research, Pedagogy, and Change

In many respects then, poorly informed conceptions of community may well contribute to poor and deficit-driven illustrations of certain learners. When researchers set out to study community as a context for learning, they must draw on both theoretical and methodological approaches to understanding learning as involving a diverse set of processes through which individuals make sense of their realities (Nasir, 2012; Nasir & Hand, 2006; Nasir & Peele-Eady, 2012; Pollock, 2005; Taylor & Dorsey-Gaines, 1988). Similar to theoretical constructs like culturally relevant pedagogy (Ladson-Billings, 1995) for example, conceptualizations of community should empower its members and underscore the richness of diversity in its own right. The growing interest in culturally relevant (Ladson-Billings, 1995), culturally appropriate (Hale, 2001), culturally responsive (Gay, 2010), culturally sustaining (Paris, 2012), and reality (Emdin, 2016) pedagogies has expanded the boundaries of community to include a focus on diversity that we consider central to studying learning in the context of community. It is from this perspective that we offer a framework for conducting research on learning in communities.

We propose a robust analysis of community as a construct independently worthy of study and as an analytical tool that both organizes and is organized by understandings of learning in cultural contexts. A useful framework highlights working across differences in beliefs, identities, and power relations and exploring the workings of the intersectionalities undergirding them. We believe such a tool will help researchers and scholars use community in more full-bodied ways that honor people and their unique experiences and histories independent of and in relation to each other. The framework we propose has four main assumptions that we consider essential and broadly applicable for conducting research on, in, and in reciprocity with learning communities:

- Communities are comprised of real people.
- Community is broad in scope.
- Community practice is social practice.
- Communities are diverse and complex.

Communities Are Comprised of Real People

Although persuaded by Anderson's (2006) notion of "imagined communities," we also recognize that communities are real to the people who live and imagine them. When researchers or teachers simplify communities as intrinsic to a particular person, place, thing, or group, these experiences evoke real consequences and feelings that have huge implications for how stories about learners get told. Put another way, how we conceptualize community has both empirical and practical implications for the people who inhabit (or imagine) the communities of their everyday lives. Indeed, we agree with Weis and Fine's (2013) assentation that community members engage in the constant work of "trying to make sense – knowingly and not – of the relations between their personal circumstances and the historic, economic, and class, ethnic, and racial relations and antagonisms within which they exist" (p. 225)—what we are calling *diversity*.

Thus, researchers need to be mindful of ideologies and language that reify community as static and homogenous. In this way, the use of community as a framework can respectfully resist romanticized notions and instead take care not to constrain and contain a community artificially.

Community Is Broad in Scope

Community is broad in scope and requires an analytic approach that recognizes its breadth. Notwithstanding notable critiques (e.g., Spencer, 2007), conceiving of community as a network resembles observations that Geertz made in his characterization of thick description.[3] Geertz (1973) writes:

> It is not against a body of uninterpreted data, radically thinned descriptions, that we must measure the cogency of our explications, but against the power of the scientific imagination to bring us into touch with the lives of strangers.
>
> *(p. 16)*

In other words, the richness of community is lost with unsolicited attempts to stabilize and romanticize it. We recognize this stabilization as a function of the research process as we have come to know it (i.e., publishing) rather than because of the researcher's intention. However, if normalized, community is a limited and potentially dangerous construction (Weis & Fine, 2013).

In learning situations, especially those occupied by students from historically marginalized and vulnerable groups, narrow conceptions of community risk treating all learners as though they are all the same. And yet, a great deal of research—at both a large and small scale—categorizes people into identity groups precisely for seeking equity and justice. Research that disaggregates data by ethnic and racial groups, for example, is meant to shine a spotlight on inequity. Research that highlights the power and potential of a given racial, class, or gender identity group serves to deconstruct stereotypic understandings of the possibilities for children in said group. And research that focuses on a particular community—however constructed or imagined—is often meant to serve that community's interest. Simultaneously however, such research may lead to reifying the community into stereotypical categories.

Decisions about research design, enactment, and representation require careful attention in the use of community as a construct; namely, to how troubling it can be, when mis- or overused. Community is not just a thing, but also a tool—a framework for understanding meaningful action, including how people learn. Rather than isolate community as a stable place or group, we urge researchers to situate learning in certain times, places, and relationships. And when community membership is presented as something unitary for challenging commonly held notions of a community, we argue that researchers should clearly name and explain such moves. Such a framework underscores that people are much more complicated than a stabilized grouping.

Communities as Contexts for Learning

This parallels with Forsey's (2010) conception of ethnography "as a process of participant listening" whereby the researcher can locate the participants' personal stories within "the broader context and issues we are seeking to describe and analyse in the formal reports of our research data" (p. 569). Moreover, to the extent that identities are shaped within cultural contexts (Lewis & Moje, 2003), context is vital to what happens in it. The same is true of learning; context is vital to where it occurs and to interpretations of it.

Romanticization and Essentialization are particularly heightened when community assignment is based exclusively on the obvious—skin color, spoken language, style of dress, or gender representation—with little to no attention to the nuances of issues embedded within. If the researcher stays just within the scope of these expressions, then these are the only representations that will emerge as interesting. Thus, this framework characterizes communities as much more intersectional than the traditional conceptions typically presented through ethnography or sociocultural theory.

Community Is a Social Practice

Community by its very nature is a social practice and therefore reflects the complexities of societal structures, many of which center on issues of power. As we have stated, studies of community must also attend to intersectionality—or the interconnected relationships among race, class, gender, age, and other dynamics that govern how power flows in and through community life. What makes a community involves both the "consequence of fundamental social change" and "a consequence of social researchers having different ideas about what constitutes a community" (Brunt, 2007, p. 80). Alas, it is not enough to designate a community by simply calling it such.

Like the words we use in our studies, the researcher's role is an important one. How we gather data—what information we consider important even—how we analyze and interpret data, and how we write up findings for dissemination to the public, are all important aspects of conducting research. Researchers and theoreticians can easily turn the real into a concept or an abstraction. Thus, a final and essential component of a framework for studying community is the understanding of what these "imagined realities" (and legacies of such) mean for the people who live in them. Only then can we have a useful and ethical construct for studying how people learn in and with the many different communities they navigate.

Communities Are Diverse and Complex

Communities are diverse and complex; and the individuals who make up communities are equally complicated. The tension facing the researcher lies in finding ways to portray difference (in the overly stabilizing medium of the written research article) while also learning from it. Collins (2012) makes the point that community provides a template for describing actual power relations as people live and conceptualize them. If we fail to complicate notions of community, we perpetuate the very problems we aim to solve and exploit the vulnerabilities that inhibit social mobility. As we theorize the value of diversity in learning, it is important to keep several things in mind. First, to borrow from Diaz de Rada and Sedano (2016), "diversity is not a one-dimensional concept" (p. 414). There exist "diverse relationships to diversity" because how diversity gets defined in a community will depend on members' interpretations.

Working across differences in beliefs, identities, and power relations requires extended time in the field. How can one look for the working of intersectionality if she is bent on homogeneity? We believe this lays the groundwork for a Pygmalion effect in learning studies, such that individuals will behave in ways they perceive the researcher expects. In their conception of "a good ethnography of schooling," Spindler and Spindler (1997) instruct the ethnographer to work *in situ*, observing things as they happen, repeatedly; observing until nothing new appears. Prolonged time in a site affords the researcher with opportunities to go deep.

The researcher's first step in identifying these nuances is to locate things that matter with the community. This means paying attention to the range of occurrences, products, documents and other data that shape members' routine life experiences. Spindler and Spindler (1997) note that "in ethnography, one is always dogged with the realization that what is happening will never happen again. The categories of happenings repeat themselves endlessly in human affairs, yet each is unique" (p. 68). Studies of community require a similar kind of attention to *uniqueness* and it is this reality that ought to govern data collection, analysis, and interpretation (Geertz, 1973).

Conclusions

In this chapter, we have argued for a new way of thinking about community, its potential, and how we can use it. As an analytical tool, the key strength of community lies in the way researchers view community and position themselves as learners within it. Like the community members they study, researchers cannot "be in the world, with the world, and with others in a neutral manner" (Freire, 2004, p. 60). Research, by nature, is political, and studying communities as contexts for learning is messy work. The researcher must assume an ideational stance that debunks an overly harmonious view of community, recognizing that an oversimplified view is not only unrealistic, but also potentially harmful to the very people whose experiences one aims to understand.

Failure to consider the construct of community at the outset of the research process threatens to alter what the researcher ultimately pays attention to during fieldwork. Because data generation carries consequences for representation, how one in turn conceptualizes these data could have major repercussions for research design and implementation. Beyond this, and probably most important, is the potential to overlook the complexity of community and the misuse of findings to misrepresent the people we study. These consequences inform every step in the research process, from design and site selection to writing up findings.

The challenge to researchers is furthering this complex view of community in relation to understanding learning across disciplines. Doing so requires the researcher to deliberately select research sites that gravitate toward understandings of communities as constellations of diverse people and perspectives (Diaz de Rada & Sedano, 2016; Jones, Nasir, & Peele-Eady, 2011). In which case, researcher interpretations may oppose the ways members of communities view themselves, so careful attention to the ways we frame communities as contexts of learning is of critical import. Finally, we want to stress that communities are not singular or rudimentary in nature. To the contrary, they are complicated, involved, and compounded. Furthermore, communities are plural—few people in the modern world live and work in just one. These factors, taken together, offer both a challenge and an opportunity for researchers who study learning in community contexts.

Notes

1 Because an extensive review is not possible here, we refer readers to comprehensive reviews already documented in the literature (see for example, McDermott & Raley, 2016; Weis & Fine, 2013).
2 See Peirce (1997) for an overview of selected works.
3 The concept of *thick description* originated with Gilbert Ryle, as cited in Geertz (1973).

References

Adger, C. T. (2003). Discourse in educational settings. In: D. Schiffrin, D. Tannin & H. E. Hamilton (Eds.), *The Handbook of Discourse Analysis* (pp. 503–517). Malden, MA: Blackwell Publishing.

Anderson, B. (2006). *Imagined Communities: Reflections on the Origin and Spread of Nationalism* (2nd ed.). London, England: Verso.

Anderson, J. D. (1988). *The Education of Blacks in the South, 1860–1935*. Chapel Hill, NC: The University of North Carolina Press.

Battiste, M. (2005). Indigenous knowledge: Foundations of first nations. *World Indigenous Nations Higher Education Consortium Journal, Indigenous Knowledge - WINHEC Journal*, 1–17. Retrieved from http://www.win-hec.org/docs/pdfs/ Journal/Marie%20Battiste%20copy.pdf

Brunt, L. (2007). Into the community. In: P. Atkinson, A. Coffey, S. Delamont, J. Lofland & L. Lofland (Eds.), *Handbook of Ethnography* (pp. 80–91). Los Angeles, LA: SAGE Publications.

Cajete, G. (1995). *Look to the Mountain: An Ecology of Indigenous Education*. Durango, CO: Kivaki Press.

Carter, P. L. (2005). *Keepin' It Real: School Success beyond Black and White*. New York, NY: Oxford University Press.

Casanova, U. (2010). *¡Si Se Puede! Learning from a High School That Beats the Odds*. New York, NY: Teachers College Press.

Cazden, C. B. (2001). *Classroom Discourse: The Language of Teaching and Learning* (2nd ed.). Portsmouth, MH: Heinemann.

Cecelski, D. S. (1994). *Along Freedom Road: Hyde County, North Carolina, and the Fate of Black Schools in the South*. Chapel Hill, NC: The University of North Carolina Press.

Champion, T. B. (2003). *Understanding Storytelling among African American Children: A Journey from Africa to America*. Mahwah, NJ: Lawrence Erlbaum Associates.

Coburn, C. E. & Stein, M. K. (Eds.) (2010). *Research and Practice in Education: Building Alliances, Bridging the Divide*. Lanham, MD: Rowman & Littlefield Publishers, Inc.

Coffey, H. (2010). "They taught me": The benefits of early community-based field experiences in teacher education. *Teaching & Teacher Education, 26*(2), 335–342.

Collins, P. H. (2012). Social inequality, power, and politics: Intersectionality and American Pragmatism in dialogue. *The Journal of Speculative Philosophy, 26*(2), 442–457.

Coppens, A. D., Silva, K. G., Ruvalcaba, O., Alcalá, L., López, A., & Rogoff, B. (2014). Learning by observing and pitching in: Benefits and processes of expanding repertoires. *Human Development, 4*(57), 150–161.

Crenshaw, K. (1991). Mapping the margins: Intersectionality, identity politics, and violence against women of color. *Stanford Law Review, 43*(6), 1241–1299.

DeVitis, J. L. (Ed.) (2016). *Popular Educational Classics: A Reader*. New York, NY: Peter Lang Publishing.

Diaz de Rada, A. & Sedano, L. J. (2016). Variations on diversity and the risks of bureaucratic complicity. In: B. A. Levinson & M. Pollock (Eds.), *A Companion to the Anthropology of Education* (pp. 408–424). Malden, MA: Wiley Blackwell.

Dyson, A. H. (1993). *Social Worlds of Children Learning to Write In an Urban Primary School*. New York, NY: Teachers College Press.

Emdin, C. (2016). *For White Folks Who Teach in the Hood…and the Rest of y'all Too: Reality Pedagogy and Urban Education*. Boston, MA: Beacon Press.

Engeström, Y. (2001). Expansive learning at work: Toward an activity theoretical reconceptualization. *Journal of Education & Work, 14*(1), 133–156. doi:10.1080/13639080020028747.

Farmer, J. L., Leonard, A. E., Spearman, M., Qian, M., & Rosenblith, S. (2016). Picturing a classroom community: Student drawings as a pedagogical tool to assess features of community in the classroom. *Action in Teacher Education, 38*(4), 299–314.

Fine, M. (1991). *Framing Dropouts: Notes on the Politics of an Urban Public High School*. Albany, NY: SUNY Press.

Foley, D. E. (1990). *Learning Capitalist Culture: Deep in the Heart of Tejas*. Philadelphia, PN: University of Pennsylvania Press.

Forsey, M. G. (2010). Ethnography as participant listening. *Ethnography, 11*(4), 558–572.

Foster, M. L. (1995). Talking that talk: The language of control, curriculum, and critique. *Linguistics & Education, 7*(2), 129–150.

Foster, M. L. (1997). *Black Teachers on Teaching*. New York, NY: The New Press.

Foster, M. L. (2000). School practice and community life: Cultural congruence, conflict, and discontinuity. In: B. A. U. Levinson et al. (Eds.), *Schooling the Symbolic Animal: Social and Cultural Dimensions of Education* (pp. 161–168). Landham, MD: Rowman & Littlefield Publishers, Inc.

Foster, M. L. & Peele, T. B. (2001). Ring my bell: Contextualizing home and school in an African American Community. In: E. McIntyre, A. Rosebery & N. Gonzalez (Eds.), *Classroom Diversity: Connecting Curriculum to Students' Lives* (pp. 27–36). Portsmouth, NH: Heinemann.

Freire, P. (2004). *Pedagogy of Indignation*. Herndon, VA: Paradigm Publishers.

Gay, G. (2010). *Culturally Responsive Teaching: Theory, Research, and Practice* (2nd ed.). New York, NY: Teachers College Press.

Geertz, C. (1973). *The Interpretation of Cultures: Selected Essays by Clifford Geertz*. New York, NY: Basic Books, Inc.

González, N., Moll, L. C., & Amanti, C. (2005). *Funds of Knowledge: Theorizing Practices in Households, Communities, and Classrooms*. Mahwah, NJ: Lawrence Erlbaum Associates.

Goodwin, M. H. (1990). *He-Said-She-Said: Talk as Social Organization among Black Children*. Bloomington, IN: Indiana University Press.

Graham, R. (1972). The school as a learning community. *Theory into Practice, 11*(1), 4–8.

Hale, J. E. (2001). *Learning While Black: Creating Educational Excellence for African American Children.* Baltimore, MD: The Johns Hopkins University Press.

Hart, B. & Risley, T. (1995). *Meaningful Differences in the Everyday Experiences of Young Children.* Baltimore, MD: Paul H Brookes.

Heath, S. B. (1983). *Ways with Words: Language, Life, and Work in Communities and Classrooms.* New York, NY: Cambridge university Press.

Heath, S. B. (1990). The children of Trackton's children: Spoken and written language in social change. In: J. W. Stigler, R. A. Shweder & G. Herdt (Eds.), *Cultural Psychology: Essays on Comparative Human Development* (pp. 496–519). New York, NY: Cambridge University Press. doi:10.1017/CBO9781139173728.019.

Hull, G. & Schultz, K. (2001). Literacy and learning out of school: A review of theory and research. *Review of Educational Research, 71*(4), 575–611.

Hull, G. A. & Stornaiuolo, A. (2014). Cosmopolitan literacies, social networks, and "proper distance": Striving to understand in a global world. *Curriculum Inquiry, 44*(1), 15–44.

Jones, A., Nasir, N. S., & Peele-Eady, T. B. (2011). Getting beyond the script: Negotiating the complexity of urban settings as research sites. In: K. A. Scott & W. J. Blanchett (Eds.), *Research in Urban Educational Settings: Lessons Learned and Implications for Future Practice* (pp. 201–222). Charlotte, NC: Information Age.

Ladson-Billings, G. (1995). Critical social theory and transformatie knowledge: The functions of criticism in quality eduacation. *Education Researcher, 33*(6), 11–18.

Latour, B. (2005). *Reassembling the Social: An Introduction to Actor-Network Theory.* New York, NY: Oxford University Press.

Lave, J. & Wenger, E. (1991). *Situated Learning: Legitimate Peripheral Participation.* New York, NY: Cambridge University Press.

Leander, K. (2002). Locating Latanya: The situated production of identity artifacts in classroom interaction. *Research in the Teaching of English, 37*(2), 198–250.

Lee, C. D. (1992). Profile of an independent Black institution: African-centered education at work. *The Journal of Negro Education, 61*(2), 160–177.

Lee, C. D. (2006). "Every good-bye ain't gone": Analyzing the cultural underpinnings of classroom talk. *International Journal of Qualitative Studies in Education, 19*(3), 305–327.

Levinson, B. A. U., Borman, K. M., Eisenhart, M., Foster, M., Fox, A. E., & Sutton, M. (2000). *Schooling the Symbolic Animal: Social and Cultural Dimensions of Education.* Lanham, MD: Rowman & Littlefield Publishers, Inc.

Levinson, B. A. & Pollock, M. (Eds.) (2016). *A Companion to the Anthropology of Education.* Malden, MA: Blackwell Publishing.

Lewis, C. & Moje, E. B. (2003). Sociocultural perspectives meet critical theories. *International Journal of Learning, 10,* 1979–1995.

Marx, D. & Pecina, U. (2016). Community: The missing piece in preparing teacher candidates for future urban classrooms. *Action in Teacher Education, 38*(4), 344–357.

McCarty, T. L. & Warhol, L. (2016). The anthropology of language planning and policy. In: B. A. Levinson & M. Pollock (Eds.), *A Companion to the Anthropology of Education* (pp. 177–196). Malden, MA: Blackwell Publishing.

McDermott, R. & Raley, J. D. (2016). The ethnography of schooling writ large, 1955-2010. In: B. A. Levinson & M. Pollock (Eds.), *A Companion to the Anthropology of Education* (pp. 34–49). Malden, MA: Blackwell Publishing.

Moje, E. B. (2000). Circles of kinship, friendship, position, and power: Examining the community in community-based literacy research. *Journal of Literacy Research, 32*(1), 77–112.

Moje, E. B. (2004). Powerful spaces: Tracing the out-of-school literacy spaces of Latino/a youth. In: K. Leander & M. Sheehy (Eds.), *Spatializing Literacy Research and Practice* (pp. 15–38). New York, NY: Peter Lang.

Moje, E. B. (2013). Hybrid literacies in a post-hybrid world: Making a case for navigating. In: K. Hall, T. Cremin, B. Comber & L. C. Moll (Eds.), *International Handbook of Research in Children's Literacy, Learning and Culture* (pp. 359–372). Oxford, UK: Wiley-Blackwell.

Moje, E. B., Ciechanowski, K. M., Kramer, K., Ellis, L., Carrillo, R., & Collazo, T. (2004). Working toward third space in content area literacy: An examination of everyday funds of knowledge and discourse. *Reading Research Quarterly, 39*(1), 38–70.

Moll, L. C. (1992). Bilingual classroom studies and community analysis. *Educational Researcher, 21*(2), 20–24.

Nasir, N. S. (2012). *Racialized Identities: Race and Achievement among African American Youth.* Stanford, CA: Stanford University Press.

Nasir, N. S. & Hand, V. M. (2006). Exploring sociocultural perspectives on race, culture, and learning. *Review of Educational Research, 76*(4), 449–475.

Nasir, N. S. & Peele-Eady, T. B. (2012). Identity and learning. In: N. Seel (Ed.), *Encyclopedia of the Learning Sciences* (pp. 1482–1484). New York, NY: Springer Science & Business Media, LLC. doi:10.1007/9781441914286.

Nussbaumer, D. (2012). An overview of cultural historical activity theory (CHAT) use in classroom research 2000 to 2009. *Educational Review*, *64*(1), 37–55. doi:10.1080/00131911.2011.553947.

Ogbu, J. (2003). *Black American Students in an Affluent Suburb: A Study of Academic Disengagement*. Mahwah, NJ: Lawrence Erlbaum.

Paris, D. (2012). Culturally sustaining pedagogy: A needed change in stance, terminology, and practice. *Educational Researcher*, *41*(3), 93–97.

Peele-Eady, T. B. (2011). Constructing membership identity through language and social interaction: The case of African American children at Faith Missionary Baptist church. *Anthropology & Education Quarterly*, *42*(1), 54–75.

Peele-Eady, T. B. (2016). The "Responsive Reading" and reading responsively: Language, literacy, and African American student learning in the Black church. In: V. Lytra, D. Volk & E. Gregory (Eds.), *Navigating Languages, Literacies and Identities: Religion in Young Lives* (pp. 85–109). New York, NY: Taylor & Francis Group.

Peele-Eady, T. B. & Foster, M. L. (2018). The more things change, the more they stay the same: African American English, language policy, and African American learners. *International Journal of Qualitative Studies in Education*, *31*(8), 652–666.

Peirce, C. S. (1997). *The Collected Papers of Charles Sanders Peirce*, Vol. Book 3, Chapter 3. Retrieved from http://library.nlx.com.proxy.lib.umich.edu/.

Philips, S. (1983). *The Invisible Culture: Communication in Classroom and Community on the Warm Springs Indian Reservation*. New York, NY: Longman.

Piselli, F. (2007). Communities, places, and social networks. *American Behavioral Scientist*, *50*(7), 867–878.

Pollock, M. (2005). *Color Mute*. Princeton, NJ: Princeton University Press.

Pratt, M. L. (1991). Arts of the contact zone. *Profession*, 33–40.

Rogoff, B. (1994). Developing understanding of the idea of communities of learners. *Mind, Culture, & Activity*, *1*(4), 209–229.

Rosaldo, R. (1993). *Culture & Truth* (2nd ed.). Boston, MA: Beacon Press.

Schieffelin, B. B. & Ochs, E. (Eds.) (1986). *Language Socialization across Cultures*. New York, NY: Cambridge University Press.

Scribner, S. & Cole, M. (1981). *The Psychology of Literacy*. Cambridge, MA: Harvard University Press.

Seymour-Smith, C. (1986). *Dictionary of Anthropology*. New York, NY: Macmillan Press.

Siddle Walker, V. (1996). *Their Highest Potential: An African American School Community in the Segregated South*. Chapel Hill, NC: The University of North Carolina Press.

Siddle Walker, V. (2000). Valued segregated schools for African American children in the South, 1935–1969: A review of common themes and characteristics. *Review of Educational Research*, *70*(3), 253–285.

Spencer, J. (2007). Ethnography after postmodernism. In: P. Atkinson, A. Coffey, S. Delamont, J. Lofland & L. Lofland (Eds.), *Handbook of Ethnography* (pp. 443–452). Los Angeles, CA: SAGE.

Spindler, G. D. (Ed.) (1997). *Education and Cultural Process: Anthropological Approaches* (3rd ed.). Long Grove, IL: Waveland Press, Inc.

Spindler, G. D. & Spindler, L. (1997). Cultural process and ethnography: An anthropological perspective. In: G. D. Spindler (Ed.), *Education and Cultural Process: Anthropological Approaches* (3rd ed., pp. 56–76). Long Grove, IL: Waveland Press, Inc.

Taylor, D. & Dorsey-Gaines, C. (1988). *Growing up Literate: Learning from Inner-City Families*. Portsmouth, NH: Heinemann.

Urrieta, L. (2013). Familia and communidad-based saberes: Learning in an indigenous heritage community. *Anthropology & Education Quarterly*, *44*(3), 320–335.

Valdes, G. (1996). *Con Respeto: Bridging the Distances between Culturally Diverse Families and Schools: An Ethnographic Portrait*. New York, NY: Teachers College Press.

Valenzuela, A. (1999). *Subtractive Schooling: U.S.-Mexican Youth and the Politics of Caring*. New York, NY: State University of New York Press.

Walby, S., Armstrong, J., & Strid, S. (2012). Intersectionality: Multiple inequalities in social theory. *Sociology*, *46*(2), 224–240.

Warhol, L. (2012). Legacies of NALA: The Esther Martinez Native American Preservation Act and implications for language revitalization policy and practice. *Journal of American Indian Education*, *51*(3), 70–91.

Weis, L. & Fine, M. (2012). Critical bifocality and circuits of privilege: Expanding critical ethnographic theory and design. *Harvard Educational Review*, *82*(2), 173–201.

Weis, L. & Fine, M. (2013). A methodological response from the field to Douglas Foley: Critical bifocality and class cultural productions in anthropology and education. *Anthropology & Education*, *44*(3), 222–233.

Wenger, E. (1998). *Communities of Practice: Learning, Meaning, and Identity*. New York, NY: Cambridge University Press.

Williams, H. A. (2005). *Self-Taught: African American Education in Slavery and Freedom*. Chapel Hill, NC: The University of North Carolina Press.

Willis, P. (1977). *Learning to Labor*. New York, NY: Columbia University Press.

Winn, M. (2011). *Girl Time: Literacy, Justice, and the School-To-Prison Pipeline*. New York, NY: Teachers College Press.

Woolley, S. W. (2012). "The silence itself is enough of a statement": The day of silence and LGBTQ awareness raising. *Anthropology & Education Quarterly, 43*(3), 271–288.

14
ADAPTIVE LEARNING ACROSS THE LIFE SPAN

Shirley Heath, Michelle J. Bellino, and Maisha Winn

Following World War II, "displaced persons" (known in some nations, including the United States, as DPs) scattered across the world. Forced from their institutional niches as well as their home nations, these individuals faced relocation and the imperative need for adaptive learning. With little readiness for taking on new habits, skills, languages, and types of employment, DPs had in most cases been forced by war to leave behind much of what had previously defined their lives. Forces far stronger than they pushed them out from their home nations. Their exits paralleled those of today's seventy million refugees and asylum-seekers fleeing war and regional strife, as well as devastation to their way of making a livelihood created by climate change.

The need to leave what has been home may also be said today of many groups within modern economies. Such groups include those incarcerated, whether for life or shorter periods; the elderly left behind when children and grandchildren move far away; foster children pushed out of foster care systems; street dwellers, young and old; and individuals whose struggle to age in place fails. While the concept of "displaced persons" or DPs was terminology used for a specific time and event, our chapter uses the concept of DPs to consider the role of learning in the lives of multiply marginalized students and families in education settings including refugees, learners who have experienced incarceration, and youth entangled in the United States foster care system. Therefore, displacement in the context of this chapter is a useful tool to think about those displaced by economic, military, political, or social forces of expulsion and exclusion.

This chapter draws from anthropology and the learning sciences to examine, albeit briefly, contributions from these fields that augment experimental studies from neuroscience. At the outset, these fields may not be viewed as "cultural." However, all contexts from classrooms to on-the-job training or arts participation reflect cultural norms and expectations (Rogoff, 2003). While this chapter provides brief accounts of opportunities for learning across the age span that can benefit learners but are often prevented from doing so, it also demonstrates the irony that for prisoners as well as refugees, their conditions and ways of entering their current situation work against provision of appropriate opportunities to learn. The authors close with a summative account of what we have learned and by troubling the notion of a "formal education."

It is important to note the limitations of the term "informal learning." Elsewhere, the authors employ terms such as "voluntary learning," "critical learning," or "adaptive learning" in strategic and purposeful ways to demonstrate that schools do not own the rights to the concept of learning or education. Instances of voluntary learning include taking up drawing or the study of trees as a pastime, hobby, or means of engaging with grandchildren. "Critical learning" that is not subject to formal education includes the types of learning parents undertake when told their child has a particular disease or disability. Parents move to methods such as studying library resources, meeting other parents whose child has the same diagnosis, consulting experts across fields, or a combination of these and other means of gaining information.

In essence, this chapter places emphasis on will and intentions as key personal bases for learning. Yet these often become thwarted by institutional rules that do not grant respect or possibility to individuals such as prisoners or refugees. Early socialization of individuals cannot and will not dictate how or what they learn across the life span. Instead, individuals tend to learn when they gain a sense of aspiration for the future and what anthropologist Arjun Appadurai calls "terms of recognition" (Appadurai, 2004). To be sure, early socialization plays a key role in building "the capacity to aspire," though substantial evidence shows that prior socialization need not always have to be in place for learner success resulting from developing driving aspirations toward a future.

In order to demonstrate how "adaptive learning" is germane to the learning sciences, this chapter provides three primary cases that illustrate points related to those living and learning in different situations of displacement including (1) a case study of political refugees attempting to escape extreme violence and persecution in their countries of origin, as well as drastic economic and environmental shifts; (2) research on incarcerated individuals whose previous life was marked by unsuccessful formal education, and who in prison sometimes have the chance to engage with learning opportunities; and, finally, (3) young people forced out of foster care or abusive homes to live on the street or in shelters, low-income families, and elders living separately from their families. Together these cases illustrate how adaptive learning is situated, negotiated, and defined by stakeholders; evolving yet connected and, therefore, can be considered more relevant and valuable to learners than learning in more traditional and monolithic school-based ways. Adaptive learning is an agentive endeavor for learners.

The learning circumstances of all these groups call for ongoing adaptive learning. The means, materials, and purposes of their new ways of learning differ markedly from features of formal education. The foremost factor is age; most are above the general leaving age of those who seek further education following secondary school. Entering mid-life and later life makes high demands for adaptive learning.

Opportunities for Lifelong Learning? A YPAR Collaboration in Kakuma Refugee Camp

This case considers youth participatory action research (YPAR) that Bellino carried out in collaboration with young people living in Kakuma Refugee Camp in Kenya. Nearly half of Kakuma's population of 180,000 refugees is comprised of school-age children and youth who access schools implemented by the United Nations High Commissioner for Refugees (UNHCR) and partners. The majority fled violence and deprivation in the neighboring countries of Somalia, Sudan, South Sudan, and the Democratic Republic of Congo (DRC), with smaller numbers from other East African nations such as Burundi, Rwanda, Uganda, and Ethiopia. Refugee camps differ across host countries, though common characteristics include geographic isolation, containment, and a level of "enforced dependency" (Crisp, 2004), given legal restrictions on spatial mobility and work within the host nation. These structural factors limit opportunities for refugees to pursue postsecondary education, employment, and non-formal learning opportunities in the camp and elsewhere in Kenya.

Yet despite these structural and legal constraints, school completion followed by tertiary education is espoused as the ideal trajectory for achieving social adulthood and a civic obligation for displaced communities with the idea that doing so contributes to regional peace and stability (Bellino, 2018). When young people transition from secondary school, the opportunities and demands they encounter deviate sharply from their expectations. The adaptive learning needed once they leave

Adaptive Learning Across the Life Span

classrooms calls on distinct skills, knowledge, and capabilities from those emphasized within the rote learning environment of their formal schooling.

How then do young people create paths for adaptive learning when school completion has failed to transform their circumstances? Here we describe one attempt to address this question. A group of young people within the refugee camp formed, with Bellino's guidance, the Kakuma Youth Research Group (KYRG). They developed a public education campaign outside the context of school, motivated by the desire to support and educate other youth. These non-citizens engaged in ongoing civic learning in spite of their lack of legal status in Kenya but in preparation for claiming rights in exile and as future citizens of as yet unknown places.

School completion ironically drew the attention of the youth to the need for ongoing voluntary or adaptive learning outside of school spaces. Once beyond school, these young people often fell in the cracks between programing aimed at ensuring educational access for school-age children and youth, out-of-school programing oriented toward basic literacy skills for adult learners, and competitive university scholarships favoring high-achieving unmarried students in their early twenties. The vast majority of school-leavers in the camp do not qualify for any of these services, having lost their footing in the camp's social structure upon school completion. Moreover, most young people enrolled in secondary school are already over-age because of disrupted learning trajectories, discontinuous certification, and the need to orient to new curricula in an unfamiliar language of instruction. Adapting to the scarce and volatile conditions of protracted exile necessitates alternative paths toward adulthood, which the KYRG collaboration aimed to explore.

In school spaces, future orientations often framed educational attainment as an antidote to painful past experiences of war and displacement. "You are here for your future," became the common refrain from teachers who hoped to move students closer to their "aspirational selves" while increasing the distance between their present and "negative possible selves" (Oyserman, 2008). The public education campaign designed by KYRG oriented Kakuma youth to their possible futures in distinct ways, differing from images and discourses that had circulated in their schools.

KYRG emphasized the likelihood of prolonged exile and called on young people to plan for multiple futures, an approach echoed within other im/migrant communities (Bajaj & Bartlett, 2017; Dryden-Peterson et al., 2019). Youth researchers identified strategies that allowed for sequential transferrable learning that could accumulate over time and space, with applications to multiple contexts.

For example, they advised young people to learn skills with utility in the host country and in one's country of origin in the case of repatriation. These strategies called for knowledge of formal and informal learning opportunities in multiple contexts, as well as economic, environmental, and social considerations, such as which crops could thrive in particular climates and appeal to local consumers.

Additionally, this approach required a flexible stance toward learning and future preparation as well as a readiness to change course when contexts shift. Traversing the multiple structures that govern the rights of, and shape opportunities for, displaced populations requires mastery over quotidian tasks such as ensuring one's name is consistent across legal documents. Moreover, refugees have to call on complex, indistinct civic literacies such as patience and readiness to adapt to conditions largely out of their locus of control (Auyero, 2011; Bellino, 2017). For the KYRG, research skills became an opportunity to enhance civic literacy, and the youth sought to share this learning with others by strategically mobilizing information as a public good. Moreover, they positioned themselves as rights-holders entitled to access information from service providers who governed their opportunity structure. Initially reluctant to ask questions of organizational actors, youth came to see self-directed learning as essential among fundamental practices beyond the learning of transferrable skills (Bellino & KYRG, 2018).

Youth researchers also sought to distinguish school, which was institutional and time-bound, from learning, which stretched along the life course and generally included intermittent contact with formal demands of work and school. KYRG designed resources that drew attention to "continuous paths of voluntary learning" (Heath, 2012, p. 9) that could possibly exist for them in multiple settings and throughout the life course. They identified non-formal trainings offered in the context of work preparation, informal on-the-job learning, and online opportunities such as massive open online coursework. They also pointed to everyday social opportunities to learn from one another's experiences through dialogue. Adaptive learning here promoted informational and practical knowledge exchanges, such as the availability of a new job in the camp, subjective evaluations of various trainings, or openings for repatriation based on perceptions of political and economic stability.

Individuals involved in this collaboration not only became inclined to shift their conceptions of learning to be distinct from formal schooling as they increased recognition of learning as continuous, but they also saw increased accessibility and autonomy as possible through working toward an ethos of voluntary learning. However, seeing true opportunities for such learning became more and more difficult. Learning across the lifespan offered little comfort to those who had been drilled to accept the value of formal credentials with transnational recognition. Moreover, continually faced with pressing economic needs, they yearned to be able to turn their schooling into income-earning opportunities. However, knowledge and skills privileged in schools were not particularly useful or relevant for these young people, but in the context of rising credentialism, the certificates that school completion represented held value regardless of the absence of useful learning they reflected. Accordingly, KYRG came to see voluntary learning as most beneficial when it led to a credential. In some cases, this value held even when the credential was not authorized by a well-recognized institution (e.g., a local driving course offered in Kakuma Town). Ideally, learners acquired useful skills as well as a credential that truly documented actual learning, but such an ideal rarely became available.

The context, strategies, and orientation of KYRG deviated in important ways from learning in both school and community contexts. Within the collaboration, young people had shared agency to shape the research process through democratic decision-making, a power rarely granted to youth in local communities, where elders traditionally held positions of power. Working across nationalities, genders, and legal status, YPAR practices emphasized the social elements of voluntary learning through discussion, debate, and cooperation. The means, materials, and purposes of these new ways of learning held no place within formal education in the camp (Mendenhall, M., et al., 2015). The YPAR group struggled to unlearn internalized practices, such as silence and conformity, often rewarded in school. Over the course of the collaboration, youth gained comfort with and began to see value in democratic practices, learning that could ideally apply to young people's future aspirations, which often included the desire to return home as active shapers of new democratic arrangements there. Yet simultaneously, they maintained a parallel set of civic norms and practices rooted in compliance to adult authority. Enhanced democratic skills came with increased fluency in reading, navigating, and adapting to particular environments with distinct affordances as well as risks that could result from active youth participation.

Accounting for experiences such as those of KYRG matters for how we theorize civic learning in contexts of forced displacement. The experiences of members of the group also carry implications for how young people moving into adulthood develop a sense of themselves and their rights and capabilities, made more urgent as unprecedented numbers of displaced peoples migrate and integrate into stable and weak democracies across the globe. For example, in 2019, efforts in Sudan to oust the oppressive dictator Omar Hassan al-Bashir demonstrated the need for ongoing civic learning in mobilizing popular demands for transition and the democratization process that could follow. Survival skills derived through experiences with violence and oppression find no rewards in schools, despite the fact that high-risk settings generate new learning (Edberg & Bourgois, 2013). Nor are they the types of informal learning experiences that global development actors are seeking to formalize, in efforts to strengthen links across living, learning, and working (e.g., UNESCO, 2015).

Throughout life, individuals must learn when and how to activate the appropriate knowledge and skills in order to survive and thrive. A critical question then is how to capitalize on the potential of all learning settings in order to enhance skill development as well as application and advancement. Answers to this and related questions become critical to survival for youth living in exile and within refugee camps. How can refugee youth and adult learners adapt to conditions that dispossess them of the power to shape their present and future circumstances without systematically lowering expectations through "adaptive preferences" (Walker, 2007, p. 183)? Members of the KYRG displayed adaptive means of acquiring skills and knowledge, while advocating for others to embrace new roles as lifelong learners prepared for continuous learning over time and space. Openness to such learning could, and we argue should, become the civic work of nation-building in exile. Almost regardless of realistic possibilities for repatriation, these youth held to their adaptive learning in the hope of building democratic governments and remaking their communities in the midst and aftermath of war.

From "School to Prison" to "Prison to School"

This next case parallels the prior case in that both groups are "encased"—closed in and thus away from open and flexible opportunities to learn to do civil or any other type of work. Here, Winn considers how, within certain prisons of the United States, injustices forcing young people within schools onto pathways to prison can sometimes, albeit too rarely, lead to schooling within prisons.

In 2013, the Asian Prisoner Support Committee (APSC) introduced, in San Quentin State Prison (in California), Restoring Our Original True Selves (ROOTS), a curriculum designed to provide incarcerated students with opportunities to engage in Ethnic Studies. Chung (2018) asserts that these efforts resulted largely in response to the punishment of life-term prisoner, Eddy Zheng, who advocated for Ethnic Studies and Asian American Studies coursework.

Recognizing that most prisoners were already privy to rehabilitation programs that focused on personal accountability, remorse, and substance abuse, ROOTS was co-designed by incarcerated Asiana and Pacific Islanders and APSC to highlight a variety of resources likely to be culturally, politically, and racially relevant for these prisoners' reentry into society. Programing ranged from academic themes under the Ethnic Studies umbrella to workshop based presentations by community based organizations around themes such as deportation, and skill building sessions addressing topics such as intergenerational trauma (Chung, 2018).

Thinking about this work "inside" the walls informs work taking place "outside the walls" in various community colleges, such as Laney (through the Restoring Our Communities ROC program) in Oakland, California and Solano Community College in Fairfield, California. Several other colleges located in California use either or both such programs as blueprints. Also in Northern California, other learning institutions that engaged in this work included Merritt College (Street Scholars) and College of Alameda (New Dream) in what has been referred to as a "prison-to-school" movement.

Universities have also taken up similar efforts. The University of California, Berkeley has the Berkeley Underground Scholars or BUS initiative that goes beyond supporting formerly incarcerated individuals academically. These efforts include advocacy and policy work such as the "Ban the Box" campaign, which worked to remove from college applications the box applicants for university jobs must check if they have prior criminal convictions. Students within the University of California, Davis established "Beyond the Stats." In preparing a class project, two students learned they both had experienced incarceration. Their discussions led to awareness that their "stats" could include their prior convictions. As sociology majors, they believed they should be able to present themselves with the "complete objectivity" most scholars taught and reflected in their research.

All these movements connect to a legacy of student and scholarly activism on campuses fueled by liberation movements from the 1960s and 1970s that led to publications such as *The Black Scholar*, which bridged the intellectual community "inside" with that on the "outside." These efforts built an education experience for incarcerated people that extended beyond remorse and "fixing" the individual toward a "self-determined" and rigorous education in which individuals could learn about contributions incarcerated individuals had made to the world (Winn, 2010).

De-carceration, or active resistance to incarceration, works to prepare the incarcerated to live dignified and productive lives and to remove unnecessary markers of imprisonment. For example, once Pell Grant funding extended to those undertaking coursework while incarcerated, such individuals began to view themselves and their futures in new ways (Harer, 1995). Much scrutinized, college-in-prison programs have persisted, largely through studies such as the Three State Recidivism Study (Steurer & Smith, 2003) and the RAND Corporation Study (Davis et al., 2013), which demonstrated that the higher the degree a prisoner received while incarcerated, the less likely that individual was to return to prison.

Meriting special attention within learning programs have been creative arts programs (Clift, 2012) such as those that included playwriting (Winn, 2011), theater (Fraden, 2001), and literary arts (Appleman, 2019). These programs have also supported incarcerated youth and adults in defining themselves in the world beyond labels. A theater company teaching incarcerated girls the art of playwriting and performance enabled the young women to redefine themselves beyond labels such as "delinquent," "promiscuous," "at-risk," or "troublemaker," and to use instead identifiers such as "writer," "artist," "actor," or even just "human."

This research challenged typical questions, such as those related to recidivism, to argue that programs led by non-profit organizations could change dimensions of inequality that disrupt progress among young women with incarceration in their past (Winn, 2011). These young women, through the "Girl Time" arts program, learned not only literacy skills, but also agency for themselves and their futures. A consistent theme in the girls' narratives reported that their schools had either rendered them invisible or hyper-visible in ways that negated their futures. Becoming writers and experiencing the power of their words came about through their adaptive learning. They saw the arts program and the performances that resulted as offering them new ways to see themselves and their future.

Similarly, Fraden's (2001) study of Rhodessa Jones' Medea Project demonstrates the power of adaptive learning through participation that leads to a sense of belonging with others to a worthwhile project. The Medea Project led incarcerated women to wish to engage in more arts work and to find ways to sustain their creativity. Fraden's ethnography details how Rhodessa Jones worked closely with a social worker in the arts workshops, understanding that arts alone could not and would not provide all that the imprisoned women needed.

Women in San Francisco County jails have had similar opportunities to tell their stories to outside audiences using performance-based arts. In doing so, they report learning that their stories raise awareness of the struggles incarcerated women face. They also affirm that this kind of participatory learning enables the women to engage in other learning experiences that provide practice and reward for public speaking as well as showing confidence and agency—internal and performative resources highly useful once these women leave prison.

Prison learning projects cited here, as well as many others, demonstrate how adaptive learning works in contexts of incarceration and ask what it means to teach freedom in spaces of confinement. Such provisions of opportunities to learn bring about strong positive effects when these formerly incarcerated individuals return to their families and communities prepared to contribute in positive ways. The Renewing Communities Initiative, a California effort to bring state officials together with representatives from a consortium of private foundations, undertook a comprehensive study of college-in-prison programs around the United States (Lagemann, 2016). What they learned led this initiative to propose statewide plans for colleges in prisons in 2015 (Mukamai et al., 2015).

This report urged several core features of such programs: they must be of high quality, exposing learners to new ideas and instilling desire for inquiry. Moreover, the learners must be viewed as learners and not as prisoners, except for the necessity of following the security regulations of each prison. Every program should meet the standards of the offering college and, to the extent possible, be identical in grading policies, requirements, and expectations. College-in-prison programs thus must match the learning demands made within colleges and universities sponsoring these offerings. Moreover, ongoing evaluation of the programs should be carried out to ensure that excellence of instruction is consistently holding to high standards.

College-in-prison programs have helped ensure that once released, former inmates return as contributing individuals to work and contribute as good workers and citizens. In other words, advocacy for college in prison amounts to advocacy for healthy communities of returnees who have, even under situations of considerable strain and tough exclusion, succeeded in both formal instruction and the related adaptive learning that prisoners must undertake to complement the formal instruction they receive. Research shows that those who have successfully managed to do both while incarcerated generally continue to do so, often as community leaders working to offer positive and yet realistic guidance to young men and women whose life circumstances lead them into gang life or drug dealing. In these situations, those who have gained a college degree while in prison can be highly effective in positive community leadership. Driven by strong intentionality, they work "on the outside" to understand what they now believe might have kept them from having to go to prison. They now adaptively learn how to help shape policies that can provide aspiration for neighborhoods mired in poverty and desperation. In doing so, these individuals report that now they continually use the adaptive learning practices they acquired in coordination with their academic study in prison. They seek out and question sources of information and work toward building for the young new and appealing experiences that enable them to learn both within and beyond their classrooms.

The culture of hyper incarceration has permeated the U.S. public school system, as evidenced by "zero-tolerance" policies (Gregory, Skiba, & Noguera, 2010; Haft, 2000), racial disparities in school discipline policies and practices (U.S. Department of Education Office for Civil Rights, 2014), and pervasive focus on controlling and managing Black and Brown bodies rather than providing robust and rigorous learning opportunities (Winn, 2018). Restorative justice or a paradigm shift from punitive ways of engaging in human relationships to one that begins with purpose, belonging, and consensus building has been imported from the criminal justice system to some U.S. schools. For example, Kennedy High School in the Midwest (Winn, 2018) began to have members of their student service staff trained in restorative justice circle processes—or a process whereby a student or students could build consensus as a community to address harm and wrongdoing. Student service staff such as social workers and the school psychologists were more engaged in these processes than content area teachers, which created a culture whereby restorative justice continued to be secondary. In the best case scenarios, content area teachers, like an English/Language Arts teacher at Kennedy, implemented a restorative justice culture and mindset in their approach with students as well as in their practices. These efforts were largely undermined by the school community and, according to the teacher at Kennedy, were too difficult to maintain in spite of the fact that she understood these efforts to be vital to multiplying marginalized students' experience of school as an environment that cultivated intellectual curiosity and engagement. Most recently, scholars are considering what it would mean to leverage restorative justice theory to create more robust learning opportunities in science (Patterson & Gray, 2019), math (Gholson & Robinson, 2019; Bullock & Meiners, 2019), social studies (Kohli, Montaño, & Fisher, 2019), digital media (Degand, 2019), and English Language Arts (de los Rios et al., 2019), or for a Transformative Justice Teacher Education (Winn & Winn, 2019 that considers the purpose of adaptive learning spaces and how the tools in these contexts can and should be taken up.

Adaptive Learning and How It Matters

Members of the two groups in the cases above had to survive in spaces often touted as being places where transition happens, albeit with different degrees of individual agency and choice available to individuals. However, circumstances in these and similarly institutionalized settings differ in the extent to which true transition or transformation may be possible. Individuals in some circumstances may decide for themselves to undertake voluntary or adaptive learning if available and as tied to future aspirations, such as exiting prison or a refugee camp in pursuit of work and service. However, these opportunities often do not come with mediating circumstances that also bring about opportunities of "going home." The sobering truth can often be that some may never have known "home" as a place to love or may not be able to return to a home they did love.

The next case differs from the prior two in that this third case provides a situation in which learning is entirely voluntary, as well as sustained in its existence. Research followed this situation for its first six years, focusing on those who took part to record effects on their daily habits related to self-regulation, aspirations for the future, and improved integrative social skills. Findings revealed that when contexts for learning such as those described for this final case are offered and sustained, individuals who maintain involvement for several years learn to draw upon specific positive changes that develop, maintain, and advance them in highly unexpected ways. This case illustrates how voluntary learning in and through the arts under high-risk situations of performance accelerates the benefits of learning (Heath, 2016).

Public Works, a drama program begun in 2013 in New York City by the Public Theater, set out to engage in intensive and high-risk dramatic performance those living with limited opportunities and hopes for a better future. The plan, devised by Heath with Oskar Eustis, Artistic Director of the Public Theater, and Lear deBessonet, Founding Director of Public Works, enlisted five community-serving organizations (one in each of the five boroughs of New York City). In these organizations, individuals could take advantage of learning through the coming year under a teaching artist who would come to their organization. In each site, the group selected what they wanted to learn on topics and skills ranging from musical theater to the works of August Wilson to acting or poetry. Over a period of nine months, a teaching artist worked with each group in their community site on their chosen area of learning. Auditions took place each May giving individuals open opportunities to perform as they wished—with a short narrative, a song, or a rehearsed piece from a play. The goal was to work toward being ready to perform with 100-plus others in a musical created for one of Shakespeare's plays or a musical version of a story from Greek mythology. On the stage of the Delacorte Theater in Central Park, the performance would take place for several days over Labor Day weekend, with critics from newspapers across the city in the audience of 2500 each evening (Heath, 2015, 2018).

Set in place in each site were principles from the learning sciences shown to be highly effective for advancing the learning of those who often feel that in their earlier lives, they have failed at learning. In the first few years of the program, the five community organizations that participated included a community organization working with those released from long stretches in prison. Other community groups included: domestic workers, a recreation center serving elders in a part of New York City especially marked by poverty; a choir of the Children's Aid Society; and a community organization providing opportunities in the arts for families and children (many immigrants) living in a particularly disenfranchised area of the city.

Individuals who chose to take part in auditions ranged in age from five to eighty-five. Individuals as well as entire families could audition, though all knew that regardless of their audition, they would hold some place in the coming production. Some would have speaking parts, while others would be engaged primarily in the musical numbers that required dance and singing. Following auditions, rehearsals generally ran from July until Labor Day weekend.

Learning principles behind the program ensured that those who volunteered to undertake the classes and the audition would be included regardless of ability or age. Rehearsals took place in the downtown location in Manhattan of the Public Theater. Riding the subway into new areas and finding a building they had never before known became an orienting part of the initial experience of those coming to the Public Theater for rehearsals. The stage manager had strict rules that required on-time and consistent attendance for rehearsals. All participants had her cell number, and a five-minute tardiness drew a phone call inquiring where each individual was, for someone would be sent to bring them to rehearsal. The clear message was that every person was needed for every rehearsal.

For participants, learning that each person's presence was absolutely needed became a transformative experience. Many said that they had never before been needed nor had they been so persistently and generously offered help in getting to where they needed to be. For many participants, rehearsals marked the first time in their lives that they knew someone cared where they were because they were needed elsewhere for good reasons. Thus, regular on-time appearances became the norm for participants. Many confessed that they had never before been able to be on time for anything, and thus they had never had jobs or taken regular classes. In rehearsals from beginning to end, performers learned about the drama being performed, heard the original music and songs created for the piece, and began to learn the sequencing and pacing of the show (Bogke et al., 2008; Schlaug, 2014; Wan & Schlaug, 2010). Each year, four or five Equity actors joined the cast, taking some lead parts. Choreographers worked during each rehearsal with members of the community cast to help them learn dances and essential ways of moving that enabled the huge cast to get onto and off the stage quickly. Individuals with speaking parts learned how to enter and exit the stage at the requisite pace.

The work was hard, and much reading, thinking, and focusing on directors' instructions and modeling was called for (Moreno et al., 2011). Young members stepped in to help older members up and down the steep stairs to the seats where cast members watched as particular scenes were rehearsed at the Public Theater. Choreographic assistants helped those who felt they needed extra work to master dance steps. For certain scenes, small groups worked with assistant directors in other parts of the Public Theater. Each person had a notebook filled with script, songs, and rehearsal schedule, and each person received almost daily updates on rehearsal content, needs, and areas needing special attention.

Throughout the long months from September into the next year when the cycle began again, individuals felt they now belonged in the Public Works group. Some became Ambassadors for Public Works, recruiting other community members to attend the show at the Delacorte. Still others worked together to create newsletters or volunteered to help distribute tickets. By the second year, monthly pot lucks began to take place at the Public Theater site in lower Manhattan. On these occasions, different community organizations or individuals proposed programs of their own works as well as ideas about questions and concerns to be covered during the business time of these dinners. In short, a coherent community resulted among the first five community organizations as well as the subsequent three organizations that joined following the first three years.

Public Works held as its goal that from community members' lessons from teaching artists, plus the stretch of summer rehearsals and end-of-summer performances, community members would gain confidence and skills essential to their daily lives and employment. Heath, a part of the Public Works "family" from the beginning, was immersed in and among community members as they rehearsed and throughout productions. She also met with them on occasion in their community organizations. She listened to conversations and documented how they reported to one another other changes they saw happening in their own lives. She asked no direct questions but only questions of clarification. Listening, joining in, and being a long-term part of the participant group made clear through quantitative and qualitative language data that participants talked most frequently about five key matters in their lives. These included the following new situations and behaviors they wanted to tell one another about again and again:

- ways that being integrated and needed within a "big" and ongoing enterprise marked a huge change in their prior lives of being alone, feeling isolated, or shut away (in prison or in life on the streets).
- how they were now so aware of their own mental and physical health and knew that to be in the show year after year, they had to "get healthy and stay that way!"
- the realization that they were now looking at themselves and deciding to do "something about myself" which meant for some going to a doctor for medical care, and for others, making new

friends, finding ways to reunite with family members from whom they had been estranged, and taking lessons or enrolling in courses or programs in their local communities.

- how they now realized they were developing positive social and conversational skills centered on the here and now and the future and no longer on their failures of the past.
- acceptance of an "I can do this" attitude leading them to take classes in other fields, seek job training, and apply with confidence for jobs.

Heath's research based on conversations among the participants showed that with each year, new positive features of daily contexts for individuals young and old came into their lives. Following year one, older individuals (those beyond age forty) who had no regular contact with a physician reported improved memory and attentiveness (Rogalski & Gefen, 2013; Taubert et al., 2010, 2012). Moreover, they now knew they had to take charge of their medical health. Those with diabetes went to be reassessed and given up-to-date medicines and exercise recommendations. Those with arthritis followed a similar process. Others resolved to lose weight, exercise more, and take voice or dance lessons.

By the end of the third year, for all those (94%) who had stayed with Public Works from the first year, just over 70% now held either full or part-time jobs, and over 65% had either taken a class or were still taking some type of ongoing learning experience beyond their work with the Public Theater (Schlaug, 2001, 2014). Perhaps most obvious from these two major outcomes was the fact that for all those over age forty, they had either begun to go to a physician or clinic. Some began to be sure they went to have regular check-ups to monitor blood-pressure, get new nutritional recommendations, and find ways to manage mobility issues or chronic conditions. Without exception, all those in the first three years, as well as those joining for the next three years, agreed that being with and in Public Works had brought them to a deep realization that they had to take responsibility for their own health. Many said openly: "Now I have something to look forward to. I know now I am needed here (within Public Works)." A key motivating factor was the knowledge that if in May of each year, they showed they could undertake the choreography, read the music, and take full part in the upcoming performance, they were likely to be on stage for the run of performances in late August and early September. Over the first six years of its existence, Public Works had to ask only a very few individuals to depart the program.

Everyone who took classes all year in their community organization wanted to be "on stage" in the following year. Thus, an additional strong learning principle behind Public Works was the fact that it was sustaining, going on from year to year. Individuals learned how to give constant evidence of commitment and membership as well as to stay in touch with others in the group to check on their well-being. Throughout the work, the clear and consistent message from staff was that "Art will never change you. It certainly cannot 'save' you. Only you can do that by taking full advantage of the learning environment the arts offers you" (cf. Levitin, 2006; Levitin & Menon, 2003; Marcus, 2012).

Directors and leaders consistently made clear that agency and strong intentionality had to rest within the participants. Thus, whatever was good, glorious, and successful came from them and not from someone else. Here again, a key design research principle comes into play. This is awareness that the best learning environments are those in which learners use their hands as well as their heads and know that quality of outcomes must depend on their commitment, participation, and ongoing assessment of how and what they are doing to make their roles in life as well as performances better and better (Pallasmaa, 2009; Reiner, 2008; Wilson, 1998).

Failed Schooling or Failing School?

An undercurrent of this chapter, as noted in all the above cases, is the need to consider how individuals see themselves as failing from and during their schooling or perhaps how schools failed them. We raise such considerations in the context of certain key features of the historic role of

Adaptive Learning Across the Life Span

formal schooling. As we do so, we recognize that schools, like other social institutions, are complex organizations. We describe in this section schooling aligned with historical structures and norms, recognizing that schools which look very different from this, and which are productive places for learning, do exist (Alim, Django, & Wong, this volume).

However, from the eighteenth century, certain key aspects of formal education have held: an adult expert instructor, pupils physically inactive and seated, wooden desks including seats and writing surfaces, instruments and other artifacts related to representation of structured symbol systems, primarily the alphabet and numerals. Beyond these features stand requirements of daily hours during certain times of the year, and attendance for a certain number of years to meet requirements for primary and secondary levels.

Today these features of formal education still hold in the policies of powerful international entities such as the United Nations and World Bank, as well as policymakers of both developing nations and modern economies. Around the world, policymakers prize certain key features of schooling in their attention to the learning of the young—those from pre-school through exit from secondary school. Doing so allows leaders to overlook or dismiss the fact that in many ways, the content, methods, and materials of traditional classroom learning continue to look very much as they did three centuries ago (Farrell, 2008). Moreover, the same approaches to schooling are prescribed, sought, and rewarded across distinct contexts, as evidenced by global educational agendas (Anderson-Levitt, 2003).

Thus policymakers around the world hold faith that for economies to become fully modern, the society must rely on those who are formally educated into and through further education toward a degree and often certification as well as licensing (determined by standardized tests) for some professions. Such state policies make evident the expectation that degree conferrals from higher education institutions lead the young into employment in sites ranging from small businesses and multinational corporations to large institutions such as hospitals and colleges and universities, as well as legal, political, and environmental employment. For such individuals, prior consistent academic achievement marks those who successfully find and hold employment that provides salaries (as well as bonuses for those working in contexts where the work of the employee is seen as advancing the wealth of the employing entity).

The reality, however, is that for many jobs, as well as for successfully handling what life can be like, formal education K–12 often does not fully or appropriately prepare individuals. In particular, even gaining entry-level work often requires more and different skills and knowledge than what can be gained through only formal education (see Roth, 2019 for an extensive analysis of these points). Moreover, for the changing needs and circumstances critical to advancement in many of the most widely needed jobs within modern economies, higher education often helps but may not be sufficient.

Furthermore, for numerous means of earning incomes, such as farming, fishing, caregiving, and maintenance occupations (e.g., auto mechanics, plumbing, electricity, pipefitting, etc.), apprenticeship is essential. In these instances, a period of hands-on learning is often capped by experiential testing and mentorship under a master. Achievement of requisite licensing becomes the primary way of entering and sustaining a steady means of gaining a paycheck, a contract for a particular task or project, or entry into a trade union through which health and liability insurance can be secured. In addition, for most of these occupations, having some formal training in financial literacy as well as shifting regulations and knowing how to take advantage of various means of staying abreast of innovations in processes, types of tools, materials, and safety regulations become essential. Beyond all these demands, wage earners must also understand legal requirements, such as local and national taxes, as well as the need to secure health insurance and to save toward retirement.

In short, those who set policy and often practices for formal education generally have little comprehensive understanding of the complex array of types of information as well as skills that wage-earning adults have to learn initially and keep abreast of in order to manage their own contracted time or small business (Collins & Halverson, 2018; Farrell, 2007). Once hired, workers who wallpaper a room, install a French drain, or power-wash and refinish the exterior of a home have to have achieved the requisite expertise. Medical caregivers, often with titles to which the label "assistant" is attached, make much medical "lab work" and preparation for surgery happen. These individuals sustain nursing homes, at-home care, and complement professional staff in hospitals across the globe.

An additional oversight resulting from the near exclusive attention to formal schooling across history has been neglectful of the nature of learning across indigenous populations around the world. These groups have long modeled what outsiders, such as anthropologists, as well as indigenous scholars, see as voluntary learning and a focus on "well-being," as well as ongoing demonstration of systems of thinking that underlie gains in skills as well as information (see Colby, 1987 for a summary; see also Huaman & Brayboy, 2017; Urrieta, 2013). Moreover, such learning has generally been closely linked to land and interactions between local history and the natural environment. Outcomes related to well-being or states of physical and mental health are generally positively associated (Kelly, Foxe, & Garavan, 2006). As far back as the 1980s, anthropologists pointed to the strong positive correlations between "adaptive potential," including the will and capacity to learn adaptively, and positive states of well-being. The uprootedness and migration of an increasing proportion of the world's populations, including many indigenous people, is forcing almost total disengagement with what is beneath the feet and in the air and sky above and also with long-standing positive effects on concern for behavioral pursuits in the natural environment.

Modernity escalates these separations—from one another across communities, races, ethnicities, age, and numerous other barriers. However, given the pace and severity of changes to the climate around the world, learning voluntarily together how to save ourselves through preserving and honoring the planet may be the most urgent type of (in)voluntary learning everyone faces (Wallace-Wells, 2019). Doing so requires knowledge and skills from the most expert and esoteric to the most mundane and everyday ways of being, thinking, and doing. In this chapter, we have identified several key principles of this kind of adaptive learning. Namely, that it is situated, negotiated, and defined by stakeholders; is evolving yet connected and, therefore, can be considered more relevant and valuable to learners than learning in more traditional and monolithic school-based ways; is an agentive endeavor for learners. These characteristics describe the learning that occurred in learning settings designed to be aligned with a set of real world learning needs, for populations that have tended not to find rich or productive learning experiences in schools. The studies we describe suggest that indeed, it may be that voluntary or adaptive learning is in reality not so utterly voluntary, and may be the planet's only route to saving humanity.

References

Anderson-Levitt, K. (Ed.) (2003). *Local Meanings, Global Schooling: Anthropology and World Culture Theory*. New York, NY: Palgrave.

Appadurai, A. (2004). The capacity to aspire: Culture and the terms of recognition. In: V. Rao & M. Walton (Eds.), *Culture and Public Action* (pp. 59–84). Chicago, IL: Stanford University Press.

Appleman, D. (2019). *Words No Bars Can Hold: Literacy Learning in Prison*. New York: W. W. Norton & Company.

Auyero, J. (2011). Patients of the state: An ethnographic account of poor people's waiting. *Latin American Research Review* 46(1):5–29.

Bajaj, M., & Bartlett, L. (2017). Critical transnational curriculum for immigrant and refugee students. *Curriculum Inquiry* 47(1):25–35.

Bellino, M. J. (2018). Youth aspirations in Kakuma Refugee Camp: Education as a means for social, spatial, and economic (im)mobility. *Globalisation, Societies & Education* 16(4):541–556.

Bellino, M. J. (2017). *Youth in Postwar Guatemala: Education and Civic Identity in Transition*. New Brunswick, NJ: Rutgers University Press.

Bellino, M. J., & Kakuma Youth Research Group. (2018). Closing information gaps in Kakuma Refugee Camp: A youth participatory action research study. *American Journal of Community Psychology* 62(3–4):492–507.

Bogke, J., et al. (2008). Training-induced brain structure changes in the elderly. *Journal of Neuroscience* 28(28):7031–7035. doi:10.1523/JNEUROSCI.0742-0802008.

Bullock, E. C., & Meiners, E. R. (2019). Abolition by the numbers: Mathematics as a tool to dismantle the carceral state (and build alternatives). *Theory Into Practice*. Published Online. doi:10.1080/00405841.2019.1626613.

Chung, R. V. (2018). Imprisoned curriculum: The Roots Program and prisoner led healing. University of California, Davis, Transformative Justice in Education (TJE) Center White Paper Series. https://tje.ucdavis.edu/sites/g/files/dgvnsk1141/files/files/page/Roger%20Viet%20Chung%20-%20Imprisoned%20Curriculum_4.pdf_.

Clift, S. (2012). Creative arts as a public health resource: Moving from practice-based research to evidence-based practice. *Perspective in Public Health*, I(3):120–127. doi:10.1177/1757913912442269.

Colby, G. (1987). Well-being: A theoretical program. *American Anthropologist* 89(4):879–895.

Collins, A., & Halverson, R. (2018). *Rethinking Education in the Age of Technology*. 2nd ed. New York, NY: Teachers College Press.

Crisp, J. (2004). *The Local Integration and Local Settlement of Refugees: A Conceptual and Historical Analysis*. Geneva: UNHCR.

Davis, L. M., et al. (2013). *Evaluating the Effectiveness of Correctional Education: A Meta-Analysis of Programs That Provide Education to Incarcerated Adults*. Washington, DC: The RAND Corporation.

Degand, D. (2019). Stereotypes vs. strategies for digital media artists: The case for culturally relevant media production. *Theory Into Practice*. Published Online. doi:10.1080/00405841.2019.1626617.

de los Rios, C., et al. (2019). Upending colonial practices: Toward repairing harm in English Education. *Theory Into Practice*. Published Online. https://www.tandfonline.com/action/showAxaArticles?journalCode=htip20

Draganski, B., et al. (2004). Neuroplasticity: Changes in grey matter induced by training. *Nature* 427(6972):311–312.

Dryden-Peterson, S., et al. (2019). The purposes of refugee education: Policy and practice of integrating refugees into national education systems. *Sociology of Education* 92(4):346–366. doi:10.1177/0038040719863054.

Eckmann, T. (2011). Exercise and the aging brain. *Journal on Active Aging* 10(6):20–28.

Edberg, M., & Bourgois, P. (2013). Street markets, adolescent identity and violence: A generative dynamic. In: R. Rosenfeld, M. Edberg, X. Fang, & C. S. Florence (Eds.), *Economics and Youth Violence: Crime, Disadvantage, and Community* (pp. 181–206). New York, NY: New York University Press.

Farrell, J. P. (2007). Education in the years to come: What we can learn from alternative education. In: M. Mason, P. D. Hershock, & J. N. Hawkins (Eds.), *Changing Education: CERC Studies in Comparative Education*, Vol. 20. Dordrecht: Springer.

Farrell, J. P. (2008). Community education in developing countries: The quiet revolution in schooling. In F. M. Connelly, M. F. He, & J. I. Phillion (Eds.), *The SAGE Handbook of Curriculum and Instruction* (pp. 369–389). Thousand Oaks, CA: Sage.

Fraden, R. (2001). *Imagining Medea: Rhodessa Jones and Theater for Incarcerated Women*. Chapel Hill, NC: University of North Carolina Press.

Gholson, M., & Robinson, D. (2019). Restoring mathematics identities of Black learners: A curricular approach. *Theory Into Practice*. Published Online. doi:10.1080/00405841.2019.1626613.

Gregory, A., Skiba, R. J., & Noguera, P. A. (2010). The achievement gap and the discipline gap: Two sides of the same coin? *Educational Researcher* 39(1):59–68. doi:10.3102/0013189X09357621.

Haft, W. (2000). More than zero: The cost of zero tolerance and the case for restorative justice in schools. *Denver University Law Review* 77:795.

Harer, M. D. (May 1995). *Prison Education Program Participation and Recidivism: A Test of the Normalization Process*. Washington, DC: Federal Bureau of Prisons Office of Research and Evaluations.

Heath, S. B. (2018). Performing risk. In: C. McAvinchey, et al. (Eds.), *Phakama: Making Participatory Performance* (pp. 246–260). London: Bloomsbury Press.

Heath, S. B. (2016). The benefits of ensemble music experience (and why these benefits matter so much in underserved communities). In: C. Witkowski (Ed.), *Music for Social Change: El Sistema beyond Venezuela* (pp. 73–94). New York, NY: The Music Sales Group.

Heath, S. B. (2015). Museums, theaters, and youth orchestras: Advancing creative arts and sciences within under-resourced communities. In: W. G. Tierney (Ed.) *Rethinking Education and Poverty*. Special issue of The Annals of the American Academy of Political and Social Science (pp. 177–200). Baltimore, MD: John Hopkins University Press.

Heath, S. B. (2012). *Words at Work and Play: Three Decades*. Cambridge: Cambridge University Press.

Huaman, E. S., & Brayboy, B. M. J. (Eds.) (2017). *Indigenous Innovations in Higher Education: Local Knowledge and Critical Research*. Rotterdam, The Netherlands: Sense.

Kelly, C., Foxe, J. J., & Garavan, H. (2006). Patterns of normal human brain plasticity after practice and implications for neuro rehabilitation. *Archives of Physical Medicine & Rehabilitation* 87(12):20–29.

Kholi, R., Montaño, E., & Fisher, D. M. (2019). History matters: Challenging an ahistorical approach to restorative justice in teacher education. *Theory Into Practice*. Published Online. doi:10.1080/00405841.2019.1626613.

Lagemann, E. (2016). *Liberating Minds: The Case for College in Prison*. New York, NY: The New Press.

Levitin, Daniel J. (2006). *This Is Your Brain on Music: The Science of a Human Obsession*. New York, NY: Penguin.

Levitin, Daniel, & Menon, V. (2003). Musical structure is processed in 'language' areas of the brain: A possible role for Brodmann Area 47 in temporal coherence. *Neuroimage* 20(4):2142–2152.

Marcus, Gary (2012). *Guitar Zero: The New Musician and the Science of Learning*. New York, NY: Penguin Press.

Mendenhall, M., et al. (2015). Quality education for refugees in Kenya: Pedagogy in urban Nairobi and Kakuma Refugee Camp settings. *Journal on Education in Emergencies*, 1(1):92–127.

Moreno, S., et al. (2011). Short-term music training enhances verbal intelligence and executive function. *Psychological Science* 22(11):1425–1433. doi:10.1177/09567976/1425-1433.

Mukamai, et al. (2015). *Degrees of Freedom*. Berkeley, CA: Institute on Law and Social Policy, UC Berkeley and Stanford University School of Law.

Oyserman, D. (2008). Possible selves: Identity-based motivation and school success. In: H. W. Marsch, R. G. Craven, & D. M. McInerney (Eds.), *Self-Processes, Learning, and Enabling Human Potential: Dynamic New Approaches* (pp. 269–288). Charlotte, NC: Information Age.

Pallasmaa, Juhani (2009). *The Thinking Hand*. New York, NY: Wiley.

Patterson, A., & Gray, S. (2019). Teaching to transform: (W)holistic Science Pedagogy. *Theory Into Practice*. Published Online. doi:10.1080/00405841.2019.1626616.

Reiner, M. (2008). The validity and consistency of force feedback interfaces in telesurgery. *Journal of Computer-Aided Surgery* 9:69–74.

Rogalski, E. J., & Gefen, T. (2013). Youthful memory capacity in old brains. *Journal of Cognitive Neuroscience* 25(1):29–36.

Rogoff, B. (2003). *The Cultural Nature of Human Development*. New York, NY: Oxford University Press.

Roth, G. (2019). *The Educated Underclass: Students and the Promise of Social Mobility*. London: Pluto Press.

Schlaug, G. (2001). The brain of musicians: A model for functional and structural adaptation. *Annals of the New York Academy of Sciences* 930:281–299.

Schlaug, G. (2014). Musicians and music-making as a model for the study of brain plasticity. *Progress in Brain Research* 217:37–55. doi:10.1016/bs.pbr.2014.11.020.

Steurer, S. J., & Smith, L. G. (February 2003). *Education Reduced Crime: Three-State Recidivism Study*. Lanham, MD: Correctional Education Association.

Taubert, M., Villringer, A., & Ragert, P. (2012). Learning-related gray and white matter changes in humans: An update. *The Neuroscientist: A Review Journal Bringing Neurobiology, Neurology & Psychiatry* 18(4):320. doi:10.1177/1073858411419048.

Taubert, M., et al. (2010). Dynamic properties of human brain structure: Learning-related changes in cortical areas and associated fiber connections. *Journal of Neuroscience* 30(35):11670–11677. doi:10.1523.JNEUROSCI.2567-10.2010.

UNESCO. (2015). *EFA Monitoring Report, 2015, Education for All, 2000–2015: Achievements and Challenges*. Paris, France: UNESCO.

Urrieta, L. (2013). Familia and comunidad-based saberes: Learning in an indigenous heritage community. *Anthropology & Education Quarterly* 44(3):514–535.

U.S. Department of Education Office for Civil Rights. (2014). *Civil Rights Data Collection: Data Snapshot School Discipline*. http://www2.ed.gov/about/offices/list/ocr/docs/crdc-discipline-snapshot.pdf.

Walker, M. (2007). Selecting capabilities for gender equality in education. In: M. Walker, & E. Unterhalter (Eds.), *Amartya Sen's Capability Approach and Social Justice in Education* (pp. 177–195). New York, NY: Palgrave.

Wallace-Wells, D. (2019). *The Uninhabitable Earth: Life after Warming*. New York, NY: Tim Duggan Books.

Wan, C. V., & Schlaug, G. (2010). Music-making as a tool for promoting brain plasticity across the life span. *The Neuroscientist: A Review Journal Bringing Neurobiology, Neurology & Psychiatry* 16(5):566–577. doi:10.1177/1073858410377805.

Wilson, Frank (1998). *The Hand: How Its Use Shapes the Brain, Language, and Human Culture*. New York, NY: Random House.

Winn, M. T., & Winn, L. T. (2019). This Issue. *Theory Into Practice*. Published Online. doi:10.1080/00405841.2019.1626621.

Winn, M. T. (2018). *Justice on Both Sides: Transforming Education through Restorative Justice*. Cambridge: Harvard Education Press.

Winn, M. T. (2011). *Girl Time: Literacy, Justice and the School-To-Prison Pipeline*. New York, NY: Teachers College Press.

Winn, M. T. (December 2010). "Betwixt and between": Literacy, liminality, and the "celling" of Black girls. *Race, Ethnicity, & Education* 13(4):425–447.

15

CULTURALLY SUSTAINING PEDAGOGY

A Critical Framework for Centering Communities

H. Samy Alim, Django Paris, and Casey Philip Wong

If particular cultural practices and belief systems allowed people of African descent in the U.S. and the diaspora to survive and thrive through enslavement and Jim Crow—America's two centuries of legal apartheid—then it seems reasonable that sustaining these practices and strategic transformations in response to changing conditions is a worthwhile goal. If belief systems and practices around relationships with the natural world among Indigenous populations in the Americas have allowed for ecological resilience (see the Menominee Nation in Wisconsin), then it seems reasonable that such practices should be sustained.

—Carol D. Lee (2017, p. 266)

Neoliberalism knows what it wants. Neoliberalism wants to produce workers—cheap sources of labor. So, when you ask the question of how to teach, think first about what you want to produce. So, whereas neoliberalism wants to produce cheap labor, culturally relevant pedagogies and culturally sustaining pedagogies want to produce critically thinking human beings. Start there.

—Gloria Ladson-Billings (2014, Lecture at Stanford University)

I told one of the teachers, I was like, 'To me, school isn't really about learning anymore. It's about being obedient... I think that the reason why the kids that are poor and of color have to be taught obedience is—it's kind of like a conspiracy. They're always going to want Blacks, Mexicans, People of Color, to stay under this rule.

—Alan, Bay Grove High School student (Wong, 2019, p. 49)

Culturally sustaining pedagogy (CSP) is a critical framework for centering and sustaining Indigenous, Black, Latinx, Asian and Pacific Islander communities[1] as these memberships necessarily intersect with gender and sexuality, dis/ability, class, language, land and more. First and foremost, CSP explicitly names whiteness (including white normativity, white racism and ideologies of white supremacy) as the problem, and thus, decentering whiteness and recentering communities is our point of departure. In the context of the United States and other nation-states living out the legacies and contemporary realities of genocide, enslavement, apartheid, occupation and various forms of colonialism, CSP recognizes that the purpose of state-sanctioned schooling has always been to forward the largely assimilationist and often violent white imperialist project. In the context of deeply entrenched, structural racial and economic inequalities, CSP is necessarily and fundamentally a critical, anti-racist, anti-colonial framework that rejects the white settler capitalist gaze and the kindred cisheteropatriarchal, English-monolingual, ableist, classist, xenophobic and other hegemonic gazes.

In the U.S. and beyond, white cultural and linguistic hegemony has had and continues to have devastating effects on the access, achievement and well-being of many communities, particularly in the context of state-sanctioned schools. These effects are multiplied when coupled with the sweeping forces of racialized settler capitalism, which as Ladson-Billings and high school student Alan mentioned above, seeks to extract young people from communities as nothing more than "obedient, cheap sources of labor." CSP reimagines education not only within the context of centuries of oppression and domination, but critically, draws strength and wisdom from centuries of intergenerational revitalization, resistance and the revolutionary love of our communities in the face of such brutality.

As Carol D. Lee argued above, in the contexts of genocide and enslavement—the foundational, settler colonial experiences of Indigenous peoples and enslaved Africans—acts of historic and cultural resistance and *survivance* (Viznor, 1994) have allowed Indigenous and African descended communities to sustain practices and belief systems (and their very lives) in the face of racialized white terror. The gravity of Lee's statement, and this perspective writ large, is laid to bear starkly by Alim and Paris (2017, p. 14) who have raised the critical question:

> Under the latest iterations of white supremacist, capitalist, cisheteropatriarchal ideologies, systems and practices, what knowledges *MUST* we sustain in order to overcome and survive when faced with a power that seeks to sustain itself above and beyond—and sometimes shot-through—our bodies?

CSP seeks to respond to the many ways that schooling (and other state-sanctioned institutions—like health and law, for example[2]) continues to function as part of a colonial project. Not only do we seek to disrupt the pervasive anti-Indigeneity, anti-Blackness and related anti-Brownness (from anti-*Latinidad* to Islamophobia) and model minority myths so foundational to schooling in the U.S. and many other colonial nation-states (Woodson, 2000; S. Lee, 2005; Lomawaima & McCarty, 2006; Alexander, 2007; Moll, 1992; Dumas, 2014, Grande, 2018; Paris, 2019), but CSP, at its core, proposes educational contexts as sites for sustaining the lifeways[3] of communities rather than eradicating them.

As we think about the kinds of teaching and learning settings required to sustain communities as part of pluralistic societies, we join other critical scholars who recognize the need to shift the function of schooling from assimilation to cultural pluralism. Toward that end, we ask a series of related questions: what would our pedagogies look like if these hegemonic gazes weren't the dominant ones? What if, indeed, the goal of teaching and learning with young people of color was not ultimately to see how closely they could perform white middle-class norms, but rather was to explore, honor, extend and, at times, problematize their cultural practices and investments? What would our educational contexts look like in a world where we owed no explanations, to anyone, about the value of our children's culture, language and learning potential? How can we move beyond these forced explanations of our worth, i.e., testing regimes, achievement expectations based on normative notions of culture, language and narrow, *white settler-gazed* (Morrison, 1998; Paris, 2019), capitalist ideas of academic success, more generally? These are the kinds of questions that motivate CSP educators and researchers.

"As goods unto themselves": The Paradigm Shift to Sustenance

Over the past decade, we have worked to offer CSP (Paris, 2012; Paris & Alim, 2014; Alim & Paris, 2015; Paris & Alim, 2017) as a needed change in stance and terminology in pedagogical theory and practice. CSP, as articulated by Paris (2012), seeks to perpetuate and foster—to sustain—linguistic, literate and cultural pluralism as part of schooling for positive social transformation and revitalization. CSP positions dynamic cultural dexterity as a necessary good, and sees the outcome of learning as additive, rather than subtractive, as remaining whole rather than framed as broken, as critically enriching strengths rather than replacing deficits. Moreover, in fundamentally reimagining the purpose of education, CSP demands a critical, emancipatory vision of schooling that redirects the focus of critique away from children (and their cultures, communities, languages, histories, etc.) and aims it squarely at the oppressive systems that frame us in *everywhichway* as marginal or deficient. As educators, we have never been interested in asking young people and families to abandon their languages, literacies, cultures and histories in order to achieve in schools. Instead, we have aimed to build a transformative, liberatory educational movement with like-minded educators and scholars interested in creating educational opportunities—from classrooms and schools, to universities, to community organizations, to family settings—that center and sustain young people and their communities.

CSP settings demand explicitly pluralist outcomes that are not centered on dominant white, middle-class, monolingual/monocultural norms of educational achievement (Paris & Alim, 2014; Alim & Paris, 2015). Whereas previous approaches sought to build upon the cultural and linguistic practices of students to support academic learning, CSPs, as Carol D. Lee (2017, p. 261) noted, "have expanded these ideas to argue that diverse funds of knowledge and culturally inherited ways of navigating the world need to be sustained *as goods unto themselves* [emphasis ours]." This fundamental shift argues that the cultural and linguistic practices and knowledges of communities of color have always been vital in their own right, and should be creatively foregrounded rather than merely viewed as resources to take learners (almost always unidirectionally) from "where they are at" to some presumably "better" place, or ignored altogether.

CSP is not interested in relegating learners' cultural and linguistic strengths as tools for advancing the learning of an "acceptable" curricular canon, a "standard" variety of language, or other "academic" skill. Rather, extending Alim's approach to critical language awareness (2005, 2010), we are interested in producing learners that can interrogate what counts as "acceptable" or "canonical," what language varieties are heard as "standard," and what ways of knowing are viewed as "academic"—and ask how did these perspectives come to be the dominant ones, even sometimes in our own communities?

While CSP represents a shift from many previous approaches to pedagogy within the research tradition, we very explicitly highlight the strengths of the research and theoretical traditions upon which we build. Inspired by the critical tradition of Black feminist thought, particularly Joan Morgan's (1999) applications of what we termed, "loving critique," CSP was conceptualized through a series of respectful and generative *loving critiques* of previous *asset* or *strength-based pedagogies*, as we sought to problematize and extend three areas of scholarship and practice: (a) previous conceptualizations and enactments of asset pedagogies; (b) asset pedagogies that consider the longstanding practices of communities of color without taking into account contemporary enactments of communities; and (c) asset pedagogies that do not critically contend with problematic elements expressed in some youth (and adult) cultural practices. Below, we trace and extend these loving critiques as we build toward the future of CSP, a future where we not only contest the white supremacist, settler, capitalist, patriarchal nature of nation-state schooling, but where we guide learners to think about ways to disrupt, dismantle and displace these oppressive ideologies and systems by imagining, revitalizing and enacting ever-more just and equitable ways of being together in the world.

Our first engagement is with previous conceptualizations and enactments of asset pedagogies, which began with an understanding of the emergence of these necessary approaches to teaching and learning. While "responsiveness" and "relevance" were developed as strategically impactful frames for thinking about how to achieve equitable schooling in the educational problem-space[4] of the 1990s and 2000s, the concepts of "sustaining" and "revitalizing" have emerged in the 2010s to grapple with the enduring salience of white settler colonial violence[5] in schooling, and the evolving communities where our children learn and live (Paris, 2012; Paris & Alim, 2017; Gay, 2000; Ladson-Billings, 1995; McCarty & Lee, 2014; Scott, 2004, p.4).

Building on the court rulings of the 1960s and 70s and the subsequent policies that required schools to take the languages and (less so) broader cultural ways of communities of color into account (e.g., *Martin Luther King, Jr. Elementary School Children v. Ann Arbor School District, Lau v. Nichols*[6]), collaborations between teachers and researchers proved the deficit approaches that were foundational to U.S. schooling to be untenable and unjust (Labov, 1972; Cazden & Legget, 1976; Smitherman, 1977; Heath, 1983; Moll, 1992). With this research as a foundation, asset pedagogies were understood and enacted in increasingly complex ways by teachers and researchers throughout the 1990s and into the 2000s (Garcia, 1993; Ladson-Billings, 1994; Lee, 1995a; McCarty & Zepeda, 1995; Moll & Gonzalez, 1994; Nieto, 1992; Valdés, 1996). These liberatory pedagogies repositioned the linguistic, literate and cultural practices of working-class communities—specifically poor communities of color—as strengths and assets to honor, explore and extend in critically accessing the white middle-class dominant cultural norms that are demanded in schools (thereby transforming those norms and academic spaces).

Taking up an "ecological framework," Lee (1993; 1995a; 1995b; 2001) theorized "Cultural Modeling" as a way to operationalize resource pedagogies. Lee, Spencer and Harpalani (2003) argued that, "It is through the experience of learning to cope *both* with the often acknowledged experience of race-linked stigmatization *and* with the more generic cultural requirements as humans that broad-based 'cultural capital' is accrued" (p. 8). Thus, through Cultural Modeling, Lee et al. (2003) noted that teachers should understand "cultural socialization" as multidimensional as they "conceptualize classrooms as sites of co-constructed knowledge" and "meaning making" (p. 8). Similarly, Gutiérrez and Johnson (2017) considered "collective zones of proximal development" and how "students learn in formal learning environments such as school, but also what they learn by participating in a range of practices outside of school" (p. 149; Vygotsky, 1978). This builds from Gutiérrez (2008) who theorized a "collective Third Space" where "students begin to reconceive who they are and what they might be able to accomplish academically and beyond" (p.148).

One of the most important pedagogical statements of this asset pedagogies movement was Ladson-Billings' (1995) landmark article *Toward a Theory of Culturally Relevant Pedagogy*. In this seminal work, Ladson-Billings outlined the three essential criteria of CRP: "(a) Students must experience academic success; (b) students must develop and/or maintain cultural competence; and (c) students must develop a critical consciousness through which they challenge the status quo of the current social order" (p. 160).[7] We, like countless teachers and researchers, continue to be inspired by what it means to make teaching and learning relevant to our communities, and we understand our work with CSP as founded upon the original formulation of CRP. Indeed, as Ladson-Billings (2014) recently wrote, "culturally sustaining pedagogy uses culturally relevant pedagogy as the place where the beat drops" (p. 76).

Ladson Billings's (1995) original formulation of CRP laid the groundwork for pedagogies that maintained the longstanding cultural practices of communities of color while students also learned to critique dominant power structures. And yet we believe much of the work being done under the umbrella of CRP comes up far short of these goals. As predominantly white teachers and teacher education programs began (mis)interpreting and (mis)appropriating CRP through the hegemonic lens of whiteness, they oftentimes unwittingly devalued the cultural and linguistic practices of students of color (Ladson-Billings, 2014). Intentionally or not, whiteness was frequently and uncritically positioned as the unmarked norm by which all others were measured. Further, as Ladson-Billings herself has noted, teachers and teacher education programs "rarely pushed students to consider critical perspectives on policies and practices that may have direct impact on their lives and communities" (p. 78). Relatedly, Ladson-Billings has critiqued white educators for gravitating toward her work on CRP, while at the same time, ignoring her work on CRT, critical race theory (see Ladson-Billings' 1998 article, "Just What Is Critical Race Theory and What's It Doing in a Nice Field Like Education?").

At the same time, it may also be true that the term "relevance" does not do enough to explicitly support the sustenance of our communities. It is quite possible to be relevant to something without ensuring its continuing and critical presence in students' *repertoires of practice* (Gutiérrez & Rogoff, 2003), and its presence in our classrooms and communities. We believe the term CRP and, just as important, the way it has been taken up in teacher education and practice, needs to be revised forward from the crucial work it has done over the past decades (and continues to do in the present day!). We make this call with deep respect for the work we have cited to this point, for it has allowed us all to move beyond rationalizing the need to include the linguistic, literate and other cultural practices (e.g., Hip Hop) of our communities meaningfully as assets in educational spaces. Rather, we begin with this as a given and ask, *for what purposes and with what outcomes?*

CSP explicitly calls for education,[8] including state-sanctioned schooling, to be a site for sustaining the cultural ways of being of communities of color. We believe the term, stance and practice of CSP is increasingly necessary in the context of the new students of color majority in U.S. public schools[9] (a majority that is of course the norm globally). As our society continues to shift, CSP must be part of a shifting *culture of power* (Delpit, 1988). We cannot continue to act as if the white, middle-class linguistic, literate and cultural ways of being that were seen as the sole gatekeepers to the opportunity structure over a quarter-century ago have remained so or will remain so as our society changes. To put it more directly, the future is (and always has been) a multilingual and multiethnic one, regardless of attempts to suppress that reality.

As we enter the education problem-space of the 2020s, the "culture wars" (Chang, 2005) have been not only revived but reinvigorated. But so has our youths' resistance to the imposition of white cultural and linguistic hegemony, as this brief case from Cliffside Park High School in New Jersey demonstrates. As of 2016, two-thirds of Cliffside Park's students identified as People of Color and over 40 languages were spoken by the student body. Despite the school's rhetoric of diversity, all 1100 students walked out of school in protest over patterns of blatant raciolinguistic discrimination faced by their Spanish-speaking students. In one particularly egregious case, captured on film by one of the students, a white teacher scolded students for speaking Spanish in class, arguing: "The brave men and women who are fighting are not fighting for your right to speak Spanish. They're fighting for your right to speak American!" In doing so, she not only reproduced oppressive, xenophobic ideologies of language, nationalism and militarism, but she implied that her students should be grateful for this linguistic liberation at the hands of the nation's armed forces.

This teacher, however, was not ready. In the video, a student can be heard talking directly back to the teacher, reading her nativist assumptions about her students' abilities: "That's racist. I can speak English!" And despite a disciplinary warning by the school's principal, they walked out in support of the expelled student. Meanwhile, the teacher was placed on administrative leave. CSP was conceived with this new, brave generation of students in mind. Sixteen-year-old Vianery Cabrera, an Afro-Latina immigrant student from the Dominican Republic, responded directly to her teacher's orders to "Speak American!":

> I laughed, because first of all, that's not a language [Laughing]. And I have the right to speak Spanish. I have the right to speak English. I have the right to speak whatever language I speak. And that's my right. There's no law in the United States that says that I should, or I must, speak English… [The teacher said] she don't wanna hear Spanish. Like, she didn't spend her time in college to listen to Spanish, because she's an English teacher.

This young person upholds all of the scholarship on "Students' Right to Their Own Language," advocated by linguists Geneva Smitherman (1981), Ana Celia Zentella and many others over the past few decades. For this student, who rejects the imposition of white monolingualism/mono-culturalism as the preferred norm, schools can be seen as oppressive, homogenizing institutions. CSP asks us to reimagine schools as sites where diverse, heterogenous practices are not only valued but sustained "as goods unto themselves," and to reimagine educational achievement by creating contexts where our students' sense of self-worth is no longer contingent upon their assimilation into the racist, white colonial project. CSP's pluralistic future is already this generation's pluralistic present.

Sustaining Dynamic Community Practices

Our second loving critique examines how contemporary research and practice too often draw over-deterministic links between languages, literacies, cultural practices and race/ethnicity. As we seek to perpetuate and foster a pluralist present and future through our pedagogies, it is crucial that we understand that the complex ways young people are enacting race, ethnicity, language, literacy and cultural forms are always shifting and dynamic. Indeed, the vast majority of asset-oriented research, and the pedagogies it documents or enacts, has been focused solely on abstract or fixed versions of the culturally situated practices of our communities.

Although these practices have historically been and continue to be the target of deficit approaches, contemporary research has pushed against the tendency of researchers and practition-ers to assume static relationships between race, ethnicity, language and cultural ways of being (Alim et al., 2016; Gutiérrez & Rogoff, 2003; Irizarry, 2007; Paris, 2011; Wyman, McCarty & Nicholas, 2014). The result has been the simplification of what teachers are seeking to sustain as only, for example, Black Language (BL) among Black students or Spanish among Latinx students (a one-to-one mapping of race and language—which also of course imagines Latinx students as not being speakers of Indigenous languages, and Blackness and *Latinidad* as discrete). And this goes, of course, beyond language, where communities of cultural practice, such as Hip Hop cultures, are assumed to be a cultural source for teaching with only Black or even with Black and Brown students. Culture, as sets of practices and systems of meaning, is far more complex than this.

To move us out of this overly deterministic rut while continuing (of course) to attend to sustaining the cultural practices that have sustained and strengthened us, CSP shifts toward con-temporary understandings of culture as dynamic and fluid, while also allowing for the "past" and "present" to be seen as merging, a continuum, or distinct depending on how young people and their communities live race/ethnicity, language, culture, place and land.[10] For example, Holmes and Gonzalez (2017) argue for the need to focus on "elder epistemologies" and practices, as they have sustained Indigenous communities for centuries. As a collective, we argue that these cultural practices and ways of knowing should of course be sustained, even as we make room for how youth of today are reworking this set of knowledges to meet their current cultural and political realities. Such understandings further push us to consider the necessary intergenerationality of CSPs and to push for teaching and learning contexts which include multiple generations (Alim & Haupt, 2017; Holmes & Gonzalez, 2017; Lee & McCarty, 2017).

As examples of these cultural reworkings, we draw from our research (Paris, 2011; Alim, 2011) in local and international contexts. In this work, we examine how young people both rehearse long-standing versions of racial/ethnic and linguistic identities and, importantly, offer new ones (Alim & Reyes, 2011; Irizarry, 2007; Martinez, 2012; Paris, 2009, 2011). In his research, Paris (2012) worked with youth in a California high school and community to explore the important ways Black stu-dents navigated identities through the longstanding practices of BL and Hip Hop cultures. What he learned was that, in addition to Black youth, many Mexicanx, Mexican American and Pacific Islander youth (born in the continental U.S. and born in Samoa, Fiji and Tonga) also navigated identities through their participation in BL and Hip Hop cultural practices. Moreover, they did so while simultaneously participating in their longstanding community practices of, for example,

Spanish or Samoan and other cultural practices (clothing, ways of believing) passed down from the elders in their ethnic communities.

In this way, much like the global youth practices documented in Alim's studies of *global linguistic flows* (2009) and *global ill-literacies* (2011), youth were fashioning linguistically and culturally dexterous ways of being Latinx or Fijian that relied on longstanding cultural practices as well as emerging ones. Therefore, our pedagogies must address the well-understood fact that what it means to be Black or Latinx or Pacific Islander (as examples) both remains rooted *and* continues to shift in the ways culture always has (see Perez et al., 2016 and Alim & Haupt, 2017 for how organic CSPs complicate and extend static ideas of culture).

These examples show that while it is crucial that we work to sustain Indigenous, Black, Latinx, Asian and Pacific Islander languages and cultures in our pedagogies, we must be open to sustaining them in ways that attend to the emerging, intersectional and dynamic ways that they are lived and used by young people and across specific contexts. Indeed applications of the most lasting frameworks for asset pedagogies—the *funds of knowledge* (Moll & Gonzalez, 1994), the *third space* (Gutiérrez et al., 1999; Gutiérrez, 2008) and *culturally relevant pedagogy*—have too often been enacted by teachers and researchers in static ways that look only to the important ways that racial/ethnic and/or Tribal membership was enacted by previous generations. As youth continue to develop new, complex and intersecting forms of racial/ethnic identification in a world where cultural and linguistic recombinations flow with purpose, we need pedagogies that speak to our shifting cultural realities.

A final caveat in our discussion of sustaining dynamic community practices: too often cultural practices, activities, ways of being and doing are invoked in ways that obscure the racialized, gendered, classed, landed, dis/abilitied, languaged (and so on) bodies of the people enacting them. We cannot separate culture from the bodies enacting culture and the ways those bodies are subjected to systemic discrimination. Further, as argued by Waitoller and King Thorius (2016), focusing on the body and intersecting oppressions allows CSP scholars and educators to form strategic alliances against exclusion.

Critical Reflexivity: Maintaining a Critical Lens Through the Inward Gaze

In our final loving critique, we seek to move beyond critiquing the dominant pedagogies that perpetuate educational injustice, and turn our gaze inward. Here, we are primarily interested in creating generative spaces for asset pedagogies to support the practices of youth and communities of color, while maintaining a critical lens vis-à-vis these practices. Providing the example of Hip Hop as a form of the cultural and community practice that pedagogies should sustain, we argue that, rather than avoiding problematic practices or keeping them hidden beyond the white gaze, CSP must work with learners to critique regressive practices (e.g., homophobia, misogyny) and raise critical consciousness. We are implicated in this final critique as we have been throughout this work; our own research on and practice of Hip Hop pedagogies have not always taken up these problematic elements in the direct ways that we put forward here.

And so we migrate further inward, to what Alim has called "ill-literacies" (Alim, 2011)—counterhegemonic forms of youth literacies—and ask: "What happens when ill-literacies get *ill*?" In other words, what happens when rather than challenging hegemonic ideas and outcomes, the cultural practices of youth actually reproduce them, or even create new ones? Most of the research and practice under the asset pedagogies umbrella view youth cultures too often through a purely "positive" or "progressive" lens. The vast majority of Hip Hop education research, for example, has focused pedagogies on the many progressive, justice-oriented aspects of Hip Hop (which has filled scholarly volumes). As we have stated, however, we build on this important work by engaging in reflexive analyses that are not bound by how educational systems that privilege white middle-class norms view the practices of communities of color.

In nearly *all* of the U.S.-based and global research on Hip Hop pedagogies, youth's texts are seen only as challenging prescriptive, restrictive and anti-democratic notions of culture, citizenship, language, literacy and education. With few important exceptions (Hill, 2009; Low, 2011; Wong, 2019; and some chapters in Petchauer & Hill, 2013), studies rarely look critically at how youth might reify existing hegemonic discourses about, as examples, gender, race, sexuality and citizenship. In other words, Hip Hop pedagogies have tended to be largely celebratory and have ignored the contradictory forces found within all popular cultural forms (Giroux, 1996). However, the simultaneously progressive and oppressive currents in these innovative youth practices must be interrogated, as has been done consistently for non-education based Hip Hop research, such as Rose (1994), Perry (2004), Neal (2006), Haupt (2008) and Alim et al. (2010, 2011). Simply put, a reading of most of the asset-based pedagogies literature would make it appear that youth practices present us with no internal inconsistencies, or as Gutiérrez and Johnson (2017) argued, no "ambivalence" (see Wong, 2018 for "strategic ambivalence"). Being participants and scholars of and with communities of color, we take it as a given that practices of youth of color often work explicitly toward social justice, but critically, we must pay attention to both the liberatory and non-liberatory currents within these practices.

Many Hip Hop pedagogies, from Alim's "Critical Hip-Hop Language Pedagogies" (2004) to Emdin's work on Hip Hop and science education (2010), for example, argue for the use of rap battles—improvised verbal duels—in classroom learning. Yet, few take up the fact that the Hip Hop battle can *sometimes* be a masculinist space that excludes young women, queer youth and young men of color who do not identify as Black (even as young women, queer youth and youth who are not Black continue to "roc the mic"). CSP must contend with the possibility that Hip Hop pedagogies that utilize rap battles (as one among many examples of Hip Hop pedagogical practices) may seemingly serve the needs of many students of color, particularly young, non-disabled, cishetero men, but may unwittingly reproduce forms of exclusion in our classrooms and communities. (For example, we rarely produce gendered analyses of classroom participation when using Hip Hop; see Wong, 2019 for a critical feminist analysis).

We must work toward CSPs that sustain the many practices and knowledges of communities of color that forward equity (like much of Hip Hop does) and help youth, teachers and researchers expose those practices that must be revised in the project of cultural justice. Our goal is to find ways to support and sustain what we know are remarkable ways with language, literacy and cultural practice, while at the same time opening up spaces for students themselves to critique the ways that they might be—intentionally or not—reproducing discourses that marginalize members of our communities. As Low (2011) has argued, the very real and difficult tensions found within youth cultures are not reasons to inhibit their use in schools, but rather, to demand their use in the development of more critical approaches.

Although we have used Hip Hop education here as an example, it is important to note again that these damaging discourses are present across *all* cultural communities and practices, including those within which we and our young people are socialized. As Tricia Rose argued in her June 2016 keynote address at Cambridge University's Hip Hop Studies Conference, in line with our notion of loving critique, "to love something is not to affirm it all the time; we need transformational love." Ultimately, sustaining those practices within our communities that promote equity across race, gender, sexuality, language, class, land and dis/ability, and revising those that don't, will help us thrive and, ultimately, will allow us to get free (Smith, 2016).

CSP: A Conceptual and Empirical Project

Like the asset pedagogies from which it builds, CSP is both a conceptual and empirical project. CSP begins with the premise that sociohistorically marginalized communities are carrying on, evolving and revitalizing what we know as effective CSP, or what Alim and Haupt (2017) referred

Culturally Sustaining Pedagogy

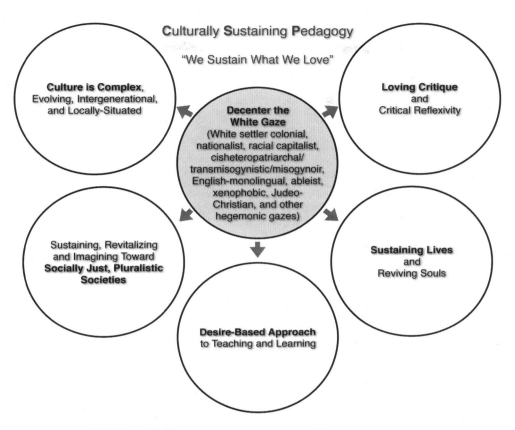

Figure 15.1 Six Principles of CSP

to as *organic forms of CSP*. That is, we know that there are—and always have been—institutions and educators across our communities who are innovating and regenerating pedagogical traditions and knowledges that sustain the lifeways of our communities, and are doing so in ways that hold implications for how we might reimagine and revitalize schooling and education. CSP is a conceptualization of practice within a long trajectory of educators who have sought to take on the ways that race, class, gender, sexuality, dis/ability, language, migration and other socially constructed axes of difference have been utilized to limit the opportunities of young people, and therefore, the societies in which we live.

While there are many consistencies across CSP-minded pedagogues and researchers, these pedagogies take on necessarily different forms across different contexts. Within this expected variation, key features across this work include a critical centering on dynamic community languages, valued practices and knowledges, student and community agency and input, historicized content and instruction, a capacity to contend with internalized oppressions, and an ability to curricularize all of this in learning settings.

Wong (2019, see Figure 15.1) has argued that six central principles that undergird the conceptualization of CSP have been consistently present. CSP researchers share the goal of sustaining the cultures, languages and lives of communities in ways that aim to:

1) decenter the white supremacist, settler, capitalist, cisheteropatriarchal/transmisogynistic/misogynoir, ableist and other hegemonic gazes;
2) recognize culture as complex, intergenerational, constantly shifting and locally situated;

3) engage in loving critique and critical reflexivity in theory and practice;
4) foster, revitalize and teach toward socially just, pluralistic societies;
5) practice a *desire-based* (Tuck, 2009) approach to teaching and learning that takes up joy alongside pain and offers a deeper love of ourselves and our young people;
6) and importantly, sustain the lives and "revive" the souls of young people and communities (Paris & Alim, 2017; Alim & Haupt, 2017), who face what Love (2019) calls "spirit murder" in compulsory schooling contexts.

A growing body of contemporary evidence indicates that CSP has been highly successful in (1) challenging the normativity of whiteness and sustaining the cultural ways of being of pluralistic communities of color; (2) revitalizing the language and lifeways of Indigenous youth in particular; (3) promoting cultural well-being among young people and communities; (4) increasing academic achievement—even on narrow white-gazed measures; and (5) promoting the linguistic and cultural dexterity of young people of color. Much of this recent research on CSP provides case studies and empirical analyses of teaching and learning contexts.

Kinloch (2017) studies an Afro-Jamaican young woman and a Black young man and their "performances of resistance." She finds that their performances are "invitations into learning" that prove powerful when sustained in literacy instruction. She argues that CSP "is necessary because it not only validates who students are and their ways of knowing, [but] it also locates students at the center of classrooms through assets-based, humanizing perspectives that lead to pluralism" (p. 38). Speaking to the power of sustaining language and culture as CSP, particularly among Latinx youth, Bucholtz, Casillas and Lee (2017) explore the translanguaging, language brokering and literacy practices of over 800 public school students from six urban, rural and suburban counties on California's Central Coast within a CSP program. They find that the predominantly working-class Latinx youth who make up the CSP program "come to understand their language in a new light: as creative and innovative rather than 'wrong,' as a powerful symbol of family and community belonging rather than as a marginalized practice" (p. 55). Likewise, Lee and Walsh (2017) engage in youth participatory action research (YPAR) as CSP and examine the impact on low-income immigrant youth at a high school in New York City. They find that "incorporating YPAR into the curriculum for immigrant students is one promising practice that builds academic competence, is culturally sustaining, and promotes justice-oriented citizenship" (p. 203).

Exploring the impact of CSP with Native youth, San Pedro's (2017) three-year longitudinal ethnographic study of a Native American literature course finds a Native student who "only" decides not to drop out because of this "sacred truth space" (p. 101). San Pedro argues that the experiences of Native students in the class "[speak] quite literally to CSP as an anti-colonial, anti-imperial project" (p. 100). Extending CSP as "culturally sustaining/revitalizing pedagogy" (CSRP), Lee and McCarty (2017) examine two case studies of schools and subsequently argue that effective CSRP requires "relentless commitment to community-based accountability" (p. 78). Further, Holmes and González (2017) study traditional elder pedagogies and practice, and remind us that "nesting, placing and locating traditional Indigenous ways of knowing and being, languages, and oral practices of intergenerational transmission at the center of a movement of reawakening creates the possibility for contemporary reflexivity and responsiveness" (p. 220).

Wong and Peña (2017) study two different teachers making use of CSP within racially and ethnically pluralistic performing arts programs at two schools. They note that reimagining and building pluralistic societies through CSP and the arts demands that we be mindful of "damage-centered narratives," and that we pay serious attention to pleasure and joy as crucial to liberation (p. 131; Tuck, 2009, p. 409–428). Likewise, exploring Hip Hop as an organic form of culturally sustaining pedagogy, Alim and Haupt (2017) study Hip Hop artist-pedagogues outside of classroom settings where they are "remixing and reclaiming history, language, and other cultural symbols to invert and subvert oppressive, colonial narratives" (p. 169).

Culturally Sustaining Pedagogy

Assessing the teacher education pedagogies "capable of producing the types of decolonial educators" needed for enacting CSRP, Domínguez (2017) argues that cultivating liberatory educators will require an epistemic paradigm shift from preparing teachers based on the terms of the colonizer to the colonized. Introducing CRP 2.0, Ladson-Billings (2017) reflects upon how what she sees in CRP classrooms rarely represents the practices that she described from her original study of eight outstanding teachers (p. 142). She further draws upon Hip Hop pedagogy and her experiences preparing teachers to argue for reconsidering how and who we admit into teacher education, reviewing how we determine teacher readiness and certification (p. 154). Lastly, drawing from his two-year ethnographic study of Latinx high school students in a participatory action research collaborative, Irizarry (2017, p. 95) extends thinking on CSP by asking: "How might understandings of culturally sustaining pedagogies be enhanced if they were informed by teaching practices developed, implemented, and refined by students themselves?" (p. 108).

CSP: An Ongoing Movement Toward the World We Need

As we continue to think through the promises and challenges of CSP, we know that we must remain vigilant, constantly making visible the ways that the white settler gaze will continue to ignore the critical role of decentering whiteness and other oppressive ideologies and systems in our pedagogies. These distortions will undoubtedly occur, as they have for CRP, and whiteness will surely find a way to uncritically devalue students' languages, cultures, experiences, histories, families, etc. Given this, supporting and sustaining our multiethnic and multilingual present and future must remain at the center of the work.

A second point concerns the need for desire-based CSP, one that moves toward a desire-based approach to teaching that takes up joy alongside pain and offers a deeper love of ourselves and our young people (Morgan, 1999; Tuck, 2009, p. 416). Wong (2019) reminds us how "sustaining lives and reviving souls," as a principle of CSP, highlights the need to always consider what is beautiful about us, and mind joy and pleasure as a prerogative alongside our concerns with addressing systemic violence and pain. As we move forward, we need to constantly question whether we are perpetuating incomplete and *damage-centered* (Tuck, 2009) narratives.

A third point is the need to constantly re-emphasize the centrality of culture (shifting cultural practices) and identity (various, evolving forms of identification) to processes of learning. The project of reimagining and revitalizing education takes for granted that we are up against centuries of oppression and domination, further enacted through discursive wars that are currently being waged through the prism of culture. As educational researchers, we have no choice but to center identities and cultures within and beyond the classroom. That may not sound particularly revolutionary, considering the dire, material conditions of many of our people, but the project of centering cultures and identities remains marginalized within educational research institutions. We must resist this marginalization and call it out for its complicity with the status quo. So, as we continue to do work that is viewed as marginal, we know that, in fact, these issues are central, not marginal, to the education enterprise—nor can they be separated from materialist realities (Flores, 2017). As the editors of this volume have argued over the years, we must constantly frame culture as central to learning, indeed as learning itself.

A fourth point is for researchers who insist that working within schools is a lost cause. Even as we know that liberatory teaching has always occurred outside of whitestream institutions (Urrieta, 2010), we would not be engaged in this work if millions of our children weren't mandated to attend public schools. Until that changes, we must shift the nihilistic way that we view schools: what if instead of merely theorizing schools as pillars of the ideological state apparatus meant to reproduce the colonial status quo, we joined the long-term work of our communities in imagining schools (and other institutions, like health care and law) as sites for potentially transforming and revitalizing societies by sustaining the languages, cultures, identities and lives of our students and communities? That is, while we understand the school to be a site of social reproduction, what kinds of possibilities are opened up if we understand the school also as a site of social resistance, resurgence and transformation? This is *not* to say that our work on CSP is limited to schools and schooling—education is a social process not a specific context. What we have learned across contexts—about community accountably within schools (Lee & McCarty, 2017), about intergenerationality and elder pedagogies beyond schools (Holmes & Gonzalez, 2017), and about organic forms of CSP in community organizations in relationship to schools (Alim & Haupt, 2017)—necessarily offers us guidance in the project of transforming and revitalizing education toward its just potential.

A final point is about what the stakes are for the work on CSP. CSP is fundamentally about sustaining communities and their lifeways and, by doing so, sustaining life—the planet, our relationship to the land. This means continuing to center, listen to and follow the lead of Indigenous people in this work. This means re-forging and continuing Black, Latinx and Asian and Pacific Islander connections to land and community well-being—and all of these must be centered beyond state sanctioned settler capitalism's commodification of and violence upon Indigenous, Black and migrant bodies and communities, who are often forced to labor on or move off the land as well as relate to each other in unsustainable ways. It is also true to some degree that all of our communities, as we have written, have internalized these unsustainable, settler capitalist ways of relating to each other and to the land (and so the *inward gaze*). As we continue to build together, we remain grateful for our CSP collective and look forward to continuing our efforts to create the world we need, with our ancestors, our young ones, our elders.

Notes

1 We understand, of course, that Indigenous, Black, Latinx, Asian and Pacific Islander communities are not monolithic or mutually exclusive communities. We also understand that these terms follow U.S.-based racial nomenclature and formations. Our work, however, extends across marginalized communities, in the U.S. and beyond, with Alim & Haupt (2017), for example, working in South Africa, and Alim & Perez (2019) working in Oaxacalifornia (across the U.S. and Mexico), as well as others taking up the work globally.

2 We are indebted to Shaheen Ariefdien's and Sharim Hannegan-Martinez's comments at the Culturally Sustaining Pedagogies Retreat (June 11th, 2019) for emphasizing the need for CSPs to work across public health, social services, youth care work, etc.

3 We learn and build with Indigenous communities in using the term "lifeways" to denote the full expression of culturally embedded practices and activities that sustain communities and the land across generations.

4 "A problem-space... is an ensemble of questions and answers around which a horizon of identifiable stakes (conceptual as well as ideological-political stakes) hangs. That is to say, what defines this discursive context are not only the particular problems that get posed as problems as such (the problem of "race," say), but the particular questions that seem worth having... " (Scott, 2004, p. 4).

5 We define settler colonialism in line with scholars like Tuck and Gaztambide-Fernández (2013, p. 73): "Settler colonialism is the specific formation of colonialism in which the colonizer comes to stay, making himself the sovereign, and the arbiter of citizenship, civility, and knowing. Patrick Wolfe (2006) argues that settler colonialism 'destroys to replace,' (p. 388) operating with a *logic of elimination*... The violence of invasion is not contained to first contact or the unfortunate birthpangs of a new nation, but is reasserted each day of occupation. Troy Richardson (2011) offers a critique of contemporary 'culture-based' models, such as multicultural education and culturally responsive pedagogy, that seek to 'include' Indigenous epistemologies which have the effect of enclosing and containing the possibility of Indigenous futures." Paris and Alim (2017) argue that CSP aims to respond to these critiques of "culture-based" models and does not seek inclusion into the white settler colonial order, but aims to sustain, build, revitalize and lovingly critique the lives and communities of students outside of the white gaze (Morrison, 1998), while refusing to "respond" or be "relevant" to white ways of knowing, being, acting, seeing and speaking.

6 Lau v. Nichols was brought and won on behalf of Chinese speaking Chinese American students in San Francisco, CA, who claimed a lack of equal educational opportunity based on language discrimination. The Supreme Court's 1974 decision for the plaintiffs relied on the 1964 Civil Rights Act, which explicitly banned educational discrimination based on race or national origin. MLK Elementary School Children

Culturally Sustaining Pedagogy

v. Ann Arbor School District, more commonly known as the 1979 "Black English Case," was brought and won by families of eleven African American students in Ann Arbor, MI, who had been diagnosed as "linguistically handicapped" by the district's speech pathologist. The families contended that the children had been misdiagnosed and miseducated as a result of their strong use of AAL (see Smitherman, 1981).

7   Other important terms and formulations that have looked to forge asset pedagogies with students of color include, but are not limited to, *culturally responsive pedagogy* (Gay, 2000), *culturally congruent pedagogy* (Au & Kawakami, 1994), *culturally compatible pedagogy* (Jacob & Jordan, 1987), *engaged pedagogy* (hooks, 1994) and *critical care praxis* (Rolón-Dow, 2005). We focus on the term and formulation of *culturally relevant pedagogies* and, less so, on *culturally responsive pedagogies* as it has become the most used, short-handed term and concept in teacher education, teacher practice, and research on teaching and learning.

8   CSP exists wherever education sustains the lifeways of communities who have been and continue to be damaged as erased through schooling. This means that while schools remain a central institutional site for CSP, as our collective research has shown, CSP occurs across teaching and learning spaces, from community organizations to family and peer settings (Paris & Alim, 2017).

9   In citing this demographic shift it is crucial of course to note that Indigenous communities have been living and learning, have been educating their children and young people for millennia on their lands, though U.S. public schooling for Native peoples has historically been one of the forced and violent loss of culture and land associated with the settler colonial nation-state (Lomawaima & McCarty, 2006, Tuck & Yang, 2014). It is also of course the case that students of color are the majority in most nations globally, though other settler colonial contexts (e.g., Aotearoa/New Zealand, Australia, South Africa) have similarly violent colonial educational histories to the U.S.

10   We are indebted to Pedro Noguera for his comments at the Culturally Sustaining Pedagogies Retreat (June 11th, 2019) about the specificity of cultural practices and their relation to place (e.g., can West Indians in the Caribbean and London be expected to share "a culture"?). We are also indebted to Kris Gutierrez, Carol D. Lee and Gloria Ladson-Billings for conversations complicating "culture" in earlier and current iterations of this work. It continues to be a beleaguered, and yet necessary and enduring, term.

References

Alexander, N. (2007). Mother-tongue education and the African Renaissance, with special reference to South Africa. In: H. S. Alim & J. Baugh (Eds.), *Talkin Black Talk: Language, Education, and Social Change* (pp. 142–152). New York, NY: Teachers College Press.

Alim, H. S. (2004). *You Know My Steez: An Ethnographic and Sociolinguistic Study of Styleshifting in a Black American Speech Community*. Durham, NC: Duke University Press.

Alim, H. S. (2005). Critical language awareness in the United States: Revisiting issues and revising pedagogies in a resegregated society. *Educational Researcher, 34*(7), 24–31.

Alim, H. S. (2009). Intro: Straight Outta Compton, straight aus München: Global linguistic flows, identities, and the politics of language in a Global Hip Hop Nation. In: H. S. Alim, A. Ibrahim & A. Pennycook (Eds.), *Global Linguistic Flows: Hip Hop Cultures, Youth Identities, the Politics of Language* (pp. 1–24). New York, NY: Routledge.

Alim, H. S. (2010). Critical language awareness. In: N. H. Hornberger & S. L. McKay (Eds.), *Sociolinguistics and Language Education* (pp. 205–231). Tonawanda, NY: Multilingual Matters.

Alim, H. S. (2011). Global ill-literacies: Hip Hop cultures, youth identities, and the politics of literacy. *Review of Research in Education, 35*(1), 120–146.

Alim, H. S., & Haupt, A. (2017). Reviving soul(s) with Afrikaaps. In: D. Paris & H. S. Alim (Eds.), *Culturally Sustaining Pedagogies: Teaching and Learning for Justice in a Changing World* (p. 157). New York, NY: Teacher's College Press.

Alim, H. S., Lee, J., & Carris, L. M. (2010). 'Short fried-rice-eating Chinese MCs and 'good-hair-havin Uncle Tom niggas': Performing race and ethnicity in freestyle rap battles. *Journal of Linguistic Anthropology, 20*(1), 116–133.

Alim, H. S., Lee, J., & Carris, L. M. (2011). Moving the crowd, 'crowding' the emcee: The production of Black normativity in freestyle rap battles. *Discourse and Society, 22*(4), 422–440.

Alim, H. S., & Paris, D. (2015). Whose language gap? Critical and culturally sustaining pedagogies as necessary challenges to racializing hegemony. *Journal of Linguistic Anthropology, 25*(1), 79–81.

Alim, H. S., & Paris, D. (2017). What is culturally sustaining pedagogy and why does it matter? In: D. Paris & H. S. Alim (Eds.), *Culturally Sustaining Pedagogies: Teaching and Learning for Justice in a Changing World* (p. 1). New York, NY: Teacher's College Press.

Alim, H. S., & Reyes, A. (2011). Complicating race: Articulating race across multiple social dimensions. *Discourse and Society, 22*(4), 379–384.

Alim, H. S., Rickford, J., & Ball, A. (Eds.) (2016). *Raciolinguistics: How Language Shapes Our Ideas of Race*. New York, NY: Oxford University Press.

Au, K., & Kawakami, A. (1994). Cultural congruence in instruction. In: E. Hollins, J. King & W. Hayman (Eds.), *Teaching Diverse Populations: Formulating Knowledge Base* (pp. 5–23). Albany, KY: SUNY Press.

Bucholtz, M., Casillas, D. I., & Lee, J. S. (2017). Language and culture as sustenance. In: D. Paris & H. S. Alim (Eds.), *Culturally Sustaining Pedagogies: Teaching and Learning for Justice in a Changing World* (p. 43). New York, NY: Teacher's College Press.

Cazden, C., & Leggett, E. (1976). Culturally responsive education: A discussion of LAU remedies II. Prepared for the U.S. Department of Health, Education, and Welfare. National Institute of Education.

Chang, J. (2005). *Can't Stop, Won't Stop: The History of the Hip Hop Generation*. New York, NY: Picador.

Delpit, L. (1988). The silenced dialogue: Power and pedagogy in educating other people's children. *Harvard Educational Review, 58*(3), 280–298.

Domínguez, M. (2017). "Se hace puentes al andar": Decolonial teacher education as a needed bridge to culturally sustaining and revitalizing pedagogies. In: D. Paris & H. S. Alim (Eds.), *Culturally Sustaining Pedagogies: Teaching and Learning for Justice in a Changing World* (pp. 225–246). New York, NY: Teacher's College Press.

Dumas, M. J. (2014). "Losing an arm": Schooling as a site of Black suffering. *Race, and Ethnicity in Education, 17*(1), 1–30.

Emdin, C. (2010). *Urban Science Education for the Hip Hop Generation*. New York, NY: Sense Publishers.

Flores, N. (2017). From language as resource to language as struggle: Resisting the Coke-ification of bilingual education. In: M. Flubacher & A. Del Percio (2017). *Language, Education and Neoliberalism: Critical Studies in Sociolinguistics* (pp. 62–81). Blue Ridge Summit, PA: Multilingual Matters.

Garcia, E. (1993). Language, culture, and education. *Review of Research in Education, 19*, 51–98.

Gay, G. (2000). *Culturally Responsive Teaching: Theory, Research, and Practice*. New York, NY: Teachers College Record.

Giroux, H. (1996). *Fugitive Cultures: Race, Violence, and Youth*. New York, NY: Routledge.

Grande, S. (2018). Refusing the university. In: E. Tuck & K. W. Yang (Eds.), *Toward What Justice? Describing Diverse Dreams of Justice in Education* (pp. 47–65). New York, NY: Routledge.

Gutiérrez, K. (2008). Developing a sociocritical literacy in the third space. *Reading research Quarterly, 43*(2), 148–164.

Gutiérrez, K., Baquedano-Lopez, P., Alvarez, H., & Chiu, M. (1999). Building a culture of collaboration through hybrid language practices. *Theory into Practice, 38*(2), 87–93.

Gutiérrez, K. D., & Johnson, P. (2017). Understanding identity sampling and cultural repertoires: Advancing learning in justice pedagogies. In: D. Paris & H. S. Alim (Eds.), *Culturally Sustaining Pedagogies: Teaching and Learning for Justice in a Changing World* (pp. 247–260). New York, NY: Teacher's College Press.

Gutiérrez, K., & Rogoff, B. (2003). Cultural ways of learning. *Educational Researcher, 35*(5), 19–25.

Haupt, A. (2008). Black masculinity and the tyranny of authenticity in South African popular culture. In: A. Hadland, E. Louw, S. Sesanti & H. Wasserman (Eds.), *Power, Politics and Identity in South African Media* (pp. 378–398). Cape Town, South Africa: Human Sciences Research Council.

Heath, S. B. (1983). *Ways with Words*. New York, NY: Cambridge University Press.

Hill, M. L. (2009). *Beats, Rhymes and Classroom Life: Hip-Hop Pedagogy and the Politics of Identity*. New York, NY: Teachers College Press.

Holmes, A., & Gonzalez, N. (2017). Finding sustenance an Indigenous relational pedagogy. In: D. Paris & H. S. Alim (Eds.), *Culturally Sustaining Pedagogies: Teaching and Learning for Justice in a Changing World* (pp. 207–224). New York, NY: Teacher's College Press.

Hooks, B. (1994). *Teaching to Transgress*. New York, NY: Routledge.

Irizarry, J. (2007). Ethnic and urban intersections in the classroom: Latino students, hybrid identities, and culturally responsive pedagogy. *Multicultural Perspectives, 9*(3), 21–28.

Irizarry, J. G. (2017). "For us, by us": A vision for culturally sustaining pedagogies forwarded by Latinx youth. In: D. Paris & H. S. Alim (Eds.), *Culturally Sustaining Pedagogies: Teaching and Learning for Justice in a Changing World* (pp. 83–98). New York, NY: Teacher's College Press.

Jacob, E., & Jordan, C. (1987). Moving to dialogue. *Anthropology and Education Quarterly, 18*(1), 259–261.

Kinloch, V. (2017). "You ain't making me write": Culturally sustaining pedagogies with Black youths' performances of resistance. In: D. Paris & H. S. Alim (Eds.), *Culturally Sustaining Pedagogies: Teaching and Learning for Justice in a Changing World* (pp. 25–41). New York, NY: Teacher's College Press.

Labov, W. (1972). *Language in the Inner City*. Philadelphia, PA: University of Pennsylvania Press.

Ladson-Billings, G. (1994). *The Dreamkeepers: Successful Teachers of African American Children*. San Francisco, CA: Jossey-Bass.

Ladson-Billings, G. (1995). Toward a theory of culturally relevant pedagogy. *American Educational Research Journal, 32*(3), 465–491.

Culturally Sustaining Pedagogy

Ladson-Billings, G. (1998). Just what is critical race theory and what's it doing in a nice field like education? *International Journal of Qualitative Studies in Education, 11*(1), 7–24.

Ladson-Billings, G. (2014). Culturally relevant pedagogy 2.0: The remix. *Harvard Educational Review, 84*(1), 74–84.

Ladson-Billings, G. (2014, April 23). Culturally relevant and culturally sustaining pedagogies: Two decades deep. In: H. S. Alim & J. Chang (Instructors), *The 5th Element: Hip-Hop Knowledges, Pedagogies, and Social Justice*. Class lecture conducted at Stanford University.

Ladson-Billings, G. (2017). The (r)evolution will not be standardized: Teacher education, hip hop pedagogy, and culturally relevant pedagogy 2.0. In: D. Paris & H. S. Alim (Eds.), *Culturally Sustaining Pedagogies: Teaching and Learning for Justice in a Changing World* (pp. 141–156). New York, NY: Teacher's College Press.

Lee, C. D. (1993). *Signifying as a Scaffold for Literary Interpretation: The Pedagogical Implications of an African American Discourse Genre*. Urbana, IL: National Council of Teachers of English.

Lee, C. D. (1995a). A culturally based cognitive apprenticeship: Teaching African American high school students' skills in literary interpretation. *Reading Research Quarterly, 30*(4), 608–630.

Lee, C. D. (1995b). Signifying as a scaffold for literary interpretation. *Journal of Black Psychology, 21*(4), 357–381.

Lee, C. D. (2001). Is October Brown or Chinese? A cultural modeling activity system for underachieving students. *American Educational Research Journal, 38*(1), 97–141.

Lee, C. D. (2017). An ecological framework for enacting culturally sustaining pedagogy. In: D. Paris & H. S. Alim (Eds.), *Culturally Sustaining Pedagogies: Teaching and Learning for Justice in a Changing World* (p. 261). New York, NY: Teacher's College Press.

Lee, C. D., Spencer, M. B., & Harpalani, V. (2003). "Every shut eye ain't sleep": Studying how people live culturally. *Educational Researcher, 32*(5), 6–13.

Lee, S. (2005). *Up against Whiteness: Race, School, and Immigrant Youth*. New York, NY: Teachers College Press.

Lee, S., & Walsh, D. (2017). Socially just, culturally sustaining pedagogy for diverse immigrant youth. In: D. Paris & H. S. Alim (Eds.), *Culturally Sustaining Pedagogies: Teaching and Learning for Justice in a Changing World* (p. 191). New York, NY: Teacher's College Press.

Lee, T. S., & McCarty, T. L. (2017). Upholding Indigenous education sovereignty through critical culturally sustaining/revitalizing pedagogy. In: D. Paris & H. S. Alim (Eds.), *Culturally Sustaining Pedagogies: Teaching and Learning for Justice in a Changing World* (p. 61). New York, NY: Teacher's College Press.

Lomawaima, K. T., & McCarty, T. L. (2006). *To Remain an Indian: Lessons in Democracy from a Century of Native American Education*. New York, NY: Teachers College Press.

Love, B. (2019). *We Want to Do More Than Survive: Abolitionist Teaching and the Pursuit of Educational Freedom*. Boston, MA: Beacon Press.

Low, B. E. (2011). *Slam School: Learning through Conflict in the Hip-Hop and Spoken Word Classroom*. Stanford, CA: Stanford University Press.

Martínez, D. C. (2012). *Expanding Linguistic Repertoires: An Ethnography of Black and Latina/o Youth Communication in Urban English Language Arts Classrooms* (Ph.D. Dissertation). University of California, Los Angeles.

McCarty, T. L., & Lee, T. (2014). Critical culturally sustaining/revitalizing pedagogy and Indigenous education sovereignty. *Harvard Educational Review, 84*(1), 101–124.

McCarty, T. L., & Zepeda, O. (1995). Indigenous language education and literacy: Introduction to the theme issue. *The Bilingual Research Journal, 19*(1), 1–4.

Moll, L. (1992). Literacy research in community and classrooms: A sociocultural approach. In: R. Beach, J. L. Green, M. L. Kamil & T. Shanahan (Eds.), *Multidisciplinary Perspectives in Literacy Research* (pp. 211–244). Urbana, IL: National Conference on Research in English and National Council of Teachers of English.

Moll, L., & Gonzalez, N. (1994). Lessons from research with language minority children. *Journal of Reading Behavior, 26*(4), 23–41.

Morgan, J. (1999). *When Chickenheads Come Home to Roost*. New York, NY: Simon and Schuster.

Morrison, T. (1998, March). From and interview on *Charlie Rose*. Public Broadcasting Service. Retrieved from http://www.youtube.com/watch?v=F4vIGvKpT1c.

Neal, M. A. (2006). *New Black Man*. New York, NY: Routledge.

Nieto, S. (1992). *Affirming Diversity: The Sociopolitical Context of Multicultural Education*. New York, NY: Longman Publishers.

Paris, D. (2009). "They're in my culture, they speak the same way": African American Language in multiethnic high schools. *Harvard Educational Review, 79*(3), 428–447.

Paris, D. (2011). *Language across Difference: Ethnicity, Communication, and Youth Identities in Changing Urban Schools*. Cambridge: Cambridge University Press.

Paris, D. (2012). Culturally sustaining pedagogy: A needed change in stance, terminology, and practice. *Educational Researcher, 41*(3), 93–97.

Paris, D. (2019). Naming beyond the white settler colonial gaze in educational research. *International Journal of Qualitative Studies in Education, 32*(3), 217–224.

Paris, D., & Alim, H. S. (2014). What are we seeking to sustain through culturally sustaining pedagogy? A loving critique forward. *Harvard Educational Review, 84*(1), 85–100.

Paris, D., & Alim, H. S. (2017). *Culturally Sustaining Pedagogies: Teaching and Learning for Justice in a Changing World*. New York, NY: Teacher's College Press.

Perez, W., Vasquez, R., & Buriel, R. (2016). Zapotec, Mixtec, and Purepecha youth. In: H. S. Alim, J. Rickford, & A. Ball (Eds.), *Raciolinguistics: How Language Shapes Our Ideas of Race* (pp. 255–272). New York, NY: Oxford University Press.

Perry, I. (2004). *Prophets of the Hood: Politics and Poetics in Hip Hop*. Durham, NC: Duke University Press.

Petchauer, E., & Hill, M. L. (Eds.) (2013). *Schooling Hip-Hop: Expanding Hip-Hop Based Education Across the Curriculum*. New York, NY: Teachers College Press.

Richardson, T. (2011). Navigating the problem of inclusion as enclosure in Native culture-based education: Theorizing shadow curriculum. *Curriculum Inquiry, 41*(3), 332–349.

Rolón-Dow, C. (2005). Critical care: A color(full) analysis of care narratives in the schooling experiences of Puerto Rican girls. *American Educational Research Journal, 42*(1), 77–111.

Rose, T. (1994). *Black Noise: Rap Music and Black Culture in Contemporary America*. Middletown, CT: Wesleyan University Press.

San Pedro, T. J. (2017). "This stuff interests me": Re-centering Indigenous paradigms in colonizing schooling spaces. In: D. Paris & H. S. Alim (Eds.), *Culturally Sustaining Pedagogies: Teaching and Learning for Justice in a Changing World* (pp. 99–116). New York, NY: Teacher's College Press.

Scott, D. (2004). *Conscripts of Modernity: The Tragedy of Colonial Enlightenment*. Durham, NC: Duke University Press.

Smith, M. D. (2016). *Invisible Man, Got the Whole World Watching: A Young Black Man's Education*. New York, NY: Nation Books.

Smitherman, G. (1977). *Talkin and Testifyin*. Detroit: Wayne State University Press.

Smitherman, G. (Ed.) (1981). *Black English and the Education of Black Children and Youth*. Detroit: Wayne State University Press.

Tuck, E. (2009). Suspending damage: A letter to communities. *Harvard Educational Review, 79*(3), 409–428.

Tuck, E., & Gaztambide-Fernández, R. A. (2013). Curriculum, replacement, and settler futurity. *Journal of Curriculum Theorizing, 29*(1), 72–89.

Tuck, E., & Yang, K. W. (2014). R-words: Refusing research. In: D. Paris & M. T. Winn (Eds.), *Humanizing Research: Decolonizing Qualitative Inquiry for Youth and Communities*. Thousand Oakes, CA: SAGE.

Urrieta, L. (2010). *Working from Within: Chicana and Chicano Activist Educators in Whitestream Schools*. Tucson, AZ: University of Arizona Press.

Valdés, G. (1996). *Con Respeto: Bridging the Distances between Culturally Diverse Families and Schools*. New York, NY: Teachers College Press.

Vizenor, G. (1994). *Manifest Manners: Postindian Warriors of Survivance*. Hanover, CT: Wesleyan University Press.

Vygotsky, L. (1978). Interaction between learning and development. *Readings on the Development of Children, 23*(3), 34–41.

Waitoller, F. R., & King Thorius, K. A. (2016). Cross-pollinating culturally sustaining pedagogy and universal design for learning: Toward an inclusive pedagogy that accounts for dis/ability. *Harvard Educational Review, 86*(3), 366–389.

Wolfe, P. (2006). Settler colonialism and the elimination of the Native. *Journal of Genocide Research, 8*(4), 387–409.

Wong, C. P. (2018). Double entendre got bodied: Strategic ambivalence and Latinx young men rappin' under the White gaze. *Journal of World Popular Music, 5*(2), 193–212.

Wong, C. P. (2019). *Pray You Catch Me: A Critical Feminist and Ethnographic Study of Love as Pedagogy and Politics for Social Justice*. Stanford, CA: Stanford University.

Wong, C. P., & Peña, C. (2017). Policing and performing culture. In: D. Paris & H. S. Alim (Eds.), *Culturally Sustaining Pedagogies: Teaching and Learning for Justice in a Changing World* (p. 117). New York, NY: Teacher's College Press.

Woodson, C. G. (2000). *The Mis-Education of the Negro*. Trenton, NJ: Africa World Press. (Original work published in 1933).

Wyman, L., McCarty, T., & Nicholas, S. (Eds.) (2014). *Indigenous Youth and Multilingualism: Language Identity, Ideology, and Practice in Dynamic Cultural Worlds*. New York, NY: Routledge.

16
MULTIPLE WAYS OF KNOWING*
Re-Imagining Disciplinary Learning

Beth Warren, Shirin Vossoughi, Ann S. Rosebery,
Megan Bang, and Edd V. Taylor

A collaborative work of thinking-writing

Canon building is empire building.

—*Morrison (1989, p. 132)*

Introduction

In her essay "Unspeakable Things Unspoken," Toni Morrison guides us into a practice of re-reading novels that have long defined the canon of American literature to make visible the "informing and determining Afro-American presence in traditional American literature" (Morrison, 1989, p. 145). She powerfully names this presence as "the unspeakable unspoken" that has been studiously avoided in the long tradition of white, Eurocentric literary scholarship. In her readings of canonical texts, she makes visible how the texts work, intellectually and linguistically, to erase African American presence, and thereby reveals their "deeper and other meanings, deeper and other power, deeper and other significances" (p. 140). As she disturbs settled forms of literary scholarship, she gives volume to the political and ethical dimensions of the literary imagination. She expands the possibilities of literature and scholarship, ways of reading the world, and, as we will highlight in this chapter, what it might mean for teachers to think of themselves as careful, expansive readers of their students and their ideas, questions, desires, and fears.

We open with Morrison's re-reading of American literature because she shines a searing light on canon building as a process of exclusion, erasure, and onto-epistemic violence that nullifies presences-assumed-not-to-exist (Morrison, 1989) in the form of white imaginings of African Americans (Gates, 1984) or settler imaginings of Native people (Smith, 2012; Vizenor, 2000). Morrison draws our attention to the necessity of analyzing "the workings as well as the work" (p. 162) in order to understand the processes and motives—racial, colonial, patriarchal—that have driven canon building as empire building in the West and in disciplinary learning and teaching in U.S. schools. She makes legible how:

> (s)ilences are being broken, lost things have been found, and at least two generations of scholars are disentangling received knowledge from the apparatus of control…it is no

---

* This material is based upon work supported by the Spencer Foundation and the National Science Foundation under Grants No. 1720578, 1713368, 1348494, 0353341, and 201900011. The opinions expressed are solely those of the authors and do not reflect those of the foundations. The authors wish to thank all the teachers, community members and children who have collaborated in the development of the work and thinking represented in this chapter. We would also like to express our gratitude to the editors for the opportunity to think, learn and write together.

longer acceptable merely to imagine us and imagine for us. We have always been imagining ourselves.

(Morrison, 1989, pp. 132–133)

In these ways, Morrison serves as a guide in imagining radically different horizons of possibility for disciplinary knowing *and* learning as the making and sharing of worlds woven with the making and sharing of selves (Morrison, 1993; Smith, 2012).

Toward Onto-Epistemic Heterogeneity

In this chapter we explore what is required of us, as researchers and educators, to disentangle received disciplinary knowledge and ways of knowing from what Morrison names as "the apparatus of control," and to enable expansive and insurgent ways of learning, being, and acting in, with, and across disciplines. We posit that engaging in liberatory forms of disciplinary learning within a framework of decolonization and onto-epistemic heterogeneity is necessary for equitable, dignified, and just forms of education that support learners in who they imagine themselves to be and might become (Espinoza & Vossoughi, 2014). By onto-epistemic heterogeneity we mean to highlight two key ideas. First, that knowing and being are inextricably tied; and second, that liberatory education ought to be deeply rooted in the pasts, presents, and futures that sustain and imagine multiple values, purposes, and arcs of human learning. This viewpoint is distinct from equity efforts organized by access paradigms that position the disciplines themselves as settled and exempt from reproach or historicity. In short, greater access to settled forms of disciplinary knowledge is not only insufficient, but functions as the newest form of assimilation and domestication into Western supremacy, perhaps more insidiously through a veneer of liberal inclusion (Melamed, 2011).

Following Morrison, and anchoring ourselves in the history of ideas around culture and learning, we argue the need for a view of disciplinary learning animated by the following political and ethical commitments: the critique and refusal of settled forms of disciplinary knowledge and practice (Tuck, 2009); epistemic delinking from colonial matrices of power (Mignolo, 2009); and the collective imagining, articulation, and enactment of alternative possibilities for human learning and relations (Espinoza, 2009). We conceptualize these as the always evolving desires and practices that give form to just learning environments. We see them as inextricably and dynamically interrelated, not sequentially ordered. Importantly, deliberation and action infused with these interrelated commitments are critically different from efforts that begin with and remain overly constrained by the critique of normative ways of knowing. Remaining solely in the mode of critique invites enclosure such that powered ways of knowing continue to set the terms (Lyons, 2000).

Indeed, the scholars with whom we are in dialogue in this chapter have sought, in a multiplicity of ways, to craft new language and tools for conceptualizing problems and possibilities in disciplinary learning uninhibited by the epistemic, ontological, and axiological assumptions of Western normativity in service of empire building. Mindful of the ways conceptions of difference are domesticated through enclosure into normative epistemologies and their assimilative demands, we work to further theorize a more radical view of difference through a re-imagining and expansion of the onto-epistemic field (Richardson, 2011). To nurture these potentialities, we focus on key efforts to re-imagine the design, enactment, and study of disciplinary learning that take seriously the "task of de-colonial thinking" (Mignolo, 2009, p. 15) and the project of onto-epistemic heterogeneity (Bang & Vossoughi, 2016; Rosebery, Ogonowski, DiSchino, & Warren, 2010).

Beyond Colonial Terms for Disciplinary Learning

All disciplines are in need of a critical re-reading of white supremacist ideology. Similar arguments for onto-epistemic heterogeneity are being advanced in the sciences, mathematics, and engineering, among other disciplines, where the dominant representation—in education and in public discourse, if not in actual disciplinary work—presumes singularity, neutrality, and an objectified universe subject to human mastery (Latour, 1988; Massey, 2005). Scholars are asking how we

Multiple Ways of Knowing

might create learning environments liberated from ethnocentrism imposed by Western science and science education (Bang, Marin, & Medin, 2018; Barton & Tan, 2018; Mensah, 2019). This ethnocentrism gives rise to a zero point epistemology of the knowing subject "disincorporated from the known and untouched by the geo-political configuration of the world" (Mignolo, 2009, p. 2; see also Anzaldúa, 1987; Grosfoguel, 2013; Smith, 2012). Forged in the Renaissance and Enlightenment, zero point epistemology melds European modernity with the imperial structure of coloniality to "map the world and its problems, classify people, and project what is good for them" (Mignolo, 2009, p. 1). Zero point epistemology enacts colonial violence by claiming the privilege of narrating what "others" are while simultaneously denying other perspectives, histories, and subjectivities.

The onto-epistemic architecture of the zero point is built continuously to mask and secure its Western supremacist origins and intentions through its claims to universality, neutrality, objectivity, egocentricity. The detached, omniscient observer is the one who "controls the disciplinary rules and puts himself or herself in a privileged position to evaluate and dictate" (Mignolo, 2009, p. 4) as well as exclude, erase, and exterminate. As Bang, Marin, and Medin (2018) argue, the myth of a culturally neutral, value free, unsituated, and anthropocentric science has and continues to motivate and justify violence. Among other harms, it contributes to the long history of erasure and marginalization of minoritized students from science, especially in its school forms, and to a distorted view of disciplinary possibility itself (Barton & Tan, 2018; Martin, 2006; Medin & Bang, 2014; Warren & Rosebery, 2011). It is therefore not enough to change the content of the conversation about disciplinary knowledge and learning; it is essential to change its terms (Mignolo, 2009; Morrison, 1989; Lyons, 2000). Without acts of epistemic disobedience, the apparatus of onto-epistemic control is not disrupted and future possibilities become newly domesticated.

In this chapter, we argue that grounding forms of onto-epistemic heterogeneity in ideas and practices that disallow conceptual flattening and colonial enclosure (e.g., heterogeneity as "multiculturalism") requires ongoing vigilance and reflexivity on the part of researchers and educators (Richardson, 2011). Further, epistemic delinking that makes possible radical disciplinary heterogeneity entails opening ourselves to living more ethically and politically responsive relations (Bang, Warren, Rosebery, & Medin, 2012; Shotter, 2006a). As the field continues to theorize and work to enact onto-epistemic heterogeneity, we posit three sensibilities crucial to liberatory forms of disciplinary learning: *multiplicity*, *horizontality*, and *dialogicality*. We argue that these sensibilities are necessarily linked to practice, that is, to creating the pedagogical conditions for enacting the political and ethical commitments discussed above.

These three sensibilities organize our chapter and push us to consider enactments and commitments to ethical praxis. New ways of seeing and attuning to students' cultural and intellectual activity, and new ways of reflecting on the implications of pedagogical language and action, become crucial to cultivating deeper forms of relationality in learning and development. These new ways of seeing and reflecting must be disentangled from ongoing legacies of oppression, deficit-thinking, and assimilation. The following sections elaborate these sensibilities, illustrate how they shift the ways we understand disciplinary knowledges and forms of knowing in literacy, science, and mathematics, and articulate key implications for the design of learning and the practice of teaching. A key challenge in enacting onto-epistemic heterogeneity is to hold multiple political and ethical commitments in ways that make practice and interaction improvisational, emergently creative, and deeply responsive to young peoples' sense-making and world-making (Philip, 2019).

Multiplicity

We begin with multiplicity. Multiplicity attunes us to the heterogeneity of knowledges and ways of knowing. It works to surface and analyze relationships among identity, history, and knowledge production (i.e., who is in the room and how they are positioned matters for the kinds of questions asked and pursued). Multiplicity centers the need for intellectual histories of disciplinary knowledge—both recognized and unrecognized. Multiplicity is therefore a principled and necessary beginning toward delinking; without it, horizontality and dialogicality are often flattened and mobilized toward settled views of the disciplines themselves.

In actuality, disciplines are always changing (Latour, 1988). For example, the microbial turn in life sciences has given rise to whole new fields of inquiry, e.g., microbial oceanography, the human microbiome, and biopolitics (Paxson & Helmreich, 2014). Novel collaborations among genomic scientists and microbiologists are leading to paradigm-shifting views of human-bacteria relationships as essential partners in a vast microbial-human ecosystem of life (Blaser, 2014). This shift away from Pasteurian "germ theory"—which revolutionized life science in the 1880s—is contributing to a radical de-settling of knowledge around health and well-being as well as representations of life which locate humans above rather than beside other organisms. In short, disciplines are in continuous movement, and shifts in the social configurations of intellectual work are consequential to disciplinary activity and understanding.

This dynamic nature of disciplinary activity is routinely invisibilized in schools, where disciplines are flattened and engaged as if they are static, known, and finalized domains. Building from Morrison (1989), the maintenance of such static conceptualizations enacts forms of control that reproduce racialized and ideological anxieties and projects (e.g., hierarchical orderings of life; acknowledging contributions of singular, "exceptional" women and people of color over collective and culturally rooted epistemologies). An understanding of multiplicity creates openings for interrupting onto-epistemic supremacy and supporting students to wrestle with the genealogies and internal tensions inherent in disciplines as a crucial facet of critiquing and delinking.

Disciplinary knowledge is also shaped by who is allowed to create the "official" knowledge in a discipline. Indeed, in many science and engineering domains there continue to be few women and people of color (NSF, 2019). Yet, in fields in which women and people of color participate with agency, dramatic intellectual revolutions have taken place. We turn again to the sciences, which are being transformed as significant numbers of women gain a professional foothold and unearth pervasive male bias (Wald & Wu, 2010). Studies of species reproductive behaviors, conducted historically by male scientists, have paid little attention to the role of females in mating, marshalling evidence for the theory that mating is initiated by the males of a species. Due in large part to research by women scientists, the field now understands that mating behaviors occur in myriad variations and reach beyond normative heterosexual constructions (Bagemihl, 1999). Less well-recognized are the forms of hostility routinely encountered by those who dare to change social configurations in disciplines, a point we carry into the discussion of multiplicity's educational implications.

As a sensibility attuned toward educational possibility, multiplicity requires a closer look at the ways disciplinary practices are narrated, framed, and enacted, including in recent reform efforts to connect disciplinary learning with professional practice. At least two questions are important here. First, how can disciplinary learning better reflect the heterogeneity of professional practice? This question requires that curricular and pedagogical efforts to connect the disciplinary activities of children and youth to those of adult professionals center the distinct intellectual histories, perspectives, debates, values, and purposes that animate disciplinary schools of thought. This privileging of multiplicity *as extant within all disciplines* can mediate deeper forms of conceptual understanding, apprentice students into habits of critiquing and refusing the treatment of knowledge as "settled," and cultivate a disposition toward concepts and practices as always reflective of culturally and politically situated ways of knowing (Bang et al., 2012; Philip, Olivares-Pasillas, & Rocha, 2016; Vossoughi, 2014). As reflected in the examples below, such onto-epistemic openness also positions students as agentive thinkers, poised to not only participate in but to imagine, articulate, and reshape disciplinary activity.

Second, how are professional disciplinary practices themselves forged and constrained by dynamics of power and erasure? Consider, for example, the ways science continues to be defined as apolitical (Harding, 1993) and distinct from affect, values, and aesthetics (Jaber & Hammer, 2016; Leander & Ehret, 2019). Dynamics of power and erasure are also present within the discursive and interactional processes of settings that aim to foreground ethics in science. In an undergraduate

Multiple Ways of Knowing

ethics course designed for engineers in training, Philip, Gupta, Turpen, and Elby (2018) analyzed the language that unfolded in a classroom discussion on the use of drones in modern warfare. Their research shows how "ideological convergence among participants constructed locally significant categories of "civilian," "terrorist," and (un)grievability, which narrowed the possible trajectories for students' disciplinary learning in engineering and engineering ethics" (p. 1). Their analysis of the ways Brown bodies were reconstituted by engineering students as disposable reminds us that, without changing the onto-epistemic terms of the conversation, the weight of hegemonic categories supporting projects of empire is easily reproduced.

Thus, the question of the role that power plays in professional disciplinary practices also problematizes reforms that limit imaginings of progressive possibilities to children's disciplinary learning that *simulates* professional disciplinary practices, in so far as those practices are treated as outside of history (McKinney de Royston & Sengupta-Irving, 2019). Indeed, the politics and ethics of scientific practice and technological innovation in the 21st century shape both official conversations in professional organizations and unofficial forms of dissent and whistle blowing (Vakil & Higgs, 2019). Designs for learning that speak to these complexities have the potential to reshape disciplinary practices and what and whom they are for. This stance also resonates with reform efforts that seek to push beyond viewing children's activity as practice for life toward viewing it as constituting life (Rogoff, 2003).

Understanding disciplinary activity as dynamic and historically developing involves attending closely to the ways disciplinary canons are forged in and through processes of epistemic violence, erasure, and resistance. One noteworthy example of such educational contestation is Cultural Modeling (Lee, 1995, 2000). In Cultural Modeling, students were apprenticed into the meanings and uses of literary forms typically valued in school (e.g., irony, symbolism, point of view) as they engaged in analyzing and making visible the interpretive power of practices of signifying, a highly valued discourse practice in African American communities (Smitherman, 2000). Gates (1988) traces signifying to its origins in slavery when survival could be determined by sharply honed language practices. With these practices, enslaved Africans voiced layered and coded counter messages in the face of domination while simultaneously reinforcing fierce bonds of resilience and caring.

In direct contrast to the persistent denigration of African American Vernacular English (AAVE), both by conservative and liberal "culture of poverty" scholars and policy-makers (Rickford, 1999), students in Cultural Modeling classrooms studied examples of their own and others' signifying dialogue. As they interpreted layered meanings in these examples, they identified formal rules for the signifying-based practices they used to generate those meanings. These rule-practices relationships, which Lee calls "cultural data sets," were then used to scaffold the interpretation of texts by Toni Cade Bambara, Zora Neale Hurston, and Alice Walker, among others. The intentional decision to connect students' cultural and linguistic practices to canonical literature within African American traditions serves as a critique and refusal of settled disciplinary expectations by positioning these practices as already central to academic genres and as always a part of a history of intellectual self-determination and resistance. Lee (2000) documented dramatic changes in the intellectual culture of the classroom as students increasingly took up and shaped their use of the formal, literary tropes. While contemporary forms of canon policing result in ongoing conflation of normative practices with rigor, an explicit valuing of multiple linguistic and literary traditions—and the specific and detailed histories they grow out of—make new forms of learning possible. These relationships actively disentangle intellectual depth and complexity from norms born of racial hierarchy and epistemic supremacy, and expose the lack of epistemic rigor required by engaging with singularly normative forms.

While epistemic critique, delinking, and imagination require a view of all disciplinary learning as interwoven with critical social analysis, they also demand that we not take the practices of critical social analysis as given or unproblematic. Critical pedagogies themselves can benefit from deep engagement with multiplicity (Vossoughi & Gutiérrez, 2016). The case of the Migrant Student Leadership Institute (MSLI) illustrates this point through pedagogical and discursive practices grounded in multiplicity.

MSLI was a summer academic program that worked to apprentice high-school-aged migrant students in decolonial and sociocritical literacies rooted in their community histories and everyday experiences (Gutiérrez, 2008; Tejeda, Espinoza, & Gutiérrez, 2003). Here multiplicity became a resource for moving beyond the ideological rigidities and forms of epistemic singularity that can be reproduced in the complex work of critical and decolonial pedagogies (Bang & Vossoughi, 2016; Smith, 2012), and toward more variegated and epistemically open forms of political education. Studies of classroom discourse in MSLI have revealed patterns of talk that were subjunctive (*what if, might be, perhaps*) (Vossoughi, 2011); modal (*may, would, could*) (Gutiérrez, 2008); and variegated (multiple question-asking patterns that were distinct from conventional I-R-E structures and roles) (Espinoza, 2009). Designing for conceptual openings within pedagogical talk, that is, ways into new concepts as well as the space to critique and imagine beyond those concepts, therefore constitutes a key practice of multiplicity.

Educators mediated the reading of social theoretical texts by crafting generative questions, analytic paths, and metaphors that invited autobiographical connections and multiple interpretations. Instructional narratives also routinely positioned students as engaging in a conversation with the authors of social theoretical texts. Thus, on any given day, one could hear MSLI educators making statements such as, "Freire is going to help us think about education as it is and as it could be" (Vossoughi, 2011). Positioning texts as tools and students as full participants in a textual conversation can help push beyond some of the more instrumentalist ways critical texts may be interpreted within the context of political education. Such moves substantiate the onto-epistemic movements and forms of intellectual history argued for above, and lay the ground for the expression of multiple meanings.

During a collective discussion of Ana Castillo's *A Countryless Woman*, Miguel, a 17-year old student who had recently arrived in the U.S. from Mexico, engaged in pedagogical leadership and forms of explication that exemplify the valuing of multiple linguistic tools and modalities within MSLI, and the often subtle and unanticipated ways students appropriated social analytic artifacts over time. Social analytic artifacts are specific discursive tools used to deepen the collective analysis of social problems, in this case *semantic sharpening* and *heteroglossic attunement*. Miguel began:

> En esa frace que dice, este, que las mujeres no tienen país, es como un tipo de metáfora… No las esta soportando la sociedad, el pais, la sociedad, y la sociedad somos nosotros. Y so no las soportamos nosotros, esta, las mujeres estan en el aire.
>
> *In this phrase that says that women have no country, it's like a type of metaphor…it is not supporting them, society, the country, society, and society is us, and if we don't support them, women are left in the air.*

Vossoughi's analysis of discourse practices in MSLI revealed that teachers frequently asked students to specify their use of general terms like "society"—often to encourage naming the role of particular social actors and policies in shaping current structural conditions. Such *semantic sharpening* involved revising one's discourse (word choice, tone, gesture) to gain analytic and political clarity (Vossoughi, 2014, p. 359). Here we see that when Miguel arrived at the word society, he recognized it as an occasion for semantic sharpening, and proceeded to specify who is meant by society in ways that compelled his peers and teachers to take collective responsibility for patriarchy. His metaphor "Las mujeres estan el aire" offers a powerful image of the vulnerabilities forced upon women and reflects the ways students felt license to work with and extend the metaphors offered by the authors (e.g., "a countryless woman"). Miguel continued:

> Nosotros siempre vamos a soportar el hombre, porque, según es más fuerte, según eso viene de la naturaleza, es el que trae el dinero a la casa, es el que cuida, es el hombre de la casa es muchas cosas que las mujeres, según no pueden hacer

Multiple Ways of Knowing

We are always going to support the man because supposedly he is stronger, supposedly this comes from nature, he's the one that brings the money home, he's the one that does the hard work, he's the one that takes care, he's the man of the house, he is many things that women supposedly cannot do.

Here we see the social analytic work of *heteroglossic attunement*: discerning the multiple historical and ideological voices shaping spoken or written texts, attending to the ways pitch, tone, word choice, and gesture index particular meanings, and recognizing dominant discourses in order to analyze, play with, or subvert them. Through the use of multiple semiotic tools (symbolism, humor, drama, using *segun* [supposedly] to ventriloquate and interrogate the idea of men as "stronger"), Miguel modeled both what it looks like to take responsibility for hegemonic discourses *and* how to enact critique and solidarity by carefully attuning to ideological echoes and apertures present in the narratives we produce. Miguel's stance was not singular; instead he expertly moved between his familiarity with patriarchal narratives and a critique of those narratives in ways that underscore the vital role of wrestling with complex and sometimes contradictory meanings within processes of socio-political learning and becoming (Tuck, 2009). In line with our prior discussions of enclosure as a colonial practice, this view also cautions against moves to enclose intellectual struggle in its many forms within critical and decolonial pedagogies.

In this section we have called for attention to the forms of multiplicity alive in students' purposes and concerns as well as the forms of multiplicity alive in disciplines. Without this dual attention, there is a heightened risk in reproducing forms of epistemic supremacy in the work of teaching through simplified interpretations of onto-epistemic heterogeneity, e.g., as multiple pathways to the same destination that effectively foreclose the development of insurgent and resurgent forms of disciplinary knowledge.

Horizontality

We turn now to horizontality, which specifically attends to the ways learning happens in and across multiple activity systems (Engeström, 1996; Gutiérrez, 2008; Vossoughi & Gutiérrez, 2014). Horizontality also attends to cultural repertoires of practice within activity systems as resources that are always available for disciplinary learning (Gutiérrez & Rogoff, 2003; Nasir, Rosebery, Warren, & Lee, 2006/2014). And it focuses attention on the contradictions—and the acts of refusal, questioning, re-visioning, re-storying—that drive boundary-crossing and the creation of new meanings, tasks, and goals (Cole & Griffin, 1980; Engeström, 1996). Horizontality highlights the boundless variety of places, cultural contexts, and practices through which people learn. In other words, learning is infinitely deeper and broader than school. In this section we consider research that focuses attention on learning as youth do life.

Learning as Doing Life Across Spatio-Temporal Scales

Funds of knowledge theorizes horizontality as fundamental to learning (Moll & Greenberg, 1992; González, Moll, & Amanti, 2005). Working with families in a predominantly Mexican working-class community in Tucson, Moll and Greenberg (1992) defined funds of knowledge as "the strategic knowledge and related activities essential to household functioning, development, and well-being...pertaining to the social, economic, and productive activities of people in a local region" (1992, p. 139). Moll (2000) documented the ways varied funds accumulated across geographical and generational frontiers, were shared within and across households, and used to respond adaptively to ever evolving circumstances of life. Moll, González and colleagues (González et al., 2005; Moll et al., 1992) then analyzed the potential of household funds of knowledge for academic learning with the intention of infusing home and community knowledge and ways of knowing with school-based ways. Collaborating with teachers and families, they developed curricular units in mathematics, science, and literacy based in the community's funds of knowledge. This work, like Cultural Modeling, highlighted the ways in which disciplinary learning was already alive in the social and intellectual activity of these families and, by extension, in *all* households, communities, and social networks. Connecting to Morrison, it also helped to expose the "workings as well as the work" of schooling designed to eradicate and exclude these living connections.

The notion that critical repertoires are alive in the varied experiences of youth is now widely recognized. By documenting the depth and breadth of learning as ongoing in the lives of youth, research across disciplines has exposed the hegemonic function of categories such as everyday/non-academic/concrete and disciplinary/academic/abstract, i.e., how they organize learning along a vertical axis that stratifies people, knowledges, and practices. Sociocultural research in mathematics, literacy, and STEM education has demonstrated the purposeful, creative, and analytic meaning-making practices in which children and youth engage across the settings of their daily lives (e.g., Barajas-López, 2104; Bell, Tzou, Bricker, & Baines, 2012; Booker & Goldman, 2016; Dubinsky & Moses, 2011; Gutiérrez, 2013; Nasir, Hand, & Taylor, 2008; Tate, 1996; Tucker-Raymond, Gravel, Kohberger, & Browne, 2017; Warren, Ogonowski, & Pothier, 2005; Wright, 2019).

For example, Taylor's (2009) study of mathematical understanding in a predominantly African American and Latinx community documented specific mathematical understandings (place value and multi-digit addition) and strategies (addition, subtraction, estimation) that young children used as they shopped for snacks in a neighborhood store. He described the distributed nature of the children's purchasing practices by analyzing the interrelatedness of their knowledge, the activities of the store clerk, the artifacts to be purchased, and the store's shopping norms. He documented the children's discourse and activity as they calculated how much money they had, added up prices, and estimated change. He also described how the clerk spontaneously supported the children to make successful purchases: reading a price aloud when they did not understand a given notational representation, and suggesting variations on the combination of items presented for purchase if a child did not have enough money.

During interviews, Taylor found that while most children were able to use their knowledge of place value to solve problems with coins, many struggled to show an equivalent understanding with base-ten blocks. He concluded that features of the environment that enabled the children to engage successfully in the store were likely also present in the coin-based assessment but not in the base-ten blocks assessment. This led him to hypothesize that mathematical understanding exhibited outside of school may not "show up" in formal settings unless intentionally invited. In this case, the assumption of greater intellectual rigor in abstracted forms of mathematical activity (base-ten blocks) speaks to the ways epistemic supremacy is built on a view of cognitive activity as separate from life.

The ways learners are positioned by the racialized and gendered narratives that circulate in disciplinary curricula and practice also negatively affects the formation of their discipline-based identities (e.g., Nasir, 2012; Martin, 2006). Like the literary canon, STEM curricula have been developed within particular histories that present these disciplines as culturally and politically neutral. Counter narratives are now being developed that reveal multiple powerful ways of knowing within and across disciplines. The field of ethnomathematics is one example (see R. Gutiérrez, 2017 for an incisive critique of mathematics education); the work of Barton, Tan, and colleagues (Barton & Tan, 2018; Tan, Barton, & Benavides, 2019) to re-envision engineering education and making spaces for girls and youth of color within justice-oriented learning is another.

To this point, this section has focused on re-thinking learning in school. We turn now to designs for learning that are reconsidering what learning is and where it happens to encompass the heterogeneity of places and times in which children do life.

Multiple Ways of Knowing

Expanding Classroom Walls: Learning as Life

Leander, Phillips, and Taylor (2010) asked what it might mean for the field to shift its "historical vision of the classroom as a container for learning" to one of the classroom "as a dynamic place-in-the-making" (p. 381)? Pursuing this idea, learning scientists have begun to focus on bodies-in-motion, reconceptualizing possible relationships among bodies, place, movement, time, and engagement in the design of learning environments (Lee, 2015; Marin & Bang, 2018; Stevens, 2012; Taylor & Hall, 2013). In the case of Walking Scale Geometry, Ma (2016) disrupted typical classroom geometry by inviting students to construct large-scale geometry figures in a soccer field. In the process, the students realized the need to invent new tools and strategies, in essence, re-placing their bodies as tools for learning geometry.

Taking a deep view of learning as living, Taylor and colleagues (Taylor, 2017; Taylor & Hall, 2013) collaborated with youth to design environments for learning-on-the-move. One outcome is a new literacy genre, locative literacies, in which youth learn to negotiate varied forms of place-based inscription along lines they make through physical (e.g., walking, riding bikes) and digital mobilities (e.g., GPS, digital maps). Locative literacies involve reading and writing varied representational forms at the scale of the city to make visible relationships that "foreground humans not merely as consumers or generators of texts but as being part of that text, literacy agents of a text they populate" (Taylor, 2017, p. 1). In this way, learning-on-the-move has the potential to re-center students' and communities' ways of knowing by theorizing learning as bodied and taking place across varied spatial-temporal scales.

In closing this section, we ask: why is re-thinking learning through a lens of horizontality important? Because it allows us to begin to critique and delink from the ways that schooling and disciplines have been structured to privilege and humanize certain ways of knowing and being over others. It forces us to recognize that learning environments are not "neutral" with respect to life, they are life. As currently constituted, schooling is structured to de-legitimate the repertoires of minoritized students and control their bodies as well as their minds in ways that prevent embodied learning in place. Horizontality is key to delinking from colonial matrices of power in the way it re-places disciplinary learning within practices of doing life, and re-centers the histories, purposes, and places integral to students' ways of being. Such horizontal attunements are critical to the design and enactment of learning ecologies in which children and youth from minoritized communities can thrive.

Dialogicality

In this section, we build from our discussion of multiplicity and horizontality to explore dialogicality as a related sensibility that attunes us to the ways in which every utterance brings into contact centralizing and centrifugal forces of language (Bakhtin, 1981). A dialogical sensibility focuses on the discursive, layered aspects of meaning-making as a critical site of refusal, delinking, and re-imagining the normative chains that structure disciplinary learning. In this light, we can think of meaning-making as bringing to life "thousands of dialogic threads" that are necessarily woven into our words and utterances, but often left unspoken and unspeakable in the dominant practices of disciplinary learning. We explore what is opened, onto-epistemically and pedagogically, when teachers and researchers engage words and utterances within disciplinary work as moving dialogical fields of other words, points of view, tones, and values.

By dialogical we mean more than structured forms of participatory talk. Indeed, as Matusov (2009) argues, while meaning-making in classrooms, like meaning-making in life, is inherently dialogic, it is often distorted and flattened by "anti-dialogic projects." Anti-dialogic projects constitute the dominant form of school discourse marked by known disciplinary destinations, finalized meanings, and images of stable expertise. In these projects, gaps in how learners and teachers are thinking about a given phenomenon—gaps in their consciousnesses, as Matusov (2009) puts it—are to be assimilated into singular, finalized understandings of what is taken to be settled disciplinary knowledge. In contrast, a dialogical sensibility entails understanding that "no living word relates to its object in a *singular* way" (Bakhtin, 1981, p. 276). It implies a form of "whole-person engagement" (Matusov, 2009) or "withness-thinking" (Shotter, 2006a) among participants in classroom talk that centers responsiveness to the already spoken and openness to the not yet spoken (Bakhtin, 1981), taking care to bring to life present, distant, and absent voices.

Dialogicality holds that there are no neutral words spoken from nowhere, detached from the varied contexts of their use (Bakhtin, 1981) as framed within zero point epistemology. Rather, words carry compressed histories (Nemerov, 1969) and suggest potential futurities. A dialogical sensibility, therefore, takes up the socially and politically saturated life of words as a necessary focus of analysis and imagination in disciplinary learning. It demands intentional engagement with the multiplicity and horizontality of discourse in moment-to-moment disciplinary learning as a way of grappling with, rupturing, and re-imagining settled concepts and perspectives.

The following example explores the meaning horizons that a dialogical sensibility brings into being. It illustrates how disciplinary language is entangled with—and can be disentangled from—a specifically Western scientific perspective. It also highlights how teachers, elders, and researchers, working concertedly, slowed down their design activity in a process of critiquing, delinking from, and re-imagining the compression of histories in the disciplinary language they were in the habit of using.

As part of a community-based design project to explore urban Indigenous land-based pedagogies, Bang et al. (2014) discuss how acts of naming can be made into sites of critical work that delink from zero point epistemology. Naming became problematized as curriculum designers—teachers, elders, and researchers—developed learning environments focused on "invasive species," with the common buckthorn (a species native to Europe and brought to North America in the early 1800s) as a focus. This experience was part of a larger endeavor to organize learning and teaching in youth programs at the American Indian Center of Chicago around the core principle of upholding land as a relative. Naming plant relatives became a dialogically focused practice that refused Western conceptions and made present Indigenous conceptions of nature-culture relations.

The design group came to question their use of "invasive species" as a conceptual anchor because of its entanglement with Western scientific values on one hand and a history of ecological imperialism on the other. The terminology, they realized, located buckthorn outside their own design principle of naming human-plant relations. And, while buckthorn may not have been *their* relative, having been transported from Europe to Chicago, it was, undoubtedly, a relative to other communities of people. Critically, the settled terminology compressed and obscured the interests of the settlers who colonized the "new lands" with European flora that profoundly shifted the ecology of Native lands. An elder in the design group gave voice to the need generated out of this tension:

> we need to express these concepts we're putting together for the kids in Indian thought… to create our own language of how we're going to express these concepts and what we want our kids to learn and understand as well as to help us to be able to become familiar with that language…because we, as Native people, we have that connection that non-Indian people are searching for…[T]hey're not to the point of recognizing any relatives… They're not talking about helping the earth heal. They're not talking about helping our relatives to survive.
>
> *(Bang et al., 2014, p. 10)*

Working from this insight, the group created a naming centered in a relational ethics. They framed buckthorn and other "invasive species" as "plants that people lost their relationships with." As a language of teaching, this way of naming was rooted in Indigenous onto-epistemic relationality,

Multiple Ways of Knowing

and at the same time invited probing of the histories of plant movements wrought by (invasive) colonialism. The group's pedagogical attunement to settled forms of scientific discourse opened up possibilities for creating insurgent language that simultaneously ruptured these forms and re-centered attention to the layers of changes in Chicago lands and waters in relationship to settler colonial and Indigenous land practices.

A sensibility toward utterances as dialogically saturated entails, as in the above example, a "relentless critical awareness of what guiding principles are structuring engagement *in moments*" (Mignolo, 2007, p. 458, our emphasis), whether among adults as designers or among adults and young people as teachers and learners. Here, as in the discussions of MSLI and Cultural Modeling, teachers and elders focused attention on the compressed, often intentionally suppressed, dialogical reverberations in the deep historical strata of disciplinary discourses. Refusing settled disciplinary lenses and engaging emergent tensions in these ways seeds possibilities for insurgent readings of disciplinary discourses.

Few things weigh as heavily in teaching as the challenge of attending to the multiplicity of meanings and horizontal layering of words and utterances in moment-to-moment interaction with students. Teachers are in the demanding, but often neither acknowledged nor supported, position of recognizing and mediating the intellectual, social, racial, and ideological tensions that arise moment-to-moment between the concepts, practices, and forms of relations that students wish to explore and those privileged in school renderings of disciplines (Bang, et al., 2012; Philip et al., 2016). With a final example, we explore the tension-filled space of a science classroom as the students and teacher wrestled with onto-epistemic heterogeneity in life sciences in the course of a seemingly straightforward curricular exercise to develop an operational definition of life.

In the classroom, seventh grade students were discussing how to categorize various phenomena—e.g., rain, jellyfish, a rocking horse, the sun—into living and nonliving (see Warren & Rosebery, 2011). The question arose as to where to place the sun in that binary space. Students expressed various points of view on the question of the sun's ontological status, its contributions to living things, and its relationship to human life.

Here we focus on an extended interaction involving Jonathan, who identified as African American, and his science teacher, Ms. V, who identified as a foreign-born U.S. citizen of Filipino and European American descent. As she reported later in her professional learning community, Ms. V worried about how best to "manage" what she viewed as Jonathan's at times "problematic" engagement in science class. As the class considered the sun's status, Jonathan wondered aloud how it is possible for a "nonliving" sun—the expected categorization—to produce a "living" flowering plant? Reasoning within a relational ecology, Jonathan shifted the ground of argument away from the settled binary logic to an ecological way of seeing the sun as a life-giving force within a complex system.

Jonathan's thinking propelled a vigorous discussion in which students expressed doubts about previously held certainties (e.g., the sun is not alive) and sought resolutions to Jonathan's complicating view. At one point, a white female student, Molly, suggested an analogy that she felt explained why the sun should be classified as nonliving: "Well, I don't know if this makes sense but like for Jonathan's we have to have water even though water is not living…we still need it like plants need the sun." Ms. V ratified Molly's analogy, endorsing it as an explanation of the relationship between the sun and plants.

Jonathan experienced Molly's analogy and Ms. V's ratification as a closure. He expressed his frustration by arguing that the water-human analogy was not in fact an *explanation* but the very same problem with the very same logic he was exploring. Rather than seeking simple answers, he was questioning the presumed coherence of the binary logic of living/nonliving for classifying physical objects like the sun on which all forms of life depend, a logic that locates the sun and a rocking horse in the same category. He was suggesting a profoundly different way of seeing the sun and its connection to life on Earth, as a living system. Working at making ecological rather than categorical sense, he was thinking from an arguably deeper place than the curriculum, one closer to contemporary scientific thinking (Pierotti, 2011) and one that refused and re-imagined the curriculum's settled, implicit ontology (i.e., the sun as nonliving object) and epistemology (i.e., binary logic).

Ms. V felt the tension rippling through the discussion, but in the moment did not recognize the specific meanings, points of view, and values being contested. Although she responded to Jonathan in ways at once open, concerned, and puzzled, she did not know how to engage with his perspective as onto-epistemically fertile ground inviting heteroglossic attunement. Rather, she affirmed Molly's response to Jonathan to settle the status of the sun as "nonliving" and re-enclose it within the normative, binary frame. For his part, Jonathan well understood the analogy being proposed—the sun is to plants as water is to humans—but did not find it responsive to his intellectual concerns.

Ms. V's response to Molly's explanation reinforced onto-epistemic hierarchies, and thereby undermined Jonathan's intellectual inquiry and desire. It also foreclosed an expansive learning opportunity for Molly and the other students. Like the school experience of many minoritized students, Jonathan experienced the systemic effects of racialized hierarchies intersecting with the logic of Cartesianism. In this moment, the thinking of a white female student was not only treated as superior, in alignment with the curriculum, but also served to suppress the dialogically generative probing of an African American male student into settled disciplinary ways of thinking, knowing, and being. Not only do these moments enact racialized experiences of onto-epistemic violence on African American students, they also teach white students to see themselves as inherently smarter, even when their thinking is being limited by reductive interpretations of disciplines.

The story of this event continued as it moved into a space of professional learning. Working a transcript of the event with other teachers and researchers, Ms. V came to see Jonathan's participation and her own response in a new light. First, as the group unpacked uses of the words *life* and *lifecycle* in both scientific and school discourses, Ms. V became aware of the heteroglossic environment in which students encountered those words in specific relation to the sun (e.g., as nonliving; as the energy source that sustains life; as having a "life cycle" like other stars). As the group attuned to the (unexpected) heteroglossia of scientific discourses, Ms. V came to see Jonathan's exploration within a larger history of school science encounters, now interpreting him as keenly attentive to consequential namings and framings in curricular representations of biological and physical worlds. The group also began to imagine how as teachers they might cultivate a sensibility toward dialogicality by intentionally engaging with the compressed histories and possible futurities of settled namings and framings in scientific and other disciplines.

As the group worked to analyze the exchange involving Molly, Ms. V also came to see that Molly's analogy was merely an extension of Jonathan's, not an explanation as she had thought in the moment:

> Yeah, looking at what he said, "that doesn't answer anything," I get she didn't explain how it works, she just gave another example. To me *at the time*, I thought he was *just being argumentative*...So he really was like, "No one understands me right now." And I didn't understand him, I was like "Why don't you understand what she said?"

Ms. V realized that in the event she credited Molly's thinking with value and, with that same gesture, discredited Jonathan's. Through sharpened sensitivity to the heteroglossia present in Jonathan's comments, the group came to understand how racialized hierarchies and ways of seeing students routinely come into contact with settled onto-epistemic namings and framings, with consequences for individuals and the class as a whole.

Finally, we note that Ms. V and her colleagues came to see the erasure of onto-epistemic heterogeneity through a critical expansion of the disciplinary frame. Importantly, inquiry that wrestles with the dialogical entanglements of racialized hierarchies with onto-epistemic framings could also emerge from attunement to the ways that racialized hierarchies are structured and reproduced interactionally in classrooms. Both flows involve teachers and researchers "thinking from an other place, imagining an other language, arguing from an other logic," in Mignolo's terms (2000, p. 313). Working from a dialogical sensibility, teachers and researchers can in the ways explored here develop into more careful, generous, and responsive readers of young people's words, ideas, questions, and desires.

In this section we have focused on work that has grappled with language and meaning-making as always actively entwined in "thousands of living dialogic threads" (Bakhtin, 1981, p. 276) at multiple scales of time and place. The examples highlight dialogicality as a critical sensibility toward language and knowledge, one that refuses a logic of neutrality and singularity, and instead propels acts of naming and framing as relational work across connected webs of other words, points of view, tones, and values. Indeed, part of what is powerful about teaching from a dialogic sensibility is that students and teachers, working together, can shift from seeing Western knowledge-making as natural, normalized, and totalizing to analyzing it as one, dominant and dominating, way of being and knowing the world. Dialogically charged openings into and beyond settled disciplinary frames make space for multiple forms of onto-epistemic movement to thrive, including learning to see what is not meant to be seen—in disciplines as in young people's ideas, questions, and desires—in the logic of Western coloniality.

Concluding Thoughts

For decades, our field has been confronting the root problem of white normativity in education, through important efforts to re-mediate difference and re-imagine learning. Educational discourse around difference has been re-theorized in importantly insightful ways, each critical gesture aimed at transforming problematic constructions of difference toward more heterogeneous conceptions of life and learning. This work has made possible the envisioning of new horizons for radical heterogeneity pursued in this chapter.

The repeated violence wrought by systems of power heightens the demand for radically new "conscientious epistemic, ethical, and aesthetical...political projects" (Mignolo, 2000, p. xvi) that move beyond reforming disciplinary learning in ways that do not dismantle its settled logic (Esmonde & Booker, 2017; Politics of Learning Writing Collective, 2017; Stetsenko, 2018). Toward this end we have put forward three sensibilities crucial to liberatory forms of disciplinary learning: multiplicity, horizontality, and dialogicality. We argue that these sensibilities constitute a new horizon for radical heterogeneity and create the pedagogical conditions for enacting the political and ethical commitments of critique, refusal, delinking, and re-imagining learning as "a genuine multiplicity of trajectories, and thus potentially of voices" (Massey, 2005, p. 55). In a world where empire building based in Western supremacy is rapidly losing intelligibility as an adequate response to the onto-epistemic devastation of our times (Lear, 2006), radical heterogeneity impels creative acts of epistemic disobedience (Mignolo, 2011) that nurture learning and thriving.

The stories of disciplinary learning and teaching featured in this chapter illustrate what becomes speakable when disciplinary discourse and activity break away from settled expectations rooted in racial, epistemic, and linguistic hierarchies (Anzaldúa, 1987; Bang et al., 2012; Rosa & Flores, 2017; Rosebery, Warren, & Tucker-Raymond, 2016). In them, we see young people rupturing matrices of power by expressing their desire for onto-epistemic heterogeneity, or by wrestling with complex, sometimes contradictory, meanings of heteroglossic texts within processes of socio-political education. Not having yet been disciplined into dominant Western ideology, or actively resisting it as a form of enclosure to their learning and becoming, they readily attune to disciplines as moving fields where a multiplicity of words, points of view, tones, and values demands attention. In these ways, young people invite us into encounters where radical heterogeneity can thrive, if we, in our roles as educators or researchers, are willing to join with their openings and not be overcome by anxieties born of Cartesian influences or the closures of zero point epistemologies (Mignolo, 2009; Shotter, 2006a, 2006b).

We also see educators taking up the disciplines as open, living entanglements with historical, present, and future heterogeneities. They wrestle with settled disciplinary namings and framings to change the terms of the conversation and engage critically with the political and intellectual histories that have shaped them. Their efforts to conjure new language and new worlds reverberate at multiple scales at once locally meaningful and world-making. Indeed, the more attentive and relationally responsive educators become to these dialogically structured openings (Shotter, 2015), the more ordinary, i.e., practiced, the work to delink from colonial matrices of power can become.

This chapter reflects our joint exploration of what could become possible when we take the interwoven sensibilities of multiplicity, horizontality, and dialogicality as movements toward creating the relational grounds for what we might think of as withness-pedagogies, building from Shotter (2015), that make expansive world-making, delinked from empire building, possible. This kind of pedagogical imaginary respects what young people are already thinking and desiring (Tuck, 2009); at the same time, it profoundly shifts the work of teaching away from oppressive languages of mastery toward insurgent, generative language that, in Morrison's (1993) words, "arcs toward the place where meaning may lie." If, as seems increasingly true, "life is outrunning the pedagogies in which we have been trained" (Fischer, 2003, p. 23), then it becomes ever more imperative that we center a relational ethics in our research and pedagogies in order to nourish visions of disciplinary practice that grapple creatively with the world as it is and imagine the world as it might be.

References

Anzaldúa, G. (1987). *Borderlands: La frontera*. San Francisco, CA: Aunt Lute.

Bagemihl, B. (1999). *Biological Exuberance: Animal Homosexuality and Natural Diversity*. New York, NY: St. Martin's Press.

Bakhtin, M.M. (1981). *The Dialogic Imagination: Four Essays*. Austin, TX: University of Texas Press.

Bang, M., Curley, L., Kessel, A., Marin, A., Suzukovich III, E.S., & Strack, G. (2014). Muskrat theories, tobacco in the streets, and living Chicago as Indigenous land. *Environmental Education Research, 20*(1), 37–55.

Bang, M., Marin, A., & Medin, D. (2018). If Indigenous peoples stand with the sciences, will scientists stand with us? *Daedalus, 147*(2), 148–159.

Bang, M., & Vossoughi, S. (2016). Participatory design research and educational justice: Studying learning and relations within social change making. *Cognition and Instruction, 34*(3), 173–193.

Bang, M., Warren, B., Rosebery, A.S., & Medin, D. (2012). Desettling expectations in science education. *Human Development, 55*(5–6), 302–318.

Barajas-López, F. (2014). Mexican immigrant students' schooling experiences and the construction of disengagement in mathematics learning contexts. *Journal of Latinos and Education, 13*(1), 14–32.

Barton, A.C., & Tan, E. (2018). *STEM-Rich Maker Learning: Designing for Equity with Youth of Color*. New York, NY: Teachers College Press.

Bell, P., Tzou, C., Bricker, L., & Baines, A.D. (2012). Learning in diversities of structures of social practice: Accounting for how, why and where people learn science. *Human Development, 55*(5–6), 269–284.

Blaser, M. (2014). *Missing Microbes: How the Overuse of Antibiotics Is Fueling Our Modern Plagues*. New York, NY: Picador.

Booker, A., & Goldman, S. (2016). Participatory design research as a practice for systemic repair: Doing hand-in-hand math research with families. *Cognition and Instruction, 34*(3), 222–235.

Cole, M., & Griffin, P. (1980). Cultural amplifiers reconsidered. In: D. Olson (Ed.), *Social Foundations of Language and Thought* (pp. 343–364). New York, NY: W.W. Norton.

Dubinsky, E., & Moses, R.P. (March 2011). Philosophy, math research, math ed research, K–16 education, and the Civil Rights Movement: A synthesis. *Notices of the AMS, 58*(3), 401–409.

Engeström, Y. (1996). Development as breaking away and opening up: A challenge to Vygotsky and Piaget. *Swiss Journal of Psychology, 55*(2–3), 126–132.

Esmonde, I., & Booker, A.N. (2017). Learning discourses of race and mathematics in classroom interaction: A poststructural perspective. In: I. Esmonde & A. Booker (Eds.), *Power and Privilege in the Learning Sciences* (pp. 68–87). New York, NY: Routledge.

Espinoza, M. (2009). A case study of the production of educational sanctuary in one migrant classroom. *Pedagogies: An International Journal, 4*(1), 44–62.

Espinoza, M., & Vossoughi, S. (2014). Perceiving learning anew: Social interaction, dignity and educational rights. *Harvard Educational Review, 84*(3), 285–313.

Fischer, M.M.J. (2003). *Emergent Forms of Life and the Anthropological Voice.* Chapel Hill, NC: Duke University Press.

Gates, H.L. (1984). *Black Literature and Literary Theory.* New York, NY: Methuen.

Gates, H.L. (1988). *The Signifying Monkey: A Theory of Afro-American Literary Criticism.* New York, NY: Oxford University Press.

González, N., Moll, L., & Amanti, C. (2005). *Funds of Knowledge: Theorizing Practices in Households, Communities, and Classrooms.* Mahwah, NJ: Lawrence Erlbaum Associates.

Grosfoguel, R. (2013). The structure of knowledge in Westernized universities: Epistemic racism/sexism and the four genocides/epistemicides of the long 16th century. *Human Architecture: Journal of the Sociology of Self-Knowledge, XI*(1), 73–90.

Gutiérrez, K. (2008). Developing a sociocritical literacy in the Third Space. *Reading Research Quarterly, 43*(2), 148–164.

Gutiérrez, K., & Rogoff, B. (2003). Cultural ways of learning: Individual traits or repertoires of practice. *Educational Researcher, 32*(5), 19–25.

Gutiérrez, R. (2013). The sociopolitical turn in mathematics education. *Journal for Research in Mathematics Education, 44*(1), 37–68.

Gutiérrez, R. (2017). Living mathematx: Towards a vision for the future. *Philosophy of Mathematics Education Journal, 32*(1), 1–34.

Harding, S. (Ed.) (1993). *The "Racial" Economy of Science: Toward a Democratic Future.* Indianapolis, IN: Indiana University Press.

Jaber, L., & Hammer, D. (2016). Engaging in science: A feeling for the discipline. *Journal of the Learning Sciences, 25*(2), 156–202.

Latour, B. (1988). *Science in Action.* Cambridge, MA: Harvard University Press.

Leander, K.M., & Ehret, C. (Eds.) (2019). *Affect in Literacy Teaching and Learning: Pedagogies, Politics, and Coming to Know.* New York, NY: Routledge.

Leander, K.M., Phillips, N.C., & Taylor, K.H. (2010). The changing social spaces of learning: Mapping new mobilities. *Review of Research in Education, 34*(1), 329–394.

Lear, J. (2006). *Radical Hope.* Cambridge, MA: Harvard University Press.

Lee, C.D. (1995). A culturally based cognitive apprenticeship. Teaching African American high school students' skills in literary interpretation. *Reading Research Quarterly, 30*(4), 608–631.

Lee, C.D. (2000). Signifying in the zone of proximal development. In: C.D. Lee & P. Smagorinsky (Eds.), *Vygotskian Perspectives on Literacy Research: Constructing Meaning through Collaborative Inquiry* (pp. 191–225). Cambridge, England: Cambridge University Press.

Lee, V.R. (Ed.) (2015). *Learning Technologies and the Body: Integration and Implementation in Formal and Informal Learning Environments.* New York, NY: Routledge.

Lyons, S.C. (2000). Rhetorical sovereignty: What do American Indians want from writing? *College Composition and Communication, 51*(3), 447–468.

Ma, J.Y. (2016). Designing disruptions for productive hybridity: The case of walking scale geometry. *Journal of the Learning Sciences, 25*(3), 335–371.

Marin, A., & Bang, M. (2018). "Look it, this is how you know": Family forest walks as a context for knowledge-building about the natural world. *Cognition and Instruction, 36*(2), 89–118.

Martin, D.B. (2006). Mathematics learning and participation as racialized forms of experience: African American parents speak on the struggle for mathematics literacy. *Mathematical Thinking and Learning, 8*(3), 197–229.

Massey, D. (2005). *For Space.* London: Sage.

Matusov, E. (2009). *Journey into Dialogic Pedagogy.* New York: Nova Science Publishers, Inc.

McKinney de Royston, M., & Sengupta-Irving, T. (2019). Another step forward: Engaging the political in learning. *Cognition and Instruction, 37*(3), 277–284.

Medin, D.L., & Bang, M. (2014). *Who's Asking? Native Science, Western Science, and Science Education.* Cambridge, MA: MIT Press.

Melamed, J. (2011). *Represent and Destroy: Rationalizing Violence in the New Racial Capitalism.* Minneapolis, MN: University of Minnesota Press.

Mensah, F.M. (2019). Finding voice and passion: Critical race theory methodology in science teacher education. *American Educational Research Journal, 56*(4), 1412–1456.

Mignolo, W.D. (2000). *Local Histories/Global Designs.* Princeton, NJ: Princeton University Press.

Mignolo, W.D. (2007). Delinking: The rhetoric of modernity, the logic of coloniality and the grammar of de-coloniality. *Cultural Studies, 21*(2–3), 449–514.

Mignolo, W.D. (2009). Epistemic disobedience, independent thought and de-colonial freedom. *Theory, Culture and Society, 26*(7–8), 1–23.

Mignolo, W.D. (2011). Epistemic disobedience and the decolonial option: A manifesto. *Transmodernity, 1*(2), 44–66.

Moll, L. (2000). Inspired by Vygotsky: Ethnographic experiments in education. In: C. Lee & P. Smagorinsky (Eds.), *Vygotskian Perspectives on Literacy Research: Constructing Meaning through Collaborative Inquiry* (pp. 256–268). Cambridge: Cambridge University Press.

Moll, L.C., & Greenberg, J. (1992). Creating zones of possibilities: Combining social contexts for instruction. In: L.C. Moll (Ed.), *Vygotsky and Education* (pp. 319–348). Cambridge: Cambridge University Press.

Morrison, T. (1989). Unspeakable things unspoken: The Afro-American presence in American literature. *Michigan Quarterly Review, XXVII*(1), 1–34.

Morrison, T. (1993). *The Nobel Lecture in Literature, 1993.* Nobel Prize.org, 1993, https://www.nobelprize.org/prizes/literature/1993/morrison/lecture/.

Nasir, N.S. (2012). *Racialized Identities: Race and Achievement among African American Youth.* Stanford, CA: Stanford University Press.

Nasir, N.S., Hand, V., & Taylor, E.V. (2008). Culture and mathematics in school: Boundaries between "cultural" and "domain" knowledge in the mathematics classroom and beyond. *Review of Research in Education, 32*(1), 187–240.

Nasir, N., Rosebery, A., Warren, B., & Lee, C.D. (2006/2014). Learning as a cultural process: Achieving equity through diversity. In: K. Sawyer (Ed.), *Cambridge Handbook of the Learning Sciences* (pp. 489–504). Cambridge: Cambridge University Press.

National Science Foundation, National Center for Science and Engineering Statistics. (2019). *Women, Minorities, and Persons with Disabilities in Science and Engineering: 2019.* Special Report NSF 19–304. Alexandria, VA. https://www.nsf.gov/statistics/wmpd.

Nemerov, H. (1969). On metaphor. *The Virginia Quarterly Review, 45,* 621–636.

Paxson, H., & Helmreich, S. (2014). The perils and promises of microbial abundance: Novel natures and model ecosystems, from artisanal cheese to alien seas. *Social Studies of Science, 44*(2), 165–193.

Philip, T.M. (2019). Principled improvisation to support novice teacher learning. *Teachers College Record, 121,* 1–32.

Philip, T.M., Gupta, A., Turpen, C., & Elby, A. (2018). Why ideology matters for learning: A case of ideological convergence in an engineering ethics classroom discussion on drone warfare. *Journal of the Learning Sciences, 27*(2), 183–223.

Philip, T.M., Olivares-Pasillas, M.C., & Rocha, J. (2016). Becoming racially literate about data and data literate about race: A case of data visualizations in the classroom as a site of racial-ideological micro-contestations. *Cognition and Instruction, 34*(4), 361–388.

Pierotti, R. (2011). *Indigenous Knowledge, Ecology, and Evolutionary Biology.* New York, NY: Routledge.

The Politics of Learning Writing Collective. (2017). The learning sciences in a new era of U.S. Nationalism. *Cognition and Instruction.* doi:10.1080/07370008.2017.1282486.

Richardson, T. (2011). Navigating the problem of inclusion as enclosure in native culture-based education: Theorizing shadow curriculum. *Curriculum Inquiry, 41*(3), 332–349.

Rickford, J.R. (1999). *African American Vernacular English: Features, Evolution, Educational Implications.* Malden, MA: Wiley-Blackwell.

Rogoff, B. (2003). *The Cultural Nature of Human Development.* New York, NY: Oxford University Press.

Rosa, J., & Flores, N. (2017). Unsettling race and language: Toward a raciolinguistic perspective. *Language in Society, 46*(5), 621–647.

Rosebery, A.S., Ogonowski, M., DiSchino, M., & Warren, B. (2010). "The coat traps all your body heat": Heterogeneity as fundamental to learning. *The Journal of the Learning Sciences, 19*(3), 322–357.

Rosebery, A.S., Warren, B., & Tucker-Raymond, E. (2016). Developing interpretive power in science teaching. *Journal of Research in Science Teaching, 53*(10), 1571–1600.

Shotter, J. (2006a). Understanding process from within: An argument for 'withness'-thinking. *Organization Studies, 27*(4), 585–604.

Shotter, J. (2006b). Participative thinking. In: Y. Haila & C. Dyke (Eds.), *How Nature Speaks: The Dynamics of the Human Ecological Condition* (pp. 106–126). Durham, NC: Duke University Press.

Shotter, J. (2015). On being dialogical: An ethics of 'attunement'. *Context, 137,* 8–11.

Smith, L.T. (2012). *Decolonizing Methodologies: Research and Indigenous Peoples.* London: Zed Books Ltd.

Smitherman, G. (2000). *Talkin That Talk: Language, Culture and Education in African America.* London: Routledge.

Stetsenko, A. (2018). Research and activist projects of resistance: The ethical-political foundations for a transformative ethico-onto-epistemology. *Learning, Culture and Social Interaction.* doi:10.1016/j.lcsi.2018.04.002.

Stevens, R. (2012). The missing bodies of mathematical thinking and learning have been found. *Journal of the Learning Sciences, 21*(2), 337–346.

Tan, E., Barton, A.C., & Benavides, A. (2019). Engineering for sustainable communities: Epistemic tools in support of equitable and consequential middle school engineering. *Science Education, 103*, 1011–1046.

Tate, W.F. (Ed.) (1996). Urban schools and mathematics reform: Implementing new standards. *Urban Education, 30*(4), 379–521.

Taylor, E.V. (2009). The purchasing practice of low-income students: The relationship to mathematical development. *Journal of the Learning Sciences, 18*(3), 370–415.

Taylor, K.H. (2017). Learning along lines: Locative literacies for reading and writing the city. *Journal of the Learning Sciences, 26*(4), 533–574.

Taylor, K.H., & Hall, R. (2013). Counter-mapping the neighborhood on bicycles: Mobilizing youth to reimagine the city. *Technology, Knowledge, and Learning, 18*(1–2), 1–29.

Tejeda, C., Espinoza, M., & Gutiérrez, K. (2003). Toward a decolonizing pedagogy: Social justice reconsidered. In: P. Trifonas (Ed.), *Pedagogies of Difference* (pp. 10–40). New York, NY: Routledge Falmer Press.

Tuck, E. (2009). Suspending damage: A letter to communities. *Harvard Educational Review, 79*(3), 409–428.

Tucker-Raymond, E., Gravel, B., Kohberger, K., & Browne, K. (2017). Source code and a screwdriver: STEM literacy practices in fabricating activities among experienced makers. *Journal of Adolescent and Adult Literacy, 60*(6), 617–627.

Vakil, S., & Higgs, J. (2019). It's about power: A call to rethink ethics and equity in computing education. *Communications of the ACM, 62*(3), 31–33.

Vizenor, G. (2000). *Fugitive Poses: Native American Scenes of Absence and Presence.* Lincoln, NE: University of Nebraska Press.

Vossoughi, S. (2011). *On the Formation of Intellectual Kinship: A Qualitative Case Study of Literacy, Learning, and Social Analysis in a Summer Migrant Education Program.* (University of California, Los Angeles). ProQuest Dissertations and Theses (p. 299).

Vossoughi, S. (2014). Social analytic artifacts made concrete: A study of learning and political education. *Mind, Culture and Activity, 21*(4), 353–373.

Vossoughi, S., & Gutiérrez, K. (2014). Toward a multi-sited ethnographic sensibility. In: J. Vadeboncoeur (Ed.), *Learning in and Across Contexts: Reimagining Education NSSE Yearbook, 113(2)* (pp. 603–632). New York, NY: Teachers College Press.

Vossoughi, S., & Gutiérrez, K. (2017). Critical pedagogy and socio-cultural theories of learning. In: I. Esmonde & A. Booker (Eds.), *Power & Privilege in the Learning Sciences.* New York, NY: Routledge.

Wald, C., & Wu, C. (2010). Of mice and women: The bias in animal models. *Science, 327*(5973), 1571–1572.

Warren, B., Ogonowski, M., & Pothier, S. (2005). "Everyday" and "scientific": Rethinking dichotomies in modes of thinking in science learning. In: R. Nemirovsky, A.S. Rosebery, J. Solomon & B. Warren (Eds.), *Everyday Matters in Science and Mathematics: Studies of Complex Classroom Events* (pp. 119–148). Mahwah, NJ: Lawrence Erlbaum.

Warren, B., & Rosebery, A. (2011). Navigating interculturality: African American male students and the science classroom. *Journal of African American Males in Education, 2*(1), 98–115.

Wright, C.G. (2019). Constructing a collaborative critique-learning environment for exploring science through improvisational performance. *Urban Education, 54*(9), 1319–1348.

PART 4

Reframing and Studying the Cultural Nature of Learning

Introduction

Understanding learning as inescapably cultural requires appreciating how learning is linked to ways of knowing, doing, and being that dynamically unfold across time and contexts, and in relation to systems of power. Disrupting the boundary between learning *and* culture as separate, yet intertwined, entities to an understanding of *learning as cultural* also means we must interrogate and rethink how we study learning. This process involves rethinking prior conceptualizations and approaches, as well as being open to novel and innovative interpretations and methods. The chapters in this section clarify what it means to engage in research when we take seriously how we think about learning as cultural for everyone, not just those who have been historically essentialized or exceptionalized via race, gender, class, ability, and other dynamics of power. By design, these chapters reach across the boundaries of disciplinary literatures—including anthropology, economics, ethnic studies, gender and women studies, linguistics, philosophy, and political science—to raise key conceptual and methodological issues that educational research must begin to address.

Annamma and Booker analyze how conceptions of diversity get wielded as a "weapon of normativity" within discussions of learning that essentialize difference. They examine how power and normativity are inscribed in discussions of learning and within learning contexts, yet can be disrupted through using intersectional analyses and practices of solidarity. Similarly interrogating long-held conceptualizations in education, Dixon-Román, Jackson, and McKinney de Royston desettle the distinction between quantitative and qualitative research by rethinking debates about nature versus nurture in the context of racialized, gendered, and otherwise "othered" bodies and realities. Also pushing on the boundaries of educational research and theory, Gutiérrez, Jurow, and Vakil examine the political and ethical dimensions of social design-based research as a methodology concerned with possible futures and "human flourishing." Foregrounding a discussion of this methodology's principles, such as historicity and prolepsis, they use two compelling cases to illustrate the dynamic and relational actions that require a researcher's constant attention to sustain the goals of this methodology.

Continuing the thread of imagining possible futures, Penuel considers the cultural and relational nature of *models of organization* that hold promise for creating equitable change within educational systems and communities. Reminding us that equity-oriented institutional change always occurs in the contexts of normative and sociopolitical challenges, Penuel takes a cultural approach to the study of organizations that seeks to understand how to construct and sustain long-term relations

Reframing and Studying the Cultural Nature of Learning

among people, tools, and settings. Finally, Gomez, Biag, and Imig examine the cross-cultural challenges of effectively preparing educational leaders capable of forming and sustaining cross-institutional connections that facilitate the learning of each and every child. The authors demonstrate how educational leaders must be encouraged to negotiate meaning and achieve "hybridity" in order to grapple with the vexing problems of education.

17

INTEGRATING INTERSECTIONALITY INTO THE STUDY OF LEARNING

Subini Ancy Annamma and Angela Booker

> How do we resist simplistic assumptions about the meaning of group membership and develop more nuanced and complex research agendas that work from a basic assumption that human beings always have agency, always have resources, and make meaning of their experiences in varied ways?
>
> —*Carol D. Lee (2003)*

In this conceptual review, we revisit how diversity was conceptualized by Nasir, Roseberry, Warren, and Lee (2006) who, "argue for a more sophisticated understanding of diversity and learning—one that shows schools they can use diversity to enhance learning, rather than simply viewing it as a problem to overcome" (p. 688). We return to this conception of diversity to (1) juxtapose how diversity continues to be taken up in educational discourse and practices in ways that maintain inequitable power dynamics; and (2) build on and expand how we respond to difference in learning contexts in both practice and research. Here we define difference as human variation in bodyminds—or "the intertwinement of the mental and the physical" (Schalk, 2018)—which is normal and expected. Carol Lee's words in our epigraph guide us through these conversations of how to organize (practice) and study (research) culture in heterogenous learning environments.

To do this, we begin with an inquiry into ways that diversity has been conceptualized as representation and how this conception yields particular forms of (re)production in practice and problem-framing when responding to difference in learning contexts. We then engage a critical interrogation of diversity projects, which we conceptualize as the *practices* that are informed by conceiving diversity as representation, as a mirror for making hegemonic forces more legible. To bring these dialogues to life, we examine school discipline as a case for recognizing the impacts of reductive approaches to diversity, and, in turn, the expansive role that conceptions of intersectionality and Disability Critical Race Theory (DisCrit, Annamma, Connor, & Ferri, 2013) can play in unseating reductive conceptions of difference as the enemy of normativity. We argue that theories of learning must explicitly identify how power is inscribed in all learning contexts in order to effectively sever difference from hegemonic conceptions of diversity where normal is situated as desirable. We conclude by emancipating difference from normativity through identifying moves toward solidarity and the ways intersectionality reveals vulnerability alongside repertoires of resistance that reveal ingenuity in the face of oppression. Ultimately, this review explores what happens when intersectional theory (Crenshaw, 1991) disrupts typical discussions of learning and identity that essentialize difference or avoid explicit articulations of power.

Conceptions of Diversity as Representation

The central proposition of this handbook is "that issues of culture are fundamental to the scientific study of learning" (Nasir, Lee, Pea, & McKinney de Royston, this issue). This proposition recognizes that culture, "the changing ways of life of societies and groups. The networks of meaning which individuals and groups used to make sense of and communicate with one another" (Hall, 1989/1992, p. 10), is infused with "ways in which the colonizing experience had indeed threaded itself through the imaginary of the whole culture, what one can only call racism" (Hall, 1989/1992, p. 13). Though Hall is specifically referring to the English context, these sentiments are applicable to the United States as well, where the foundation of segregation was built on viewing Black and Indigenous people as deficient and white people as superior. Whiteness was set as the norm in which all others were measured (Ladson-Billings, 1998).

When schools became less racially homogenous during "second-class integration" (Walker, 2009) wherein the firing of Black teachers meant, "the destruction of a system that both sought to eradicate injustice and foster psychological resilience in the face of overt oppression within black boys and girls" (p. 273), white teachers were forced to educate multiply marginalized—those at the intersections of multiple and cumulative systemic injustices (e.g., racism, ableism) (Cyrus, 2017)—children of color[1]. What often occurred was both a forcing of multiply marginalized Black children to act more like white children and punishing them when they did not (Tyack, 1974). This became a narrow yet popular conception of diversity, as Maxine Greene (1993) noted,

> I become somewhat obsessive about what diversity ought to signify in a democracy. At once, I keep pondering the meanings of inclusion and wondering how it can occur without the kind of normalization that wipes out differences, forcing them to be repressed, to become matters of shame rather than pride.

Decades later, we ponder similar questions about diversity to those that Greene (1993) and Nasir and colleagues (2006) did. When is diversity something substantive that can mediate a recognition of "learning to be a culturally heterogeneous process of engagement in repertoires of practices" (Nasir et al., 2006, p. 699) and when is it wielded as a weapon of normativity, aiming to punish difference?

Why Diversity?

It is essential to note that diversity is not the only term we could have examined in relationship to how to take seriously the study of culture within heterogenous learning environments. Conceptions of inclusion (as noted in Greene's quote above) or equity, which have gained increased use, could also be explored in relationship to difference in learning contexts. What we take seriously is how these conceptions are imbued in practice and research in learning contexts and how these discourses reify instantiations of power. We focus on the conception of diversity specifically because it continues to be (mis)used as a way to position:

> nondominant students and communities as different or deficient...From this viewpoint, the proper way to address diversity is to help nondominant groups become more like dominant groups. In this chapter, we reject this historically dated view and argue for a more sophisticated understanding of diversity and learning—one that shows schools they can use diversity to enhance learning, rather than simply viewing it as a problem to overcome.
>
> *(Nasir et al., 2006, p. 688)*

Hence, conceptions of diversity—within a view of learning that focuses on making the multiply marginalized more like the powerful—ignores the ways power is inscribed in learning contexts and the resulting damage. We also focus on diversity because it is an active, catch-all conception of difference (and related institutional projects) and what role difference plays in learning contexts.

We posit that difference, as a conceptual idea, is broader than diversity. Difference is constantly emerging, with experiences of difference being deeply dynamic. By contrast, diversity projects—the practices that align with narrow conceptions of diversity—often essentialize difference, assuming experiences of those categorized as different are the same (Harris, 1990). This gives rise to politicized experiences of diversity, where change is a risk to be mitigated through signs of assimilation of those marked as different, while institutions maintain stratifications of power (Lee, 2003). Diversity projects can require a recalibration back to the norm, situating the powerful as the right kind of diverse. For example, bilingualism can be prized and celebrated in white people while being shunned and discouraged for people of color. These raciolinguistic ideologies contribute to people of color being "constructed as linguistically deviant even when engaging in linguistic practices positioned as normative or innovative when produced by privileged white subjects" (Flores & Rosa, 2015, p. 150). Thus, diversity does the work of triage rather than transformation. The wounds are cognitive, social, and historical—the blight of accepted injustice. These wounds harm *all* involved, though awareness of harm varies by socio-historical position. Our concern here is why and how educators and scholars can contend with this dynamic, persistent, and urgent set of conditions, as we hold responsibility for designing learning contexts. We argue that if educators and scholars resisted a structurally favored norm, difference would not be equated with deficiency; instead variation would be expected and welcomed.

Creating Deviance Out of Difference

In describing the origins of cultural studies, Stuart Hall (1989/1992) indicted the ways difference has been the underlying root of power disparities and the responsibility society has in response:

> If you go to analyze racism today in its complex structures and dynamics, one question, one principle above all, emerges as a lesson for us. It is the fear—the terrifying, internal fear—of living with *difference*. This fear arises as the consequence of the fatal coupling of difference and power. And, in that sense, the work that cultural studies has to do is to mobilize everything that it can find in terms of intellectual resources in order to understand what keeps making the lives we live, and the societies we live in, profoundly and deeply anti-humane in their capacity to live with difference.
>
> *(italics in original, p. 17–18)*

Hall referred to the myriad symbolic, material, geographic, and discursive ways in which access to power has been concentrated and inscribed as an inverse function of normativity and deficiency (Hall, Segal, & Osborne, 1997). Said differently, the closer to the norm (e.g., white, male, able, straight, cisgender) one is perceived, the more property and therefore power to which one is allowed access (Harris, 1993; Leonardo & Broderick, 2011).

Learning is a collective and communal endeavor, requiring persistent ethical and open-eyed engagements with power relations that flow through people, activity, and learning environments (Freire, 1970; Lave & Wenger, 1991; Cole, Engeström, & Vasquez, 1997; Gutiérrez, 2008; McDermott, 2014; Esmonde & Booker, 2016). However, when ongoing conceptions of diversity remain shallow and synonymous with essentialization and assimilation that (re)produce power relations, reductive prescriptions for extending access to problematic learning contexts for the under-represented tend to emerge. Diversity projects that yield counts of types of people but stop short of conceiving shared responsibility for learning to change and be changed by one another tend to prioritize stable and hierarchical power dynamics. In turn, diversity projects are susceptible to being applied as reductive tools that obscure the fullness of human experience and hinder learning—which is, at the root, an ongoing act of communication and contribution.

Fortunately, there has been a historical arc of scholarship and literature in theory, method, and practice that challenges the misuse of diversity in learning and organizes, in its place, fully conceived relations among people, environment, cultural history, and forms of knowledge that support difference. This work rendered power relations visible through accounts of subtle and insidious reduction of human practice into categories of normative and deficient through classed, gendered, racialized, and other separations of difference that divide neighborhoods, schools, jobs, and the always varying activities of daily life (Willis, 1977; Heath, 1983; Eckert, 1989; Varenne & McDermott, 1998). "[R]outine cultural contexts," were theorized in relation to "different developmental domains" that ranged from the cultural historical to the microgenetic (Cole, Engeström, & Vásquez, 1997). Learning and the ongoing circulation of knowledge were rendered as legible cultural and socio-historical processes rooted in communities and shared practices (Lave & Wenger, 1991; Gutiérrez & Rogoff, 2003; González, Moll, & Amanti, 2005). In each case, the work has moved well beyond a minimally conceived idea of diversity as acceptable normativity. Despite this robust body of work, difference has continued to be understood as deficiency, thus we take seriously the difficulty of reinforced power relations that follow thin, representational understandings of diversity and their constraining force in learning contexts.

Conditions emerging from diversity's misconception in learning contexts present a critical opportunity to take on ethical responsibility for learning and power (Torres, 2005; Booker, 2016; Zavala, 2018). In this chapter, we focus on one way the concept of diversity has been misused to constrain learning as a collective and justice-oriented practice. We will not trace the lineage of critiques of racialized and classed hierarchies, as that has been done thoroughly elsewhere and is beyond the scope of this chapter (for excellent reviews see Lee, 2003; Nasir & Hand, 2006; and McDermott, 2014). Our concern is with how practice works and how research responds when diversity as a discourse gets leveraged as a representational answer or a solution to a responsibility problem in which power is not considered as an organizing aspect of learning.

Practices of Diversity That Reinscribe Power

What work does diversity do? We ask this question specifically in the context of learning. Diversity projects—those that move institutions toward superficially including difference, particularly along historically stratified lines of normative categories (e.g., white, male, heterosexual)—mark out a space for noting difference *while* masking the interdependence between normativity and the Other that maintains a status quo and exercises power over difference (Hall, 1989/1992). A limitation of diversity projects is insufficient attention to power dynamics that are infused with the very same supremacist logics that gave rise to the need for such projects at the outset. These supremacist logics find the Other as different and therefore deficient in bodyminds; an ableist view. Campbell (2014) states, "An ableist imaginary tells us what a healthy body means – a normal mind, the pace and tenor of thinking and the kinds of emotions and affect that are suitable to express" (p. 80). Hence supremacist logics (e.g., racism, deficit thinking, cultural deprivation) are infused with ableism.

These biological or cultural supremacist logics, at minimum, set limits on learning and learners from the start. Whether learning is conceived as a process of changing cognitive capacity or changing access to participation, supremacist logics suggest learning is contestable in the face of fixed capacity. What would such a system have to learn from the so-called Other? At minimum, a diversity project in such a system is in danger of organizing practices that establish a form of unintentional charity rather than solidarity (Freire, 1970; Hall, 1992).

Yet robust understandings of the dynamics of culture and the ongoing relational negotiations of environment, experience, and meaning frame learning as reciprocal, resourceful, and agentic. Change through practice and reflection—individual and collective—is the foundation of learning rather than the fixed capacities of individual minds as separated from bodies. A rigid and resistant environment, then, is not a natural phenomenon providing evidence of supremacy but rather a set of complex activities persistently connoting difference as the necessary enemy of power. And potential enemies must be constantly proving themselves loyal, constantly surveilled, carefully controlled, and sometimes eliminated. In learning environments, these are devastating constraints.

Learning in this context focuses on demonstrations of developmental likeness. Successful instantiations of diversity programs seek to reveal students, who have been marked as in some way diverse, to be capable of what normatively marked students are also capable (Nasir et al., 2006). People become proofs of their potential for normative likeness, even as their diverseness "become[s a matter] of shame rather than pride" (Greene, 1993, p. 212). If, on the other hand, the diverse student fails, it is branded as individual failure without indicating anything other than personal fault. This type of learning context is hazardous for the marked subject, but the system seeking to instantiate the diversity project of counting representation remains seemingly unscathed. All of the exposure to risk is embodied by the marked subject when normativity is used to define change as representational, and no demand for reciprocal learning or structural or institutional change is sought or met.

This diversity project is a good systemic bet for institutions, school systems included. The exposure is low, and the potential payoff is high. It looks good for the institution, aesthetically and philosophically, to include a few bodies noticeably marked by difference without changing the institutional structures. For example, college brochures have been found to provide images of diversity to prospective students that were significantly different than the actual student population (Pippert, Essenburg, & Matchett, 2013). Simultaneously, efforts at increasing the enrolment of students of color is being fought even by the Department of Justice (see *Students for Fair Admissions, V. Harvard*). When students of color fail under these circumstances, a mismatch between skills and expectations is blamed instead of the institutions, which refuse to support these learners (Jackson, 2011). Responsibility to open a visible pathway for diverse groups asks little in terms of institutional change in learning contexts—in fact, it can be something an institution fights against while using the discourse of diversity—and in turn, little change in power relations occurs. It is clear that educators and scholars need tools to persist, ethically and productively, in this change effort together, in mutually transformative ways.

Diversity as an idea is itself not horrible, but can be put to work for a few specific aims. The work most prominently undertaken does only part of the necessary labor (though even this is limited by slow speed and minimal progress). That part is to crack open various ports of entry to individuals acquired as representationally "diverse" (McDermott, 1993) through necessary critiques. What happens next is historically predictable and indicative of how responsibility was conceived and distributed among people living out the material and conceptual impacts of our active conceptions of diversity. People are counted, percentages are reported, critics argue people's displacement or exclusion, and the newly included are pressed to conform to existing systems and to share some form of accrued credit with the institution organizing the diversity project or to drop out (taking on full responsibility for failure). If this diversity project does not sound like contribution or collective continuance, it is because a hierarchical and bureaucratic system is sustained, relatively unchanged (Weber, 1978) while people are either poorly sustained or sustained at unaccountable cost. The diversity project here is representational without the requisite implications of the concept: the system responds to a societal necessity, but it is not sufficient. Things *look* different and, in a meaningful way, they *are* different because a handful of the less powerful are present and potentially included. The people, and our embodied experiences, have shuffled. Possibility has arrived.

Diversity as a Measuring Stick of Learning in Pedagogical Practice

As the possibility of diversity arrived and began to be put forward as a measure of success to support difference in learning contexts, it became equated with specific pedagogical moves. Specifically, in practice, diversity became a curricular overlay, a set of learning styles, and corresponding pedagogical strategies. Measuring diversity projects, and gathering evidence of its sightings in research, began to reduce participation rights. This was achieved through a set of moves that organized counts of diverse markers, then argued the goal had been reached, thereby eliminating the need for correctives like affirmative action and disciplinary developments like ethnic studies (e.g., California's passage of Proposition 209 in 1996 prohibiting consideration of racial/ethnic identity and gender in public education, and Arizona's 2010 effort to ban ethnic studies in public schools through HB 2281). These approaches toward diversity projects are not undertaken with an openness to *being changed by* the presence of people with a broader range of experiences, either institutionally or curricularly.

Yet, when multiply marginalized communities of color experienced repeated erasure from curricula, diversity was presented as the solution. As diversity projects became the answer to an all-white curriculum, educators and researchers often imagined diversity as minimal representation wherein examples of different identities in the classroom were all that was needed (Au, Brown, & Calderón, 2016). Reading an article about Martin Luther King or Rosa Parks was enough to honor Black History Month. Mentioning Sally Ride as the first female in space or Katherine Johnson (especially since the movie *Hidden Figures* came out) as a Black mathematician checked off box(es) of representation. Yet this overlaying of Black and Brown stories on top of a curriculum rooted in whiteness does little to disrupt the ways white superiority was imbued within curriculum overall. Instead, this curricular overlay superimposes singular identities on top of the curriculum to illustrate exceptional successes without disrupting the hegemony beneath. Consequently, the diversity project of curricular overlay is a transparent covering, leaving nothing altered.

While some theorists responded to heterogenous learning contexts with reframed logics of diversity such as learning styles and strategies to address difference in styles—a reductive notion of learning—critical learning theorists sought to conceptualize full participation through cultural practices and honoring cultural ways of knowing and learning as inherently cultural. Still, processes of reduction predictably persist because these practices are tuned to individual identities rather than collective positionalities and because they ask little in the way of systemic or institutional change in power relations. In practice, then, we argue that diversity projects have been leveraged and deployed as a process of containment and assimilation as it is trapped within a view of learning that centers representation and thus, renders power relations invisible.

This is a fear that people express when it comes to diversity in particular—that it means we all must change. Yet, that is precisely what we ask of learners. Let us consider these complex challenges and ideas as an invitation for change—change that is both reciprocal and responsive to what newcomers and people grappling with marginalization on multiple scales bring to learning contexts. How do we make these changes together? This work requires us to establish and sustain a shared project of recognizing power relations inscribed within learning. Where we fail to meet these challenges together—for they are always met but often only by those who bear the historically levied costs—we produce diversity projects as acts of containment.

Diversity as a Process of Containment and Assimilation

When diversity is reduced to learning styles met with reductive strategies, teaching to and through (Gutiérrez & Larson, 1994) diversity projects becomes a process of containment of difference and assimilation into the normative. As Tuck and Gaztambide-Fernández (2013) write:

a language of diversity…can more fully be reoccupied by white subjects. Under the banner of "we are all the same because we are different," the language of diversity completes the replacement, positioning white people as the true diverse subjects, the new natives, and protectors of the value of human difference.

(p. 82)

That is, diversity projects become a way to identify both white people as the norm, and yet also diverse in the way that is desired. For example, Apple's first vice president of diversity and inclusion exemplified this when she publicly stated, "there can be 12 white, blue-eyed, blonde men in a room and they're going to be diverse too because they're going to bring a different life experience and life perspective to the conversation." We found the comment, and her later firing, concerning because the comment can be used to resituate the powerful as diverse AND the company's lack of diversity can now be blamed on a Black Woman, and no change needed to occur within the company. There are multiple instantiations of this narrative where diversity of thought and diversity of experience are being substituted for disrupting homogenous spaces. In this case, the powerful are diverse and yet so close to the desired norm that they continue to set both the norm and acceptable variance that qualifies as diversity. In other words, diversity projects in this form equate diversity with difference, regardless of the type of difference being indexed. In this way, diversity has become flattened and does not address power relations or systemic oppression; in fact, it recalibrates back to the white norm (see many examples of employing diversity of thought as the most important type of diversity).

Simultaneously, the differences from the norm that students of color "possess" are positioned as undesired and demands to change accompany the label of different (Erevelles & Minear, 2010). The non-dominant are imagined as needing remediation, wherein one is trapped in learning ecology focused on fixing the damage of difference (Gutiérrez, Morales, & Martinez, 2009). To remediate refers back to the initial act of mediation. That is, to be "placed in the middle." Remediate, then, comes to mean to pull toward the middle, or directs to remedial which is to offer a remedy which, in turn, means "to heal and cure" ("Remediate," OED, 2009). Considering that the interposing or placing in the middle has no explicit direction, we argue that without interrogation this implicit placing in the middle will always be unidirectional and follow the flow of power. Said differently, the less powerful will always be pulled toward the middle through curing and healing.

Hence, remediation is equated with learning to assimilate, to be cured of the problematic difference. The less powerful will be understood to contain the problem within, and in turn, will need to be contained (Nasir et al., 2006). This containment can be focused on a particular grouping of students (e.g., slow readers, disabled students), curricula (e.g., remedial math, direct instruction), or geographic space (e.g., homogeneous groups, segregated classrooms, alternative schools, youth prisons). Said differently, the remedy to difference is to ideologically and/or spatially restrict and unlearn that difference. This ideology of normal, which sustains difference as deficit discursively and materially (Annamma, Boelé, Moore, & Klingner, 2013), forecloses access in ways that peel away the strengths in an attempt to assimilate or contain the difference until it is minimized, and ignore the vulnerability of those who experience oppression. Ultimately, this foreclosure maintains power relations while domesticating difference.

Weaponizing Diversity through Disciplinary Practices

This domestication of difference is evidenced in the ways people positioned as different from the ideal norm are more likely to be labeled as deviant and disabled, and lose access to equitable education opportunities (McDermott, Goldman, & Varenne, 2006). For example, youth of color are more likely to be disciplined than white peers (Office for Civil Rights, 2016), despite little evidence for behavioral differences (Carter, Skiba, Arredondo, & Pollock, 2017). However, despite minimal evidence of behavioral differences, some scholars *search for* deviance of Black and Brown youth as the root cause of these disciplinary disparities. Using early teacher reports of prior "problem behaviors" for students of color as correlation with later discipline, Wright, Morgan, Coyne, Beaver, and Barnes (2014) argue, "the association between school suspensions and blacks and whites reflects long-standing behavioral differences between youth and that, at least in the aggregate, the use of suspensions may not be as racially biased as many have argued" (p. 8). Regardless of the fact that these early teacher reports are just as subjective and inculcated with the punishment of difference as the later disciplinary actions, the authors use the language of "pre-existing behavioral problems" (p. 7) to argue that it is behavioral differences, not racism, that have caused the overrepresentation of youth of color in disciplinary actions. In other words, these scholars claim Black and Brown kids act out more and that is why they are disciplined more. The researchers aver educators, administrators, schools, and society that they are not to blame, the kids are—a reassuring finding for those committed to a color-evasive meritocracy, one where color is invoked but racism is not named in the failure of multiply marginalized youth (Annamma, Jackson, & Morrison, 2017).

The belief that multiply marginalized youth of color act up more and so are punished more allows a justification for the links between schools and prisons (Meiners, 2007). That is, domestication of diversity positions this foreclosure of access to equitable education as inevitable; multiply marginalized youth of color deserve to be punished and whatever impacts the punishment has on their own trajectory is the result of refusing to minimize or erase their differences. When diversity is weaponized in this way, its projects are the sorting of the "bad kids", while keeping just enough "good kids" in classes to (re)produce the meritocratic narrative based on the exceptional success (e.g., the one Black gifted student in class, Barack Obama, Oprah: if they can succeed, it proves the system is not racially organized).

Given that Education Secretary Betsy DeVos recently used Wright et al.'s work as a rationale for rescinding Obama-Era Guidelines on reducing racial disproportionality in school discipline (see chapter 8 of Final Report on Federal Commission on School Safety, 2018), it is clear how when scholars target those who fall outside of the boundaries of "normal," these ideas are sedimented through scholarship and policy, leading to a narrative of deviance imbued in the language of inherent behavioral problems (Waitoller, Artiles, & Cheney, 2010). Diversity becomes weaponized because this flattened version of diversity required no change from those with power. This is why we argue that when we center diversity projects as a measure of success in response to the question "How do we support difference in learning contexts?", we end up with domesticated diversity as processes of assimilation and containment.

Emancipating Difference from Diversity

Examples like the racial gap in discipline described above abound in schools and are why we argue that conceptions of difference as diversity within a view of learning that centers representation ignore the ways power is inscribed in all learning. That is, "wherever we find social relations, variability of experience and practice, or evaluation of knowledge and learning, we also find dynamics of power" (Esmonde & Booker, 2016, p. 1). To effectively emancipate difference from the simultaneously invisibilized and idealized norm in learning contexts, theories of learning must center the ever-present dynamics between power and learning that unfold in microinteractions. In the last third of this chapter, we operationalize intersectionality, beyond multiple identities or embodied markers of diversity, as a method to excavate converging vectors of oppression (Combahee River Collective, 1977; Crenshaw, 1991). We then use Disability Critical Race Theory (DisCrit; Annamma, Connor, & Ferri, 2013) to illustrate a specific example of how intersectionality can support learning theorists in unmasking interlocking oppressions and forms of resistance in learning contexts while addressing persistent processes of domestication infused in environments that prioritize stable power relations over equity. Finally, we argue that when the vulnerability of human learning (and learners) is exposed, the demands of responsibility for organizing humanizing processes of education research are more clearly asserted (Paris & Winn, 2014). By claiming this responsibility, scholars, educators, and communities can build solidarity with multiply marginalized students, a necessity to effectively support learning as an integral process for persistently recalibrating uneven socio-historical relations.

Using Intersectionality to Unmask Oppression and Resistance in Learning Contexts

Intersectionality has been misused to highlight the carving up of identities to address limited population segments and to erase oppressions particular groups do not feel comfortable naming (Roberts & Jesudason, 2013). Intersectionality is about understanding and analyzing how multiple oppressions co-occur and amass through systemic processes and interpersonal discursive practices (Matsuda, 1989). In other words, intersectionality, as conceptualized by Black and post-colonial feminists, has never been solely focused on identity. Since Crenshaw's (1991) early conceptions of intersectionality, she has highlighted Black women as "multiply burdened" (p. 140), exploring "intersectional aspects of their subordination" (p. 148). Note here that the bodies, lives, and identities of Black women are not identified as intersectional; instead the structures that are proximal or distal to power are what are being presented as intersecting. Prior to that, Black women from Anna Julia Cooper (1892/1988) to Audre Lorde (1984) have articulated the multiple oppressions they experienced. Hence, intersectionality is about identifying converging vectors of oppression—a tool to name the ways multiple marginalizations manifest in the lives of specific people (Comabahee River Collective, 1977; Crenshaw, 1991). It is within this view of intersectionality that we believe it can unmask the ways the multiply marginalized are especially vulnerable to systemic and interpersonal inequities in learning contexts.

DisCrit: Emancipating Difference from Normativity

Continuing the example from above of overrepresentation of students of color in disciplinary actions, DisCrit—an intersectional sibling of Critical Race Theory—can help untangle the ways in which oppression and resistance are invisibilized within the discourse of inherent behavioral problems in schools (Annamma, Connor, & Ferri, 2013; Annamma, Ferri, & Connor, 2018). DisCrit begins with the recognition that racism and ableism are mutually constitutive. The interdependence of racism and ableism allows for just such a conclusion as Wright and colleagues reached, that there is simply something markedly different about Black and white kids' behavior and that is why Black kids are disciplined more. Wright et al. (2014) draw parallels between disciplinary actions in schools and the legal system when they state, "Similar to prior studies, Beaver et al. (2013) found that black males were more likely to be arrested and incarcerated than white males. However, the racial gap in criminal justice processing was accounted for by self-reported lifetime violent behavior and IQ." (p. 7). Consequently, here the interdependence of racism and ableism are more explicitly articulated when the authors cite literature that argues violent behavior is directly linked to the (lack of) intelligence of Black people. Scholars and educators who engage Wright's argument believe that there is something inherently different about Black children, that they are simply less able to control themselves in classrooms. Those who believe Black children are unable to control themselves whether due to biological or cultural differences, have argued they are rightfully excluded from learning environments (see Jeff Sessions, Annamma, 2017).

DisCrit argues that what is also significant is how these views get sedimented into the practices of classrooms and schools; the material realities of being socially constructed through the intersecting oppressions of racism and ableism matter. Okonofua and Eberhardt (2015) studied the ways teachers responded to behavioral infractions by race. The authors found that with identical behaviors reported:

1. "Teachers felt more troubled after the second infraction committed by a Black student than after the second infraction committed by a White student" (p. 4).
2. "Teachers thought the Black student should be disciplined more severely after the second infraction" (p. 4).
3. "Teachers were significantly more likely to imagine themselves suspending the Black student in the future" (p. 5).
4. "The Black student was significantly more likely...than the White student...to be labeled a troublemaker" (p. 5).

Given that racial disciplinary disparities are consistently found to begin in the classroom, both through quantitative (Anyon et al., 2014) and qualitative analyses (Annamma, 2016), Okonofua and Eberhardt's (2015) findings illustrate how racial disciplinary inequities occur in teachers' differential reactions to the same behaviors in learning environments (Varenne, Goldman, & McDermott, 1998). Consequently, as Ferguson (2000) documented, Black students are vulnerable to punishment for the same behaviors that white youth are forgiven for repeatedly.

Moreover, in a recent study of the processes which animate disciplinary disparities for girls of color, Annamma, Handy, Miller, and Jackson (accepted) found that these inequities were often rooted in academic interactions, not just behavioral. The authors noted:

> Educators required that students engage in appropriate, non-disruptive, help-seeking behaviors (i.e., raising their hands or waiting for their turn). Our findings highlighted how, despite engaging in these appropriate classroom practices, Girls of Color did not receive educational support in meaningful ways. In other words, Girls of Color reported the ways in which teachers withheld academic support. Specifically, Girls of Color discussed: (a) being ignored, (b) receiving adverse responses, and (c) having rewards withheld.

This work further elucidates the practices which result in the vulnerability of girls of color to inequitable power dynamics along vectors of intersecting marginalizations (e.g., racism and whiteness,[2] ableism, cis-heteropatriarchy[3]) that is revealed in learning contexts. Here, problematic practices are understood to present additional challenges that girls of color face when trying to participate in the academic life of the classroom. It is not only their behaviors that are read as suspect, but their academic interactions which are, at times, met with suspicion or derision. What these diversity projects do is to include the girls in class, and yet (re)produce static power relations where girls of color are only allowed as passive members of the classroom; girls of color cannot ask questions or actively participate in ways that are imagined as anything but problematic, which forecloses access to learning. Consequently, this diversity project is ableist because the underlying assumption is that girls of color cannot appropriately express themselves, that their emotions and affect are unsuitable. In other words, it positions girls of color as abnormal, relying on supremacist logics that define difference as deficient. These examples illustrate how racism and ableism are interdependent in learning contexts, how other oppressions expose multiply marginalized youth to additional burdens, and how there are material realities to being constructed as outside the boundaries of "normal." Hence, intersectionality that accounts for the interdependence of racism and ableism reveals learning contexts as dangerous spaces and the processes of learning within as vulnerability for multiply marginalized youth of color.

Intersectionality and Fugitivity Reveals the Responsibility of Humanizing Processes

As shown in the example above, learning is revealed to be a vulnerable process when intersectional theories are engaged—they expose the foreclosures that occur along the myriad vectors of oppressions multiply marginalized youth face in learning contexts. What is clear is that learning happens in these spaces and one question that arises is, "What is learned?" From the research discussed previously, it is evident that power dynamics and vulnerability are imbued in learning contexts, and multiply marginalized youth learn they are not welcome in the academic life of the classroom—their behavior will be surveilled, their learning labeled, and their variance from the script of diversity as representation will be punished (Annamma, 2018). Difference is locked into a hierarchal relationship with normativity wherein normal is powerful and difference is deficient.

When the vulnerability of human learning (and learners) is exposed, the demands of responsibility for organizing humanizing processes of education research are more clearly asserted (Paris & Winn, 2014). Returning to the question, "How do we support difference in learning contexts?", we have witnessed how narrow notions of diversity have resulted in a process of assimilation and containment that isolates and harms through diversity projects. This is not necessarily because of the failure of conceptualizations of diversity itself, but because of the failure to articulate or adopt commitments to unequal distributions of power in learning as the root of what diversity was trying to address. We could trace a multitude of shifts in answers to this question—multiculturalism (Au et al., 2016), Critical Race Theory (Tuck & Gaztambide-Fernández, 2013)—where radical roots are severed.

However, it is essential to note that students do not simply succumb to vulnerability and quit learning. Instead, multiply marginalized students consistently create, "invented spaces of insurgency and resistance" (Miraftab, 2004, p. 4). These invented spaces are ones where multiply marginalized youth continually get their needs met in learning contexts through creating and engaging Strategies of Resistance, ones in which they navigate multiple vectors of oppression with savvy and ingenuity (Annamma, 2016). This employment of Strategies of Resistance is learning within vulnerable contexts and is a fugitive practice, one that happens despite efforts to consistently discourage, monitor, and punish (Patel, 2016) in academic life. Researchers and educators must shift our questions. Patel (2019) does this when she queries "I ask the reader to consider how often learning has been undertaken in this settler society as an act of fugitivity" (p. 4). Once these acts of fugitive learning are recognized for the savvy responses to oppression that they are, researchers and educators can rethink the questions they ask.

This is essential because though we do recognize the ways intersectionality reveals vulnerability, and fugitivity reveals ingenuity in learning contexts, "resistance comes at tremendous cost to both the individual and the community" (Grande, 2004, p. 85). Each moment multiply marginalized students spend creatively navigating oppressions in learning contexts takes energy and brings the potential for additional oppressions coming in a pedagogy of pathologization rooted in surveillance, labeling, and punishment (Annamma, 2018). Researchers and educators must recognize the ways answers to this persistent question, "How do we support difference in learning contexts?", such as diversity, often ignore systems of power. When we disregard or are silent about the ways systems of power are refracted in learning contexts, the result is harm of multiply marginalized youth. And this harm radiates outward, threatening integrity and justice in communities and society. Once we understand the existence, cause, and impacts of this harm, educators must ask ourselves, "How do we repair this damage our refusal to explicitly name power has caused?" Below are some specific places that first educators, and then researchers, can engage these inquiries.

Educators

As realization of the vulnerability multiply marginalized youth face in learning contexts permeated with power, educators can ask different questions and claim responsibility for disrupting when they can. By claiming responsibility, educators can build solidarity with multiply marginalized students, one in which we seek to recognize and alleviate power dynamics in learning contexts, a necessity to effectively support learning as an integral process for persistently recalibrating uneven sociohistorical relations. We believe that recognizing responsibility for addressing power in the classroom means educators must shift our practices away from diversity projects. If responsibility is accepted by educators, then solidarity is the practice we undertake.

Solidarity means understanding that student actions that occur in the classroom are related to unequal power dynamics and that student resistance, in whatever form, is expected and welcomed in the classroom (Annamma, 2018). Solidarity, then, allows educators to (re)conceptualize the roles of themselves and their students in the classroom. Educators can refuse their prescribed roles that ignore and therefore (re)produce power.

Researchers

> From this perspective, diversity is not a problem to be solved; it becomes a pedagogical asset…Our perspective is much deeper and more transformational than the simple idea that schools should treat everyone equally and should value everyone's culture. We contend that particular configurations of race, ethnicity, and class require that youth wrestle with pervasive challenges (Spencer, 1999) and that designing learning environments must address multiple (and often neglected) elements of learning, including identity and affect.
>
> *(Nasir et al., 2006, p. 699)*

Ultimately, Nasir and colleagues recognize the vulnerability of youth and the responsibility of researchers to generate knowledge within, and explicitly name, this context of power. When designing learning contexts then, intersecting vectors of oppression must not be ignored; they must be explicitly identified and strategically resisted.

In order to unwed power from normativity, educators and researchers must recognize, articulate, and interrupt the power conceptions of normal hold. Intersectionality provides an opportunity to untangle the ways a myriad of oppressions land in the lives of our students and participants. Our ontologies, epistemologies, methodologies, and pedagogies must be driven by an axiological commitment to emancipate difference from hegemonic arrangements that place power within the normative. This allows us to move away from thin representational ideas infusing conceptions of diversity projects and toward emancipation of difference.

Discussion

Societies as a whole take credit for evolving beyond our pasts, while neglecting present indicators of persistent injustices (Bell, 1980). It is that particular historical condition, often invisible yet always circulating, that informed general calls for diversity to address inequality (Leonardo, 2005). The response to these calls generates responsibility for equality, one where everyone is treated the same, which is both rhetorical and dutiful. But efforts toward a vague equality are diffused and unaccountable, and it is simultaneously specifically and narrowly targeted. That is, when inequality is felt or experienced, it falls to specific less-powerful persons or groups to identity it and offer legible solutions that recommend the same treatment for everyone and therefore, do not make the powerful uncomfortable. Naming and resisting power dynamics imbued within nominal conceptions of diversity as a general, moral position becomes a duty to name inequity and generate solutions toward equity. To whom does this duty fall? And how shall we know when the duty has been fulfilled?

If we follow Stuart Hall's (1989/1992) words above, researchers must focus on mobilizing all "intellectual resources to go on understanding *what keeps making the lives we live and the societies we live in profoundly and deeply anti-humane in their understanding and capacities to live with difference*" (emphasis added). It is a shared political and ethical responsibility to relate humanely with difference when the forms of difference are historically and currently conceived as justification for varied forms of subjugation, enclosure, and exclusion. Difference as a mobilized tool for inscribing "antihumane" power relations (Hall, 1992) must be understood through Lee's "basic assumption that human beings always have agency, always have resources, and make meaning of

Integrating Intersectionality into the Study of Learning

their experiences in varied ways." Supremacist logics are false and displace and obscure power in learning contexts.

Cultural variation and learning become tools for establishing and/or restoring our capacities for critical reflection. While Lee (2003) has called on educational scholars to reconceptualize race and ethnicity through complex analyses and attention to deep variation within assumed groupings, Hall (1992) spent his career working to make current experience available for critical reflection. Both point the way toward just, human, and equitable relationships with difference through careful attention to active production and circulation of meaning. The dynamic complexities, and the tension between their lack of fixity yet perceived static group categorization, push us beyond representation. Consequently, it is the combined forces of Lee and Hall that push us toward understanding difference as expected and welcomed and to consider intersectional oppressions.

If we choose to be responsible for the shared world(s) we inhabit, what is the importance of our labor to responding to difference in substantive ways that do not require an adherence to the norm from the less powerful? Critical practices are implied including: silence, listening, and critical practices for attunement (Vossoughi, 2014), preparation and skilled practice as critical processes for anticipating breakdown and reproducing problems (Jackson, 2014; Booker & Goldman, 2016), and a human drawing-forth of diverse ways of knowing and being as critical practices for responsible people and systemic integrity (Gutiérrez & Rogoff, 2003; González, Moll, & Amanti, 2005). Repair is always specific, contextual, and must be responsive to changing conditions, predictable and unpredictable.

We end where we began, returning to Carol Lee's words in our epigraph:

> How do we resist simplistic assumptions about the meaning of group membership and develop more nuanced and complex research agendas that work from a basic assumption that human beings always have agency, always have resources, and make meaning of their experiences in varied ways?

Lee reminds us as scholars of the potential for us to engage an intersectional epistemological framing, which allows us to reveal the vulnerability of learning for multiply marginalized youth. As researchers, we have an opportunity to collaborate with youth of color at the intersections of a myriad of oppressions to center their knowledge in how learning contexts sediment or disrupt power dynamics inscribed in moment-to-moment interactions, institutional policies, and systems of education. Researchers can also engage solidarity, refusing the ways our fields encourage us to stay silent on issues of power, systemic oppression, and intersectional injustice.

Patel (2019) states, "I aver that educators have much to learn about learning itself and that much of that learning must come from beyond brick and mortar schools" (p. 4). What we are also doing is inviting educators to engage in learning ourselves. We cannot erase all manifestations of power, but we can learn about, expose, and disrupt when power is reinscribed in our own practices. Small practices of solidarity are as simple as taking data in our classrooms on who we call on, how often we discipline, how often we shut down a conversation, or how we cede responsibility in our classrooms or learning environments. Changing pedagogy, curricula, and relationships in the classroom can shift the entire classroom ecology to center multiply marginalized youth (Annamma & Morrison, 2018; Gutiérrez, 2008). It is about educating ourselves as individuals so our students, their families and communities are not more burdened with the labor of educating the educators too. Solidarity means speaking up when we witness injustice in individual cases, the local policies and practices of learning contexts, and national issues that are spilling onto the streets. None of these acts on their own are solidarity, but they all move toward taking responsibility for hegemony, adding up to practices that can reduce power disparities in learning contexts. Yet we refuse to simplify solidarity to individual actions.

We also invite educators and scholars to recognize that we do not have the capability to undertake all of this alone and encourage collective community building. Building collectives within local learning contexts means educating each other and being open to feedback when we are held accountable for our failures. Because we are all going to fail, but we seem so scared of failure. But learning is a risk we ask our students to take daily in dangerous contexts. Consequently, we invite educators and scholars to engage intersectional theories, recognize the vulnerability and fugitivity taking place in learning contexts, and build solidarity with multiply marginalized youth. We certainly will fail but the imperative of learning requires us to do so in order to grow.

Notes

1 We are aware of the concerns with the term People/Children of Color, as Lee (2003) notes, it can insinuate that white people do not have a color, therefore reinforcing their normativity and the Otherness of raced bodyminds. However, we draw from Ross (2011) who described it as "a solidarity definition, a commitment to work in collaboration with other Women of Color who have been minoritized…a political destination…we self-named ourselves. This is a term that has a lot of power for us." We center these coalitional politics infused through the original term Women of Color in this discussion.

2 Maitas and Liou (2015) name "the centrality of Whiteness in teaching by questioning what constitutes normalcy and how teachers implicitly and explicitly participate and reproduce it" (p. 610).

3 Alim, Lee, Carris, and Williams (2017) define cis-heteropatriarchy as, "an ideological system that naturalizes normative views of what it means to 'look' and 'act' like a 'straight' man and marginalizes women, femininity, and all gender non-conforming bodies that challenge the gender binary" (p. 59)

References

Alim, H. S., Lee, J., Carris, L. M., & Williams, Q. E. (2018). Linguistic creativity and the production of cisheteropatriarchy: A comparative analysis of improvised rap battles in Los Angeles and Cape Town. *Language Sciences*, *65*, 58–69.

Annamma, S. A. (2016). Disrupting the carceral state through education journey mapping. *International Journal of Qualitative Studies in Education*, *29*(9), 1–21.

Annamma, S. A. (2017). Not enough: Critiques of Devos and expansive notions of Justice. *International Journal of Qualitative Studies in Education*, *30*(10), 1047–1052.

Annamma, S. A. (2018). *The Pedagogy of Pathologization: Dis/Abled Girls of Color in the School-Prison Nexus*. New York, NY: Routledge.

Annamma, S. A., Connor, D., & Ferri, B. (2013). Dis/ability critical race studies (DisCrit): Theorizing at the intersections of race and dis/ability. *Race, Ethnicity and Education*, *16*(1), 1–31.

Annamma, S. A., Ferri, B. A., & Connor, D. J. (2018). Disability critical race theory: Exploring the intersectional lineage, emergence, and potential futures of DisCrit in education. *Review of Research in Education*, *42*(1), 46–71.

Annamma, S. A., Handy, G. T. , Miller, A., & Jackson, E. (accepted). Animating discipline disparities through debilitating practices: Girls of Color & withholding in the classroom. *Teachers College Record*, *123*(1).

Annamma, S. A., Jackson, D. & Morrison, D. (2017). Conceptualizing color-evasiveness: Using dis/ability critical race theory to expand a color-blind racial ideology in education and beyond. *Race Ethnicity and Education*, *20*(2), 147–162. doi:10.1080/13613324.2016.1248837

Annamma, S. A., & Morrison, D. (2018). DisCrit classroom ecology: Using praxis to dismantle dysfunctional education ecologies. *Teaching and Teacher Education*, *73*, 70–80.

Au, W., Brown, A. L., & Calderón, D. (2016). *Reclaiming the Multicultural Roots of US Curriculum: Communities of Color and Official Knowledge in Education*. New York, NY: Teachers College Press.

Bell Jr, D. A. (1980). Brown v. Board of Education and the interest-convergence dilemma. *Harvard Law Review*, *93*, 518–533.

Booker, A. (2016). Ethical commitments in community-based research with youth. *Mind, Culture, and Activity*, *23*(1), 15–27.

Booker, A., & Goldman, S. (2016). Participatory design research as a practice for systemic repair: Doing hand-in-hand math research with families. *Cognition and Instruction*, *34*(3), 222–235.

Integrating Intersectionality into the Study of Learning

Campbell, F. K. (2014). Ableism as transformative practice. In: Cocker, C., & T. Hafford-Letchfield (Eds.), *Rethinking Anti-Discriminatory and Anti-Oppressive Theories for Social Work Practice* (pp. 78–92). New York: Palgrave Macmillan.

Carter, P. L., Skiba, R., Arredondo, M. I., & Pollock, M. (2017). You can't fix what you don't look at: Acknowledging race in addressing racial discipline disparities. *Urban Education, 52*(2), 207–235.

Cole, M., Engeström, Y., & Vasquez, O. A (1997). Introduction. In: Cole, M. D. (Ed.), *Mind, Culture, and Activity: Seminal Papers from the Laboratory of Comparative Human Cognition.* Cambridge: Cambridge University Press.

Combahee River Collective. (1977). A black feminist statement. In: Guy-Sheftall, B. (Ed.), *Words of Fire: An Anthology of African American Feminist Thought* (1995) (pp. 232–240). New York, NY: New Press.

Cooper, A. J. (1892/2000). Woman vs. Indian. In: Lemert, C., & E. Bhan (Eds.), *The Voice of Anna Julia Cooper: Including A Voice from the South and Other Important Essays, Papers, and Letters* (pp. 88–108). Lanham: Rowman & Littlefield Publishers.

Crenshaw, K. (1991). Mapping the margins: Intersectionality, identity politics, and violence against women of color. *Stanford Law Review, 43*(6):1241–1299.

Cyrus, K. (2017). Multiple minorities as multiply marginalized: Applying the minority stress theory to LGBTQ people of color. *Journal of Gay and Lesbian Mental Health, 21*(3), 194–202.

Eckert, P. (1989). *Jocks & Burnouts: Social Categories and Identity in the High School.* New York, NY: Teachers College Press.

Erevelles, N., & Minear, A. (2010). Unspeakable offenses: Untangling race and disability in discourses of intersectionality. *Journal of Literary and Cultural Disability Studies, 4*(2), 127–145.

Esmonde, I., & Booker, A. N. (2016). *Power and Privilege in the Learning Sciences.* New York, NY: Routledge.

Ferguson, A. A. (2000). *Bad Boys.* Ann Arbor, MI: University of Michigan Press.

Flores, N., & Rosa, J. (2015). Undoing appropriateness: Raciolinguistic ideologies and language diversity in education. *Harvard Educational Review, 85*(2), 149–171.

Freire, P. (1970). *Pedagogy of the Oppressed* (Ramos, M. B., Trans.). New York, NY: Herder and Herder.

Gonzalez, N., Moll, L., & Amanti, C. (Eds.) (2005). *Funds of Knowledge.* New York, NY: Routledge.

Grande, S. (2004). *Red Pedagogy: Native American Social and Political Thought* (1st edition). Lanham, MD: Rowman & Littlefield.

Greene, M. (1993). Diversity and inclusion: Toward a curriculum for human beings. *Teachers College Record, 95*(2), 211–221.

Gutiérrez, K. D. (2008). Developing a sociocritical literacy in the third space. *Reading Research Quarterly, 43*(2), 148–164.

Gutiérrez, K., & Larson, J. (1994). Language borders: Recitation as hegemonic discourse. *International Journal of Educational Reform, 3*(1), 22–36.

Gutiérrez, K. D., Morales, P. Z., & Martinez, D. C. (2009). Re-mediating literacy: Culture, difference, and learning for students from nondominant communities. *Review of Research in Education, 33*(1), 212–245.

Gutiérrez, K. D., & Rogoff, B. (2003). Cultural ways of learning: Individual traits or repertoire of practice. *Educational Researcher, 32*(5), 19–25.

Hall, S. (1989). *The Origins of Cultural Studies.* Media Education Foundation. MEF Stuart Hall Collection. Accessed transcript May 4, 2019, www.mediaed.org/transcripts/Stuart-Hall-the-Origins-of-Cultural-Studies-Transcript.pdf.

Hall, S. (1992). Race, culture, and communications: Looking backward and forward at cultural studies. *Rethinking Marxism, 5*(1), 10–18.

Hall, S., Segal, L., & Osborne, P. (1997). Interview Stuart Hall: Culture and power. *Radical Philosophy, 86*, 24–41.

Harris, A. P. (1990). Race and essentialism in feminist legal theory. *Stanford Law Review, 42*(3), 581–616.

Harris, C. (1993). Whiteness as property. *Harvard Law Review, 106*(8), 1709–1791.

Heath, S. B. (1983). *Ways with Words: Language, Life and Work in Communities and Classrooms.* Cambridge, UK: Cambridge University Press.

Jackson, D. D. (2011). Sander, the mismatch theory, and affirmative action: Critiquing the absence of praxis in policy. *Denver University Law Review, 89*(1), 245–268.

Jackson, S. J. (2014). Rethinking repair. In: Gillespie, T., P. Boczkowski, & K. Foot (Eds.), *Media Technologies: Essays on Communication, Materiality and Society* (pp. 221–239). Cambridge, MA: MIT Press.

Ladson-Billings, G. (1998). Just what is critical race theory and what's it doing in a nice field like education? *International Journal of Qualitative Studies in Education, 11*(1), 7–24.

Lave, J., & Wenger, E. (1991). *Situated Learning: Legitimate Peripheral Participation.* Cambridge, UK: Cambridge University Press.

Lee, C. D. (2003). Why we need to rethink race and ethnicity in educational research. *Educational Researcher, 32*(5), 3–5.

Leonardo, Z. (2005). Through the multicultural glass: Althusser, ideology and race relations in post-civil rights America. *Policy Futures in Education, 3*(4), 400–412.

Leonardo, Z., & Broderick, A. (2011). Smartness as property: A critical exploration of intersections between whiteness and disability studies. *Teachers College Record, 113*(10), 2206–2232.

Lorde, A. (1984). *Sister Outsider.* Trumansburg, NY: Crossing.

Matsuda, M. J. (1989). When the first quail calls: Multiple consciousness as jurisprudential method. *Women's Rights Law Reporter, 11*(1), 7–10.

McDermott, R. (1993). The acquisition of a child by a learning disability. In: Chaiklin, S., & J. Lave (Eds.), *Understanding Practice: Perspectives on Activity and Context* (pp. 269–305). Cambridge, UK: Cambridge University Press.

McDermott, R. P. (2014). Ethnicity and race. In: Phillips, D. C. (Ed.), *Encyclopedia of Educational Theory and Philosophy* (pp. 301–304). Los Angeles, CA: Sage Publications, Inc.

McDermott, R., Goldman, S., & Varenne, H. (2006). The cultural work of learning disabilities. *Educational Researcher, 35*(6), 12–17.

Meiners, E. R. (2007). *Right to Be Hostile: Schools, Prisons, and the Making of Public Enemies* (1st edition). New York, NY: Routledge.

Miraftab, F. (2004). Invited and invented spaces of participation: Neoliberal citizenship and feminists' expanded notion of politics. *Wagadu, 1*(Spring), 1–7.

Nasir, N. S., & Hand, V. M. (2006). Exploring sociocultural perspectives on race, culture, and learning. *Review of Educational Research, 76*(4), 449–475.

Nasir, N. S., Rosebery, A. S., Warren, B., & Lee, C. D. (2006). Learning as a cultural process: Achieving equity through diversity. In: Sawyer, R. K. (Ed.), *The Cambridge Handbook of the Learning Sciences* (pp. 489–504). New York, NY: Cambridge University Press.

Office of Civil Rights Civil Rights Data Collection (CDRC). (2016). First look report. http://www2.ed. gov/about/offices/list/ocr/docs/2013-14-first-look.pdf.

Okonofua, J. A., & Eberhardt, J. L. (2015). Two strikes: Race and the disciplining of young students. *Psychological Science, 26*(5), 617–624.

Paris, D., & Winn, M. T. (2014). *Humanizing Research: Decolonizing Qualitative Inquiry with Youth and Communities.* Thousand Oaks, CA: Sage.

Patel, L. (2016). Pedagogies of resistance and survivance: Learning as marronage. *Equity and Excellence in Education, 49*(4), 397–401.

Patel, L. (2019). Fugitive practices: Learning in a settler colony. *Educational Studies, 55*(3), 253–261.

Pippert, T. D., Essenburg, L. J., & Matchett, E. J. (2013). We've got minorities, yes we do: Visual representations of racial and ethnic diversity in college recruitment materials. *Journal of Marketing for Higher Education, 23*(2), 258–282.

Remediate. (December 2009). *Oxford English Dictionary* (3rd edition). http://www.oed.com/view/ Entry/162119.

Roberts, D., & Jesudason, S. (2013). Movement intersectionality. *Du Bois Review: Socialscience Research on Race, 10*(02), 313–328.

Schalk, S. (2018). *Bodyminds Reimagined: (Dis) Ability, Race, and Gender in Black Women's Speculative Fiction.* Durham, NC: Duke University Press.

Tyack, D. B. (1974). *The One Best System: A History of American Urban Education.* Cambridge: Harvard University Press.

Torres, M. (2005). "Doing Mestizaje": When epistemology becomes ethics. In: Keating, A. (Ed.), *EntreMundos/ AmongWorlds* (pp. 195–203). New York, NY: Palgrave Macmillan.

Tuck, E., & Gaztambide-Fernández, R. A. (2013). Curriculum, replacement, and settler futurity. *Journal of Curriculum Theorizing, 29*(1), 72–89.

Varenne, H., Goldman, S., & McDermott, R. (1998). Racing in place. In: Varenne, H., & R. McDermott (Eds.), *Successful Failure: The School America Builds* (pp. 106–128). Boulder, CO: Westview Press.

Varenne, H., & McDermott, R. (1998). *Successful Failure: The School America Builds.* Boulder, CO: Westview Press.

Vossoughi, S. (2014). Social analytic artifacts made concrete: A study of learning and political education. *Mind, Culture, and Activity, 21*(4), 353–373.

Waitoller, F. R., Artiles, A. J., & Cheney, D. A. (2010). The miner's canary: A review of overrepresentation research and explanations. *The Journal of Special Education, 44*(1), 29–49.

Walker, V. S. (2009). Second-class integration: A historical perspective for a contemporary agenda. *Harvard Educational Review, 79*(2), 269–284.

Weber, Max (1978). *Economy and Society: An Outline of Interpretive Sociology.* Berkeley, CA: University of California Press.

Willis, P. (1977). *Learning to Labour: How Working Class Kids Get Working Class Jobs*. New York: Columbia University Press.

Wright, J. P., Morgan, M. A., Coyne, M. A., Beaver, K. M., & Barnes, J. C. (2014). Prior problem behavior accounts for the racial gap in school suspensions. *Journal of Criminal Justice, 42*(3), 257–266.

Zavala, M. (2018). *Raza Struggle and the Movement for Ethnic Studies: Decolonial Pedagogies, Literacies, and Methodologies* (pp. 163–173). Bern, Switzerland: Peter Lang US.

18

RECONCEPTUALIZING THE QUANTITATIVE-QUALITATIVE DIVIDE

Toward a New Empiricism

Ezekiel J. Dixon-Román, John L. Jackson, Jr., and Maxine McKinney de Royston

The traditional divide between quantitative and qualitative methods in educational research reifies a dualistic perspective about what can be known and how it can be known that obscures the complexity of human diversity, discursively forms essentialist notions of race, culture, and learning, and limits possibilities for critical inquiry. Undergirding this splitting of research methods into two broad camps—quantitative *or* qualitative—are recurring sets of dualistic logics that rely upon the false separation between mind and body, biology and culture, nature and nurture, and so on. These recurring binaries, however reductionist, cumulatively and continually reproduce conceptualizations of the human being, of human learning, and for studying human activity that get taken up through discourse and practice in everyday life, schooling, and in educational research. This is despite distinct dualisms, such as the split between nature and nurture or object/ive and subject/ive, having been disproved by sociological and humanistic theories of the human and of learning and development.

When these reductionist dualisms get iteratively instantiated rather than challenged, the conceptualization of the human subject remains contingent upon inherited logics of the post-Enlightenment; that is, an assumption of natural human difference and racialized hierarchies (Chakrabarty, 2000; da Silva, 2007; Roberts, 2011). The global historical record offers great evidence that these essentialized and racialized constructions of the human, more often than not, get hegemonized as European, male, heterosexual, ableist, and Christian, rendering all others inferior, primitive, and even outside of the scope of humanity (i.e., non-human). In this way, reductionist dualisms such as the nature/culture binary discursively shape and are shaped by the racialized formations they construct, which in turn are socially and politically reinscribed through commonsensical beliefs, institutional and societal policies, everyday practices, and even scholarly research methods.

In this chapter, then, we consider what it would mean to rethink classic nature/nurture debates anew as a way to de-settle contemporary approaches to educational research and policy. For instance, how might challenging the ostensible fault line between nature and nurture (a trope for culture) impact the study of education in the twenty-first century, particularly in the context of powerful racializing forces and concerns about educational equity that span the globe? How might this reconceptualization of the human have implications for the conventional social scientific distinctions that continue to be drawn between quantitative and qualitative methods?

This inquiry leans upon work in feminist new materialisms that fundamentally interrogate these complex dualistic entanglements. We begin by unpacking what a new materialist deconstructionist

Reconceptualizing the Quantitative-Qualitative

analysis is and what it offers us toward better understanding research methods. We then engage in this kind of analysis through revisiting some widely engaged literature on culture and learning (e.g., Boesch & Tomasello, 1998; Cole & Scribner, 1974; Holland, Lachiotte, Skinner, & Cain, 2001; Lave & Wenger, 1991; Vygotsky, 1978) and the ways in which educational research, particular that which focuses on culture and learning, has rested on these haunting dualisms that assume the identity and difference of mind and body, biology and culture. Finally, we end our chapter by discussing how critical inquiry might better account for what Barad (2007) calls an onto-epistemology—or a dynamic and entangled conception of *knowing in being* in the world—that does not rely upon reductionist and binary logics but assumes the researcher is always already entangled with and part of the object of inquiry, an object that is not passive but actively acting on/with the researcher, precisely because the cultural has always been biological and vice versa (Dixon-Román, 2017a; Kirby, 2011). In short, we will analyze the sociopolitical formations of the human, what this means for educational research, as well as proffer thoughts toward a new empiricism.

Deconstructionist Analyses: Questioning Tensions and Hierarchies

The analyses in this chapter aim to situate dualistic notions within a history of philosophy and de-settle the hegemonic constructions of the quantitative and qualitative research paradigms we rely upon in educational research. While there are many ways to do this, the analytical move made here is to interrogate the inherent dualisms and hierarchies within how we conceptualize culture and learning that underlie our research methods and that frequently un-fold on themselves in tense if not contradictory ways. We take up Barad's (2007) and Kirby's (2011) new materialist rethinking of Derrida's (1974/1984) deconstructionism, a form of philosophical and literary criticism, to question commonsensical and traditional assumptions and modes of being and thought. Deconstructionism has a long history within the humanities and social sciences, including in philosophy, literature, anthropology, feminist studies, and political science.

Deconstruction, such as that which we later do with nature (biology) and nurture (culture), seeks to interrogate the assumptions that undergird the conceptual distinctions often made in texts through creating logical binaries or oppositions and through the hierarchical ordering of particular notions or ideas, however indirectly or implicitly (Derrida, 1974/1984; Dixon-Roman, 2017a). These binary oppositions often have a history and this type of analysis shows how discourses, tensions, and hierarchies are the cultural construction of a given text. Text here is understood not simply as a written text but in a more general sense of the objects of the world, where "there is no outside of text." Derrida (1974/1984) pushed for the undoing or decomposing of discourses as they are constructed within texts and effectively operate as material (read ideologically tangible) constructions that shape how we conceive of reality and activity, including that of our own becoming. Deconstruction is not a method or model, but a process of closely reading the assumed irreducible differences that may undergird the logic of a text. It is a provocation toward understanding how discourses represent what has come to be understood and iteratively sedimented as truth. Through analyzing written texts—a medium through which discourses get conceptually solidified, communicated to others, and taken up—deconstructionist analyses interrogate foundational notions that we hold true and the identity of which we rarely disrupt. In so doing, deconstructionism offers an opportunity to explore how the explication and instantiation of discourses into language and practice can result in the subversion of the original meanings in ways that may not be intentional, foreseen, or endorsed by the authors.

Deconstruction via new materialisms (e.g., Barad, 2007; Kirby, 2011; Dixon-Román, 2017a) rethinks Derridean deconstruction in relation to material phenomena wherein matter and discourse are understood as inseparable. A new materialist deconstruction works to deconstruct material and discursive phenomena to illuminate the differences that matter or make a difference. Like Derridean deconstruction, new materialist deconstruction is not a method or model, but rather

315

a close reading or analysis that is focused not on what the assumed irreducible difference may be of a text but rather what are the produced differences that have material significance, such as the enabled access and exclusion to selective higher education due to SAT scores.

It is important to note that deconstruction is a non-linear process and does not presume to unfold in chronological or sequential ways. Instead, the focus is on understanding how discourses get layered onto one another, where historicity is not equivalent to linearity. Barad (2007) discusses how new materialist deconstructionist analyses put different strands of thought or discourses into direct contact with one another, not by employing a hierarchical methodology but by dialogically reading texts "through one another" (p. 30). In this way, what was theorized or articulated before is not completely rejected; instead the foundations of that thinking are re-purposed to think anew and to consider alternate and creative possibilities that may not rest upon or center extant or dominant logics. Instead, non-dominant discourses or ways of thinking and knowing, including those from other disciplines, can also be brought in and explored. Specifically, new materialist deconstruction asks, what are the presumptions that a text is written on? What are the dualistic assumptions that it rests upon? Through a close reading, assumptions and presumptions that create binarism are identified and questioned. Here the move is to draw out the possibilities for multiplicity and dynamism rather than static binaries that lead to essentialisms and ignore the shifting referents of discourses.

Understanding the genealogy of particular discursive constructs, as we do later in this chapter with nature and culture, is a deconstructionist move that points to specific rupturing events that become forces in producing discourses. These rupturing events operate as discursive apparatus' that then get leveraged by others to, in turn, create additional discourses. For example, when Piaget's stage theories about intellectual development were taken up by Western scholars in the United States and Europe, these scholars went on to engage in cross-cultural studies in contexts around the globe that led to various discourses not only about individual child development, but also about the intelligence and capacity of particular persons or communities, normative child development versus retardation, the effects of illiteracy and schooling on the intellectual development of adults, and so forth. (Rogoff & Chavajay, 1995). While Piaget himself went on to revise his own stance on the generality of his stages and how they aligned with specific ages, contexts, and domains, the discursive damage was already done. Piaget's work continues to be leveraged, frequently in Eurocentric and racialized ways, to determine normative development versus that which is deviant or problematic. In this way, we can begin to see how the discourses set forth by Piaget's work operate as discursive apparatus of learning and development that themselves create and reproduce new material relations of power that get instantiated into institutional modes of thought and practice that have day to day consequences for persons, communities, and even whole societies.

Deconstructing Nature (Biology) and Nurture (Culture)

A radical division between nature and culture has long persisted in social science theory and philosophy. The instituted assumptions and seemingly self-evidential distinctions of nature and culture go back to early philosophical thinkers such as Descartes, Plato, and Newton, among others. For example, Descartes' mind/body dualism argued that there is a radical split between the body and mind; that these are co-joined and possibly interacting entities that nonetheless exist independent of each other and are fundamentally distinct in composition and function. The mind, as an entity, is pure and indivisible and does not rely upon a material or physical presence. The mind just is. This is best represented by Descartes' the *cogito* [I think, therefore I am].

The mind, under this logic, is a distinct thinking object that is undeniable because without it we cannot exist. In distinct contrast and opposition to the mind is the body. The body is composite—i.e. it is material or made up of matter—and is therefore divisible. The body is not a thinking object, it is a subject that is often, but not always, controlled by the mind. This dualistic logic constructs a

Reconceptualizing the Quantitative-Qualitative

separation in composition (mind is immaterial, body is material) and function (mind is for thinking, the body for feeling), as well as a hierarchical power relation between the mind and body. This mind/body dualism is visible in Descartes (2017) use of analogies:

> Nature likewise teaches me by these sensations of pain, hunger, thirst, etc., that I am not only lodged in my body as a pilot in a vessel, but that I am besides so intimately conjoined, and as it were intermixed with it, that my mind and body compose a certain unity.
>
> *(p. 113)*

Descartes' words codify the mind and body as essentially different realities and identities, but also instantiates a relationship between the two wherein the mind, as pilot, can control or steer the body, the vessel. Here, the discourses of experiencing, teaching, and learning are made visible. While the body can experience things like pain, hunger, and thirst, biological reactions to a corporeal reality, it is the mind that is learning these lessons that are being taught by nature. Nature, under this configuration, is pure and undeniable and the mind has access to this in a way that is distinct from the experiential feelings of the body. By contrast, the body, insofar as it engages in feeling, but not in thinking, does not have direct access to the natural world.

This modernist philosophy of the conception of human/corporeal materiality and mind immateriality suggests fixed and uniform properties that create a binary between human ontology (ways of being) and epistemology (ways of knowing). The social sciences inherited these modernist assumptions as evidenced by Comte's philosophical and political project of positivism. The "social physics" that Comte developed was situated in the Cartesian split between biology and culture, and understandings of matter as "corporeal substance constituted of length, breadth, and thickness; as extended, uniform, and inert" (Coole & Frost, 2010). These logics, and their reliance upon fixed definitions of matter and of dualisms and hierarchies, came to constitute how we discursively represent human engagements with the natural world and the basis of social theory that aims to make sense of human thinking and behavior over time and space.

Figure 18.1 is a representation that roughly traces the discursive trajectory of dualistic and hierarchical logics in the social sciences as they get reified and reinscribed through an evolving set of conceptualizations rooted in the mind/body distinction. We assert that this representation is itself inherently reductive and lacks the discursive complexity of the literature. This is precisely the point, however, as Figure 18.1 illustrates how discourse becomes material whether or not we believe it to be fundamentally true, and despite the existences of other discourses that contradict it. If a discourse gets taken up reductively in the literature, our move analytically is to reveal that reductionism and how it gets iteratively reified and reproduced as other discourses develop that are based upon that initial discursive apparatus or pivot. In highlighting these reductionisms, we can then interrogate the assumptions they rest on, and eventually disrupt them, imagine, and create alternative and creative possibilities that do not rest upon these same logics.

The study of human learning and development has long rested on the radical separation between nature and nurture, such as the Darwinian inspired studies of the evolution of the human, the phylogenetic analyses of Piaget that distinguish the development of cognitive schema based on interaction with the natural and physical world, or Vygotsky's notion of development as biological maturation as distinguished from learning that is stimulated through social and cultural interaction (c.f. Piaget, 1973; Vygotsky, 1978). Although Darwin's theories continue to influence human development, Piagetian and Vygotskian discourses are more prominent within educational research and serve as a departure from more biological deterministic arguments.

Piaget and Vygotsky take an interactionist perspective, which assumes that although the human is born with some genetic information, that genetic structure interacts with the environment to shape human development (Dixon-Román, 2017a). This is especially seen in works that on the one hand acknowledge the existence of genetic structures, but on the other focus their inquiry on

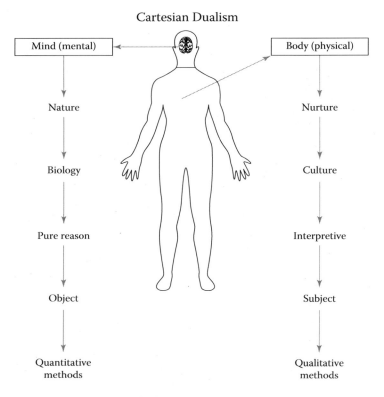

Figure 18.1 Cartesian dualist logics.

what can be changed in the environment in order to influence human learning and development. Although this perspective treats the "natural" or biological processes of the body as in interaction with social and cultural processes, the identity and difference between the two are maintained. For example, for Piaget this binary nature and nurture can be seen in the "unbridgeable dualism between the individual and the social" (Matusov & Hayes, 2000, p. 217). Piaget describes the young child as an "egocentric" and independent thinker who experiences the social world but is not yet structured by it. If anything it constrains them:

> during the sensory–motor period preceding language, one cannot yet speak of the socialization of intelligence. In fact, it is only during this period that one may speak of anything like a purely individual intelligence. True, the child learns to imitate before knowing how to speak. But he only imitates gestures the he already knows how to execute by himself or of which he has acquired, by himself, sufficient understanding.
>
> *(Piaget, 1995, p. 143)*

In this view, the social and cultural world, which is distinct from the mind or biology of the child, shapes the child's activity only insofar as to present options to them to employ their own thinking. These social and cultural interactions do not yet "penetrate the essential structures of the child's thinking" (Matusov & Hayes, 2000, p. 218) until later in childhood when they are presumed to engage in cooperative activity with others. As with Descartes, for Piaget the thinking mind of the child is in direct contact with nature, and thus can engage in pure reason that is unencumbered by the socializing or "nurturing" aspects of childhood that the child's body encounters through interacting with family, communities, and cultural and historical artifacts.

Reconceptualizing the Quantitative-Qualitative

This dualistic maintenance of the identity and difference between mind and body, nature and nurture, and biology and culture (see Figure 18.1), is also reinscribed in Vygotsky's research. While some argue that in Vygotsky's work "human subjectivity is conceptualized as originating from, and subordinate to, the collective exchanges and material production" (Stetsenko, 2005, p. 74), others suggest that Vygotsky privileges the mastery of the body by the mind (Lerman, 2000). In either case, like Piaget, Vygotsky maintains the mind/body distinction and a hierarchical nature to this distinction. For example, Lerman (2000) points out that Vygotsky continues this dualistic hierarchy through focusing on the internalization or intrapsychological plane of the individual as distinct from the social (interpsychological) plane (Vygotsky, 1978). Moreover, Vygotsky exceptionalizes human learning and development given this distinction, which he views as unique to our species because of language (1978):

> The specifically human capacity for language enables children to provide for auxiliary tools in the solution of difficult tasks, to overcome impulsive action, to plan a solution to a problem prior to its execution, and to master their own behavior. Signs and worlds serve children first and foremost as a means of social contact with other people. The cognitive and communicative functions of language then become the basis of a new and superior form of activity in children, distinguishing them from animals.
>
> *(p. 28–29).*

In this way, Vygotsky continues to leverage dualistic logics in relation to the mind and body split, the distinction between nature and nurture, biology and culture, as well as between human and non-human interactions.

Even those scholars, like Minick (1987) and Lerman (2000), who credit Vygotsky with laying the foundation for a unified analysis of mind and body—of consciousness and behavior—indicate that at the time of Vygotsky's untimely death, this work required further elaboration to move beyond dualistic tensions and hierarchies. We see this come through in work by Boesch and Tomasello (1998) who, in expanding upon Vygotsky, clarify that culture is not monolithic and that there are many cultural phenotypic similarities between, for instance, the human and chimpanzee. Nonetheless, these perspectives maintain dualisms and hierarchies (as represented in Figure 18.1) by exceptionalizing the human over the chimpanzee through privileging the human's capacities of transmitting information and engaging in cumulative cultural evolution.

These anthropocentric views have been widely shared and accepted in the social sciences, especially from those influenced by Modernist thought and Darwin's evolutionary ideas. The Modernist inherited dualistic conceptions of mind as immaterial and body as matter, as well as those about the nature/nurture binary. This, however, was challenged in the mid-twentieth century by work in the sociology of science (e.g., Berger & Luckman, 1967) and postmodern philosophy. Deconstruction and post-structuralism, in particular, interrogated the binary between nature and culture, calling into question conceptions of matter, the body, truth, and the accompanying metanarratives. For example, Derrida questions the possibility of truth and objectivism with the aphorism that "there is no outside of the text," or nothing, even the mind or nature, that is outside of interpretation. Foucault (1990) recast this thesis as there is no outside of power/knowledge (notation between power and knowledge symbolizing integration rather than contra-distinction), with Butler (1993) arguing that there is no outside of cultural performance.

Each of these postulations suggest that even things understood to be the objects of nature become signifiers of interpretation that are always contaminated or obscured by culture and power. For example, the assumed "natural" division of the sexes becomes a bodily signifier for the cultural and political construction of gender. These discursive moves reconfigure the epistemological possibilities and render binaries like nature and nurture, biology and culture incomprehensible and indefensible. Moreover, these moves call into question the discursive progeny of these dualities and hierarchies such as the positivistic purity and veracity of models, instrumentations, and "objects" of science.

These deconstructionist moves have begun to find a place through those who study the cultural nature of human learning and development (e.g., Bourdieu, 1990; Bourdieu & Passeron, 1977; Cole & Scribner, 1974; Gutiérrez & Rogoff, 2003; Lave & Wenger, 1991; Lee, 2001; Rogoff, 2003). This work is necessarily interdisciplinary and influenced by cultural psychology as well as critical theory and cultural studies. Although these interdisciplinary interventions have extended the limits of culture, making everything a symbolic aspect of a cultural landscape, they ultimately did not interrogate the identity and ontology (or way of being) of nature. Scholars (e.g., Holland et al., 2001; Stentsenko, 2005, 2008) point out that these culturalist and constructivist perspectives of human learning and development still need to push beyond reductionist dualisms and hierarchies. Nature remains ontologically preserved as that which is fixed with essential characteristics yet epistemologically inaccessible due to the ubiquity and inescapability of culture. Thus, the Cartesian logics, while challenged, were not sufficiently deconstructed and eradicated in these discursive turns.

Feminist new materialists, however, offer some productive insights. Kirby (2011) raises the following provocative question: "To what extent is nature culture and culture nature?" Re-appropriating Derrida's aphorism, Kirby points to the possibility that "there is no outside of nature." In this thesis, she makes two important arguments: (1) nature has always engaged in cultural processes of communicating, meaning making, and decision making; and (2) the human organism is one of infinite expressions of Earth's ontology. Both of these arguments reconfigure the ontological and epistemological entanglements of nature and culture. Other feminist new materialist thinkers have taken seriously the remarkable developments across disciplines, including in the natural and physical sciences. While educational research (e.g., Vygotsky and those building from this work) claims that symbolic consciousness and language are what separate the human from the non-human/animal, work in biosemiotics (e.g., Hoffmeyer, 2008) points toward the communicative and interpretive processes of nature and the forming, storing, and passing of information, such as that which occurs with DNA. Previously it was argued that DNA determined phenotype, psychic, or behavioral characteristics. We now understand that DNA is merely passive codes of information or instructions. The actors, readers, and translators of these passive codes are the membranes of egg cells which do the interpreting of the coding system of genetic structures as contingent on the temporal and spatial context in which the interpretation takes place, which results in material effects that occur in often unpredictable ways. Even genetic code is not singular; it is based on interplay and message exchange. These developments challenge conceptions of the corporeal body and the materiality or immateriality of aspects of the human. To assume fixed, uniform, and pre-scripted bodily or biological substances misses the creative subtleties of humans and their covariations and adaptations that shift with the material conditions of socioeconomic, racial, gendered, disabled, or sexualized structural relations, among others.

The example of DNA is but one that feminist new materialists pull from. Other works discuss developments and discoveries in quantum physics, chaos theory, and complexity theory (Barad, 2007; Coole & Frost, 2010; Dixon-Román, 2017a; Kirby, 2011). There is a raft of natural and physical science theories and research that continue to challenge the Modernist conceptions that the social sciences continue to rest upon. The materiality of nature is not fixed, stable, or simply subject to causal forces. Likewise, the assumption of fixed material context overlooks the ontologies of place and space. Not only do we learn from new materialisms that that which constitutes biology and culture is vibrant, active, and acting, but that these materialisms are indistinguishable and inseparable from each other. This observation has also long been made in indigenous and African philosophies (Kawagley, 2006; Mbembe, 2017; Tuck & McKenzie, 2015). The ontologies of context push the social sciences to reconsider the bodily, cultural, and ecological contexts and dimensions of learning and development as well as how they are entangled with the ontologies of time, space, and matter. The deconstructive argument here around nature (biology) and nurture (culture) suggests that such a duality is false, that hierarchies across these dualities are equally unfounded, and finally that culture is not unique to the human organism but is an ontological expression of Earth's becoming, in which the human organism is an heir (Dixon-Román, 2017b; Kirby, 2011).

The Human and Racializing Assemblages

Given that the category of the human was conceived based on a radical division between nature and culture (see Figure 18.1) and various sets of dualistic discourses that relied upon it, the deconstruction of nature and culture as distinct also reconfigures the understanding and study of the human, human activity, and human learning and development. Before talking about how, we need to reconfigure the study of the human in educational research away from dualistic logics; we first need to reconceive of the human outside of these logics. Work in Black studies and Black literary feminism has long interrogated the construction of the human while also theorizing about the ontology of racial logics to account for the nature/culture binary and rethink the study of these processes in relation to the biopolitics of whose bodily capacities are enabled or constrained through this material and discursive formation.

Hegel developed a conceptualization of the human as a self-determining and self-conscious subject in relation to human difference that evolves from national and geographic context and time (da Silva, 2007). This conceptualization of the subject became known as the liberal subject of Modernism and was constituted by dualistic logics of "natural" human difference and racialized hierarchies (Chakrabarty, 2000; da Silva, 2007; Roberts, 2011). The development of reason and the subject in the post-Enlightenment was hegemonized as European, male, heterosexual, ableist, and Christian, rendering all others as inferior, primitive, or non-human. These constructions placed the bodies *and* minds of all "others" closer to (if not synonymous with) nature and animals without, paradoxically (see Figure 18.1), bringing them closer to reason or to the "human" scope of thinking (da Silva, 2007; Weheliye, 2014; Wynter, 2007). The Christian white male was able to engage in the high-cognitive, disembodied work of reason that could be understood as *cultured* without being cultural, while all "others" were understood to be more embodied, affective, impulsive, and animalistic, thus less human or even non-human. As such, the biology/culture binary influenced and was influenced by the racialized formations of the subject.

Race and gender have long been treated as social and political constructions, and work in Black studies and Black literary feminisms has long interrogated the ontology of the human. In *Habeas Viscus* ("you shall have the flesh"), Alexander Weheliye (2014) brings into focus the theoretical work from Black literary feminists that more richly account for the processes of power and the racializations of the material body/flesh. For Weheliye, racialization cannot be reduced to race or racism. Instead, it is the process of embedding differentiation and hierarchization into discourse that produces the entangled race, gender, class, sexuality, and dis/ability into the social categories of "others." He argues that posthumanist and anti-humanist theories assume that everyone equally occupies the space of humanity, without accounting for the ongoing historicity of sociopolitical and racialized logics of colonialism and how political violence has been constitutive of the hierarchy of humanity.

Situating his theory of racialization within sociopolitical assemblages, Weheliye leans on the work of two Black feminists, Sylvia Wynter and Hortense Spillers. For Wynter (2001), neurobiology provides a theoretical route to explain how racializations become part of the ontologies of the body via neurochemical processes that reconfigure (the experience of) the self. Wynter argues that sociogenic (or narratives of the sociopolitical constitution of the huMan and difference) become ontogenic (or biological explanations of being and development) via the flesh. As a product of sociopolitical forces, race is not inherent to anatomical ontologies; instead those ontologies *become* racialized through encounters of/with racialized events, situations, or acts in and across time and space. Weheliye further states,

Consequently, racialization figures as a master code within the genre of the human represented by Western Man, because its law-like operations are yoked to species-sustaining physiological mechanisms in the form of a global color line—instituted by cultural laws so as to register in human neural networks—that clearly distinguishes the good/life/fully-human from the bad/death/not-quite-human.

(p. 27)

The "master code" that Weheliye posits points to the reality that processes of racialization express and nurture the capacities of certain bodies, while at the same time suppressing and hindering the expression and development of like capacities within other bodies. As an example, consider the decisions racially minoritized parents make in having the "race talk" with their children in order to ensure their safety by helping them make informed decisions about not only where to play, but what toys to play with depending on where you are playing (e.g., Tamir Rice). The "talk" is both a practice of racialization that disciplines and hinders the expression available to the body of the racialized as "other" child, just as it preserves the bodily expression of childhood for the child racialized as "normative."

Weheliye's theory of racializing assemblages—the racialized, classed, gendered, queered, and disabled shaping and forming of human, more than human, and non-human bodies—also draws upon Spillers' (2003) theorizing of the "flesh" as profoundly sociopolitical rather than biological. Spillers states "before the 'body' there is 'flesh,' that zero degree of social conceptualization and the discourse or the reflexes of iconography…" (as quoted by Weheliye, 2014, p. 39). Spillers argues that the formation of the flesh, itself a discourse, is historically and politically bound by the markings or traces of violence that designate a hierarchy of humanity. These markings or traces—aka the "hieroglyphics of the flesh"—are produced from the instruments or acts of violence such as slave masters' whips, police brutality, mass shootings, or more subtly from the silence in speech acts. These "hieroglyphics" are transmitted to future generations even as they remain obscured through that which is narrativized to be pathological or biological explanations of hierarchies of "difference." It is this violence and disciplining that designates bodies as full humans, not-quite-humans, and non-humans, rendering certain bodies as exceptional and others as disposable (Weheliye, 2014).

Racializing assemblages are empirically demonstrated, for instance, in the research on stereotype threat where there is an immediate situational affect of being exposed to or primed by a negative group stereotype and the produced anxiety of self-fulfilling that negative stereotype or being evaluated or judged by it, particularly when you want to disprove it. Steele and Aaronson (1995) found that these processes suppress performance on standardized educational tests. Here, the sociogenic "master code" that works to align Blackness with a negative group stereotype produces already (re-)programed neurobiological processes of anxiety and subsequently the suppression of performance on tests. Eudell (2015) argues:

stereotype threat can be positioned in a broader intellectual context as being neither an individual nor an arbitrary phenomenon, but rather can be understood as an organizing and integrating principle of the realization of what it means to Be Human in the present governing terms of biocentrism.

(p. 239)

Thus, stereotype threat is not an individual phenomenon of being primed by a negative group stereotype, but a discourse and politics of the body that manages and controls racialized populations.

Likewise, social epidemiology research indicates that racism and perceived discrimination become embodied and materialized in racial health disparities (Gravlee, 2009; Krieger, 2005; Williamson & Mohammed, 2009). Included in these racial health disparities are learning disabilities, developmental delays, mental health, exposure to lead, stress, and the onset of asthma, each empirically found to impact human learning and development. These studies make clear that power relations do not just exist in sociopolitical relations or in well-informed concerns about possible harm, but are actually already part of the corporeal matter of the body, forming and shaping how we preconsciously act and intra-act in the world as well as our material well-being—leaving more than just "traces" on otherwise discretely fleshy bodies, but reconstituting those bodies as racialized at the cellular level through and through.

The forces of racialization similarly occur in the discourses of schooling through disciplinary practices and students' interactions with schoolteachers and administration. Smith and Harper (2015) found that in 13 Southern states, Black students in K–12 public school were disproportionately suspended or expelled at higher rates. In 84 school districts in the South, Black students made up 100% of those students suspended. Ladson-Billings (2011) has also discussed how Black male behaviors in the classroom are feared and not tolerated whereas their white or Asian American counterparts' behaviors are much more tolerated. Others have found that school administrations respond differently to Black parents' engagement with the school, regardless of class (Lareau & Horvat, 1999), and parental meetings or conferences with school teachers have been found to, on average, have a negative effect on achievement growth for Black males (Dixon-Román, 2013). These racialized discursive practices of schooling discipline the bodies of students differently, encouraging for some greater space for risks and creative exploration and others less risk and greater practiced constraint.

Racializations also include the structural arrangement of space and resources and material conditions of space. Black families are disproportionately overrepresented in neighborhoods of urban poverty, and the impact of urban neighborhood poverty on contextual mobility has been more deleterious for Black families than for white families. For Black adults, on average 72% of those who reside in poor urban neighborhoods were raised by parents who resided in poor urban neighborhoods (Sharkey, 2011). This was only 40%, on average, for their white adult counterparts. In addition, Sharkey and Elwert (2011) empirically demonstrate that the degree of contextual mobility is consequential for education. They found that being raised in a high-poverty neighborhood in one generation has a substantial negative effect on child cognitive ability in the next generation. This is particularly alarming as research indicates that school desegregation trends halted in the early 1970s and that the reterritorialized boundaries of recent redistricting have not only been on racial lines but also have produced curricular differences as a result of resegregating processes and policies (Reardon & Yun, 2003; Rosiek & Winslow, 2016). These are but a few examples of how the conceptualizations of the human and the racialization of humans *matter*. These examples highlight how "master codes" become materialized in institutional policies and practices and in the forming and shaping of bodily capacities.

The Quantitative-Qualitative Divide and the Ethnographic Imagination

A commitment to reconceiving the human away from reductionist dualisms and toward understanding how racial logics operate in relation to the biopolitics of those whose bodily capacities are enabled or constrained by particular discursive constructions has broad and deep implications for how we reconfigure and think anew about the study of human and human activity in educational research. "Quantitative" research has long been assumed to have privileged and unbiased access to "nature," to pure reason, and factual evidence devoid of subjective interpretation. "Qualitative" research, by contrast, has been assumed to be the province of "social" and "cultural" phenomena or the study of "cultural" (read non-white, non-Western, non-affluent) persons which brought forth the ethnographic imagination. Insights from feminist new materialists around the entanglements between biology and culture suggest that each of these methods could be studying material and discursive processes and producing different forms of mutually constitutive data, thus creating the potential for "new empiricisms" (Clough, 2009).

Inheriting positivism from the Enlightenment, the "truths" of the social, cultural, and psychological world were understood to be lodged in the materiality of human phenomena. As part of the natural world, the material manifestations of human behavior are said to be fixed, pre-scripted, and prior to human symbolic consciousness and sociality. The material of human phenomena includes not just the solid, inert forms of physical matter but also the corporeality of human social behavior. Building from the Cartesian split between biology and culture, and understandings of matter as "corporeal substances," Comte's positivist philosophy forged what later became known as the quantitative imperative in the social sciences.

The quantitative imperative suggested that in order to unlock the "truths" of the world and to be considered a science, the discipline needed to employ the instrumental reason of quantification and demonstrate the ability to access objectivity. This imperative affected all of the disciplines of the social sciences including sociology, economics, psychology, anthropology, political science, linguistics, and history. For instance, the development of psychophysics, psychometrics, experimental psychology, mathematical psychology, and quantitative psychology each came about as different responses from the discipline of psychology to the quantitative imperative. Despite Comte specifically calling for mathematical reasoning and disagreeing with the lack of *determinism* in the probabilistic reasoning of statistics, much of the quantitative imperative for the social sciences became built on probability and statistics, now integral to the algorithms that underlie global social media platforms used by billions of people (e.g., Noble, 2018). The quantitative imperative was based on an alignment of quantitative reasoning with the study of nature and the objectivism of pure reason.

By contrast, the social scientific method that has long been understood for the study of culture is via the ethnographic imagination. Ethnographic practice has long been offered up as an approach to empiricism that ostensibly captures nuances of human thought and action supposedly distinct from the logics of quantification, logics that reduce the sloppiness of social life to the hard and fast numbers emerging from carefully crafted equations. The ethnographer's conventional path is typically conceived as a long journey from outsider to insider, from stranger to trusted/trustworthy interlocutor. The kind of knowledge gained from long-term, immersive "deep-hanging out" is meant to produce a kind of "thick description" (Geertz, 1973) of cultural practices that provides insights into communities, insights impossible to capture with the naked eye (that is, with weak forms of empiricism that don't appreciate how cultural practices are not fully comprehensible without a rich sense of sociocultural and historical context).

While anthropologists did not create ethnography, they worked to make it a systematic and routinized method acceptable to the academy. Before figures such as Bronislaw Malinowski affirmed the centrality of long-term field research, participant-observation, to anthropological knowledge production, "armchair anthropologists" used the observational work of priests, sailors, and others to ground their theories and contentions about human beings as a species. Unlike forms of cultural analysis not predicated on intensive and immersive cohabitation over months and even years (and with scientific aspirations different from the diarists and journalists who deploy similar field tactics), ethnography is recognized as a kind of empirical project that captures more of the intangible and tangible stuff of everyday culture than any news headline or regression analysis can muster. Of course, even though ethnographies are hardly one-size-fits-all in their embrace of positivist assumptions, there is a sense that recent anthropological investments in "the ontological turn," as well as recuperations of demonized forms of "thin description," are readable as emergent efforts to challenge some of the obvious assumptions of culture's ontological and heuristic ends/contours (Graeber, 2015; Jackson, 2013). Some of these emergent efforts include approaches to quantifying the quotidian processes of life via agent based modeling or the dynamic processes of the body with biomarker or forensic measurement. Even still, ethnography is fundamentally a genre organized to understand culture on its own terms (terms deemed distinct from nature) and with a fine-grained sensitivity to the particularities of culture that are both shared with others and distinct to the specific community being studied.

Reconceptualizing the Quantitative-Qualitative

The above discussed alignment of quantitative reasoning with nature and ethnography with culture is based on at least two false assumptions. First, the construction of mathematics as a discipline made both ideological and theological assumptions about mathematics and the universe. It was posited and believed that the language and logic of the universe was mathematics (aka the "book of the universe") and that its "universal" properties made it objective and distinct from language. The second assumption was that mathematics was understood to be of nature and not a discursive formation like language. Where language was understood to be culturally constructed by the human, mathematics was the provenance of nature.

As historians of statistics (e.g. Hacking, 2006) and cultural studies of mathematics (Kirby, 2011; Rotman, 2000) scholars have argued, prior to the Renaissance, probability was not understood to be evidence but rather opinion. In the same way, mathematics was understood as a cultural practice that does not have universal characteristics but rather discursive formations. Likewise, the gaze of the ethnographic has always observed and studied nature, material conditions, and materiality. From Geertz's classic example of the material performative act of the "wink" to Kohn's "anthropology beyond the human" and Campt's haptic inquiry into listening to images, ethnography has always studied the matter and materiality of nature. A more recent example is in Jason de Leon's *Land of Open Graves* where he studies the spatial arrangement, material conditions, and discursive practices of migration across the US Southern border. He employs the theories and methods from four subfields of anthropology, including forensics, in order to study the process of bodily decay in the elements of the open desert. His ethnographic approach among others provides profound new insight into the dynamic and vibrant acts of non-human and material objects and a great instantiation of how power works with the more-than-human to do its work of maintaining and reproducing power relations. Thus, both quantitative and ethnographic methods have always studied material and discursive processes, nature, and culture, yet have, over time, come to produce different forms of mutually constitutive data about human phenomena and the cultural world.

If the ethnographic imagination is an ethos and genre built for representing the nuances of cultural difference with a long-formed commitment to observational granularity, then quantification is a special case of the ethnographic imagination that takes its cues from similar logics of empirical essentialism and specificity—only all the more hallowed (in some circles) because of the would-be elegance and absolutism of its numeracy. The quantitative social sciences become only more hegemonic with the advent and ascendancy of "big data" as a way to reinforce assumptions about the power and force of quantifiable possibility. With various forms of computational methods, the unit of analysis becomes even smaller than the individual, purporting to capture tensors, flows, energy, and intensities of the body in ways that often circumvent the conditioning acts of subject formation. In computational cultures, the subject is often no longer asked any questions, the extraction of information from the datafied body is all that is needed and of interest. The ethnographer might study the data scientist, the latter interrogating matter with more granularly grand ambitions than ever. But the true power of big data might ultimately be in its backdoor challenge to the very distinction between quantity and quality. We see this quite literally where algorithms are designed to capture information based on unstructured data that was formerly of the domain of the non-quantifiable, culture, and the studies of the ethnographic, literature, art, or humanities (e.g., written or spoken speech, paintings, or photos). In big data's relentless commitment to re-scaling the known in ways that make aspirations of bigness (like thickness) unintelligible except with recourse to a vast and receding horizon of data points, the data scientist might be likened to an ethnographer's all-encompassing gaze. This is an ethnographer who was always raced, classed, and gendered despite all attempts at presuming a universal subject position beyond the particularities of identity, politics, and culture. Ultimately, this is an ethnographer that is in a field that has the observational granularity of a participant observer and of the deluge of big data.

Toward a New Empiricism

In light of the aforementioned onto-epistemological shifts and theoretical developments, we proffer thoughts toward a new empiricism by considering what emergent models of research these developments might suggest and what new methodological postures and possibilities might be employed. In contradistinction to the logical empiricist/positivist Western social science tendency to treat data as self-evident, we posit the profound importance for theory- and concept-driven research. Not only are data phenomena and events that provisionally emerge from a multiplicity of forces, affects, and intensities, they are also imbued with varying degrees of sociopolitical relations (Dixon-Román, 2017b). As Sharpe (2016) reminds us, the "wake" of colonialism and slavery continues to materialize in contemporary events of anti-Black sociopolitical violence. Here, wake is not just a metaphor for the disturbance and tracks left in a body of water or air from the movement of a body or ship (e.g., a slave ship), the wake is also to be understood as an analytic for examining anti-Black, hierarchizing, and differentiating reverberating forces of sociopolitical violence. This is not a phenomenological inquiry of "what is" but rather an examination of the becoming of how the events of sociopolitical violence come to be. What are the various affective becomings of those events? What might be the social formations (or machines) that are regularly generative of these events? Again, theory- and concept-driven inquiry, such as critical race and ethnic studies informed theories and concepts that interrogate and reimagine the complicated nature of sociopolitical violence, are necessary for examining these events of racializing assemblages and processes of becoming. Without careful theorizing and (re-)conceptualizing, researchers can reify racializing assemblages.

In addition, there is the need for a radical rethinking of new forms of empiricism. Clough's "The New Empiricisms" argues with Steinmetz (2005) that post-World War II United States produced a silent and even haunting epistemology that was dominated by methodological positivism. The post-World War II moment and the relationship between the government and the economy led to the prioritizing of the instrumental reason of quantitative sociology, while the non-positivist methodological approaches privileged the critical epistemological possibilities of qualitative inquiry. This, in part, was a reaction to the quantitative imperative of the social sciences, an imperative born out of logical empiricism/logical positivism that designated what was inclusive of scientific inquiry (Dixon-Román, 2017a). Thus, qualitative methods made an interpretive then phenomenological turn in order to critically distance themselves from the scientific reductionism of logical empiricism/logical positivism (Clough, 2009; St. Pierre, 2016). This more phenomenological move placed greater focus on the voice and experience of the marginalized subject by allowing their voice to be centered in research rather than that of theoretical narrative interpretation. Unfortunately, this shift in qualitative inquiry reinscribed the liberal all-knowing subject of Modernism while also re-introducing through the backdoor assumptions of data as self-evident from logical empiricism/logical positivism (Clough, 2009; St. Pierre, 2016). Thus, critical inquiry had reached a crossroads. Clough also describes how the digitization of society has enabled cultural critics to engage in an empiricism that examines not the given event or outcome but rather the conditions of external relations that produced the event's emergence, the study not of what *is* but of its *becoming*. As Clough and St. Pierre argue, this radically different form of empiricism, as put forth by Deleuze, necessitates new modes of inquiry, as a process of empiricism. These must be modes of inquiry that are not bounded by method, but begin from a philosophical question about in-process phenomena in a world that is constantly in motion, and in which one creatively imagines how we might engage those phenomena in order to begin to make sense of those processes in relation to our becoming. Such a process of inquiry is not prescribed, and as such, it would not close off work that allows new assemblages to emerge. Although this kind of inquiry is difficult, it should not be paralyzing.

Among the many approaches that might be proffered as a way to move forward, there are a few that we believe are paramount: multi-method and multi-modal. Multi-method includes multiple

Reconceptualizing the Quantitative-Qualitative

different methods of capturing and analyzing data, whereas multi-modal refers to approaches to inquiry that utilize different media to capture different forms of data such as oral, visual, etc. While we agree with Deleuze, Clough, and St. Pierre that method and mode should not drive inquiry, we do also believe that the creative approach of inquiry on generative conditions of becoming will often necessitate multiple and varied methods and modes of inquiry. These methods may include, for example, new forms of measurement (e.g., wearable biotechnology) or the social network analysis of social media, for instance. The process may also be multi-modal by way of using visual forms of documenting, performance/dance ethnography, or other forms of arts-based inquiry. Here, the inquiry is not aiming to be representative or to verify the identity of predetermined concepts and ideas; those are closed-ended processes that make it difficult for something different or new to emerge about learning. Instead, multiple methods and modes of inquiry attend to open-ended generative conditions of becoming to focus on tensions and contradictions that make a difference. As each method and mode illuminates something different about phenomena of inquiry, the tensions and contradictions become productive toward further illuminating and complicating the phenomena of interest (see Dixon-Román, 2017a for further explanation and examples). This is a process that is fundamentally interested in that which is ontologically new and different, and on understanding the complexity of ever-evolving human diversity and difference rather than essentializing human activity and performance.

Inseparable from the ontological and epistemological shifts of such an alternative approach for critical inquiry in educational research is the ethical. With the study of the generative conditions of emergent racializing events of learning and the forming and shaping of bodily capacities is also a debt and conditions of responsibility and answerability. As Harney and Moten (2013) argue, "We owe it to each other to falsify the institution, to make politics incorrect, to give the lie to our own determination" (p. 20). This radically different form of empiricism recognizes the inescapable links between tying true and false to right and wrong in ways that are justifiable, inescapable, and humane.

References

Barad, Karen (2007). *Meeting the Universe Halfway: Quantum Physics and the Entanglement of Matter and Meaning.* Durham: Duke University Press.

Berger, P., & Luckmann, T. (1967). *The Social Construction of Reality: A Treatise in the Sociology of Knowledge.* Garden City, NY: Anchor.

Boesch, C., & Tomasello, M. (1998). Chimpanzee and human cultures. *Current Anthropology*, 39(5), 591–604.

Bourdieu, P. (1980/1990). *The Logic of Practice.* Stanford, CA: Stanford University Press.

Bourdieu, P., & Passeron, J. C. (1977). *Reproduction in Education, Society, and Culture* (4th ed.). Thousand Oaks, CA: Sage Publications.

Butler, J. (1993). *Bodies That Matter: On the Discursive Limits of "Sex".* New York, NY: Routledge.

Chakrabarty, D. (2000). *Provincializing Europe: Postcolonial Thought and Historical Difference.* Princeton, NJ: Princeton University Press.

Chetty, R., Friedman, J. N., Hendren, N., Jones, M. R., & Porter, S. R. (2018). *The Opportunity Atlas: Mapping the Childhood Roots of Social Mobility* (No. w25147). Cambridge, MA: National Bureau of Economic Research.

Clough, P. (2009). The new empiricism: Affect and sociological method. *European Journal of Social Theory*, 12(1), 43–61.

Cole, M., & Scribner, S. (1974). *Culture and Thought.* New York, NY: Wiley.

Coole, D., & Frost, S. (2010). *New Materialisms: Ontology, Agency, and Politics.* Durham, NC: Duke University Press.

da Silva, D. F. (2007). *Toward a Global Idea of Race.* Minneapolis, MN: University of Minnesota Press.

Derrida, J. (1974/1984). *Of Grammatology* (G. C. Spivak Trans.). Baltimore, MD: Johns Hopkins University Press.

Descartes, R. (2017). *Descartes: Meditations on First Philosophy: With Selections from the Objections and Replies.* New York, NY: Cambridge University Press.

Dixon-Román, E. (2013). The forms of capital and the developed achievement of Black males. *Urban Education*, 48(6), 828–862.

Dixon-Román, E. (2017a). *Inheriting Possibility: Social Reproduction and Quantification in Education*. Minneapolis, MN: University of Minnesota Press.

Dixon-Román, E. (2017b). Toward A hauntology on data: On the sociopolitical forces of data assemblages. *Research in Education*, 98(1), 44–58.

Eudell, D. (2015). "Come On Kid, Let's Go Get The Thing": The sociogenic principle and the being of being black/human. In: Katherine McKittrick (Ed.), *Sylvia Wynter: On Being Human As Praxis* (pp. 226–248). Durham: Duke University Press.

Foucault, M. (1990). *The History of Sexuality: An Introduction*. New York, NY: Vintage.

Geertz, C. (1973). *The Interpretation of Cultures*. New York, NY: Basic Books.

Graeber, D. (2015). Radical alterity is just another way of saying 'reality': A reply to Eduardo Viveiros de Castro. *The Journal of Ethnographic Theory*, 5(2), 1–41.

Gravlee, C. C. (2009). How race becomes biology: Embodiment of social inequality. *American Journal of Physical Anthropology*, 139(1), 47–57.

Gutiérrez, K., & Rogoff, B. (2003). Cultural ways of learning: Individual traits or repertoires of practice. *Educational Researcher*, 32(5), 19–25.

Hacking, I. (2006). *The Emergence of Probability: A Philosophical Study of Early Ideas About Probability Induction and Statistical Inference* (2nd ed.). New York, NY: Cambridge University Press.

Harney, S., & Moten, F. (2013). *The Undercommons: Fugitive Planning & Black Study*. New York, NY: Minor Compositions.

Hoffmeyer, J. (2008). *Biosemiotics: An Examination into the Signs of Life and the Life of Signs*. Scranton, PA: University of Scranton Press.

Holland, D. C., Lachicotte, W., Skinner, D., & Cain, D. (2001). *Identity and Agency in Cultural Worlds*. Cambridge: Harvard University Press.

Jackson, J. (2013). *Thin Description: Ethnography and the African Hebrew Israelites of Jerusalem*. Harvard: Harvard University Press.

Kawagley, A. O. (2006). *A Yupiaq Worldview: A Pathway to Ecology and Spirit* (2nd ed.). Long Grove, IL: Waveland Press. Inc.

Kirby, V. (2011). *Quantum Anthropologies: Life at Large*. Durham: Duke University Press.

Krieger, N. (2005). Embodiment: A conceptual glossary for epidemiology. *Journal of Epidemiology and Community Health*, 59(5), 350–355.

Ladson-Billings, G. (2011). Boyz to men? Teaching to restore Black boys' childhood. *Race, Ethnicity and Education*, 14(1), 7–15.

Lareau, A., & Horvat, E. M. (1999). Moments of social inclusion and exclusion: Race, class, and cultural capital in family-school relationships. *Sociology of Education*, 72(1), 37–53.

Lave, J., & Wenger, E. (1991). *Situated Learning: Legitimate Peripheral Participation*. New York, NY: Cambridge University Press.

Lee, C. (2001). Is October Brown Chinese? A cultural modeling activity system for underachieving students. *American Educational Research Journal*, 38(1), 97–142.

Lerman, S. (2000). The social turn in mathematics education research. In: J. Boaler (Ed.), *Multiple Perspectives on Mathematics Teaching and Learning* (pp. 19–44). Westport, CT: Ablex.

Massumi, B. (2002). *Parables for the Virtual: Movement, Affect, Sensation*. Durham: Duke University Press.

Matusov, E., & Hayes, R. (2000). Sociocultural critique of Piaget and Vygotsky. *New Ideas in Psychology*, 18(2–3), 215–239.

Mbembe, Achille (2017). *Critique of Black Reason*. Durham, NC: Duke University Press.

McKinney de Royston, M., & Sengupta-Irving, T. (2019). Another step forward: Engaging the political in learning. *Cognition and Instruction*, 37(3), 277–284. doi: 10.1080/07370008.2019.1624552

Minick, N. (1987). The development of Vygotsky's thought an introduction. In: R. W. Rieber, & A. S. Carton (Eds.), *The Collected Works of L. S. Vygotsky* (Vol. 1, pp. 17–36). New York, NY: Plenum Press.

Noble, S. U. (2018). *Algorithms of Oppression: How Search Engines Reinforce Racism*. New York, NY: NYU.

Piaget, J. (1973). *To Understand Is to Invent: The Future of Education*. New York, NY: The Viking Press.

Piaget, J. (1995). In Smith, I. *Sociological Studies* (2nd ed.). (Smith et al., Trans.). London, New York, NY: Routledge (Original work published 1977).

Reardon, S. F., & Yun, J. T. (2003). Integrating neighborhoods, segregating schools: The retreat from school desegregation in the South, 1990–2000. *North Carolina Law Review*, 81(4), 1563–1596.

Roberts, D. (2011). *Fatal Invention: How Science, Politics, and Big Business Re-Create Race in the Twenty-First Century*. New York, NY: The New Press.

Rogoff, B. (2003). *The Cultural Nature of Human Development*. New York, NY: Oxford University Press.

Rogoff, B., & Chavajay, P. (1995). What's become of research on the cultural basis of cognitive development? *American Psychologist*, 50(10), 859.

Rosiek, J., & Kinslow, K. (2016). *Resegregation as Curriculum: The Meaning of the New Racial Segregation in the US Public Schools*. New York, NY: Routledge.

Rotman, B. (2000). *Mathematics as Sign: Writing, Imagining, Counting*. Stanford: Stanford University Press.

Sharkey, P. (2011). *Stuck in Place: Urban Neighborhoods and the End of Progress Toward Racial Equality*. Chicago, IL: University of Chicago Press.

Sharkey, P., & Elwert, F. (2011). The legacy of disadvantage: Multigenerational neighborhood effects on cognitive ability. *American Journal of Sociology*, 116(6), 1934–1981.

Sharpe, C. (2016). *In the Wake: On Blackness and Being*. Durham, NC: Duke University Press.

Smith, E. J., & Harper, S. R. (2015). *Disproportionate Impact of K–12 School Suspension and Expulsion on Black Students in Southern States*. Philadelphia, PA: University of Pennsylvania, Center for the Study of Race and Equity in Education.

Spillers, H. (2003). *Black White and in Color: Essays on American Literature and Culture*. Chicago, IL: University of Chicago Press.

St. Pierre, E. A. (2016). The empirical and the new empiricisms. *Cultural Studies-Critical Methodologies*, 16(3), 111–124.

Steele, C. M., & Aronson, J. (1995). Stereotype threat and the intellectual test performance of African Americans. *Journal of Personality and Social Psychology*, 69(5), 797–811.

Steinmetz, G. (2005). The epistemological unconscious of U.S. Sociology and the transition to post Fordism: The case of historical sociology. In: J. Adams, E. Clemens, & A. Orloff (Eds.), *Remaking Modernity Politics, History and Sociology* (pp. 109–160). Durham, NC: Duke University Press.

Stetsenko, A. (2005). Activity as object-related: Resolving the dichotomy of individual and collective planes of activity. *Mind, Culture, and Activity*, 12(1), 70–88.

Stetsenko, A. (2008). From relational ontology to transformative activist stance on development and learning: Expanding Vygotsky's (CHAT) project. *Cultural Studies of Science Education*, 3(2), 471–491.

Swimme, B. T., & Tucker, M. E. (2011). *Journey of the Universe*. New Haven, CT: Yale University Press.

Tuck, E., & McKenzie, M. (2015). *Place in Research: Theory, Methodology, and Methods*. New York, NY: Routledge.

Vygotsky, L. (1978). *Mind in Society* (M. Cole, V. John-Steiner, S. Scribner, & E. Souberman, Eds.). Cambridge, MA: Harvard University Press.

Weheliye, A. (2014). *Habeas Viscus: Racializing Assemblages, Biopolitics, and Black Feminist Theories of the Human*. Durham, NC: Duke University Press.

Williams, D., & Mohammed, S. A. (2009). Discrimination and racial disparities in health: Evidence and needed research. *Journal of Behavioral Medicine*, 32(1), 20–47.

Wynter, S. (2001). Towards the sociogenic principle: Fanon, identity, the puzzle of conscious experience, and what it is like to be Black. In: A. Gomez-Moriana, & M. Duran-Cogan (Eds.), *National Identities and Sociopolitical Changes in Latin America* (pp. 30–66). New York, NY: Routledge.

Wynter, S. (2007). Human being as noun? Or being human as praxis? Towards the autopoetic turn/overturn: A manifesto. Available at: https://www.scribd.com/document/329082323/Human-Being-as-Noun-Or-Being-Human-as-Praxis-Towards-the-Autopoetic-Turn-Overturn-A-Manifesto#from_embed (last accessed May 19, 2017).

19

SOCIAL DESIGN-BASED EXPERIMENTS

A Utopian Methodology for Understanding New Possibilities for Learning

Kris D. Gutiérrez, A. Susan Jurow, and Sepehr Vakil

Introduction

Social design-based experiments (SDBEs) are a new design methodology in education. The approach is gaining traction as a way of studying and organizing for equity and learning in complex, real-world situations. Social design-based experiments foreground the political and ethical dimensions of design research and our theories of learning. Doing so raises questions about issues including the kinds of problems that are best suited for SDBE methodology, the role of the researcher and their participants over the arc of a project, and the desired impact of an intervention(s) that is situated in dynamic historical and cultural contexts. In this chapter, we offer an introduction to SDBE methodology. We begin by describing its relation to other design methodologies for studying learning and explain how it is distinct from these approaches. In the second section, we illustrate how we have organized SDBEs to address community-based problems, highlighting some of the tensions around doing this work in practice.

Defining Social Design-Based Experiments and Their History

This chapter elaborates an approach to design-based research that seeks to co-design learning ecologies in which learning is made equitable and consequential for youth from nondominant communities. As we have written in Gutiérrez and Jurow (2016, p. 2):

> Social design methodology combines traditions of design-based research (Design Based Research Collective, 2003) and democratizing forms of inquiry that seek to make the design experimentation process a co-construction between different institutional stakeholders (Cole & the Distributed Literacy Consortium, 2006). Social design research shares important theoretical and methodological features and aims with sociocultural approaches to design, including formative interventions (Bronfenbrenner, 1979; Engeström, 2011) and ecologically valid experimentation (Cole, Hood, & McDermott, 1982; Scribner & Cole, 1981). Social design research also complements the context-sensitive, problem-focused, and iterative approach of design research (Brown, 1992; Sandoval & Bell, 2004) and is compatible with the goals of the design-based research community as advanced

by Collins, Joseph, and Bielaczyc (2004), Cobb, Confrey, diSessa, Lehrer, and Schauble (2003), and Anderson and Shattuck (2012).

Informed by cultural historical activity theory and ecological and critical approaches to inquiry, SDBEs involve proleptic forms of design organized around a utopian ideal and methodology (Brown & Cole, 2001; Levitas, 2013)—that is, imagining and designing an ideal ecology and outcome. However, these outcomes are not fixed but instead are better understood as moving horizons of possibility. Thus, rather than static or stable, SDBEs utopian ideal pulls collectives forward in a process through which goals are necessarily reimagined and modified. Social design-based experiments, as a utopian methodology, are concerned with possible futures (Gutiérrez, 2008) and robust conceptions of "human flourishing in [the contexts of] those possible futures" (Levitas, 2013, p. xi). Our approach to SDBEs thus envisions utopia as both method and goal, recognizing that they are inextricably related to each other through the design of ecologies that support robust learning and becoming.

Our work on SDBEs has been developed in relation to conceptions of utopia as method and goal with roots in traditions of inquiry in sociological (Levitas, 2013) and cultural historical activity theory (Engeström, 1987; 2001; Cole & Engeström, 1993; Leont'ev, 1981). There are a number of ways to think about utopia. Our work finds resonance with Levitas' conception of utopia "as the expression of the desire of a better way of being or of living, and as such is braided through human culture" (p. xii). This conception of utopia is affective and cognitive, one that moves between the present and the future and as such sustains the tension between "re-reading the present from the standpoint of the future, transforming it into the history of the future" (Levitas, 2013, p. 218). This future orientation is linked to a commitment to developing a historicized view of the present to engage in newly imagined projections of learning and becoming in the future. We argue that how the past is indexed in the present helps us develop as well as design our futures as individuals in collectives. This attention to history helps open up the process of prolepsis—an important design principle in the development of people's future selves and a future-oriented agenda (Gutiérrez, 2016; 2018). We build on these insights and extend them by focusing directly on learning and conceptual development as drivers of systemic change and movement toward utopian ideals. A central premise of SDBEs is that learning is organized as a formative anticipation of a possible future (Vossoughi, 2011), that is, "the realization of a potential, through a process of prolepsis, a mediated representation and nascent experience of the future in the present" (p. 184).

The practice of utopian thinking as part of social design-based experimentation moves us from abstract notions of the ideal to concrete processes of what utopian designs mean, what Bloch (1986) refers to as *docta spes,* i.e., "informed or educated hope" (Levitas, 2013, p. 5)—"a move from the purely fantastical to the genuinely possible" (p. 6). This focus on possible horizons is thus tightly aligned with SDBEs' proleptic orientation and imagination. Following Wartofsky (1979), this process necessarily involves learning to see historically in which "representation" is replaced with "imagination," and relating this process to the activities of "picturing and modeling" new social futures (Gutiérrez, 2016, p. 189). Thus, the utopian character of SDBEs is tied to a social imagination about the design of learning systems or ecologies that are equitable, resilient, sustainable, future oriented, and necessarily contextualized in participants' meaningful life activities.

Part of utopian method, metaphorically and analytically, is learning to see possibility and ingenuity in people's everyday practices to imagine and design new forms of learning and schooling that rupture educational and social inequality and invite new forms of participatory inquiry that have transformative potential for vulnerable communities (Gutiérrez et al., 2017). These new approaches involve a reconceptualization of what it means to partner with nondominant communities toward the design of new technologies and infrastructure that support the production of knowledge, with an emphasis on what participants collectively deem valuable. This is exceedingly important as rapidly growing infrastructures are reproducing and expanding inequality.

Drawing on insights from science studies and critical feminist sociology of science perspectives, our analyses at work in SDBEs help us focus on how the world gets built materially, symbolically, and culturally to advance some forms of knowledge and not others (Bowker & Star, 2000; Hall, Stevens, & Torralba, 2002). As Shea and Jurow (under review) explain in their analysis of changing infrastructure to support social transformation:

> Star and Ruhleder (1996) uses the term "infrastructure" to describe the fundamentally relational network of people, practices, and technologies that constitute the classification systems, procedures, and physical materials on which society runs. [It] is nearly "invisible" when it is functioning well. When it breaks down or is seen as getting in the way of desired goals, we can become aware of how it is put together, whom it serves well, and who suffers as a result of its constitution.

Of relevance to the method of collaborative work we do with colleagues, attention to how people's lives get organized requires a focus on all facets of infrastructure, as it helps us understand what gets valued and by whom; such analysis should also orient us to what Soja (1989, 2010) calls geographies of consequentiality, including issues of who has transportation and health care, how cities are planned, and so forth. Social design-based experiments, then, are concerned with how the world gets built to advance some view or practice and not others—a perspective that orients the design of our interventions to the re-mediation of failing and inequitable systems with attention to a system's reorganization and all aspects of the ecology (Gutiérrez, 2016; 2018). This points to one of the challenges in doing relevant empirical work: understanding that "seeing" is socially situated, power-laden, and historically constituted (Goodwin, 1994).

Design Principles

Social design-based experiments begin from a place of hope and possibility, stemming out of the material reality that there are many groups of people who have been, and continue to be, oppressed as a result of systemic injustice. Central to this approach, we work *with* the people who have faced these injustices in order to understand and directly address their experiences of oppression and understand their remarkable individual and collective agency. Social design-based experiments were first developed as a way of systematically addressing urgent problems of practice relevant to redressing educational inequities for vulnerable student populations and communities. The orienting principles of SDBEs emerged as a concrete response to the material conditions created by social and educational inequality, and through a process of reading, theorizing, and deep empirical work across multiple research and practice sites.

We briefly describe these early programs to explain how the methodology developed out of dialogic engagement with community problems, social theory, and pedagogical innovations. The long-standing ecologies from which the SDBE approach was developed were deeply collaborative with community partners, school administrators, students, and researchers. Through engagement with these various stakeholders, participants gained deep understanding of the problems facing communities. Relationships characterized by trust and mutual relations of exchange, in terms of division of labor, goals, and ideas, supported joint work around imagining a better future. The main sites out of which social design-based experimentation emerged were an innovative, intensive pre-collegiate summer academic institute for high school youth who shared migrant farmworker backgrounds (the Migrant Student Leadership Institute/MSLI) and several after-school community collaboratives (*Las Redes* and *El Pueblo Mágico*), for K–5 youth from nondominant and immigrant communities, largely Latinx.

Social Design-Based Experiments

The impetus for SDBEs was motivated by a desire for educational justice in environments and communities of interest in which learning for youth from nondominant communities could become meaningful and consequential, expanding their social futures. The MSLI and the after-school community collaboratives were designed to counter persistent problems of educational inequity and harm for nondominant communities. They offered alternative ways of organizing learning, teaching, and educational possibilities for young people who had not been served well by the infrastructural organization of public schooling. The MSLI was a learning ecology in which conventional conceptions of disciplinary learning and instruction were contested and replaced with syncretic forms of learning (Gutiérrez, 2014) that privileged and were contingent upon students' sociohistorical lives, both proximally and distally (Gutiérrez, 2008; Gutiérrez & Jurow, 2016; Vossoughi, 2014; Espinoza, 2009). Within the MSLI, translanguaging practices, the conscious use of social theory, the playful imagination, and historicized disciplinary learning in which students could re-imagine themselves as historical actors (Gutiérrez & Becker et al., 2019) were normative. As cross-institutional partnerships, *Las Redes* and *El Pueblo Mágico* were educational designs that privileged intergenerational collaboration and foregrounded the agency of learners in ways that are distinct from the agency of designers and policymakers. These collaborative experiments promoted new forms of engagement mediated by novel technologies and divisions of labor in which learning was reorganized to create space for experimenting pedagogically across institutional settings—the university and community (Cole, 1996; Cole & Griffin, 1980; Gutiérrez, Bien, & Selland, 2011; Vasquez, 2003). At their best, SDBEs like the MSLI, *Las Redes*, and *El Pueblo Mágico* had the potential to become lived arguments for the possible, what Wartofsky referred to as tertiary artifacts, "imaginative artifacts that color the way we see the 'actual' world, providing a tool for changing current practice" (Cole, 1996, p. 121). The dual goals of equity and transformative learning in SDBEs were brought together in the organization of newly imagined ecologies in which such goals were viewed as interrelated.

This utopian design method necessarily involved bringing together robust conceptions of learning and culture, while foregrounding foundational concepts of justice and social transformation. We drew on cultural historical activity theory (Engeström, 1987; 2011; Cole & Engeström, 1993; Vygotsky, 1978), democratizing forms of inquiry (Freire, 1970; 1998), and later, a resilience thinking framework (Walker & Salt, 2006) to make visible design principles for modeling resilient and equitable learning ecologies. The core principles of SDBEs require: (a) deep attention to history and historicity, including how they relate to resilience, sustainability, and equity; within activity theory, historicity helps make visible previous cycles of the activity system, as well as spaces of constraint and possibility "against their historical background" (Engeström, 1991, p. 14–15); (b) a focus on prolepsis, the "cultural mechanism," as Cole (1996) has written, "that brings the past into the present" (p. 183); (c) vigilance to making equity central across design cycles in which the construct of equity is understood as both an ideal and material, and an actionable tool; (d) a focus on re-mediating activity which reorganizes the functional system, rather than on "fixing" individuals (see Cole & Griffin, 1986; Gutiérrez, Morales, & Martinez, 2009 for further elaboration)—a move that helps to make visible and challenge deficit and reductive notions of learners and their potential; (e) employing a dynamic model of culture with an understanding that cultural and other forms of diversity are key resources for the sustainability of ecologies, and where attending to cultural regularity and heterogeneity is essential; (f) an emphasis on resilience and change, where change implicates the individual, the collective, and the ecology, and where resilience encompasses ecological thinking about social and environmental systems; and (g) an end goal of transformation and sustainability (See Gutiérrez, 2016, p. 192). Here, drawing on Walker and Salt (2006), transformability involves the "capacity to create a fundamentally new system when ecological, social, economic, and political conditions make the existing system untenable" (p. 62) and sustainability enhances the resilience of social-ecological systems, rather than fixing isolated components of the system (p. 9) (see Figure 19.1).

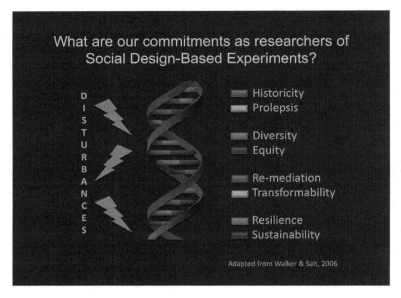

Figure 19.1 Design Principles for Social Design Experiments. Adapted from Walker and Salt 2006, Gutiérrez, 2016).

Although these principles work hand-in-hand to conceive of and implement social design-based experiments, particular emphasis is given to those design elements related to justice and transformation. In previous work, we have illustrated some key dimensions of enduring resilient ecologies, such as diversity, transformability, and sustainability (Walker & Salt, 2006), and mutual relations of exchange with partners to make the case for consequential design interventions for youth and families from nondominant communities (Gutiérrez, 2016; Gutiérrez & Jurow, 2016). This focus on changing systems and infrastructure is tied to particular notions of equity, resilience, and change. As Levitas (2013, p. xii) notes, however, "It is the nature of [that] change that is in question." She elaborates:

> We need to think about what kind of social and economic system can deliver secure and sustainable livelihoods and ways of life for all. For those who still think that utopia is about the impossible, what really is impossible is to carry on as we are, with social and economic systems that enrich a few but destroy the environment and impoverish most of the world's population. Our very survival depends on finding another way of living.
>
> (p. xii)

Thus, social design-based research's utopian methodology and commitments to transformative change must engage and experiment with how diversity and equity are intertwined with the design and sustainability of resilient ecologies in which learning and becoming are made just. Paraphrasing Wartofsky (1979), we ask: what perceptions of equity and justice underlie our research and design-based interventions and what is their role in advancing a more expansive social and pedagogical imagination for all youth across all schools and communities?

Equity as Ideal and Material

Design-based research aims to generate new visions, theories, and technological tools for teaching and learning that can advance change in educational settings. Social design-based experiments share these aims, but are distinct from design-based research efforts (Brown, 1992; Collins, 1992) in their focus on joining equity and learning goals. It is through pursuing these goals as linked that SDBEs aim to transform inequitable institutions. As a form of proleptic design, SDBEs are focused on organizing new trajectories for learning and identity development and working side-by-side with community partners to identify those needs that are the most urgent for nondominant communities. This approach centers people's lived experiences as the driver of possibilities for learning such that participants become intentional designers of their own futures. They become what Espinoza (2003) and Gutiérrez et al. (2019) refer to as conscious "historical actors" who can manage everyday dilemmas, challenge the impact and intentions of systems and the people who created them, use and develop tools toward different ends, and strive to address social and political inequities. This attention to the challenges that communities face demands analysis of their everyday practices and the creativity therein to design for new forms of learning and development that can be consequential for participants across scales.

Shining the light on inequitable systems and their practices is an important first step in addressing problems of oppression and white supremacy (Kendi, 2019). Yet, we are concerned that much of education research has been devoted to the moral side of equity, where equity is the goal or the rationale for projects and interventions. Significant attention has been given (understandably) to developing ideal notions of equity (i.e., equity as a just and righteous goal). We have also made good headway in addressing equity materially through curriculum and pedagogy. We need, however, much more work on the material side of equity such as has been developed in legal scholarship (e.g., Haney-López, 2003) and through the law (e.g., Williams v. California, Brown v. Board of Education) to advance educational justice in the courts.

In our design work we treat equity as both an ideal and material tool; equity is our miner's canary (Guinier & Torres, 2002), that is, a tool for making visible and monitoring the materiality of in/equity across design cycles by monitoring the health, well-being, and resilience of the entire ecology for all participants, but especially those who are in subordinate positions within these communities. For example, Gutiérrez developed a set of indices as part of operationalizing an equity framework with school partners to track, over time, the material conditions of emergent bilinguals' everyday schooling experiences. In monitoring opportunity to learn, Gutiérrez in partnership with school teachers and administrators developed the following indices: (a) the degree of separation emergent bilinguals experienced academically and socially; (b) their rates of school mobility; (c) access to courses required for college admission whose practices were organized around meaningful learning and participation; (d) access to credentialed, experienced, and well-prepared teachers; (e) ongoing opportunity to develop dynamic and multiple learning and career pathways; (f) opportunity to use their language repertoires to learn and make meaning; and (g) opportunity to appropriate a robust set of college-going practices (Gutiérrez & Jurow, 2016). By viewing equity's ideal and pragmatic and material dimensions, we are able to organize work toward equity as a social interactional achievement and a pragmatic imperative of SDBEs. Social design-based research strives to develop and employ a more complex and nuanced conception of inequity grounded in people's lived and felt experiences of oppression. Toward this end, inequity must be understood and addressed systemically across spatial, temporal, and social scales of action. This allows us to understand inequities dynamically and as experienced differentially by people and communities, rather than as uniformly experienced. Further, the nature of inequity is that it is intersectionally compounded. It is complicated by race, gender, sexual orientation, social class, citizenship status, and employment, for example, and by the resources and constraints of the ecology and the cumulative history of oppression shared by nondominant communities (Lee, 2010).

Social design-based experiment's cultural historical theoretical underpinning and attention to equity orients researchers to seek deeper understanding of the following: (a) the resources and constraints of the ecologies that constitute people's everyday lives; (b) the full range of people's practices understood across at least several activity systems; (c) people's repertoires of practice, including the history of those practices (Gutiérrez & Rogoff, 2003); and (d) people's participation in and movement within and across activity systems, as well as what takes hold in that movement (Gutiérrez, 2008). While this approach benefits from mixed methods, it privileges multi-sited ethnography (drawing in part from Marcus, 1995) to develop an appreciation of community members' categories and experiences and broader understanding of the ecology, its resources and constraints, and the complexity and diversity of the various activity systems of which people are a part. This "multi-sited ethnographic sensibility" helps make visible how learning is made consequential in people's movement across practices, as well as which tools might facilitate and constrain that movement (Vossoughi & Gutiérrez, 2014).

Radical Openness and Possibility

Designing research that lifts up the practices of nondominant communities requires a different kind of design-based research; it requires attention to the everyday, to how people's repertoires of practice get constructed and are made consequential in and across sociopolitical and sociohistorical contexts. We seek to bring to the fore, in our collaborative work with communities, an awareness of infrastructures and how our worlds are constructed materially, symbolically, and culturally (Bowker & Star, 2000), as well as how these infrastructures can be transformed. In this chapter, we thus engage in a discussion about how social design-based experimentation can be employed as a utopian method. We ask: how can we design for spaces of radical openness and possibility in the study of learning? We use the phrase "radical openness and possibility," following hooks (1990), as a way of enriching how we talk about equity in the study of learning and in SDBEs in particular (Jurow, 2018). Designing for radical openness and possibility is a way of challenging the political and social order as a way to develop theories of learning that can embody "lived arguments for the possible" (Gutiérrez & Jurow, 2016).

hooks (1989) describes what it means to imagine the possible from the position of marginality and oppression. She writes:

> I am located in the margin. I make a definite distinction between that marginality which is imposed by oppressive structures and that marginality one chooses as site of resistance—as location of radical openness and possibility.

For hooks, the margin is not a place to "…give up or surrender as part of moving into the center—it is a site one stays in, clings to even, because it nourishes one's capacity to resist…to imagine alternatives, new worlds" (p. 150). Radical openness and possibility thus signifies a generative space for freedom, a space alive with continual engagement, play, and the re-making of cultural and historical relations that can create flourishing ways of being and becoming. Radical openness and possibility is fundamentally about learning, without bounds and without end. This type of learning has a deeply ethical dimension; it is about creating new forms of collective life and ways of being with care and compassion for others in the world.

Introduction to the Cases

In this section, we present two examples of social design-based experimentation to illuminate how cultural practices mediate new forms of learning and becoming. Prior research on cultural-historical practices has detailed how they are lived in people's varied forms of engagement in recurrent activities across space and time (Eckert, 1989; Gutiérrez & Rogoff, 2003; Nasir, 2011); are dynamic and creative (Holland & Eisenhart, 1990; Saxe, 2012); vary within groups (e.g., ethnic, racial) and not only between groups; and, are intricately connected to power (Abu-Lughod, 1991; Anzaldúa, 1987). Expanding upon this literature, within these cases we foreground how social design-based experiment methodology builds on insights about cultural-historical practices and learning to transform oppressive systems.

In the first case, which is grounded in ongoing activism in relation to the food justice movement, Jurow focuses on the sensitivities to historicity, resilience, and sustainability that guide engagement in SDBEs. She writes specifically about what we notice and how this shapes how we organize consequential change. The second case focuses our attention on how the interplay between historicity and re-mediation in social design experiments deepens our vision of, and expectations for, innovations in education premised on notions of educational equity. In this instance, the case is grounded in Vakil's multi-year collaboration with a high school computer science teacher to design Computer Science (CS) learning opportunities grounded in complex interactions between technology, ethics, and power. We show how an SDBE lens surfaces critical tensions otherwise obscured, specifically related to politicized trust, across multiple activity systems. We present these cases to underscore how SDBEs help us theorize learning as mediated by cultural-historical practices and are thus deeply linked to considerations of community desires for organizing their own futures.

A Case of Social Design-Based Experimentation: Beginning with Food Justice

The Learning in the Food Movement[1] project was organized to contribute to how scholars study social practice theories of learning. The project was: (1) intentionally focused on the development of new cultural forms of knowledge and identity in contentious, collective action; and (2) centered on community-led efforts to organize justice (Jurow & Shea, 2015). The Learning in the Food Movement team worked with the non-profit Impact[2] for five years. Impact was founded by two white men who grew up in the state where the non-profit is located and who wanted to improve the quality of life for their city's most marginalized populations. Impact situated their efforts in South Elm, a historically immigrant neighborhood marginalized by city policies and lack of economic investment, but resourceful in terms of community activism.

At the time of the study, the co-founders of Impact served as the non-profit's Executive Director and the Director of Operations for the organization. Impact's staff also included eight *promotoras*, seven women and one man from the community. The *promotoras* were recent immigrants from Mexico who were primarily Spanish speakers—though they all spoke some English. The Impact website describes the *promotora* model in this way:

> Community health workers can be found in every nation and culture. The *promotora* model has been used extensively in Latin America, and has recently—since the 1950s— been applied in the United States to bridge gaps between people and resources in rural and underserved communities. From personal to environmental health, [*promotoras*] are advocates for change and work to create thriving, resilient communities for their families and neighbors.

The founders of Impact recognized the value of using an asset-based approach wherein they could use the *promotora* model in South Elm to leverage the shared cultural practices and language backgrounds between *promotoras* and residents to facilitate desired health and economic goals. Impact focused their energies on improving access to healthy food in South Elm. The U.S. Department of Agriculture had categorized South Elm as a "food desert" because the residents did not have easy geographical access to buying healthy and affordable food.

Impact's most successful and long-standing initiative is its backyard garden program. Through this initiative, residents are supported in designing and growing their own backyard vegetable gardens with educational and material support from the non-profit. The *promotoras* plan the gardens with the residents, prepare the ground for the gardens, and regularly attend to the gardens to help the residents grow a wide variety of vegetables and fruits. On their regular visits to the gardens, *promotoras* get to know their neighbors, the problems they are facing, and how they might assist them either directly or through recruiting resources from the non-profit and other community organizations. This was a particularly important function as the neighborhood was one without a lot of resources and financial means. The residents thus had needs that were not met by established infrastructure. Since Impact began the backyard garden program (ten years ago at the time of this writing), they have established more than 2000 backyard gardens. Residents have produced over 500,000 pounds of organic produce for themselves and their neighbors. From a structural change perspective, Impact has worked with city, private, and national funders along with residents to develop a cooperative market where neighbors can sell their produce to others in South Elm and to residents in other parts of the city. This has changed the physical organization of the neighborhood *and* the understanding of "community" as a concept that mediates how people interact with each other, materials, and ideas (Hall & Jurow, 2015).

Over the five years during which the Learning in the Food Movement team collaborated with the non-profit, the organization grew and its needs shifted. Relatedly, Jurow (the Principal Investigator of the project) played many different roles. She was a researcher, a professional development designer and leader, and on request of the *promotoras* and the non-profit leadership, a member of the Impact Board of Directors. The story of this SDBE, the neighborhood's changing circumstances, and the shifting roles the researchers played in relation to the work were interrelated; they mediated each other. Understanding these shifts—why they took place and how they changed the collective work of the project—is a critical, but under-investigated dimension of design research that can illuminate learning and processes of cultural change (Teeters, Jurow, & Shea, 2016).

Designing for Radical Openness and Possibility

Designing for radical openness and possibility in SDBEs demands sensitivity to historicity as embodied in people's lived experiences as well as the organization of infrastructure, the sustainability of designs, particularly as they leverage diverse forms of expertise to imagine new possibilities (Gutiérrez & Jurow, 2016), and resilience as evidenced in individuals' ingenuity in increasingly "tight" (McDermott, 2010) circumstances (McDermott, 2010). Three themes organize these sensitivities[3]:

- what we notice and our choices regarding with whom we stand;
- how we organize consequential change;
- and, the need to recalibrate our designs and responsibilities in response to the shifting nature of oppression.

What We Notice and Our Choices Regarding with Whom We Stand

The Learning in the Food Movement project began with an ethnographic overview of the food movement in a three-city metropolitan area. This allowed us to historicize our understanding of people's lived experiences, how infrastructural relations shaped what was valued in communities facing food injustice, and what this might mean for our research designs. The team noticed that there were many groups focused on healthy and sustainable eating and fewer organized around food justice. According to the Lexicon of Food, food justice refers to "a wide spectrum of efforts that address injustices within the U.S. food system. Weak forms of food justice focus on the effects of an inequitable food system, while stronger forms of food justice focus on the structural causes of those inequities" (https://lexiconoffood.com/recipe/definition-food-justice).

A year into the ethnographic phase of the project, the university-based research team made a decision to focus on groups committed to strong forms of food justice as we, like the people we

Social Design-Based Experiments

were studying, recognized the need to organize for lasting structural changes to the food system. The team spent about another six months analyzing the food justice dimension of the food movement to understand its variations and contradictions. The research team also began to get to know the people who were part of the different groups, assessing their willingness to allow us to learn more about their work, and getting a sense of where our contributions might be useful. Based on systematic comparison across groups and writing about what we were learning, the team decided to collaborate with Impact. The team partnered with Impact because they were the only group that, at that time, was leveraging the assets of the community they were serving to generate solutions to collective problems. Other groups were focused on what Guthman (2008) describes as "bringing good food to others"—wherein people, working in "white cultural spaces" and from a missionary stance, aim to educate poor people of color about a particular set of valued "food practices" and bring them healthy food to which they believe poor people of color would not otherwise have access. The orientation of Impact, in contrast, viewed the community as part of a solution aimed at structural reorganization.

The choices made in this phase of our project shaped the direction of the research and designs. The team identified a group of people and a set of practices that were already working toward radical openness and possibility. We joined in with them because we both wanted to learn how they were doing this work and how we might collaborate with them to deepen what they were doing across scales.

How We Organize Consequential Change

In the work with Impact, the university research team focused on the experiences and work of the *promotoras*. We did this not only because our entry to the organization was focused on enhancing the professional development of the *promotoras*, but also because we noticed the ways in which the *promotoras* were working hard with minimal resources, for little money, and with significant positive effect on building trust and social change in the neighborhood. The *promotoras* noted that the complexity of their work was not fully understood by the directors at Impact. This led to tensions around different ways of understanding the nature and purpose of "the work" that they were doing in terms of community organizing, what kinds of support were needed to do this work well, and how the *promotoras'* efforts should be valued by the organization.

With the *promotoras*, we used art and political theater activities as well as more typical forms of data generation to understand the organization of Impact's and the *promotoras'* work, tensions between the *promotoras'* and the non-profit leadership's views on approaches to effective and responsive community organizing, and how these tensions could be productively re-mediated. The research team and the *promotoras* leveraged their diverse forms of expertise and networks to engage in this joint work. The university team used their disciplinary training and professional experiences as designers, researchers, and teachers to organize interventions with the *promotoras*. They strategically drew on their academic networks across disciplines, financial resources from grants, and their social and cultural capital to enact responsive and sustainable plans. The *promotoras* drew on their networks of influence across the city and their expertise as gardeners and community advocates to initiate and revise designs for improving their professional practices.

Designing for radical openness and possibility involved using strategies that built on our assumptions about how the organization of social and material infrastructure makes particular knowledge, skills, and identities consequential. Our aim was to organize designs in which the *promotoras* could develop ways of knowing and becoming that support their increased capacities for self-determination. We co-designed the *Promotora* App, a tablet-based application, in collaboration with colleagues in the department of Information Communication Technology and Development to make visible the routine, yet not fully appreciated relational dimensions of the *promotoras'* work. What the *promotoras* were doing in the community was not new. Engaging in reciprocal relations of care and commitment with community is foundational to the *promotora* model. What was critical in our work with the *promotoras* was that we were documenting their work and making it visible in spaces of power, authority, and decision-making.

Based on what we learned about issues that mattered to the *promotoras* and the non-profit leadership, we decided to design a dynamic data collection tool—the *Promotora* App—that could facilitate systematic data collection on a variety of activities, data sharing, and analysis. Prior to the use of the App, the *promotoras* were using low-technologies—pen and paper—to collect data on vegetable growth in the gardens and then giving this information to one of the non-profit's directors who input the data in an Excel file located on the sole computer in the office. Because the *promotoras* were not responsible for using Excel or for coordinating the data, they were also not learning office, analytic, and management skills that they were very interested in gaining. The *promotoras* believed that these skills could help them to get higher paying jobs and take greater leadership in their careers.

The data sources that used to be collected prior to the use of the *Promotora* App were restricted to information related to vegetable production in the gardens, leaving out the robustness of the *promotoras'* extensive work in, for instance, connecting community members to health care resources and responding to sexual violence. The *Promotora* App was designed to allow for information about the *promotoras'* community advocacy to be collected and used to inform the non-profit's initiatives in the neighborhood. Combining traditional practices with new technical practices is what we describe as a "syncretic" approach to design—a strategy that leverages historically valued community practices and extends them into the future to create new possibilities (Gutiérrez & Jurow, 2016).

Before we started our project, the nearly "invisible work" of the *promotoras* was not officially discussed in the organization, it was not sufficiently valued, and it was not supported with professional development (Jurow, Teeters, Shea, & Van Steenis, 2016). The *promotoras* wanted to design a tool like the App to help them collect information about how they were interacting with neighborhood residents and what resources they could use to advance that work. Since the introduction of the *Promotora* App into the *promotoras'* daily practices, they have harnessed the opportunities supported by the App to secure new community grants for their advocacy work. The first they were awarded focused on ending domestic violence in South Elm.

The *promotoras'* and our experiences designing and using the *Promotora* App resonate with hooks' (1990, p. 24) notion of radical openness and possibility when she writes:

> We come to this space through suffering and pain, through struggle. We know struggle to be that which pleasures, delights, and fulfills desire. We are transformed, individually, collectively, as we make radical creative space which affirms and sustains our subjectivity, which gives us a new location from which to articulate our sense of the world.

Recognizing and Responding to Compounding and Shifting Forms of Oppression

For people facing oppression, the ground is always shifting and thus freedom is a "constant struggle" (Davis, 2016) that draws out communities' resourcefulness and resilience. With reference to Rittel and Webber (1973), SDBEs intentionally focus on "wicked problems" or social and cultural problems that are difficult to solve because:

- their boundaries are blurry so their scope is hard to define;
- the contexts in which the problem emerges are difficult to recognize and are constantly shifting;
- the problem's roots are vast and tangled;
- and, there is no necessarily "right" answer to the problem under consideration; there are, however, better and worse efforts to tame the problem.

Social Design-Based Experiments

Wicked problems like food insecurity and housing injustice are multiplying problems as experienced by those from historically nondominant groups. For those who are vulnerable because of social characteristics such as race, gender, religious affiliation, sexual orientation, and immigration status, the social and material infrastructure of society is precarious (Ahmed, 2017). It privileges some and exacerbates the suffering of others. The nature of oppression has significant implications for our roles as researchers and partners in SDBEs and for our designs. It demands that we engage in ongoing analysis of what is consequential to communities and how we must, in response, adapt and recalibrate our work with community partners.

As an example: since the start of the Learning in the Food Movement project, the South Elm neighborhood has changed both physically and in the imagination of the city and country. As a result of the collective work of community organizers (including Impact), local and federal foundations, and collaborations with university partners across multiple disciplines, South Elm now has a lot of beautiful and productive gardens, a cooperative grocery store that sells the produce grown in the gardens, improved thoroughfares that include bike lanes and street lights, a community arts hub, and a profusion of murals along main streets that were inspired by the community's pride and hope for their future.

The city in which South Elm is located has also changed during this time. New flows of money, people, and ideas have contributed to the growth of the city to become a major destination for migration in the U.S. and for urban development and revitalization. South Elm—a largely immigrant neighborhood with limited resources, but just 15 minutes from the city's downtown—has become newly attractive to people who would not have considered living in the neighborhood before. Gentrification has become a serious threat to the community's survival.

Following the election of Donald Trump as U.S. president, the problem of gentrification was intensified by new concerns with deportation and community safety. As members of a largely undocumented Mexican population, South Elm residents' experience with housing is increasingly perilous. Through our relationships in the community, we began to hear heartbreaking stories of corrupt landlords preying on residents because of their undocumented and unprotected status. This is just one example meant to highlight how oppression experienced in the community not only shifted, but was compounded by political and economic forces.

As the nature of what was consequential to the community shifted, our research designs and our role in relation to the community members needed to shift as well. The flexibility of our design was enabled because of our relationships *de confianza*—understood as relationships of "mutual trust, respect, and commitment" (Teeters & Jurow, 2016, p. 86)—with the *promotoras* and Impact. We university researchers had come to be seen as trusted colleagues and friends who could recruit resources to support community-led action. While the *Promotora* App was one of the more "spectacular" ways in which we responded to the tensions and problems that the *promotoras* were trying to address, we—in relation with community partners—found other ways to develop understanding of residents' lives, to build solidarity with them around shared concerns, and to care for each other.

We were profoundly influenced by the theories, analyses, and actions of the *promotoras*, a group that represents a community that are the most affected by oppressive policies and practices, but among the least seen and heard. By working with them, we learned to listen in a way that was similar to how they listened to residents. We listened in order to act. Our actions were guided by the *promotoras* in a dialogue between what they believed they needed and how we thought we could respond. Given the community's increasing concerns with housing insecurity, they invited the university team to work in collaboration with *promotoras*, residents, and pro-bono lawyers on a new "Housing Campaign" initiative that would centrally focus on immigrant rights. In this way, new agendas and new forms of participation in the life of the community emerged and developed.

The shifting nature of our research and designs was a mirrored response to the shifting nature of injustices facing the community. This movement within the project speaks to what it means to work toward radical openness and possibility in an SDBE.

A Case of Social Design-Based Experimentation: Toward Radical Openness and Possibility in Computer Science Education

We describe in this case a series of closely related social design-based experiments carried out by Vakil in collaboration with Mr. Mayson, a computer science teacher within a technology academy of a large urban public high school in Oakland, CA. We situate the SDBE in the cultural-historical and geographical specificity of the San Francisco Bay Area, as well as in the exceedingly rapid proliferation of the Computer Science for All movement that has powerfully gripped the education space in recent years. We begin with a brief description of the project's history to frame a discussion on how careful attention to historicity as well as re-mediating activity in design and analysis can simultaneously facilitate radical openness and possibility, while also revealing political tensions across multiple scales that can ultimately compromise ethical aspirations of educational interventions.

Mr. Mayson founded the Computer Science and Tech academy at Bay Prep High School over 25 years ago. He is originally from Nigeria and holds advanced degrees in physics and computer science. He came to Oakland and to Bay Prep specifically to serve as a mentor to students of color, though his initial placement was within a tracked Advanced Placement Physics course enrolling an abysmally low number of African-American and Latinx students. This was the backdrop to the founding of the Computer Science and Technology (CST) academy: Mr. Mayson designed and founded this academy the year after he arrived at Bay Prep to increase the number of Black/Latinx students in technical career pathways. His own children attended and graduated from the CST academy. Vakil met Mr. Mayson in 2008 when they collaborated around a project to design the Oakland Science and Mathematics Outreach (OSMO) project, a STEM-focused afterschool program created in partnership with the Boys and Girls Clubs of Oakland (Vakil, 2014). His collaboration and relationship with Mr. Mayson evolved to include several collaborative projects including the sequence of social design experiments discussed here, and persists into the present.

This historicity of partnership mediated their design work in complex and consequential ways. For example, the long-standing relationship with his classroom led to a more formalized ethnographic study of his academy, which was part of a larger multi-school study of race, learning, and identity in the district (Nasir & Vakil, 2017). A key finding there was that not only were Black and Latinx students severely underrepresented in all advanced and honors pathways offered through the academy system (adopted and touted by the district as an equity system), but that there were powerful alliances and creative equity initiatives underway often led by students themselves. In short, we learned that there was a deep and powerful resistance to inequity that included the voices of students, teachers, and parents. This expanded understanding of how issues of race and equity were *actually* being interpreted, experienced, and resisted at the school level deeply informed the curriculum Mr. Mayson and Vakil designed together for his Introduction to Computing class, offered primarily to entering 10th graders in the academy.

A History of Co-Design

Their previous work together with OSMO had explored ways to connect CS learning to cultural practices at the individual and community level, particularly those that intersect with questions of opportunity and power. For example, OSMO students had identified a key community issue as unsupervised after-school time; namely the disparities between white and wealthy students, many of whom are shuttled off to private tutoring, and low-income students of color, who often can't afford private tutors. Historicity, in this instance, is embodied in the histories of racialized and classed subjugation, and modern-day conditions of racialized poverty and structural disadvantage in the city of Oakland. In this way, lack of opportunity in the after-school hours compounds the racialized disadvantage students of color already endure *during* the school day. Yet, students also keenly noted that their city has a particularly strong legacy of community-based, youth-centered, and justice-oriented afterschool programs designed to meet the needs and desires of the most vulnerable students in the city. With this in mind, OSMO students designed, coded, and user-tested a mobile app that aimed to expand awareness of these resources by connecting students and parents to the plethora of opportunities in their community. Similar to the syncretic approach of the *promotoras* discussed earlier, OSMO students leveraged newly acquired CS learning (UI design, client/server relationships, AppInventor) to amplify existing cultural practices in their community, and in the process honed a sense of self that elegantly braided together their identities as learners and activists. This is the historicity that not only characterized the intellectual and design partnership work between Vakil and Mr. Mayson in the past, but was a precursor for the kind of work they would do together in the future. This, together with the ethnographic insights about the depth of awareness of and resistance to racialized inequity, directly informed the design of a ten-week CS unit where students designed technological artifacts to address equity issues they were especially passionate about at their school (Vakil, 2016).

Toward Radical Openness and Possibility: Politicized Trust as a Cautionary Tale

The pedagogical and political aspiration of the design was to re-mediate the extant system of CS learning at the school—to pivot away from an access or "STEM pipeline" frame to one where CS learning is couched within, and fused to, questions of ethics and power, grounded in a philosophical commitment to radical openness and possibility (Vakil & Higgs, 2019).

In the process of re-mediation, we may encounter unexpected tensions inherent in the overlapping activity systems students often simultaneously (and contradictorily) inhabit. In this case, a tension we "discovered" was that while the CST academy was a model academy through the lens of racial equity—with an equitable racial/ethnic representation with regard to the school demographics—subtle but ultimately insidious racial divides existed between students in the class. Drawing on earlier research focused on trust between researchers and communities (Vakil, McKinney de Royston, Nasir, & Kirshner, 2016), we analyzed student interactions through the lens of *politicized trust* and found that lack of trust between white students and students of color ultimately constrained learning/design possibilities in the class (Vakil & McKinney de Royston, 2019). We theorize trust as political and politicized here to highlight how its formation and sustenance are inextricably linked to dynamics of race and power, and are enacted interactionally through student discourse including talk, emotions, engagement, and participation patterns.

Following the thread of politicized trust, we highlight yet another tension in the activity systems related to CS education, race, and equity in racially diverse urban cities like Oakland—one that is entirely missing from scholarship on diversity and equity in computing (and STEM more broadly). Computer Science for All is a movement that has in recent years spurred hundreds of calls for proposals, new initiatives in schools of education focused on preparing future CS teachers, and bountiful research funding and political support. The "for all" is a gesture to the overt equity commitments of this educational movement—the justifiable notion that access to coding and computational literacies is a civil rights issue. That to fully participate economically, culturally, and politically in the twenty-first century (and beyond), a solid foundation in CS is mandatory and therefore a matter of justice. Yet, in the case of Oakland and the CST academy, an SDBE approach highlights a core tension in the casual coupling of increased access to CS courses in urban high schools to an ethical commitment to radical openness and possibility. We call here for a more sensitive, scrutinizing examination of how equity projects in CS education mediate and implicate near-adjacent activity systems, including the interwoven ecologies of schools, corporations, and the state (Giroux, McLaren, & Peter, 1989).

In *Race After Technology*, Benjamin (2019) notes the growing disaffection for high profile technology companies in communities all across the country, stemming from recent abuses as well as their role in gentrification processes (which have become almost synonymous with the cultural context of the SF Bay Area). Meanwhile, these companies are also centrally positioned in the Computer Science for All movement (Vakil, 2018). Probing into how politicized trust mediated the activity system for students in the CST academy, we learned that many students questioned the unmentioned political agendas inherent in the rollout of their school's and district's partnership with Intel, a regional and international technology enterprise. This was despite civil rights leader Jesse Jackson's heralding the partnership, culminating in a speech he delivered to students urging them to "stop the violence" and "learn how to code" (Vakil, 2018). There was a range of interpretations of Jesse Jackson's speech and the school's partnership with Intel, and a number of students we interviewed expressed questions, doubts, or concerns about the surrounding ethics and politics of their learning. These tensions both emerged from, and contributed to, an erosion of trust between students and their school, and highlight the obscured relationship between the activity system of the classroom and school, and those at the level of city, state, and industry. A focus on re-mediation, a core principle of SDBEs, is critical in that it brings into focus tensions at multiple scales of an activity system. In this way, the SDBE approach is well suited to conceptualizing the linkages of activity systems and the resulting implications for learning and learners, which sometimes may jeopardize pursuits of radical openness and possibility. As such, SDBEs work to deepen, clarify, and ultimately make more accountable our theories and language for equity and justice in education.

Conclusion

Social design-based experiments have developed as a methodology through the mutual engagement of community, theory, and pedagogy. The principles grounding social design-based research efforts—historicity, prolepsis, diversity, equity, re-mediation, transformability, resilience, and sustainability—intentionally name dynamic and relational actions that require our continuous attention if we are to move toward our utopian goals. As we have underscored in this chapter, the utopian aims of social design-based research to advance a more just social world require attention to ideological, historical, and cultural practices as well as how these become embodied in the materiality of people's lives.

Our empirical cases illustrate that a commitment to equity is only a first step for SDBEs. As a next step toward embodying what hooks (1990) describes as "radical openness and possibility," we must use our nuanced understanding of how people live culturally across scales of practice to re-mediate relations between people and as part of dynamic infrastructures. As illustrated in the cases of the *promotoras* and the young people in Oakland, the arc of social design-based work fundamentally depends on communities, our relationships with them, and the contexts in which we locate our work together, defined in part by the histories and material needs of the specific ecologies and their participants. Attending to the complexity and diversity of these systems and people's practices illuminates the tensions that enliven them. Following the tenets of cultural historical theory, identifying these tensions and contradictions is central to the ongoing analyses and design iterations of social design-based research projects, and they must be recognized as constraints *and* drivers of what is possible, both for design and people's possible futures

The syncretic designs that we are able to generate through our social design-based work provide practical means through which we can work toward radical openness and possibility, such that we and our collaborators can develop new forms of being as historical actors. As we develop new forms of agency, what becomes possible is less predictable and, guided by our ethical commitments to supporting our capacities for self-determination, becomes more hopeful.

Notes

1 Central members of the Learning in the Food Movement team included Jurow, Leah Teeters, and Molly Shea. Doctoral students and faculty across multiple disciplines (education, engineering, and business) also helped support our work with community members.

2 All proper names in the reported study are pseudonyms.
3 The ideas written here were originally developed as part of a keynote lecture by Jurow in October, 2018 (see Jurow, 2018).

References

Abu-Lughod, L. (1991). Writing against culture. In: R. Fox (Ed.), *Recapturing Anthropology: Working in the Present* (pp. 137–162). Santa Fe, NM: School of American Research Press.

Ahmed, S. (2017). *Living a Feminist Life*. Durham, NC: Duke University Press.

Anderson, T., & Shattuck, J. (2012). Design-based research: A decade of progress in education research. *Educational Researcher, 41*(1), 16–25. doi:10.3102/0013189X11428813.

Anzaldua, G. (1987). How to tame a wild tongue. In: *Borderlands/La Frontera: The New Mestiza* (pp. 75–86). San Francisco, CA: Aunt Lute Books.

Benjamin, R. (2019). *Race After Technology: Abolitionist Tools for the New Jim Code*. Hoboken, NJ: John Wiley & Sons.

Bloch, E. (1986). *The Principle of Hope* (N. Plaice, S. Plaice, Paul Knight, & Basil Blackwell, Trans.). Cambridge, MA: MIT Press..

Bowker, G.C., & Star, S.L. (2000). *Sorting Things Out: Classification and Its Consequences*. Cambridge, MA: MIT Press.

Bronfenbrenner, U. (1979). *The Ecology of Human Development: Experiments by Nature and Design*. Cambridge, MA: Harvard University Press.

Brown, A.L. (1992). Design experiments: Theoretical and methodological challenges in creating complex interventions in classroom settings. *Journal of the Learning Sciences, 2*(2), 141–178. doi:10.1207/s15327809jls0202_2.

Brown, K., & Cole, M. (2001). A Utopian methodology as a tool for cultural and critical psychologies: Toward a positive critical theory. In: M. J. Packer, & M. B. Tappan (Eds.), *Cultural and Critical Perspectives on Human Development* (pp. 41–66). New York, NY: SUNY Press.

Cobb, P.A., Confrey, J., diSessa, A.A., Lehrer, R., & Schauble, L. (2003). Design experiments in educational research. *Educational Researcher, 32*(1), 9–13. doi:10.3102/0013189X032001009.

Cole, M. (1996). *Cultural Psychology: A Once and Future Discipline*. Cambridge, MA: Belknap.

Cole, M., & The Distributed Literacy Consortium. (Eds.) (2006). *The Fifth Dimension: An after-School Program Built on Diversity*. New York, NY: Russell Sage.

Cole, M., & Engeström, Y. (1993). A cultural-historical approach to distributed cognition. In: G. Salomon (Ed.), *Distributed Cognitions: Psychological and Educational Considerations* (pp. 1–46). Cambridge, England: Cambridge University Press.

Cole, M., & Griffin, P. (1980). Cultural amplifiers reconsidered. In: D. Olson (Ed.), *Social Foundations of Language and Thought* (pp. 343–364). New York, NY: Norton.

Cole, M., & Griffin, P. (1986). A sociohistorical approach to remediation. In: S. de Castell, A. Luke, & K. Egan (Eds.), *Literacy, Society, and Schooling: A Reader* (pp. 110–131). Cambridge, England: Cambridge University Press.

Cole, M., Hood, L., & McDermott, R. (1982). Ecological niche picking. In: U. Neisser (Ed.), *Memory Observed: Remembering in Natural Context* (pp. 366–373). San Francisco, CA: Freeman.

Collins, A. (1992). Toward a design science of education. In: E. Scanlon, & T. O'Shea (Eds.), *New Directions in Educational Technology* (pp. 15–22). New York, NY: Springer-Verlag. doi:10.1007/978-3-642-77750-9_2.

Collins, A., Joseph, D., & Bielaczyc, K. (2004). Design research: Theoretical and methodological issues. *Journal of the Learning Sciences, 13*(1), 15–42. doi:10.1207/s15327809jls1301_2.

Davis, A.Y. (2016). *Freedom Is a Constant Struggle: Ferguson, Palestine and the Foundations of a Movement*. Chicago, IL: Haymarket Books.

Design-Based Research Collective. (2003). Design-based research: An emerging paradigm for educational inquiry. *Educational Researcher, 32*(1), 5–8, 35–37.

Eckert, P. (1989). *Jocks and Burnouts: Social Categories and Identity in the High School*. New York, NY: Teachers College Press.

Engeström, Y. (1987). *Learning by Expanding*. Cambridge, UK: Cambridge University Press.

Engeström, Y. (1991). Activity theory and individual and social transformation. *Multidisciplinary Newsletter for Activity Theory*, No.7/8, 14–15.

Engeström, Y. (2001). Expansive learning at work: Toward an activity theoretical reconceptualization. *Journal of Education and Work, 14*(1), 133–156. doi:10.1080/13639080020028747.

Engeström, Y. (2011). From design experiments to formative interventions. *Theory and Psychology, 21*(5), 598–628.

Espinoza, M. (2003). *UCLA Statewide Migrant Student Institute curriculum*. Los Angeles: University of California, Los Angeles.

Espinoza, M. (2009). A case study of educational sanctuary in one migrant classroom. *Pedagogies: An International Journal, 4*(1), 44–62.

Freire, P. (1970). *Pedagogy of the Oppressed*. New York, NY: Seabury.

Freire, P. (1998). *Teachers as Cultural Workers: Letters to Those Who Dare Teach* (D. P. Macedo, D. Koike, & A. Oliveira, Trans.). Boulder, CO: Westview.

Goodwin, C. (1994). Professional vision. *American Anthropologist, 96*, 606–633.

Giroux, H.A., McLaren, P.L., McLaren, P., & Peter, M. (Eds.) (1989). *Critical Pedagogy, the State, and Cultural Struggle*. New York, NY: Suny Press.

Guthman, J. (2008). Bringing good food to others: Investigating the subjects of alternative food practice. *Cultural Geographies, 15*(4), 431–447.

Gutiérrez, K. (2008). Developing a sociocritical literacy in the third space. *Reading Research Quarterly, 43*(2), 148–164.

Gutiérrez, K. (2014). Integrative research review: Syncretic approaches to literacy learning: Leveraging horizontal knowledge and expertise. In: P. Dunston, L. Gambrell, K. Headley, S. Fullerton, & P. Stecker (Eds.), *63rd Literacy Research Association Yearbook* (pp. 48–61). Alamonte Springs, FL: Literacy Research Association.

Gutiérrez, K. (2016). Designing resilient ecologies: Social design experiments and a new social Imagination. *Educational Researcher, 45*(3), 187–196.

Gutiérrez, K.D. (2018). Social design–based experiments: A proleptic approach to literacy. *Literacy Research: Theory, Method, and Practice, 66*(2), 1–23.

Gutiérrez, K.D., Becker, B., Espinoza, M., Cortes, K., Cortez, A., Lizárraga, J.R., Rivero, E., & Yin, P. (2019). Youth as historical actors in the production of possible futures. *Mind, Culture, and Activity*. doi:10.1080/1 0749039.2019.1652327.

Gutiérrez, K., Cortes, K., Cortez, A., DiGiacomo, D., Higgs, J., Johnson, P., Lizárraga, J., Mendoza, E., Tien, J., & Vakil, S. (2017). Replacing representation with imagination: Finding ingenuity in everyday practices. *Review of Research in Education, 41*, 30–60. doi:10.3102/0091732X16687523

Gutiérrez, K., Bien, A., & Selland, M. (2011). Polylingual and polycultural learning ecologies: Mediating emergent academic literacies for dual language learners. *Journal of Early Childhood Literacy, 11*(2), 232–261.

Gutiérrez, K., & Jurow, A.S. (2016). Social design experiments: Toward equity by design. *The Journal of the Learning Sciences, 25*(4), 1–34.

Gutiérrez, K., Morales, P.L., & Martinez, D. (2009). Re-mediating literacy: Culture, difference, and learning for students from non-dominant communities. *Review of Research in Educational Research, 33*(1), 212–245.

Gutiérrez, K., & Rogoff, B. (2003). Cultural ways of learning: Individual traits or repertoires of Practice. *Educational Researcher, 32*(5), 19–25.

Hall, R., & Jurow, A.S. (2015). Changing concepts in activity: Descriptive and design studies of consequential learning across time, space, and social organization. *Educational Psychologist, 50*(3), 173–189.

Hall, R., Stevens, R., & Torralba, T. (2002). Disrupting representational infrastructure in conversations across disciplines. *Mind, Culture, and Activity, 9*(3), 179–210.

Haney-López, I. (2003). *Racism on Trial: The Chicano Fight for Justice*. Cambridge, MA: Belknap/Harvard University Press.

Holland, D.C., & Eisenhart, M.A. (1990). *Educated in Romance: Women, Achievement, and College Culture*. Chicago, IL: University of Chicago Press.

Holland, D.C., Fox, G., & Daro, V.E.F. (2008). Social movements and collective identity: A decentered, dialogic view. *Anthropological Quarterly, 81*(1), 95–126.

hooks, B. (1990). Choosing the margin as a space of radical openness. In: b. hooks (Ed.), *Yearnings: Race, Gender, and Cultural Politics* (pp. 145–153). Boston, MA: South End.

Jurow, A.S. (October 13, 2018). *Designing for Radical Openness and Possibility in the Learning Sciences*. Keynote at the Learning Sciences Graduate Student Conference. Nashville, TN: Vanderbilt University.

Jurow, A.S., & Shea, M.V. (2015). Learning in equity-oriented scale-making projects. *The Journal of the Learning Sciences, 24*(2), 286–307.

Jurow, A.S., Teeters, L.A., Shea, M.V., & Van Steenis, E. (2016). Extending the consequentiality of "invisible work" in the food justice movement. *Cognition and Instruction, 34*(3), 210–221.

Kendi, I.X. (2019). *How to Be an Antiracist*. New York: One World.

Lee, C.D. (2010). Soaring above the clouds, delving the ocean's depths: Understanding the ecologies of human learning and the challenge for education science. *Educational Researcher, 39*(9), 643–655.

Leont'ev, A. N. (1981). *Problems of the Development of the Mind*. Moscow: Progress.

Levitas, R. (2013). *Utopia as Method: The Imaginary Reconstitution of Society*. New York, NY: Palgrave Macmillan.

McDermott, R.P. (2010). The passions of learning in tight circumstances: Toward a political economy of the mind, In: W. R. Penuel & K. O'Connor (Eds.). *Learning Research as a Human Science. National Society for the Study of Education Yearbook, 109*(1), 144–159.

Nasir, N. (2011). *Racialized Identities: Race and Achievement among African American Youth.* Stanford, CA: Stanford University Press.

Nasir, N.I.S., & Vakil, S. (2017). STEM-focused academies in urban schools: Tensions and possibilities. *Journal of the Learning Sciences, 26*(3), 376–406.

Rittel, H.W.J., & Webber, M.M. (1973). Dilemmas in a general theory of planning. *Policy Sciences, 4*(2), 155–169.

Sandoval, W.A., & Bell, P. (2004). Design-based research methods for studying learning in context: Introduction. *Educational Psychologist, 39*(4), 199–201.

Saxe, G.B. (2012). *Cultural Development of Mathematical Ideas: Papua New Guinea Studies.* New York, NY: Cambridge University Press.

Scribner, S., & Cole, M. (1981). *The Psychology of Literacy.* Cambridge, MA: Harvard University Press.

Soja, E.W. (1989). *Postmodern Geographies: The Reassertion of Space in Critical Social Theory* (Radical Thinkers). New York, NY: Verso.

Soja, E.W. (2010). *Seeking Spatial Justice.* Minneapolis, MN: University of Minnesota Press.

Star, S.L., & Ruhleder, K. (1996). Steps toward an ecology of infrastructure: Design and access for large information spaces. *Information Systems Research, 7*(1), 111–134.

Teeters, L.A. (2017). Developing social alongside technical infrastructure: A case study applying ICTD tenets to marginalized communities in the United States. *Journal of Community Informatics, 13*(1), 193–209.

Teeters, L.A., & Jurow, A.S. (2016). Relationships *de confianza* and the organization of collective social action. *Ethnography and Education, 13*(1), 1–16.

Vakil, S. (2014). A critical pedagogy approach for engaging urban youth in mobile app development in an after-school program. *Equity and Excellence in Education, 47*(1), 31–45.

Vakil, S. (2018). Ethics, identity, and political vision: Toward a justice-centered approach to equity in computer science education. *Harvard Educational Review, 88*(1), 26–52.

Vakil, S., & Higgs, J. (2019). It's about power: A call to rethink equity and ethics in computing education. *Communications of the ACM, 62*(3), 31–33.

Vakil, S., & McKinney de Royston, M. (2019). Exploring politicized trust in a racially diverse computer science classroom. *Race, Ethnicity and Education, 22*(4), 545–567.

Vakil, S., McKinney de Royston, M., Nasir, N.S., & Kirshner, B. (2016). Rethinking race and power in design-based research: Reflections from the field. *Cognition and Instruction, 34*(3), 194–209.

Vásquez, O.A. (2003). *La Clase Mágica: Imagining Optimal Possibilities in a Bilingual Community of Learners.* Mahwah, NJ: Erlbaum.

Vossoughi, S. (2011). On the formation of intellectual kinship: A qualitative case study of literacy, learning, and social analysis in a summer migrant education program (Doctoral dissertation). University of California, Los Angeles, CA. Retrieved from https://search.proquest.com/docview/894116618?pq-origsite.gscholar.

Vossoughi, S. (2014, October). Social analytic artifacts made concrete: A study of learning and political education. *Mind, Culture and Activity, 21*(4), 353–373. doi:10.1080/10749039.2014.

Vossoughi, S., & Gutiérrez, K. (2014). Toward a multi-sited ethnographic sensibility. In: J. Vadeboncoeur (Ed.), *Learning in and across Contexts: Reimagining Education NSEE Yearbook Volume 113(2)* (pp. 603–632). New York, NY: Teachers College Press.

Vossoughi, S., & Gutiérrez, K. (2016). Critical pedagogy and socio-cultural theories of learning. In: I. Esmonde, & A. Booker (Eds.), *Power and Privilege in the Learning Sciences: Critical and Socio-Cultural Theories of Learning* (pp. 139–161). New York, NY: Routledge.

Vossoughi, S., & Gutiérrez, K. (2016). Lifting off the ground to return anew: Mediated praxis, transformative learning, and social design experiments. *Journal of Teacher Education, 61*(1–2), 100–117.

Vygotsky, L. (1978). *Mind in Society.* Cambridge, MA: Harvard University Press.

Walker, B., & Salt, D. (2006). *Resilience Thinking: Sustaining Ecosystems and People in a Changing World.* Washington, DC: Island Press.

Wartofsky, M.W. (1979). Perception, representation, and the forms of action: Towards an historical epistemology. In R.S. Coher, & M.W. Wartofsky (Eds.), *A Portrait of Twenty-Five Years* (pp. 215–237). Dordrecht, the Netherlands: Springer.

20

PROMOTING EQUITABLE AND JUST LEARNING ACROSS SETTINGS

Organizational Forms for Educational Change

William R. Penuel

Introduction: Models of Organization as Cultural Tools

A key contribution of sociocultural research has been to separate the concept of learning from that of education. When the two are conflated, it makes it difficult for us to imagine how learning is an aspect of all participation in social practice (Lave & Wenger, 1991). It also makes it nearly impossible to see how, when young people do not meet externally defined benchmarks of success, the education system is producing failure in ways that reproduce inequalities in society (Varenne & McDermott, 1998). Instead, we become obsessed with "gap gazing" (Rodriguez, 2001), pondering how best we can close achievement test score gaps between White, economically advantaged students and students from nondominant communities, and justifying social inequality on the basis of students' effort or ability.

Seeing learning and contemporary educational organizations as distinct allows us to imagine radically new possibilities for more caring, inclusive, and sustainable ways of relating to one another and the planet now and in the future. We can look, for example, for inspiration to settings where the learning that takes place allows for more supportive relationships between newcomers and old-timers in practice. We can look for settings where patterns of participation in activity are not predictable from knowing a student's race, gender, or home language, and where queer and gender queer youth feel welcomed, safe, and supported. And, we can look to settings where multi-generational assemblies of people are re-making their relationship with the land where they live. These settings could be anywhere—in schools, families, community organizations, or spaces in between.

A cultural approach to the study of organizations is needed if we are to transform these identified sites of possibility into new institutional arrangements in communities. Such a perspective would help us "see" how and why these settings differ from classrooms and schools with respect to participants' opportunities to contribute to and make changes to activities. It would also help us understand how people can stabilize, resource, and legitimate new forms of organization that make use of what we learn from studying settings where relations are more caring, inclusive, and sustainable. Finally, it would give us a framework for changing the ways that educational organizations structure opportunities for participation and link to families and communities.

In this chapter, I develop the idea that *models of organization* that are culturally and experientially available to participants can help us understand possibilities for bringing about equitable change within educational systems and communities. Models of organization are "templates for arranging relationships with an organization and sets of scripts for action culturally associated with that type of organization" (Clemens, 1993, p. 758). As models, these templates can be used not just to represent the world but also for "*picturing* and *modeling* a future" (Wartofsky, 1979, p. 189). Models of organization focus specifically on those aspects of the world that pertain to how relations among people, tools, and settings are constructed and maintained. Their analysis can also help us see how new forms of organization can emerge when existing forms are combined in novel ways by different associations of people working together over a sustained period of time—typically many years—and across different spatial scales.

The chapter is organized as follows. First, I introduce and elaborate on the basic idea of models of organization as cultural tools, locating it within a tradition of scholarship that sits at the intersection of institutional theory and the study of social movements. Then, I name some elements of the cultural toolkit for organizing that are familiar in education and that hold promise as resources for bringing about equitable educational change. This section includes brief descriptions of projects in which these elements or forms of organization have been appropriated for different purposes. Finally, I describe some emerging approaches to research and development that support organizing for new models of organization within existing educational organizations (e.g., schools) and for changing relations between existing organizations and the community.

Developing the Idea of Models of Organization for Studying Institutional and Organizational Change in Education

In a seminal article that critiqued the view of culture adopted in much research on learning, Gutiérrez and Rogoff (2003) foreground the need to attend to learners' "linguistic and cultural-historical repertoires for participation in practice." They explain:

> By "linguistic and cultural-historical repertoires," we mean the ways of engaging in activities stemming from observing and otherwise participating in cultural practices. Individuals' background experiences, together with their interests, may prepare them for knowing how to engage in particular forms of language and literacy activities, play their part in testing formats, resolve interpersonal problems according to specific community-organized approaches, and so forth.
>
> *(p. 22)*

For them, focusing on individuals' repertoires gives researchers a language for describing regularities across individuals' and cultural communities' ways of doing things, without reducing culture to a single "social address." And, it provides ways to identify experiences of continuity and discontinuity that arise when individuals draw on repertoires developed in one setting, in a different setting. At a very general level, it also provides a framework for describing how individual actors can bring about change within cultural practices through their contributions to ongoing activity.

I also draw on the idea of a "repertoire" in this chapter, but my focus is on repertoires of organization. Whereas Gutiérrez and Rogoff's purpose was to use the concept to understand how practices contribute to learning and development, my purpose is to understand variation and regularities in the very ways that those practices are organized. In that sense, it is inspired by Rogoff and colleagues' (Rogoff, 2014; Rogoff et al., 2007) related efforts to characterize the social organization of learning arrangements in different cultural communities, but it draws directly from a different line of scholarship that has investigated the cultural tools that social movement organizations in the past have used to effect broad political and social change. This choice is purposeful: my aim is to provide conceptual tools for analyzing and bringing about changes to organizations and societal institutions and their relations, tools that might be particularly useful within the emerging forms of intervention research that I describe in the concluding part of this chapter.

Models of Organization as Cultural Tools for Change

Sociologist Elisabeth Clemens (1993) proposed the concept of *models of organization* as a way to help explain how women's groups in the late nineteenth and early twentieth centuries helped to transform American politics. During this period, women's associations, many of which began initially as social clubs, evolved into powerful lobbying organizations that won multiple legislative victories and, ultimately, the vote. Further, their strategic actions, along with those of other Progressive groups, served to transform American politics in ways that we recognize today as organized around legislative activity and bargaining by interest groups. What unsettled American political institutions was the women's movement's strategic use of familiar organizational forms—of social clubs, unions, corporations, and parliaments—in new ways. At the time, the appropriation of "social club" by women was novel and unfamiliar: most women's groups that drew attention were affiliated with religious groups and charitable societies. Though a recognizable model of organization, its appropriation by women was culturally counter-normative, but it proved successful and was adopted by women's organizations across the country.

Models of organization are part of "the cultural tool kit of any society," Clemens (1993, p. 771) argues. They "comprise both templates for arranging relationships within an organization and sets of scripts for action culturally associated with that type of organization" (Clemens, p. 758). Critically, they are recognizable forms to people in a society, and societies draw on *multiple* forms to organize groups for different purposes. Those multiple forms constitute the "repertoires of organization" that are culturally available to participants in the society, according to Clemens. And as Clemens illustrates in the case of the women's movement, when familiar forms are deployed in novel ways by unfamiliar groups—that is, groups for whom it would be counter-normative to deploy the model of organization—then both changes to organizations and new relations among organizations can emerge.

Although we are accustomed to thinking of schools as having a durable form of organization, famously described by Tyack and Cuban (1995) as a kind of "grammar of schooling" that is robust to efforts to change it, there are examples today of groups from outside established decision making bodies for education (e.g., school boards) engaged in strategic action to introduce familiar forms in novel ways to change schools. For example, in the past two decades, large philanthropic organizations appropriating a familiar organizational practice—grant making—in novel ways, by funding a small set of new intermediary organizations to work toward similar aims, have strengthened these nonpublic actors' abilities to influence education through the resources they are able to offer to schools and districts (Reckhow & Snyder, 2014). These funding agencies, moreover, use their powerful position as funders of new organizations to direct the activities of those organizations (J. Scott & Jabbar, 2014). Understanding the shifting power of philanthropies and new intermediary organizations such as charter management organizations has been a focus of critical scholarship in education policy (Lubienski, Scott, & DeBray, 2011) and illustrates Clemens' proposition that the deployment of familiar models of organization in novel ways by unfamiliar actors can bring about changes in a field such as education.

What is different in the example above, however, is that philanthropic organizations may have been marginal in education policy in the past, but they are not at all comparable in their position to the status of women activists in the late nineteenth century. These organizations, moreover, have yet to show evidence that their actions are beneficial to students, families, and their communities, in terms of achieving goals of educational equity and justice (J. Scott, Lubienski, DeBray, & Jabbar, 2014). In the following sections, I name some repertoires for organizing that might be deployed to achieve goals of equity and socio-ecological justice, by a different set of unfamiliar actors, groups that rarely have a voice in, and have more limited resources for, shaping educational change efforts.

Promoting Equitable and Just Learning Across Settings

Following Hwang and Colyvas (in press), I treat actors here as abstractions, that is, not as concrete individuals but as archetypes at the association level of society, and as types of "central actors" as characterized in social movement theory (Kim & Bearman, 1997; McCarthy & Zald, 1977). I do so in order to enhance the communicability of the ideas presented and provide some initial conjectures that could be put in harm's way by learning scientists.

Models of Organization for Promoting Equitable Change in Education

Below, I describe some of the models of organization that could serve as resources for groups engaged in equity-focused change efforts. By no means is this list of models an exhaustive list of the practices, routines, and roles that make up the cultural tool kit of organizing that is possible. Rather, the list is focused on models of organization that are in some sense *familiar* to a wide range of individuals and groups in education today—that is, both their experiential availability to groups who wish to deploy them and their recognizability by others. Table 20.1 below summarizes the

Table 20.1 Cultural Forms of Organization in Education That Can Be Appropriated to Promote Equitable Change in Education

Organizational Form	Actor Type (Level of Association of Individuals)	Adherents and Constituents	Novel Purposes
Internship	Education coalition	Adherents: interns, teachers, school leaders. Constituents: philanthropic organizations, corporate sponsors, state	Systemic implementation of learning opportunities to prepare all students for both college and careers
Afterschool Program	Collaborative design team	Adherents: elders, researchers, youth. Constituents: university, community-based organization, funding agency	Creating experiences to help students navigate everyday and disciplinary ways of knowing
Parent–Teacher Group	Collaborative design team	Adherents: researchers, teachers, parents. Constituents: university, private foundation	Support meaningful parent engagement that counteracts deficit views of families
Student Organization	Online network	Adherents: undocumented youth, activists. Constituents: technology providers, activist organizations	Promote "coming out" as a way to build support for DREAM Act
Leadership Development Program	Planning and implementation team	Adherents: students, university faculty, youth and family advocates. Constituents: university center, activist coalition	Build critical consciousness to inform youth action to expand opportunities to learn
Research–Practice Partnership	Team representing an advocacy organization, a university, and a school district	Adherents: Student and family advocates, researchers, education leaders. Constituents: national teacher's union, national advocacy group	Promote district-wide implementation of program to reduce racial disparities in discipline

forms reviewed and the examples presented in this section. In this table, following the resource mobilization theory of social movements (McCarthy & Zald, 1977), two kinds of central actors are identified who are adherents of the initiative, that is, people who believe in and contribute to the goals of the change effort, as well as actors who are constituents, that is, who provide resources to support the initiative. Often in social movements—as reflected in this table—there is overlap between interest groups and those who hold resources; however, this is not always the case (Kim & Bearman, 1997).

Internship

Internships are an organizational form in which students have the opportunity to become part of a workplace for a limited period of time. Internships have a long history in U.S. education, and they are at least partly inspired by Dewey's (1997) call for a method of learning through doing, in which students learn how to apply ideas from the curriculum by embodying them in practical activity. Internships are increasingly common experiences for students who complete four-year degrees in college: today, three-fifths of students graduating from college have had an internship at some point in their educational career (National Association of Colleges and Employers, 2017). In contrast to Dewey's expectation that learning by doing would not be tied to preparation for specific jobs in industry (DeFalco, 2010), many of today's formal internship arrangements between schools and workplaces entail a tight coupling with industry and vocational tracks in schools (e.g., career academies, Kemple & Willner, 2008). Such arrangements can provide students with a sense of hope and possibility, but access and implementation are often uneven in ways that reproduce rather than reduce inequities in opportunity (Conchas & Clark, 2002).

At their best, internships provide young people with exposure to a different form of learning than "assembly line" learning typical in schools. When they engage students in tasks that are part of the core work practices of an organization, they provide students with a means to apprentice into a mature work practice as what Lave and Wenger (1991) call a "legitimate peripheral participant" in the practice (Richmond & Kurth, 1999). Well-structured internships can also provide young people with opportunities to work side-by-side with adults in a way that positions them as knowledgeable, competent contributors to practice (Gupta & Negron, 2017). Finally, internships can provide young people with access to different kinds of spaces and windows into pathways into careers, windows that can help them develop a clearer sense of their career goals (Penuel, Van Horne, DiGiacomo, & Kirshner, 2016).

The work of the Linked Learning Alliance in California is an example of how this particular organizational form—the internship—can be appropriated to advance equitable educational change at the scale of a state. This coalition of school districts, employers, and community organizations was formed in 2008 to create certified pathways for young people to in turn create more equitable access to the kinds of learning opportunities described above. While coalitions are increasingly familiar actors in education, many focus primarily on advocacy activities and not on supporting and studying what the Alliance refers to as "systemic implementation." Supporting systemic implementation within the Alliance has entailed "engaging a wide range of stakeholders in expanding and sustaining a menu of high-quality Linked Learning pathways, accessible to any student wanting this kind of pathway" (Hoachlander, McGlawn, & Stam, 2017, p. 93).

Notably, although the Alliance's efforts relied on the wide political support and significant external funding from the state, philanthropy, and corporate sources for better pathways for school to career among broader publics, the Linked Learning Initiative entailed much more than ensuring all students had access to high-quality internships. The Alliance established quality standards through a certification process for 46 different pathways, ensuring a diversity of possible pathways for participants. It supported changes to instruction in classrooms to make them more meaningfully related to student internships, as well as strategies for aligning in-school activities with out-of-school and

Promoting Equitable and Just Learning Across Settings

summer learning opportunities (Hoachlander et al., 2017). The nine districts that were part of the program developed "Graduate Profiles" that named competencies of graduates that would be prepared for both college and career. It supported schools in using other increasingly common forms of organization in education, such as block scheduling and dual enrollment programs, to expand student access and learning time. Teacher learning was supported by "externships," where they got to become legitimate peripheral participants themselves in work practices and enjoy a different relationship to their students. The outcomes, as measured in an external evaluation of the Linked Learning Initiative, showed promise with respect to the Alliance's equity goals: English learners and African American students in particular earned 10 more credits on average and were significantly more likely to go to a four-year college than were their counterparts in traditional high schools (Warner et al., 2016).

The power of the Linked Learning Initiative as an example of a familiar organizational form being adopted by an intermediary organization and for different purposes derives not just from its technical innovations, though. As Valladares and Welner (2017) state, new advocacy organizations were formed to build political power and will across the different sectors and communities within the state. These organizations helped secure strong support from funding organizations, policy changes, and even helped to expand the initiative beyond the state (Warner et al., 2016).

Afterschool Program

Structured programs that take place outside of regular school hours—in schools, community-based organizations, and faith-based organizations—are commonplace in the United States today. As of 2014, they served roughly 10 million children, or 18 percent of the United States population (Afterschool Alliance, 2014) and are supported through a variety of federal, state, and private funding streams and thousands of volunteer hours. In addition to their ubiquity, afterschool programs enjoy relatively strong political support from a wide variety of constituencies, including, and especially, working parents who depend on them for organizing workable daily routines. A large body of research (Durlak, Weissberg, & Pachan, 2010) showing the benefits of afterschool programs buttresses their legitimacy as well.

Afterschool programs serve a wide variety of purposes—keeping young people safe, providing enrichment opportunities, training youth in specific skills, and supporting academic success—and this variety has given afterschool programs:

> Room to be a different kind of child development institution—one that mostly avoided pathologizing low-income children and one that can identify gaps in children's lives and try to fill them. It has allowed after-school programs to be adult-directed institutions where the adult agenda is relatively modest. And it has allowed them to be responsive to changing needs and circumstances in the lives of low-income children.
>
> *(Halpern, 2002, p. 179)*

Not surprisingly, then, afterschool programs are often sites for experimentation for new models of education that seek to engage young people and adults in new ways of relating to one another (e.g., DiGiacomo & Gutiérrez, 2016), in structuring engaging entry points for youth into disciplinary forms of learning (e.g., Subramaniam, Ahn, & Waugh, 2015), supporting interest discovery (e.g., Ito, 2009), and in supporting young people's identity development (e.g., Blackburn, 2005).

One particularly transformative appropriation of this organizational form is a program developed for youth at the American Indian Center (AIC) in Chicago. The AIC is a cultural center serving the Native American community in the city; residents representing many different Indigenous peoples of North America participate in activities there. A collaborative team of elders, parents, teachers, community content experts, youth, and other community members designed and studied the program, called Urban Explorers (Bang, Medin, & Cajete, 2009). The developers refer to the program as a curriculum that has the aim of helping students come to see science as a historically evolving, cultural practice for studying and making sense of the world and to navigate between their own communities' epistemologies and ways of knowing the world with those of Western science (Bang & Medin, 2010).

The core idea animating the program was that humans, other animals, and plants are all related. Students explored this idea through a variety of field experiences in which students made careful observations and were encouraged to establish direct relationships with plants and animals, as well as through culturally based stories that focus on relations among plants, animals, humans, and the land. Evidence gathered by researchers indicated that young people in the program came to see the community—not just school—as a significant context for learning science, and to view science as "a set of knowledge-making activities done in school and community by Native people" (Bang & Medin, 2010, p. 1022).

Several aspects of this appropriation of the afterschool form make it a good example of the kind of appropriation that Clemens (1993) identified as creating conditions for change at the inter-organizational level. First is the matter of who the educators were in the program: in this effort, Indigenous community members were directly involved in designing, leading, and studying the program. Critical to AIC team members was the need to reclaim *sovereignty* over the educational process of Indigenous youth, given the history of U.S. educators in using schooling as a means to separate Indigenous children from their families and eradicate their cultures (Bang, Faber, Gurneau, Marin, & Soto, 2016). The purposes were also different from either traditional school science's focus on "culturally neutral" content in its emphasis on science as cultural practice, and from afterschool science's more typical short-term, activity-focused nature (see Lundh, House, Means, & Harris, 2013) in its emphasis on building sustained relationships with one another and the land through the curriculum. The collaborative design and implementation of this afterschool program—including the direct engagement of community elders in the process—was doubly restorative: of agency in the process of educating children and youth and of the value of cultural ways of knowing their relation to the land, other animals, and plants that the community sought to sustain. In addition, the fact that resources to support the work flowed to both the university and community organization ensured that its key adherents were also in some sense constituents, or resource providers in the effort.

Parent-Teacher Group

Parent-teacher groups are a ubiquitous feature of American schools. Parent-Teacher Associations and Parent-Teacher Organizations are membership organizations that host meetings and events, advocate for resources for schools and the children they serve, and sometimes have a formal governance role within schools. Most of these groups' primary purpose is to support parent involvement in the workings of the school. For many school staff, parent involvement is a means to a larger end, improving student achievement. By involving parents in activities that bring them into the school, the hope is that they become more active in supporting their child's learning, a key contributor to improved achievement (Epstein, 1991; Jeynes, 2003). A problem with this instrumentalist approach is that it forces parents to take a largely uncritical stance toward the workings of schools, or what Shirley (1997) has called an *accommodationist* form of family engagement. In its place, he suggests that what is needed is more parent engagement that "designates parents as citizens in the fullest sense—change agents who can transform urban schools and neighborhoods" (Shirley, p. 73).

There is a strong desire among many parents and teachers for more democratic relationships characterized by mutual trust and regard, even if that is not the experience of many parents and teachers. A study of parents and teachers in three Chicago elementary schools, for example, found that both groups shared a common investment in the school community and desired more direct communication with one another (Miretsky, 2004). At the same time, parents and teachers each described the other as periodically defensive and not doing enough to communicate with the other. As students get older, the emphasis on disciplinary learning puts everyday expertise in a "marginalized status and in a position of acquiescence, alienation, and subordination" to school staff (Goldman, 2006, p. 71). Dynamics of race and class further contribute to the marginalization of parents in their interactions with school staff (Dyrness, 2009; Fine, 1993). The result is that when parents and teachers come together, they do so not as partners, but as people with an inequitable distribution of power and voice in shaping children's education.

Ishimaru and colleagues (Barajas-López & Ishimaru, 2020; Ishimaru & Takahashi, 2017) sought to provide a context for disrupting typical patterns of relations between parents and school staff by changing the approach to organizing opportunities for parent involvement. With external funding from a private foundation and the support of their university, they appropriated methods of participatory design—commonly used in the design of workplace technologies in Scandinavia for decades (Ehn, 1992)—to engage teachers and parents in developing a series of workshops for parents that would replace the school-adopted curriculum used in a "parent academy" for the district. The design process re-positioned parents from nondominant communities as key decision makers, naming parents explicitly as "the experts on their own children and their own learning priorities and processes," (Ishimaru & Takahashi, p. 353) and the researchers as facilitators of the process who "privileged families' stories and lived experiences as *tools*" for highlighting gaps between what the schools ostensible goals for parent engagement were and its practices (Ishimaru & Takahashi, p. 354). To do so, they had to allow parents and teachers to meet both separately and together: separately, for parents to develop a collective sense of their own purposes, and together, in order to present their perspective in a way that demanded responsiveness of teachers.

The team also engaged in an activity common within a practice used in sociocultural intervention research called the Change Laboratory (Engeström, Virkkunen, Helle, Pihlaja, & Poikela, 1996), in which interactions are mirrored back to participants for reflection on the contradictions evident within them. Teachers and parents met separately to review transcripts of an early meeting of the group, and parents and teachers both noticed ways in which parents' ideas had not been taken up in the discussion, particularly when the principal spoke up. The group continued to work together, but without the principal as an active member of the design team, and at the conclusion of the process reflected on how the experience expanded their sense of possibilities for how the school could change, even in the face of constraints from current policies and leadership practices.

In this example, both the actors and the organizational form are relatively familiar, but the different sets of actors are positioned very differently with respect to one another and to accomplish different aims. Parents and teachers are both implicated in parent-teacher workshops, but not typically as co-equal participants. In this project, parents took on a new and counter-normative role of co-designer of workshops designed to foster greater parent involvement. And while the explicit purpose of the workshops themselves might be recognizable as fitting within the bounds of traditional parent involvement strategies, the design activity itself explicitly challenged deficit framings of parents as incapable and as uninterested in supporting their children's education through involvement in the school. The co-design process further amplified their voices and helped both groups feel more of a sense of their own power to make change in their school.

Student Organization

Student organizations, particularly in secondary schools and in higher education settings, are voluntary groups that students join at least in part on the basis of a desire to affiliate with peers with similar interests and identities. School-sponsored organizations are just one type of student organization; community- and faith-based organizations also sponsor student organizations. Where participation in school-sponsored student organizations has often been studied for its contribution to student outcomes such as increased achievement and prosocial behaviors (e.g., Eccles & Barber, 1999; Jordan, 1999), student organizations serve broader functions than just contributing to adults' goals for students. For example, organizations that serve students from racially minoritized groups can provide a source of social support for participants, especially on campuses where White cultural practices predominate (Guiffrida, 2003). Such organizations offer avenues for self-expression and sociopolitical development as well (Harper & Quaye, 2007). Student organizations for LGBTQ youth, such as Gay-Straight Alliances (GSAs), function similarly: not only providing a safe context for youth to gather in a supportive environment, but also serving as a base from which youth can explore ways to become advocates for LGBTQ youth in their schools and communities. In fact, evidence suggests that the advocacy function is a key contributor to an enhanced sense of agency experienced by participants in GSAs (Poteat, Calzo, & Yoshikawa, 2016). In this sense, student organizations can function much like affinity groups do in contemporary social movements, providing support to groups with similar interests and identities within a broader coalition that allows members of those groups to stand up in public forums for their perspectives and positions (Poletta, 2002).

Today, many young people are finding affinity groups online, rather than in physical spaces. Gee (2005) calls these *semiotic social spaces,* because they are grounded in common meanings rather than in a shared place, and he highlights the functions online networks play today in bringing young people together who might otherwise feel isolated because of their interests or identities. Online spaces afford youth the opportunity not just to consume mainstream media that include messages targeting communities with which they identify but also to produce their own, thereby promoting political change "through social and cultural mechanisms rather than through established political institutions," in spaces "where citizens see themselves as capable of expressing their political concerns—often through the circulation of media" (Jenkins, 2016, p. 2). Such networks can provide a space outside the one on the ground, a space of freedom where youth activists and their allies can imagine alternatives, generate new symbols, choreograph simultaneous protests across different communities, and spread, test, and refine protest tactics and memes quickly, as has been illustrated many times within the Black Lives Matter movement in recent years (Kedhar, 2014). While not replacing the need to gather in person together, the "digitized" affinity group has become a powerful force in mobilization in both progressive and far right movements for social change.

Gamber-Thompson and Zimmerman's (2016) analysis of the "Youth Coming Out of the Shadows Week" campaign illustrates the power of this new form of mobilization. During this campaign, undocumented youth posted their stories online on a variety of platforms from Vimeo to YouTube, challenging dominant media narratives about them through direct public messaging. Hundreds of videos were produced, and these not only provided a means for self-expression and countering narratives, but also mobilized a distributed network of support for youth who have come to call themselves DREAMers, because of their campaign's specific focus on passage of the DREAM Act. Gamber-Thompson and Zimmerman argue:

> Sharing stories through various social and digital media platforms has allowed youth to challenge and, at times, supplant mass media representations though more locally constructed and participatory forms of messaging. The practice has also given undocumented youth the opportunity to identify and connect with one another online.
>
> *(p. 203)*

The form of many of these stories was that of a *testimonio,* a cultural practice involving a first-person narrative told for its ties to broader social and political struggles (Reyes & Rodríguez, 2012). As such, it embodies what Jenkins (2016) refers to as a "cultural" turn in youth organizing, one that embraces a wider diversity of community practices of expression within movements, from spoken word poetry to media "mash-ups."

Promoting Equitable and Just Learning Across Settings

The transformation of the student organization into an online space for mobilizing what have come to be called "networked publics" (Varnelis, 2012) to refer to the ways that the Internet—and social media in particular—connects people with common interests across wide geographic spaces, offers an opportunity to connect educational change efforts across different communities. These publics do not replace local efforts or other means of communication, and they also benefit from the support of formal organizations like DreamActivist.org, which emerged from early transmedia mobilization efforts. Still, the DREAMers' success in raising the consciousness of citizens and politicians regarding educational opportunity is striking. Though their campaign has not yet been successful in achieving its primary objective, it illustrates the cultural and political potential of appropriating the student organization for explicitly equity-oriented advocacy for expansion of opportunity.

Leadership Development Program

Youth-led organizing initiatives like those of the DREAMers typically involve some formal leadership development programming for participants (Delgado & Staples, 2008). Youth organizing—as all community organizing—requires the development of participants' critical consciousness, their skill in facilitating meetings and developing strategic action plans, and in both democratic deliberation and direct action (Boehm & Staples, 2006; Shirley, 1997; Warren, Mapp, & the Community Organizing and School Reform Project, 2011). Developmental goals supported through such programs include fostering productive, reciprocal relationships with both peers and adults and building skill in navigating organizations and societal institutions (Edelman, Gill, Comerford, Larson, & Hare, 2004; Larson & Hansen, 2005; Wheeler, 2003). Many other youth leadership programs are not activist oriented, though, and may be focused on building character or promoting individual development. In their widely cited text on youth leadership and development, van Linden and Fertman (1998) describe "leaders as individuals (both adults and adolescents) who think for themselves, communicate their thoughts and feelings to others, and help others understand and act on their own beliefs" (p. 17). Programs with these goals—such as Boy Scouts and 4-H—have long been available to youth in many communities and have strong constituencies. Leadership development programs are, in that sense, familiar organizational forms within education.

The Futures Project illustrates a creative appropriation of leadership development to more activist ends. Facilitated by researchers working in collaboration with teachers and youth at a Los Angeles high school, the Futures Project was a project that sought simultaneously to support individual youths' pathways into higher education, create more equitable learning opportunities at the school, and develop knowledge about conditions needed for equity-oriented school reforms to succeed (Oakes & Rogers, 2006). As part of the project, a group of some 30 low-income youth engaged in social inquiry over a three-year period into the "tracks" or pathways youth could take in their high school. Notably, and by design, the youth came from the non-college preparatory track. The research team hoped that their investigations would lead them to commit to pursue more ambitious education pathways themselves, as well as yield systematic evidence that could be used to advocate for better access to advanced coursework in their school. As part of the project, they met as part of class during the regular school year, and they also participated in a summer leadership program where they read sociological texts that focused on social stratification and inequality in schooling (Rogers, Morrell, & Enyedy, 2007). At the program, they apprenticed to faculty at UCLA who were studying urban education, and faculty and other staff supported them to develop research designs to carry out their own social inquiry, not just within their school but also within the community. For example, one young woman developed a study focused on how journalists chose stories involving youth and represented them.

As Oakes and Rogers (2006) concede, the project was only partly successful. On the one hand, young people who participated did, for the most part, embark on pathways that the low-track classes they began in had not prepared them for. They took AP and honors classes, and by graduation, 25 of the original 30 had been accepted into a four-year college or university. Additionally, young people took on leadership roles within the school in student government and in the community on race relations. Some founded a new student organization at the school focused on supporting Indigenous students. And, they turned regularly to one another for academic and social support. But the school policies did not immediately change, and youth found their own voices squelched by administrators and board members when they sought to advocate for improved access to advanced coursework. Only a few years later did the principal at the school create reforms to broaden access by committing to a college preparatory pathway for all students and to additional academic and social supports for students.

This particular approach does illustrate the power of harnessing youth leadership programs for activist means as a way to promote individual and collective change, even when it does not result in significant organizational change. The bonds created in the program were powerful resources to youth, and their own pathways shifted significantly in ways that differed from their peers (Oakes & Rogers, 2006). It's also likely that the students' efforts and own successes shifted what Renée, Oakes, and Welner (2009) have called the "zone of mediation" within the school, that is, the zone of politically feasible solutions to educational problems, in ways that help explain subsequent shifts in the school's policies and programs. In addition, by appropriating another organizational form of social inquiry—Youth Participatory Action Research (Cammarota & Fine, 2008)—within a school context, the project both provided students with concrete research skills and also a process for turning inquiry into action and advocacy.

Research-Practice Partnership

The research-practice partnership is an emerging form of organization in education that is rapidly expanding, thanks in part to increased calls for evidence use in education and a growing awareness of the need for research to become more relevant to practice (Coburn & Penuel, 2016). The Futures Project described above is an example of a kind of research-practice partnership involving researchers at a university, teachers in a school, and students. But today's partnerships often include entire school districts as partners, and they tackle problems of educational inequity at the level of systems and communities (Coburn, Penuel, & Geil, 2013; Penuel & Gallagher, 2017). Research-practice partnerships pursue a range of goals, from supporting more evidence use in district-level decision making, changing policies and practices, to improving teacher and student outcomes (Henrick, Cobb, Penuel, Jackson, & Clark, 2017). Though they are constructed to be mutualistic among partners, their success in addressing issues of equity very much depends on the inclusiveness of the partnership of the voices of youth, families, and the community, as well as a willingness to name and address specific inequities, such as those linked to race (Barton & Bevan, 2016; Penuel, 2017).

One such research-practice partnership stretches the very idea of "who" can be a partner by including as a key partner an advocacy organization that has actively and publically fought against district leadership regarding racial disparities in discipline. For decades, the advocacy and activist organization Padres y Jóvenes Unidos in Denver has fought for educational justice for the community's growing Latinx community (see Warren et al., 2011, chapter 4, for one account). For years, the group worked with a national group, the Advancement Project, to call attention to unfair discipline practices within the district, and eventually was successful in securing a change to district policies. They joined with researchers at the Graduate School of Social Work at the University of Denver, the Denver Classroom Teachers Association, Denver Public Schools, and the National Education Association to form the Denver School-Based Restorative Justice Partnership, to support ongoing study and support for implementation of new restorative policies in the district, with the aim of eliminating racial disparities in discipline. The partnership, funded by a national teachers' union and national advocacy group, is studying the implementation of the initiative, applying

Promoting Equitable and Just Learning Across Settings

critical race theory perspectives to interrogate obstacles in publications co-authored by district leaders (Annamma, Anyon, Joseph, Downing, & Simmons, 2019), and they are also studying the impacts of the initiative (Anyon et al., 2016). At present, this partnership is working to develop a more robust intervention support system within the district, grounded in work done in three different district schools.

What is unusual here is not the form of organization itself—research-practice partnership—but rather the ways that Padres y Jóvenes Unidos engages in multiple ways with the district, both as an advocacy organization fighting against unjust practices in the Denver Public Schools and the practices of the Denver Classroom Teachers Association, and as a partner with the district and union. Throughout, the organization has maintained its role as outside advocate for Latinx children in the schools and in the community. This approach has long been employed in grassroots organizing campaigns to improve schools, which often involve a push-pull relationship between community leaders and school staff but require cooperation between the community and school system to successfully implement more equitable policies and secure additional resources for schools (Shirley, 1997; Warren et al., 2011). The expansion of research-practice partnerships as an organizational form to include advocacy organizations in the community will no doubt require substantial rethinking of what partnerships can accomplish and investigations of their potential for promoting more inclusive approaches to policy development and equitable outcomes in education (Kirshner, Pacheco, Sifuentes, & Hildreth, 2018; Tseng, Fleishman, & Quintero, 2018).

Emerging Approaches to Supporting and Studying the Appropriation of Repertoires of Organizing for More Equitable Educational Systems

Above, I have outlined examples of appropriation of repertoires of organizing in education by novel groups of actors and for different purposes. As Clemens (1993) did for the women's movement, I have sought to show how this pattern of appropriation points to new possibilities for institutional change in education. The efforts described above, however, remain too few and far between, and most can claim only partial success at a project level to effect organization-level changes that resulted in more equitable opportunities for all. All—by virtue of being equity-oriented reforms—face considerable headwinds in the face of logics of scarcity, deficit, and merit that characterize education (Oakes & Rogers, 2007). Importantly, all of them attempt to address these head-on; the examples above involve recruiting culturally familiar forms of organizations to challenge other normative aspects of the culture of education that reproduce failure systematically in ways that are gendered, raced, and classed. As such, they are potential models to learn and build from.

Common to the examples, too, is a different way of organizing research and development efforts that are focused on supporting equitable change, ones that adopt a relational approach to power consistent with contemporary social movements. A relational approach sees political interests—including self-interest—as "developing in and through relationships with others" and views leadership in social movements as needing to "balance authority with accountability" (Poletta, 2002, pp. 183–184). Collective inquiry and social action are powerful means to achieve transformation from this relational perspective, occurring as organizing groups bring individuals, communities, and organizations into relationship and action (Warren et al., 2011, p. 30).

Still, we need to develop a broader repertoire of forms of organizing for educational change than are currently available, and this will require new, collaborative approaches to research and development that many of the examples above embody. Just as in social movement organizing for social justice, "[e]ffective organizational forms are necessarily hybrids, [and] the problem for movement groups is that they have such an impoverished menu of options from which to assemble such hybrids" (Poletta, 2002, p. 221). In addition, we will need to become more precise in our description of actors in these efforts, specifying the level of society for actors (e.g., individuals, association, groups), as well as prototypes and roles of individuals and organizations, in order to inform and study change efforts (cf., Hwang & Colyvas, in press). Below, I outline three promising but still emerging approaches to research and development that seek to accomplish this aim: (1) Design-Based Implementation Research; (2) Community-Based Design Research; and (3) Social Design Experiments.

Design-Based Implementation Research

Design-Based Implementation Research (DBIR; Penuel, Fishman, Cheng, & Sabelli, 2011) is an approach to research and development within research-practice partnerships that integrates the iterative, collaborative approach to developing and testing innovations in the practice of design research with theories and methods of policy and organizational research in education. It seeks not just to describe whether innovations work, but to create conditions for scaling and sustainability of equity-oriented change efforts. Equity is central to DBIR efforts in three respects: (1) in its commitment to including all key stakeholder groups in the process of design; (2) in its focus on creating conditions for equitable implementation of innovations within educational systems and communities; and (3) in its commitment to studying equity of implementation and outcomes (Fishman & Penuel, 2018). The Linked Learning Initiative, as well as the work of the Denver School-Based Restorative Justice Partnership, are examples of research that have integrity to the key principles of DBIR, which emphasize collaborative goal definition and design, and the study and support of systemic implementation of equity-oriented reforms.

Community-Based Design Research

Like DBIR, Community-Based Design Research is committed to inclusive, participatory design of innovations (Bang & Vossoughi, 2016). Unlike DBIR, it is centered more in the community than in schools and districts, as illustrated by the Urban Explorers program (Bang et al., 2016), though CBDR often does directly engage with school systems, as is the case with Ishimaru and colleagues' work to co-design a new parent involvement curriculum in an elementary school. CBDR centers questions related to both power (e.g., "Who designs?") and persistent inequality (e.g., "Why do inequalities of opportunity persist for racially minoritized students?") (Bang et al., 2016; Booker & Goldman, 2016; Le Dantec & Fox, 2015). As with other forms of participatory and community based research, CBDR places strong emphasis on values, social justice, promoting the agency of participants in research, and accountability to participants in research (Campano, Ghiso, & Welch, 2015).

Social Design Experiments

The aim of a social design experiment is to develop new tools and practices that produce novel cross-organizational learning arrangements, especially for students from nondominant communities (Gutiérrez & Jurow, 2016; Gutiérrez & Vossoughi, 2010). The goals of a social design experiment are to design and test "theoretically grounded and practical educational interventions, the social agenda of ameliorating and redressing historical injustices, and the development of theories focused on the organization of equitable learning opportunities" (Gutiérrez & Jurow, p. 565). For individuals, the goal of a social design experiment is to promote the goal of transformative agency (Virkkunen, 2006), where participants collectively envision and explore new possibilities for consequential learning and more just social futures. In a social design experiment, there is also always a goal of changing institutional relationships to be more equitable, particularly to leverage and recognize the expertise, contributions, and dignity of people from nondominant communities. The Learning Futures project is a good example of a social design experiment in which a key aim, in Oakes and Rogers' (2006) words, was to use "the method

Promoting Equitable and Just Learning Across Settings

for examining how constructing settings for participatory social inquiry might help us understand the intersection of the larger political and social context of schooling and specific efforts to make schools more educative and equitable for low-income students of color. We use 'social' to emphasize the vital role of participants in shaping the purpose and character of our shared work" (p. 42).

Each of these approaches requires a supportive infrastructure and broad expertise from the community, families, educators, researchers, and policy makers to succeed. Their complexity is a reminder that equity-oriented change always faces significant normative and sociopolitical challenges and that change requires drawing on and adding to the repertoires for organizing for educational change.

References

Afterschool Alliance. (2014). *America after 3pm: Afterschool Programs in Demand.* Washington, DC.

Annamma, S. A., Anyon, Y., Joseph, N. M., Downing, B., & Simmons, J. (2019). Black girls and school discipline: The complexities of being overrepresented and under studied. *Urban Education, 54*(2), 211–242.

Anyon, Y., Gregory, A., Stone, S., Farrar, J., Jenson, J. M., McQueen, J., Downing, B., Greer, E., & Simmons, J. (2016). Restorative interventions and school discipline sanctions in a large urban school district. *American Educational Research Journal, 53*(6), 1663–1697.

Bang, M., Faber, L., Gurneau, J., Marin, A., & Soto, C. (2016). Community-based design research: Learning across generations and strategic transformations of institutional relations toward axiological innovations. *Mind, Culture, and Activity, 23*(6), 28–41.

Bang, M., & Medin, D. (2010). Cultural processes in science education: Supporting the navigation of multiple epistemologies. *Science Education, 94*(6), 1008–1026.

Bang, M., Medin, D., & Cajete, G. (2009). Improving science education for Native students: Teaching place through community. *SACNAS, 12*(1), 8–10.

Bang, M., & Vossoughi, S. (2016). Participatory design research and educational justice: Studying learning and relations within social change making. *Cognition and Instruction, 34*(3), 173–193.

Barajas-López, F., & Ishimaru, A. M. (in press). "Darles el lugar": A place for nondominant family knowing in educational equity. *Urban Education, 55*(1), 38–65.

Barton, A. C., & Bevan, B. (2016). Leveraging RPPs to address racial inequality in urban school districts. Retrieved from http://wtgrantfoundation.org/leveraging-rpps-address-race-reduce-inequality-urban-school-districts.

Blackburn, M. V. (2005). Co-constructing space for literacy and identity work with LGBTQ youth. *Afterschool Matters, 4*, 17–23.

Boehm, A., & Staples, L. (2006). Grassroots leadership in task-oriented groups: Learning from successful leaders. *Social Work with Groups, 28*(2), 77–96.

Booker, A., & Goldman, S. V. (2016). Participatory design research as a practice for systemic repair: Doing hand-in-hand math research with families. *Cognition and Instruction, 34*(3), 223–235.

Cammarota, J., & Fine, M. (2008). *Revolutionizing Education: Youth Participatory Action Research in Motion.* New York, NY: Routledge.

Campano, G., Ghiso, M. P., & Welch, B. (2015). Ethical and professional norms in community-based research. *Harvard Educational Review, 85*(1), 29–49.

Clemens, E. S. (1993). Organizational repertoires and institutional change: Women's groups and the transformation of U.S. politics. *American Journal of Sociology, 98*(4), 755–798.

Coburn, C. E., & Penuel, W. R. (2016). Research-practice partnerships in education: Outcomes, dynamics, and open questions. *Educational Researcher, 45*(1), 48–54.

Coburn, C. E., Penuel, W. R., & Geil, K. (2013). *Research-Practice Partnerships at the District Level: A New Strategy for Leveraging Research for Educational Improvement.* Berkeley, CA and Boulder, CO: University of California and University of Colorado.

Conchas, G. Q., & Clark, P. A. (2002). Career academies and urban minority schooling: Forging optimism despite limited opportunity. *Journal of Education for Students Placed at Risk, 7*(3), 287–311.

DeFalco, A. (2010). An analysis of John Dewey's notion of occupations: Still pedagogically valuable? *Education and Culture, 26*(1), 82–99.

Delgado, M., & Staples, L. (2008). *Youth-Led Community Organizing: Theory and Action.* New York, NY: Oxford University Press.

Dewey, J. (1997). *The Collected Works of John Dewey, 1882–1953.* Charlottesville, VA: InteLex.

DiGiacomo, D., & Gutiérrez, K. D. (2016). Relational equity as a design tool within making and tinkering activities. *Mind, Culture, and Activity, 23*(2), 141–153.

Durlak, J. A., Weissberg, J. A., & Pachan, M. (2010). A meta-analysis of after-school programs that seek to promote personal and social skills in children and adolescents. *American Journal of Community Psychology, 45*(3–4), 294–309.

Dyrness, A. (2009). Cultural exclusion and critique in the era of good intentions: Using participatory research to transform parent roles in urban school reform. *Social Justice, 36*(4), 36–53.

Eccles, J. S., & Barber, B. L. (1999). Student council, volunteering, basketball, or marching band: What kind of extracurricular involvement matters? *Journal of Adolescent Research, 14*(1), 10–43.

Edelman, A., Gill, P., Comerford, K., Larson, M., & Hare, R. (2004). *Youth Development and Youth Leadership: A Background Paper.* Washington, DC. National Collaborative on Workforce and Disability for Youth.

Ehn, P. (1992). Scandinavian design: On participation and skill. In: P. S. Adler, & T. A. Winograd (Eds.), *Usability: Turning Technologies into Tools* (pp. 96–132). New York, NY: Oxford University Press.

Engeström, Y., Virkkunen, J., Helle, M., Pihlaja, J., & Poikela, R. (1996). Change laboratory as a tool for transforming work. *Lifelong Learning in Europe, 1*(2), 10–17.

Epstein, J. L. (1991). Effects on student achievement of teachers' practices of parent involvement. *Advances in Reading/Language Research, 5,* 261–276.

Fine, M. (1993). [Ap]parent involvement: Reflections on parents, power, and urban schools. *Teachers College Record, 94*(4), 682–710.

Fishman, B. J., & Penuel, W. R. (2018). Design-based implementation research. In: F. Fischer, C. E. Hmelo-Silver, S. R. Goldman, & P. Reimann (Eds.), *International Handbook of the Learning Sciences* (pp. 393–400). New York, NY: Routledge.

Gamber-Thompson, L., & Zimmerman, A. M. (2016). DREAMing citizenship: Undocumented youth, coming out, and pathways to participation. In: H. Jenkins, S. Shresthova, L. Gamber-Thompson, N. Kligler-Vilenchik, & A. M. Zimmerman (Eds.), *By Any Media Necessary: The New Youth Activism* (pp. 186–218). New York, NY: New York University Press.

Gee, J. P. (2005). Semiotic social spaces and affinity spaces: From the age of mythology to today's schools. In: D. Barton, & K. Tusting (Eds.), *Beyond Communities of Practice: Language, Power, and Social Context* (pp. 214–232). New York, NY: Cambridge University Press.

Goldman, S. V. (2006). A new angle on families: Connecting the mathematics of life with school mathematics. In: Z. Bekerman, N. C. Burbules, & D. Silberman-Keller (Eds.), *Learning in Places: The Informal Education Reader* (pp. 55–76). New York, NY: Peter Lang.

Guiffrida, D. A. (2003). African American student organizations as agents of social integration. *Journal of College Student Development, 44*(3), 304–319.

Gupta, P., & Negron, J. (2017). There is no "Off Button" to explaining: Theorizing identity development in youth who work as floor facilitators. In: P. G. Patrick (Ed.), *Preparing Informal Science Educators* (pp. 153–168). Dordrecht, the Netherlands: Springer.

Gutiérrez, K. D., & Jurow, A. S. (2016). Social design experiments: Toward equity by design. *Journal of the Learning Sciences, 25*(4), 565–598.

Gutiérrez, K. D., & Rogoff, B. (2003). Cultural ways of learning: Individual traits or repertoires of practice. *Educational Researcher, 32*(5), 19–25.

Gutiérrez, K. D., & Vossoughi, S. (2010). Lifting off the ground to return anew: Mediated praxis, transformative learning, and social design experiments. *Journal of Teacher Education, 61*(1–2), 100–117.

Halpern, R. (2002). A different kind of child development institution: The history of after-school programs for low-income children. *Teachers College Record, 104*(2), 178–211.

Harper, S. R., & Quaye, S. J. (2007). Student organizations as venues for Black identity expression and development among African American male student leaders. *Journal of College Student Development, 48*(2), 127–144.

Henrick, E. C., Cobb, P., Penuel, W. R., Jackson, K., & Clark, T. R. (2017). *Assessing Research-Practice Partnerships: Five Dimensions of Effectiveness.* New York, NY: William T. Grant Foundation.

Hoachlander, G., McGlawn, T., & Stam, B. (2017). Linked learning: Making the best of time for all students. In: M. Saunders, J. Ruiz de Velasco, & J. Oakes (Eds.), *Learning Time in Pursuit of Educational Equity* (pp. 89–109). Cambridge, MA: Harvard Education Press.

Hwang, H., & Colyvas, J. A. (in press). Ontology, levels of society, and degrees of generality: Theorizing actors as abstractions in institutional theory. *Academy of Management Journal.* doi: 10.5465/amr.2014.0266.

Ishimaru, A. M., & Takahashi, S. (2017). Disrupting racialized institutional scripts: Toward parent-teacher transformative agency for educational justice. *Peabody Journal of Education, 92*(3), 343–362.

Ito, M. (Ed.) (2009). *Hanging Out, Messing around, and Geeking Out: Kids Living and Learning with New Media.* Cambridge, MA: MIT Press.

Jenkins, H. (2016). Youth voice, media, and political engagement: Introducing the core concepts. In: H. Jenkins, S. Shresthova, L. Gamber-Thompson, N. Kligler-Vilenchik, & A. M. Zimmerman (Eds.), *By Any Media Necessary: The New Youth Activism* (pp. 1–60). New York, NY: New York University Press.

Jeynes, W. H. (2003). A meta-analysis: The effects of parental involvement on minority children's academic achievement. *Education and Urban Society, 35*(2), 202–218.

Jordan, W. J. (1999). Black high school students' participation in school-sponsored sports activities: Effects on school engagement and achievement. *The Journal of Negro Education, 68*(1), 54–71.

Kedhar, A. (2014). "Hands up, Don't shoot!": Gesture, choreography and protest in Furguson. Retrieved from http://thefeministwire.com/2014/10/protest-in-ferguson.

Kemple, J. J., & Willner, C. J. (2008). *Career Academies: Long-Term Impacts on Labor Market Outcomes, Educational Attainment, and Transitions to Adulthood*. New York, NY: Research Alliance for New York City Schools.

Kim, H., & Bearman, P. J. (1997). The structure and dynamics of movement participation. *American Sociological Review, 62*(1), 70–93.

Kirshner, B., Pacheco, J., Sifuentes, M., & Hildreth, R. (2018). Rethinking "the community" in university-community partnerships: Case studies from CU Engage. In: B. Bevan, & W. R. Penuel (Eds.), *Connecting Research and Practice for Educational Improvement: Ethical and Equitable Approaches* (pp. 85–99). New York, NY: Routledge.

Larson, R. W., & Hansen, D. (2005). The development of strategic thinking: Learning to impact human systems in a youth activism program. *Human Development, 48*(6), 327–349.

Lave, J., & Wenger, E. (1991). *Situated Learning: Legitimate Peripheral Participation*. Cambridge, MA: Harvard University Press.

Le Dantec, C. A., & Fox, S. (2015). Strangers at the gate: Gaining access, building rapport, and co-constructing community-based research. In: D. Cosley, A. Forte, L. Ciolfi, & D. McDonald (Eds.), *CSCW '15: Proceedings of the 18th ACM Conference on Computer Supported Cooperative Work & Social Computing* (pp. 1348–1358). Vancouver, BC, Canada: Association for Computing Machinery.

Lubienski, C., Scott, J., & DeBray, E. (2011). The rise of intermediary organizations in knowledge production, advocacy, and educational policy. *Teachers College Record*. Retrieved from http://www.tcrecord.org ID Number: 16487.

Lundh, P., House, A., Means, B., & Harris, C. J. (2013). Learning from science: Case studies of science offerings in afterschool programs. *Afterschool Matters, 18*, 33–41.

McCarthy, J. D., & Zald, M. N. (1977). Resource mobilization and social movements: A partial theory. *American Journal of Sociology, 82*(6), 1212–1241.

Miretsky, D. (2004). The communication requirements of democratic schools: Parent-teacher perspectives on their relationships. *Teachers College Record, 106*(4), 814–851.

National Association of Colleges and Employers. (2017). *Student Survey Report: Results from NACE's Annual Survey of College Students, Executive Summary*. Bethlehem, PA.

Oakes, J., & Rogers, J. (2006). *Learning Power: Organizing for Education and Justice*. New York, NY: Teachers College Press.

Oakes, J., & Rogers, J. (2007). Radical change through radical means: Learning power. *Journal of Educational Change, 8*(3), 193–206.

Penuel, W. R. (2017). Research–practice partnerships as a strategy for promoting equitable science teaching and learning through leveraging everyday science. *Science Education, 101*(5), 520–525.

Penuel, W. R., Fishman, B. J., Cheng, B., & Sabelli, N. (2011). Organizing research and development at the intersection of learning, implementation, and design. *Educational Researcher, 40*(7), 331–337.

Penuel, W. R., & Gallagher, D. (2017). *Creating Research-Practice Partnerships in Education*. Cambridge, MA: Harvard Education Press.

Penuel, W. R., Van Horne, K., DiGiacomo, D., & Kirshner, B. (2016). A social practice theory of learning and becoming across contexts and time. *Frontline Learning Research, 4*(4), 30–38.

Poletta, F. (2002). *Freedom Is an Endless Meeting: Democracy in American Social Movements*. Chicago, IL: University of Chicago Press.

Poteat, V. P., Calzo, J. P., & Yoshikawa, H. (2016). Promoting youth agency through dimensions of gay–straight alliance involvement and conditions that maximize associations. *Journal of Youth and Adolescence, 45*(7), 1438–1451.

Reckhow, S., & Snyder, J. W. (2014). The expanding role of philanthropy in education politics. *Educational Researcher, 43*(4), 186–195.

Renée, M., Welner, K., & Oakes, J. (2009). Social movement organizing and equity-focused educational change: Shifting the zone of mediation. In: A. Hargreaves, A. Lieberman, M. Fullan, & D. Hopkins (Eds.), *Second International Handbook of Educational Change* (pp. 158–163). London: Kluwer.

Reyes, K. B., & Rodríguez, J. E. C. (2012). Testimonio: Origins, terms, and resources. *Equity and Excellence in Education, 45*(3), 525–538.

Richmond, G., & Kurth, L. A. (1999). Moving from outside to inside: High school students use of apprenticeships as vehicles for entering the culture and practice of science. *Science Education, 36*(6), 677–697.

Rodriguez, A. J. (2001). Sociocultural constructivism, courage, and the researchers gaze: Redefining our roles as cultural warriors for social change. In: A. Calabrese Barton, & M. D. Osborne (Eds.), *Teaching Science in Diverse Settings* (pp. 325–345). New York, NY: Peter Lang.

Rogers, J., Morrell, E., & Enyedy, N. (2007). Studying the struggle: Contexts for learning and identity development for urban youth. *American Behavioral Scientist, 51*(3), 419–443.

Rogoff, B. (2014). Learning by observing and pitching in to family and community endeavors: An orientation. *Human Development, 57*(1), 69–81.

Rogoff, B., Moore, L., Najafi, B., Dexter, A., Correa-Chavez, M., & Solis, J. (2007). Children's development of cultural repertoires through participation in everyday routines and practices. In: J. E. Grusec, & P. D. Hastings (Eds.), *Handbook of Socialization: Theory and Research* (pp. 490–515). New York, NY: Guilford Press.

Scott, J., & Jabbar, H. (2014). The Hub and the spokes: Foundations, intermediary organizations, incentivist reforms, and the politics of research evidence. *Educational Policy, 28*(2), 233–257.

Scott, J., Lubienski, C., DeBray, E., & Jabbar, H. (2014). The intermediary function in evidence production, promotion, and utilization: The case of educational incentives. In: K. S. Finnigan, & A. J. Daly (Eds.), *Using Research Evidence in Education: From the Schoolhouse Door to Capitol Hill* (pp. 69–92). New York, NY: Springer.

Scott, W. R. (2008). *Institutions and Organizations: Ideas and Interests* (4th ed.). Thousand Oaks, CA: Sage.

Shirley, D. (1997). *Community Organizing for Urban School Reform*. Austin, TX: University of Texas Press.

Subramaniam, M., Ahn, J., & Waugh, A. (2015). The role of school librarians in enhancing science learning. *Journal of Librarianship and Information Science, 47*(1), 3–16.

Tseng, V., Fleishman, S., & Quintero, E. (2018). Democratizing evidence in education. In: B. Bevan, & W. R. Penuel (Eds.), *Connecting Research and Practice for Educational Improvement: Ethical and Equitable Approaches* (pp. 3–16). New York, NY: Routledge.

Tyack, D., & Cuban, L. (1995). *Tinkering Toward Utopia: A Century of Public School Reform*. Cambridge, MA: Harvard University Press.

Valladares, M. R., & Welner, K. (2017). Expanding learning time within the zone of mediation. In: M. Saunders, J. Ruiz de Velasco, & J. Oakes (Eds.), *Learning Time in Pursuit of Educational Equity* (pp. 219–234). Cambridge, MA: Harvard Education Press.

van Linden, J. A., & Fertman, C. I. (1998). *Youth Leadership: A Guide to Understanding Leadership Development in Adolescents*. San Francisco, CA: Jossey-Bass.

Varenne, H., & McDermott, R. P. (1998). *Successful Failure: The School America Builds*. New York, NY: Westview Press.

Varnelis, K. (Ed.) (2012). *Networked Publics*. Cambridge, MA: MIT Press.

Virkkunen, J. (2006). Dilemmas in building shared transformative agency. *Activités, 3*(1), 43–66.

Warner, M. T., Caspary, K., Arshan, N., Stites, R., Patel, D., Park, C. J., & Adelman, N. (2016). *Taking Stock of the California Linked Learning District Initiative. Seventh-Year Evaluation Report*. Menlo Park, CA: SRI International.

Warren, M. R., Mapp, K. L., & the Community Organizing and School Reform Project. (2011). *A Match on Dry Grass: Community Organizing as a Catalyst for School Reform*. New York, NY: Oxford University Press.

Wartofsky, M. (1979). *Models: Representation and the Scientific Understanding* (Vol. 4). Dordrecth, Holland: Riedl.

Wheeler, W. (2003). Youth leadership for development: Civic activism as a component of youth development programming and a strategy for strengthening civil society. In: R. M. Lerner, F. Jacobs, & D. Wertlieb (Eds.), *Handbook of Applied Developmental Science: Promoting Positive Child, Adolescent, and Family Development through Research, Policies, and Programs* (Vol. 2, pp. 491–405). Thousand Oaks, CA: SAGE.

21

LEARNING AT THE BOUNDARIES*

Reconsidering University-District Partnerships for Educational Change

Louis M. Gomez, Manuelito Biag, and David G. Imig

Across the United States, school leaders are being asked to reshape their work away from serving as managers of schools toward leaders of learning organizations. School boards are asking superintendents to create schools where teachers hone their practice within learning communities and encourage children to engage in collaborative learning with their peers. At the same time, superintendents are turning to schools of education and asking them to prepare more leaders who can lead in these new ways. However, more often than not, school districts struggle to establish organizations that are top to bottom learning communities, and schools of education have yet to figure out how to nurture leaders with the requisite knowledge, skills, and dispositions to build and lead thriving learning communities (Darling-Hammond, LaPointe, Meyerson, Orr, & Cohen, 2007). In this chapter, we explore what it means for school districts and schools of education to share problems like these. We define sharing as extending beyond idiosyncratic, individually based working relationships that cross institutional boundaries. Instead, we examine what animates the formation of sustainable and systemic cross-institutional connections. We argue that forming these connections poses a problem that is cultural in nature.

Leadership in a New Light

School leadership forms the backdrop for an exploration of what can engender institutions and organizations, from different sectors (or different parts of the same sector), to examine their core customs, social behaviors, and foundational ideas. Studies indicate that after teachers, leadership matters most for effective schools (Cruickshank, 2017; Leithwood, Louis, Anderson, & Wahlstrom, 2004). Effective leaders are defined as those skilled at orchestrating the intellectual, structural, cultural, and social resources for educating students. Yet what we expect of leaders, and thus leadership preparation, has changed palpably in recent decades.

In the decades leading up to the 21st century, school leadership was largely seen as a matter of the acquisition and deployment of school resources—from food to books, buses to band uniforms. Essentially, the hiring of teachers, financial stewardship of the school, and a smattering of teaching and learning consumed much of the time and effort of most school leaders (Hess & Kelly, 2005; Levine, 2006). Then, the field experienced a "paradigm shift" (Murphy, 2002) driven partly by political and popular calls to educate people to master things such as "21st century skills" (Ananiadou & Claro, 2009; Dede, 2010), and to achieve "deeper learning" (Martinez &

---

* The authors would like to thank the Carnegie Corporation of New York for their support of the iLEAD network and the writing of this manuscript.

McGrath, 2014) that is fully cognizant of the social-emotional aspects of what it means to learn. Overarching these increasingly greater ambitions was the aspiration to accomplish these aims equitably and universally. Yet most school leaders lacked these skills.

Leadership and the ecology that supports it, including schools of education, now need to be considered in a different light. In this chapter, we posit that the task of preparing and supporting today's leaders is a cross-cultural challenge that encourages key actors in local education agencies (LEAs) and institutions of higher education (IHEs) to interrogate and redesign traditional structures and ways of operating to find more productive means to work together in the service of preparing leaders capable of helping all children to learn, regardless of their background. Indeed, practitioners and scholars alike argue that these university-district partnerships will serve communities by getting powerful ideas from scholarship and practice into action faster and more effectively. It is no wonder that school districts and universities are increasingly forming partnerships where they can, together, learn how to prepare leaders of this sort (Miller, Devin, & Shoop, 2007; Orr, 2012; Young, Petersen, & Short, 2002).

In this vein, Dawes, Creswell, and Pardo (2009) note that the critical need to share ideas and responsibility across organizational boundaries in the public sector can put organizational context and social practice in relief for mutual interrogation. As in the proverbial two sides of a coin, this can pose interaction and coordination challenges, and also has the benefit of making visible subtle aspects of organizational boundaries related to ideology, professional norms, and institutional divisions. In our judgment, traversing these organizational boundaries, seen this way, are emblematic of culture, cultural negotiation, and cultural learning.

Animating Notions of Culture

A comprehensive rendering of culture—its definitions and characteristics—is beyond the scope of this chapter. We do, however, extract notions of culture from the myriad treatments of the subject that might further this inquiry. We draw from those that are helpful as we work toward a preliminary understanding of what enables postsecondary institutions, districts, and schools to form new working arrangements in the service of leadership preparation.

Culture Unfolds at Multiple Levels

The first notion that undergirds this discussion is that culture unfolds at multiple levels (Van Herk & Fischer, 2017); this notion seems a convenient shorthand because the issue of "place" is prominent in this and other characterizations of culture (e.g., Cole, 1998; Lave & Wegner, 1991). For our treatment, culture unfolds at the macro-level where it is constituted by arrangements like the nation state, as well as groupings with this nation state such as regions and ethnically and racially distinct sub-populations. Culture also exists at the meso-level (Fine, 2012), where it is comprised of groups of various sizes, which can include place-based groupings like school districts and universities. Cultures at this level are partially constituted by place and shaped by the macro-cultural contexts. Moreover, culture has coherent micro-expression in the actions of individual agents and small groups of individuals such as families (Cole & Packer, 2019). The stable presence of coherent cultural activity at the meso-level is particularly important to our discussion—meaning that we can anticipate coherent regularity in action that is discernible in the work of LEAs and IHEs. We may also ascribe such regularities to evolving cross-cultural organizational formations.

Culture Is Agentive

A second underlying aspect of culture, pertinent to our discussion, is that culture is accomplished through human action. For example, psychologists Cole and Packer (2019) describe culture "as a

Learning at the Boundaries

dynamically changing environment that is transformed by the artifacts created by prior generations, extending back to the beginning of the species. As we employ the term, an artifact is an aspect of the material world that has been modified over the history of its incorporation into goal-directed human thought and action (p. 245)." From a sociologist's perspective, Archer (1996) argues that culture is made and remade by people. These and other scholars draw attention to human *action* as the linchpin in the formation of culture. Our takeaway is that we have to attend to the separate doings in organizations of IHEs and LEAs, as well as their actions jointly, to understand their cross-organization formation as cultural.

Culture Is Malleable

The foregoing perspectives underscore a third important characteristic of culture relevant for discussion: culture is malleable. Once shaped, culture is not fixed. We can therefore ask about what, and how, over time, the activities of key actors in LEAs and IHEs are shaping and reshaping their shared cultural environment.

Culture Develops in Activity Systems

A fourth key idea is the notion of activity system. Engeström, Miettinen, and Punamäki (1999) define an activity system as a multi-voiced formation. An activity system has a complex mediational structure that captures the intellectual work of people in contextually bound ways. The mediational aspects of activity systems aid us in seeing how people, as they engage in work using material objects such as tools, move toward achieving a particular objective. This "multivoicedness" expressly aims to represent collective action; it shows, among other aspects of work, how activity is divided and coordinated among different actors. For this chapter, activity systems as a matter of representation help us see the work of LEAs and IHEs collectively in an intra-organizational sense. For example, the notion of an activity system helps us view the work of school leadership as distributed (Spillane, Halverson, & Diamond, 2001). In addition, seen through the lens of activity, we understand that the same work can be differently and similarly organized at different schools. Scholars who take this perspective (e.g., Harris 2012; Spillane, Camburn, & Stitziel Pareja, 2007) find that successful leadership, especially instructional leadership, involves collaborative performances that in the words of Spillane and colleagues (2001) "is stretched across" multiple school role groups.

Following Engeström (2001), activity systems, in their most recent formulations, are seen in network relations to other activity systems. In fact, most activity systems occur in multiples that are in a dialectic. This opens up the possibility of seeing work as mutually supportive within and across organizations via dialogue among activity systems. In this way, the activity system becomes a vantage point to see work both within, and across, IHEs and LEAs.

Culture as Learning and Knowing

Bearing in mind the dialectical nature of activity systems, we highlight one final way culture animates the perspectives on leadership we bring forward here. Activity in activity systems is the centerpiece of intra- and inter-organizational learning. Learning is accomplished in processes that unfold through mediated behavior, as they are executed in activity systems (Engeström, 2001). As mediated action unfolds, organizations learn. As actors participate in activity, they learn. Knowing is not a precondition to action; rather it is purposeful action in context that is the essence of learning and knowing.

Further, the interconnected nature of activity systems underscores inter-organizational learning, especially fueled when contradictory or discordant activity is placed in relief at the boundaries of activity systems. Consider, for example, an activity system aimed at the execution of empirical research where an LEA actor is also a student at the IHE. On the one hand, the research project, in the context of the IHE, is an element of a certification system aimed at making a judgment of competence. On the other hand, this research project from the LEA perspective may be a key element in moving forward on resolving a problem of practice. Perceived in this way, the project may serve somewhat contradictory purposes when these purposes intersect. However, it is at points like these that actors can come to see new, possibly merged forms of activity. Here, for instance, the IHE might modify an evaluation process so that its elements value productive steps toward a resolution of the LEA's problem of practice.

Taken together, these elements of culture allow us to study institutions working in partnership. Also, these foundational notions help us understand why scholarly adherents (whether in research or practice) to distributed organizational perspectives find that they cannot account for leadership behavior by only appealing to the content knowledge and intellectual resources owned by the principal. They have to appeal to tools (e.g., schedules) found in the environment, and also to the expert knowledge of others (e.g., counselors, youth providers). School leaders are prime examples of actors making, and remaking, organizational culture. Distributive perspectives embrace learning through action as the mechanism that allows communities of leaders to create organizations where people help and trust each other by relying on collaboration to achieve instructionally effective schools (Bryk & Schneider, 2002).

We use these notions of culture to characterize the leadership challenges that school districts and universities face as they learn to jointly prepare leaders and determine the appropriate sets of experiences and pedagogies for the modern challenges of schooling and education (Tozer, Zavitkovsky, Whalen, & Martinez, 2015). In what follows, we examine the increasing use of partnership as a central strategy in addressing enduring problems in education and to support innovation and change. We explore how these partnerships try to bring their activity systems and working arrangements into closer proximity. In particular, we examine research-practice partnerships (RPPs; Coburn, Penuel, & Geil, 2013), focusing on networked improvement communities (NICs; Bryk, Gomez, Grunow, & LeMahieu, 2015) as one type of organizational arrangement that structures activity for cross-organizational learning, and which vitalizes deeper and more systemic relationships between universities and school districts. We attend to how these arrangements lay the groundwork for mutually beneficial relationships between IHEs and LEAs that break down common siloed arrangements between them.

We draw attention to how learning occurs at the organizational boundaries within these partnerships. We examine an historic sampling of university-district partnerships to characterize the relationships and learning they aimed for, and what they were able to accomplish. We close the chapter by discussing the Carnegie Foundation's Improvement Leadership Education and Development (iLEAD) network to explore the dynamic in which an organization, that has characteristics of both an RPP and a NIC, might be well-positioned to spur cross-organizational and collaborative learning, and produce the types of program designs and organizational relationships that better equip leaders with the know-how to redress enduring inequities in educational opportunities and outcomes.

The Reemergence of Partnerships to Prepare School Leaders

Partnerships as a strategy have reemerged to address longstanding problems in education and as a key form of activity to support innovation and change. The formation, and use, of partnerships have come and gone, for nearly a century, in multiple rounds with limited success. Apart from transactional arrangements such as providing training venues for leaders and other professionals, as well as contexts for grant funded research to be executed, universities and K–12 systems persistently remain siloed from one another. Research-practice partnerships may step into this void to help create compacts that vitalize deeper and more systemic relationships between these two types of institutions.

Learning at the Boundaries

Characteristics of Research-Practice Partnerships

Research-practice partnerships are distinguished, by a number of characteristics (Coburn et al., 2013), from other ways that universities and schools have previously worked together. First, RPPs aim to be long-term; they are not oriented as episodic short-term engagements. Second, they are meant to address important and genuinely central problems that the organizations in the partnership face. These arrangements take significant effort to get off the ground and, as such, are only worth the effort when focused on critical problems of practice. Third, RPPs are mutually beneficial partnerships because the work of the partnership is animated by genuine concerns held by all partners involved. In mutualistic relationships, two or more parties come together, in a dependency, for the benefit of both. Fourth, from a design perspective, mutual benefit requires intentional strategies to engender close collaboration among the partners. It is through this close working association that partners learn how to accomplish tasks that they might not be able to accomplish in isolation. Accomplishment at this level requires participants to explore one another's identities constructed through work and work roles. Finally, research-practice partnerships are structured to produce original analyses aimed at advancing extant knowledge.

Networked improvement communities (NICs) are a growing type of research-practice partnership. For the past decade, the Carnegie Foundation for the Advancement of Teaching has been advancing a new relationship between practice and research through the use of improvement science principles, methods, and tools enacted through NICs (Bryk et al., 2015; Russell et al., 2017). With its roots in management theory (Deming, 1993), improvement science employs disciplined inquiry to solve a specific problem of practice (Langley et al., 2009). Improvement science bloomed in healthcare during the 1990s and has spread rapidly to other sectors including education (Lewis, 2015). NICs are distinguished by four characteristics:

1. focused on a well-specified common aim;
2. guided by a deep understanding of the problem, the system that produces it, and a shared theory of improvement (i.e., an understanding of what to do about the problem);
3. disciplined by the rigor of improvement science; and,
4. coordinated to accelerate the development, testing, and refinement of interventions along with their more rapid diffusion out into the field and effective integration into varied educational contexts.

The Carnegie Foundation has been and continues to test this approach through its own NICs and with a range of partners, such as Tennessee's Early Literacy Network (Bradford, Fillers, McLeroy, McManus, & Wells, 2019) and the Carnegie Math Pathways (Hoang, Huang, Sulcer, & Yesilyurt, 2017).

Mutualism: The Secret Sauce of Partnerships?

While forms of mutualism existed in previous university-district partnerships, perhaps the attribute of research-practice partnerships and networked improvement communities that make them most distinctive is that they are committed to mutualism (Coburn et al., 2013), in that aspects of their organizational mission are commonly shared and more likely to be reached if they join together in partnership. In the case of educational leadership, the task of effectively leading schools that face challenges like crushing poverty and high mobility, engendered by homelessness and foster care in the student population, is something that the parties can only do by working together. This work requires a new kind of social partnership between organizations—one that is mutualistic.

Both universities and school districts have a social learning challenge where their goal has to be to provide opportunities for aspiring leaders through organizational coordination. They both have to recognize that they serve as mutually dependent stakeholders in leader learning. Core to this accomplishment is developing shared sense-making mechanisms (Eddy-Spicer, 2019) such as new routines and participation structures that stretch across their organizations. Their aim is thus to create a kind of third space (Bhabha, 1990, 2004; Gutiérrez 2008; Martin, Snow, & Torrez, 2011; Zeichner, 2010) where new hybrid practices (Gutiérrez, Rymes, & Larson, 1995) emerge from the interweaving of elements of both school and university culture. In this in-between space, hybridity is both privileged and celebrated (Bhabha, 1990) and is where "translation" and "negotiation" occur as efforts are made to create a new learning environment. In leadership preparation, the university and school district are an informally merged organization where participants knit together an infrastructure that provides novel opportunities to learn to better enable new leaders to take on local and complex problems. This is the essential mutualism-based social learning problem of the formation of RPPs that we tackle in this chapter.

Providing leaders with new forms of learning opportunities in a mutualistic environment is a multi-level problem-solving endeavor. School districts and universities, for instance, need to recognize professional accreditation expectations that call for "the co-construction of mutually beneficial arrangements" to prepare leaders to confront local problems (Council for the Accreditation of Educator Preparation [CAEP], 2013). At this level, aspiring leaders ought to encounter problems that school districts deem important, and utilize pedagogies determined by university colleagues to be efficacious for those problems. This type of coordination extends beyond the classroom to seeing district and university governance in new ways.

Given these stretched arrangements, universities might need to see the allocation of faculty time and responsibility differently. For a professor to genuinely understand how expertise, honed over many years, can be applied to the local context is in itself a problem that requires time to solve and a financial structure at the university to account for the time expenditure. Similarly, school districts will need to re-think their infrastructure. For example, districts may challenge employees pursuing advanced degrees to tailor their training to focus explicitly on local organization problem imperatives or consider new mechanisms to assist aspiring leaders with the cost of preparation.

Cross-organizational partnerships that establish mutualism represent an extraordinary opportunity to make progress on longstanding and vexing problems by offering a way to surmount the troubling history that may have created an organizational gulf between universities and districts. These relations have been fraught with power imbalances and conflict born of a lack of mutual understanding (Cross, Ernst, & Pasmore, 2013). Recently, competition has made its way into the relationship with school districts and charter management organizations taking on some of the leadership preparation tasks that had been, virtually, the sole province of institutions of higher education until the 1980s. While effective collaboration grows from self-interest motives (Thomson & Perry, 2006), organizations in successful partnerships find ways to establish mutualism. According to Googins and Rochlin (2000), the path of working effectively together lies in learning how to: (1) define clear goals; (2) obtain senior level commitment; (3) engage in frequent communication; (4) assign professionals to lead the work; (5) share a commitment of resources; and (6) evaluate progress/results. This is the sort of learning that gets beyond simple transactional relationships to the mutualism we are seeking.

Boundaries as Spaces and Opportunities for Learning

Akkerman and Bakker (2011) define boundaries as "sociocultural differences leading to discontinuities in action and interaction" (p. 152). According to this framing, the people, the objects they use, and their patterns of communication exist at the nexus of two systems with distinct activity structures and routines. From the perspective of mutualism, the aim of learning at the boundary is to bring cohesion and continuity across the boundary. The ability to define clear goals is a boundary condition because, among other things, aspiring partners do not, at the start, have a common

Learning at the Boundaries

language to express what they want to happen in the partnership. In the case of leaders-as-learners, a boundary condition can be created by something as, ostensibly, straightforward as defining what successful learning looks like. In the university context, success may be largely tied to what happens in circumscribed classroom activities while in the school district success might be tied to the ability to exhibit skills that move district priorities forward.

We are in the habit of thinking about boundaries as barriers. From a mutualism perspective, LEA and IHE actors at the boundary have to reframe their perception of boundaries, and see them instead as opportunities to connect. In short, they have to learn how to create tools that serve as boundary objects and they have to develop mutualistic participation structures and routines that we call boundary practices that enable organizations to work together (Eddy-Spicer 2019; Eddy-Spicer & James, 2018; Thomson & Perry, 2006).

Four Learning Mechanisms at the Boundaries

In their review of the literature, Akkerman and Baker (2011) derive four learning mechanisms that allow these sorts of tools and practices to form in a partnership:

1. *Identification*, where the learning brings sharper demarcation to organizational boundaries;
2. *Coordination*, a type of learning that seeks procedures which provide the means for diverse organizational practices to cooperate (it is important to note that the emphasis here is on sustaining workflows across organizations and not necessarily broad cross-organizational consensus);
3. *Reflection*, a type of learning that allows actors in different organizations to recognize and perhaps name explicit differences in practices between organizations, thus allowing for consideration of local practices and those of the partner organizations; and
4. *Transformation*, where the form of learning, in the words of Akkerman and Bakker (2011), results in "…profound changes in practice, potentially even the creation of new, in-between practices" (p. 146).

These cross-organizational opportunities for learning often occur at the nexus of organizational functions, for example when organizations accomplish the same task with different organizational structures, or expertise, as in different pockets of technical skill to work on a problem (Yip, Ernst, & Campbell 2016).

Mutual benefit is learning to knit the organizations at these boundaries, wherein the knitting together of these partnerships is a multi-process learning accomplishment. Minimally, the partners will engage in each of the stages of learning outlined above. First, universities and school districts identify the boundary conditions that make them different. They then look for places to coordinate. Having done so, they engage in the deep, reflective work necessary to take on the perspective of their partner organization, and similarly, they must find ways to make it easy for their partner organization to do the same. Finally, they must confront a shared problem and build routines and social infrastructures to transform, at least with respect to that problem of practice, into what we call a stretched organization. What might this look like?

Take the ethos of caring as an example. IHEs and LEAs probably see one another as organizations that care deeply for the welfare of the children and youth in a community. In all likelihood, universities and districts have evolved functions in their respective spheres to discharge their caring ethos. The challenge is that these approaches to discharging their caring ethos are distinctive and produced by different, within-group, mindsets. These siloed mindsets make it difficult to see these demarcations in processes. When organizational partnerships find it difficult to see the demarcations in process, it is difficult to align work operations for coordination. We suggest that meaningful reflection on what might transform their organizations is a precondition for, in this case, executing care in collaborative and transformative ways to produce maximum results.

Recognizing the existing boundaries, cultivating recognition that boundary spanning is necessary, and building a cross-organizational mindset to realize a particular aim, are steps in a process. Achieving mutual benefit and the mechanisms to negotiate across complex partner organizations at the boundaries is no small task. In our judgment, in the past, when IHEs and LEAs have confronted these boundaries, they have treated them as barriers rather than as opportunities for knitting new, stretched organizations. Further, we conjecture that when partnerships have had to tackle problems that demanded transformational learning, yet relied on misaligned efforts, they were only able to achieve coordination rather than the transformation necessary to accomplish a stretched organization. Below we discuss some seminal moments in recent university-district partnerships and consider their accomplishments through the lens of levels of learning required relative to the problem they undertook, and the level they reached.

"Partnerization"

Bullough (2014) suggests that reform-minded educators and policy makers episodically promote university-school partnerships. He highlights efforts to foster school university partnerships and sees them as a recurring theme in efforts to transform schools. Bullough cites time and space, turnover and commitment, resource scarcity, and cultural difference as major barriers to realizing the kind of mutualism envisioned here. Each of these factors have been overlooked in the efforts to build viable and lasting university-district partnerships, despite being promoted over the course of the past hundred years to now influence the work described below. RPPs are just the latest example of the field's efforts at some form of "partnerization" that brings together divergent voices from schools and universities to address persistent problems in new ways. RPPs hold promise in large measure because we have the opportunity to learn from earlier change efforts; however, the matter of helping two complex organization forms, like school districts and universities, is a challenge that has been under-appreciated from a learning perspective.

Early Efforts at Boundary Spanning

Throughout the 20th century there were persistent efforts to feature the schooling of educators in different forms—with stark divides between initial training and continuing education. Schools and, then, school systems functioned side-by-side with colleges and universities. Many of today's urban universities often functioned as city normal schools, integral to and part of the local school system, with which they shared a common vision. Their realized forms of mutualism were in part achievable because they belonged to parts of a single system; yet belonging to a common system did not ensure that a boundary-free relationship existed. In all likelihood, the mere fact that normal schools and public schools had different responsibilities meant that different activity systems existed.

The inter-play between normal schools (later, state teachers' colleges), flagship universities, school systems, and laboratory schools in the early decades of 20th century America is largely undescribed. The Carnegie Foundation's report on the condition of teacher education in one state is relevant to this description because of the failures by political and education leaders to successfully bridge boundaries and to find common purposes (Learned et al., 1920). The Foundation's Bulletin 10 documents early efforts at bridging disparate elements of a state-wide school and university system and offers insight into the challenge of bringing together multiple stakeholders with varying socio-political priorities. Dewey's Laboratory School at the University of Chicago became a boundary object by being situated between a school system and a university (Benson et al., 2007). Boundary objects conceived in this way have persisted and, in terms of learning, suggest that these partnerships produced boundary facilitated coordination learning but often failed to lead to sustained transformation of either the school or university.

Thirty-five years later, the National Teacher Corps, a Great Society school reform effort premised on deep engagement between schools and universities, was formed to build "successful" school-university partnerships (Eckert, 2011; Rogers, 2009). While the Teacher Corps focused on preparing teachers for urban settings, efforts at cultural understanding and boundary spanning were integral to this engagement between schools and universities. Meeting the needs of teachers who could address changing school demographics and an accelerated school curriculum prompted a decade of efforts at transforming both schools and universities.

Professional Development Schools (PDSs)

Many of the reform efforts in the 1980s and 1990s were efforts to promote deep engagement of universities in schools. A particular form of such partnership was the Professional Development School (Dolly & Oda, 1997; Zimpher, 1990), placed at the junction between a school and university as a replacement for more insular laboratory schools and in response to the needs of local schools as sites for student teaching, professional development, and scholarly inquiry. The effort to establish PDSs was premised on sets of assumptions not dissimilar to those now articulated by leaders for RPPs.

Perhaps the most compelling of late-20th century efforts at building partnerships was John Goodlad's National Network for Educational Renewal (NNER)—which initially included ten university-school partnerships in ten states to serve as "proofing sites." Similar to the Holmes Group (1995), Goodlad (1994) emphasized that school-university partnerships in general, and partner schools in particular, were the essential vehicles for bringing about school transformation. Goodlad (2000) insisted that collaboration within a partnership structure was the means to promote both school renewal and the revitalization of educator preparation programs; he saw the concept of *simultaneous renewal* or "mutually beneficial learning" as the aim of such partnership efforts. We argue that Goodlad's and the parallel Holmes Group's transformative efforts were forms of reflective learning because they were centered on helping both schools and colleges see inside one another's operations and using these as insights to rejuvenate their respective activity systems.

Partnership Examples of Learning at the Boundaries
Identification

An example of the Akkerman and Bakker description of creative identification learning was the effort by a visionary dean of education who found ways to both fund and legitimize the concept of "hanging out" for his faculty. With local foundation funding, he supported faculty "being in schools" with no assigned purpose other than to familiarize themselves with the school culture and promote potential ways of partnering on a range of activities (Whitford & Gaus, 1988). The task was to better understand existing boundaries and to sharpen skills as boundary spanners or brokers between the university and the several schools in the district. As a result, faculty and school leaders were successful in building an enduring partnership based on social interactions and identified professional needs that persists nearly a half-century later.

Coordination

Coordination, or the efforts at better aligning the needs of universities with those of a school system, can be seen in early college and dual-enrolment schemes which require the integration of systems and processes into the fabric of both school system and university. An equally compelling example of efforts to promote such coordination is the relationship established by a university coordinator and district human resource representative for educator preparation programs. In many cases, this coordinator holds a joint appointment between school and university and negotiates intern placements, defines good mentoring, maintains a "pool" of exemplary teachers with whom to place interns, deals with calendar differences, and ensures that experiences conform to state requirements. They are able to express needs and expectations across the two systems and serve as a "communicative connector" or "translator" with the goal of regularizing processes.

Reflection

The existing CAEP (Council for the Accreditation of Educator Preparation) standards call for "providers" (IHEs) to ensure that effective partnerships between IHEs and LEAs are established and share responsibility for the "continuous improvement" of preparation programs. They are an example of efforts to promote reflective learning at the boundary between university and school district (CAEP, 2013). Professional accreditation standards for universities and schools seek common "cultures of evidence" with deep reflection regarding effective forms of preparation. CAEP's self-studies and team reports document the seriousness with which representatives of the intersecting worlds of schools and colleges reflect on current practices and seek transformative forms of educator preparation.

Transformation

We return to Goodlad's *A Place Called School* (1984) and his subsequent books on educator preparation and school leadership as an effort at transformative learning. Goodlad called for partner schools, new curricula, better alignment between schools and colleges, meaningful partnerships between schools and universities, and Centers of Pedagogy. He successfully formed dozens of enduring partnerships, articulated a set of postulates still used to guide this work, and prepared transformative school leaders. The Center concept positioned educator preparation at the juncture between school and university (Patterson, Michelli, & Pacheco, 1994), with the aspiration that such locations for educator preparation would serve local needs and promote mutuality (Goodlad, 1990). Successful in his efforts, he inspired two generations of adherents to pursue ways to provide greater access to knowledge, engage in educational renewal, and transform schools and colleges. Similarly, Boyer in his *Scholarship Reconsidered: Priorities of the Professoriate* (1990) called for revamping promotion and tenure practices to place more emphasis on practitioner focused scholarship and engagement with schools. His was a call for the re-culturing of the university but as with Goodlad's efforts at transformation, the Boyer initiative was widely embraced by reform-minded education school faculty but produced little change in university policies and practices. Why such calls for transformation and change go unheeded is the stuff of organizational differences, cultural discontinuities, and boundary demarcations unsuccessfully bridged.

Negotiating the Cultural Divides between LEAs and IHEs

The literature on partnerships raises questions regarding whether partnerships can be more than "acts of cooperation"—represented by parallelism or "parallel play"—or genuine "acts of collaboration" or realizations of "interdependence" and "mutualism" (O'Hair & Odell, 1994) working within and across cultures. Many of the reports of successful partnerships highlight particular pathways pursued with particular milestones (Jones et al., 2016), while others offer theories of action or ways of achieving given purposes for the partnership (Schön & McDonald, 1998).

There are a host of advocacy pieces that describe the "fundamental characteristics of successful university-school partnerships" (Thorkildsen & Stein, 1996), which repeat expectations for participant commitment, mutual trust and respect, external support, shared decision-making, a clear focus,

Learning at the Boundaries

information sharing, a manageable agenda, strong leadership, clearly defined objectives and goals, specific deliverables, and a willingness to adapt and change. Overall "partnerization" continues more or less unabated and efforts at building new partnerships are ongoing.

Still, confronting the cultural gulf that exists between school and university remains a perplexing problem that is often overlooked. Recognition of the cultural differences between schools, universities, and professional schools, is longstanding. Knight and colleagues (1992) observed three decades ago that "university culture values reflection, analysis, and scientific research; the professional school culture values application of knowledge to practical situations to prepare future teachers, administrators and researchers; [while] the school culture values action and experience based knowledge that can immediately be applied to local teaching and learning" (p. 271).

Knight et al. speculated that such cultural differences could serve as a barrier and an opportunity to enhance collaboration and partnership as university faculty seek to promote inquiry into practice on the part of schools and schools draw university faculty into the nature and immediacy of practical problems. The "siloed-activities" of universities and their separation from schools caused by different funding streams and governance structures continue to serve as obstacles to the easy transition of students through the different levels of schooling (Davis & Hoffman, 2008). States have sought to overcome the divides with recognition that K–12 schooling embraces universality, a common mission, and uniform standards while higher education champions selectivity, mission diversity, and focused program standards (Walsh, 2007). More recently, states have championed a K–16 or P–20 movement to eliminate barriers and promote alignment across the span of a student's formal education (Loss & McGuinn, 2016). Whether the convergence of schools and colleges will proceed and the possible influence this will have on the attainment of mutualism remains to be seen.

Partnerships Opening Up a Third Space

Earlier we noted that the coming together often begins in a "third space" (Bhabha, 1990; Gutiérrez, 2008; Zeichner, 2010), located between university and school. It is in this space where partnerships are formed—sometimes building on existing transactional relationships—with participants from both school and university meeting as peers to consider new ways of addressing old problems. It is in the intersection between schools and universities where there is a willingness to engage in collaborative ways, to recognize the "sociocultural differences" that often divide, and a determination to identify and overcome the boundaries that often separate (Akkerman & Bakker, 2011). Participants are encouraged to negotiate meaning and to achieve "hybridity" in both the analysis of, and the proposed solution to, big vexing problems. There can be recognition of the discontinuities that often exist between the two activity systems and, hopefully, a willingness to concede that this is "unfamiliar territory," where hubris is replaced with humility (Martin, Snow, & Torrez, 2011).

There is also a determination that in the act of coming together, there is meaningful dialogue regarding ways the "other" learns and the system functions. Successful partnerships seem to privilege "listening" rather than "pontificating," and promote understanding rather than obliviousness. It is our assumption that just as in learning a new language, one becomes more aware of the structures in the primary or first language, so it is the case that in the act of learning about the "other," participants better understand their own system as well as effective ways of approaching and comprehending the other system. As participants pursue these efforts, there is also the anticipation that the acknowledgment of the differences between schools and universities becomes a vital force for learning and development.

Several years ago, Corderio's (1996) *Boundary Crossing: Educational Partnerships and School Leadership* called for new forms of school leadership that resonate today with those attempting to build enduring school-university partnerships. She highlighted the need for "boundary crossers," "boundary workers," "bridge builders," and "brokers" who could navigate effectively between the two activity systems—schools and universities—and who possessed "the ability to manage and integrate divergent discourses and practices across social boundaries." She championed forms of school leader development that embraced boundary spanning and she advocated for boundary spanning leadership in schools and universities.

Attending to Context in Educational Leadership Preparation

Reforms in educator preparation programs have sought to better train leaders to attend to context-specific conditions and dynamics. One entailment has been to bring greater instructional focus, so that future leaders can better guide the technical core of instruction in schools (Browne-Ferrigno & Knoeppel, 2005). Universities prominently feature courses that acquaint leaders with the latest advances in instruction, from digital learning and reliance on high leverage practices to instructional coaching and the use of professional learning communities to promote collaborative teaching (Davin & Troyan, 2015; DuFour & Eaker, 2009; DuFour, DuFour, Eaker, & Many, 2006). Along with these strategies, preparation programs are advancing new ways to support professional learning through clinical practice, including its connection to restorative justice, cultures of care, and social justice (Brown, 2004; McKenzie et al., 2008).

Although these and other advances help move education leadership away from a sterile managerial focus, too often programs remain disconnected from the communities they serve and the problems that confront them. Most programs operate with the notion that their institution's graduate students (i.e., those preparing to be leaders) are their central "customers," rather than the K–12 students and the communities in which many of these leaders will end up working. In essence, this can be characterized as the challenge of "place," where what leaders need to learn and understand is divorced from the needs of the contexts in which they will serve. Since graduate students are treated as the primary customer, programs are loosely coupled to the dilemmas that are faced by nearby schools and districts. As a result, programs often do not situate the continuous improvement of local school systems as the practical and intellectual focus of their programmatic work. This, in turn, can be characterized as the challenge of "problem"; that is, aligning the problem focus of IHE leadership programs with those that are of chief concern to local LEAs.

University-District Partnerships Attending to Problem and Place

Establishing working relations between IHEs and the community districts and schools they serve is a central approach in ensuring that educational leaders are attending to issues of "problem" and "place" (Miller et al., 2007; Young et al., 2002). As noted above, for the past century, university-district partnerships have been a catalyst for program innovation (Young et al., 2002), and philanthropic organizations including the Wallace Foundation have supported efforts to more actively involve districts in the redesign of leadership preparation (Orr, 2012). Supporters of these partnerships contend that intentional and well-designed collaborations between IHEs and LEAs help link theory to practice by involving leaders in the authentic work of improving students' performance in school (Perez et al., 2011; Pounder, 2011; Young et al., 2002). Evidence suggests that leaders prepared in this way are able to cultivate an "ecology of expertise," which brings together the knowledge of communities, teachers, administrators, and universities (Zeichner & Payne, 2013).

The Improvement Leadership Education and Development (iLEAD) Network

Driven by the theory that well-designed, locale focused, partnerships between IHEs and LEAs are critical in preparing leaders with the competencies to lead continuous improvement efforts in schools and school systems, the Carnegie Foundation launched the iLEAD network in September

Learning at the Boundaries

2017. With support from the Carnegie Corporation of New York, iLEAD seeks to bolster the efforts of university-district partnerships committed to localizing leadership preparation through the use of improvement science principles, methods, and tools.

iLEAD supplants notions that leadership preparation can have a generic one-size-fits-all model. Instead, the network contends that effective leaders are those who understand the nuances of particular problems and the settings in which they occur. Fundamental to iLEAD's formation is the belief that leaders, teachers, and other stakeholders need to find ways to embed sustained improvement in the core fabric of their practice, where they live an improvement discipline as they enact their work each and every day. Drawing on the insights of Deming (1993), this means those directly engaged in the work of helping young people learn and thrive in school are central to the improvement of that practice. The discipline of improvement science and working in improvement partnerships (Bryk et al., 2015) must play central roles in the conceptual and methodological preparation of aspiring leaders.

Such an improvement ethic demands new working relations between IHEs, where this preparation has traditionally occurred, and the school districts where individuals serve and learn to practice the art and science of continuous improvement. Working together means that faculty in schools of education partner with local districts in practical problem solving. By doing so, both institutions build directly applicable scholarship with an aim to accumulate practice-based evidence to solve complex dilemmas and advance learning in the field so as to accomplish more at greater scale. Further, jointly confronting these shared high-leverage problems allows partnerships to foster an in-between or "boundary practice," forcing the intersecting worlds of IHEs and LEAs to "seriously reconsider their current practices and the interrelations" (Akkerman & Baker, 2011, p. 146) in making sure that aspiring leaders have the wherewithal to lead continuous improvement in the service of equitable outcomes for all children.

iLEAD: A Means for Re-Culturing

At present, iLEAD is comprised of 13 partnerships—from universities and schools across the United States—that seek to learn from and with one another as they create programs and opportunities that are collaborative in design, organized by improvement science as a shared methodology, and sustained through a joint commitment to address high-leverage dilemmas in the community. Through a competitive application process, these partnerships were identified as having: a strong commitment to improvement science as a central approach in tackling local educational challenges; support from leadership and peers within their respective institutions; and a willingness to build and sustain a collaborative community where learnings, materials, and resources are actively shared. Through networked and collaborative activities, the past two years have demonstrated the commitment of these partnerships in strengthening the capabilities of institutions as well as aspiring educational leaders to make progress on a broad base set of challenges aimed at achieving more equitable systems, and in building a practice-centric scholarship around this work that can guide and inform the field.

At the time of this writing, iLEAD partnerships have strengthened IHE-LEA relations, enhanced leadership commitment to this work, and produced preliminary knowledge, tools, and resources that support improvement-based partnerships. The network structure of iLEAD, with its shared focus on improving leadership preparation and working together on common problems, has afforded collaborative opportunities for districts and universities alike. What's more, these activities have allowed members to closely examine and re-culture the ways they pursue their routines, norms, and practices in partnership with others. For example, partnerships have deepened their individual and collective relationships through twice-yearly, in-person network convenings hosted at rotating sites—with each convening requiring significant pre-meeting preparation (e.g., documenting and assessing current progress) and post-meeting "action period" work (e.g., testing ideas of change to influence key system drivers). Activities during these convenings afford cross-site learning, joint planning, increased learning about local improvement efforts through site visits, and collaborative problem solving on important dilemmas such as building will among institutional leaders, securing and sustaining funding, and developing curricula and other professional learning opportunities.

Additionally, partnerships have generated a range of artifacts that document the development and evolution of their vision, strategy, and progress within the IHE, LEA, as well as in their partnership. These artifacts include future-state "storyboards" that conceptualize measures of success; public narratives that convey the values and priorities of partnerships (Greene & Tichenor, 1994); and presentation materials shared with network members during convenings to draw attention to both progress and challenges. Consistent with iLEAD's aspirations to transform the field, university and school partners have also co-developed multiple improvement resources, including presentations and papers for professional audiences. Together, these convenings and activities strengthen the foundation for relationship building within and across each partnership. In all, the network structure affords many opportunities for "hybridization" and "crystallization" where new cultural forms can emerge and be made formal through shared routines and practices (Akkerman & Bakker, 2011).

In addition to iLEAD's regular convenings, senior fellows from the Carnegie Foundation check in regularly with their assigned partnership sites. In this capacity, fellows serve as thought partners, improvement coaches, and connect the partnerships with supports that bolster their local improvement efforts. For instance, to build their capabilities in the practice of continuous improvement, participants from both the IHEs and LEAs have enrolled in the Carnegie Foundation's mediated online course. Network members are also downloading and utilizing curriculum materials from Carnegie's Teaching Commons—an online repository of instructional resources (e.g., lesson plans, PowerPoint slides) that advance quality and rigor in the teaching of networked improvement science. Additionally, partnerships have leveraged senior fellows, as well as other Carnegie executives, to build legitimacy with leaders in their respective contexts including with state policymakers, deans, school boards, and superintendents. In fact, a Deans and District Leaders Council, comprised of iLEAD members, has been formed to further advocate for this work with other stakeholders operating in higher education and K–12 systems.

With strong interest and engagement from network members, an iLEAD Steering Committee was formed to directly engage one IHE and one LEA representative at each of the dozen partnerships in the ongoing process of co-design and to advance the evolving vision and mission of iLEAD. The Committee helps distribute the governance of iLEAD such that, much like a Networked Improvement Community, it is a community owned by and for its members. Among other responsibilities, the Committee: serves as a key liaison representing the needs and interests of the broader iLEAD community; advises and engages in the planning and facilitation of network convenings; represents the interests and insights of their partnership as well as evangelizes the work to external stakeholders; provides leadership to new activities that might emerge aiming to expand the learning opportunities for the iLEAD community; and offers guidance and expertise for building a broader funding base for iLEAD.

iLEAD's Developmental Progressions

Perhaps the most important accomplishment to date that defines iLEAD is the Developmental Progressions, a framework that aims to create a common language to anchor and define the work in which partnerships engage. Network members collaborated and co-constructed these Progressions during a series of facilitated group discussions at the second network convening in January 2018. Together, members identified 24 critical areas of work, at the IHE, LEA, and partnership levels, that must be addressed to build productive partnerships. These areas include institutional leadership commitment, professional development of staff, and strengthening partnership relations. Rather

Learning at the Boundaries

than a precise plan to be implemented across sites with fidelity, the Progressions offer a common way to organize the work of the partnerships and the learning mechanisms that happen at the boundaries. Table 21.1 provides an overview of a subset of these Progressions.

With the number of institutions involved in the network, the work of iLEAD is very much a study in diversity and variation. While some iLEAD members are well along in the co-creation of new leadership programs that more meaningfully incorporate the ideas and aspirations of both the LEA and IHE (i.e., they are "institutionalizing and sustaining the work" as defined by the Progressions), others are at the early stages of their work together, where they may be engaged in exploratory meetings to ascertain one another's aspirations and priorities (i.e., they are "exploring change ideas"). Network members understand that they will excel in some areas of the Progressions, and in others they will fall short. In this way, the framework offers partnerships a means to periodically self-assess where they are in their work, and the extent to which they are making progress in critical areas.

The Progressions are a work-in-progress and are designed to be refined periodically to ensure that they capture and effectively guide the efforts of members. Although the Progressions are consistently used in network-wide activities, partnerships differ in how they use the framework to guide their work. While some use the Progressions to take stock of their progress at certain points in time, others more actively use them to guide their planning, activities, and strategies. Nonetheless, the Progressions represent a mechanism to help transform how LEAs and IHEs collaboratively conceive, structure, and support leadership development in place-based, problem-focused, and student-centered ways. The framework brings into focus the kinds of competencies at the institutional, partnership, and individual levels that help ensure that leaders have the knowledge, skills, and dispositions to orchestrate improvement work to redress systemic inequities in educational outcomes and opportunities.

Why Partnership Now? What's Different?

Why the recommitment of time and resources to university-district partnership building? What is different from past times when partnerships offered much possibility but were only modestly successful in their accomplishments? If we are to pursue meaningful and mutually beneficial partnerships now, how do we avoid the shortcomings of the past? How do we make partnerships more than a recurring theme in the century-old, ongoing efforts to improve schooling?

Our contention is that a number of things have happened or are happening that hold great promise for the future. The promise of improvement science and the possibilities of networked improvement communities to address longstanding vexing problems are new (Bryk et al., 2015; Conklin, 2006; Head, 2008). We also think that the explicit attention to mutualism by RPPs is a genuine advance in the field's approach.

We believe that the iLEAD network is a significant attempt to foster "mutualism" between schools and higher education and that it holds much promise for guiding the efforts of others as they pursue ways to champion university-district partnerships. The Developmental Progressions Framework makes growth toward mutualism explicit. Heretofore we have not had such a co-constructed framework to guide partnerships in their improvement efforts.

Also new is the press for P-20 alignment and the blurring of boundaries between schools and colleges (Loss & McGuinn, 2016). We are also seeing accreditation standards for professional schools of education that promote continuous improvement and greater collaboration between universities and schools (CAEP, 2013) as well as standards to guide the design of principal preparation programs (National Policy Board for Educational Administration, 2018) that make continuous improvement and effective partnerships central to the conduct of all programs. For many institutions, accreditation is a powerful lever. We suspect these next generation perspectives on accreditation will create new social protocols that will require activity systems in both IHEs and LEAs to evolve.

Table 21.1 Examples of Developmental Progressions at the Partnership, LEA, and IHE Levels

Level	Specific Dimension or Area of Work	Progress Status			
		"Exploring Change Ideas"	*"Small Change Implementation"*	*"Integrating Improvement Science (IS)/NICs Into the Core Work"*	*"Institutionalizing and Sustaining the Work"*
Partnership	Partnership relationships	Initial explorations and commitments make it possible to apply to become a member of the iLEAD community. A landscape analysis is initiated of past and existing partnership efforts between LEA–IHE as a basis for learning how to work productively together going forward.	Regular meetings and possible other activities are occurring and provide a basis for exploring working relationships. Success and shortcomings from past partnership efforts have been identified and now inform emerging new partnership commitments.	*Active joint work is occurring between IHE and LEA staff, and positive attitudes characterize the work.*	*A strong bond of trust and respect has formed and provides the basis for even difficult conversations to happen.*
Local Education Agencies (LEA)	Professional Development of District Staff	Select district participants are learning about IS principles, tools, and methods, as well as the work of NICs.	A district iLEAD group is deepening their learning about IS/NICs. Professional development offerings are appearing to introduce knowledge about IS/NICs to LEA staff.	*IS/NICs training for teachers and leaders has become a regular part of the professional development offerings of the district.*	*IS/NICs training is also integrated into the onboarding process of new hires, including teachers and leaders.*
Institution of Higher Education (IHE)	Institutional Leadership Commitment	Faculty members, program chair, and Dean are engaged with the iLEAD Program by applying in partnership with a local LEA.	Dean/Program Chair is aware of the initiative and is providing seed resources to get the initiative off the ground (e.g., professional development for faculty; release time for course and program development; travel support to iLEAD community meetings).	*Dean/Dean's Cabinet expresses support for this with faculty across the school and with senior university leaders.*	*Dean/Dean's Cabinet continues to actively express support. University communications recognizes this as a distinctive and "innovative" contribution.*

Learning at the Boundaries

Finally, also "new" is a return to and expansion of clinical practice for all educator preparation programs—with yearlong, school-situated residencies—that demand greater collaboration, coordination, and partnership between universities and schools to create and sustain (American Association of Colleges for Teacher Education, 2018). Requirements like long-term situated residences make it almost impossible for the resident not to confront local activity systems in a deep way. Similarly, the emphasis in the *Every Student Succeeds Act* on continuous improvement cycles, deeper learning, and school classification demands university engagement (Jimenez & Sargrad, 2017; O'Day & Smith, 2019—particularly the engagement of research faculty in RPPs (Penuel & Farrell, 2017). It is always the case that the policy's spirit has to make it to practice. We posit that if local actors and policy advocates take up continuous improvement and partnership even with a mild degree of serious action, it will engage learning at the boundaries of the organizations involved. Serious engagement at the boundary will spur people of multiple stripes in LEAs and IHEs to "do" differently and to remake what it means to act in concert—in sum, they will learn how to remake organizational cultures.

References

Akkerman, S. F., & Bakker, A. (2011). Learning at the boundary: An introduction. *International Journal of Educational Research, 50*(1), 1–5.

American Association of Colleges for Teacher Education [AACTE]. (2018). *A Pivot Toward Clinical Practice, Its Lexicon, and the Renewal of Educator Preparation: A Report of the AACTE Clinical Practice Commission.* Retrieved from www.aacte.org.

Ananiadou, K., & Claro, M. (2009). 21st century skills and competences for New Millennium learners in OECD countries. *OECD Education Working Paper, No. 41.* Paris: OECD Publishing.

Archer, M. S. (1996). *Culture and Agency: The Place of Culture in Social Theory.* Cambridge, UK: Cambridge University Press.

Benson, L., Harkavy, I. R., & Puckett, J. L. (2007). *Dewey's Dream: Universities and Democracies in an Age of Education Reform: Civil Society, Public Schools, and Democratic Citizenship.* Philadephia, PA: Temple University Press.

Bhabha, H. K. (1990). The third space: Interview with Homi Bhabha. In J. Rutherford (Ed.), *Identity, Community, Culture and Difference* (pp. 207–221). London, UK: Laurence & Wishart.

Bhabha, H. (2004). *The Location of Culture.* London and New York, NY: Routledge.

Boyer, E. L. (1990). *Scholarship Reconsidered: Priorities of the Professoriate.* Lawrenceville, NJ: Princeton University Press.

Bradford, S., Fillers, B., McLeroy, M., McManus, R., & Wells, M. K. (2019). The story of the Tennessee Early Literacy Network. Retrieved from www.tn.gov

Brown, K. M. (2004). Leadership for social justice and equity: Weaving a transformative framework and pedagogy. *Educational Administration Quarterly, 40*(1), 77–108.

Browne-Ferrigno, T., & Knoeppel, R. C. (2005). Training principals to ensure access to equitable learning opportunities in a high-need rural school district. *Educational Considerations, 33*(1), 8–14.

Bryk, A. S., Gomez, L. M., Grunow, A., & LeMahieu, P. G. (2015). *Learning to Improve: How America's Schools Can Get Better at Getting Better.* Cambridge, MA: Harvard Education Press.

Bryk, A., & Schneider, B. (2002). *Trust in Schools: A Core Resource for Improvement.* New York, NY: Russell Sage Foundation.

Bullough Jr, R. V. (2014). Toward reconstructing the narrative of teacher education: A rhetorical analysis of preparing teachers. *Journal of Teacher Education, 65*(3), 185–194.

Coburn, C. E., Penuel, W. R., & Geil, K. E. (2013). *Research-Practice Partnerships: A Strategy for Leveraging Research for Educational Improvement in School Districts.* New York, NY: William T. Grant Foundation.

Cole, M. (1998). *Cultural Psychology: A Once and Future Discipline.* Cambridge, MA: Harvard University Press.

Cole, M., & Packer, M. (2019). Culture and cognition. In K. D. Keith (Ed.), *Cross-Cultural Psychology: Contemporary Themes and Perspectives,* 2nd edition (pp. 243–270). Chichester, UK: Wiley Blackwell.

Conklin, J. (2006). *Wicked Problems & Social Complexity.* San Francisco, CA: CogNexus Institute.

Corderio, P. (1996). *Boundary Crossing: Educational Partnerships and School Leadership: New Directions for School Leadership.* New York, NY: John Wiley & Sons.

Council for the Accreditation of Educator Preparation [CAEP]. (2013). The CAEP standards. Retrieved from www.CAEP.org.

Cross, R., Ernst, C., & Pasmore, B. (2013). A bridge too far? How boundary spanning networks drive organizational change and effectiveness. *Organizational Dynamics, 42*(2), 81–91.

Cruickshank, V. (2017). The influence of school leadership on student outcomes. *Open Journal of Social Sciences, 5*(9), 115–123.

Darling-Hammond, L., LaPointe, M., Meyerson, D., Orr, M.T., & Cohen, C. (2007). *Preparing School Leaders for a Changing World: Lessons from Exemplary Leadership Development Programs.* Stanford, CA: Stanford University, Stanford Educational Leadership Institute.

Davin, K. J., & Troyan, F. J. (2015). The implementation of high-leverage teaching practices: From the university classroom to the field site. *Foreign Language Annals, 48*(1), 124–142.

Davis, R. P., & Hoffman, J. L. (2008). Higher education and the P-16 movement: What is to be done? *Thought and Action, 24,* 123–134.

Dawes, S. S., Cresswell, A. M., & Pardo, T. A. (2009). From "need to know" to "need to share": Tangled problems, information boundaries, and the building of public sector knowledge networks. *Public Administration Review, 69*(3), 392–402.

Dede, C. (2010). Comparing frameworks for 21st century skills: 21st century skills. *Rethinking How Students Learn, 20,* 51–76.

Deming, W. E. (1993). *The New Economics.* Cambridge, MA: Massachusetts Institute of Technology. Center for Advanced Engineering Study.

Dolly, J. P., & Oda, E. A. (1997). Toward a definition of professional development schools. *Peabody Journal of Education, 72*(1), 178–186.

DuFour, R., DuFour, R., Eaker, R., & Many, T. (2006). *Learning by Doing: A Handbook for Professional Learning Communities at Work.* Bloomington, IN: Solution Tree.

DuFour, R., & Eaker, R. (2009). *Professional Learning Communities at Work: Best Practices for Enhancing Student's Achievement.* Bloomington, IN: Solution Tree Press.

Eckert, S. A. (2011). The national teacher corps: A study of shifting goals and changing assumptions. *Urban Education, 46*(5), 932–952.

Eddy-Spicer, D. H. (2019). Where the action is: Enactment as the first movement of sensemaking. In B. L. Johnson, & S. Kruse (Eds.), *Educational Leadership, Organizational Learning, and the Ideas of Karl Weick: Perspectives on Theory and Practice* (pp. 94–118). New York, NY, London: Routledge.

Eddy-Spicer, D. H., & James, C. (2018). Boundary perspectives on schools as organizations. In M. Connolly, D. H. Eddy-Spicer, C. James, & S. D. Kruse (Eds.), *The SAGE Handbook of School Organization* (p. 228). London, UK: SAGE Publications.

Edwards, G., Tsui, A. B. M., & Stimpson, P. (2009). School-university partnership and theories of learning. In G. Edwards, A. Tsui, & F. Lopez-Real (Eds.), *Learning in School-University Partnership: Sociocultural Perspectives* (pp. 3–24). New York, NY: Routledge.

Engeström, Y. (2001). Expansive learning at work: Toward an activity theoretical reconceptualization. *Journal of Education and Work, 14*(1), 133–156.

Engeström, Y., Miettinen, R., & Punamäki, R. L. (Eds.) (1999). *Perspectives on Activity Theory.* Cambridge, UK: Cambridge University Press.

Fine, G. A. (2012). *Tiny Publics: A Theory of Group Action and Culture.* New York, NY: Russell Sage.

Goodlad, J. I. (1990). *Places Where Teachers Are Taught.* San Francisco, CA: Jossey-Bass, Inc.

Goodlad, J. I. (1994). The national network for educational renewal. *The Phi Delta Kappan, 75*(8), 632–638.

Goodlad, J. I. (2000). Education and democracy: Advancing the agenda. *Phi Delta Kappan, 82*(1), 86–89.

Googins, B. K., & Rochlin, S. A. (2000). Creating the partnership society: Understanding the rhetoric and reality of cross-sectoral partnerships. *Business and Society Review, 105*(1), 127–144.

Greene, P., & Tichenor, M. (1999). Partnership on a collaborative continuum. *Contemporary Education, 70*(4), 13–19.

Gutiérrez, K. D. (2008). Developing a sociocritical literacy in the third space. *Reading Research Quarterly, 43*(2), 148–164.

Gutierrez, K., Rymes, B., & Larson, J. (1995). Script, counterscript, and underlife in the classroom: James Brown versus Brown v. Board of Education. *Harvard Educational Review, 65*(3), 445–472.

Harris, A. (2012). Distributed leadership: Implications for the role of the principal. *Journal of Management Development, 31,* 7–17.

Head, B. W. (2008). Wicked problems in public policy. *Public Policy, 3*(2), 101.

Hess, F. M., & Kelly, A. M. (2005). *Learning to Lead? What Gets Taught in Principal Preparation Programs.* Washington, DC: American Enterprise Institute for Public Policy Research.

Hoang, H., Huang, M., Sulcer, B., & Yesilyurt, S. (2017). *Carnegie Math Pathways 2015–2016 Impact Report: A Five-Year Review. Carnegie Math Pathways Technical Report.* Stanford, CA: Carnegie Foundation for the Advancement of Teaching.

Holmes Group. (1995). *Tomorrow's Schools of Education: A Report of the Holmes Group.* East Lansing, MI: Author.

Jimenez, L., & Sargrad, S. (2017). *ESSA: A New Vision for School Accountability*. Washington, DC: Center for American Progress.

Knight, S. L., Wiseman, D., & Smith, C. W. (1992). The reflectivity-activity dilemma in school-university partnerships. *Journal of Teacher Education, 43*(4), 269–277.

Langley, G. J., Moen, R. D., Nolan, K. M., Nolan, T. W., Norman, C. L., & Provost, L. P. (2009). *The Improvement Guide: A Practical Approach to Enhancing Organizational Performance*. Hoboken, NJ: John Wiley & Sons.

Lave, J., & Wenger, E. (1991). *Situated Learning: Legitimate Peripheral Participation*. Cambridge, UK: Cambridge University Press.

Learned, W. S., Bagley, W. C., McMurry, C. A., Strayer, G. D., Dearborn, W. F., Kandel, I. L., & Josselyn, H. W. (1920). *The Professional Preparation of Teachers for American Public Schools: A Study Based Upon an Examination of Tax-Supported Normal Schools in the State of Missouri (No. 14)*. New York, NY: Carnegie Foundation for the Advancement of Teaching.

Leithwood, K., Louis, K. S., Anderson, G., & Wahlstrom, K. (2004). *How Leadership Influences Student Learning: A Review of Research for the Learning from Leadership Project*. New York, NY: The Wallace Foundation.

Levine, A. (2006). *Educating School Teachers*. New York, NY: The Education Schools Project.

Lewis, C. (2015). What is improvement science? Do we need it in education? *Educational Researcher, 44*(1), 54–61.

Loss, C. P., & McGuinn, P. J. (2016). *The Convergence of K-12 and Higher Education: Policies and Programs in a Changing Era*. Cambridge, MA: Harvard Education Press.

Martin, S., Snow, J., & Torrez, C. (2011). Navigating the terrain of the third space: Tensions with/in relationships in school-university partnerships. *Journal of Teacher Education, 62*(3), 299–311.

Martinez, M., & McGrath, D. (2014). *Deeper Learning: How Eight Innovation Public Schools are Transforming Education in the Twenty-First Century*. New York, NY: The New Press.

McDonald, J. P., Domingo, M., Jeffrey, J. V., Pietanza, R. R., & Pignatosi, F. (2013). In and of the city: Theory of action and the NYU partnership school program. *Peabody Journal of Education, 88*(5), 578–593.

McKenzie, K. B., Christman, D. E., Hernandez, F., Fierro, E., Capper, C. A., Dantley, M., & Scheurich, J. J. (2008). From the field: A proposal for educating leaders for social justice. *Educational Administration Quarterly, 44*(1), 111–138.

Miller, T. N., Devin, M., & Shoop, R. J. (2007). *Closing the Leadership Gap: How District and University Partnerships Shape Effective School Leaders*. Thousand Oaks, CA: Corwin Press.

Murphy, J. (2002). Reculturing the profession of educational leadership: New blueprints. *Educational Administration Quarterly, 38*(2), 176–191.

National Policy Board for Educational Administration [NPBEA]. (2018). Educational leadership preparation program recognition standards. Retrieved from www.npbea.org.

O'Day, J., & Smith, M. S. (2019). *Opportunity for All: A Framework for Quality and Education*. Cambridge, MA: Harvard Educational Press.

O'Hair, M. J., & Odell, S. J. (1994). *Partnerships in Education (No. 2)*. Belmont, CA: Wadsworth Publishing Company.

Orr, M. T. (2012). When districts drive leadership preparation partnerships: Lessons form six urban district initiatives. *AASA Journal of Scholarship and Practice, 9*(3), 3–17.

Patterson, R. S., Michelli, N. M., & Pacheco, A. (1994). *Centers of Pedagogy: New Structures for Educational Renewal*. San Francisco, CA: Jossey-Bass.

Penuel, W., & Farrell, C., (2017). *ESSA: An Opportunity for RPPs to Support Districts and States*. Boulder, CO: National Education Policy Center.

Perez, L. G., Uline, C. L., Johnson Jr, J. F., James-Ward, C., & Basom, M. R. (2011). Foregrounding fieldwork in leadership preparation: The transformative capacity of authentic inquiry. *Educational Administration Quarterly, 47*(1), 217–257.

Pounder, D. G. (2011). Leader preparation special issue: Implications for policy, practice, and research. *Educational Administration Quarterly, 47*(1), 258–267.

Rogers, B. (2009). "Better" people, better teaching: The vision of the national teacher corps, 1965–1968. *History of Education Quarterly, 49*(3), 347–372.

Russell, J. L., Bryk, A. S., Dolle, J., Gomez, L. M., LeMahieu, P., & Grunow, A. (2017). A framework for the initiation of networked improvement communities. *Teachers College Record, 119*(7), 1–36.

Schön, D. A., & McDonald, J. P. (1998). *Doing What You Mean to do in School Reform*. Providence, RI: Annenberg Institute.

Smedley, L. (2010). Impediments to partnership: A literature review of school-university links: Teachers and teaching: *Theory and Practice, 7*(2), 189–209.

Spillane, J. P., Camburn, E. M., & Stitziel Pareja, A. (2007). Taking a distributed perspective to the school principal's workday. *Leadership and Policy in Schools, 6*(1), 103–125.

Spillane, J. P., Halverson, R., & Diamond, J. B. (2001). Investigating school leadership practice: A distributed perspective. *Educational Researcher, 30*(3), 23–28.

Thomson, A. M., & Perry, J. L. (2006). Collaboration processes: Inside the black box. *Public Administration Review, 66*(s1), 20–32.

Thorkildsen, R., & Stein, M. R. (1996). Fundamental characteristics of successful university-school partnerships. *School Community Journal, 6,* 79–92.

Tozer, S. E., Zavitkovsky, P., Whalen, S., & Martinez, P. (2015). Change agency in our own backyards: Meeting the challenges of next generation programs in school leader preparation. In G. Khalifa, & A. Witherspoon (Eds.), *Handbook for Urban Educational Leadership* (pp. 480–495). New York, NY: Rowman & Littlefield.

Van Herk, H., & Fischer, R. (2017). Multi-level cultural issues. In H. van Herk, & C. J. Torelli (Eds.), *Cross Cultural Issues in Consumer Science and Consumer Psychology: Current Perspectives and Future Directions* (pp. 191–211). New York, NY: Springer.

Walsh, E. J., (2007). *P-16 Policy Alignment in the States: Findings from a 50-State Survey: Claiming Common Ground.* San Jose, CA: National Center for Public Policy and Higher Education.

Whitford, B. L., & Gaus, D. M. (1988). Collaboration for action and inquiry: Some effects of an ethnographic stance. Paper presented at the annual meeting of the American Educational Research Association Conference, Toronto, Canada.

Yip, J., Ernst, C., & Campbell, M. (2016). *Boundary Spanning Leadership: Mission Critical Perspectives from the Executive Suite.* Greensboro, NC: Center for Creative Leadership.

Young, M. D., Petersen, G. J., & Short, P. M. (2002). The complexity of substantive reform: A call for interdependence among key stakeholders. *Educational Administration Quarterly, 38*(2), 137–175.

Zeichner, K. (2010). Third space theory: Rethinking the connections between campus courses and field experiences in college and university-based teacher education. *Journal of Teacher Education, 61*(1–2), 89–99.

Zeichner, K., & Payne, K. (2013). Democratizing knowledge in urban teacher education. In J. Noel (Ed.), *Moving Teacher Education into Urban Schools and Communities* (pp. 3–19). New York, NY: Routledge.

Zimpher, N. L. (1990). Creating professional development school sites. *Theory into Practice, 29*(1), 42–49.

PART 5

Implications for Practice and Policy

Introduction

Complex and expanded notions of learning, that take seriously the cultural and contextual nature of learning, undoubtedly have significant implications for policy and practice. The way teacher education is organized, and the kinds of policies that are enacted at the local, state, and federal levels are all informed by how learning is conceptualized, and the kinds of learning that are determined as the goal. The two chapters in this final section articulate a vision for what teacher education and educational policy would look like if we honored the kinds of robust notions of learning described in the chapters in this volume. Ball and Ladson-Billings examine both traditional and alternative certification programs in what they identify as a "two-tiered system" of teacher education. They imagine how understanding cultural practices might be more effectively integrated into teacher education programs, and what this would mean for structures, pedagogies, and practice. Darling-Hammond lays out a vision for the kinds of learning that an approach that puts children in their cultural and community contexts at the center would support, and the implications for the design of education systems and policies of enacting such a vision. She argues that equitable systems of education understand learning as connected to the developmental needs of students, and that designing for learning and equity are mutually supportive.

22

EDUCATING TEACHERS FOR THE 21ST CENTURY

Culture, Reflection, and Learning

Arnetha F. Ball and Gloria Ladson-Billings

Introduction

Teacher education is undergoing some rather dramatic changes that make attempting to talk about teacher education as a unilateral process near impossible. For decades, the majority of teachers were prepared in college and university settings where students entered professional training after receiving either a liberal arts education (for elementary teachers) or subject matter preparation, e.g. English, mathematics, science, social studies, etc. (for secondary teachers). Typical professional education preparation includes courses in history of education, philosophy of education, sociology of education, and educational psychology along with child or adolescent development. These foundational courses are followed by methods courses focused on how to teach specific subjects and skills (e.g. mathematics, reading, science, etc.). The final aspect of most typical teacher education preparation is an opportunity for field experiences, e.g. practica and student teaching. Different programs may adjust these three components—longer or integrated field experiences or different sequencing of courses—but the components are recognizable despite these changes. What is clear in most teacher education programs is the lack of attention to the concept of culture (Kozleski & Handy, 2017).

Some programs argue that students are required to take a "diversity" course but most such courses fail to help students understand culture as a fundamental aspect of human existence. Instead diversity courses are aimed at attempting to teach students about "the other" and may create a sense of the exotic, particularly for white, middle class, English speaking teacher candidates. Often such approaches treat culture as a static or fixed set of artifacts or behaviors. Instead of learning how culture impacts the way everyone thinks and operates in the world, many teacher education programs fail to interrupt the stereotypes that candidates have about students and families racially, ethnically, economically, linguistically, religiously, and of national origins different from their own.

The failure to address culture as an important aspect of learning means that teachers who intend to teach in communities serving students and families unlike their own will exit teacher education programs that send teacher candidates out unprepared to be successful in classrooms serving diverse learners. In this chapter we attempt to discuss the two distinctly different ways that teacher learning and teacher preparation is taking place in the United States.[1]

The traditional path: The majority of the nation's teachers receive their teacher education in university-based programs that are approved and sanctioned by local state agencies. According to the Department of Education (2015), 1,023 Institutions of Higher Education (IHEs) offer teacher certification through traditional routes only. Another 456 IHEs offer alternative teacher certification routes with 432 of the IHEs offering both traditional and alternative routes to certification. Only 34 IHEs offer only alternative routes to certification and 219 non-IHEs (e.g. school districts, private entities, etc.) offer alternative programs. Of all teacher preparation programs, 7,187 (29 percent) were alternative route programs, which enrolled 62,961 (10 percent) of all teacher preparation candidates and accounted for 29,212 (14 percent) of all program completers. By comparison, traditional certification programs comprised 17,592 of teacher education programs with 551,166 teacher candidates.

On the surface it may appear that the numeric dominance of traditional teacher education programs means that we should expect teaching to continue as a profession primarily developed in colleges and universities. However, the distribution of alternatively certified teachers is an issue that bears greater scrutiny.

Alternative certification: Using alternative methods to certify teachers is not a new idea. Whenever the nation was concerned with teacher shortages it found ways to provide an alternative route to becoming a teacher. The National Teacher Corps was a program established by the United States Congress under the Higher Education Act of 1965 to improve teaching in economically disadvantaged or low-income communities in urban areas. The difference in the alternative certification of 1965 to those of today is that the Teacher Corps model required the preparation to be conducted in IHEs in conjunction with local school districts.

Studies comparing traditional and alternative certification programs have shown some strengths and some weaknesses for each type of program. For example, Legler (2002) found that scholars enrolled in alternative programs reported more intensive mentoring support than traditional programs. Legler's (2002) study showed that the urban teacher residency teachers had a higher retention rate inside high need schools as compared to teachers trained by other routes. Zeintek (2006) also found that positive mentoring experiences influenced novice teachers' perceptions and sense of preparedness for the classroom. Legler (2002) reported that the main supporting argument for alternative programs is that they require less coursework and requirements before becoming the teacher of record; thus they make the teaching profession more accessible to career changers and candidates who are interested in teaching but do not have adequate funds to pay for prolonged education. Legler also found that alternative programs may increase the number of minority teachers, increase the number of teachers in shortage areas, produce teachers that demonstrate similar classroom performance and student outcomes to traditionally certified teachers, and provide intensive mentoring and support, which contributes to the development of alternatively certified teachers.

The main supporting argument for traditional certification programs was that the extensive coursework, field experiences, and mentoring required before becoming the teacher of record produces teachers who are more qualified and confident about their preparedness to teach (Darling-Hammond, 2003). Similarly, Guyton, Fox, and Sisk (1991) found that teachers who had completed traditional certification programs were perceived by principals and themselves as better prepared to teach than those who had completed alternative certification programs. In addition, Darling-Hammond (1999) found that traditional certification programs seem to have higher entry and retention rates compared to alternative certification programs and that they actually cost less when considering the costs of certification, recruitment, induction, and replacement resulting from attrition. The main argument against traditional programs is that their additional requirements do not necessarily provide teachers who are better prepared for the classroom. Otherwise, Bowe et al. concluded that alternative and traditional programs were similar in many ways. Easton-Brooks and Davis (2009) reported on a large national study of 4,400 early elementary children from the Early Childhood Longitudinal Study, which examined achievement gaps and teacher qualifications using value-added methods and found one important difference between traditional and alternative certification programs. The report found that students who had a certified teacher for most of their early school experience scored significantly higher in reading than students with uncertified or alternatively certified teachers. Students with fully certified teachers for at least two of the three grade levels studied averaged 1.5 IRT units greater growth per year. Teacher certification accounted for 8 percent of the growth in reading achievement and was particularly influential in predicting growth for African American students. Having fully certified teachers narrowed the academic gap between African American students and European American students across the early elementary grades.

Bowe et al. summarized much of the research literature when they reported findings demonstrating that most teacher education program scholars in their study from alternative and traditional programs were similar in most demographics, in their affective characteristics, in their levels of commitment to teaching, and in their perceptions regarding their programs. In contrast, they differed in background experiences, beliefs about teaching, mentoring experiences, and teaching location. Moreover, the data suggest that alternative routes might attract more candidates who are more likely to teach in high need schools. Finally, intensive mentoring opportunities, and coursework and fieldwork that have a strong urban emphasis, appear valuable for teacher candidates who intend to teach in high need settings. Therefore, Bowe et al. suggested that all teacher preparatory programs might want to consider incorporating both intensive mentoring and a strong urban emphasis to better prepare all teacher candidates for working in high need schools.

Today alternative and traditional certification can occur within or beyond IHEs and by for-profit or non-profit entities. However, the commonality among the alternative certification models of the 1960s and those of today is their almost exclusive focus on preparing teachers who will work in communities serving poor students, and especially poor students of color. This two-tiered system—one for mostly middle class white students and the other for poor students and students of color—is one focus of this chapter. The central questions of this chapter are how learning about culture is incorporated in these two approaches to teacher education, what are some implications of current approaches to teaching culture, and what are some suggestions for how teacher education programs can help teachers understand culture better.

What We Mean by Culture

Culture is a concept that is simultaneously simple and complex. It is a ubiquitous concept that covers almost every aspect of human endeavor. As the central concept in the field of anthropology, it has at least 50 accepted definitions (see Seelye, 1993 and Tang, 2006). Commonly accepted definitions include what anthropology terms "KBAMLCS" (pronounced "kabamlics")—knowledge, beliefs, art, morals, language, customs, and any other capabilities and habits acquired by humans as members of society (Tylor, 2016 [1871], p. 1). However, that omnibus definition challenges most people in ways that almost render the term meaningless. Culture is everything but may seem like nothing. It is like the air we breathe—all around us but invisible. For members of a dominant group, culture is that which other people have. Their foods, their language, their beliefs, all seem strange or foreign to the dominant group.

Because culture may be deemed as anything that is deviant or different from the mainstream, it is not unusual for dominant group members to mistakenly describe behaviors or actions as culture when they are not. In the article "It's not the culture of poverty, it's the poverty of culture: The problem with teacher education," Ladson-Billings (2004) argues that much of the discussion about Black and poor children being a part of a "culture of poverty" (Payne, 2013) erroneously identifies the outcomes of social policies as "culture." For example, in the U.S. when changes in the social welfare program such as Aid to Families with Dependent Children (AFDC) prohibited the distribution of benefits to families with adult males in the household we saw a major increase in female-headed households among Black families. This was not a "cultural" phenomenon; it was a social policy that created a socially constructed phenomenon.

The comprehensive nature of culture makes it a difficult concept with which to work. We are bound to mistake all types of behaviors and activities for cultural ones. We must also understand that people participate in culture to varying degrees. A person with a Latinx family background may not speak Spanish. This does not mean they are not a part of Latinx culture. Thus, rather than universally ascribing culture to people based on physical attributes or phenotype (e.g. racial/ethnic characteristics, hair texture, etc.), in this chapter we employ Gutierrez and Rogoff's (2003) notion of cultural practices:

> People's varied *participation* in the practices of dynamic cultural communities can be distinguished from *membership* in ethnic groups, which often is treated in an all-or-none, static fashion. Individuals participate in varying and overlapping ways that change over their lifetimes and over historical change in a community's organization and relationship with other communities....
>
> By focusing on the varied ways people participate in their community's activities, we can move away from the tendency to conflate ethnicity with culture, with assignment to ethnic group made on the basis of immutable and often stable characteristics.
>
> *(p. 21)*

When we speak of culture in this chapter we look at the degrees to which individuals participate and share in aspects of a home culture. With this framework we attempt to avoid over generalizing culture as a worldview, set of beliefs, language, customs, etc. that all individuals participate in because they share genetic and phenotypic commonalities. This chapter looks at how teacher education engages with (or fails to engage with) the notion of cultural practices in order to adequately prepare teachers to become successful with **all** students.

Additionally, scholars like Moll and Gonzalez (1997) and Gonzalez, Moll, Tenery et al. (1995) have described the multidimensional aspects of culture that function dynamically within individuals, households, and communities. Their work points to the need for pre-service teachers to have opportunities to learn *from* (as opposed to learn *about*) communities comprised of members with backgrounds different from that of white, monolingual English-speaking, Christian, middle income women. We could find little evidence of this approach in either traditional or alternative approaches to teacher preparation.

After conducting a review of the research literature on preparing teachers for culturally and linguistically diverse classrooms, Liu and Ball (2019) found that the 1969 Smith Report was one of teacher education's earliest acknowledgments of students' cultural diversity. In that report, Smith noted that reform was needed on how teacher education programs teach teachers about culture because students who are not taught by teachers who have a good understanding of culture often turn out to be stigmatized as disadvantaged, are sometimes excluded from broader cultural activities because they do not learn how to interact with others well, or are often denied inter- and intra-personal competencies and segregated from the larger society. In too many cases, these students are even labeled as socially or emotionally disturbed if they protest against the inequity of the situation (1969, p. 3–4). Even after fifty years of subsequent calls concerning the need for teacher education programs to adequately prepare teachers who have cultural skills, competencies, knowledge, and dispositions concerning appropriate teaching and learning of cultural practices needed to become successful with _all_ students, we find that most teacher education programs, whether traditional or alternative, do not effectively integrate this information into their programs. However, it is important that teachers be taught how to meet the needs of culturally diverse students, because, as Morrier et al. (2007) found, their study supports previous research demonstrating that "teachers' lack of cultural awareness leads to reduced academic achievement by minority students" (Hickling-Hudson & Ahlquist, 2003; Serwatka, Deering, & Grants, 1995; Thompson et al., 2004).

Why Culture Is Important in Teacher Education

A decade ago, it was projected that by 2020, 50 percent of the student population would be students of color with no projected increase in teachers of color (Gollick & Chinn, 2009). The rapid fulfillment of this projection is a strong indication that education departments need to take more seriously the need to provide experiences and pedagogy concerning culture to their predominantly white pre-service and in-service teaching force. With this goal in mind, education departments around the United States should be taking aggressive steps to prepare their teachers to work successfully with racially and ethnically diverse populations of students and parents. Within this context, according to Krummel (2013), "[t]here is a need for pre-service teachers to understand how to work with students who are racially diverse" (p. 1). As outlined by Metcalf-Turner (2009), "[o]ne of the recurring and most daunting (threats) is the continued slow or little progress that has occurred in student achievement, particularly for poor and minority students" (p. 464). This lack of progress can be linked to teachers' inability and lack of desire to understand and build on students' cultural practices. Pre-service teachers appear to be ill-prepared to work with minority students because they lack the skills and oftentimes the desire to implement multiple instructional strategies in order to reach different types of students, especially students from different racial, cultural, and economic backgrounds (Metcalf-Turner, 2009).

Researchers have also found that many teachers entering the field of education feel uncomfortable addressing the idea of diversity. They may express fear and anxiety in working with communities that are extremely different from their own upbringing and background (Ford & Quinn, 2010; He & Cooper, 2009). The majority of pre-service teachers and in-service teachers in the United States are white, middle class females who identify as Christian and who come to teaching with little knowledge or experience regarding cultural and linguistic diversity (Liggett & Finely, 2009; Silverman, 2010). Mosley and Rogers (2011) found that the white pre-service teachers remained silent when the issue of multiculturalism or diversity arose in their classrooms. Silverman (2010) discussed this same silence as a mentality that someone else will take on the responsibility of educating students on multicultural topics.

One of the more difficult topics subsumed under the category of culture is race. The two concepts are not synonymous; however, much of the data on student academic performance, student behavior, special education assignment, and curriculum opportunities are rendered in terms of race, not culture (Ladson-Billings & Tate, 1995). Thus, it is imperative that we make some mention of the way race impacts the way teachers think about their work. Almost 30 years ago, King (1991) identified the issue that pre-service teachers wrestle with as "dysconscious racism." According to King (p. 135), "dysconsciousness is an uncritical habit of mid (including perceptions, attitudes, assumptions, and beliefs) that justifies inequity and exploitation by accepting the existing order of things as given...Dysconcious racism is a form of racism that tacitly accepts dominant White norms and privileges." We contend that not only are pre-service teachers subject to dysconsciousness, this phenomenon is also present among teacher educators, most of whom are members of the dominant culture. Teacher educators and teachers regularly conflate race and culture and the perception that there are no alternatives to the status quo force novice teachers to attempt to "save" or "rescue" students from their cultural backgrounds.

Pre-service teachers of color, on the other hand, have been found to "bring a commitment to multicultural teaching, social justice, and providing children of color with an academically challenging curriculum" (Amos, 2010, p. 31). Amos (2010) found that while pre-service teachers of color were ready and willing to learn about multicultural education, they were in a state of fear concerning the retaliation and ostracism they would receive from their white classmates who were in denial of their whiteness. The denial by the white pre-service teachers was forcing the pre-service teachers of color to become silent (Amos, 2010). The pre-service teachers of color did not feel part of the community, especially when their white classmates would not recognize or acknowledge their white privilege and were not open to discussing diversity in the classroom settings. According to Krummel (2013), both groups of pre-service teachers silenced themselves and each other. This was the pattern of behavior that one of the authors also observed in an elite teacher education program she worked in. Throughout this whole process, the white teacher educators in the program pretended not to notice this behavior and, thus, it was allowed to persist.

According to the Southern Poverty Law Center (2018), honoring students' cultures and experiences supports student learning. The Center reported that students who feel their cultural experiences are unwelcome, judged, stereotyped, disrespected, or invisible find it extremely difficult to engage in classroom activities and discussions in meaningful ways (p. 6). On the other hand, those whose stories and voices are heard and reflected in the classroom are more likely to engage with the curriculum and translate their learning into positive actions. When pre-service teachers know about students' cultural practices and value them, this can provide opportunities for building on that knowledge in the development of caring student/teacher relationships that support effective teaching and positive identity development on the part of students.

While it is important to teach teachers about culture and specifically cultural practices, Zeichner and Conklin (2005) posited that—rather than focusing on culture—studies of teacher preparation indicate that most programs focused largely on program structures, such as hours of clinical practice, number of credits, or regurgitating meaningless information rather than on specific design features and substantive program elements that can prepare them to integrate successful cultural practices into their classrooms. According to Zeichner and Conklin (2005), these programs have little potential to explain much of the variation in what graduates know and can do. For example, knowing how many hours a candidate works with a cooperating teacher may be less useful to understanding a program's impact than focusing on the quality and impact of the interactions between the candidate, the cooperating teacher, and their students. Howard's (2010) prediction that the "demographic divide" between the increasing numbers of minority students entering the classrooms and the homogeneous teaching force will continue to expand, is an indication that teachers need adequate experiences and preparation in order to "face the reality that they are most likely to come into contact with students from cultural, ethnic, linguistic, racial, and social class backgrounds different from their own" (Howard, 2010, p. 40). Since U.S. schools are continuing to become increasingly heterogenous learning spaces where the teachers are predominantly white, female, monolingual, and middle class and the student populations are becoming increasingly diverse students of color, who come from culturally and linguistically diverse and low-income backgrounds, teachers will need to be prepared to understand culture and will need to interact successfully with a mostly heterogeneous student population.

Missing from both forms of preparation (traditional and alternative) is a serious interrogation of one's own cultural beliefs and practices. Because white, middle class cultural practices are presumed to be the "default," teachers regard those practices as "normal" and universal. Such practices may be rendered invisible to pre-service students and those things different from them are seen as deviant. For example, teachers may presume celebrations of particular holidays (e.g. Halloween, Thanksgiving, Christmas, etc.) are "normal" activities and rather than describe them as a cultural practice in which some people engage, students who do not participate are presumed to have "cultural deficits."

Teacher education programs can easily ask teacher candidates to explore practices in which their own families participate as a way to bring into high relief the cultural nature of their everyday behaviors. The point is not to have students denigrate their home practices but to recognize that they are indeed their cultural practices—not necessarily shared by all.

Some Approaches That Traditional and Alternative Programs Use

While some researchers and universities claim they are adequately educating pre-service teachers on the topic of culture (Bleicher, 2011; Bodur, 2010; Davis, Beyerbach, & London, 2008; Kang, 2010),

Educating Teachers for the 21st Century

other professionals and researchers have found teacher education program graduates are "without adequate knowledge, skills, and dispositions to teach diverse students" (Benton-Borghi & Cheng, 2011, p. 29). While several studies agree that education departments need to adequately prepare pre-service teachers to teach students from diverse cultural and linguistic backgrounds effectively, for the last decade teacher education programs have drawn primarily on two approaches—reflection and service learning—in teaching about culture (Chang, Anagnostopoulos, & Omae, 2011). Self-reflection is a common professional practice among teachers and teacher candidates as a way to reflect on experiences, thoughts, as well as challenging one's own preconceived views. In teacher education programs around the country, pre-service teachers are asked to reflect on their reactions to articles and/or books, classroom assignments, discussions in class, and/or actual experiences in diverse classrooms (Chang et al., 2011). Service-learning involves going into urban and/or diverse settings and engaging with students who live and/or learn in those environments (Carter Andrews, 2009). Cooper (2009) found that combining these two experiences led to favorable outcomes and changing dispositions regarding diversity among pre-service teachers. Although the teacher educators seldom go into these urban environments for sustained periods of time, they offer mentoring in collaboration with the cooperating teachers and provide support through oral or written feedback, and they sometimes offer examples of quality teaching and emotional support. Watson's (2011) research suggests that mentoring and modeling are two essential supports that should be provided during service-learning along with content courses. It is hoped that through reflections, service-learning experiences, and modeling and mentoring, previously held biases and negative preconceived perceptions concerning poor students from culturally and linguistically diverse backgrounds (that teacher candidates may have developed as a result of their exposure to negative images in the media or negative attitudes expressed by family or community members) can be changed or at least challenged using these relatively passive approaches. However, since research shows that most candidates leave teacher education programs feeling that they have inadequate knowledge, skills, and training to teach students from diverse backgrounds effectively, we would do well to revisit and re-evaluate the efficacy and the adequacy of the approaches that we have been using.

In a recent exploration of how pre-service teachers come to understand a social construct like race, Ladson-Billings (2018) argued that despite the scientific evidence that debunks the notion of race, most teacher education students come to their professional training with the idea of race "fully funded" because of 19–20 years of considering it a real and stable concept. Thus, the major task for teacher educators is to help pre-service teachers "unlearn" what they think they know about a concept that is central to how U.S. society is organized.

In this final section, we recommend some additional approaches and frameworks, which teacher education programs should seriously consider, that expand upon and go beyond their current practices of reflection and service-learning by attending to contextualizing culture, critical reflection, and generative learning.

Contextualizing Culture

Teacher education programs can support pre-service teachers in acquiring the knowledge, skills, training, and dispositions needed to teach students from diverse cultural and linguistic backgrounds effectively by embedding the learning of culture throughout and within the teaching and learning of other contextualized materials that students must learn. According to Metcalf-Turner (2009), through the integration of information about a wide range of cultural practices into all courses, pre-service teachers would be able to fully understand the "issues of diversity within the context of making pedagogical decisions that lead to increased academic achievement" on the part of their students (Metcalf-Turner, 2009, p. 464). Dema and Moeller (2012) provide an excellent example of how this can be accomplished by integrating culture into foreign language courses. Since language emerges from societal interactions, teachers and students can learn language *and* acquire knowledge

393

about the culture *together* when learning the core objectives in the foreign language classroom. Dema and Moeller (2012) describe effective pedagogical practices that can be integrated into the language curriculum in ways that engage learners actively in the acquisition of culture. Research findings confirm that language and culture learning are inextricably linked and can be taught effectively through authentic, collaborative, and contextualized learning tasks (Maor & Roberts, 2011). When teachers integrate culture into their instruction through powerful technological tools, students are empowered to personally interact with real data and solve real open-ended problems. This learner-centered approach places the majority of responsibility for negotiating meaning into the hands of the learners and allows them to build their own understanding of cultural practices. The integration of content, pedagogy, and instructional technology when constructing knowledge promotes a rich and engaging learning environment for all learners (p. 76).

Practices discussed in Oxana and Moeller (2012) may also serve as a model that teacher education programs can emulate in their efforts to support pre-service teachers in acquiring teaching skills, knowledge about students' cultural practices, and dispositions needed to teach students from diverse cultural and linguistic backgrounds effectively. Oxana and Moeller present effective pedagogical practices that can be integrated into the teacher education curriculum as an enhanced approach for teaching cultural practices to novice teachers. They present an inquiry-based teaching approach to teaching culture utilizing instructional technology, which promotes student motivation and engagement that can help overcome past issues of stereotyping and lack of intercultural awareness. Using this approach, teacher candidates come to recognize the need to incorporate more cultural activities in order to promote students' cultural and intercultural understanding to "help combat the ethnocentrism that often dominates the thinking of our young people"—including students and classroom teachers as well (National Standards in Foreign Language Education Project, 1999, p. 47).

Embedding examples of how teachers might teach and learn about cultural practices within the curriculum and organizing that information around five main goals (Communication, Cultures, Connections, Comparisons, and Communities) helps teachers to articulate the essential skills and knowledge needed to support students' needs and their expanding understandings. An example of how teachers and teacher educators can embed the learning of cultural practices into the curriculum can be found in the National Standards in Foreign Language Education Project (1999). The foreign language standards define "'culture'…as the philosophical perspectives, the behavioral practices, and the products – both tangible and intangible – of a society" (p. 47). In this context, cultural practices are "patterns of behavior accepted by a society" or, in other words, "what to do where and when" (Lafayette, 1988, p. 213), as well as other forms of procedural aspects of culture (e.g. rites of passage, use of the forms of discourse, etc.). Cultural perspectives can be described as popular beliefs, values, attitudes, and assumptions held by the members of the target culture. The most significant improvement of the framework is the expansion of the definition of culture to include how a specific culture behaves and interacts. Similar to Gee's (1990) use of the notion of "Big 'D' Discourse" ("Discourse" spelled with a capital "D"), which is meant to capture the ways in which people enact and recognize socially and historically significant identities (through well-integrated combinations of language, actions, interactions, objects, tools, technologies, beliefs, and values), and his use of "Little 'd' discourse" (language in use among people), Lange (1999) spoke of culture practices in terms of "Big 'C' Culture" and "Little 'c' culture." According to Lange (1999), defining culture as such avoids "the common, overworked conflict between C and c by interweaving the formal and informal aspects of daily life, as one normally lives it in any culture" (p. 60). This re-conceptualized approach to culture shifts the focus of teaching culture to a study of underlying values, attitudes, and beliefs, rather than simply learning about cultural products and practices. One of the major goals for a teacher is to create inquiry questions that provoke interest in learning about the target culture and will lead to important discoveries about the culture and the people and thus, to develop an understanding of cultural differences. According to Short, Harste, and

Educating Teachers for the 21st Century

Burke (1996), "curriculum as inquiry is a philosophy, a way to view education…Inquiry is more than problem solving…inquiry suggests alternate answers," (p. 51). A number of researchers (Allen, 2004; Grittner, 1996; Tavares & Cavalcanti, 1996) state that teaching about cultural practices is most effective when students *discover* aspects of the target culture, rather than having information delivered. Tavares and Cavalcanti (1996) propose that the main aim of teaching culture is "to increase students' awareness and to develop their curiosity toward the target culture and their own, to make comparisons among cultures" (p. 19). Thus, an inquiry approach to teaching allows students and teachers to ask questions that are relevant or particularly interesting to them, collect necessary information, create answers by investigation, generate a theory, present their findings to others, and then formulate new questions that are derived from the original questions. Using technology in teaching about cultural practices has changed the nature of instruction and learning. Teachers and students are exploring digital technologies to make learning more effective and to engage students actively. Technology promotes socially active language in multiple authentic contexts due to its "accessibility, flexibility, connectivity speed and independence of methodological approach" (Gonzalez, 2009, p. 62). Through the use of interactive media, learners become less dependent on the printed word and more engaged with learning about authentic cultural practices that they can access and explore freely, because they have more control over the selection and investigation of multimedia materials and resources. These numerous resources and materials allow teachers to tailor digital media to make learning about cultural practices more relevant and accessible to the students in their classrooms (Moore, 2006). With the incorporation of technology into the curriculum, both the teacher and the students become part of the interactive learning environment.

Critical Reflection

Liu and Ball (2019) have challenged the simplistic notion that reflection is enough to prepare teachers for the classrooms they will be entering and propose that a more complicated notion of critical reflection and generativity are needed if teachers' reflections are to have a transformative impact on teachers' understanding of cultural practices and their effective teaching in classrooms. Critical reflection is a hermeneutic approach that involves repeated reexamination of one's assumptions about cultural knowledge and understanding, particularly those that are socially, politically, or culturally based (Liu & Ball, 2019). Mezirow (1990, 2000) and other scholars like Brookfield (1995) and Habermas (1970) have pointed out that reflection alone cannot lead to transformative learning—it is the emancipatory *action*, the *praxis* based upon reflective insight, that leads to transformative understandings of culture and cultural practices. Simple reflection alone is not enough. Liu (2015), working from Brookfield's stages of critical reflection (1995), developed a full hermeneutic model of critical reflection for transformative learning, which included a cycle of six steps that progress from assumption analysis to reflection on reflection-based action, and assert an ultimate goal of learning about culture as a transformative practice that leads to educational equity (see Figure 22.1, from Liu & Ball, 2019).

Liu (2017) provides an example of how the use of multiple stages of critical reflection resulted in a deeper understanding of the cultural practices and needs of a student of color in a pre-service teacher's classroom as well as transformative actions that had not previously been considered. This research highlights the pedagogical significance of dialogic spaces in supporting critical reflection and transformative learning among prospective teachers in the United States. It illustrates how systematic observation and careful follow-up dialogue with teacher educators can stimulate deep reflection to springboard transformative learning, and to improve their teaching practice. Liu points out that to be effective in enabling professional growth, prospective teachers' reflections should go beyond the technical concerns of minute-to-minute classroom management and reach for critical reflection. As proposed by Liu (2015): "Critical reflection is a process of constantly analysing, questioning, and critiquing established assumptions of oneself, schools, and the society about teaching

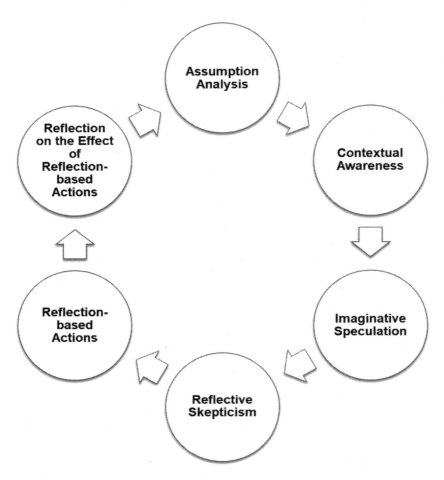

Figure 22.1 The hermeneutic cycle of critical reflection for transformative learning

and learning, and the social and political implications of schooling, and implementing changes to previous actions that have been supported by those established assumptions for the purpose of supporting student learning and a better schooling and [a more just] society for all children" (p. 10–11). Liu's (2017) recounting of Anne's critical reflections illustrates her changing perspectives over time. Anne was a pre-service teacher who initially thought that her African American student, Rebecca, "just didn't want to concentrate in classes." A recounting of her critical reflections illustrate how she came to understand her students' lived experiences, how her voice became modulated with understanding and empathy over time, and how the practice of critical reflection can be linked to the goal of transformative learning on the part of pre-service teachers. Anne's dialogue with her supervisor, the cooperating teacher, and Rebecca's parents helped her drop her initial polyphonic narrative of the classroom with its imagined Rebecca who just "didn't want to concentrate." At the same time, Anne's videos of her interactions with Rebecca preserved the polyvocality of the social text within the classroom, allowing Anne to analyze, question, and critique her prior assumptions concerning Rebecca and to reflect on them again. Anne's critical reflections show her growing awareness of the value of Rebecca's authentic voice, not just for her own learning but for that of her classmates as well. Anne uploaded her video together with her reflections into her ePortfolio to make it available to herself for future review, analysis, questioning, and critique for her cooperating teacher and her peers. The supervisor's role in this process is to assist the prospective teacher

Educating Teachers for the 21st Century

in creating a coherent narrative that supports their transformative learning by putting the texts in conversation with each other and revealing the rich variety of voices in them, while preventing the prospective teacher from omitting problems and challenges, and thereby short-circuiting the potential for transformation.

This close study illustrates how prospective teachers and their university supervisors use critical reflection within the context of an ePortfolio as a dialogic space for reflective conversations, and the impact of this on prospective teachers' teaching and learning, which can lead to transformative learning and transformative actions on the part of teacher educators and pre-service teachers in teacher education programs.

Generative Learning

The theme running throughout the literature on generativity over the last seventy years conceives of generativity as a formal, predictive theory of creative behavior or activity that leads to transformative action on the part of individuals. Building on this research, Ball (2009) proposed that theories of generativity provide an excellent framework to explain how teachers can engage in transformative change that can make a difference in the lives of students from diverse cultural and linguistic backgrounds in their classrooms. Teacher education programs that are based on the Model of Generative Change work to instill the expectation in teachers that they must become generative thinkers. When these programs prepare teachers to become generative thinkers, they are preparing them to apply creative problem solving to the teaching and learning activities they plan—activities that can lead to transformative action in their classrooms. Ball defines generativity as

> an individual's ability to *continually add* to their education knowledge by connecting their personal and professional knowledge with the knowledge they gain from their students, from the students' communities, and from their teaching experiences within the classroom context, in order to *produce new knowledge* that is useful to them in pedagogical problem solving and in meeting the needs of the students in their 21st Century classrooms.

Since most teachers do not feel that they know enough about their students' culture in order to teach them effectively, they must think in generative ways about how they can learn more about the students' culture from the students and along with the students.

Given the reality that almost 40 percent of teachers entering classrooms report that they do not feel adequately prepared for the challenges that await them, we need to look to generativity theories to guide teachers and teacher educators in their transformation of program practices. Building on the work of Erickson, Epstein, and Franke et al., and influenced by Bandura's (1977, 1997) self-efficacy theories, Ball (2009) combined generativity theory and teacher efficacy in a model designed to prepare teachers who believe in their potential ability to effect positive change in the lives of their students, and who also think in generative ways to incorporate creative transformative action in their classroom practices in order to meet the needs of 21st century students. A teacher's sense of efficacy is critical to his or her generation of effective strategies in bringing transformative practices into the classroom. A teacher has a greater chance of developing a sense of efficacy concerning the work they are doing with a student if they understand the students' culture and their cultural practices. Therefore, the teachers in Ball's research developed a deep appreciation for their students' cultural backgrounds as they engaged with new perspectives, new ideas, new theories, and new voices through carefully selected assigned readings, the sharing of their stories, critical reflective writing, teacher research projects, and required interactions with diverse learners to facilitate metacognitive awareness, ideological becoming, and internalization. The outcome was pre-service teachers who entered the classroom with an increased sense of metacognitive awareness concerning their students' cultural and linguistic practices. Carefully designed program activities were introduced to facilitate pre-service teachers' sense of agency, advocacy, and efficacy and their use of generative practices within their classrooms. The model below illustrates a series of stages through which individuals move from metacognitive awakening to their own sense of efficacy in their journeys toward becoming transformative intellectuals (Giroux, 1988), able to reshape curriculum and pedagogy motivated by their increasing understanding of their students' cultural lives and experiences, resulting in new relationships between teachers and students, and schools and communities (see Figure 22.2).

Ball (2000, 2009) provides an illustration of a program based on the Model of Generative Change and designed to facilitate the development of teachers who are generative thinkers, who are pedagogical problem solvers, and who are developing a commitment to teaching students from culturally and linguistically diverse backgrounds effectively. An analysis of teachers' developing discourses and observations of their classroom practices over a decade revealed transformative changes in teaching practices and engagement with their students. This study revealed how teachers' developing perspectives, practices, and their commitment to teaching students from diverse cultural and linguistic backgrounds can be facilitated through carefully designed teacher education programs.

Niko was a student who came to the course with preconceived notions about literacy and diversity and her interest in the course was piqued by the realization that all students do not receive the type of education she had; as a result, she was developing a deep interest in working with some of our society's needier populations. She was open to considering new ideas and perspectives. Niko began the course by sharing narrative reflections that served to increase her metacognitive awareness of their own literacy experiences. The biographical activities served as readiness exercises that prepared teachers to consider different theoretical perspectives and new visions for generative literacy practices they could try with the students in their own classrooms. Following the sharing of autobiographical literacy narratives and their students' biographies, the teachers were exposed to

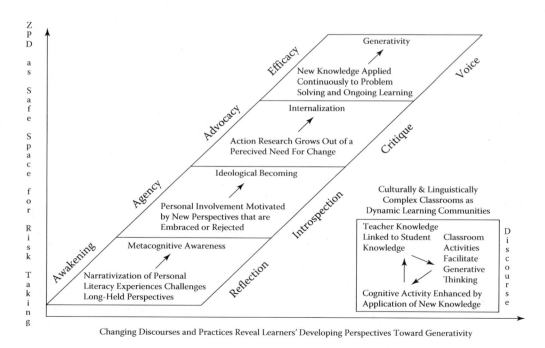

Figure 22.2 Model of generative change: the process through which teachers develop voice, generativity, and efficacy in their development toward transformative change. *Source*: Ball, A.F., *Am Educ Res J* 2009;46:45–72.

Educating Teachers for the 21st Century

carefully selected readings that were written by sociocultural and critical theorists along with practical teaching strategies that were based on these theories. The readings were selected to broaden previously held views on cultural practices, literacy, and classroom practice.

Through much discussion of the ideas represented in these texts and the ideas of other authors, teachers began to consider which, if any, of these ideas would become a part of their own discourses. Through this process, teachers began the initial stages of developing their own voices on issues related to preparing teachers to work with students from culturally and linguistically diverse backgrounds. The readings were coupled with assigned observations and authentic teaching experiences and gave assignments that used writing as a pedagogical tool for inquiry in order to facilitate their ideological becoming. Later, the teachers completed action research projects. These activities served as the catalyst needed to motivate a sense of agency, advocacy, and efficacy on the part of these teachers as they began making plans about how the course information would influence their work with students.

By the end of the term it became evident that Niko and other teachers in the course were beginning to use generative thinking in planning their classroom teaching. I also noted that they were drawing on the instructional approach that was used in the professional development course to plan and structure their own classroom teaching. Their classroom discourses reflected an awakening to the important role that cultural practices and literacy practices play in their lives and in the lives of their students. As this awakening occurred, noticeable changes were detected in their perspectives toward teaching diverse students and in their teaching practices. After demonstrating increased metacognition and a sense of awakening in their reflective writing, a sense of agency was reflected in their introspective writing, and a sense of advocacy was emerging in their critiques and future plans. Not only was Niko becoming a generative thinker, she was becoming a more confident, more effective teacher as she applied the knowledge she learned in our professional development course to learn new information about her students. As she asked her students to write about their interests, concerns, and experiences, she was able to apply that knowledge in her interactions with students and she integrated that knowledge into her content materials. In doing so, she was able to solve instructional and pedagogical problems in her classroom by making the materials more engaging for the students and more relevant to their interests. Niko's ultimate goal was for her students to generate plans of action to address some of the pressing social issues that existed in their own community. Thus, the knowledge she gained in the professional development course became generative knowledge as she saw the need to integrate this new knowledge with her existing knowledge and she continually reconsidered that knowledge in light of the needs of her students.

Niko's decision to interactively engage with the theory and activities that were planned for her in the course, to participate in the online tutoring project, the face-to-face mentoring activities, and her own tutoring and peer counseling activities, served as a catalyst that helped her to seriously consider the challenges of teaching students from diverse cultural, linguistic, and economic backgrounds, which was displayed in her developing discourses, in her curriculum planning and classroom teaching practices, and in her generative thinking and planning.

Teachers who come into the classroom from teacher education programs that are based on the Model of Generative Change realize that they must learn from the students what they need to know in order to teach the students effectively; they must skillfully draw on the students' experiences to enrich the curriculum. In other words, teachers realize that they must learn more about the students' cultural practices along with the students, from the students, and from the students' communities. Through teachers' authentic interactions with their students, and their students' parents and communities, they will come to understand that cultural practices are dynamic rather than static entities. At the community level, it is important to understand neighborhood demographics, strengths, resources, concerns, conflicts, and challenges. It is also important to understand that, like students themselves, these dynamics may change frequently.

Conclusion

Changing demographics indicate that historically minoritized populations are expanding at rates greater than previously expected (Brown, 2004; Wainer, 2004). When we situate the learning of culture by pre-service teachers in teacher education programs within a much more complex context that expands upon and goes beyond the current practices of reflection and service-learning to include contextualizing culture, critical reflection, and generative learning, then we stand a much greater chance of preparing teachers who have the cultural knowledge, skills, training, and dispositions needed to teach all students effectively. In order to support these teachers, however, it is our responsibility to constantly work toward transforming teacher education so its conceptions of learning about culture become a transformative practice that leads to educational equity. It is also our responsibility to work toward the elimination of the two-tiered system that these teachers must currently work within—one for mostly middle class white students and the other for poor students and students of color.

What we know about most alternative certification programs is that, in general, they offer a shorter pathway to licensure. This means that some of the work we have referenced is unlikely to occur because of time constraints. We also know that, in general, they place a premium on practice versus theory. Thus, novice teachers in alternative certification programs often lack the understanding of child and/or adolescent development as well as an appreciation for the history of education innovations (or failures) that can inform their curriculum decision-making and pedagogical strategies. In the more truncated programs novice teachers are treated like technicians whose primary task is to follow pre-determined curricula and scripts. Most university based traditional programs encourage novice teachers to make their own curriculum and pedagogical decisions. Since alternatively certified teachers are disproportionately assigned to schools and districts serving poor, minoritized students we see how systems of inequity are reproduced and maintained.

When we are able to eliminate this two-tiered system that shackles both students and teachers, then perhaps we can replace it with a system that truly embraces culture as an essential component of what it means to be human and rewards individuals based on the content of their character and the generativity exercised through their God-given abilities.

Note

1 Although teacher education takes place throughout the world, we are specifically focused on the process of preparing teachers in the United States.

Reference

Allen, M. (2004). *Eight Questions on Teacher Recruitment and Retention: What Does the Research Say?* Denver: Education Commission of the States.

Amos, Y. T. (2010). "They don't want to get it!" Interactions between minority and white pre service teachers in a multicultural education class. *Multicultural Education, 12*(4), 31–37.

Ball, A. F. (2000). Preparing teachers for diversity: Lessons learned from the U.S. & South Africa. *Teaching and Teacher Education, 16*, 491–509.

Ball, A. F. (2009). Toward a theory of generative change in culturally and linguistically complex classrooms. *American Educational Research Journal, 46*(1), 45–72.

Bandura, A. (1977). Self-efficacy: Toward a unifying theory of behavioral change. *Psychological Review, 84*, 191–215.

Bandura, A. (1997). *Self-Efficacy: The Exercise of Control.* New York, NY: Freeman.

Benton-Borghi, B. H., & Chang, Y. M. (2011). Critical examination of candidates' diversity competence: Rigorous and systematic assessment of candidates' efficacy to teach diverse student populations. *Teacher Education, 27*(1), 29–44.

Berry, B., Montgomery, D., Curtis, R., Hernandez, M., Wurtzel, J., & Snyder, J. (2008). Creating and sustaining Urban Teacher Residencies: A new way to recruit, prepare, and retain effective teachers in high-needs

Educating Teachers for the 21st Century

districts. Retrieved April 11, 2009, from http://www.aspeninstitute.org/sites/default/files/content/docs/pubs/ FINAL.CRE ATINGANDSUSTAININGUTR.PDF.

Bleicher, E. (2011). Parsing the language of racism and relief: Effects of a short-term urban field placement on teacher candidates' perceptions of culturally diverse classrooms. *Teaching and Teacher Education, 27*(8), 1170–1178.

Bowe, A., Liou, P.Y., & Lawrenz, F. (2009). University of Minnesota evaluation of the Robert Noyce teacher scholarship program, final report section five: Combined analysis of the Robert Noyce Teacher Scholarship Program using ORC Macro and UMN evaluation data. Retrieved May 5, 2011, from http://www.cehd.umn.edu/EdPsych/NOYCE/Reports/default.html.

Bodur, Y. (2010). Reader's response: Motivating graduate students. *International Journal for the Scholarship of Teaching and Learning, 4*(2), Article 27.

Brown, E. L. (2004). The relationship of selfconcepts to changes in cultural diversity awareness: Implications for urban teacher educators. *The Urban Review, 36*, 119–145.

Brookfield, S. (1995). *Becoming a Critically Reflective Teacher.* San Francisco: Jossey Bass.

Carter Andrews, D. J. (2009). The hardest thing to turn from: The effects of service-learning on preparing urban educators. *Equity & Excellence in Education, 42*(3), 272–293.

Chang, S., Anagnostopoulos, D., & Omae, H. (2011). The multidimensionality of multicultural service learning: The variable effects of social identity, context and pedagogy on pre-service teachers' learning. *Teaching and Teacher Education, 27*(7), 1078–1089.

Clewell, B., & Villegas, A. (2001). *Absence Unexcused: Ending Teacher Shortages in High-Need Areas: Evaluating the Pathways to Teaching Careers Program.* Washington, DC: The Urban Institute. (ERIC Document Reproduction Service No. ED460235).

Cooper, C. W. (2009). Performing Cultural work in demographically changing schools: Implications for expanding transformative leadership frameworks. *Educational Administration Quarterly, 45*(5), 694–724.

Darling-Hammond, L. (1999). *Teacher Quality and Student Achievement.* Centre for the Study of Teaching and Policy, Seattle: University of Washington.

Darling-Hammond, L. (2003). Keeping good teachers: Why it matters, what leaders can do. *Educational Leadership, 60*(8), 6–13

Davis, R. D., Ramahlo, T., Beyerbach, B., & London, A. (2008). A culturally relevant teaching course: Reflecting pre-service teachers' thinking. *Teaching Education, 19*(3), 223–234.

Dema, O., & Moeller, A. J. (2012). Teaching culture in the 21st century language classroom. Faculty Publications: Department of Teaching, Learning and Teacher Education. 181. Retrieved from http://digitalcommons.unl.edu/teachlearnfacpub/181

Department of Education. (2015, June). *Highly Qualified Teachers Enrolled in Programs Providing Alternative Routes to Teacher Certification or Licensure.* Washington, DC: United States Department of Education.

Easton-Brooks, D., & Davis, A. (2009). Teacher qualification and the achievement gap in early primary grades. *Education Policy Analysis Archives, 17*(15). Retrieved from http://epaa.asu.edu/ojs/article/download/17/17.

Epstein, R. (1996). *Cognition, Creativity, and Behavior.* Westport, CT: Praeger.

Erickson, E. H. (1963). *Childhood and Society* (2nd ed.). New York, NY: Norton.

Ford, T. N., & Quinn, L. (2010). First year teacher education candidates: What are their perceptions about multicultural education? *Multicultural Education, 17*(4), 18–24.

Franke, M., Carpenter, T., Levi, L., & Fennema, E. (2001). Capturing teachers' generative change: A follow-up study of professional development in mathematics. *American Educational Research Journal, 38*(3), 653–689.

Fraser, J. (2007). *Preparing America's Teachers: A History.* New York, NY: Teachers College Press.

Gee, J. P. (1990). *Social Linguistics and Literacies: Ideology in Discourses.* London: Falmer Press.

Giroux, H. (1988). *Teachers as Intellectuals: Toward a Critical Pedagogy of Learning.* Granby, MA: Bergin & Garvey Publishers.

Gollnick, D. M., & Chinn, P. D. (2009). *Multicultural Education in a Pluralistic Society* (8th ed.). Upper Saddle River, NJ: Pearson.

Gonzalez, L. (2009). Teaching math for social justice: Reflections on a community of practice for high school math teachers. *Journal of Urban Mathematics Education, 2*(1), 22–51.

Gonzalez, N., Moll, L. C., Tenery, M. F., Rivera, A., Rendon, P., Gonzales, R., & Amanti, C. (1995). Funds of knowledge for teaching in Latino households. *Urban Education, 29*(4), 443–470.

Grittner, F. M. (1996). Editor's introduction to special issue on culture. *Foreign Language Annals, 29*(1), 17–18.

Gutierrez, K., & Rogoff, B. (2003). Cultural ways of learning: Individual traits or repertoires of practice. *Educational Researcher, 32*(5), 19–25.

Guyton, E., Fox, M., & Sisk, K. (1991). Comparison of teaching attitudes, teacher efficacy, and teacher performance of first year teachers prepared by alternative and traditional teacher education programs. *Action in Teacher Education, 13*(2), 1–9.

Habermas, J. (1970). Towards a theory of communicative competence. *Inquiry: An Interdisciplinary Journal of Philosophy, 13*(1–4), 360–375.

He, Y., & Copper, J. E. (2009). The ABCs for pre-service teacher cultural competency development. *Teaching Education, 20*(3), 205–322.

Hickling-Hudson, A., & Ahlquist, R. (2003). Contesting the curriculum in the schooling of indigenous children in Australia and the United States: From Eurocentrism to culturally powerful pedagogies. *Comparative Education Review, 47*(1), 64–89.

Howard, T. C. (2010). *Why Race and Culture Matters in Schools: Closing the Achievement Gap in America's Classrooms.* New York, NY: Teachers College Press.

Kang, R., & Hyatt, C. (2010). Preparing preservice teachers for diversity: The power of multicultural narratives. *SRATE Journal, 19*(1), 44–51.

King, J. (1991). Dysconscious racism: Ideology, identity and the miseducation of teachers. *Journal of Negro Education, 60*(2), 133–146.

Kozleski, E. B., & Handy, T. (2017). The cultural work of teacher education. *Theory into Practice, 56*(3), 205–213.

Krummel, A. (2013). Multicultural teaching models to educate pre-service teachers: Reflections, service-learning, and mentoring. *Current Issues in Education, 6*(1), 1–6. Retrieved from http://cie.asu.edu/ojs/index.php/cieatasu/article/view/1059.

Ladson-Billings, G. (2004). It's not the culture of poverty, it's the poverty of culture: The problem with teacher education. *Anthropology & Education Quarterly, 37*(2), 104–109.

Ladson-Billings, G. (2018). The social funding of race: The role of schooling. *Peabody Journal of Education, 93*(1), 90–105.

Ladson-Billings, G., & Tate, W. F. (1995). Toward a critical race theory of education. *Teachers College Record, 97*(1), 47–68.

Lange, D. L. (1999). Planning for using the new national culture standards. In J. Phillips, & R. M. Terry (Eds.), *Foreign Language Standards: Linking Research, Theories, and Practices* (pp. 57–120). Lincolnwood, IL: National Textbook & American Council on the Teaching of Foreign Languages.

Legler, R. (2002). Alternative certification: A review of theory and research. Retrieved November 1, 2009, from http://www.ncrel.org/policy/pubs/html/altcert/index.html.

Liggett, T. (2011). Critical multicultural education and teacher sense of agency. *Teacher Education, 22*(2), 185–197.

Liggett, T., & Finley, S. (2009). "Upsetting the apple cart": Issues of diversity in pre-service teacher education. *Multicultural Education, 16*(4), 33–38.

Liu, K. (2015). Critical reflection as a framework for transformative learning in teacher education. *Educational Review, 67*(2), 135–157.

Liu, K. (2017). Creating a dialogic space for prospective teacher critical reflection and transformative learning. *Reflective Practice, 18*(6), 805–820. doi:10.1080/14623943.2017.1361919.

Liu, K., & Ball, A. F. (2019). Critical reflection and generativity: Toward a framework of transformative teacher education for diverse learners. *Review of Research in Education, 43*(1), 68–105.

Maor, D., & Roberts, P. (2011). Does the TPACK framework help to design a more engaging learning environment? In *Proceedings of World Conference on Educational Multimedia, Hypermedia and Telecommunications 2011* (pp. 3498–3504). Chesapeake, VA: AACE

Metcalf-Turner, P. (2009). Realizing the democratic ideal: A call for an integrative approach to inclusion of multicultural course content in teacher education programs. *Teacher Education and Practice, 22*(4), 464–467.

Mezirow, J. (1990). *Fostering Critical Reflection in Adulthood: A Guide to Transformative and Emancipatory Learning.* San Francisco: Jossey Bass.

Mezirow, J. (2000). *Learning as Transformation: Critical Perspectives on a Theory in Progress.* San Francisco: Jossey Bass.

Moll, L. C., & Gonzalez, N. (1997). Teachers as social scientists: Learning about culture from household research. In P. M. Hall (Ed.), *Race, Ethnicity, and Multiculturalism* (pp. 89–114). New York, NY: Garland.

Moore, Z. (2006), Technology and teaching culture: What Spanish teachers do. *Foreign Language Annals, 39*, 579–594.

Morrier, M. J., Irving, M. A., Dandy, E., Dmitriyev, G., & Ukeje, I. C. (2007). Teaching and learning within and across cultures: Educator requirements across the United States. *Multicultural Education, 14*(3), 32–40.

Lafayette, R. C. (1988). Integrating the teaching of culture into the foreign language classroom. In A. J. Singerman (Ed.), *Toward a New Integration of Language and Culture* (pp. 47–62). Middlebury, VT: Northeast Conference on the Teaching of Foreign Languages.

Mosley, M., & Rogers, R. (2011). Inhabiting the 'tragic gap': Pre-service teachers practicing racial literacy. *Teaching Education, 22*(3), 1, 303–324.

Educating Teachers for the 21st Century

National Standards in Foreign Language Education Project. (1999). *Standards for Foreign Language Learning in the 21st Century*. Yonkers, NY: Department of Teaching, Learning and Teacher Education at DigitalCommons@ University of Nebraska-Lincoln.

Oxana, D., & Moeller, A. (2012), *Teaching Culture in the 21st Century Language Classroom*. University of Nebraska-Lincoln Faculty Publications: Department of Teaching, Learning and Teacher Education, p. 181.

Payne, R. (2013). *A Framework for Understanding Poverty* (5th revised ed.). Highlands, TX: Aha! Process Inc.

Salinas, J. P. (2002). The effectiveness of minority teachers on minority student success. Proceedings of the National Association of African American Studies & National Association of Hispanic and Latino Studies: 2000 Literature Monograph Series, 24. Retrieved November 3, 2009, from the ERIC database. (ERIC Document Reproduction Service No. ED455235).

Schulte, A. K. (2009). The demographics of teaching and teacher education: The need for transformation. In A. K. Schulte (Ed.), *Seeking Integrity in Teacher Education: Self Study of Teaching and Teacher Education* (Vol. 17, pp. 23–31). Dordrecht: Springer.

Seelye, H. N. (1999). *Teaching Cultural Strategies*. New York: National Textbook Company.

Serwatka, T. S., Deering, S., & Grant, P. (1995). Disproportionate representation of African Americans in emotionally handicapped classes. *Journal of Black Studies, 25*(4), 492–506.

Short, K. G., Harste, J. C., & Burke, C. (1996). *Creating Classrooms for Authors and Inquirers*. Portsmouth, NH: Heinemann.

Silverman, S. (2010). What is diversity?: An inquiry into pre-service teacher beliefs. *American Educational Research Journal, 47*(2), 292.

Southern Poverty Law Center. (2018). *Critical Practices for Anti-Biased Education*. Montgomery, AL: Teaching Tolerance.

Tang, S.Y., Hung Cheng, M. M., & Wing Mui So, W. (2006). Supporting student teachers' professional learning with standards-referenced assessment. *Asia-Pacific Journal of Teacher Education, 34*(2), 223–244.

Tavares, R., & Cavalcanti, I. (1996). Developing cultural awareness. In *English Teaching Forum* (Vol. 34, no. 3-4, pp. 19–23). Washington: The United States Information Agency.

Thompson, S., Greer, J. G., & Greer, B. B. (2004). Highly qualified for successful teaching: Characteristics every teacher should possess. *Essays in Education, 10*(1), 5.

Tylor, E. B. (2016/1871). *Primitive Culture*, Vol. 1. London, UK: Dover Publications, Inc.

Ullucci, K. (2009). "This as to be family": Humanizing classroom management in urban schools. *The Journal of Classroom Interaction, 44*(1), 13–28.

United States Department of Education. (2016). *The State of Racial Diversity in the Education Workforce*. Washington, DC: Office of Planning, Evaluation & Policy Development.

Wainer, A. (2004). *The NEW LATINO South and the Challenge to Public Education: Strategies for Educators and Policymakers in Emerging Immigrant Communities*. Los Angeles, CA: The Thomas Rivera Policy Institute. Retrieved February 20, 2005, from http://www.troi.org.

Weiss, I., Banilower, E., McMahon, K., & Smith, P. (2001, December). *Report of the 2000 National Survey of Science and Mathematics Education*. Chapel Hill, NC: Horizon Research, Inc. Retrieved August 8, 2009, from http://2000survey.horizon-research.com/reports/status/complete.pdf (Note: When I used the URL you gave, I found no report, just links. This document has the closest title and is by the authors you list. Is it the document you cite in your text?).

Watson, D. (2011). "Urban, but not too urban": Unpacking teachers' desires to teach urban students. *Journal of Teacher Education, 62*(1), 23–34.

Zeichner, K. (2014). The struggle for the soul of teaching and teacher education in the USA. *Journal of Education for Teaching, 40*, 551–568.

Zeichner, K. M., & Conklin, H. G. (2005). Teacher education programs. In M. Cochran-Smith, & K. M. Zeichner (Eds.), *Studying Teacher Education: The Report of the AERA Panel on Research and Teacher Education* (pp. 645–736). Mahwah, New Jersey: Lawrence Erlbaum Associates Publishers.

Zeintek, L. (2006, December). Do teachers differ by certification route? Novice teachers' sense of self-efficacy, commitment to teaching, and preparedness to teach. *School Science and Mathematics, 106*(8), 326–327.

23

CULTURE, LEARNING, AND POLICY

Linda Darling-Hammond

Seriously addressing the cultural nature of human learning and development described in this Handbook requires deep rethinking by policymakers and practitioners about how we support learning. This includes the knowledge and skills required for generative teaching; the institutional supports needed to develop, support, and sustain this kind of teaching; the school designs needed to build strong relationships among students and adults (both educators and families) that support personalized, culturally grounded teaching and learning; the complementary sources of support needed to remove obstacles to learning; and the systems changes—ranging from resource allocations to school and program assignment practices—that allow us to move beyond the deficit assumptions about cultural variation that are so deeply entwined in our schools.

The knowledge provided by the sciences of learning and development, understood through a lens that incorporates social and cultural contexts, offers a framework for supporting children's health and welfare across the wide range of contexts they experience. This knowledge base indicates the importance of rethinking classrooms, schools, and social institutions designed a century ago based on factory-model conceptions of organizations that privileged standardization and minimized relationships. These organizations were also designed to select and sort students into different opportunities based on unidimensional, and often racially biased, assumptions about children's capacities and their later roles in society. These assumptions, in turn, were implicit in many training systems for teachers and leaders, which were grounded in both low expectations for educators and low expectations for many students.

Research indicates that schools and child-caring services must be organized around: strong, developmentally supportive relationships; coherent and well-integrated approaches to supports, including home and school connections; well-scaffolded instruction that intentionally supports the development of social, emotional, and academic skills, habits, and mindsets; and culturally competent, personalized responses to the assets and needs of each child.

To achieve these goals at scale, we need a holistic vision for youth development in which all the elements that impact students' social, emotional, cognitive, and identity development are designed in ways that support their learning. These elements especially include positive school cultures that connect to and affirm children's home cultures. This vision should inform policies that enable and encourage schools to personalize instruction within supportive school environments that help students grow along all of the developmental pathways that will ensure their self-actualization and success as contributing members of families and communities, as well as in pursuit of their passions and vocations.

Culture, Learning, and Policy

In this chapter, I discuss policy that can prepare educators for culturally connected and responsive teaching, and enable supportive school designs and personalized supports—both academic and non-academic—that remove barriers to learning for students. I also discuss system designs that enable equitable, culturally informed practice.

Educator Preparation

Perhaps most important for achieving culturally informed teaching are educators' understandings, knowledge, and skills. The practices described in the preceding chapters require serious investments in educator development. Teaching is a particularly complex profession: it is never routine, has multiple goals that need to be addressed at the same time, involves students who are diverse along many different dimensions and unique in their combinations of experiences, and demands multiple kinds of knowledge to be synthesized in a way that allows teachers to make sense of their students' worlds (Lampert, 2001).

Because each child's learning journey is unique, teaching cannot be fully routinized and standardized. As a consequence, many kinds of policy are problematic for teaching: in particular, policies that seek to prescribe the acts of teaching in highly specific ways—through rigid curriculum and testing requirements accompanied by pacing guides and scripted lessons—actually prevent teachers from addressing the particular needs of individual students. Furthermore, such policies—which are typically rooted in a notion of how the "average" student should learn—deny the reality that learning is rooted in cultural experiences and contexts that are, by definition, multidimensional and varied.

Teaching challenging content in ways that promote deep understanding to learners who bring very different experiences and conceptions cannot be pre-packaged or "teacher-proofed." It depends on the capacity of practitioners to create powerful learning experiences that connect to what students know and how they most effectively learn. The alternative to prescriptive teaching policy is what some have called "professional policy"—that is, a policy approach that leverages the development of deep knowledge and expertise on the part of educators so that they can be trusted to make good decisions that meet the needs of the children they serve (Elmore & Fuhrman, 1993). I begin with this important genre of policy because it is essential to culturally responsive teaching and no other aspect of educational improvement can succeed without it.

What Kind of Expertise Do Teachers Need?

Teachers must develop ***adaptive expertise*** to make non-routine judgments about what to do based on both general and specific knowledge of learners and their paths to learning, as well as curriculum goals (Darling-Hammond & Bransford, 2005). This adaptive expertise requires strong knowledge of development and learning as well as strong metacognitive capacities; it enables teachers to learn to think pedagogically, plan based on students' prior knowledge and needs, reason through dilemmas, and analyze student understandings to develop appropriate learning experiences that create connections for diverse learners.

Because learning is embedded in the linguistic, cultural, and developmental experiences of students, teachers must learn how to discern these experiences, so they can plan in light of their students' needs and to support their progression along several developmental pathways—physical, social, emotional, cognitive, linguistic, and psychological. They need ways to learn about their students' different ways of learning, prior experiences and knowledge, and cultural and linguistic capital. For example, teachers need to learn *how* to learn about the strengths and needs of individual students through careful observation and listening, as well as such techniques as regular check-ins and class meetings, conferencing, journaling, and classroom surveys.

Creating identity safe classrooms that support the education of the whole child relies on teachers understanding the view and experiences children bring to school, including, for example, how students communicate in their communities (Lee, 2007; 2017). Such teaching uses a disposition toward developing classroom practices that capitalize on the funds of knowledge that are abundant in children's households and communities (Lee, 2007; Moll, Amanti, Neff, & Gonzalez, 1992; Nasir, Roseberry, Warren, & Lee, 2014) rather than a deficit-based orientation. Teachers need culturally sensitive listening and questioning skills to use when meeting with parents as authentic partners. These skills can enable teachers to learn about their students' lives and learning strategies and to create more coherent learning opportunities between home and school. This helps them create environments where students feel culturally respected as well as emotionally and intellectually safe (Carter & Darling-Hammond, 2016; Villegas & Lucas, 2002).

Furthermore, meeting students' needs depends on knowing how to take them into account while undertaking a purposeful curricular journey supporting students' deep understanding of subject matter. Central to this work is an understanding of curriculum design and skill in developing lessons and units of instruction that can achieve worthwhile learning objectives while connecting to students' experiences in and outside of school (Nasir, Roseberry, Warren, & Lee, 2014). When teaching these lessons and units, teachers need well-developed skills for scaffolding the learning process through the choice of materials, design of tasks, and use of helpful questions and supports to guide the learning process.

Behind the scenes, teachers must also be keen diagnosticians, deeply reflective about what they see happening with students each day, to respond to the dynamic process of learning for understanding. Preparing teachers who can learn *from* teaching, as well as learning *for* teaching, is a key challenge for teacher education today (Darling-Hammond et al., 2006).

How Can Teachers Learn in these Ways?

Helping teachers learn to practice in these ways requires both coursework and clinical work that, together, help teachers understand students and how they learn while also developing skills and tools to organize and manage these kinds of rich, culturally connected learning experiences. Studies have found that teacher education programs that have a greater impact on the initial conceptions, practices, and effectiveness of new teachers connect theory and practice in coherent ways and blend theory and practice around a vision of teaching that supports empowering learning for all students (Darling-Hammond & Bransford, 2005).

Furthermore, well-prepared teachers and principals feel more efficacious, experience less stress in their jobs, and are more likely to stay in the profession, providing students with the stability they need. They are also more likely to have skills that enable them to understand students' experiences more deeply and thus treat them more fairly and support them more effectively (for reviews, see Darling-Hammond & Bransford, 2005; Darling-Hammond et al., 2009).

Educator preparation programs for both teachers and school leaders should offer a thoughtful, science-based course sequence that centers on understanding child and adolescent development and learning, addressing implicit bias, creating culturally responsive classroom communities, and advancing equity as well as crafting engaging instructional units that connect to students' experiences and move them toward deeper learning outcomes. To shape practice, this training must include a strong clinical component interwoven with this coursework, in which candidates integrate theory and practice with the guidance of experienced and effective educators in schools that model practices supportive of student development.

Training should include how to support children's social, emotional, and identity development as well as their academic success, how to develop classroom communities that enable productive adult and peer relationships, how to use educative and restorative behavior supports, and how to work effectively with families in a diverse community.

Culture, Learning, and Policy

Policy for Changing Professional Education

A key lever for changing practice in professions is by enacting **standards for professional licensing and program accreditation** that reflect these practices and are universally enforced. Standards are a strong lever in medical, legal, and other areas of professional education. However, when Abraham Flexner conducted his famous 1910 study of medical education that eventually led to its overhaul, there were no serious standards for the field. Programs ranged widely—from a three-week course of study in which doctors memorized a list of symptoms and "cures" to Johns Hopkins University's purposeful coursework in the sciences of medicine coupled with clinical training in the school's newly invented teaching hospital.

In his introduction to the Flexner Report, Henry Pritchett, president of the Carnegie Foundation for the Advancement of Teaching, noted that, although there was a growing science of medicine, most doctors did not get access to this knowledge because of the great unevenness in medical training. He observed that

> very seldom, under existing conditions, does a patient receive the best aid which it is possible to give him in the present state of medicine...[because] a vast army of men is admitted to the practice of medicine who are untrained in sciences fundamental to the profession and quite without a sufficient experience with disease.
>
> *(Flexner, 1910)*

Similarly, few students—especially in the neediest schools—receive the quality of education that is possible given what is known from educational research today, in substantial part because so many of their teachers have not had the opportunity to learn what is known about how to teach them effectively.

Flexner's identification of successful models stimulated the reform of medical education, which occurred over the next two decades through the use of licensing and accreditation standards to ensure that doctors would get the best training the field had to offer. Now, doctors all over the world are trained with a common introduction to the sciences of medicine and clinical training through internships and residencies in teaching hospitals.

Teaching standards are the foundation for this kind of reform. In education, the strongest examples have emerged from the work of the National Board for Professional Teaching Standards, which was founded in 1987 and began certifying veteran accomplished teachers in the 1990s. The National Board built on research about learning and teaching—and the wisdom of highly respected practitioners—in developing standards articulating what expert teachers should know and be able to do. The standards—and the associated performance assessments, which include teacher plans, classroom videotapes, commentaries about practice, and evidence of student learning—support a view of teaching as complex and responsive to students' diverse experiences and needs. This was a major break from the view of teaching as the implementation of standard routines, irrespective of what students bring to the classroom.

Although more than one hundred thousand teachers have been certified through the Board's assessment, and many studies have since found that the Board's assessment process identifies teachers who are more effective (National Research Council, 2008), this voluntary process has reached only about 3% of the teaching force. Applying these kinds of standards and assessments in the licensing process for beginning teachers can have much more systemic effects. In the early 1990s, the National Board's standards were carried into initial teacher licensing standards by the Interstate New Teacher Assessment and Support Consortium (INTASC), a consortium of state education agencies and higher education institutions.

The standards developed by the National Board and INTASC take into explicit account the need for teachers to respond to a student body that is multicultural and multilingual and that learns in diverse ways. They define teaching as a collegial, professional activity that responds to considerations of subjects and students. The INTASC standards have been adopted or adapted by more than forty states and integrated into licensing and accreditation standards for candidates and programs. They were revised nearly a decade ago to incorporate the implications of new student standards across the United States and are slated for further revision in the next year or so. It is important that this process pay particular attention to the socio-cultural foundations of learning; the integrated nature of social, emotional, and academic development; and the need for educators to be knowledgeable about and thoughtfully connected to families and communities.

As much as standards focus a field on common goals, much more is needed to change actual practice in preparation programs. One key tool is the use of ***performance assessments*** for evaluating beginning teachers. Unlike the bevy of multiple-choice licensing tests that have accrued since the 1980s, these kinds of assessments, like those of the National Board, can incorporate expectations for culturally responsive teaching and have been found to predict teachers' effectiveness in promoting student learning (Darling-Hammond, 2010; Goldhaber, Cowen, & Theobald, 2016; Wilson, Hallam, Pecheone, & Moss, 2014); they also have less disparate pass rates for teachers of color than most other teacher tests. Most important, the assessments shape program design in ways that strengthen clinical practice focused on teachers' abilities to respond to the needs and experiences of students as they teach.

Typically these kinds of assessments require teachers to document their plans and teaching for a unit of instruction, taking into account their students' prior knowledge and experiences; adapt the lessons for English learners, students with disabilities, and other students requiring particular attention; videotape and analyze the lessons, offering commentary about their teaching decisions; and collect and evaluate evidence of student learning, outlining what should happen to support the learning of different students in the future. Studies have found that these performance assessments help beginning teachers develop a more learner-centered practice, and shape practice in ways that continue after the assessment experience has ended (Chung, 2008; Lustick & Sykes, 2006; Sato, Chung, & Darling-Hammond, 2008). Currently, about 20 states use performance assessments as the basis for initial teacher licensing, and have begun to see changes in teacher education as a result (Darling-Hammond et al., 2019).

A second means to enforce standards is through ***performance-based accreditation for preparation programs***. Accreditation, designed a century ago as a process in which institutions describe their work in relation to common questions and standards (typically at great length) and display it in brief site visits, has value as a means for guiding self-assessment and reflection. However, in most states and nationally, it has not been a powerful tool for setting a floor on the quality of teacher education or for moving the field forward on a common path toward more powerful practices.

While all states approve programs and a few require or encourage national accreditation, neither process has incorporated and enforced clear requirements for the kinds of practices we have described here: demonstrated coherence around a vision of practice grounded in what is known about learning and development; modeling of powerful teaching practices in university coursework, along with the provision of concrete strategies and tools for practice; demonstrated connections between theory and practice and between coursework and clinical work; extended, well-planned, carefully supervised clinical training in sites that also instantiate these practices. Even when these practices are present in some universities' programs, those same universities often operate other, weaker programs that do not offer the same features. Despite the fact that the achievement of goals is not universal across programs, accreditors commonly approve the program provider, allowing low-quality programs a free pass.

Two needed changes in accreditation, then, are the much clearer incorporation of these features of successful programs into the requirements for approval, and the application of these standards universally to all programs. For example, in California, a newly launched accreditation system will take into account: candidate pass rates on the new performance assessments that examine what

Culture, Learning, and Policy

candidates can *do* to support the learning of their diverse students, rather than merely what courses they have taken; results from graduate surveys about whether they have experienced strong learning opportunities like those described earlier; and results from surveys of mentors and employers. The new system will examine the conditions of clinical work—including the kinds of supports, coaching, and learning opportunities provided—as well as the specific content of courses, including candidates' views of their quality. Already, some programs have changed substantially as a result of the new approach.

Another critical policy element is ***state and federal funding for professional development school partnerships.*** As noted earlier, the invention of the teaching hospital was a key element in the capacity of the medical profession to dramatically improve practice. The analog of the teaching hospital has been fully implemented in Finland, where all teachers are prepared in partner schools that are tightly connected to universities (Darling-Hammond et al., 2017). The teachers in these partner schools are especially selected for their expertise and capacity to mentor; they also engage in research on practice with the teacher candidates and the university professors. The school-based teachers have appointments in the university. University faculty also work directly in the schools. Theory and practice are tightly linked. These efforts are funded by the national government, through the universities.

Finally, achieving stronger standards of professional knowledge and skill requires strategies to address teacher shortages and to recruit and retain an adequate supply of diverse, well-prepared teachers. Recurring teacher shortages result in a large number of untrained teachers in classrooms, typically concentrated in communities of color (Sutcher, Darling-Hammond, and Carver-Thomas, 2016). Not only are such teachers less effective than those who have been fully prepared, they are more than twice as likely to leave soon after entry, creating disruption and churn that also undermine achievement (Ingersoll, Merrill, & May, 2014; Sutcher, Darling-Hammond, & Carver-Thomas, 2016). Research also indicates that there is a relationship between high student suspension rates and a higher than average number of novice teachers or those without preparation (Losen, 2015). Investments that expand the pool of well-prepared teachers will help provide schools with a more stable workforce that can transform school climate and culture.

In addition, proactive strategies for recruiting underrepresented students to prospective careers in teaching and school leadership can help build the kinds of school environments that feature cultural pluralism and communicate safety and belonging to all students. Growing evidence documents the benefits to students of color of having at least one teacher of the same race, including higher achievement and graduation rates, as well as a greater likelihood of aspiring to higher education (Dee, 2004; Gershenson, Hart, Lindsay, & Papageorge, 2017). It is likely that the affirming messages and supports these teachers give their students have long-term effects on students' identities as learners and their experience of school. A diverse educator workforce also brings more experiences and perspectives to the table, enabling greater mutual exchange among professionals about how to understand and meet the needs of their students.

Although many school districts are beginning to recognize the desirability of having a teaching staff that is more representative of the student body, the lack of teacher diversity is a growing concern in the United States. While recruitment has increased, there is still a major challenge in retaining teachers of color once they have entered the profession. This is often because they have had less access to high-quality preparation and mentoring, and because they typically teach in the most challenging school environments (Carver-Thomas, 2018).

Policy for Teacher Recruitment and Retention

Efforts to recruit and retain racially underrepresented individuals to become teachers and school leaders can pay great dividends for other educators as well as for students. The most successful strategies offer forgivable loans and scholarships to offset the costs of preparation; high-quality, affordable entry pathways such as teacher and leader residencies that offer excellent preparation for high-need urban and rural schools at little cost to candidates; and supportive mentoring in collegial environments (Carver-Thomas, 2018).

Federal and state *service scholarships or loan forgiveness programs* to attract candidates to the fields and locations where they are needed most are paid back with several years of service in public schools. The most successful approaches, like the North Carolina Teaching Fellows program, completely underwrite a student's education in exchange for a commitment to teach in the state for at least four years. The Fellows program recruits disproportionately larger numbers of candidates of color, math and science teachers, and male teachers into the profession, and it has high rates of retention, with more than 75% still teaching after five years, and other graduates having moved into school administration. These fellows are also among the most effective teachers in the state (Henry, Bastian, & Smith, 2012).

Teacher residencies, which prepare and retain well-trained teachers where they are most needed, provide another strategy for solving teacher shortages and recruiting a diverse, well-prepared teaching force. In these models, universities partner with districts to recruit residents who are career switchers or recent college graduates who want to teach in high-need urban or rural schools. Many residencies have created partnerships with schools that exemplify culturally responsive approaches to deeper learning and equity and focus their training on these understandings and skills (Darling-Hammond & Oakes, 2019). The residents apprentice alongside an expert teacher in one of these teaching schools for a full academic year. They take closely linked coursework from a partnering university that leads to a credential and a master's degree at the end of the residency year. They receive living stipends and tuition support as they learn to teach, plus two years of early career mentoring after they start teaching. In exchange, they commit to teach in the district for three to five years beyond the residency. This model fosters tight partnerships between local school districts and teacher preparation programs. Residencies recruit teachers to meet district needs—usually in shortage fields. Then they rigorously prepare them and keep them in the district.

Initial research suggests that these programs produce a strong pool of diverse, effective teachers. Nationally, about twice as many candidates in teacher residency programs are teachers of color as in the entering teaching force generally, and in many programs they are a majority of candidates (Guha, Hyler, & Darling-Hammond, 2016).

Learning Supports for Generative Teaching

Once educators enter the workforce, the cultures and professional communities they encounter and create in schools influence both how they teach and how they receive, implement, and redefine policy (Coburn & Stein, 2006). Such cultures and communities are an inescapable feature of life in schools, and arise organically as well as by administrative contrivance. As recent research has illustrated, the possibilities for teacher learning and school effectiveness increase greatly as professional communities move from individualistic or "balkanized" cultures to "collaborative" cultures, and ultimately to what can be described as "learning communities" (Hord & Sommers, 2008; Kraft & Papay, 2014)

Teachers who are part of productive professional learning communities—within and beyond their schools—can continually develop their skills and work on the many problems of practice they confront in their work. Teaching teams and networks can create professional communities in which teachers observe one another, share practices, develop curriculum plans together, and solve problems collectively. It is important that the framework for these efforts does not frame students as the problem, but enables teachers to more deeply understand their students and learn new approaches they can try and refine with their colleagues.

Productive educational opportunities for adults build on what we know about adult learning: they connect to learners' goals and provide them with new experiences that encompass problem-solving in real-life contexts. Highly impactful or "transformational" adult learning that dramatically changes how individuals see the world and act within it takes place when earlier experiences or views are seen in a different light with new meaning (Mezirow, 1991). Perspective transformation—the mechanism by which transformation occurs—is the process by which one's perspective of oneself and the world shifts with greater understanding of the perspectives of others. It occurs when learners are faced with a dilemma which cannot be solved without looking at an issue through the eyes of someone else.

In educator development, for example, it is crucial that participants understand the perspectives and experiences of their students, as well as the impacts of those experiences, on their development and learning (Cantor, Osher, Berg, Steyer, & Rose, 2018). In professional communities, this is sometimes accomplished through family outreach and community study as well as community-embedded internships and other experiences, shared planning for classroom meetings and discussions that leave room for students to share their experiences and views, use of authentic assessments that allow for students' reflections and insights, case studies and two-way pedagogical practices that involve observing and interviewing children and parents, and child reviews conducted by teaching teams to share their knowledge of children with each other to develop more effective strategies.

Professional communities that work on curriculum development and implementation with feedback, reflection, and coaching can support deeper learning in content areas. A review of the research on teacher development programs that produce changes in teachers' practices and student outcomes found that the programs: incorporate active learning, directly engaging teachers in analyzing practice, as well as designing and trying out teaching strategies; support collaboration, typically in job-embedded contexts, creating space for teachers to share ideas, learn together, and create communities that positively change the culture and instruction of their entire grade level, department, school, and/or district; use models and modeling of effective practice; provide coaching and expert support involving the one-on-one sharing of expertise; offer opportunities for feedback and reflection, such as built-in time for teachers to intentionally think about, receive input on, and make changes to their practice by facilitating reflection and soliciting feedback that can be put into action (Darling-Hammond, Hyler, & Gardner, 2017).

To support generative teaching, teachers' own social-emotional competence should be part of an ongoing learning agenda. Consistent with the biological evidence that relationships impact brain development and learning, increasing evidence points to the importance of teachers' social-emotional wellness for students' success (Jennings & Greenberg, 2009; Meiklejohn et al., 2012). Creating an environment in which all students are respected, nurtured, and safe depends not only on teachers' classroom management skills but also on their social-emotional skills (Jones, Bouffard, & Weissbourd, 2013). Furthermore, teachers' roles in cultivating students' social-emotional skills is accomplished through modeling of those skills, as well as direct instruction and the creation of strong teacher-student relationships (Hamre & Pianta, 2001).

In order to support the development of social and emotional skills in children, teachers themselves need to learn and embody the social and emotional skills for managing adversity, directing energy in productive ways, and the ability to interact positively with others. This includes (a) the skill for cultivating empathy and caring for all their students, particularly for recognizing and supporting students that have experienced trauma; (b) the skills for affirming students' identities and academic progress in ways that support both student self-confidence and -competence; and (c) the interpersonal skills to address students' needs to the extent possible within the classroom and to build with care and discretion on outside-of-classroom resources that may also be needed (Darling-Hammond et al., 2019).

These skills can be cultivated by learning how to take a strengths-based approach that recognizes how students' feelings and experiences can cause them to behave and that illustrates how teachers can maintain good relationships even in the face of conflict. Research has demonstrated how this framework can lead to reduced levels of implicit bias, lower levels of punitive discipline, and greater respect from students (Okonofua, Paunesku, & Walton, 2016).

Learning strategies to develop an understanding of commonalities teachers and students share has also been shown to improve teachers' relationships with historically underserved Black and Latino students, sharply reducing the achievement gap (Gehlbach et al., 2016). There are many practices communities of teachers can deploy that enable them both to learn about and develop commonalities that strengthen relationships fundamental to teaching.

Policy for Ongoing Educator Learning

States and districts can organize and fund professional learning that supports professional learning communities and reflects the features of effective programs which enable marked improvement in school functioning, teachers' skills, and students' outcomes. Policies need to attend not only to funding for professional development costs and educator time that is regularly available and job-embedded, but also to the design of professional learning opportunities, which can be shaped through the criteria used to fund programs as well as the preparation of mentors and coaches who support professional learning.

A study of four states with exceptionally strong professional development found that they shared some common strategies, including developing professional development standards to guide re-licensing and professional development offerings; establishing district and school committees to oversee professional development at the local level; establishing means to monitor professional development quality; requiring mentoring or induction programs for beginning teachers; and leveraging collegial strategies involving staff collaboration as a means for professional learning, often in the form of professional learning communities. All four states sought to move professional development from the individual "sit and get" model to a more collective model embedded in the work teachers do with their students and with one another (Jaquith, Mindich, Wei, & Darling-Hammond, 2010). These findings also point to the importance of administrator training that enables principals to create such collegial, supportive school environments, which reduce teacher stress, support teacher engagement and ongoing learning, and improve teacher effectiveness (Kraft & Papay, 2014).

Designing Environments That Support Learning and Development

Children learn best when they can connect what happens in school to their cultural contexts and experiences, when their teachers are responsive to their strengths and needs, and when their environment is "identity safe," (Steele & Vargas, 2013), reinforcing their value and belonging. Students need a sense of physical and psychological safety for learning to occur because fear and anxiety undermine cognitive capacity and short-circuit the learning process.

This is especially important given the societal and school-based aggressions many children, especially those living under adverse conditions, experience. For all these reasons, and because children develop through individual trajectories shaped by their unique traits and experiences, teachers need to know them well to create productive learning opportunities.

Warm, caring, supportive student-teacher relationships, along with strong school and family relationships, are linked to better school performance and engagement, greater social competence, and willingness to take on challenges (Osher et al., 2018). Students who are at higher levels of risk for poor outcomes can benefit especially from nurturing relationships with teachers and other adults, which can increase student learning and support their development and wellness, especially when these relationships are culturally sensitive and responsive (Hammond, 2016). Such relationships help develop the emotional, social, behavioral, and cognitive competencies foundational to learning.

Designing Schools That Support Strong Attachments and Relationships

Developing these relationships can be difficult in schools where organizational structures minimize opportunities for personalized relationships that extend over time, as is often the case in schools designed a century ago for efficient batch processing of masses of students (Tyack, 1974). Unlike schools in many countries, where teachers often stay with their students for two or three years (what in the U.S. is referred to as "looping"), U.S. schools adopted the Prussian age grading model that typically moves students to another teacher each year and to as many as seven or eight teachers daily in secondary schools. Secondary teachers may see 150 to 200 students per day in short 45-minute blocks, and, despite their best efforts, are unable to know all of their students or their families well. This reduces the extent to which teachers can build on personal knowledge in meeting students' needs. Counselors are assigned to attend to the personal needs of hundreds of students, also an unmanageable task, and students who experience adversity may have no one to turn to for support (Eccles & Roeser, 2009).

Ecological changes that create personalized environments with opportunities for stronger relationships among adults and students can create more productive contexts for learning. For example, small schools or small learning communities with personalizing structures—such as advisory systems in which advisors work with a small group of students over multiple years, teaching teams that share students, or looping with the same teachers over two years or more—have been found to improve student achievement, attachment, attendance, attitudes toward school, behavior, motivation, and graduation rates (Bloom & Unterman, 2014; Darling-Hammond, Ross, & Milliken, 2006; Felner, Seitsinger, Brand, Burns, & Bolton, 2007). Similarly, schools that keep students together for longer numbers of years (e.g., K–8 or 6-12 structures) have been found to produce stronger achievement and student confidence than those that require students to change schools and disrupt their community more frequently (Schwerdt & West, 2013).

These strategies allow educators to create a community within the school where caring is a product of individuals knowing each other in multiple ways. Teachers in such personalized settings report a heightened sense of efficacy, while parents report feeling more comfortable reaching out to the school for assistance (Felner, Seitsinger, Brand, Burns, & Bolton, 2007).

Part of this rethinking should be the creation of schedules that provide time for teachers to regularly meet together for planning and collaboration around curriculum and students. The factory model school design also leaves U.S. teachers with more teaching time and less planning time than nearly all other countries in the world (OECD, 2013). Schools that have reorganized themselves to recapture this time have shifted the composition of their staff, program design, and uses of time to do so (Noguera, Darling-Hammond, & Friedlaender, 2017).

Policies for Redesigning Schools

To create more productive school designs, policies can reframe regulations and adjust financial incentives in order to:

- design and build smaller schools and buildings that host smaller learning communities;
- eliminate state and district rules that have accrued over time which hold the factory model in place in terms of how time is used, adult roles are configured, and adult-student relationships are structured;
- create opportunities and incentives, including funding and technical assistance, to encourage educators to design new schools that include personalizing features, as well as time for professional collaboration among adults, as New York City did in the 1990s with much improved outcomes for students (Darling-Hammond, Ancess, & Ort, 2002; Unterman & Haider, 2019).

- train school leaders about why and how school designs can be constructed to support more in-depth learning and relationships for students and teachers, and train teachers to work productively as advisors and team members within these new designs.

Structures are important to set the stage for the kinds of coherent, consistent, continuous relationships children need to support their development, but the nature of those relationships and the resulting educational experiences are not a given. They depend on: the attitudes, skills, and capacity of staff; the school climate, including norms for interactions; and the practices and procedures that are adopted for instruction, classroom management, school discipline, and more.

Policies for Designing Schools That are Identity Safe and Culturally Competent

It is well-known that teachers influence student learning in part through their beliefs and the feedback they provide to their students. Their perceptions of students shape expectations that often predict student achievement apart from prior ability (Dweck, 2000; Ladson-Billings, 1995; 2009). Unfortunately, many teachers attribute inaccurate characterizations of academic ability and behavior to students based on race and ethnicity (Irvine, 2003). On average, White teachers have lower expectations of Black and Latino/a students and interact with them less positively than White students (Gershenson, Holt, & Papageorge, 2016; Tenenbaum & Ruck, 2007), and they are more likely to label Black students as "troublemakers," punishing them more harshly than White students for the same offenses (Okonofua & Eberhardt, 2015). While the vast majority of teachers enter the profession with a passion for fostering children's learning, growth, and development, implicit bias can nonetheless color how they interact with their students.

While this issue is often discussed in terms of the beliefs and behaviors of individual teachers, schools foster or impede these behaviors to the extent that they group or track students in ways that convey messages about perceived ability, deliver stereotypic messages associated with group status, or engage in punitive and discriminatory discipline practices, which are widespread in American schools (Skiba et al., 2012). Thus, schools need to be designed to support culturally competent practices that result in greater equity and achievement for students.

Teachers and school leaders need to understand how school policies as well as staff attitudes shape students' views of their own capacity and what students ultimately learn. Students who have received societal or school-delivered messages that they are less capable as a function of race, ethnicity, language background, gender, economic status, learning differences, or other status will often translate those views into self-perceptions of ability. These social identity threats induce a form of toxic stress that triggers reduction in working memory and focus, leading to impaired performance (Schmader & Johns, 2003).

Schools can exacerbate or reduce social identity threats by the ways in which their policies and practices send implicit and explicit messages that communicate how students are valued and viewed. Studies of many schools that show dramatic improvements in achievement and attainment for students of color point out that they consciously communicate value for all students by equalizing access to high-status knowledge by reducing or eliminating tracking, offering a range of readily available supports for achievement, adopting grading policies that support a growth mindset by encouraging ongoing revision of work, and adopting restorative disciplinary practices, as described further below (Hamedani, Zheng, Darling-Hammond, Andree, & Quinn, 2015; Noguera, Darling-Hammond, & Friedlaender, 2015).

Policies for Designing Schools for Inclusion rather than Exclusion

A key area for policy leverage is reducing rates of student suspension and expulsion, and the overuse of these exclusionary tools with students of color, which typically begins a process of successive

Culture, Learning, and Policy

failures for students and dramatically increase the likelihood of dropping out (Raffaele Mendez, 2003). Both because of implicit bias and cultural misunderstandings, students of color and those with disabilities are disproportionately suspended for the same behaviors their White and nondisabled peers engage in (U.S. Department of Education Office for Civil Rights, 2016). When students are regularly removed from the classroom, they fall behind in their classwork and they experience a social and emotional distancing and disengagement from school (Hirschfield, 2008; Skiba et al., 2003). The more time students spend out of the classroom, the more their sense of connection to the school wanes, along with their ability to succeed academically (Hemphill, Toumbourou, Herrenkohl, McMorris, & Catalano, 2006). This distance promotes disengaged behaviors, such as chronic absenteeism and antisocial behavior (Hemphill et al., 2006), which in turn contributes to the widening achievement and opportunity gap.

Policies that can disrupt these patterns include those that incentivize interventions such as replacing zero-tolerance strategies with more effective strategies, such as social-emotional learning programs and restorative practices which educate both students and educators in how to recognize and manage their emotions and behaviors and give them tools for interpersonal interactions, problem solving, and conflict resolution. Research has found that in-service training that improves classroom environments, such as that associated with social-emotional learning programs, promotes greater teacher efficacy, more positive attitudes toward teaching, and teaching practices that are supportive of students (see, e.g., Rimm-Kaufman & Sawyer, 2004), as well as positive academic and behavioral outcomes for students (Brock et al., 2008).

Recognizing the need to reduce the use of exclusionary disciplinary practices and to improve student engagement, 29 states not only fund these trainings, they are also including a measure of suspension and/or expulsion in their statewide accountability and improvement systems (Kostyo, Cardichon, & Darling-Hammond, 2018). When these measures are used as school quality and student support (SQSS) indicators under ESSA, they must be disaggregated by race and other student characteristics. Research indicates that tracking suspension and expulsion data by student groups can help highlight racially disparate practices and promote positive behavioral interventions that can improve student engagement and academic success (Skiba et al., 2012).

Policy for Developing and Assessing Positive Learning Environments

Policies are increasingly focused on improving school environments. Under the Every Student Succeeds Act (ESSA, 2015), local educational agency plans must be designed to "strengthen academic programs and improve school conditions for student learning." ESSA's requirement that states adopt an accountability indicator of "school quality or student success" opens the door to measures of school quality that reveal students' experiences and opportunities to learn.

Under ESSA, eight states are using school surveys to measure school climate as one of their indicators of school quality, and 12 more states will make school climate data available so that schools can evaluate how they are doing and work to strengthen their supports for students. Sixteen additional states are working to improve school climate in schools identified for support and improvement or as part of a broader statewide effort. Eleven states explicitly mention providing resources and support to schools to improve students' social and emotional learning (Kostyo, Cardichon, & Darling-Hammond, 2018). In addition to sponsoring surveys, states and districts can also support educators in using measures of school climate to improve school environments by providing time and training to use data from surveys and other sources to inform school improvement initiatives and the use of professional development resources.

For example, Maryland is using school climate surveys of students and educators as an accountability indicator, evaluating safety, engagement, and environment. To respond to the data provided by school climate and other indicators, the Maryland Department of Education will develop and implement a multi-tiered system of support that will include partnerships between schools and community members to further sustainable conflict resolution programs, reduce and eliminate disproportionality in discipline, provide a Youth Mental Health First Aid curriculum for staff, and implement wraparound services for students dealing with substance abuse and other issues. Ultimately, this work should shape every aspect of school design to support an inclusive and positive climate (National Center on Safe and Supportive Learning Environments, n.d.).

A System of Supports for Students

Effective school environments take a systematic approach to promoting children's development in all facets of the school and its connections to the community. Science has found that stress is a normal part of healthy development, but excessive stress in any context—at home, at school, or in other aspects of the community—can undermine learning and development and have profound effects on children's well-being. Well-designed supports, including specific programs and interventions that buffer children against excessive stress, can enable resilience and success even for children who have faced serious adversity and trauma.

A key aspect of creating a supportive environment is a shared developmental framework among all of the adults in the school, coupled with procedures for ensuring that students receive additional help for social, emotional, or academic needs when they need them, without costly and elaborate labeling procedures standing in the way. Many schools are adopting multi-tiered systems of support (MTSS) to accomplish this (Adelman & Taylor, 2008; Osher et al., 2016). The first tier, for all students, uses teaching strategies grounded in universal designs for learning that are broadly successful with children who come to school with different experiences and prior knowledge, including social-emotional learning and positive behavioral support strategies that are culturally and linguistically competent.

Tier 2 services and supports address the needs of students who are at some elevated level of risk or who need some additional support in particular areas. The risk may be demonstrated by behavior (e.g., number of absences) or be due to having experienced a known risk factor (e.g., the loss of a parent.). These services may include academic supports, such as tutoring, or family outreach, counseling, or behavioral supports. Schools may operate counseling groups to support students who have experienced loss or violence, who are managing traumatic events, or who need mental health supports. They may use social workers to help students—and sometimes their families—access supports and services. Tier 3 services, such as one-on-one mental health supports and effective special education, involve intensive interventions for students who are at particularly high levels of risk or whose needs have not been met by tier 2 strategies.

Often these services are provided through integrated student support (ISS) programs which aim to remove barriers to school success by connecting students and families to service providers in the community, or bringing those services into the school. A synthesis of well-controlled studies of ISS models found significant positive effects on student progress in school, attendance, mathematics and reading achievement, grades, and graduation rates (Gravel, Opatrny, & Shapiro, 2007).

Providers should recognize that students have strengths in many areas, building upon student assets, and services should be implemented in a child- and family driven manner that is culturally competent. This can maximize engagement and minimize errors that occur when students, families, or teachers are not asked about their context and needs. These supports often benefit from collaboration with local service agencies and community-based organizations with communication feedback loops to school-based staff. Key is that a whole child approach is taken; students are dealt with in connected rather than fragmented ways, and care is personalized to the needs of individuals (Darling-Hammond, Flook, Cook-Harvey, Barron, & Osher, 2019).

Helping staff and parents better understand child development is critical so that they can use information about children in productive ways to foster their deeper attachment and growth. When staff and parents work together from a developmentally informed framework, substantial improvements occur for children. The School Development Program (SDP), launched by James Comer in 1969, is an example of this approach (Comer, 2004; Darling-Hammond, Cook-Harvey, Flook, Gardner, & Melnick, 2018). Building a shared school culture to address six developmental pathways—social-interactive, psycho-emotional, ethical, cognitive, linguistic, and physical—the program establishes collaborative working relationships among principals, parents, teachers, community leaders, superintendents, and health care workers, teaching them about child development and grounding collective action in a shared developmental framework for multi-tiered supports. Research on the SDP shows that it helps reduce absenteeism and suspension, improves school climate and relationships among students and teachers, increases student self-competence and self-concept, and strengthens achievement (Borman, Hewes, Overman, & Brown, 2002; Cook, Murphy, & Hunt, 2000; Darling-Hammond, Cook-Harvey et al., 2019).

Policy for Student Supports

In order to provide a multi-tiered system of student supports, states need to ensure that there is an adequate supply of qualified teachers for all districts, including learning specialists, who are well-prepared to teach diverse students. They must also ensure an adequate supply of counselors and social workers to provide intensive supports where they are needed. States and districts must provide high-quality training for all staff in diagnostic and responsive approaches if multi-tiered strategies are to work. This includes resources that underwrite candidates to acquire this training— a particularly important element of developing a diverse, well-prepared workforce.

In addition, states and local communities need to make it possible for schools and community-based health, mental health, and social service organizations to work productively together. In addition to adequately funding these services, this requires coordinating and aligning services and funding streams, as well as streamlining eligibility for children and families, so that schools can help ensure that students are served as needed.

This integration of education and supports can also be accomplished by creating community schools, which integrate health and social services into the school itself. Community schools represent a place-based strategy in which "schools partner with community agencies and resources to provide an integrated focus on academics, health and social services, youth and community development, and community engagement." (Coalition for Community Schools, n.d.). Many operate year-round, from morning to evening, and serve both children and adults. They typically offer integrated student supports, expanded learning time and opportunities, family and community engagement, and collaborative leadership and practices. A recent review of research on such initiatives concluded that well-implemented community schools improve student and school outcomes ranging from achievement scores and grades to behavior and graduation rates (Oakes, Maier, & Daniel, 2017). The research meets the ESSA standard that qualifies community schools as an "evidence-based" intervention, so that federal Title I funds can be spent to enact this approach in low-performing schools.

In New York, this kind of investment is quite direct. A community schools set-aside in the Foundation Aid portion of the state budget provides formula funding to high-need school districts for creating and operating community schools. In 2017–18, the state set aside $150 million for 233 school districts that were identified as high-need, with an additional allocation for schools with extraordinarily high levels of student need. These kinds of policies are fundamental to ensuring that all students can come to school ready and able to learn each day.

Designing Systems for Learning and Equity

All of these strategies in support of learning require financial and human resources, yet U.S. schools are among the most inequitably funded in the industrialized world. The wealthiest states spend about three times what the poorer states spend (Baker, Farrie, Johnson, Luhm, & Sciarra, 2018), and in many states, the wealthiest districts spend two to three times what the poorest districts can spend per pupil (Adamson & Darling-Hammond, 2012). Furthermore, the high child poverty rate in the United States—one in four children live in poverty—means that more children experience food and housing insecurity, lack of health care, and other adverse conditions.

These challenges require schools to provide more services, which in turn requires greater school funding. However, as of 2015, the most recent year for which data are available, only 12 states had progressive funding distributions that provide at least 5% more funding to districts in which student poverty is high as compared to districts in which there is little or no poverty. And of these, only five states—Delaware, Massachusetts, Minnesota, New Jersey, and Wyoming—also funded education at a level of adequacy that enables students to receive the resources they need (Baker et al., 2018).

Adequate and equitable funding is needed to ensure all students have opportunities to learn from highly qualified teachers and school leaders in well-resourced schools. Many studies have found that in states that have achieved both equity and adequacy, student achievement and attainment are substantially higher, especially for those historically underserved (Baker, 2017). One national study found that children from low-income families in states that spent 20% more on them over the 12 years of school experienced graduation rates 23 percentage points higher than similar children without this benefit. The benefits carried on in later life: household income for these students as adults increased by 52%, and the gap in adult poverty rates between them and their more affluent peers was eliminated (Jackson, Johnson, & Persico, 2015).

Furthermore, it is critically important to reverse the growing segregation of African American and Latino/a students in high-poverty schools, which are also generally under-resourced. A large body of research on the impact of school racial and socioeconomic composition on academic outcomes shows that racially segregated, high-poverty schools have a strong negative association with students' academic achievement. A summary of research filed by 550 scholars as an amicus brief in the Seattle case which challenged desegregation efforts concluded:

> …[M]ore often than not, segregated minority schools offer profoundly unequal educational opportunities. This inequality is manifested in many ways, including fewer qualified, experienced teachers, greater instability caused by rapid turnover of faculty, fewer educational resources, and limited exposure to peers who can positively influence academic learning
>
> *(Parents Involved in Community Schools v. Seattle School District No. 1, 2007).*

Meanwhile, substantial evidence demonstrates academic, cognitive, and social benefits for students attending racially and socioeconomically integrated schools (Potter, Quick, & Davies, 2016; Wells, Cox, & Cordova-Cobo, 2016; George & Darling-Hammond, 2019). In a study of the effects of court-ordered desegregation on students born between 1945 and 1970, economist Rucker Johnson (2019) found that graduation rates climbed by 2 percentage points for every year a Black student attended an integrated school. A Black student exposed to court-ordered desegregation for 5 years experienced a 15% increase in wages and an 11 percentage point decline in annual poverty rates, while there was no decline in outcomes for Whites. The difference is tied to the fact that schools under court supervision benefited from higher per-pupil spending and smaller student-teacher ratios, among other resources.

Studies also show that, beyond student achievement, integrated education contributes to: improving critical thinking skills; improving educational attainment; promoting tolerance; developing cross-cultural understanding; eliminating bias and prejudice; and promoting civic participation in a diverse global economy (Eaton, 2011a; Eaton, 2011b). These advantages can, if educationally

Culture, Learning, and Policy

supported in the ways described in this Handbook, support the creation of a more culturally responsive and supportive society as well as more educative schools.

Policy for Providing Adequately Resourced Education in Diverse School Settings

There is much that federal and state governments can do to make a difference in achieving greater equity and adequacy in school funding, and to reduce segregation by race and income. The federal government can:

- require states that receive federal funds to report not only on student achievement progress but also the state's movement toward adequacy and equitable access to education resources—for example, the availability of well-qualified teachers, strong curriculum opportunities, books, materials, and equipment (such as science labs and computers), and adequate facilities—as well as a plan for further progress;
- enforce the rules in the Every Student Succeeds Act that require a balance of qualified and experienced teachers across schools serving more- and less-advantaged students;
- re-establish federal grant programs that support voluntary state and local efforts to create more diverse schools by, for example, revising school boundaries, expanding innovative programs to attract diverse students from outside a local area, supporting magnet schools, and hiring and training diverse educators.

Meanwhile, states can:

- redesign school finance plans to focus on funding on pupil needs, for example, through weighted student formulas that add additional funds for pupil characteristics such as poverty, limited English proficiency, foster care or homeless status, and special education status;
- ensure high-quality preschool for children who may have fewer learning opportunities or greater learning needs before they enter school—for example, children from low-income families, new English learners, and children with disabilities. This closes much of the gap that would otherwise be present at entry to kindergarten and reduces the need for costly supports such as special education services;
- enable districts to hire and keep well-prepared educators in under-resourced schools through stronger educator preparation, induction and mentoring for novices, and ongoing professional learning, as well as comparable salaries and working conditions;
- act to equalize and improve the opportunity indicators required by ESSA—including equity in school funding and teacher qualifications, as well as the degree of student integration in schools and classrooms by race, ethnicity, language, and disability status, developing settings in which equity is enacted through inclusion as well as the provision of resources.

Summary of Policy Implications

This growing knowledge and practice base suggests that, in order to create schools that support healthy development for young people, policymakers and educators should, at minimum:

1. focus accountability, guidance, and investments on developmental supports for young people, including a positive, culturally responsive school climate and supportive instruction and services;
2. design schools to provide settings for healthy development, including secure relationships, coherent, well-designed teaching for 21st century skills, and services that meet the needs of the whole child;

3. provide educators with the knowledge and skills to enable them to work effectively to offer successful instruction to diverse students from a wide range of contexts.

1. Focus the System on Developmental Supports for Young People

States guide the focus of schools and professionals through the ways in which accountability systems are established, guidance is offered, and funding is provided. To ensure developmentally healthy school environments, states, districts, and schools can:

- provide **adequate and equitable school funding** based on pupil needs, to support a well-prepared and supported professional staff, programmatic and curriculum resources, and integrated student supports to ensure all children have what they need to learn effectively;
- incorporate educator competencies regarding knowledge of culturally responsive and culturally competent practices, support for students' social, emotional, and cognitive development, and support for restorative practices, into **licensing and accreditation requirements** for teachers and administrators, as well as counseling staff;
- include measures of school climate, social-emotional supports, and school exclusions in **accountability and improvement systems**, so that these are a focus of schools' attention, and data are regularly available to guide continuous improvement;
- adopt **standards** or other guidance for social, emotional, and cognitive learning that clarifies the kinds of competencies students should be helped to develop and the kinds of practices that can help them accomplish these goals;
- replace zero-tolerance policies regarding school discipline with **discipline policies** focused on explicit teaching of social-emotional strategies and restorative discipline practices that support young people in learning key skills and developing responsibility for themselves and their community;
- provide **funding** for school climate surveys, social-emotional learning and restorative justice programs, and revamped licensing practices (including appropriate assessments) to support these reforms. As suggested below, additional investments are needed for multitiered systems of support, integrated student services, extended learning, and professional learning for educators to enable progress within schools.

2. Design Schools to Provide Settings for Healthy Development

Within a productive policy environment, schools can do more to provide the right kinds of supports for students if they are also designed to foster strong relationships and provide a holistic approach to student supports and family engagement. To provide settings for healthy development, educators and policymakers can:

- design schools for **strong, personalized relationships** so that students can be well-known and supported, by creating small schools or learning communities within schools, looping teachers with students for more than one year, creating advisory systems, supporting teaching teams, and organizing schools with longer grade spans—all of which have been found to strengthen relationships and improve student attendance, achievement, and attainment;
- develop schoolwide norms and supports for **safe, culturally responsive classroom communities** that provide students with a sense of physical and psychological safety, affirmation, and belonging, as well as opportunities to learn social, emotional, and cognitive skills;
- ensure **integrated student supports** are available to promote students' health, mental health, and social welfare through community school models or community partnerships, coupled with parent engagement and restorative justice programs;
- create **multitiered systems of support (MTSS)**, beginning with universal designs for learning and personalized teaching and continuing through more intensive academic and

non-academic supports, to ensure that students can receive the right kind of assistance when needed, without labeling or delays;

- provide **extended learning time** to ensure that students do not fall behind, including skillful tutoring and academic supports, such as Reading Recovery, and additional support for homework, mentoring, and enrichment;
- design **outreach to families** as part of the core approach to education, including home visits and flexibly scheduled student-teacher-parent conferences to learn from parents about their children; outreach to involve families in school activities; and regular communication through positive phone calls home, emails, and text messages;

3. Ensure Educator Learning for Developmentally Supportive Education

Educators need opportunities to learn how to redesign schools and develop practices that support a positive school climate and healthy, whole child development. To accomplish this critical task, the state, counties, districts, schools, and educator preparation programs can:

- design **pre-service preparation programs** for both teachers and administrators that provide: a strong foundation in child and adolescent development and learning; knowledge of how to create engaging, effective instruction that is culturally responsive; skills for implementing social-emotional learning and restorative justice programs; and an understanding of how to work with families and community organizations to create a shared developmentally supportive approach. These should provide supervised clinical experiences in schools that are good models of developmentally supportive practices that create a positive school climate for all students. Administrator preparation programs should help leaders learn how to design and foster such school environments;
- offer widely available **in-service development** that helps educators: continually build on and refine student-centered practices; learn to use data about school climate and a wide range of student outcomes to undertake continuous improvement; problem solve around the needs of individual children and engage in schoolwide initiatives in collegial teams and professional learning communities; and learn from other schools through networks, site visits, and documentation of successes;
- invest in educator **recruitment and retention**, including forgivable loans and service scholarships that support strong preparation, high-retention pathways into the profession—such as residencies—that diversify the educator workforce, high-quality mentoring for beginners, and collegial environments for practice. A strong, stable, diverse, well-prepared teaching and leadership workforce is perhaps the most important ingredient for a positive school climate that supports effective whole child education;
- invest in **educator wellness** through strong preparation and mentoring that improve efficacy and reduce stress, mindfulness and stress management training, and social-emotional learning programs that benefit both adults and children.

The emerging sciences of learning and development make it clear that a culturally grounded, whole child approach to education, which begins with a positive school climate that affirms and supports all students, is essential to support academic achievement as well as healthy development. Research and the wisdom of practice offer significant insights for policymakers and educators about how to develop such environments. The challenge ahead is to assemble the whole village—schools, health care organizations, youth and family serving agencies, state and local governments, philanthropists, and families—to work together to ensure that every young person receives the benefit of what is known about how to support his or her healthy path to a productive future.

References

Adamson, F., & Darling-Hammond, L. (2012). Funding disparities and the inequitable distribution of teachers: Evaluating sources and solutions. *Education Policy Analysis Archives, 20,* 37.

Adelman, H. S., & Taylor, L. (2008). School-wide approaches to addressing barriers to learning and teaching. In B. Doll & J. Cummings (Eds.), *Transforming School Mental Health Services: Population-Based Approaches to Promoting the Competency and Wellness of Children* (pp. 277–306). Thousand Oaks, CA: Corwin Press.

Baker, B. D. (2017). *How Money Matters for Schools.* Palo Alto, CA: Learning Policy Institute.

Baker, B., Farrie, D., Johnson, M., Luhm, T., & Sciarra, D. G. (2018). *Is School Funding Fair? A National Report Card* (7th edition). Newark, NJ: Education Law Center.

Bloom, H. S., & Unterman, R. (2014). Can small high schools of choice improve educational prospects for disadvantaged students? *Journal of Policy Analysis and Management, 33*(2), 290–319.

Borman, G. D., Hewes, G. M., Overman, L. T., & Brown, S. (2002). *Comprehensive School Reform and Student Achievement: A Meta-Analysis (No. 59).* Baltimore, MD: Center for Research on the Education of Students Placed at Risk (CRESPAR).

Brock, L. L., Nishida, K. K., Chiong, C., Grimm, K. J., & Rimm-Kaufman, S. E. (2008). Children's perceptions of the social environment and social and academic performance: A longitudinal analysis of the *Responsive Classroom* approach. *Journal of School Psychology, 46,* 129–149.

Cantor, P., Osher, D., Berg, J., Steyer, L., & Rose, T. (2018). Malleability, plasticity, and individuality: How children learn and develop in context. *Applied Developmental Science.* doi: 10.1080/10888691.2017.1398649

Carter, P., & Darling-Hammond, L. (2016). Teaching diverse learners. In D. H. Gitomer & C. Bell (Eds.), *Handbook of Research on Teaching, 5th Edition* (pp. 593–638). Washington, DC: American Educational Research Association.

Carver-Thomas, D. (2018). *Diversifying the Teaching Profession: How to Recruit and Retain Teachers of Color.* Palo Alto, CA: Learning Policy Institute.

Chung, R. R. (2008). Beyond assessment: Performance assessments in teacher education. *Teacher Education Quarterly, 35*(1), 7–28.

Coalition for Community Schools. (n.d.). *What Is a Community School?* Retrieved from http://www.communityschools.org/aboutschools/what_is_a_community_school.aspx

Coburn, C. E., & Stein, M. K. (2006). Communities of practice theory and the role of teacher professional community in policy implementation. In M. I. Honig (Ed.), *New Directions in Education Policy Implementation: Confronting Complexity* (pp. 25–46). Albany, NY: State University of New York Press.

Comer, J. P. (2004). *Leave No Child Behind: Preparing Today's Youth for Tomorrow's World.* New Haven, CT: Yale University Press.

Cook, T. D., Murphy, R. F., & Hunt, H. D. (2000). Comer's school development program in Chicago: A theory-based evaluation. *American Educational Research Journal, 37*(2), 535–597.

Darling-Hammond, L. (2010). *Evaluating Teacher Effectiveness: How Teacher Performance Assessments Can Measure and Improve Teaching.* Washington, DC: Center for American Progress.

Darling-Hammond, L., Ancess, J., & Ort, S. W. (2002). Reinventing high school: Outcomes of the coalition campus schools project. *American Education Research Journal, 39*(3) 639–673.

Darling-Hammond, L., & Bransford, J. (Eds.) (2005). *Preparing Teachers for a Changing World: What Teachers Should Learn and Be Able to Do.* San Francisco, CA: Jossey-Bass.

Darling-Hammond, L., Burns, D., Campbell, C., Goodwin, A. L., Hammerness, K., Low, E-L., McIntyre, A., Sato, M., & Zeichner, K. (2017). *Empowered Educators: How High-Performing Systems Shape Teaching Quality Around the World.* San Francisco, CA: Jossey-Bass.

Darling-Hammond, L., Cook-Harvey, C., Flook, L., Gardner, M., & Melnick, H. (2018). *With the Whole Child in Mind: Insights from the Comer School Development Program.* Alexandria, VA: ASCD.

Darling-Hammond, L., Flook, L., Cook-Harvey, C., Barron, B., & Osher, D. (2019). Implications for educational practice of the science of learning and development. *Applied Developmental Science, 1*–45.

Darling-Hammond, L., Hyler, M. E., & Gardner, M. (2017). *Effective Teacher Professional Development.* Palo Alto, CA: Learning Policy Institute.

Darling-Hammond, L., Meyerson, D., LaPointe, M., & Orr, M. T. (2009). *Preparing Principals for a Changing World: Lessons From Effective School Leadership Programs.* San Francisco, CA: Jossey-Bass.

Darling-Hammond, L., Oakes, J., Wojcikiewicz, S. K., Hyler, M. E., Guha, R., Podolsky, A., Kini, T., Cook-Harvey, C. M., Jackson Mercer, C. N., & Harrell, A. (2019). *Preparing Teachers for Deeper Learning.* Cambridge, MA: Harvard Education Press.

Darling-Hammond, L., Ross, P., & Milliken, M. (2006). High school size, organization, and content: What matters for student success? *Brookings Papers on Education Policy, 2006/2007*(9), 163–203.

Dee, T. (2004). Teachers, race and student achievement in a randomized experiment. *The Review of Economics and Statistics, 86*(1), 195–210, 15.

Dweck, C. S. (2000). *Self-Theories: Their Role in Motivation, Personality, and Development*. New York, NY: Psychology Press.

Eaton, S. (2011a). *School Racial and Economic Composition & Math and Science Achievement*. Washington, DC: National Coalition on School Diversity.

Eaton, S. (2011b). *How the Racial and Socioeconomic Composition of Schools and Classrooms Contributes to Literacy, Behavioral Climate, Instructional Organization, and High School Graduation Rates*. Washington, DC: National Coalition on School Diversity.

Eccles, J. S., & Roeser, R. W. (2009). Schools, academic motivation, and stage-environment fit. In R. M. Lerner & L. Steinberg (Eds.), *Handbook of Adolescent Psychology* (pp. 404–43). Hoboken, NJ: John Wiley & Sons.

Elmore, R., & Fuhrman, S. (1993). Opportunity to learn and the state role in education. In *The Debate on Opportunity-to-Learn Standards: Commissioned Papers*. Washington, D.C.: National Governors Association.

Every Student Succeeds Act, Pub. L. No. 114–95, § 1112(b)(1)(D), 129 Stat. 1802 (2015).

Felner, R. D., Seitsinger, A. M., Brand, S., Burns, A., & Bolton, N. (2007). Creating small learning communities: Lessons from the project on high-performing learning communities about "what works" in creating productive, developmentally enhancing, learning contexts. *Educational Psychologist, 42*(4), 209–221.

Flexner, A. (1910). *Medical Education in the United States and Canada: A Report to the Carnegie Foundation for the Advancement of Teaching*, Bulletin No. 4. New York: Carnegie Foundation for the Advancement of Teaching.

Gehlbach, H., Brinkworth, M. E., King, A. M., Hsu, L. M., McIntyre, J., & Rogers, T. (2016). Creating birds of similar feathers: Leveraging similarity to improve teacher–student relationships and academic achievement. *Journal of Educational Psychology, 108*(3), 342.

Gershenson, S., Hart, C. M. D., Lindsay, C. A., & Papageorge, N. W. (2017). *The Long-Run Impacts of Same-Race Teachers*. Bonn, Germany: IZA Institute of Labor Economics.

Gershenson, S., Holt, S. B., & Papageorge, N. W. (2016). Who believes in me? The effect of student–teacher demographic match on teacher expectations. *Economics of Education Review, 52*, 209–224.

George, J., & Darling-Hammond, L. (2019). *The Federal Role and School Integration*. Palo Alto, CA: Learning Policy Institute.

Goldhaber, D., Cowan, J., & Theobald, R. (2016). "Evaluating Prospective Teachers: Testing the Predictive Validity of the edTPA" (CALDER Working Paper No. 157).

Gravel, J., Opatrny, L., & Shapiro, S. (2007). The intention-to-treat approach in randomized controlled trials: Are authors saying what they do and doing what they say? *Clinical Trials, 4*(4), 350–356.

Guha, R., Hyler, M. E., & Darling-Hammond, L. (2016). *The Teacher Residency: An Innovative Model for Preparing Teachers*. Palo Alto, CA: Learning Policy Institute.

Hamre, B. K., & Pianta, R. C. (2001). Early teacher–child relationships and the trajectory of children's school outcomes through eighth grade. *Child Development, 72*(2), 625–638.

Hamedani, M. G., Zheng, X., Darling-Hammond, L., Andree, A., & Quinn, B. (2015). *Social Emotional Learning in High School: How Three Urban High Schools Engage, Educate, and Empower Youth*. Stanford, CA: Stanford Center for Opportunity Policy in Education.

Hammond, Z. (2016). *Culturally Responsive Teaching and the Brain: Promoting Authentic Engagement and Rigor Among Culturally and Linguistically Diverse Students*. Thousand Oaks, CA: Corwin Press.

Hemphill, S. A., Toumbourou, J. W., Herrenkohl, T. I., McMorris, B. J., & Catalano, R. F. (2006). The effect of school suspensions and arrests on subsequent adolescent antisocial behavior in Australia and the United States. *Journal of Adolescent Health, 39*(5), 736–744.

Henry, G. T., Bastian, K. C., & Smith, A. A. (2012). Scholarships to recruit the 'best and brightest' into teaching. *Educational Researcher, 41*(3), 83–92.

Hirschfield, P. J. (2008). Preparing for prison? The criminalization of school discipline in the USA. *Theoretical Criminology, 12*(1), 79–101.

Hord, S. M., & Sommers, W. A. (2008). *Leading Professional Learning Communities: Voices from Research and Practice*. Thousand Oaks, CA: Corwin.

Ingersoll, R., Merrill, L., & May, H. (2014). *What Are the Effects of Teacher Education and Preparation on Beginning Teacher Attrition?* (Consortium for Policy Research in Education, University of Pennsylvania, CPRE Report #RR-82.)

Irvine, J. (2003). *Educating Teachers for Diversity: Seeing With a Cultural Eye*. New York, NY: Teachers College Press.

Jackson, C. K., Johnson, R. C., & Persico, C. (2015). The effects of school spending on educational and economic outcomes. *Quarterly Journal of Economics, 131*(1), 157–218.

Jaquith, A., Mindich, D., Wei, R. C., & Darling-Hammond, L. (2010). *Teacher Professional Learning in the United States: Case Studies of State Policies and Strategies*. Stanford, CA: Stanford Center for Opportunity Policy in Education.

Jennings, P. A., & Greenberg, M. T. (2009). The prosocial classroom: Teacher social and emotional competence in relation to student and classroom outcomes. *Review of Educational Research, 79*(1), 491–525.

Jones, S. M., Bouffard, S. M., & Weissbourd, R. (2013). Educators' social and emotional skills vital to learning. *Phi Delta Kappan*, *94*(8), 62–65.

Kostyo, S., Cardichon, J., & Darling-Hammond, L. (2018). *Making ESSA's Equity Promise Real: State Strategies to Close the Opportunity Gap*. Palo Alto: Learning Policy Institute.

Kraft, M. A., & Papay, J. P. (2014). Can professional environments in schools promote teacher development? Explaining heterogeneity in returns to teaching experience. *Educational Effectiveness and Policy Analysis [Internet]*, *36*(4), 476–500.

Ladson-Billings, G. (1995). Multicultural teacher education: Research, practice, and policy. In J. A. Banks & C. M. Banks (Eds.), *Handbook of Research in Multicultural Education* (pp. 747–759). New York, NY: Macmillan.

Lampert, M. (2001). *Teaching Problems and the Problems of Teaching*. New Haven, CT: Yale University Press.

Lee, C. D. (2007). *Culture, Literacy, and Learning: Taking Bloom in the Midst of the Whirlwind*. New York, NY: Teachers College Press.

Lee, C. D. (2017). Integrating research on how people learn and learning across settings as a window of opportunity to address inequality in educational processes and outcomes. *Review of Research in Education*, *41*(1), 88–111.

Losen, D. J. (2015). *Closing the Discipline Gap: Equitable Remedies for Excessive Exclusion*. New York, NY: Teachers College Press.

Lustick, D., & Sykes, G. (2006). National board certification as professional development: What are teachers learning? *Education Policy Analysis Archives*, *14*(5). Retrieved June 10, 2008 from http://epaa.asu.edu/epaa/v14n5/

Meiklejohn, J., Phillips, C., Freedman, M. L., Griffin, M. L., Biegel, G., Roach, A., & Saltzman, A. (2012). Integrating mindfulness training into K-12 education: Fostering the resilience of teachers and students. *Mindfulness*, *3*(4), 291–307.

Mezirow, J. (1991). *Transformative Dimensions of Adult Learning*. San Francisco: Jossey-Bass.

Moll, L. C., Amanti, C., Neff, D., & Gonzalez, N. (1992). Funds of knowledge for teaching: Using a qualitative approach to connect homes and classrooms. *Theory into Practice*, *31*(2), 132–141.

Nasir, N. S., Rosebery, A. S., Warren, B., & Lee, C. D. (2014). Learning as a cultural process: Achieving equity through diversity. In R. K. Sawyer (Ed.), *The Cambridge Handbook of the Learning Sciences* (pp. 686–706). New York: Cambridge University Press.

National Center on Safe Supportive Learning Environments. (n.d.). School climate measurement. https://safesupportivelearning.ed.gov/topic-research/school-climate-measurement

National Research Council. (2008). *Assessing Accomplished Teaching: Advanced-Level Certification Programs*. Washington, DC: National Academies Press.

Noguera, P., Darling-Hammond, L., & Friedlaender, D. (2015). *Equal Opportunity for Deeper Learning*. Students at the Center: Deeper Learning Research Series. Boston, MA: Jobs for the Future.

Oakes, J., Maier, A., & Daniel, J. (2017). *Community Schools: An Evidence-Based Strategy for Equitable School Improvement*. Boulder, CO: National Education Policy Center and Palo Alto, CA: Learning Policy Institute.

OECD. (2014). *TALIS 2013 Results: An International Perspective on Teaching and Learning*. Paris, France: OECD Publishing. http://dx.doi.org/10.1787/9789264196261-en.

Okonofua, J. A., & Eberhardt, J. L. (2015). Two strikes: Race and the disciplining of young students. *Psychological Science*, *26*(5), 617–624.

Osher, D., Cantor, P., Berg, J., Steyer, L., & Rose, T. (2018). Drivers of human development: How relationships and context shape learning and development. *Applied Developmental Science*. doi: 10.1080/10888691.2017.1398650

Osher, D., Kidron, Y., DeCandia, C. J., Kendziora, K., & Weissberg, R. P. (2016). Interventions to promote safe and supportive school climate. In K. R. Wentzel & G. B. Ramani (Eds.), *Handbook of Social Influences in School Contexts* (pp. 384–404). New York, NY: Routledge.

Parents Involved in Community Schools v. Seattle School District No. 1. 551 U.S. 701. Supreme Court of the United States. 2007.

Potter, H., Quick, K., & Davies, K. (2016). *A New Wave of School Integration*. New York, NY: The Century Foundation.

Raffaele Mendez, L. M. (2003). Predictors of suspension and negative school outcomes: A longitudinal investigation. In J. Wal & D. J. Losen (Eds.), *Deconstructing the School-to-Prison Pipeline* (pp. 17–34). San Francisco, CA: Jossey-Bass.

Rimm-Kaufman, S. E., & Sawyer, B. E. (2004). Primary grade teachers' self-efficacy beliefs, attitudes toward teaching, and discipline and teaching practice priorities in relation to the *Responsive Classroom* approach. *The Elementary School Journal*, *104*, 321–341.

Sato, M., Chung Wei, R., & Darling-Hammond, L. (2008). Improving teachers' assessment practices through professional development: The case of National Board Certification. *American Educational Research Journal*, *45*, 669–7000.

Culture, Learning, and Policy

Schmader, T., & Johns, M. (2003). Converging evidence that stereotype threat reduces working memory capacity. *Journal of Personality and Social Psychology, 85*(3), 440.

Schwerdt, G., & West, M. R. (2013). The impact of alternative grade configurations on student outcomes through middle and high school. *Journal of Public Economics, 97,* 308–326.

Skiba, R.., Chung, C., Trachok, M., Baker, T., Sheya, A., & Hughes, R. (2012). Parsing disciplinary disproportionality. *American Educational Research Journal, 51*(4), 640–670.

Skiba, R., Simmons, A., Staudinger, L., Rausch, M., Dow, G., & Feggins, R. (2003). *Consistent removal: Contributions of school discipline to the school–prison pipeline.* Paper presented at the School to Prison Pipeline Conference, Cambridge, MA.

Steele, D. M., & Cohn-Vargas, B. (2013). *Identity Safe Classrooms: Places to Belong and Learn.* Thousand Oaks, CA: Corwin Press.

Sutcher, L., Darling-Hammond, L., & Carver-Thomas, D. (2016). *A Coming Crisis in Teaching?* Palo Alto, CA: Learning Policy Institute.

Tenenbaum, H. R., & Ruck, M. D. (2007). Are teachers' expectations different for racial minority than for European American students? A meta-analysis. *Journal of Educational Psychology, 99*(2), 253.

Tyack, D. B. (1974). *The One Best System: A History of American Urban Education* (Vol. 95). Cambridge, MA: Harvard University Press.

Unterman, R., & Haider, Z. (2019). *New York City's Small Schools of Choice A First Look at Effects on Postsecondary Persistence and Labor Market Outcomes.* New York, NY: MRDC Policy Brief.

U.S. Department of Education Office for Civil Rights. (2016). 2013–2014 Civil Rights Data Collection: A First Look. Key data highlights on equity and opportunity gaps in our nation's public schools. Washington, DC: U.S. Department of Education.

Villegas, A. M., & Lucas, T. (2002). *Educating Culturally Responsive Teachers: A Coherent Approach.* Albany: State University of New York Press.

Wells, A.S., Fox, L., & Cordova-Cobo, D. (2016). How racially diverse schools and classrooms can benefit all students. New York, NY: The Century Foundation.

Wilson, M., Hallam, P. J., Pecheone, R. L., & Moss, P. A. (2014). Evaluating the validity of portfolio assessments for licensure decisions. *Education Policy Analysis Archives, 22,* 6.

INDEX

Note: Page numbers in italics indicate figures and those in bold indicate tables.

21st Century ERI Working Group 69
5th Dimension Project 38

ableism 268, 300, 305, 306, 415
"academic identity" 62, 127, 129
academic language *see* racialized bilingual learners and academic language
academic success, notions of 262
access and learning pathways 198, 205–206
access and marginalization 208
accommodationist form of family engagement 354
accommodation processes 62–63, 72
Achebe, Chinua 142, 151
Aché birthing traditions 8
achievement gap 62, 65, 412
action research 168
active intermodal mapping (AIM) 30
active pedagogy 185
activity systems 198
activity theory 234
adaptive expertise 405
adaptive learning across the life span 247–260; and failure of schools 256–258; overview 247–248; in prisons 251–253; through Public Works drama program 254–256; and YPAR Collaboration in Kakuma Refugee Camp 248–251
additive and subtractive bilingualism 182
ADHD spectrum 170
adolescent development 51–58
adult learning 410–411
adultcentrism 193, 212–216
Advancement Project (national group) 358
AERA 122
African American (or Black) students and communities: and "becoming Black" 67; children's storytelling practices in 236; and culturally sustaining pedagogy 261, 262; and erasure in literary scholarship 277; and ethnic-racial identity 66–69; ethno-mathematic study in 37; Goodwin's work with children in 219, 225; and high-poverty neighborhoods 323; and independent Black institutions (IBIs) 232; language practices in 181, 219; and learning disabilities 163–164; and Learning Lab model 171; and Linked Learning Initiative 353; and punishment in schools 303–306, 323, 358, 414; and school funding 418; and Shoptalk study 145, 149; and signifying 281; and STEM education 342–344; and stereotypes 64–67; Taylor's study of mathematical understanding in 284; and teacher certification 389; trauma among 47–48; White teachers' expectations of 414
African American Vernacular English (AAVE) 281
African heritage pride (in Brazil) 55–56
African philosophies on biology and culture 320
Africans: and colonization xviii–xix; Diop on xxiv; and scientific racism xx
afterschool programs **351**, 353–354
agency: and active intermodal mapping 30; and adaptive learning 253–254; among Black youths 71, 73; among youths in Argentina, Peru, and Brazil 49–56, 58; of children 220; defined 49; in educational process for Indigenous youth 354; and learning pathways perspective 200; and Public Works drama program 256; in *Las Redes* and *El Pueblo Mágico* educational designs 333
agendas 124, 125, 127
agroecology 84
Aid to Families with Dependent Children (AFDC) 389
Akkerman, S. F. 370, 371, 373
Alim, H. S. 152, 207, 262, 263, 267–270, 272n1, 310n1, 310n3
Allen, W. 48

Index

Al-Tamimi, K. 143
Altschul, I. 68–69
Amanti, C. 235
American Eugenics Society xix
American Indian Center (AIC) (Chicago) 353–354
American Indian Center of Chicago 286
American Psychological Association xix
Amos, Y. T. 391–392
analytic induction 123
analytic lens on learning 119, 121–124, 131, 137–138
Anderson, B. 233, 240
Anderson, K. 123
Anderson, T. 331
anthropocentrism xxvi
anthropology of children 216
"anthropology of experience" 217, 219
anti-dialogic projects 285–286
anti-racism 262
Appadurai, Arjun 248
Apple (company) 303
apprenticeships 168–169, 238, 257
Argentina youth 49–51
argumentation in literature and science for K–12 classrooms 141–159; and building relationships 150; canonical disciplinary understandings of 146, 148–149; and curiosity, attending to 151; hybrid model for 141–142, 145–146, *146*, 150, 155; Majors' framework 145–146, 149; and narratives, creating 154; and norms, disrupting 151–152; overview 141–142; perspectives on 143–144; and play 153–154; and ready-made argumentation 147–148; and tools, appropriating and adapting 152–153; Toulmin's model 144–146, 149
Ariefdien, Shaheen 272n2
"armchair anthropologists" 324
armed conflict 52
Aronson, J. 322; SAT exam study 65
artifacts 11–12, 172
arts education 256
Asian communities xxvi
Asian Prisoner Support Committee (APSC) 251
asset pedagogies 263–264, 267–269, 273n7, 411–412, 416
assimilation beliefs (among Black students) 69
assimilationist models of instruction 146, 299, 302–303
The Association for the Study of Classical African Civilization xxiv
The Association of Black Psychologists xxiv
Atran, S. 91
Attneave, Carolyn xxv–xxvi
Atwood, Margaret 150
Azibo, D. A. Y. xxiii

Babies (documentary film) 26
Baker, W. D. 123–124, 130–132, 138n5, 138n7
Bakker, A. 370, 371, 373
Bali, child development in 100
Ball, Arnetha 390, 395, 397–398

Bambara, Toni Cade 281
Bandura, A. 397
Bang, M. 279, 286
"Ban the Box" campaign 251
Barad, Karen 315–316
Barnes, J. C. 304
Barone, D. 122, 131
Barron, B. 203
Barton, A. C. 284
al-Bashir, Omar Hassan 250
basketball and dominoes studies 203
Bates, E. 31, 103
Bateson, Gregory 100, 107, 110, 116n3, 116n11
Bateson, W. 116n11
Battiste, M. 80, 233
Bauman, Richard 180; *Ethnography and Education* 213
bay odyans (Haitian-Creole argumentation practice) 144
Bay Prep High School (Oakland) 342
Beaver, K. M. 304, 305
becoming, processes of 67, 214, 218–219, 326
Befu, Harumi 116n6
Bell, P. 141
Bellino, Michelle J. 248, 249
belonging 25; *see also* identity and identity processes
Benjamin, R.: *Race After Technology* 343–344
Bennett, Lerone xxiv
Berkeley Underground Scholars (or BUS initiative) 251
Berland, L. K. 148
Berlin, Isaiah xxvii–xxviii
Bernstein, Basil 183
Bertrand, M. 168
Bethune, Mary McLeod xxiv
bias 46–47
BICS (basic interpersonal communication skills) 179, 182, 183, 186
Bielaczyc, K. 331
big data 325
"Big 'D' Discourse" 394
Bilingual Baby curriculum 34
bilingualism *see* multilingualism and bilingualism; racialized bilingual learners and academic language
bio-culture, defined 161; *see also* learning disabilities and bio-cultural perspective
biological determinism 25
biological evolution 4
biological processes 25, 27, 99
Birdwhistell, Ray 108–109
Birkenstein, C. 149
Bishop, D. V. 165
Black Caucus of the Society for the Study of Child Development xxiv
"Black English Case" (1979) 273n6
Black feminist thought 263
Black Language (BL) 266–267
Black Lives Matter movement 356
Black (or African-centered) psychology xxiii–xxv

428

Index

The Black Scholar publication 251–252
Black studies and Black literary feminism 321
blind adults and echolocation 26
Bloch, E. 331
Bloom, L. 31
Bloomer, M. 197
body movement as communication 116n3
Boesch, C. 319
Bolt, Andrew 152
book clubs 150, 151, 153
borders: and cultural communities xxii
boundaries 370–373
Bowe, A. 388–389
"the box problem" 26
Boyd, R. 10
Boyer, E. L.: *Scholarship Reconsidered: Priorities of the Professoriate* 374
the brain 163; *see also* neurobiology (and the brain)
Braudel, Fernand 109
Brayboy, Bryan xxv
Brazil: intercultural inductive education 79
Brazil youth 53–56
Brice Heath, Shirley 213
Bricker, L. A. 141
Briggs, C. 180
Broca's area 18
Brock, C. 123
brokering 204–205
Bronfenbrenner, U. 45, 47, 197
Brookfield, S. 395
Brookins, Geraldine K. 48
Brooks, R. 102
Brown, R. 31
Bruner, J. 154
Bucholtz, M. 270
Bullough, R.V., Jr. 372
Burke, C. 395
Burundi, refugees from 248
Butler, J. 319
Bybee, D. 68–69

Cajete, Greg xxv
California, accreditation system in 408–409
CALP (cognitive academic language proficiency) 179, 182, 183, 186
Camaioni, L. 103
Campt 325
capitalism 19, 178–179, 262–263, 272
Capitol High School study 71
caregivers 13–14
Carnegie Foundation 369, 372; *see also* Improvement Leadership Education and Development (iLEAD) network
Carraher, D. xxix
Carraher, T. N. xxix
Carris, L. M. 310n1, 310n3
Carruthers, Jacob xxiv
Carter, D. 72
Cartesianism 288, 290, *318*, 324; *see also* Descartes
Casey, B. J. 57

Casillas, D. I. 270
Casta War 85
Castellino, D. R. 71–72
Castillo, Ana: *A Countryless Woman* 282
Caswell County Training School (CCTS) (North Carolina) 232
Caudle, K. 57
Cavalcanti, I. 395
Center concept 374
"central actors" (in social movement theory) 351
Champion, T. B. 37
Change Laboratory 355
Charter Freedom School 237
Chavous, T. 68
Chemical Oceanography Outside the Laboratory (COOL) project 153
Cherokee communities 83–84
Children; *see also* infants: agency of 220; as "beings" and "becomings" 214, 218–219; and "cultural invention" xxviii–xxix; culture of 215–219; in extended ontogenetic systems 13–14; and imitative learning 27–30; inclusion of 81, 87
Children's Defense Fund 237
children's interests and concerns 212–229; and adultocentrism 213–216; and children's culture 215–219; and Early Learning Across Contexts (ELAC) 219–220; ethnographic approach to 216–217; example cases 220–225, *222–223*; interaction analysis (IA) approaches to 217–219, 225, 226–227n1; and limits of current research 212–213; overview 225–226
chimpanzee reproduction 7
Chinese American students 272–273n6
Chomsky, Noam 31, 109
chronosystem 45–47
Chung, R.V. 251
"chun qiang she jian" ("cross verbal swords") 143
cis-heteropatriarchy 306, 310n3
civic identity 49, 52–53
Civil Rights Act 272–273n6
Clark, Kenneth and Mami 66–67
class-related issues *see* economic inequalities
classroom-based research 167–169, 232, 234, 236
classroom-based schooling 15, 285
Clemens, Elisabeth 350, 354, 359
Cliffside Park High School (New Jersey) 265
climate change 258
clinical interviews 214
Clough, P.: "The New Empiricisms" 326–327
Cobb, P. A. 331
code approach to language 183
Coffey, S. 237
the *cogito* 316
cognitive revolution (1950s) 11, 120
cohort 197
Cole, Michael xxix, 38, 99, 333, 366–367
collaborative activities 103, 128
collaborative strategic reading (CSR) 167
collective community building 310
college-in-prison programs 252–253

College of Alameda (California) 251
Collins, A. 331
Collins, K. M. 168–169
Collins, P. H. 241
colonialism: and anti-Black sociopolitical violence 326; and Indigenous languages 180; and knowledge systems 278–279, 282–283, 285–287, 289–290; in Mayan communities 84–91; and the "Other" 142; in Papua New Guinea xviii–xix; and state-sanctioned schooling 261–262, 264, 265; and white supremacy xviii–xix
Colyvas, J. A. 351
Comer, James 417
Common Core State Standards 185
Common Core State Standards (United States) 185
common ground 103
communities as contexts for learning 182, 230–246; apprenticeship approaches 238; and community concept 193; and defining communities 231; difference and agreement within 230–231, 234–237; framework for 239–242; and intersectionality 239; multidimensionality of 232–234; overview 230–231, 242; place and space 232; research on 235–236; and research-practice partnership (RPP) 237–238
communities of practice 239
Community-Based Design Research (CBDR) 360
community cultural wealth frameworks 237
community schools 417
computational cultures 325
computer programming 199–200, 206; see also Oakland Science and Mathematics Outreach (OSMO) project
Comte, A. 317, 324
conception 13
Condon, W. 116n9
Confrey, J. 331
Conklin, J. 392
Conrad, Joseph: *Heart of Darkness* 142, 151, 154
consciousness see mind/body dualism
constitution, ontogenesis as 5–6
context: and positioning 128
context-dependent learning trajectory 198
conversation analysis (CA) 138nn6–7, 218, 226–227n1
Cooper, Anna Julia 305, 393
coping 50–51, 57–58
coping strategies: among Black youth 64
Corderio, P.: *Boundary Crossing: Educational Partnerships and School Leadership* 375–376
corn, origin of 84
Corsaro, W. A. 215
Cotuc, Marta Navichoc 83
Council for the Accreditation of Educator Preparation (CAEP) 374
Coyne, M. A. 304
craniology xix, 24
Crenshaw, K. W. 305
critical care praxis 273n7
critical language awareness 263

critical learning 247–248
critical literacy 151
critical pedagogies 237, 281, 282
critical race theory (CRT) 265, 326
critical reflexivity 267–268, 395–397, *396*
critical repertoires 284
Cross, William 67
Cuban, L. 350
cultural capital 264
"cultural data sets" 281
cultural evolution theory xxvii, 7, 11
cultural historical activity theory 333
cultural historical time xvii, 170
culturally compatible pedagogy 273n7
culturally congruent pedagogy 273n7
culturally relevant pedagogies 273n7
culturally responsive pedagogy 273n7
culturally sustaining pedagogy (CSP) 193–194, 207, 237, 239, 261–276; across domains 272n2, 273n8; and community practices 266–267; and critical reflexivity 267–268; intrinsic value of 262–263, 266; Ladson–Billings on 264–265; principles of 268–271, *269*; promises and challenges of 271–272; terminology 272n1; in white supremacist context 261–262
culturally sustaining/revitalizing pedagogy (CSRP) 270, 271
Cultural Modeling research 37, 281, 284, 287
cultural nature of learning, reframing 295–296
cultural pluralism 263
cultural responsiveness (CR) 171–172
"cultural socialization" 264
cultural studies 299
"cultural" turn in youth organizing 356
culture and cultural practices: centrality of 271; and coherence xxi; defining 11–12, 298, 366–368, 389–390; and development 45; within families xxii; as "parliament of prodigals" 115; race, ethnicity, and language informing 266; relationality of xxv; in space and time xvii; temporal and spatial dimensions of 26
"culture of poverty" xx
"culture wars" 265
Cummins, J. 182
cuneiform writing 15
cycles of activity 132, 138n6

"damage-centered narratives" 270, 271
Daniel, A. 47
Danish, J. A. 153–154
Darity, W., Jr. 71–72
Darling-Hammond, Linda 388
Darwin, Charles xix, 11, 319
Darwinism xx, 317
Davies, B. 119–121, 129
Davis, A. 388–389; "Child Socialization and the School" 44
Dawes, S. S. 366
Dayton, A. 82–84
deafness and deaf children 26, 34–35

Index

deBessonet, Lear 254
de-carceration 252
declarative and procedural knowledge 105
decolonial pedagogies 278, 282
deconstructionism 315–321
decontextualization 214
deep critique 132, 134–137
deficit theories: and African-American communities
219, 238; and eugenics movement 24–25; or
racialized bilingual communities 181; and
racialization 239, 264; and scientific racism 38
deictic gestures 102, 115n1
Delaware, educational funding in 418
Deleuze, G. 326–327
delinking 278–281, 285–286, 289
Deloria, Vine xxv
Dema, O. 393
Deming, W. E. 377
Democratic Republic of Congo (DRC), refugees
from 248
democratizing forms of inquiry 333
"demographic divide" 392
Denver School-Based Restorative Justice
Partnership 358–360
deontic affordances 13
deontic niches 3, 9–11, 14
deontic powers 10–12
deontology, defined 10
deportation fears 341
Derrida, J. 315, 319–320
Descartes 316–318; see also mind/body dualism
Design-Based Implementation Research
(DBIR) 360
desire-based approach 270
determinism 324
Detroit Tigers (baseball team) 232
development see human development
developmental niches 13
developmental psychology 212, 214, 216
developmental social neuroscience 27
developmental systems theory 5–6
deviance 299–300
DeVos, Betsy 304
Dewey, John 51, 104–106, 109, 116n3, 116n5, 149,
372; on learning through doing 352
dialogicality 279, 285–290
diary studies 31–32
Diaz de Rada, A. 241
dichotomous vs. non-dichotomous views of
language 187–188
difference 230–231, 234–237, 297–301, 303–308;
hierarchies of 322
digital space and media 232, 253
dimensional approach 68
Diop, Cheik Anta: The Cultural Unity of Black
Africa xxiv
disabilities see learning disabilities
Disability Critical Race Theory 304
disciplinary learning and multiple ways of knowing
277–293; and dialogicality 279, 285–290; and

erasure 277–278, 288–289; and horizontality 279,
283–285, 289–290; and multiplicity 279–283,
289–290; and onto-epistemic heterogeneity
278–279
disciplinary practices see punishment and
disciplinary practices
discourses 315–317, 394; see also positioning theory
and discourse analysis
discrepancy model 163
discursive turn and processes 120–121, 137; see also
positioning theory and discourse analysis
DiSessa, A. 205, 331
dis-identification 71
displaced persons 247, 258; see also refugees
disproportionate minority contact (DMC) 57
distributed nature of learning 205
diversity (as principle for SDBEs) 333–334
"diversity" courses 387
diversity of developmental pathways xxvii, xxix,
25–26, 38, 170, 172–173
diversity projects and intersectionality 297–313;
and containment and assimilation processes
302–303; and difference 304–306; and DisCrit
analysis 305; and humanizing processes 306–308;
importance of 308–310; and inclusion 298; and
normativity 305–306; and oppression in learning
contexts 305; overview 297; in pedagogical
practice 302; and power dynamics 298–307; in
research 213; and researchers, role of 308–309;
and responsibility of institutions 301, 305, 307;
and thought vs. experience 303; and weaponizing
diversity 303–304
diversity within communities 240
DNA, role of 320
docta spes 331
"doll studies" 66–67
"double consciousness" 66
double stimulation 171, 174n2
dragon fruit farming in Mexico 86–87
DREAMers 356
dual inheritance theory 7
dualistic logics see mind/body dualism; nature/
culture binary; the quantitative-qualitative,
reconceptualizing
Du Bois, W.E.B. xix, xxiv, 66
Duncan-Andrade, J. M. R. 154
Durand, E. S. 168
Dynamical Systems theories 84
"dynamics without motion" 82–83
"dysconscious racism" 391
dyslexia 160, 163, 165, 169

Early Childhood Longitudinal Study 388–389
Early Learning Across Contexts (ELAC) 219–220
Early Literacy Project (ELP) 168
earthworms 11–12
Easton-Brooks, D. 388–389
eavesdropping 27, 29
Eberhardt, J. L. 305–306
echolocation 26

Index

ecological framework 264
economic inequalities: and educational success 17, 19; and language ideologies 179–180
Edelsky, C. 182
educational linguistics 178–179, 188
educational psychology 212
education and schools; *see also* learning and development: community contexts for 235; among displaced communities 248–249; Eugenicist influence in xx–xxi; formal 257–258; and "grammar of schooling" 350; and holistic development xxiv; and Indigenous ways of learning 79–80; and institutionalization 14–18; multilingual experiences in 184; and racial gap in discipline 303–304; and racialization 323; transformation within 271–272; violence perpetuated by 261–262, 264, 272, 273n9, 289; Western perspectives on xxv
educator preparation program (EPP) 237
Einstein, Albert 153
Elby, A. 280–281
Elder, G. 197
Elder, Glen: "Children of the Great Depression: Social Change in Life Experience" 44
elders 90, 248, 266, 270, 286–287, 353–354
electroencephalography (EEG) techniques 30
El Hogar de los Jóvenes program 50, 51, 58n1
Elizaga, R. A. 65
Ellen, R. F. 123
"embedded achievement" 69
embodiment 30–31; *see also* "how to mean" and embodiment in cultural practices
embryology 99
emotional experience 22, 29, 57, 184, 411, 413
empathy 31
empathy and reading fiction 154
enculturation 101–104, 213
"enforced dependency" 248
engaged pedagogy 273n7
Engeström, Y. 367
engineering programs 201–202, 206
English as a second language (ESL) 178
English language 143–144
English Language Arts 253
Enlightenment xxvii–xxviii, 324
environmental niches 4, 11, 13, 20
Enyedy, N. 153–154
epigenetics 35
epistemic violence 277, 281, 289
ePortfolios 396–397
Epstein, J. L. 397
equity 58, 163, 178, 333–336
erasure of marginalized communities 277–278, 288–289
Erickson, E. H. 397
Erickson, F. 124, 213
Eriksonian, E. H. 45
Espinoza, M. 335
ethical issues 300, 327; in science 280–281
Ethiopia, refugees from 248

ethnic-racial identity (ERI) 66–73
Ethnic-Racial Identity Development Model 67
ethnic studies ban (Arizona, 2010) 302
ethnocentrism 213–214, 216, 278–279, 394
ethnography: and ethnographers as learners 131–132, 138n5; Forsey on 241; Heath's approach to 255–256; and "multi-sited ethnographic sensibility" 336; and prediction 116n12; and quantitative reasoning 324–325
ethnomathematics 37–38, 284
ethnomethodology 116n3
Eudell, D. 322
Eugenics movement xix–xxi
European bourgeoisie 180
Eustis, Oskar 254
Evans, K. 123
Every Student Succeeds Act (ESSA) 381, 415, 417, 419
evolution 6; institutional foundations of 4–9; and reproduction 7–9
evolutionary psychology 7
executive function 29
"expert infant" study 28
explanatory theory 97, 119, 122, 123, 131
Extended Evolutionary Synthesis (EES) 4–6, *6*

failure 310
families 354; *see also* elders; parents and families
fanfiction communities 151, 154
Fanon, Franz xxiv, 180
feminist new materialists 320
Ferguson, A. A. 306
Fertman, C. I. 357
"fictive kinship" concept 71, 72
Fingerson, L. 215
Finland, partner schools in 409
"flesh" as sociopolitical 322
Flexner, Abraham 407
Flores, N. 178, 179
flux notion 82–83
Fodor, J. A.: *Modularity of Mind* 31
"folk linguistics" 179
folklore 213
food deserts 337
food justice 338–339; *see also* Learning in the Food Movement
forced sterilizations 24
Fordham, Signithia 71
formal education 257–259
"forms of life" 145
Foss, S. K. 143
foster care 248
Foucault, M. 179, 319
Fox, M. 388
fractal relationships 83–84
Fraden, R. 252
Franke, M. 397
Freyre, Gilberto 54, 55
Fu construct xxix
fugitive learning 306–308, 310

Index

funds of knowledge 237, 267, 283, 406
future-binding character of institutions 10
Futures Project (L. A.) 357–358, 360–361

Galaburda, A. M. 164–165
Gallimore, R. 197
Gamber-Thompson, L. 356
game theory 10
"gap gazing" 348
Garfinkel, H. 215
Gates, H. L. 281
gaze direction 225
gaze following 102, *102*
Gaztambide-Fernández, R. A. 272n5, 302–303
Gearing, F. O. 124, 127
Gee, J. P. 37, 356, 394
Geertz, R. 240, 325
gender and sexuality 217, 219, 268, 319–320; *see also* men; women
generative learning and change 397–399, *398*
genetic and epigenetic inheritance 4
genocide 261, 262
Genovese, E. D.: *Roll, Jordan, Roll: The World the Slaves Made* 64
gentrification 341, 343–344
geographies of consequentiality 332
"germ theory" 280
Gillett, G. 120
Gilligan, Carol 64, 219
Gintis, H. 10
girls of color 306
"Girl Time" arts program 252
globalization 174, 185
global linguistic flows and global ill-literacies 267
goal-oriented, collective activity systems 161
Gobineau, Arthur de: *Essay on the Inequality of the Human Race* xix
Goddard, Henry xx
godparents 8
Goffman, E. 116n15
Goldenberg, C. 197
Gonzalez, L. 390
González, N. 235, 266, 270, 283–284, 390
González, T. 168
González Jácome, A. 84
Goodlad, John 373; *A Place Called School* 374
Goodwin, Charles 102, 110, 115; *Co-operative Action* 225
Goodwin, Marjorie 198, 217; *He-Said-She-Said* 219
Googins, B. K. 370
Gottlieb, G. 35
Gould, Stephen Jay xxvii
governmentality 179–181
Graff, G. 149
Green, J. L. 138n6
Greenberg, J. 283
Greene, Maxine 298
Greenfield, P. xxix, 196–197
Griesemer, James 5
Griffin, C. L. 143

Grossman, P. L. 147
Guidi, L. G. 165
Gupta, A. 280–281
Guthman, J. 339
Gutiérrez, K. 335, 349, 390
Gutiérrez, K. D. 26, 38, 141, 264, 273n10, 330
Guyton, E. 388

Habermas, J. 395
Hall, Stuart 299, 308, 309
Hall, T. E. 166, 298
Halliday, Michael 183–184
Hammer, D. 148
Hannegan-Martinez, Sharim 272n2
Hardman, Charlotte 216
Harney, S. 327
Harper, S. R. 323
Harré, R. 119–121, 128, 129, 138n2
Harris, P. 123–124, 128, 131
Harste, J. C. 394–395
Hart, B. 235
Hasan, R. 184, 185
Haupt, A. 268–270, 272n1
Havighurst, R. J.: "Child Socialization and the School" 44
head-touch imitation study 28
health and positive learning experiences 256
Heath, S. B. 180–181, 235, 254–256
Hegel, G. 321
Henderson, A. 227n1
Herder, Johann Gottfried von 180; *Ideas about the Philosophy of History of Mankind* xxvi–xxvii
Hernstein, Richard: *The Bell Curve* xx
Herskovits, M. J. 11
heteroglossic attunement 282, 283
hidden curriculum 17
Higher Education Act (1965) 388
Hilliard, Asa xxiv
Hip Hop cultures 266–268, 270
historicity 333, 337–338
history, perspectives on xxviii
Hodkinson, P. 197
Hoff, E. 34
holistic perspective xxiv, 81, 88, 218, 233, 404, 420
Holmes, A. 266, 270
Holmes Group 373
home, notions of 254
home language practices 181–183
homelessness: in Argentina 49–51
hooks, bell 336, 340, 344
horizontality 279, 283–285, 290
horizontal organization 88, 91
Horton, W. S. 37
Horvat, E. M.: *Beyond Acting White: Reframing the Debate on Black Student Achievement* 72
Houston, Drusilla Dunjee xxiv
Howard, T. C. 392
"how to mean" and embodiment in cultural practices 99–118; and Japanese bowing tradition *100–101*, 100–102, 106–112, **108**, *111–112*,

Index

113, *114*, 115, 116n6, 116n9, 116n15; overview 99–100, 112, 115; and semiotic function 101–104; and vocabularies of learning 104–106, 108, 109, 115, 116n3
Hudicourt-Barnes, J. 144
Hull, G. 232
human cognition, uniqueness of 103
human development: and race xviii–xix
human nature xxvii
human sciences 180
hunter-gatherer societies 8–9
Hurston, Zora Neale 281
Hutchins, Pat 127–128
Hwang, H. 351
hybrid argumentation *see* argumentation in literature and science for K–12 classrooms
hyper-incarceration culture 253

IDEA regulations 160
identity and identity processes; *see also* ethnic-racial identity: academic 62, 127, 129; in Argentina, Peru, and Brazil 49–56, 58; centrality of 271; and community, understanding 233–235, 238; within contexts 241; coping strategies affecting 51; diversity among 68; and first person plural, use of 232; and identity safe classrooms 406, 412, 414; and language ideologies 179–180; and learning xxi–xxii; and learning pathways 195, 197–199, 202–203; and meaning making 45–46; as pathway 62; and racial identity formation 45, 66–69; as relational xxiv, xxv; and teachers of color 409; and trajectories of identification 197
identity potentials 119
Iknal platform 85–90
"ill-literacies" 152, 267
"imagined communities" 240
imitative learning 27–30, 100
Impact (organization) 337–341
implicit learning 27, 32
Improvement Leadership Education and Development (iLEAD) network 368, 375–379, **380**
improvement science 369
inclusive learning environments 66, 81, 87, 236, 414–415
independent Black institutions (IBIs) 232
indexical terms 134, 136, 137
Indigenous students and communities; *see also* specific communities: and colonialism xviii–xix, 142–143; and culturally sustaining pedagogy 261, 262, 272n3; and formal schooling 258; knowledge systems of xxv, 258; and land-based pedagogies 286; language issues affecting 180; language revitalization in 233; and learning disabilities 163–164; and nature/nurture philosophies 320; portrayals of 277; and scientific racism xx; and Urban Explorers program 353–354
Indigenous ways of learning 79–95; co-construction of 91–92; history of 273n9; innovation and

continual change as features of 82–84; and LOPI framework 81–82, 87–89, 92; in Mayan communities 84–91; overview 79–80; research on 81
inequality; *see also* economic inequalities; power and privilege: in Brazil 53–56; in education xx–xxi; identity-based approach to 45–46
infant gesture types 103
infants 28–35; and cultural practices, building blocks for 112, 115
informal learning 247–250
infrastructure 332
inheritance 11
innovation 82–84, 89
inquiry-based teaching approach 394–395
inscriptions 15
institutional foundations 3–23; and brain development 18–20; and culture, defining 11–12; of evolution 4–9; and human ontogenesis 12–14; and institutions, defined 9–11
Institutionalized Public Basic Schooling (IPBS) 16
institutional rules 248
institutions of higher education (IHEs) 366–368, 371–372, 374–381, 387–388
integrated education 418–419
integrated student support (ISS) programs 416
Intel (company) 344
intent community participation (ICP) 238
interactional synchrony 107, 116n9
interaction analysis (IA) 217–219, 225, 226–227n1
interactionist perspective 317–318
interactive and reflexive positioning 127
intercultural education 79, 89–91
"interest episodes" 205
intergenerational learning environments 131, 266, 269, 270, 272; *see also* elders
intergenerational transmission of trauma (ITT) 47
International Dyslexia Association 160
internships **351**, 352–353
inter-organizational learning 367–368
interpretive reproduction 215
intersectionality xxii, xxix, 26, 72, 207, 267, 269, 335; *see also* diversity projects and intersectionality
intersections 24
Interstate New Teacher Assessment and Support Consortium (INTASC) 407–408
invasive species and ecological imperialism 286–287
invitations (during social interactions) 218
inward gaze 267, 272
IQ testing xxi, xxv
Irish communities 26
Irizarry, J. G. 271
Ishimaru, A. M. 355

Jackson, Jesse 344
Jakobson, Roman 109
James, Allison 217; "Confections, Concoctions, and Conceptions" study 216

Index

Japanese bowing tradition *100–101*, 100–102, 106–115, **108**, *111–112*, **113**, *114*, 115, 116n6, 116n9, 116n15

Jenkins, H. 215, 217

Jenkins, S. 356

Jenks, C. 216, 217

Jensen, Arthur: "How Much Can We Boost IQ and Scholastic Achievement" xx

Jernigan, M. M. 47

Jewish communities xx

Johns Hopkins University 407

Johnson, P. 264

Johnson, Rucker 418

joint attention 103–104, 115–116nn1–2

Jones, R.: *Handbook of Tests and Measurements for Black Populations* xxv

Jones, Rhodessa: Medea Project 252

Jordan, B. 227n1

Joseph, D. 331

The Journal of Black Psychology xxiv

Jurow, A. S. 330, 332, 337–338, 344n1

Kafka, Franz 111, 116n14

Kakuma Youth Research Group (KYRG) 248–251

Karenga, Maulana xxiv

Kawagley, Oscar xxv

"KBAMLCS" 389

Kelly, G. 138n6

Kemetic tradition xxiv–xxv

Kendon, A. 115n1

Kennedy High School (midwestern U.S.) 253

Kenya, refugees in 248–251

"kets" study 216

Kidwell, Marti 218, 219

Kimmerer, Robin W. 143–144

King, J. 391

Kinloch, V. 270

kinship networks xxvi, 3; among hunter-gatherer societies 8–9

Kirby, V. 305, 320

Klingner, J. 167–168

Knight, S. L. 375

knowledge and knowledge systems xxv–xxvi, 105; *see also* disciplinary learning and multiple ways of knowing

Kohn, E. 325

Krummel, A. 391, 392

Kuhn, D. 144

Laboratory School (University of Chicago) 372

Ladson-Billings, Gloria 261, 262, 271, 273n10, 323; "It's not the culture of poverty, it's the poverty of culture: The problem with teacher education" 389; on teacher education 393; *Toward a Theory of Culturally Relevant Pedagogy* 264–265

Lakoff, G. 143

Laland, Kevin 4

land, role of xxvi

Laney College (Oakland, California) 251

Lang, Berel 105

language; *see also* discourse; monolingualism and monoglossic language ideologies; multilingualism and bilingualism; positioning theory and discourse analysis; racialized bilingual learners and academic language: acquisition theories of 31–35; and argumentation 143–144; in foreign language classrooms 393–394; having *vs.* doing 179; and literacy 18, 235; and mathematics 325; and nationalism 265; and reification of communities 240; role of xxvi; scientific 184; "standard" 263; as symbol of family and community 270; Vygotsky on 319; written 165–166

language-as-entity paradigm 179, 181, 187–188

language revitalization 79, 233

Latinx students and communities xxvi, 167, 171, 184, 235; and culturally sustaining pedagogy 267, 270, 271; and Migrant Student Leadership Institute 332; Moje's study 232; and school funding 418; and STEM education 342–344; Taylor's study of mathematical understanding in 284; White teachers' expectations of 414

Latour, B. 147

Lau v. Nichols (1974) 272–273n6

Lave, J. 352

leadership and university-district partnerships 365–384; and boundaries 370–373, 375–376; contextual considerations 376; and coordination 373–374; and cultural divides, negotiating 374–375; and culture 366–368; and iLead Network 368, 375–379, **380**; and mutualism 369–372; overview 365–366; and "partnerization" 372, 374; and partnerships as third space 375–376; and professional development schools 373; and reflection 374; and research–practice partnerships 368–370, 372–373, 381; and transformation 374

leadership development programs **351**, 357–358

Leander, K. 285

learning and development; *see also* education and schools: as collective 300; as cultural process xxi; as cultural processes 14; and identity 49; and institutionalization 14–18; meaning-focused view of 120; and potential xxv; and "real" purposes 81; and resistance, learning as 64; sociocultural contexts for xxi–xxii, 25; temporality of 104–105

learning by doing 88

"learning careers" 197

learning community concept 230, 236; *see also* communities as contexts for learning

learning disabilities and bio-cultural perspective 160–177; and cultural considerations 164; definitions 161, 163; and diagnosis 164, 172; and fluid nature of disability 172–173; overview 161–162; plurality of approaches to 173; research on 162–172; and situated model of learning and competence 173–174

Learning in Formal and Informal Environments (LIFE) Center 199

Learning in the Food Movement (South Elm) 337–341, 344n1

Learning Lab studies 171–172

learning pathways 193, 195–211; case studies 199–202, 205; characteristics of 202–206; culturally informed 196–199, 204–205; and local learning interactions 195, 205; overview 207–208
learning sciences 212, 213, 226–227n1, 247
Lee, C. D. 37, 142, 149, 162, 232, 261, 270, 273n10, 281, 297, 310n1; on cis-heteropatriarchy 310n3; on Cultural Modeling 264; on difference 308–309; on group membership 297, 309; on white terror 262
Legler, R. 388
Lehrer, R. 331
Leon, Jason de: *Land of Open Graves* 325
Leontiev, Aleksei xxvi
Lerman, S. 319
Leslie, A. M. 101
Levine, S. 37
Lévi-Strauss, Claude 109
Levitas, R. 331, 334
LGBTQ youth 356
licensing standards and program accreditation 407
"lifeways" 272n3
"Like-Me" social-developmental framework 30, 31
linguistic hegemony 262
linguistic mismatch 180–181, 184
Linked Learning Alliance (California) 352–353, 360
Liou, P.Y. 310n2
literacy 3; and the brain 18; as gateway 17; and Harris's case study 125; and language 18, 235; and ontogenesis 6; and Positioning Theory 122; and restorative justice practices 38; and schooling, institutionalization of 14–18; and situated approach 173; whole-language approach to 182
literary scholarship, erasure within 277
literature *see* argumentation in literature and science for K–12 classrooms
Little Bear, L. 82–83
Liu, K. 390, 395–397
lived experiences 335, 338
loan forgiveness programs 410
local education agencies (LEAs) 366–368, 371–372, 374–381
Locke, John 180
logic-of-analysis 124, 131
logic of elimination 272n5
Lomawaima, Tsianina xxv
"looking glass self" (or reflected appraisal) 66, 67
LOPI framework 81–82, 87–89, 92, 238
Lorde, Audre 305
Love, B. 270
loving approach 270
loving critiques 263
Low, B. E. 268
Luria, Aleksandr xxiv, xxvi, xxix, 29

Ma, J.Y. 285
"MAAT" virtues 232
MacSwan, J. 182
magnetic resonance imaging (MRI) 35
magnetoencephalography (MEG) 35

Majors, Yolanda 145–146, 149
Malinowski, Bronislaw 219
marginality 336
marginalization 193, 196
marginalized youth 47–48
Marin, A. 154, 279
Markman, K. D. 65
Martin, C. K. 204
Martin, J. 183–184
Martin-Jones, M. 182
Marx, D. 237
Marx, Karl xxviii
Maryland Department of Education 415–416
Massachusetts, educational funding in 418
"master codes" 322, 323
mastery of academic registers 184
mathematics 200–201, 204, 206, 325
Matusov, E. 285–286
May, Francisco 85
Mayan communities (Yucatan region, Mexico) xxix–xxx, 84–91
Mr. Mayson 342–343
McCarty, T. L. 270
McClintock, B. 153
McDermott, Ray xxi, 116n6, 169, 213
McKinney de Royston, M. 142
Mead, Margaret 100
Meaney, M. J. 25, 35
meaning making 45
mediating structures 170
Medicine, Bea xxv
Medin, D. L. 91, 279
Mehan, H. 162–163
Meltzoff, A. N. 30, 102
men and boys; *see also* patriarchy and patriarchal narratives: incarceration among Black 305; in science professions 280; stereotypes and identity formation among 70
mentoring and modeling (in teacher education) 393
Merritt College (California) 251
message units 138n7
metapositioning 129
Metcalf-Turner, P. 391, 393
Mexican American students 178–179, 266–267
Mexican-origin students 188
Mexico, intercultural education in 79; *see also* Mayan communities
Mezirow, J. 395
microbial turn in life sciences 280
micro-genetic moments of learning 193
microgenetic time xvii
micro-genetic time scale 168–169
micro-stories 154
Miettinen, R. 367
Mignolo, W. D. 289
Migrant Student Leadership Institute (MSLI) 281–283, 287, 332–333
Migrant Student Project (UCLA) 38
Miller, D. 197–198
Mills, Charles: *The Racial Contract* xix

Index

mind/body dualism 316–321, *318*
Minick, N. 319
Minnesota, educational funding in 418
minoritized groups 57, 164; *see also* specific communities
Mitchell, C. J. 123
MLK Elementary School Children v. Ann Arbor School District (1979) 272–273n6
"model minority" discourse 206
models of organization 348–364; and afterschool programs 353–354; and Community-Based Design Research 360; as cultural tools for change 350–351; and Design-Based Implemntation Research 360; developing idea of 349–350; and emerging approaches 359–360; and equitable change in education **351**, 351–352; and internships *351*, 352–353; and leadership development programs 357–358; overview 348–349; and parent-teacher groups 354–355; and research-practice partnerships 358–359; and social design experiments 360–361; and student organizations 355–357
modernity and modernist thought 258, 317, 319–320, 326
Modern Synthesis 4–6, *6*
Moeller, A. 393–394
Moghaddam, F. 120, 128, 138n2
Moje, E. B. 232, 237–238
Moll, L. C. 235, 283–284, 390
monolingualism and monoglossic language ideologies 179–181, 263, 266
moralistic approach to literary texts 147
moral order and implications 127–130
'More Bad Thing' Game 222–225
Morgan, J. 304
Morgan, Joan 263
Morrell, E. 154
Morrier, M. J. 390
Morrison, Toni 278–280, 284, 290; *The Bluest Eye* 154; "Unspeakable Things Unspoken" 277
Mosley, M. 391
Moten, F. 327
motivation xxii, 25
motivational processes 203, 208
Multidimensional Model of Racial Identity (MMRI) 67–69
Multiethnic Model of Ethnic Identity 67
multilingualism 184
multilingualism and bilingualism 34, 37, 123, 299, 335; *see also* racialized bilingual learners and academic language
multi-method and multi-modal approaches 326
multiple inheritances 4, *6*
multiplicity 279–283, 289–290
"multi-sited ethnographic sensibility" 336
multi-tiered systems of support (MTSS) 163, 416
mu rhythm 30
Murray, Charles: *The Bell Curve* xx
musical parenting 198
mutualism 369–372, 374, 379

narrative as sense-making 37
Nasir, N. 70, 142, 202; on diversity 297, 298; dominoes study 37
Nas (rapper) 154
The National Association of Black School Educators xxiv
National Black Child Development Institute xxiv
National Board for Professional Teaching Standards 407
National Center for Culturally Responsive Educational Systems (NCCRESt) 170
National Council of Teachers of English 149
National Instructional Materials Accessibility Standard (NIMAS) 173
national languages 179–180
National Network for Educational Renewal (NNER) 373
National Research Council 149
National Teacher Corps 373
National Teacher Corps program 388
National Writing Project 131
nation-building in exile 251
nation-state/colonial governmentality 179–181
Native American literature course (case study) 270; *see also* Indigenous students and communities; Indigenous ways of learning
natural selection theory xix
nature/culture binary 314–320
Nazi regime xix
NCCRESt 170–171
Neal, M. A. 268
negro identity (in Brazil) 56
neoliberalism 261
networked improvement communities (NICs) 368, 369
"networked publics" 357
networks within communities 234–236
neural pathways 35
neurobiology (and the brain) 24–25, 162–163, 165–167; and literacy 18, 19
neurodiversity 152
neurological processes xvii
neuro-physiological processes and cultural practices 24–43; biological role in 35–36; and diversity of pathways 38; and emotions 29; and everyday knowledge 36–37; and imitative learning 27–30; and infant embodiment 30–31; and language learning 31–35; links between 25–27; overview 24–25, 36; and social organization of learning environments 37–38; and tool use 29
neuroplasticity 25, 32, 35
New Concept Development Center (NCDC) (Chicago) 232
Newell, G. 149
New Jersey, educational funding in 418
new materialist deconstruction 315–316
New York, community schools in 417
niche construction theory (NCT) 4, *6*
Nocutzepo, Mexico 84
Noguera, Pedro 273n10

Index

non-dominant communities 38
nonintrusive approaches 81
nool-iknal (elders) 90
normativity 301, 308
North Carolina Teaching Fellows program 410

Oakes, J. 357–358, 360–361
Oakland Science and Mathematics Outreach (OSMO) project 342–344
Obama, Barack 304
obedience 261
objectivity 180, 186–187, 324
observational learning 27–29, 32, 88–89
occupational identity 49
O'Connor, C.: *Beyond Acting White: Reframing the Debate on Black Student Achievement* 72
O'Connor, Flannery 153
Odawa community 150, 154
Ogbu, John 71
Ogston, W. 116n9
Okonofua, J. A. 305–306
Oksapmin of Papua New Guinea xxix, 37
online communities 199–200, 356–357
onto-epistemic heterogeneity 278–279, 289
onto-epistemology 315
ontogenesis 3–7, 12–14, 162
ontogenetic niches 13
ontogenetic time xvii
open-ended learning encounters 125, 127
Opie, I. A. 215–216, 218
Opie, P. 215–216, 218
Oppositional Identity Theory 70–72
oppression and oppressive systems 263, 340–341
Oprah 304
optimal learning environment (OLE) project 168
oral memory 15
the "Other" and othering xviii, 142–143, 300
Oxana, D. 394
Oyserman, D. 68–69

P-20 (or K-16) movement 375, 379
Pacific Islander communities xxvi, 266–267
Packer, M. 366–367
Padres y Jóvenes Unidos (organization) (Denver) 358–359
pan ethnic identities 162
parallelism 374
parallel reproduction 8–9
parda and *amarela* identities (in Brazil) 55
Pardo, T. A. 366
parentese (or motherese) 33
parents and families: and brokering 204–205; practices within xxii, 198–199, 200–201; racial socialization practices 203
parent-teacher groups **351**, 354–355
Paris, D. 262, 266
Park, J. 186–187
Parsons, Talcott 109
participant observation 138n5
"partnerization" 372, 375

Patel, L. 307, 309
pathways, defined 196–197
patriarchy and patriarchal narratives 64, 282–283
Pea, R. 99, 116n4, 142
Pecina, U. 237
Peele-Eady, T. B. 238
peer-mediated approaches 167–168
Pell Grant funding 252
Peña, C. 270
Pennington, B. F. 166
People/Children of Color (as term) 310n1
Perez 272n1
performance, learning through 254
performance assessments 408
performance-based accreditation for preparation programs 408
"performances of resistance" 270
performance standard concept 45
performance styles 119, 120
Pericean semiotics 238
Perry, I. 268
perspective transformation 411
Peru youth 51–53
phenomenological variant of ecological systems theory (PVEST) 46; case studies 48–56
philanthropic organizations 350, 376
Philip, T. M. 280–281
Phillips, D. C. 285
philosophical perspectives xxiii
Phinney, Jean 67
phonetic structure of language 35
phylogenetic time xvii
physiological processes xvii
Piaget, Jean 25, 99, 101, 109, 115, 316–318; critique of 214; phylogenetic analyses of 317
Piagetian theory 30
pigudofadimepigulatu study 32–33
Piselli, F. 236
Plath, David 115, 197, 203
play 216, 222–225
playful imagination 333
playing the dozens 223
pleasure reading 147
pointing 102–103, 107, 110–112, 115n1, 116n8
policies 404–425; and educator preparation 405–408; for equity and learning 417–419; and generative teaching, learning supports for 410–412; overview 404–405, 417–421; and system of supports for students 416–417; and teacher recruitment 409–410
political theater activities 339
Polman, J. L. 197–198
positioning, acts of 119, 122, 131; *see also* positioning theory and discourse analysis
positioning theory and discourse analysis 119–140, 199; case study 1 (Charlie) 124–131, *125–126*; case study 2 (studio art) 130–137, **133**, *135–136*; definitions and origins of 119–121; in education 122–123; overview 137–138; and role of discourse 120–121

Index

positivism 317, 324
post-conflict countries 52
post-Enlightenment period 314
posthumanist and anti-humanist theories 321
post-structuralism 319
Post-Traumatic Stress Disorder (PTSD) 47; *see also* trauma and stress
Potawatomi language 143–144
poverty 37, 163, 323; *see also* economic inequalities; and "culture of poverty" xx, 164, 281, 389; statistics on 418
power and privilege; *see also* intersectionality; white privilege: and argumentation 142–146; and the body 323; and colonialism 278; and culturally organized learning pathways 196; Foucault on 319; in human institutions 10; and institutions of power xx–xxi; Jason de Leon on 325; and language revitalization 233; and learning pathways perspective 201, 202, 205–208; Lévi-Strauss compulsory education and 17–18; in parent-teacher interactions 355; relational approach to 359; in scientific practice 280–281; and social design-based experiments 332; and societal norms 45
practical skills 81
pragmatism 186
prefrontal cortex development 57
pretend play 101
print disabilities 173; *see also* learning disabilities and bio-cultural perspective
prisons, schooling within 248, 251–253
"prison-to-school" movement 251
Pritchett, Henry 407
privilege 57, 180–181; *see also* power and privilege
problem-space concept 263–265, 272n4
professional development schools (PDSs) 373
progress and play, rhetoric around 216
Progressions Framework 378–379, **380**
Project on Ethnicity and Race in Latin America (PERLA) 54
prolepsis 197, 331, 333
*promotora*s 337–341, 344
Proposition 209 (California) 302
proto-imperatives and *proto-declaratives* 103
Prout, A. 216, 217
Prussian age grading model 413
"pseudo-argumentation" 148
psychological processes and approach 163, 172
public critique 130–137
Public Works drama program (New York) 254–256
Punamäki, R. L. 367
punctuality 254–255
punishment and disciplinary practices 303–306, 323, 358, 414–415, 420
Pygmalion effect in learning studies 241

the quantitative-qualitative, reconceptualizing 314–329; and empiricism, new forms of 326–327; and ethnographic imagination 323–325; and hierarchies 315–317, 319–321; and humans and racializing assemblages 321–323; and nature and nurture, deconstructing 316–321; overview 314–315
queer romance genre 151
Qvortrup, J. 214

race: in Brazil 53–56; defined xix–xx; and disability 171, 172; and identity formation 45, 66–69; and ideologies of human development xviii–xix; post-Enlightenment logics on 314; and racial context of learning 46–47, 289; and racial democracy ideology 54; and racial socialization practices 203; and teacher education 391; and trauma 47–48
racialization 72, 171, 189n1, 321–323; and student organizations 356
racialized bilingual learners and academic language 178–191; and accommodation *vs.* reconfiguration 185–188; and cognitive framing 181–183, 187–188; and educational linguistics 178–179; and functional framing 183–185, 187–188; and linguistic solutions 178, 185–186; and nation-state/colonial governmentality 179–181; overview 97–98; and raciolinguistic ideologies 180–181; terminology 189n1
racism; *see also* anti-racism; scientific racism; stereotypes: and ableism 305–306; and the body 262, 267, 272; and colonial project 262; and health disparities 322–323; and human development perspective 47; and identity formation 66–69; in literature 142–143, 151; and obedience 261; as political discourse xxxin1; in school discipline policies 253; Stuart Hall on 299
radical openness and possibility 336, 338–341, 343–344
RAND Corporation Study 252
Raphael, T. E. 123
reactive coping 50–51
"reading brain" 165–166
reading disabilities 160–161, 165; *see also* dyslexia; learning disabilities and bio-cultural perspective
reciprocal causation 5
recognition of extraordinary contributions 89
reconceptualizing learning xvii–xxxi; and limiting conceptions xviii–xxi
reconfiguration-oriented theory of social change 185–188
Las Redes and *El Pueblo Mágico* educational designs 332–333
reflexive turn in social sciences 123
refugees 171; *see also* displaced persons; Kakuma Youth Research Group
reification of communities 239, 240
relationality of learning 25, 203
religion xx
remediation 303, 333–334, 337
Renée, M. 358
Renewing Communities Initiative (California) 252–253
reparations 46; *see also* slavery

repertoires for organizing 349–350
repertoires of practice 265
reproduction, modes of 5–9, *6*
researchers, cultural background of 144; *see also* ethnography
research–practice partnerships (RPPs) 237–238, **351**, 358–359; *see also* leadership and university-district partnerships
resilience xxiv, 91, 333–334, 338
resilience thinking framework 333
resistance approach 64, 72, 73, 307–308
response to intervention (RTI) 163
restorative justice 253, 415
Restoring Our Original True Selves (ROOTS) 251
restricted and elaborate codes (of language) 183
revitalization of communities 270–272
Richerson, P. J. 10
risks and supports, evaluating xxiii
Risley, T. 235
Rittel, H. W. J. 340
Robinson, T. 64
Rochlin, S. A. 370
Roediger, D. 46
Rogers, B. 357–358, 360–361, 391
Rogers, L. O. 69–70
Rogoff, Barbara xxi, xxix–xxx, 26, 82–83, 349, 390
Romaine, S. 182
Rosado-May, F. J. 81–82
Rose, M. 38
Rose, Tricia 268
Rosebery, A. S. 297
Rosenblatt, L. M. 149
Ross, N. 91
Ruhleder, K. 332
Rwanda, refugees from 248
Ryle, Gilbert 242n3

Sacks, Harvey 116nn13–14, 218, 221
"sacred truth space" 270
Salt, D. 333
Samoan communities 266–267
sampling bias xxv
San Francisco County jails 252
San Pedro, T. J. 270
San Quentin State Prison (California) 251
SAT exam study 65
SAT scores 316
Saxe, G. B. xxix, 70; mathematical problem solving study 37
"saying back" pattern 136–137
Schauble, L. 331
Schleppegrell, M. J. 184, 185
school climate surveys 415–416, 419–420
School Development Program (SDP) 417
school discourses 147; *see also* education and schools
school quality and student support (SQSS) indicators 415
Schumm, J. S. 167–168
Schutz, A. 203

science education 253; *see also* argumentation in literature and science for K–12 classrooms
Science through Technology Enhanced Play (STEP) project 153–154
scientific language 184
scientific racism xix–xx, xxiii
Scribner, Sylvia xxix, 38
Searle, John 10, 11
"second-class integration" 298
Sedano, L. J. 241
segregation 181, 272–273n6, 298, 418
selective imitation 29
self and other 26, 30–31, 64, 115, 122, 196, 199, 202, 204–205; Wynter on 321
self-discipline 88
self-efficacy 397
self-reflection 393
Sellers, R. M. 67–68
semantic sharpening 282
semilingualism 182
semiotic function 101–104
semiotic social spaces 356
sensemaking 147
serial reproduction 7
Serpell, R. xxix
service scholarships 410
settler colonialism xxvi, 262–264, 269, 271–272, 273n9, 277, 287, 307; *see also* colonialism; defined 272n5
sexuality in literature 151
Seymour-Smith, C. 231
shame 301
Sharpe, C. 326
Shattuck, J. 331
Shea, Molly 332, 344n1
Shining Path (Maoist guerrilla) 52
Shirley, D. 354
Shklovsky, V. 154
Shoptalk 145
Short, K. G. 394–395
"showing off" (infant gesture type) 103
signifying 281
sign languages 34
signs, use of 120
Silverman, S. 391
Silvers, Ronald 214
Sisk, K. 388
situated research perspective 162
Skinner, B. F. 31, 32
slavery xix, 46, 142, 261, 326
Smalls, C. 68
Smith, E. J. 323
Smith, J. P. 147
Smith, Linda xxv
Smitherman, Geneva 265–266
Smith Report (1969) 390
social change 97–98, 168, 178–179, 182–184, 187–188
social-class identity 49; *see also* economic inequalities
social cognition research 26–27

Index

social Darwinism 24

social design-based experiments (SDBEs): computer science case study 342–343; defining 330–332; design principles for 332–334, *334*, 344; and equity as ideal and material 334–336; food justice case study 336–338; and radical openness and possibility 336, 338–341, 343–344

socialization models 215, 248, 264

social justice approach 151, 238, 268

social media 238

social movement theory 351–352

social relationships xxiii

social studies 253

social theory, conscious use of 333

Society of Indian Psychologists (SIP) xxv–xxvi

sociocultural LD research 167

Sociocultural Positioning in Literacy: Exploring Culture, Discourse, Narrative, and Power in Diverse Educational Contexts 122

socio-economic status (SES) 33, 216, 220; *see also* economic inequalities; poverty

sociology 212

Soja, E. W. 332

Solano Community College (Fairfield, California) 251

solidarity 295, 297, 300, 305, 307–309

Somalia, refugees from 248

Southern border migration (U.S.) 325

Southern Poverty Law Center 392

South Sudan, refugees from 248

Spanish communities 266, 267

"Speak American!" incident 265

Spencer, Herbert xviii, 24

Spencer, M. B. 48, 71

Spillers, Hortense 321, 322

Spindler, G. D. 241–242

Spindler, L. 241–242

"spirit murder" 270

Spradley 138n5

St. Pierre, E. A. 326–327

Star, S. L. 332

state and federal funding for professional development school partnerships 409

Steele, C. M. 322; SAT exam study 65

Steinmetz, G. 326

STEM fields and education 122, 205, 206, 284; *see also* Oakland Science and Mathematics Outreach (OSMO) project

Sterelny, Kim 4

stereotypes 46, 57, 62–78, 414; and critique of research 73; defined 63–64; and ethnic-racial identity (ERI) 66–70; and narrative of resistance 64; and Oppositional Identity Theory 70–72; overview 62–63; and stereotype threat 322; and *Stereotype Threat* (ST) 65–66

Stevens, R. 196

Stornaiuolo, A. 232

storylines 121

Strategies of Resistance 307

strength-based pedagogies *see* asset pedagogies

stress and well-being 416

structure and context 106, 109, 115; *see also* context

The Strum Thing (case study) 220–222, *222*

student organizations **351**, 355–357

"Students' Right to Their Own Language" 265–266

"sturm und drang" model 57

subjunctive patterns of talk 282

Sudan, refugees from 248, 250

supremacist logics 300, 306, 309; *see also* white supremacy

survival skills 250

sustainability 333–334, 338

Sutton-Smith, Brian 214–216

symbolic violence 214

synchronization (or being "in synch") 30

syncretism 141

systemic change 170–172

Tadzhikistan and Uzbekistan, education in xxix

Tajfel, H. 63

TA model 171

Tan, E. 284

Tanda practice 204

tardiness 254–255

Tavares, R. 395

Taylor, E. V. 37, 284

Taylor, K. H. 285

teacher education and professional development 122, 170–171, 387–403; *see also* leadership and university-district partnerships; and contextualizing culture 393–395; and critical reflection 395–397, *396*; and cultural awareness, need for 390–391; and culture, defining 389; and generative learning 397–399, *398*; policies for 405–408; and teachers of color 391–392; traditional *vs.* alternative pathways for 387–389, 392–393, 400

teacher residencies 410

technical assistance (TA) centers 170

technologies for learning 161, 394–397

technology fluency 203

Teeters, Leah 344n1

"Television Without Pity" (online site) 153

Tenery, M. F. 390

Terman, Lewis xix

"terms of recognition" 248

tertiary artifacts 333

testimonio 356

"test-wiseness" 182

theater, playwrighting, and literary arts 252; *see also* Public Works drama program

thick description 240, 242n3, 324

third space 264, 267

Thompson, Anderson xxiv

Thompson, C. 147

Thorndyke, Edward xix

Thorne, B. 216; *Gender Play* 217

Three State Recidivism Study 252

Thunberg, Greta 152

Index

time and timing xvii, 81, 104–106, 115; and communities, study of 233–234; of pathways 197
"time embeddedness" 108
Tinto, V. 68–69
together-and-apart approach 217, 225–226
Tomasello, M. 31–33, 103, 319
tool use 29
Toulmin, Stephen 144–146, 149
trajectories of identification 197–198
"transactional" approach to literary reading 149
transcript approach 138n6
transformability 333–334
Transformative Justice Teacher Education 253
translanguaging practices 333
transnational community codes 236
transparency and accountability 89
Traub, James: "What No School Can Do" xx
trauma and stress 46–48, 57
Trump, Donald 341
trust, political and politicized 343–344
truth and objectivism 319, 324
Tuck, E. 272n5, 302–303
Turpen, C. 280–281
Tyack, D. B. 350
Tyson, K. 71–72

UCLA 357
Uganda, refugees from 248
Umaña-Taylor, Adriana 67
"underground economy of food and objects" in elementary school 216
United Nations 248, 257
Universal Design for Learning (UDL) 166, 169–170
universal truths 145
Universidad Intercultural Maya de Quintana Roo (UIMQRoo) 85–87, 89–90
University of California, Berkeley 251
University of California, Davis 251
Urban Explorers (AIC program) 353–354, 360
Urrieta, L, Jr. 82, 238
U.S. Department of Agriculture 337
U.S. Department of Education 387–388
utopian methodology 331–332, 334

Vai community (Liberia) xxix
Vakil, S. 337, 342
Valladares, M. R. 353
van Emeren, F. H. 143
van Langenhove, L. 122, 128
van Linden, J. A. 357
Vaughn, S. 167–168
Vico, Giambattista xxvi–xxviii
violence: and human hierarchies 322
"violent science" 214
Visual Word Form Area of the brain (VWFA) 18, 165–166
Volterra, V. 103
voluntary learning 247, 249–250, 254, 258
Vossoughi, S. 282

vulnerability 56–58
Vygotsky, Lev xxiv, xxvi, 99, 161–162; and mind/body dualism 317, 319; on tools 29

Waddington, C. H. 25, 35
Walker, Alice 281
Walker, B. 333
Walker, Siddle 232
Walking Scale Geometry 285
Wallace Foundation 376
Wallat, C. 138n6
Walsh, D. 270
Ward, J. V. 64
Warhol, L. 233
Warren, B. 297
Wartofsky, M. W. 331, 333, 334
Watson, D. 393
Way, N. 69–70
Webber, M. M. 340
Wee, L. 186–187
Weheliye, Alexander: *Habeas Viscus* 321–322
WEIRD backgrounds 213
well-being xxv, 91, 258, 416
Welner, K. 353, 358
Wenger, E. 352
Western perspectives: individual focus of xxv
whistle blowing 281
White, R. 68
white male academics 148, 151
white men in literature 151
whiteness 261–262, 264–265, 271, 298, 310n2
white privilege 46, 57, 265, 392
white supremacy: and culturally sustaining pedagogy 261; and disciplinary learning 278; ideologies of xviii–xix, 24–25, 142–143; and stereotypes 64
white terror 262
whole-language approach to literacy 182
wicked problems 340–341
Wilhelm, J. D. 147
Williams, Q. E. 310n3
Wilson, August 254
Winn, M. 38, 251
"withness-thinking" 286
Wittgenstein, L. 120, 145
Wolfe, Patrick 272n5
women; *see also* Girls of Color: incarcerated 252; intersectionality experienced by Black 305; in science professions 280; and social clubs 350; stereotypes affecting 65; trauma among 48
Women of Colour 310n1
Wong, C. 207, 269–271
Woodson, Carter G. xxiv
World Bank 257
Wortham, S. 203
Wright, C. G. 304, 305
written language 165–166
Wynter, Sylvia xxiv, 321
Wyoming, educational funding in 418

xenophobia 178, 265; *see also* racism

Index

Yerkes, Robert xix
"Youth Coming Out of the Shadows Week" campaign 356
Youth Mental Health First Aid curriculum (Maryland) 416
youth participatory action research (YPAR) 270, 358
YPAR Collaboration in Kakuma Refugee Camp 248–251
Yumbuyo, Hector Sueyo 81

Zapatista Maya rebellion (Chiapas, Mexico) (1994) 85
Zeichner, K. 392
Zeintek, L. 388
Zentella, Ana Celia 265–266
zero point epistemology 279, 286, 290
"zero-tolerance" policies 253, 415, 420
Zheng, Eddy 251
Zimmerman, A. M. 356

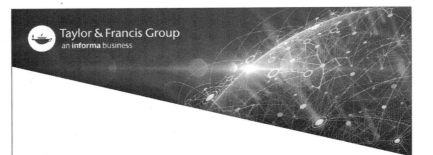